THE VOICES OF GUNS

The Voices

by VIN McLELLAN

# of Guns

The definitive and dramatic story
of the twenty-two-month career of
the Symbionese Liberation Army—one of the most bizarre
chapters in the history of the American Left

and PAUL AVERY

G. P. PUTNAM'S SONS, New York

SBN: 399–11738–5

Library of Congress Cataloging in Publication Data

McLellan, Vin.
   The voices of guns.

   Includes index.
   1. Symbionese Liberation Army.   2. Hearst, Patricia,
1954–   I. Avery, Paul, joint author.   II. Title.
F866.2.M24   1976   322.4′2′0924   75–43752

Lines from "Las Vegas Tilt," by Lawrence Ferlinghetti,
copyright © 1974. Published by New Directions.

PRINTED IN THE UNITED STATES OF AMERICA

Acknowledgments

Regretfully, many of the key sources for this book must remain anonymous. Our greatest debt must be to the friends of the SLA members, those who came to trust us, talked with us, and often convinced others to talk with us. Our commitment was to untangle the personalities from the politics, cut through the sensationalism, and reconstruct the SLA experience in human perspective. We have tried to live up to that trust. Most of those who talked with us demanded anonymity, afraid of retribution, personal embarrassment, and sometimes, criminal prosecution. And it was, besides, a story that tossed off a lot of random fear and paranoia.

We worked the story for over two years, almost continuously from the time of the Hearst kidnapping. Although we strenuously tried to avoid becoming involved in the actual police investigation, our independent research occasionally made us part of the story. It was, for instance, the authors who first located the hideout, the kidnap car, and the infamous closet in which Patricia Hearst was held captive for the first month and a half.

Among the families of the SLA members, the DeAngelises, the Wolfes, the Soliahs, Gary Ling, and Fred Soltysik were all extraordinarily helpful. We gratefully acknowledge the cooperation of the San Francisco office of the FBI, in particular, Special Agent in Charge Charles Bates; and the Berkeley, Oakland, San Francisco, and Los Angeles police departments. In each case, individual officers were particularly helpful, but they would prefer to remain unnamed. Assistant U.S. Attorneys Steele Langford and David Bancroft; U.S. Attorney James Browning; Alameda County District Attorney Lowell Jensen, and his investigator, Don Jones; and Berkeley police Inspectors Dan Woelke and Steve Engler were all helpful. The director of the California Department of Corrections, Raymond Procunier, now retired, was of considerable assistance; and CDC spokesman Phil Guthrie handled his difficult job with unfailing patience.

Randolph Hearst and William Randolph Hearst III were generous and cooperative, repeatedly. The Black Unity House in Cleveland, the United Prisoners' Union of California, and the two San Francisco chapters of the Vietnam Veterans Against the War/ Winter Soldier Organization have our respectful gratitude. Special thanks must go to Steven Weed, Colston Westbrook, and Thero Wheeler; to Robert Blackburn, the late Wilbur "Popeye" Jackson, Michael Bortin, and Pat Jean McCarthy—all key figures in the story who were unusually helpful.

Elinor Langer's brilliant 1973 essay, "Notes for the Next Time: A Memoir of the 1960s" (in the fall issue of *Working Papers*), left a significant impression on the book's perspective, and the early advice and suggestions of Bo Burlingham, Jerry Borst-Lee, Michael McCain, Fred Hapgood, Dan Segal, and, particularly, Marilyn Katz helped shape its scope and tone. For the final product, none but the authors hold blame—but credit must be widely shared.

By chance, geography, and sheer tenure on the case, the authors' files became something of an informal clearinghouse for dozens of journalists working the Hearst/SLA story across the country—in the exchange of information, we gained at least as much as we gave out. We owe thanks to our former editors and colleagues at the San Francisco *Chronicle*, the Boston *Phoenix*, *People* magazine, and the Philadelphia *Inquirer*, for whom we covered parts of the story. And among the reporters who cooperated with us, we would specifically like to thank Leroy Aarons, Rick Beban, John Bryan, Ken Dowdell, Tim Findley, Warren Hinckle, Joyce Hoffman, Robert Joffee, Art Kevin, Sally Kibbee, Marshal Kilduff, Joanne Lee-Borst, David McQueen, Miles Microft, Jim Mitchell, Carol Pogash, Andrew Ross, Mark Schwartz, Nancy Stevens, Peter Weisser and Arthur Zich.

This was a first book for both authors, and it took longer and was more difficult than we had ever expected. Without the inspiration of Bill Gross it would never have been begun; without the faith of our agents, Michael Larson and Elizabeth Pomada, we might not have continued; without the enthusiasm of our editor, John Dodds, we might never have finished. Without the sweatshop labors of Sandra Katzman, our researcher, the task would have been immeasurably more difficult. (Katzman's contributions to the effort included several key interviews, one of which produced the lead that enabled us first to locate the kidnap hideout in which the transformation of Patricia Hearst occurred.) And our gratitude also goes to Yola Jurzykowski and Katy Raddatz, typists extraordinaire. The burden of those two years on our friends and those we love was great; for those who stood by us, we can never be grateful enough.

For Mary
—v.b.m.
For Charlé and Cristin
—p.a.

Contents

THE EMBLEM of the Symbionese Liberation Army is 170,000 years old, and it is one of the first symbols used by people to signify god and life. The two bottom heads on each side of the Cobra represent the four principles of life: the sun, the moon, the earth, and the water. The three center heads represent god and the universe, and are called the god head. The number seven as embracing all the universal forces of god and life can be traced to the Egyptian temples and their seven pillars, to the seven candles of the pre-zionist, North African religions, to the Buddhist and Hindu religions, and to the North and South American Indian religions. This is because the seven principles explain the interrelationships of life, of the family and the state, of the human anatomy and the universe. And because the basic principle behind any kind of union and series of relationships must be equally accessible to all concerned, we see why the seven heads of the cobra have but one body. The thoughts and purpose in each of the seven heads of the cobra penetrates its common body and soul, and from this we see how the source of the cobra's survival lies not in any individual head, but rather in the relationship and unity of all the heads to each other.

The Symbionese Liberation Army has selected the Seven-Headed Cobra as our emblem because we realize that an army is a mass that needs unity in order to become a fighting force, and we know that true unity among people must be based upon a concern that is universal. It is a revolutionary unity of all people against a common oppressor enemy of the people. This unity of seven heads in one body defines the essence of co-operation and socialism in the great undertaking of revolutionary war. Through the puritan capitalist ethics of competition, individualism, fascism, racism, sexism and imperialism the enemy is attacking us. This enemy functions by means of attacking one race or group among us in an attempt to force us into submission and division and isolation from each other. From these attacks, we have learned that our common enemy will not stop until we come together to stop him, for he lives off the

13

murder and oppression of our divided and therefore defenseless people.

—from an SLA leaflet

We'll mass what people we can; perhaps that won't be the whole lower class. We'll mass ourselves and any ally we may be able to draw from the whole class structure, and we'll attempt to wage a war on property and property rights. . . . But if we cannot draw the support that is necessary for such a war, then we see a positive benefit for the majority of the world's people in the reduction of this whole country to a vast wasteland, and a graveyard for two hundred million of history's most damnable fools!

—GEORGE JACKSON, *Blood in My Eye*

. . . a blood stained inanity of so fatuous a kind that it was impossible to fathom its origin by any reasonable or even unreasonable process of thought. For perverse unreason had its own logical process. . . .

—JOSEPH CONRAD, *The Secret Agent*

THE VOICES OF GUNS

1

The Story

THEY called themselves the Symbionese Liberation Army and declared the Revolution come. As their emblem, the sign of the new order, the mark of the SLA, they chose the writhing seven-headed cobra, the *naga,* hoary symbol of the serpent god of occult myth. They were a tiny band of political terrorists, made in America, organically grown, and in a frantic 682-day career they wrote one of the most bizarre chapters in the history of the American Left.

Enigmatic and fey, they seemed to burst from the past into the fall of 1973; bewildering, ruthless, puerile, and tragic. Loose from nearly all contemporary moorings. As distanced from any common American zeitgeist as their *naga* from the bald eagle. There were but a handful—no more than a score actually took up arms—but through that somber winter and into spring, 1974, their inspired guerrilla theater captured a niche of American consciousness, projecting a brash farce and gothic melodrama that seemed an oddly appropriate counterpoint to the righteous and dour dramatics of the unfolding Watergate crisis.

The SLA was neither the first nor the strangest of the freak revolutionary cults to bounce screaming from the California fringe, but they exploded in a spectacle wildly out of scale. Perhaps it was an inevitable marriage of Charles Manson's insane dune-buggy fascism and the arrogant proto-Marxist terrorism of the early Weathermen—the final degradation of the New Left in which the center gave way completely. Perhaps it was much less: a human implosion of frustration, futility, and fantasy. Psychodrama. The Revolution as therapy.

They were neither cannibals nor imbeciles. Few would identify with these Symbionese, but many could recognize them: the proprietary sense of mission, the desperate sense of urgency, the barely restrained hysteria. The SLA was a shard of the past, a be-

17

lated tremor from the sixties. And individually, at least, there was something painfully familiar about them.

The SLA had a virtual genius for the public theater. They burst into the headlines on page 1, on network-news prime time, cover stories in magazines. They seized the media with sensationalism and clung tight, baiting, always with a new surprise—rising to claim all the stature of an American fedayeen. Their fate was sealed, their plot insane, their image fit all the expectations of a public primed.

In a matter of months the Symbionese Liberation Army achieved a notoriety and visibility unparalleled among the extremist minisects, dominating the political extreme, imprinting the whole of the fringe with their own quixotic image. It was they, finally, who gave a wholly American root to the word "terrorist," succeeding where so many others had failed. And they introduced it into the domestic political lexicon with a full freight of riddle and absurdity—all the sad, silly irrelevance that has haunted the potential of terrorism as a political tactic.

Had they been merely political and less the eerie cobra cult, had they been more the cult and less the fevered revolutionists, their grasp on our imaginations might have been less. But the image they seized was precisely crafted, grotesque enough to vivify the canty politics, political enough to invest the grotesquerie with a bizarre secular relevance.

The Symbionese set out to unleash "the most devastating revolutionary violence ever imagined," sure in their heady innocence that there was a nation ready to follow in mass insurrection, sure that principled suicide was preferable to complacency. They called themselves "Children of the Wind" and touted their leader, General Field Marshal Cinque, as not only a military genius to lead us but a spiritual prophet to save us. Cinque was Donald David DeFreeze, a thirty-one-year-old escaped convict who, like many black nationalists, had renounced his Christian "slave name" to affirm his African heritage and deny the slave tradition. He called himself Cinque Mtume—Cinque from the name of an enslaved Wendji chief who led a famous revolt on the slave ship *L'Amistad* in 1839; Mtume from the Swahili word for "apostle" or "disciple."

Cinque Mtume: *"The name means Fifth Prophet,"* explained an SLA communiqué, *"and Cin was many years ago given this name because of his keen instinct and senses, his spiritual consciousness, and his deep love of all the people and children of this earth. . . .*

"Now, once again, the people have brought forth another prophet and leader"—a black brother who *"to us and to all oppressed people is the instilled hope and spirit of his people and all peoples."*

DeFreeze entered California's prison system in 1970, virtually apolitical, a ghetto punk and petty hood. When he escaped after serving three and a half years of a five-to-life sentence for armed robbery, he had undergone a powerful transformation. In the intense, bitter atmosphere of the highly politicized California prisons he had become a revolutionary, a cellblock communist. He had *become* Cinque, acquiring a new personality, a new persona.

DeFreeze as Cinque was a magnetic, charismatic figure—but the SLA that gathered around him was more than just a personality cult. Only gradually did Cin become more than the first among equals; and it is unclear even now how much of his deification was self-conscious theater. Cinque had not the mesmerizing hypnotic qualities of a Manson; those who followed him were more self-willed and independent than the burned-out cripples who followed Manson. The chemistry of the SLA was more complex.

DeFreeze was a black man sought out to lead the SLA because he was a black man. The soldiers of his tiny army were white—upper-middle-class dropouts from the fringe of privilege, college-educated radicals who believed any successful revolution had to be led by a black, preferably a black convict. Each had sworn to follow only black or nonwhite leadership.

This was to be a black revolution, a neo-Maoist *Helter Skelter,* the triumph of the nonwhite over the bourgeois white capitalists. The rise of the oppressed against the oppressors—and of course it would be led by a black convict, a man from the ranks of the most oppressed of the oppressed. But the first platoon would be this band of "conscious whites," reclaimed children of the oppressor who would show the way, as it were.

"Contrary to what many of us may think, the special privileges white men as a group have gained for themselves through the oppression of all other people has never secured for us the freedom we desire. White men must understand that they will live under the threat of death as long as they continue to oppress the members of any class or group who have the strength and determination to fight back. White men themselves have only one avenue to freedom and that is to join in fighting to the death those who are and those who aspire to be the slave masters of the world. . . ." The SLA credo; the gospel according to Teko.

Teko was the "reborn name" of William Taylor Harris, the SLA's second in command. General Teko, thirty years old, white, a Vietnam veteran from Carmel, Indiana, with a master's degree in urban education.

"Many of us have been 'bold' enough to intellectualize about revolution, but far too chickenshit to get down and help make it. Most of us have been nearly fatally stricken with the vile sickness of racism. Again, most of us have been immobilized by our sexist egos and have watched and done nothing as our sisters have rushed by us into battle. We have fooled ourselves into believing that Madison Avenue piggery will bring us eternal bourgeois happiness. If we haven't bought into the racist, sexist, capitalist, imperialist program, we have 'greened out' in Mendocino and New Hampshire. To black people, who lead our struggle to freedom, we have proved to be the racist punks of the world when we kick back and live off the blood and lives of the people."

The SLA was not a voice from the ghetto—despite such excessive empathetics as faked black accents. The SLA was born in white suburbs, nurtured in affluence, schooled in the protest politics of the civil rights movement and Vietnam War. They were young radicals who had defined themselves as revolutionaries in the late sixties, when the horizon seemed full of possibilities. They had then been caught treading water as tension waned with quieter years. Finally they had reached the point where they had to vitalize the dream with their own lives, their own bodies, or at last surrender the heroic self-image for the more mundane role of a middle-class survivor.

It was revolution as an act of will; ahistorical, individualistic rather than socialistic, a personal more than political process. Nothing so consumed the SLA as personal identity. Nothing so marked them individually as the effort to transform themselves, to free themselves from the bourgeois stain. *"We know that we have a long way to go to purify our minds of the many bourgeois poisons, but we also know that this isn't done through bullshitting and ego tripping— it is done by fighting and as the Comrade has taught us, 'by stalking the pig, seizing him by the tusks, and riding his pig ass into his grave.'"* The word "Symbionese" they coined from "symbiosis," an esoteric term from biology which refers to unlike organisms coexisting in harmony for mutual benefit. It was to be a rejection of race labels; a new race label, a revolutionary nation of mingled skin color.

Not only DeFreeze but all members of the SLA adopted the black-nationalist ritual, renouncing christened names for "reborn" names. The white SLA, far more than Cin, had a heritage to disclaim. It was more than ceremony. It was the culmination of their desperate struggle to cut away all traits of culture, class, and race they associated with their parents. The names they chose were plucked from fantasy and history; the names of black heroes, Indian heroes. The rhythm of their roll call must have sounded like an incantation: *Fahizah . . . Teko . . . Yolanda . . . Cujo . . . Bo . . . Gabi . . . Zoya . . . Osceola. . . .*

Redemption and Revolution.

"Death to the fascist insect that preys upon the life of the people!"

All through the sixties there had been a freaky fringe on the New Left, tiny sects of unruly overbelievers, but while there was a mass movement, the dominant voice of the moderate Left had stood to challenge them. By the time the SLA emerged there was no longer a marketplace of American radicalism in which the freak extremists had to measure themselves against the center.

The sixties were dead. Even with sloppy overlap into the early seventies, the mood of trauma, the era of drastic challenge and constant change had passed. A generation of self-righteous young rebels withdrew into their individual lives, idealism battered, spirit subdued. They failed no one so much as themselves, challenged nothing so much as the fabric of their own lives.

The retreat from the mass consciousness, the dissolution of "the Movement," was a discrete process, difficult to generalize, but central to the disaffection of many was the slow realization that the Movement had developed no language of challenge that did not alienate the vast majority of their countrymen. As the moral imperative of Vietnam receded, they were left with a structural challenge to the establishment, aware of the inequities in the distribution of power; but they had no plan, no plot for change that could convincingly relate to their neighbors. The democratic Left had sought to lead America rather than capture it, and for that they had not yet the tools. Out of the Movement, most of the New Left veterans retreated to seek within themselves and write notes for next time.

Yet there were those who could not or would not draw back. There were those who could not endure integration back into the middle-class white world from which they had so fiercely broken; those who had been so long and so fiercely alienated from the traditional American conceits that their identities were wholly bound up in the radical anticulture. And the most crippled among these were those still infatuated with the Revolution, still locked into the idea of imminent cataclysmic change, the heroic opportunity—even as the phrase became a stock facetious idiom.

The story of this tiny Symbionese rebellion was marked with the crosscurrents of the culture, the conflict of generations, and the confusions of future shock. It was rooted in the intense undercurrent of idealism and adolescent arrogance that molded the sixties, but the SLA was never more than a caricature of the past. Yet because it involved so many of the same powers, so many of the same passions, trapping and compressing them into such a bizarre and arcane story, it seemed to reveal some of the more subtle threads in the social dynamic. Sex and sexuality, gender and role—questions of identity, alienation; affirmation; the unresolved crisis of femininity confronted with feminism, the backlash tremor of masculinity—this was much more than a story of politics, dogma, destruction, and retribution, yet it encompassed all that.

From conception to conclusion, the SLA was a phenomenon smothered in sensation, but nothing so captivated the bewildered and mystified public than the climax of this brash and unwieldy crusade—the conversion of a kidnap victim, the transformation of Patricia Campbell Hearst.

Patty was the SLA's most famous victim, their only convert, a nineteen-year-old California heiress who had been kidnapped by the SLA in February, 1974, and somehow flipped and remodeled into Tania, the Symbionese terrorist princess. The Hearst story had a peculiar magic. There had been a brutal logic to the girl's choice: The complicated and escalating demands of the SLA had made her ransom virtually impossible, but the niceties of the situation might well have escaped her. Held under death threat in a captivity described by the SLA itself as particularly brutal, Patricia Hearst simply learned that she was not to be ransomed. Whatever accommodation she made with her captors might have been excused—almost was excused, at first—but then it became clear that she had gone beyond accommodation. Survival was part of her story, but there seemed to be more.

Rebellion, romance, revenge? Patty Hearst alone made this one of the most sensational mystery stories of the century, an epic that gripped a worldwide audience. Perhaps as well as any other gauge, the seven *Newsweek* cover photos (a record of sorts, for either victims or outlaws) serve as a measure of the "Pattymania" fascination—and trace as well the arcane two-year cycle of the tale:

**In February, 1974, Patty's sun-brushed smiling face, beaming teen innocence, shared its first cover with Alexander Solzhenitsyn, the Russian author then expelled from the Soviet Union. A red banner—"Terror and Repression"—angled across the page, and the two faces were labeled. Hearst: "The Captive." Solzhenitsyn: "The Exile."

**April, 1974: Tania and the transformation. Patty posed in beret and jump suit, dead eyes, dour face, holding a machine gun. The photo accompanied Patty's conversion message from the SLA underground, and the cover design put the scaly outline of the seven-headed cobra behind her, enveloping her—and over it a boldprint caption for the new myth: "The Saga of Patty Hearst."

**May, 1974: another red-banner label, "Patty Hearst: After the Shoot-out." The picture captured Patty the enigma. It was a prekidnap lover's photo, a romantic close-up of the pensive face, eyes averted. Most of the SLA was dead, trapped and killed by Los Angeles police, but Patty and two others had escaped and disappeared—and only Tania could address the haunting mystery that remained.

**A year and four months later, September, 1975, headlines in scores of languages trumpeted the capture around the world, and the *Newsweek* cover caught a famous glimpse of Patty-Tania the day after her San Francisco arrest: giggling a defiant grin; one fist raised for the photographer: the glint of a steel handcuff at the wrist. The photograph would be entered as evidence at her trial, for it was virtually the last of Tania.

**After five months in a jail cell (her family having decided not to post bond, denying ransom again, "for Patty's own good"); five months of being counseled and analyzed by a battery of psychiatrists; five months of conferring with a whole coterie of attorneys, Patricia Campbell Hearst went on trial in San Francisco charged with bank robbery. But the defendant, now, was a yet-again transformed Patricia Hearst. *Newsweek* detailed the courtroom action in three cover stories. The first, February, 1976, was headlined "Patty on Trial." The artist caught the face of a wan ex-debutante, jail-cell pallor, red-brown hair stiff and unstyled. There would be no clenched fist, no grins; only this vulnerable face with the wounded eyes. The media had labeled the Hearst case yet another "trial of the century," and *Newsweek*'s March 1 cover—"Patty's Defense"—framed the expectation more than the reality. It was a painted portrait of an aristocratic Miss Hearst, the witness-stand microphone jutting up in front of her, the angle of the jaw and the tilt of the head conveying all the impervious defiance expected of the very wealthy in situations where lesser folk seem only desperate.

**The March 29 issue splashed the verdict bold—*GUILTY!*—
across a black-orange cover photo of the woman damned; a tight
blowup of the shallow face marked with defeat and despair, the
features nearly faded out in a red wash over the portrait news
photograph.

Who *was* this woman? Who was Tania? Who was tried, and for
whose crimes was she convicted? The questions were not simple,
but they seemed horrendously pertinent—and none was answered in the trial. Nor the verdict. The search for truth and the
struggle for justice should be compatible, but in the Hearst trial
they seemed to vie at strange cross-purpose. It was the misfortune
of Patricia Hearst—and of the millions who sought so eagerly to
understand—that her lawyers presented a trial defense out of the
1950's, to a jury of the 1970's, to explain an experience that came
out of the 1960's.

The result was another masquerade—the last masque of the
SLA, an explanation that simply did not address the reality of
what happened.

The verdict simply meant that the jury could not believe Patricia Hearst, could not believe her lawyers, could not accept contradictions in the legal and psychiatric package offered as the
Hearst defense case. Legally, that defense boiled down to a claim
that Patricia Hearst had been "coerced" at gunpoint or by fear of
death for the nearly twenty months of her SLA experience, but in
the courtroom arguments of the defense, nothing was reduced to
the simple legalities.

Was it a crime trial, as billed, or was it, as it seemed, a political
trial? Perhaps the strangest thing about the courtroom debate was
the careful and deliberate effort of both the prosecution and the
defense to skirt the political context of the crime—the eagerness
with which both rushed to define the SLA as cartoon characters,
despicable but incomprehensible. A San Francisco jury in 1976
was capable of understanding a much more complicated reality,
but the Hearst defense seemed confined and limited by its own
narrow perspective. The Cold War politics for which both the
Hearst family and their chief defense attorney, F. Lee Bailey of
Boston, were noted seemed to provide the only underpinning for
the defense case.

It was a case, as many law professors put it, "that had to be
tried"—a situation that called into question so many of the crucial
and fundamental issues of law, that challenged so many significant concepts of responsibility, free will, and mental disability that

only a jury verdict could be reasonably trusted to weigh the social will. The verdict was rendered (and either way would have become subject to controversy), but the case debate in the courtroom had tangled so many issues so maladroitly that it confused and raised more questions than it resolved.

Patricia Hearst was convicted not of the bank robbery for which she was tried; Patricia Hearst was convicted of having become Tania, of having "converted to the SLA." The crux of the case, the issue of whether there were factors in the conversion that rendered it illegitimate, was confronted indirectly, if at all, for the threat of the defense was to deny that there had been any Tania transformation.

Mr. Bailey is a courtroom orator whose flair has always seemed to be flamboyant more than brilliant, and the structure of the defense case he developed seemed to rely more on his skill for slick verbal argument than on any deep or profound analysis of the issues raised. Bailey's defense seemed schizophrenic; inherently contradictory, at times virtually incoherent. On one hand, Bailey put psychiatrists and POW experts on the witness stand to explain Korean War-style "brainwashing" and argued that Patty had been subjected to some vague and mechanical form of "mind control," yet on the other, he insisted that this Symbionese mind control process had only been partially successful: that Patty had to be "coerced" in virtually every case where she did something illegal—but more, in every instance where she wrote something, or said something, or did anything that seemed to indicate latent sympathy or open camaraderie with the SLA. It was, as both the prosecutor's argument and the verdict made clear, "too big a pill to swallow." The jury simply could not believe Patricia Hearst's sworn testimony that she had never "voluntarily" supported the SLA at any time during her long sojourn in the radical underworld.

The government's evidence to the contrary was impressive: witnesses, documents, even a tape recording secretly made of a conversation between the defendant and a visitor after her arrest. If none of it actually proved her willful participation in the bank robbery for which she was charged, in the nature of the case as it evolved in court, the bank heist became only the fulcrum for judgment. The jury vote weighed the uncontested fact of the kidnapping, and the trauma and terror of her captivity, against the government's evidence of her invested involvement in the year-and-a-half Tania odyssey.

Yet the blunt facts of the conviction remain rather stunning: Patricia Hearst, kidnapped and unransomed; having been locked in a tiny bedroom closet of the SLA's tract-house hideout for at least six weeks (according to unchallenged SLA documents introduced as case evidence); having been reduced during that period to such physical state (again, according to the SLA's version) that she could not stand unassisted; blindfolded for so many weeks that she could not see but with a hallucinogenic blur of vision—this teenage girl allegedly freely and responsibly enlisted with her captors and became Tania. About four weeks later (perhaps but two weeks later; Hearst claimed she was held closet captive for eight, not six, weeks) Tania Hearst marched into a bank with an SLA assault squad and robbed it for the Symbionese Revolution. And the verdict announced the jury certain "beyond a reasonable doubt" that she robbed that bank of her own free and unfettered will.

Legalistically, Bailey's "coercion" line may have looked viable for the bank robbery case; it was even a likely argument with the bank job being the first Tania crime, coming so on the heels of the bizarre announcement that Patty was no longer a captive but a comrade of the SLA. But in such a sensational and politically sensitive case it was a law school argument that didn't approach the scope of the case. There is no brainwash defense in law, although the claim might be approached through a mix of modified insanity pleas. Bailey, however, was determined to use coercion, apparently because it provides a conventional bedrock defense. But to have clung to it, to have molded his defendant's carefully staged testimony to support it, seemed legal suicide after the trial judge, in a hotly disputed decision, ruled that the government could introduce evidence to document and describe Patty's behavior during the seventeen-month period between the bank robbery and the arrest.* Evidence which undercut the whole defense with a picture of Patty acting independently, seemingly a willful, swaggering warrior of the revolutionary underground.

---

*The decision of Federal Judge Oliver Carter to allow the scope of the case to so expand may well be the focus of any appeal brief, but well before the trial began, Bailey knew that Carter was noted for an expansionist view of case evidence. And Bailey himself, in both his out-of-court media blitz and his comments in pretrial court appearances, had underscored the question of Patty's "state of mind"—an issue which, once raised, the government has a traditional right to ex-

Bailey tried to justify his strategy amid the considerable criticism that followed the trial: "The jury was going to consider her a kidnap victim trying to survive," he argued, "or they were going to consider a very bad girl who had been doing bad things for a year and a half after her trauma. . . . We knew that was the choice." It was a simplistic, even naïve, perspective, but the statement aptly captured the tone of his argument, which reflected little of the complexity of the case, which in fact almost insulted the intelligence of the earnest and troubled jury that brought in the verdict. After the trial, several of those jurors spoke of feeling "let down" by Bailey, by the shallowness of his defense. "Every single one of us would rather have acquitted her," said one juror. Another complained that Bailey hadn't offered a shred of solid evidence with which to buttress the strong inclination of several to acquit. When the secret ballots were tallied for conviction, several jurors began to weep. Another had to vomit.

What was it in the story of Patricia Hearst that created such certainty of guilt, yet such reluctance to punish? What are the varieties of guilt? "There were some sensationally exciting questions about the borderland between volition and involition in human behavior," mused one law professor. "We could have learned a lot from this case about human behavior." That those questions were avoided and not explored is perhaps part of the ultimate tragedy of the Hearst case—all the more so, if those questions were not openly raised as the result of a defense strategy that simply didn't trust the jury to comprehend the complex truth.

Vincent Hallinan is a seventy-eight-year-old San Francisco attorney, a socialist presidential candidate several decades back, and patriarch of a feisty Irish clan that has produced conspicuously leftist lawyers the way others produce generations of policemen or naval officers. Hallinan had bitterly attacked the SLA early on, and the Hearsts had retained him for the defense team while Patty was still on the run. Vince Hallinan was one of the first people to hear Patty's story directly from her right after her arrest, and

---

plore by highlighting and backlighting the incident subject to trial. The appeal issue would rest on the question of whether the probative value of the evidence the judge allowed before the jury sufficiently outweighed its considerable prejudicial impact. (Judge Carter died on June 14, 1976, of a heart attack, and sentencing of Hearst was postponed until October 1976, while a new judge reviewed the case.)

one of his lawyer sons, Terrence "Kayo" Hallinan, was Patty's own first choice to be her defense counsel. Both were eventually edged out of the case by Bailey and the Hearsts, but after the trial Vince Hallinan delivered a scathing public denunciation of Bailey. "No amount of mischance, negligence, stupidity, or idiocy could have loused up the case worse than it was loused up!" he said. With obvious anger and scorn, he added, "If you're going to *give* a client a story to tell, for Christ's sake, give them one that can be believed."

There were evidently some major discrepancies between the story Miss Hearst and Bailey put before the jury and the version Patty told the Hallinans. "They missed the whole point," complained Kayo, who was the first person Patty opened up to after the arrest. "The jury heard the Hearst parents' version. The family just couldn't accept that she *had* become Tania. That the SLA had twisted and turned her in a very brutal way—but that she had *changed*. When Bailey put her on the stand to say she hadn't, that it was all because they had a gun to her head, it just didn't make any sense. The jury was begging for a reason to acquit her, and Bailey had her story so full of contradictions they couldn't find one."

And yet what of Patricia? Was she or had she ever been more than a marionette? This girl who had turned twenty locked in a closet begging her parents to ransom her, who had turned twenty-one a terrorist in the underground, cursing her family and sketching little seven-headed cobras; who turned twenty-two in a tiny maximum-security jail cell, betraying old lovers, friends who had risked themselves for her, former comrades in this strangest of revolutions.

The trial in any case would have been a difficult place to unravel her story. The tale of Tania is inextricably interwoven with the story of the SLA. Denied the context—stripped and removed from the peculiar psychological, emotional, and political vision that defined the separate reality of the Symbionese—even the whole of Patty's story was but a piece of the puzzle.

To comprehend at all, it seems necessary to plunge into that separate reality, to delve for the roots and trace the evolution of the vision, the gathering of personalities. It is a sad, sometimes profound study, almost a leap from one culture to another. It is a study of disintegration, of politics and personalities, ideals sinking into decadence.

The SLA was a relic of the sixties, a projection of dislocated expectations and possibilities. America in the seventies will have its rebels, certainly its revolutionaries, probably its terrorists, but the SLA was a specter of the past; conceived not out of any possibility of success, but simply in the vacuum of options, the Left's cloistered atmosphere of futility and failure. And of all the beleaguered enclaves from which it might have so predictably emerged, certainly none was so likely as the Bay Area of San Francisco—and in the Bay Area, the quaint and notorious city of Berkeley.

Berkeley is the ghost town of the Movement, the morgue of the New Left. It is a city dominated by the huge University of California Berkeley campus; a college town uniquely caught up in its own peculiar atmosphere in which swift, turbulent currents of the sixties still swirl, settling well outside the American mainstream. Once the premier capital of the counterculture, Berkeley is still mecca for those seeking to discover or re-create the angry, hopeful anarchism that surged across the nation in the youthful rebellion of the last decade.

If there was a geographical locus for that rebellion, it was the Bay Area: Berkeley, San Francisco, and the heavily black ghetto city of Oakland, the three unlikely sister cities that abut San Francisco Bay. Elegant San Francisco, with its heritage of precious arty subcultures, saw the crystallization of the New Bohemia: flower children, the Haight, beads, baubles, Zen and the art of acid tripping. Oakland, long dominated by white conservatives, gave birth to the Black Panther Party and a whole new generation of black militancy. And Berkeley—in 1964—launched the campus rebellion. Berkeley's renegade Free Speech Movement established the campus as a weather vane of student activism. It held that distinction through the most desperate and hopeful years of the sixties.

It was a tumultuous decade, full of angst and seismic change, but the tide receded everywhere, even in Berkeley. The annual spring migrations that had made the Bay Area the carnival of hip did not cease, but now the migrants were often older, and where once there were only kids hungry for experience, now many who came sought only shelter. And as the student culture became more passive and conventional, the center of Berkeley's radical subculture shifted from the university to a large transient enclave of dropouts and free-lance radicals.

The counterculture went sour, the workers voted for Nixon, and Telegraph Avenue went commercial—but in Berkeley a huge community of young white radicals, veterans of campus wars, walled themselves off from the middle-class world. It became the largest garrison of vintage New Left radicals anywhere in the nation. It was a subculture scattered through low-rent suburbs, but it remained curiously centered behind the spiritual barricades of Berkeley. Here the Revolution never failed, it merely fell into limbo.

For many it was simply a refuge for an eccentric life-style, but the common tongue of the streets became a singsong hip-Marxist rhetoric. There were coalitions of factions in niggling debates of theory and tactics; little Red Armies of textbook revolutionaries. Richard Nixon's election and massive reelection simply washed away the fantasy of some elemental revolutionary impulse bursting from the heart of the nation. The stature of the most authoritarian Marxist ideologues—Lenin, Mao, even Stalin—rose as the romantics drifted into cynicism. The innocent humanism that had been the lifeblood of the Movement faded into a militant, bitter chauvinism.

Yet there were enough so that among themselves they created a time warp, an enchanted-village effect in which much of what constitutes time seems frozen in 1969. Ideologies of "armed struggle" still dominate political debate, and Marx is still mixed with odd portions of the occult mysticism that so enchanted the freak theosophists. There is something still of the open, warm camaraderie of the street-demo veterans, a gloss of flower power, and much of the old drug culture. Street people are still called that. Revolutionaries make a distinction between themselves and mere radicals.

In radical Berkeley the Revolution is a profession, and alienation is still a social virtue. Yet there is always a tension, ever more so: a chill sense that the scheme of the world is changing drastically, in ways they do not comprehend, rendering, perhaps, even their revolt irrelevant.

The SLA dropped into a time-honored slot in the Bay Left; militarism has always been popular, a necessary accouterment in the sectarian rivalry over who is the more revolutionary. The Bay Left had coalesced around the Black Panthers in the late sixties, when the Panthers were still a paramilitary group, and young white radicals organized dozens of groups to mirror the Panthers' "armed struggle" ideology, often in tribal or cultish collectives. There were the White Panthers, the Rainbow Party, the Southern Patriots, the Red Feather Party—only a few among the myriad collectives and communes which paraded guns and theories of "armed struggle against the institutional violence of the state."

The joy of revolt was gone by 1969. SDS, the national coalition of Students for a Democratic Society, was torn in bitter schism. The best organized of the radical student Left, calling themselves Weathermen, went underground, dropping into defensive anonymity to launch a spree of terrorist bombings. (The early attacks abated after a bomb factory in a New York town house exploded, killing three Weather terrorists. The group went into a year-long depressive midpassage, winnowing a theory of "armed propaganda," a tactic of protest rather than murder.) On the Black Left, the Panthers, under deadly police attack nationally, tried to reorganize in a more classical Marxist posture. Leadership split, however, and a splinter faction formed the Black Liberation Army, a secret terrorist group linked to the murder of several police officers. The Weather Underground impinged on folklore; ubiquitous, invisible. Among the Bay Left they claim a general sympathy. Weather leader Bernardine Dohrn, one of the FBI's most wanted fugitives for years, can still issue proclamations on Bay Area civic affairs—obviously close by, but sheltered in the impenetrable thickets of the radical underworld.

The liturgy of Revolution had been reduced to the merely military options for social change; distorted until it conferred on only the soldier the dignity Marx had offered the worker. Annually new cadres emerge, flail about, then sink into oblivion. Yet on warm weekends odd squads of revolutionaries still maneuver in the mountains to the south, studying guerrilla warfare.

Only months before the SLA emerged, members of a Berkeley radical commune called the Tribal Thumb Collective were arrested in a bank heist, and a mysterious, still-anonymous group called the August Seventh Guerrilla Movement was linked with several murders, bizarre communiqués, and a Marx Brothers caper in which a Yellow Cab was hijacked and the driver kidnapped, held for a while, then released with a demand that all San Francisco cabbies strike to force the release of radical convicts.

And although it emerged unannounced, the SLA did not drop into the Bay Area unattached and without pedigree. Most recruits had long histories of radical activism. The group as a whole can trace a spin-off association with Venceremos, a large Maoist organization and for several years the most influential voice in the Bay Left until it splintered in mid-1972. Several SLA people had been Venceremos prison organizers, liaison to radical inmate gangs, particularly the Black Guerrilla Family—one of the several major California prison gangs—an inmate revolutionary group founded by George Jackson, the brilliant, bitter black author killed in San Quentin on August 21, 1971. Venceremos was torn on several issues, prominent among them the classic revolutionary debate between a gunslinger faction leaning toward "armed propaganda" and terrorist violence and a party faction that wanted grass-roots organizing for a new communist party.

In what could be seen as a dress rehearsal for the SLA, another Venceremos splinter group shot its way into the headlines in October, 1972. They ambushed a prison convoy and freed convict Ronald Beaty, a Venceremos inmate organizer. Two cars with three armed men and a young woman cut off and captured the unmarked prison car carrying Beaty and two unarmed guards. They used bolt cutters to remove Beaty's chains, handcuffed the two correctional officers, then shot both at point-blank range.

This Bay Left is a unique environment. What passes here for realism and urbane left politics is a never-never land, a cloister of nihilism in which there is often little or no distinction between sense and nonsense. Yet a public becomes inured even to this. In the Bay Area the SLA appeared at first to be just another carnival under the big top—deadly and more flamboyant than most, but nothing to send shivers through the community.

Yet, even as the SLA claimed the national limelight, there was a palpable fear on the streets of San Francisco as the so-called Zebra Killers—allegedly a black Islamic kill cult called the Death Angels—stalked white victims at random, murdering fourteen and seriously wounding seven others before police made four arrests that seemed to stop the spree. The Zodiac Killer, an anonymous psychopath who has butchered at least six victims in the Bay Area over the past several years (he claims thirty-seven), wrote the San Francisco *Chronicle,* pointing out that the word *sla* is an old Nordic verb meaning "to kill." Such is the scale and proportion that sometimes passes for reality in what is undeniably one of the most beautiful and generally benign communities in the United States.

Out of this milieu the SLA was born—recruited from limbo, a splinter of a faction of the radical subculture. The SLA emerged on November 6, 1973, ambushing and murdering Dr. Marcus Foster, the school superintendent of Oakland. Foster, a charismatic black liberal with a huge personal following, was the first black superintendent in that ghetto city. The murder had a trademark flair—Foster was shot with cyanide-laced bullets—but it seemed senseless; inexplicable when the SLA proclaimed it a blow to the vitals of the fascist power structure. The Foster murder drew little national attention—and that merely as another bewildering assassination by some anonymous group of California crazies.

The year waned. There was no word from the SLA, but the promise lingered that more would be heard from them. The Symbionese had ambitious plans for 1974: the Year of the Soldier, they called it. The Foster investigation stalled for two months. Then, ten days into the new year, there was a break. An early-morning traffic stop erupted into a gunfight between a police officer and two young white men. They were captured and identified as Joseph Remiro, twenty-seven, and Russell Little, twenty-four—the SLA's Bo and Osceola. Ballistics linked Remiro's gun to the Foster murder after police found a stack of SLA leaflets in the van the men drove. Hours later an attempted arson led police to an SLA hideout, a house full of traceable clues that began to identify some of the faces behind the cobra.

But it was February before the SLA seized the national stage, kidnapping the nubile teenage heiress Patricia Campbell Hearst from the Berkeley apartment she shared with her fiancé. It was the Hearst case that made the SLA an international sensation. On February 4 nineteen-year-old Patty Hearst was dragged nearly naked from her apartment near UC Berkeley. Her abductors were described as a young white woman and two black men, all armed, who brutally beat her fiancé before fleeing, shooting up the neighborhood as they drove off.

The scenario was inspired. Patty Hearst was pretty and rich, young but ripe, naïve but not innocent. In taking her, the SLA loosed all the feelings aroused by a child kidnapping—and then, as a lingering afterthought, there were the titillating possibilities of sex. The case could hardly have been more volatile. The two blacks were soon tentatively identified as escaped convicts—DeFreeze, one; the other a former Venceremos prison leader, Thero Wheeler. Cellblock revolutionaries. As the rest of the gang was slowly identified, they resembled nothing so much as a band of renegade hippies: young white Berkeley dropouts, self-declared commie freaks, warpath feminists, determined lesbians, and culture-shocked Vietnam vets primed with guilt and Maoist religion. It was a political kidnapping, terrorism of a type and scale rare in the United States, an attack on the aristocrats instead of the usual bullet through the third-floor window of a police station. And the Hearsts were a most prominent family: long identified with conservative politics, heir to one of the great American fortunes, "rul-

ing class" status. Patty's father, Randolph Apperson Hearst, son
of the legendary tycoon William Randolph Hearst, was president
and editor of the San Francisco *Examiner* and chairman of the
board of directors of the Hearst Corporation, which controls the
Hearst media empire of newspapers, magazines, and broadcast
stations scattered across the country. His wife, Catherine, was herself both socially and politically prominent as an outspoken conservative on the University of California Board of Regents.

The Hearsts are the first family of California, Prussian blue
among the Milquetoast blue bloods. And it was an epic kidnapping. For two months the girl was held hostage under death
threat. The ransom negotiations, such as they were, were confused and incredibly difficult. From the beginning it was clear
there would be no simple transaction, no straightforward ransom;
this was to be more than a mere kidnapping—this was to be the
symbolic debasement of the imperial "ruling class." These were
criminals with designs on history. The SLA issued long rhetorical
communiqués, one after another, diatribes and vague dialectics
that filled page after page of the nation's daily newspapers. (The
first demand had been general publication of their political
screeds.) But it seemed that no two messages set the same price or
demanded the same terms. And always the demand was for a
"good-faith gesture"—a "preliminary ransom" in the form of millions of dollars' worth of food to be distributed to California's
poor. Never did the SLA set a final ransom price that would free
Patricia.

Randolph Hearst distributed $2 million in foodstuffs. The SLA
scorned that as mere "crumbs for the people" and demanded tri-
ple the amount—still only to prove good faith. Days slipped into
weeks of garbled debate, and time created its own tense dynamic.
Finally Hearst tried to force the issue. The Hearst Corporation
announced it would put up another $4 million for food distribu-
tion—but only if and when Patty was released unharmed. The
SLA balked and withdrew. For two weeks there was no further
word.

When the terrorists spoke next, the script had changed, and in
the most bewildering and dramatic way. The communiqué came
with a tape-recorded statement from Patricia Hearst herself, now
captive more than a month. Speaking with anger and an eerie certainty, she bitterly accused her family of being too miserly to buy
her freedom. She declared her conviction that the FBI was plotting to murder her to smear the righteous reputation of the SLA.
She said she was learning a lot in captivity.

There was widespread doubt the words were her own, willingly spoken. Speculation was rampant. For three weeks there was no word. Then, in quick succession, a memo that she would be freed—then the most startling message of all.

The victim had joined her kidnappers. It was a formal SLA communiqué with another recording: Patricia Hearst now declared she was the latest recruit for "the People's Army." The SLA had offered her liberty, she said, but "I have decided to stay and fight."

In accordance with SLA custom, she chose a "reborn name." She called herself Tania, after the nickname of Haidee Tamara Burke, an Argentine Communist who died with the guerrilla forces of Che Guevara in Bolivia.

Fraud? Conversion? Coercion? Brainwashing? What had happened? Virtually any opinion seemed viable. The most popular theory, tempting in its simplicity, packaged the whole scam as a setup: a phony kidnapping, the little brat plotting all the while for Daddy's loot. Popular but irrelevant; all fact and evidence weighed against it—and police, not for lack of trying, finally dismissed the possibility. The runner-up theory had Patty making the announcement under duress: a false conversion that would find the girl soon dead, a "martyr" for the new movement. With subsequent events, only the family clung to that long.

Two weeks after the Tania announcement Patty and Donald DeFreeze stalked into a bank in a quiet residential section of San Francisco. The Field Marshal, Tania, and three other SLA women warriors spread-eagled the customers, emptied cash drawers, and escaped, spraying bullets. Two old men walking into the bank were mercilessly shot down. Photos snapped by security cameras captured Tania Hearst poised in the middle of the bank lobby, an automatic rifle slung from her shoulder.

Victim into killer: Patty into Tania. Mirror play. Reflections or distortions? What was real and what was not? Incredibly, both Patty-as-victim and Patty-as-Tania appeared genuine; an incomparable coup of guerrilla theater, but the mystery overshadowed the spectacle. If the girl had been "converted," was there not a strange taint to the process? Patty's most intimate friends had been astounded. Cynics noted that the rich contribute many times their quota into the ranks of the radical cults. (An old joke on the Left claimed the Weather Underground required a credit check on parents before enlisting new recruits.) But it was not Tania's new politics, however bizarre—it was the nature of the change, the flip-flop, so quick and under such mysterious circumstances, that discredited Tania among thousands who typically had edged into radicalism painfully and slowly, in a prolonged process of confrontation and synthesis. She had not simply "changed her mind." In two months of isolated captivity a conventionally liberal teenage girl had been completely transformed, brought to the point where she was apparently willing to kill and smirk. So great a leap—and into such an aberrant state of mind—seemed more like a religious conversion than the tortuous process of personal reassessment it purported to be.

The kidnapping *had* been real. Suspicious police and private sleuths scoured the private life of Patricia Hearst—an oddly quiet, sheltered life easily documented and cross-checked—searching for some link, some association, some sympathy with the SLA's brand of politics. Her lover, her most constant companion, had been quizzed and grilled and even given a lie-detector test. Against all inclinations, the FBI, police, and finally even the Hearst family had to conclude that Patty had been converted—somehow. Clearly the key to understanding what had happened was more psychological than political. But, then, it had been more than politics that had brought all the recruits to the SLA, that put the desperate edge to their commitment.

What did Patricia Hearst find in the SLA? What did she escape? How was she led? How was she taught? It was an incredible mystery, a gothic romance: the ultimate dream of submission, surrender, death, and rebirth. The story of Tania was the stuff of fantasy—or perhaps the edge of nightmare. It was a story that quickly escaped the facts, a story that is even now perhaps more the domain of the novelist, poet, or satirist than those who merely chronicle. Yet fable mocks the merely mortal, and the human story behind the SLA begs perspective.

The image of the SLA was conjured more of shadow than of substance. Even as they so adeptly exploited the media, they were themselves captured within it; mythified yet diminished, celebrated even as they were reduced to spectacle. The disconcerting impression that these Symbionese were, individually, not so unlike many thousands who shared a similar experience and background was buried early in the cult hunt.

On May 17, 1974—a month after the bank robbery, three and a half months after the kidnapping—Cinque and five others, the greater part of the Revolution, were surrounded and trapped by police in a cottage in a black neighborhood of Los Angeles. Pressured by the intense hunt in San Francisco, the SLA had fled south to LA—but outside the Bay Area they had neither support nor credibility. The Los Angeles police picked up their trail from a series of clumsy mistakes, then tips from neighbors targeted the hideout. Encircled and hopelessly outgunned, the Symbionese refused to surrender and opened fire with automatic weapons when police lobbed tear gas. At the height of the shoot-out, the cottage caught fire. Inside, those who were not shot burned to death, but they kept fighting to the end, and their only surrender was to the flames.

Perhaps it could have ended no other way—perhaps they would have wished it no other way, for self-destruction was not a negligible factor in the SLA psyche—but the Symbionese, defiant in their pyre, claimed homage in death denied them in life. Alive, the Fifth Prophet had been an embarrassment among the revolutionary Left; safely dead, he became a martyr, at least a symbol. And to die with the grandeur of a televised coast-to-coast *auto-da-fé,* with the walls and blazing roof caving in, surrounded by 400 police officers, the LAPD SWAT teams in full battle dress, was something more than defeat.

It was a peculiarly American denouement. A predictable police response to the SLA rampage, perhaps, but it would have been an official atrocity in many other nations, could not have happened in many other U.S. cities, and was nonetheless demeaning for all congratulatory bleachers cheers that echoed across the land. The grim determination with which the Los Angeles police, having surrounded and secured the area, brushed aside alternatives and proceeded so methodically to exterminate this trapped and motley band of misfits set up its own reaction. What could have been a civilized finale to the SLA became instead the end of a cycle and the beginning of another.

Certain only after they had checked dental records to identify the six charred bodies, police seemed relieved to announce that Tania had not been among the victims. Patty Hearst and two others—William and Emily Harris, the SLA's Teko and Yolanda—had escaped. But now the context had changed. In the aftermath of Los Angeles there came a torrent of radical leftist sympathy and new respect for the SLA. Channels of escape and support previously unavailable now opened for the three refugees. The quasi network of the radical underground—a widespread and loose association of friends and comrades from the decade of resistance, a fringe of conventional society now so ubiquitous as to be virtually invisible—opened and swallowed the three.

Shortly after the shoot-out, from the Bay Area where they hid with newfound friends, there was another message from the survivors—a tirade of fury and mourning laced with hysteria, but that was the last message from what called itself the Malcolm X Combat Unit of the SLA. They were regrouping, they said; and Tania announced that Teko was now general . . . of an army of three. With that, the SLA faded into a long silence. Now, for the first time, connected with the underground, the Harrises and Patty Hearst were carted across the country on the modern equivalent of the old Underground Railroad that had hidden escaped slaves from the sheriff.

It would be a year and a half later before the law would catch up with them, nearly two before Patricia Hearst would go on trial to tell her story. Although the FBI launched its biggest manhunt since the days of Dillinger, it would be seven months before the authorities got their first solid lead, and that only a hideout abandoned five months before. In February, 1975, the FBI found a farmhouse in rural Pennsylvania where Teko, Yolanda, Tania, and several others had spent part of the summer before. The feds identified the people who had rented the farm; they were even able to track down people who had visited with the SLA at their country refuge, but the remnant SLA had slipped away, wending west, back to California, back to the front lines. A fingerprint found at the farm identified a fourth member of the peripatetic cadre, Wendy Yoshimura—a thirty-year-old Japanese-American woman, one of that small minority of American citizens born in the squalor of American concentration camps in California during World War II, a Berkeley radical who had been a fugitive on bomb charges since 1972.

Pennsylvania gave the cops a small packet of clues, but there was no trail, and none of the leads seemed particularly hopeful. There was a great howl in the media for results, and the FBI was under enormous pressure to deliver the elusive Tania, but for most of the year it was stymied. The public's fascination still kept every hint, every rumor, in the front pages: Tania was the prodigal daughter, albeit with a machine gun, and even in the near vacuum of fact, there was something about the story that gnawed a worry in most every home. The Hearsts had seemed the least likely of candidates to become the most pitied family in America, yet briefly they had been no less than that. And Randolph Hearst, rich and aristocratic, had come to represent a generation of middle-class parents at a loss before their children. (Yet then it seemed, the daughter measured against the father, the elder generation had not come out so badly. Perhaps it took something like the SLA to refurbish the much-maligned image of the bourgeois American daddy.)

The period between the departure of the SLA from their Pennsylvania garrison in September, 1974, and the arrests in September, 1975, came to be called "the lost year of the SLA," a phrase used by the prosecuting U.S. attorney in the Hearst trial. The Symbionese had returned to California, slipping again through the dragnet, but now they burrowed in. They recruited new allies, armed themselves again, even took up a new name. The SLA, bereft of black leadership, had become the New World Liberation Front. And through Northern California and in the Bay Area—in the fall of 1974 and through nearly the whole of the following year—there had been a long unsolved series of several dozen bombings claimed by the mysterious NWLF. Yet there was none of the daring, taunting, suicidal style of the first SLA—this "second team" was less pretentious, more conscious of their mortality, if not their fallibility. What plots, what dreams, now motivated the Symbionese? What ideals led to what results? Who led and who followed . . . and where? The first answers, such as they were, had to await the dramatic leap of hindsight that followed the bloodless capture of the four fugitives, and one other, by FBI agents on September 18, 1975, twenty-two months after the murder of Dr. Marcus Foster.

Then, from the stacks of evidence the SLA had again so helpfully collected in their two final hideouts, the cops began to list the recent unclaimed crimes of the SLA. There were the bombings—but there was much more. Now the FBI tied in two bank robberies in the Sacramento area—in one of which a woman customer, a churchwoman delivering the week's offerings for her pastor, had moved too quickly or not quickly enough and had been blown apart by a close-range shotgun blast. There was evidence of other plots, some half formed and discarded, some meticulously planned and timed for execution—diagrams of various banks; a murderous scheme for an apparent police massacre at a coffee shop frequented by cops; a detailed plan for a bloody assault on a county jail with automatic weapons.

There was still more, documents and diaries and notes and letters which began to describe the internal dynamic of the "lost year" in the underground. The first and original SLA had charged for doom with such a heady rush, defining their career with such concentrated fury, that they were able to carry un-resolved a whole slew of contradictions in their politics and prac-tice. In the SLA's second cycle the new people were but a little less isolated, barely less incestuous—and all the contradictions explod-ed in rivalries, self-doubt, and a chaotic clash of infallible dogmas.

This was the political context never mentioned at the Hearst tri-al. Whatever produced Tania from Patricia Hearst dropped her into the last weeks of the first SLA's frantic crusade; with the shoot-out she was pushed into an abyss of despair and defeat. And then, in the second cycle of the SLA, she was caught up in the evolution of a new self-critical perspective within the SLA—a per-spective informed first by common sense, then by self-respect, then codified as "revolutionary feminism." The very day of the ar-rests, Wendy Yoshimura, Patty's roommate and closest comrade at the end, wrote a friend, an old lover in prison:

> Ever since the group came together around those people a little over a year ago, we've had a very trying time. The security was a big factor but there was the sensationalized media play on those people affecting our heads, in effect making us unable to think clearly of them as people with strengths and weaknesses but as "the leaders" who knew *everything*. My experience during the summer made me realize that they (two [Bill and Emily Harris] in particular—not P.H. [Patty Hearst]) in fact are very different from me and personally I did not much like them. In spite of it I decided to stick with it because of their fierce dedication, my knowing that there were others waiting to work together, and I was under their spell.
>
> Unfortunately the other people were also spellbound into sub-missiveness and there began a mass of confusion touched up with fucked up interpersonal dynamics between some of the people.

The "second team" of the SLA came to involve at least twenty-two people. Perhaps a half dozen were just trying to avert a sec-ond LA massacre, but with the NWLF renaissance, the samaritans dropped out and the "combat cadre" shaped ranks. General Teko, Bill Harris, commanded by right of his inherited rank, and he led his dozen "front line fighters" in a minispree of crime be-fore his little army splintered.

> To show you how confusing it was, it began with—some ready to go underground (expecting it to get hot next week) to some pushing for jobs, staying cool and normal; some pushing for

totally isolated communal living to some demanding normal separate living arrangements; some demanding fucked up interpersonal relationships be dealt with, to some seeing it as totally unnecessary; some wanting to off pigs to some totally disagreeing. . . . We finally were able even to do a couple of actions . . . then it began to get obvious that the security that seemed to be existing was due to total repression, politically as well as personally.

"The group," she wrote, "has literally ceased to be a group." She, Patty Hearst, and several others had decided to split off, to go their own way separately, and they were bitterly conscious of how far astray they had been led. "On the surface it seems as though we all agree and believe in the same thing, but after working with [the Harrises], we've come to the realization that we do in fact disagree politically very drastically." She went on to condemn the SLA as sexist, racist ("And are they so racist that they must put Blacks on a pedestal to even consider them worthy?")—so politically limited they could only respect their own gunstock brand of politics; so guilt-ridden that they had to write off virtually the whole of white America as expendable racists. The vision, the ideal that motivated the SLA, she wrote, "is very different from what motivates me and the others. It's very different."

I wish that I could talk to you and tell you in every detail about everything. Some day I will. I tell you this is an experience I'll never forget! It was horrendous but at the same time I've learned a hell of a lot. Now I understand more clearly my political views, and, oh, the sense of myself I've gotten out of this ordeal—I wouldn't exchange it for anything! I think most of us have come out ahead. I hope you'll have the chance to meet P.H. She is incredible! She amazes me! I swear only the toughest could have come out of it as she did. What an ordeal she went through!! What an ordeal all of us went through!! I can write a book about it.

When an FBI agent burst through the back door of the San Francisco apartment shared by Wendy Yoshimura and Patty Hearst, the two women were seated at the kitchen table. On the table in front of them, apparently just written, was this letter. It was, perhaps, the most informed judgment that was delivered upon the SLA, a condemnation from former comrades—and it was a document that all but proclaimed the liberation of Patricia Hearst from the ghost of Tania.

Five months later, when the kidnap victim Patty went on trial for the crimes of the terrorist princess Tania, she seemed to have been again transfigured, transformed—and perhaps in the attempt to reconcile her three pasts (the prekidnap Patty, Tania, and Patricia the "revolutionary feminist") she had been. Wendy Yoshimura may have discovered herself in the maelstromlike final months of the SLA—but which self could Patty Hearst salvage? Perhaps it was only this story of that "lost year" that could have explained Patty Hearst—a story the jury never heard—but could a mere explanation justify her? Would it not convict her as well, if not for the first bank robbery, then for other, some more serious crimes? Five months after she had flashed the clenched-fist salute for *Newsweek*, after she had signed in as an "urban guerrilla" when booked in jail, a then-again transformed Ms. Hearst appeared before her federal court jury, demure and distraught, to claim she had been tortured and terrorized in two months of closet captivity, had joined the SLA only to stay alive, and had then slid into some perverted psychological reality that trapped her in role.

The jury had ample evidence that something strange had happened, that even the "torture" claim was not unfounded. But the high-priced legal talents the Hearst family arrayed before the court set up a defense—in the most literal sense—that simply didn't gibe with the defendant's plea of innocence. She begged the jury for sympathy and mercy, yet she refused to tell all— refused to answer, on the grounds of self-incrimination, any questions about a full year of her experience in the underground— and it was obvious that whatever the truth of her kidnap horror story, she had found love and loyalties in the underground as well.

The jury convicted her, the judge provisionally sentenced her to the maximum, thirty-five years (promising to review and lessen the sentence, taking into account her "cooperation" with police authorities, and the results of another analysis of her psyche by government psychiatrists), and then the enormous force of the legal system began methodically and righteously to grind away at those last loyalties.

It was perhaps a wonder that she had any will left to crush, but she did not withstand the pressure long. The day of her sentencing she began to talk, filling reel after tape-recorded reel with the story of her past in daily FBI interrogations that ceased only temporarily when her body failed her, a spontaneous lung collapse that required hospitalization and recuperation, then immediately began again.

If their *naga* had seven heads, the cobra caged had as many versions of its past, more even. Each of the Symbionese seized offered different stories, and the versions cut one against the other, depending on their faction. The stories came to contradict earlier versions by the same people. For those who tried to follow the jailhouse proclamations from the caged Revolution, past and present quickly blurred and truth became a Möbius-strip creation, a continuous double circle twisted in upon itself, the schematic diagram for human systems. But nearly all screamed betrayal as Patty began to talk.

Dr. Jolian West, one of the defense psychiatrists at the trial, the chairman of the Psychology Department of the University of California at Los Angeles, whose impassioned advocacy had seemed less than objective to many of the jurors, bitterly remarked that Patty in the hands of the law had fared little better than when first kidnapped by the SLA. "She's been confined, cross-examined, interrogated . . . held by hostile persons obviously intent on destroying her life, who don't care about her as a person, who are just using her, smashing her, for their own purposes.

"She's one of the least understood people I've ever encountered," he said. "Everybody's talking about an imaginary person. They don't know her. She doesn't know herself. I see her as very fragile, very much in danger in every way. I think she is one of the saddest evidences of the ubiquity of human cruelty that I've ever run across. And," he added, "if she teaches us anything, it is that the notion that it helps to be a child of the rich and powerful when you're facing the power of a group to be cruel, well, that's just one more fiction."

Perhaps from the very bottom, we can best see the top, the beginning. This is a story full of victims; some utterly innocent, some distinctly less than innocent—with more than a few difficult to categorize. Its confusions will haunt any history, perhaps because the story of Tania Hearst reflects some very human ambiguities, and the story of the Symbionese Liberation Army reverberates with some of the larger contradictions in the contemporary American reality. Perhaps sure answers to the many questions will come with time. More likely, all absolute certainty is locked in the past, despite any alleged "explanations" forthcoming from any of the survivors. Yet there is much that can be dredged from the past, the lessons of a story largely untold.

For all their righteous fury, the SLA never escaped the tinge of farce. They came to exemplify the baneful adolescence that had corrupted the political idealism of the American New Left. With the *naga* and their Fifth Prophet they established a standard beyond the pale—at a distance from even the Left terrorists—and by the measure of that standard they give a desperately sought perspective to a dim quadrant of the political spectrum.

There seemed a curious design to the career of the SLA that unwittingly illustrated all that had been simplistic, shallow, and self-centered in the rhetoric of the New Left. Domestic fascism was for them a pervasive and absolute reality; "military dictatorship" was our state of government. Such terms may have had a certain metaphorical validity in protest rhetoric, but the SLA took them as perversely literal. And there was something autistic about a group of men and women in their late twenties and early thirties referring to themselves as "enlightened youth"—as if they dared not relinquish the prerogatives of adolescence to the new generations that had come up behind them. Teenagers and the college generation saw the SLA as a comedy of manners. It seems America not only had endured the sixties, but had outgrown them.

Perhaps it was only the generation of their peers who could follow the convoluted patterns of the SLA thought, and then with references and benefit of a sheepish *déjà vu*. Veterans of the Movement are invariably proud of their experience; it reasserted a dimension of ethics into politics that had become pragmatic and jingoistic. Yet few are blind to its many failings: the anti-intellectualism, the youthful arrogance, and in the frustration of their isolation, the flirtation with totalitarianism.

The isolation of the New Left was as much a symptom as a cause. It was not that they attempted to engage the political process and failed—they passed it by, scorning process, demanding to be recognized because they were "right." The middle-class renegades who were the backbone of the Movement feared nothing so much as the conclusion that they must work among the middle class to effect change. Chic radicalism became charity; vicarious identification with the oppressed and the victims of American imperialism. To be a revolutionary became rumpled elitism. It meant that one did not have to compromise or mingle much with the body politic: the unclean, the middle class.

People of personality and complex life patterns were reduced to cyphers. Black family men were defined simply as latent revolutionaries; housewives were defined as nothing more than oppressed women. According to the formulas, all were ripe for sedition. But the formulas were too neat, too impersonal. The covenant of the New Left became imbued with a muddled lowercase marxism; but it was a romantic attachment, reflecting little study of Marx and virtually none of Lenin (the authoritarian architect of modern Communism). It was only in the years that followed the great failure and the dispersal of the Movement, in places like Berkeley, that Lenin's work became the bible of resistance.

But through the sixties to the present, in leaning so heavily on Marx and then on Lenin, young American radicals trapped themselves in the Marxist class analysis. Bourgeois themselves, they felt discredited by privilege. Virtually innocent of the experience of labor, they realized themselves incapable of being the proletariat "agent of change" their revolutionary formulas required. Perhaps it was as much caste guilt as the Marxist imperative, for the same sense of "classless status" pervaded the entire Movement.

The entire New Left period was characterized by a frenetic, desperate, and deadly serious search for the "revolutionary vanguard"—some new class, group, or subculture with the moral authority and class validity to "lead us." It was a fantastic Ferris wheel of theory that pushed one candidate group after another to the top of the Movement (and then, as mechanically as they had been elevated, dropped them down again). There were "students as workers" and "students and professionals"; welfare families, radical professionals, striking workers, nonunion labor, and prison inmates. They tried the blacks, the Chicanos, the Indians—and finally fragments of themselves: antiwar veterans, militant feminists, radical homosexuals.

Predictably, it was futile. Nothing discovered or created had the constancy or mass appeal to serve their purpose. Yet in the prisons, among the newly politicized convicts, there was a powerful connection made. Black-nationalist groups had just fought a struggle for racial equality in many state prisons. They were militant, organized, and reinforced by street kids fresh from the ghetto. Already the cellblocks, particularly in California, had produced the most articulate and bitter voices of black power: Cleaver, Newton, Malcolm X, and "the Comrade," George Jackson. And prisons had begun to mark a rise in political consciousness among young white inmates. Locked in the fascistic routine of prison life, inmates were desperate for beliefs which affirmed their individual purpose and identity. The culture of resistance offered dignity to men who had shared little.

And as the New Left withered, the search for the class agent of Armageddon became less ambitious, the potential for mass appeal became less important, and an unspoken priority of mutual reinforcement evolved that was particularly appropriate for the prisons. The Left supported and touted the radical prison movement, giving the convicts an urgently needed "outside connection." And the prison revolutionaries adopted and legitimized the "bourgeois" revolutionary Left.

The chemistry was predictable. Middle-class whites have always been infatuated with violent men, fascinated by black men, and where better to recruit the shock troops of the Revolution? Within the prison walls revolutionaries found a subculture as isolated as their own from daily concerns and responsibilities of family, job, etc.—isolated from all the petty realities that had so often undermined and diluted grand abstractions. Prisons became *the* issue of the Left, particularly in California, where prisons had been radicalized early. A dangerously indiscriminate credo evolved: that prison convicts, by virtue of their suffering alone, make the perfect revolutionary vanguard. And black convicts—"the most oppressed of the oppressed"—became the elite cadre.

2

Prison Politics: The Cellblock Connection

I

THE most heavily populated of the fifty united states, California gives home to nearly 10 percent of America. And in 1974 nearly one-sixth of all imprisoned Americans were jailed in the Golden State.

The California state prison system, although it holds only half of the state's incarcerated population,* has more prisoners than the U.S. federal prison system, more than most nations. Indeed, the California Department of Corrections (CDC) claims to be larger than any other unified prison system in the world—save only the national systems of China and the Soviet Union. In early 1969 the CDC inmate population reached a high of 29,000 men and women; it dropped below 20,000 briefly in 1970, then began again to rise steadily. By the time the SLA was born in 1973 the cell count had pushed again over 23,000. With 7,500 full-time employees, the CDC spends an annual budget of $140 million administering twelve security institutions, eighteen minimum-security camps, and fifty parole offices up and down the state.

Prisons are difficult to describe. Pictures of massive walls, steel bars, concrete cells, and electronic gates give an image of solidity and stability that blatantly misleads; reports of daily violence, ruthless inmates, sadistic guards, institutional racism, and the politicization of convicts are all half-truths, valid but still misleading. With a history of failed promise, the contemporary prison contains a whiplash crosscurrent of conflicting realities that confine and confound both prisoners and prison administrators. The prisons of California had been for several decades the American model for a progressive technocratic penal system—yet in the past

---

*County and city jails claim the rest. In California felony sentences of less than one year are served in county jails.

47

twenty years the changing facts of our society and its growing crisis of consensus have created a fundamental paradox in the prisons, and nowhere has it exploded more bitterly or violently than in the cellblocks of California.

Over the past fifteen years the California inmate population has become steadily younger, "blacker," and—partially because of reform programs to divert "nonaggressive" offenders into community-based parole and probation programs—more violent. Between 1961 and 1971 the proportion of male felons under twenty-five in the California prisons rose by about one-third (from 34 percent to 44 percent). In the same period the proportion of black inmates jumped by a full 50 percent (from 21 percent to 31 percent). The trend was nationwide. Black people make up about 12 percent of the U.S. population, but account for nearly 40 percent of all federal, state, and local prisoners.

The California prisons are 50 percent nonwhite—about 30 percent black and nearly 20 percent Chicano. "I guess it says something about our society," acknowledged CDC spokesman Phil Guthrie, "but prisons don't recruit. We're like a hotel that can't control the reservation desk."

The racial shift and the mid-sixties program to divert nonviolent convicts have profoundly changed the nature and function of the California prisons. By 1971 fewer than 10 percent of adults convicted of felonies in California were being sentenced to state prison. According to the CDC, over half its inmate population now stand convicted of homicide or violent crimes against individuals (robbery, forcible rape, aggravated assault). Over 80 percent of the convicts coming into the system now have to be placed in medium or maximum security. "In our jargon," explained Guthrie, "that means cell housing and an armed perimeter."

It was inevitable that a new political sensitivity take seed in the prisons; the younger convicts, so many from the *barrio* and the ghetto, were drawn from an increasingly polarized society. Yet the first maxim of the convict—*do your own time*—might have held sway longer had not a series of Orwellian reform measures (touted to liberals with sugared phrases, in the guise of the "rehabilitation" ethic) rapidly escalated the level of repression within the walls. In the tradition of the Gideon Bible, convicts were to be given counseling and "therapy"—and the wardens suddenly claimed authority to keep a man behind bars until he was properly penitent, until they were certain he was no longer "antisocial." It was an arcane twist to the American folk myth of the proud, tough convict; it denied privacy, courage, and self-respect. Perhaps it could only have happened in the echo of *Sputnik* and the growing shadow of Freud, but the new penology was marked with a frightening hubris.

The revisionist issue in contemporary American penology is whether prisons should continue to seek a prisoner's rehabilitation or content themselves to confine and punish—whether to try to "cure" the criminal habit, the "criminal personality," or instead accept the idea of prisons merely as detention, penalty. The issue is revealed more deeply in the general failure of prison "rehab" programs (albeit seldom realized, with constraints of budget, manpower, and initiative) and a belated modesty on the part of the psychiatric technocrats who have begun to acknowledge that their medical analogy—the idea that prison is like a hospital and, given sufficient time, criminals could be "cured"—was false and unfounded.

"We assumed we knew how to treat criminality, but we found out we don't know how," explained prison consultant Richard McGee, retired after twenty-three years as director of the California prisons. "The trap is we let people believe we know when a prisoner should be let go . . . we thought that the longer we had a prisoner, the better we could predict when he would be released with the probability that he would not commit crimes anymore." After years of test, McGee concluded, "nothing we have [statistically] shows we can do that prediction any better."

Rehabilitation? McGee believes a man "is sent to prison as a penalty, and that is the only, *only* reason." Government has a self-interest in educating and training convicts so they can "make it" on the outside, he said, but "if we want to educate him, rehabilitate him, teach him a trade, why, all those things can be done much better outside than they can in prison."

(The flip side of the rehabilitation issue is unlikely to be draconian measures or the abolition of prison work-skill education. For both liberal and conservative critics, the issue turns on the inflated expectations and arbitrary power coded into the rehabilitation ethic.) In California, as well as in several other states, the "cure" theory justified the *indeterminate sentence*—to many convicts perhaps the single most punishing and detestable aspect of the prison experience.

Under the indeterminate-sentence procedure, the law sentences a convict for an indefinite period (for example, one year to life), and then a state parole board annually reviews the convict's behavior, habits, and "attitude"—consulting with guards, administrators, and psychiatric therapists—to decide if a convict may be safely released. The law may provide for a minimum sentence, but usually it is only the whim and "clinical" judgment of the parole board that set the maximum. "It leaves you dangling in limbo, usually for years," said one bitter ex-con, "while they've got some sort of mythical brain meter on you."

In practice, the parole board, the wardens, and the psychiatrists are all hesitant to certify a convicted criminal "cured." Statistically, indeterminate sentences are considerably longer per crime than the average sentence handed down by judges. "Roughly twenty-four to forty months more time for the prisoner," noted McGee. Some men never get out. And angry politics is easily confused with criminal attitude.

Crime is not inherently political; convicts have traditionally been patriotic and politically conservative. Most criminals do not want to overthrow the system; they just want to step outside it, take a shortcut, then climb back in to enjoy a higher status. Virtually all convicts were jailed for criminal rather than for political acts, yet in the California state prisons today virtually all inmates are at least vaguely politicized. The psychiatric rehabilitation programs demanded that inmates adopt a "sick person" role (in contrast, the "bad" role was always more attractive, offering peer support as well as romance)—but the status of *political prisoner* offers more yet: pride, idealism, a rationalization for past behavior, sometimes the possibility of a new, heroic identity. "Rebirth."

The U.S. criminal codes make no reference to political motivation, but the concept of "political prisoners" is deeply rooted in European jurisprudence, in which the law has long specified that political offenders are to be treated less harshly than ordinary criminals. The concept of political prisoners is narrowly defined in common law in terms of the motive of the criminal—a "political crime" being a violation of law for "public" rather than distinctly "private" reasons, incidental to a bona fide struggle for political power—and while dictionaries and law texts have generally held to that standard, in common language the definition has been broadened and the focus shifted. The claim of sovereignty, the right of a government to determine what is or is not a violation of civil law, is fundamental to all systems of national law. But in the contest of ideologies, and amid conflicting claims of legitimacy, it has been this concept of sovereignty that has been challenged in the broader definitions of "political prisoner," definitions which turn on the "injustice" of the state's outlawing or compelling a given act under criminal sanctions. The challenge to sovereignty leaves the concept of the political prisoner rooted not in law but in a moral or ideological context—often framed in terms of civil liberties or "human rights"—but essentially subjective, contested by conflicting and self-justifying value schemes.

The concept of political prisoner now popular in American prisons was forged in the turmoil of the 1960s—molded first by black nationalism, then tempered with vague communism—and its expression was primarily an act of self-definition, part of the search for black identity in a nation of white law. It was less a label than an explanation, and it put aside the question of criminal motive. Whereas the political prisoner was traditionally defined by the politics of his act, the new definition was an explanation and justification of the prisoner in terms of the corrupt politics of the *society* which had pushed him to desperation and crime. The jailers told prisoners they were sick; the revolutionaries told them they were oppressed and argued that it was middle-class racist white America that was sick. Particularly among blacks—who had a heightened sensitivity and vivid documentation of racial injustice from the civil rights movement—the revolutionaries had a compelling argument.

It was in 1963–64 that—particularly among the Black Muslims, a fiercely isolationist black Islamic sect that described whites as "blue-eyed devils"—convicts began to define themselves as political prisoners, no matter what crime they had been convicted of. The Muslims used the term in both a religious and a political sense (their faith being a mingled philosophy), but the phrase was quickly adopted by other black nationalists. The moral structure of the theory—the transfer of guilt from the convict to the society—created an almost metaphysical option: an instant of realization at which one no longer had to deny or excuse past behavior, a moment of purity as at birth, at which a convict could reclaim moral virtue and character. It became a vehicle for enormous personal transformation.*

*The Muslims—Elijah Muhammad's Nation of Islam—recruited extensively in the U.S. prisons and gained considerable stature in the ghettos for their ability to convert tough black hoodlums and bring them back into the communities as proud, disciplined nationalists—impeccably dressed, unfailingly courteous. Malcolm X became their most famous ex-con minister, although he later split with the Muslims before he was murdered, in 1965, allegedly by Muslims.

Even among the nonreligious black nationalists the concept of rebirth, the potential of transformation, was crucial. Criminals who had been raping and mugging in the ghettos could—and did—redefine themselves with political idealism and moral dignity. The Watts ghetto riots of Los Angeles in 1965 had shaped a vision of black rage and frustration in America that went far beyond the civil rights movement in the Southern states, and the new generation of black spokesmen were more often ex-convicts than ministers. In California the black power movement split as it began to crest; a crisis of black nationalism left the Los Angeles-based United Slaves (US), organized by ex-con Ron Karenga, favoring "defensive isolation" of black America, and the Oakland-based Black Panther Party, again organized by ex-convicts, arguing for a multiracial socialist revolution.

But the concept of the black "political prisoners" had become crucial to black politics; the objective definition had become the key to subjective politics. The process of "understanding" and the practice of transformation came to seem entwined, and even as the concept became more secular, more distinctly revolutionary, the turning point of realization remained defined in fundamentalist religious terms: to be "reborn."

In the intense, claustrophobic, bitter, violent world within the walls, racial tensions flamed almost out of control through the late sixties and early seventies—race more than politics was and remains the prime factor in prison violence. The radicalization of the California convicts is still a half-truth. The big inmate gangs in the prisons—the Mexican Mafia, the New Family, the neo-Nazi Aryan Brotherhood—are criminal, not political. Yet the number of convicts, particularly black convicts, committed to political revolution—members of groups like the Black Guerrilla Family—has risen steadily. And because of the nature of their commitment, forged in such a racist and fascistic environment, it has been this relatively small number of men who have set the mood and defined the recent history of the California prisons.

As the racial and age selections of the California prisons shifted, as the convicts became more often poor, more often barely educated, the cellblocks became meaner, more violent places. The prison guards, largely lower-class whites, reacted to their tougher clients with the brutality that has always been the final police function—and they administered it with traditional racism.

Prisons had operated with a consensus between the jailed and the jailers, and when this crumbled, there was a daily struggle between control and chaos.

In the decade of the sixties there were 266 guards assaulted by inmates. In the first four years of the seventies there had already been 368 CDC guards assaulted by convicts. In the first five years of the 1960s there were 33 inmates and 1 guard murdered in California prisons. In the second half of the decade, 55 inmates and 1 guard. Between 1970 and 1973 there were 93 inmates and 11 guards murdered in the prisons.

As the Attica Commission, probing the gory 1971 uprising in New York's Attica state prison, concluded: "The inmate who refuses to regard himself only as a criminal simply could not relate in any meaningful constructive manner with a prison staff who could not regard him as anything else."

"Inside," explained one savvy California ex-con, "many guys turn to revolutionary political theory as the only explanation for what has happened in their personal experience, their race experience, their class experience." The model is the "urban guerrilla," the revolutionary terrorist. Criminals and convicts, "accustomed to living and moving around in a situation where anything said or done can mean life or death, living on the edge of violence," become cautious and self-disciplined. And "this training, this violent revolutionary potential, is sometimes seen as the only worthwhile thing about themselves. It's the only plus they can draw from their life experience. . . . Look what it did for George Jackson. Before he began writing about his politics, he was nothing. Not even a person."

In the revolutionary creed of the prisons, George Lester Jackson is the black Lazarus. Reborn in the cellblock tombs, Jackson's convict eloquence and passion for vengeance gave a bitter, bloody edge to the new prison consciousness. A man now myth; his very death—he was shot down in a suicidal rush to the wall after leading a savage uprising in San Quentin in which three guards and two white inmate "trustys" were butchered and murdered (three guards survived cut throats)—only seemed to secure his status among black Americans, invoking the enraged tradition of John Brown's raid and Nat Turner's slave uprising.*

Convicted as an accomplice in a 1960 gas-station holdup,

---

*John Brown's raid on the Virginia state arsenal at Harpers Ferry in 1859 was an attempt to arm a slave uprising. Unsuccessful, he was captured, tried, and executed, yet the Brown raid polarized public opinion on slavery and presaged the Civil War. Nat Turner—like Brown, a religious mystic—led the most bloody and the most savagely repressed American slave revolt, in Southampton County, Virginia, in the summer of 1831. He was also captured and hanged.

George Jackson was jailed at eighteen and spent the rest of his life in the California prisons. He studied Marx, Engels, Lenin, Trotsky, Fanon, Mao, grasped the subtleties and power of words and ideas; he became the major black leader among the political convicts, dire prophet of genocide or rebellion. It is difficult to credit one man among so many as a focal point, but certainly Jackson, in the two years before his death, instigated the most violent stage of the prison rebellion,* and since his death—on August 21, 1971—he has remained, through his books and others' memory, the inspiration and epitome of the black prison revolutionary. His two books, *Soledad Brother* and the posthumous *Blood in My Eye*, etch a history of black oppression and scream rebellion and retri-

---

*Soledad, CDC's "model" prison, was where the California convict rebellion evolved and erupted. In April, 1968, black prisoner Clarence Causey was murdered, knifed by Chicano inmates after he was inexplicably sent out—alone—to exercise among them in the usually segregated main yard. Black convicts believed "racist" guards had deliberately set up the kill situation. Eight months later black inmate William A. Powell died of an officially reported "heart attack" hours after guards had teargassed and clubbed him in his cell; convict hospital workers claimed a skull fracture had killed Powell.

Other violent incidents followed, but none compared with what occurred on January 13, 1970. After years of racially segregated exercise periods the policy was suddenly changed that day; seven blacks and eight whites were put together in the maximum-security-unit yard. A scuffle broke out, and gun-tower guard Opie G. Miller, a Texas-born white, instantly opened fire with a semiautomatic carbine. Three black inmates fell, fatally wounded. One was W. L. Nolen, a convict leader, avowed revolutionary, one of George Jackson's closest friends. Three nights later white guard John V. Mills was beaten senseless and hurled to his death from a third-floor tier in the maximum-security cellblock.

George Jackson, John Cluchette, and Fleeta Drumgo, who came to be called the Soledad Brothers, were charged with Mills' murder. Their case focused attention on conditions in California prisons, and joining in nationwide support of their defense were such disparate and feuding leftist organizations as the (U.S.) Communist Party, the Huey Newton faction of the Black Panther Party (which bestowed the rank of field marshal on Jackson), and the Eldridge Cleaver-oriented Black Liberation Army. On August 7, 1970, while the Soledad Brothers were being held in San Quentin awaiting trial, Jackson's seventeen-year-old brother, "man-child" Jonathan Jackson, seized a Marin County courtroom, freed and armed three black convicts, and took several hostages, who were to be held in exchange for the release of the Soledad Brothers. As they attempted to flee in a panel truck, CDC guards began shooting; young Jackson, two of the escaping convicts, and hostage Judge Harold J. Haley died in the exchange of fire. Angela Davis, a prominent black Communist romantically linked to George Jackson, was later tried and acquitted of charges that she had been part of the Marin courtroom plot. A year later Jackson led the bloody San Quentin uprising in which he died. Cluchette and Drumgo subsequently were found not guilty of the murder of the Soledad guard.

bution. His became the archetypal vision from the cellblocks, cramped and limited by a decade behind bars; extrapolating the gruesome fascistic reality of prison life to the outside world, measuring the nation by its cells.

It was a twisted vision, blind to the very different scale, the more political nature, of "the struggle" outside the walls—yet among convicts, among extremist young whites so alienated from middle America that they could identify only with the pain of the underclass and the victims of the *truly* fascist dictatorships U.S. democracy chose as allies, from Greece to Spain and around the world to Vietnam—it was a vision of flaming clarity. It was the voice of "Comrade George," the embittered politics of the cellblocks, that energized the SLA, that laid out and justified their maddened role.

II

The California Medical Facility at Vacaville is the medical and psychiatric treatment center for the California prison system. Looking like a cross between a military base and a state mental hospital, the prison sits back about a mile and a half from California's Interstate 80, amid apple orchards and onion fields in the Sacramento Valley. Vacaville is a small town, fifty-five miles north of San Francisco, precisely forty-one miles from Berkeley.

Encircled by two fifteen-foot fences (with a five-foot no-man's-land between them) and guard towers, the sleek stone building looks very modern, very clean, very cold. Yet CMF-Vacaville is a fairly comfortable medium-security prison (doors and gates between sections of the prison remain open, although they can be closed and locked electronically), and when they compare the discipline at other CDC security prisons, convicts consider Vacaville an "easy" hitch.

In 1972 Vacaville had an average population of 1,340: 299 on administrative assignment as "workers," the rest in a variety of treatment programs.* Group psychotherapy, the largest, had an average of 538 convicts in a year-long program using gestalt, encounter, and the more confronting "attack therapy." There were also separate programs for "effeminate" homosexuals (42 in-

*The CDC Guidance Center for Northern California, a separate isolated wing of the institution, is used for orientation and "diagnostic testing" of new inmates coming into CDC prisons. CMF statistics do not include guidance center inmates.

mates); medical cases (47); "psychotics in remission" (96); "psychiatric observation" (88); and a "stress assessment" program for (42) convicts with a history of disciplinary problems or violence, up for parole but requiring "further clinical evaluation." The Maximum Psychiatric Diagnostic Unit, the focus of a lot of critical attention on Vacaville, confines a small number of heavily drugged convicts (the average is 56) under cramped, maximum-security conditions.

Except for MPDU inmates—who range from the hallucinating insane to "hysterical uncontrollables" sent to Vacaville from the maximum-security prisons—and a few on treatment assignment, most CMF inmates are on good-behavior "voluntary" assignment. Disruptive convicts get kicked out, sent to other less pleasant prisons. The majority are in on their first conviction. At Vacaville the warden is a psychiatrist, and the institution often seems more hospital than prison. CMF inmates have privileges rare in the prisons: liberal visiting rights, phone privileges, more personal liberty. They can decorate their rooms, even have personal stereos. Vacaville assignment is sometimes used to reward prison "snitches" and is seldom available to tough or militant cons until they have "laid down their guns" and agreed to accept prison routine.

"It's the kind of place you can easily manipulate from," explained one experienced ex-con, "that's why so few old-timers get put there."

A black inmate group called the Black Cultural Association (BCA) was founded at Vacaville in 1968—to offer "alternatives to the Black Offender in his apathy and to [deal with] the unique problems that confront him inside the prisons." The BCA was not a particularly militant or radical organization; within the context of black militancy in the sixties, the program of social gatherings, self-help educational tutoring, and discussion groups was almost meek in tone. Prison authorities formally recognized the group in 1969 and—in response to widespread unrest in the prisons and public concern—approved a plan by which outsiders, women as well as men, could attend BCA meetings. There were several similar programs—part of a general push to provide more public access to the prisons.

The BCA was deeply into ritual ceremony—the culture of an African past. BCA meetings began with a clenched-fist salute to the flag of the Republic of New Africa and a Swahili chant. The group was heavily flavored with black nationalism; the 1972 program director was an outspoken member of United Slaves, Karenga's LA-based nationalists. Many BCA members had ceremonially cast off their American "slave names" and taken African "reborn" names, often laden with symbolism and romance. The weekly program was written half in English and half in Swahili, and among several subjects there were regular classes in Swahili.

A black UC Berkeley graduate student and teaching assistant, Colston Westbrook, became involved with the BCA in 1971 and was appointed outside coordinator, a quasi-official though unpaid position. Taking advantage of the outside-visitors policy, Westbrook imported volunteers to expand the BCA's educational program. He set up both remedial-elementary and more advanced classes in math, reading, and writing, brought in tutors, and organized courses in art, history, political science, black sociology, and African heritage.

The BCA peaked in the summer of 1972, when it was one of the most popular inmate programs at Vacaville, with some 130 inmates involved. The program then had thirty outside tutors and ten inmate tutors. The BCA usually met twice weekly: once for the educational tutoring program and again for a general meeting, a cultural program. "Usually about sixty inmates would show up," said one regular visitor, "and usually about fifteen outsiders, although sometimes it went as high as thirty." The outsiders included a scattering of whites, but the great majority of visitors were black. "Usually," he added with a chuckle, "there were a lot of women on the make, a lot of black sisters on the catch."

It was in March of 1972 that a young, lanky nineteen-year-old white named William Wolfe began attending BCA meetings through a prison-activities program sponsored by the UC Berkeley Afro-American Studies Department. "Willie was taking a class at Berkeley," explained his friend David Gunnell, "and he had to do a term-paper project. From someone he got the idea of going in as a visitor to the BCA and doing his project on them. Willie went up to Vacaville and came back and told me about it. He was excited about the BCA. He was going to go back and then I started going with him." Later "Willie the Wolfe," as Vacaville prisoners came to call him, brought in his buddy Russ Little; Little's girlfriend, Robyn Steiner; and a half-dozen other white Oakland radicals. The whites, said Westbrook, all seemed fascinated by the BCA's ritual trappings.

Although he had originally approved of Wolfe and his friends as tutors, Westbrook soon found himself under attack from them and their inmate friends. Westbrook simply was not sympathetic to Willie Wolfe's kind of revolution. At first it was just a whispering campaign. "Russ Little was the sneakiest little son of a bitch," remembers Westbrook. "There would be weeks when he wouldn't talk to me. And then he'd be whispering with an inmate and he'd stop—pointedly—whenever I came near." Westbrook dismisses Wolfe as "just an immature little kid."

Nevertheless, the political currents stirred by the young outsiders were to reshape the BCA, and Westbrook was powerless to avert it. The BCA was founded as an inmate self-help group, inmates trying to remake themselves—one prisoner told Westbrook, "You tell us what kind of nigger they want out there and we'll mass-produce the motherfucker!"—but in the end, the possibility of remaking society itself came to seem the more exciting, more hopeful goal.

Gunnell, Wolfe, Little, and several of the others were then living in a rambling house Gunnell had purchased in a multiracial neighborhood in north Oakland, a loosely organized commune nicknamed Peking House—both for the Berkeley sidewalk vending cart (of the same name) operated by Gunnell's Chinese girlfriend and as a tongue-in-cheek reference to the Maoist politics popular in the debates around the large rough-hewn coffee table in the living room. Gunnell, his girlfriend, Wolfe, Remiro, and Little were all closely associated with Venceremos,* a militant Chinese-oriented communist group that at the time held "vanguard" status in the Bay Left—although perhaps only Remiro had actually become a member.

Venceremos, for the previous two years, had been the largest, most activist radical group in northern California; a committed revolutionary group which was in the forefront of Bay Area demonstrations against the war in 1971, particularly around military research at Stanford University, then moved into a program of multifaceted agitation. The group sponsored scattered protests about police policy, as well as tenant, prison, and factory organizing. Venceremos described itself as a "disciplined fighting organization guided by Marxism-Leninism-Mao Tse-tung thought," and the Venceremos cadres seemed to relish their street-fighting clashes with police and their reputation as considerably less than gun-shy.†

---

*The name "Venceremos" came from Fidel Castro's rallying cry during the Cuban Revolution: *"Patria o muerte, venceremos!"* As literally translated: "Nation or death, we shall triumph!"

†Venceremos was founded in 1970 with the merger of a splinter group from the militant Chicano Brown Berets and a split faction from the Revolutionary Union (RU), which itself had been a "moderate" spin-off from the 1969 SDS

Venceremos was already beginning to factionalize bitterly in the spring of 1972—resentment over leadership style of key figures, debate about building a national base, and the perennial Maoist question of terrorism versus mass organizing were creating strains that a year later would force Venceremos into yet another shatter of splinter groups of the sort that has marked the disintegration of the New Left since the late sixties. Although the members were predominantly young and white, the Venceremos creed demanded that the white and student Left submit to dominant black and minority leadership, and chartered their own organization to guarantee a nonwhite elite. Rival leftists called it reverse racism, but Venceremos argued that a multiracial revolution could happen only with nonwhite leadership.

Venceremos published no membership rolls, and "fellow traveler" status became more popular as the internal debates raged, but most of the Peking House habitants were regularly involved in Venceremos-sponsored activities. At the Vacaville BCA the influx of this small group, Wolfe and his friends, had a noticeable impact on the whole tenor of the program over a period of months. They quickly established ties with inmates who considered themselves revolutionaries, and the BCA became a Venceremos liaison with the militant convicts.

The general meetings of the BCA were both social and educational affairs. Gathering in the prison library, the group often brought in guest speakers or developed an entertainment program for the week with poetry readings, music, sometimes a rented film. In the latter part of the meeting the group would break up into committees to work on various projects. There was a publication committee (which published a bimonthly magazine), pro-

---

schism. RU, Venceremos, and the several splinter groups, including the SLA, that evolved from Venceremos were all nominally "Maoist"—defined by a subtle philosophical distinction that, as illustrated by the evolution of one group to another, turns on a shifting balance from the class-conscious Marxism to the more pragmatic maxims of Mao (activist theory that stresses military practice and revolutionary strategy over class organizing).

Marxist class analysis applies awkwardly in the United States, if only because there is still enough social and economic mobility—cynics claim the illusion of mobility—so that Americans do not define themselves primarily by class. Yet, because Mao gave heed to Marx and Lenin, the "Maoist" issue lies in the balance of the two priorities: primarily in the question of whether the "working class" (or the more broadly defined "proletariat") is yet ready for armed struggle, sufficiently aware to support a revolution against capitalism in its interest.

Relative opinions on how soon the revolution can begin define the spectrum of Maoist organizations in the United States.

gram committees, a committee to oversee the education program, and an inmate-assistance group which briefed inmates scheduled for release and provided the necessities for black convicts in the MPDU segregation block.

As the BCA grew in numbers, there was more strife within the organization, more struggle for control. "There were at least two major splits within the group, two factions," explained a prison source. "First, there were the more militant Marxist-oriented inmates, who believed the group should be more active politically, and secondly, there were the black nationalists, who wanted to concentrate on black self-awareness and who resented the presence of the whites." A third block, as large as each of the other two, was uncommitted, more interested in the social aspects of the BCA.

As was happening throughout the politicized California prison system, the solace and hope offered by the revolutionary analysis took sway. Infiltration of vaguely radical groups has always been fairly easy for the disciplined cadres from more ideological leftist groups. The more dogmatic Left can offer a certainty to believers, a structured analysis to those who only hesitantly challenge the system. The Vacaville library, impossible to search, came to be commonly used as a drop for contraband smuggled in during BCA meetings—particularly popular books like *Blood in My Eye*, Taber's *The War of the Flea*, and Stalin's *Thesis on Lenin*.

"It wasn't that they came to control the BCA," explained Westbrook, "it was more that they gained influence, particularly with key people in the group. In any group that size you have maybe ten or fifteen men who are more respected than others and have a good deal of influence with the rest of the group. Those Maoists were just particularly good at identifying that sort of man and getting close to him."

Inmate groups at Vacaville were required to hold elections every six months. It is a way to keep inmate leadership fluid, an attempt to block convict leaders from getting a support base. The six-month term of the BCA officers ended in June, 1972, and the elections that month caused a stir among the BCA factions. The influence of the outsiders was not particularly felt yet. Wolfe, in his notebook, jotted down that one of the nominated inmates was a con named "DeFriese," misspelling the name, and underlined the name of Cecil Moody, another candidate, a black nationalist, who won the election.

Inside the prison Donald "Cinque" DeFreeze, serving a term of from five years to life for robbery and a shoot-out with police, was not considered "heavy" politically. Prison politics is particularly Byzantine, with shifting blocks supporting candidates for confusing reasons, often personal. Even inmates could not explain the power blocks in that BCA election. Reportedly under pressure from the black-nationalist inmates and outside black women visitors, Robert Jackson, the outgoing BCA chairman, took it upon himself to block DeFreeze's candidacy.

According to prison officials, Jackson declared DeFreeze ineligible for election because he had not attended as many meetings as required of potential officers by the BCA constitution. DeFreeze, furious, first complained to the administration that Jackson's ruling was an injustice. Jackson retaliated by putting out the word that DeFreeze was a "snitch," an informer. (Bringing the administration into convict affairs is unusual and impolitic.) The conflict simmered awhile, but the "snitch jacket" Jackson had put on DeFreeze effectively killed DeFreeze's chances for election.

"Right after the election it was apparent to everyone that the thing about DeFreeze being an informer wasn't true," explained one ex-inmate. "Everyone realized it had just been an election ploy by Bojack [Jackson] and the rumor stopped right there."

Either before or just after the election DeFreeze threatened to sue the BCA in the state courts, charging that the rule under which he was excluded from the election was illegal. He even went so far as to draw up a writ, but it was never filed. A compromise was worked out, with the intercession of Westbrook, and the BCA executive committee agreed to allow DeFreeze to set up his own discussion group, named Unisight. Although the original concept was that it would focus study on the black family, by the time it was organized it had taken up an additional task.

The BCA pamphlet introducing new inmates to the group described Unisight as "a community-prison information service that serves the interests of the black need for insight into what is happening around them and why. We have what we call our C.S.I.A. or the unit for Community-Situation-Information-Analysis, which is fully responsible for formulating and investigating and researching and giving analysis of all information and supplying the [outside black and prison communities] with its findings.

"The Unisight Committee is also responsible for the BCA family re-organization and education classes, which purpose it is to re-assimilate and re-educate the black male to the needs and responsibility of the black family and to give the black female an understanding of her past and the relationship between the black male and herself."

The Unisight "family re-organization" classes touched on DeFreeze's primary interest. His own experiences with women and marriage had been painful, and his vision of the great changes needed in the society focused as much on personal relationships as it did on the economic politics of the colonial black ghettos. "These classes will be formed of inmates and females of the community . . . [and] will work in the areas of understanding the fear-sex-insecurity in the black home, the black church, and community organizations [and] the psychological attitudes of the black male to female relationship and the male to male relationship of our men."

When the group was officially organized in late 1972, Wolfe and Little were already involved with Unisight.* Although he sat in on the "family re-organization" meetings—which drew about fifteen persons, ten inmates and five outsiders, including Westbrook's wife and sister—Wolfe's primary interest was the CSIA. Wolfe had already been active bringing in outside radical speakers to talk about racial problems and Oakland politics. During the summer Wolfe and DeFreeze had become friends. White Willie Wolfe was reportedly the first of BCA outsiders DeFreeze asked to join with Unisight.

The paranoia endemic to the radicals had found its counterpart in the fears of the Vacaville inmates. Westbrook was caught in the squeeze. He felt control of the BCA slipping away from him.

The position of outside coordinator is time-consuming and enervating. There is no financial reward, and those who take on the task and put themselves into it—as Westbrook did with zeal—do it as a labor of love. With the two regular weekly meetings, and often a third with the executive board, the BCA was a demanding hobby. Westbrook is a man who thrust himself into the renaissance of black culture, a boisterous, barrel-chested man with extensive knowledge of the history of the African homeland; but he is, as he says, a "bourgeois black." As the political wing of the BCA moved into ascendancy, the air of mystery, the rumors of a past with "heavy" connections that Westbrook had probably cultivated

*During this period, on October 23, 1972, Russ Little wrote a letter to the Adult Authority urging that convict DeFreeze be paroled. The letter was filed, but parole consideration was not possible at that time; DeFreeze by then had served only three years of a minimum five-year sentence.

himself were turned back on him. "People began to hear that Westbrook was an ex-CIA agent, a pig, you know," said an ex-inmate.

Westbrook's past offered a skeleton to fit the rumor. He had an academic background in linguistics, spoke Italian, French, German, Korean, and Japanese, and had served seven years in the military (three in the Army, four in the Air Force). In 1965, as a civilian, he went to Saigon and signed on with an American construction firm and spent five years "doing all sorts of things" in Vietnam and, later, Cambodia. Westbrook said he had not done any work for the CIA. It was not, however, the sort of accusation you can deny away.

In December, 1972, the executive board of the BCA voted to request Westbrook's resignation as outside coordinator. Prison officials said they understood the rejection to be the inmates' reaction to Westbrook's insistence on a more structured agenda focused on education. Westbrook, however, explains it was "the CIA shit and all that." He said he had been trying to reorient some of the classes, particularly the two political science classes, which "the Maoists" had "taken over."

In Westbrook's place the BCA took in a young Oakland man, Jim Mayfield, who described himself as a graduate student in ethnic studies at UC Berkeley, according to the prison superintendent. (Although Mayfield's wife, Norma, also active in the BCA, was an undergraduate in the Berkeley ethnic-studies program, Mayfield was not a student in the department. There is no graduate program for ethnic studies.) Mayfield, who served six months as BCA outside coordinator, was more in tune with the new direction of the group.

In the late fall there had been a sudden change in the tone of radical prison organizing, a shift reflecting imminent possibilities of "armed struggle." On October 6 a splinter group of longtime Venceremos members ambushed a prison convoy, shot two unarmed and helpless guards (killing one), and freed Venceremos convict organizer Ron Beaty, a thirty-five-year-old stickup artist. The exultation of the new mood primed a reaction of confusion and depression when Beaty was recaptured, in the company of a member of the Venceremos central committee, on December 12—free but two months. And the depression was honed with fury when Beaty, immediately after arrest, turned canary.

(Beaty told police all he knew—and considerably more than he knew. He later acknowledged in court that he had lied repeatedly to police, trying to make himself more valuable by bearing witness against as many key Venceremos leaders as he could remember. At one point he had even offered to have the FBI insert a tiny electronic radio transmitter beneath his skin, through surgery, so that he might "escape" and become a walking "bug" in the high councils of Venceremos. Beaty is an enormously untrustworthy witness, but the later versions of his story had a certain coherence. He had, he said, been freed specifically to set up an underground terrorist wing for Venceremos.

("The first thing we were going to do was set up a training camp wherein we could train small teams of volunteers from the Venceremos organization and from escaped prisoners that we assisted," Beaty told State Senate investigators. "We had planned on stopping CDC buses en route, commandeering them with weapons, freeing specific prisoners that we knew were being transferred, and attempting to recruit others on the spot with reward of their freedom there. We would have a training camp where we would take these people and train them in illegal activities: sabotage, assassination, kidnap, robbery. . . ." The "camp" would produce a ten-man terrorist squad every sixty to ninety days, trained for a specific assignment. Upon completing their "assignment" (for example, assassination), they would split into two five-man teams, move on to different cities, and set up their own "camps." "Over a period of a year . . . you can see how fast we intended to multiply," said Beaty.)

The day before Beaty was recaptured, on December 11, 1972, DeFreeze was routinely transferred from Vacaville to Soledad (the name means "loneliness" in Spanish) prison. When he left, another inmate, Thero Wheeler—a key Venceremos prison organizer—briefly took over Unisight. Wheeler was a well-known prison militant, a black revolutionary who had been the first convict member of Venceremos. Wheeler had just been transferred to Vacaville in November, but he was considered politically "heavy" because he had been in so long and because he was "tight with Venceremos."

Inmate friends of Wheeler remember his saying he knew Beaty. When Beaty turned state's evidence, "Thero said he just couldn't believe the guy had snitched. He thought he knew him and it just bummed him out."

(In Venceremos the sense of betrayal and bewilderment created by Beaty's turnabout cracked the seams of the organization. It was not guilt or failure that gutted Venceremos. The Beaty case—four

Venceremos members were convicted on murder charges, although charges were dropped against several others Beaty had implicated—prompted an internal debate, a reassessment of how prepared the nation was to accept out-front revolutionaries, and it was on this issue that Venceremos floundered.* The two separate Beaty-case trials illustrated the factions: In the first the Venceremos "defense committee," of which Emily Harris was a key member, tried to organize around the trial politically, attempting to convert the jury, to vindicate the defendants on the grounds of their politics. The second trial, much chastened, used a more classic "civil liberties" defense—arguing that Beaty was a police agent, a provocateur.)

Prison officials said Wheeler seemed much more political than DeFreeze. "DeFreeze was never a leader of men at Vacaville. Wheeler didn't have a big following, but he was persuasive and articulate and other inmates listened to him."

*H. Bruce Franklin, a white Stanford professor, the leading Venceremos luminary despite his black-dominance theory, led the 1970 Venceremos split from the Revolutionary Union, arguing that RU was too conservative in scheduling the revolution for 1985, demanding a shorter timetable: perhaps urban guerrilla war by 1973. Yet when the SLA and the Beaty-case commandos attempted to keep his revolution on schedule, Franklin and most of Venceremos were extremely critical of their impetuous "adventurism"—striking a stance remarkably similar to that of the RU leadership against Franklin in 1970, counseling patience and more "mass organizing."

The debate reflected more than unsynchronized chronometers. The dilemma of class-based Marxism in the "non-class-conscious" United States had prodded much of the New Left—the Black Panthers, RU, Venceremos—into redefining the "proletariat," on which the timing of the revolution was to depend. Marx's definition (the industrial working class) seemed too racist, too "middle class" in the American context. The popular revision in the New Left was to lop off the top of the salaried working class (as sellouts to middle-class values) and then to include the "underclass"—the unemployed and the *lumpenproletariat* Marx scorned as untrustworthy, frenzied, and anti-intellectual (the unemployables, the hopeless, jobless, criminals, welfare dependents, and the brooding anarchists among the counterculture "street people.")

A "Maoist revolutionary Left" was created from upper-middle-class recruits, involved through conscience, and the underclass—the fodder of the "political prisoner" syndrome—who saw only the desperate need that surrounded them. In the series of splits and schisms that followed, the operative dynamic was that an individual's perception of the social situation is dependent on *his* position, *his* "class" (a precept of Marx; axiomatic in sociology). Time and again the *lumpen* wing of a group would split from its more middle-class parent group—certain from *their* range of experience that the "proletariat"—the people—were ready, sufficiently desperate, sufficiently "conscious" to support armed uprising.

And so it was, in the birth of the SLA.

Wheeler was first convicted in 1962 of second-degree armed robbery in San Francisco, sentenced to one to life, and did five years before being paroled. A year later he was recalled on a return warrant and sent to Vacaville for two months' psychiatric treatment. His wife called the police because she was afraid he would hurt her. Temporarily held in the San Francisco county jail, Wheeler turned suicidal. He hurled himself against the walls, smashing his head. He knocked himself unconscious once, then picked himself up and charged the wall again. After treatment he was released, but two years later, in October, 1970, he was convicted of attacking a police officer in Los Angeles and was recommitted on another one-to-life sentence.

Wheeler, twenty-eight in January, 1973, married in Las Vegas in 1968. He had a young son. His younger brother, Fay, was in San Quentin prison, and his older brother, Bill, a police officer, has been a jailer in the San Francisco city prison for many years. "Thero," said Bill Wheeler, "has a hell of a mind. Pretty close to a genius."

In December, 1971, Wheeler escaped from Soledad prison, but was recaptured three days later. Faced with a trial on the charge, Wheeler told prison authorities he felt he was justified in trying to escape because he had been denied parole so many times—and he then set out to get some support from the "outside." He first contacted a black militant newspaper, which took up his cause and connected him with white radicals in Venceremos who formed the Thero Wheeler Defense Committee. He was convicted nonetheless and given an additional six months to five years and returned to Soledad. By this time he was known through the system as a prison-movement organizer and "jailhouse lawyer."

After turning down his parole request several times, the State Adult Authority (parole board) offered him a term in the stress program. He accepted and was transferred to Vacaville. The Stress Assessment Unit at Vacaville is designed to place "violent offenders" with a history of aggressive behavior in a test-tube situation where they will be subjected to clinically administered pressure to see if they are able to control themselves. Inmates are required to participate in the group confrontation sessions five days a week. On paper the SAU is voluntary. In fact, it becomes mandatory when the Adult Authority makes SAU a preparole condition. To refuse to enter the stress program "voluntarily" is to sign a long-term lease on a cell.

Wheeler was bitterly critical of the whole concept of guards with "brain meters" who were testing his "aggressiveness." In a letter to friends in Venceremos he described the SAU group confrontation sessions as designed "to take a little bit of your humanity— manhood—every day. Instead of helping, they try to destroy you. To see if you can take the B.S. If you can cry and bow and snivel, you are released (at least the people with these characteristics are the only ones I have seen leave in the three months I have been on the program). To remain human and a man is to be denied parole as being overly aggressive and a menace to society."

The BCA made a special effort to get the stress-program convicts involved because the inmates assigned to stress were largely convicts in for long stretches with some sort of reputation and influence in the system. But Wheeler did not need much convincing. He had thought the early BCA was a waste of time, but when the BCA became a Venceremos connection, he became a faithful regular.

When Venceremos became involved in the prison movement, the group organized a sophisticated system for interprison communication, using both "human pigeon" delivery and their own illicit mail network. Rules forbid inmates from writing to one another at different prisons, so a "drop" was set up in San Francisco to which a letter could be mailed, the message rewritten, and the letter sent along to a contact at the other institution. A young Venceremos couple, only two years out of Indiana, Bill and Emily Harris, had a key role in that operation. Bill Harris, using phony identification, opened a Berkeley post-office box in the name of Jonathan Mark Salamone, which was used as the drop. Friends said the Harrises spent long hours rewriting and forwarding inmates' letters.

In Oakland the Black Panther Party was running Bobby Seale for mayor. In April, 1973, Seale took second place—forcing a runoff with the incumbent—when he received 19 percent of the vote. Seale was defeated in the runoff, but he got 35 percent of the vote, certainly an impressive showing for one of the most fiery and outspoken black militants of the sixties. There must have been a good deal of "struggle" within the BCA analyzing those results and what the Panthers' entry into traditional politics meant. The "Maoist" line condemned the Oakland-based Panthers as "revisionist," over the split between Eldridge Cleaver and Huey Newton. Newton, when he got out of prison and assumed control of the Oakland Panthers in 1970, alienated the Cleaver faction and the Maoists, who argued for "armed struggle now," when he declared the Panthers' future role was to be in mass organization and political education rather than as the armed vanguard.

Another thrust of the radical Left into Oakland politics—one that drew considerable attention and reinforcement from the same radicals involved with the BCA—focused on the Oakland schools. They had been filled with dissension for years, as a young black population crowded into a system administered by whites. The 1970 appointment of Marcus Foster—a black man from Philadelphia—as superintendent of schools had quieted much of the grass-roots anger about education in the black community with an extensive program of community involvement. When Foster first came to Oakland, there was widespread fear in the black community that he was an "Oreo cookie," black on the outside, white on the inside. He had, after all, been hired by the white power structure. Three years of Foster had dissipated most of that feeling, except in the eyes of a small fringe group of outspoken Oakland leftists.

The primary voice for this perspective was a group called the Coalition to Save Our Schools. As an organization the coalition at one time had roots going back to a broadly based group affiliated with the black church structure in north and east Oakland, but since the appointment of Foster the group had atrophied until no one knew just whom it represented. Its spokespersons became the most antagonistic and distrustful critics of the Foster Administration and appeared to be heavily influenced by a couple of ex-student activists who had graduated from Berkeley to Oakland.

The circle of radicals who were connected with the BCA had strong personal and political ties to the coalition leaders, and at least three coalition activists, Vera Silverman, Bobbie Johnson, and Reese Erlich, a longtime Berkeley and Bay Area activist, were personally involved with the BCA. (Willie Wolfe, in turn, had briefly been active with the coalition.)

The school situation developed within the context of an emerging oppressive state. It is the classic nightmare of American radicals. On the one hand, there is the incipient police state readying its technological wonders for complete population control; on the other hand, there is the local bureaucrat taking small steps to control local problems. When Oakland issued student ID cards, the possibilities of the program were immediately extrapolated into the latest Orwellian scheme.

As the situation was presented to the BCA, and through the BCA to the whole Vacaville inmate community, the line between the expected and the proposed blurred, and little flourishes were added. Not only was Foster going to set up an ID program, in-

mates were told, he was going to have all the students fingerprint-
ed. By the summer of 1973, according to several prisoners, "everyone in Vacaville knew Foster as the Black Judas in Oakland."

"I talked with Thero Wheeler and other people in the BCA
about Foster as early as July," said one influential prison activist
later, "and it was really an emotional subject. Prisoners can handle
the oppression that comes down on them individually, but it's very
different for them to accept that their children are to be subjected
to similar kinds of oppression.

"The idea of identification cards is an emotional thing for prisoners. Inmates carry all sorts of ID cards, and everyone has to
have them with them at all times. Picture cards, you know, just
like they were talking about for the kids. There was this whole scenario built up around those cards. Police on campus and fingerprints. Everyone said, 'Jesus! Fingerprinting the kids! What do
they need fingerprints for?' Everyone was thinking about kids
smoking in the toilets and 'the Man' busting in and then all being
expelled. All the blacks here—and the whites who came up from
Oakland—were angry."

Writing for the Venceremos newspaper and being touted as
Venceremos convict cadre, Thero Wheeler had become something of a cause célèbre in the radical community, particularly in
the Palo Alto–Redwood City area south of San Francisco, a Venceremos stronghold.

The Wheeler Defense Committee organized letter-writing cam-
paigns on his behalf and—when CMF medics stalled on giving
him needed surgery for a serious intestinal inflammation—
launched a lawsuit and held rallies demanding better medical
care. But the furor raised by his friends worked against Wheeler
when it came to his parole. In the last period of the stress program
an inmate is given a minimum-security job assignment, but because of Wheeler's Venceremos connection, the Vacaville
superintendent was unwilling to place him in one. After his re-
classification was twice delayed, Wheeler was told by a friendly
guard that he was going to have a problem as long as he was associated with Venceremos. Wheeler, of course, sat right down and
wrote out a "letter of resignation." It sounded sincere. The prison
censors thought so, and perhaps the Venceremos Central Committee did, too, for it set up a special subcommittee to investigate
his criticisms.

But certainly Wheeler's Venceremos contacts, whom he saw
regularly at the BCA meetings, knew something more was going

on. When DeFreeze escaped from Soledad in March, 1973, Wheeler was the first inmate at Vacaville to learn of it, and he learned because he received a message from Venceremos through the BCA.

"When DeFreeze split," explained a knowledgeable source, "he made his way to Palo Alto, where he contacted someone in Venceremos. He asked for help, but they said they didn't know him and couldn't trust him. They gave him a place at which to recontact them in one week and then they got a message in to Wheeler, asking him if this guy had escaped and whether he was cool.

"Now, Wheeler didn't really know DeFreeze well, so he asked a few of the political inmates what they thought of the guy and they said that he had been pretty cool at Vacaville. Then he had some of his friends get through to an inmate clerk with access to records who was able to check and verify that DeFreeze had really escaped.

"When he had done this, and talked with people about DeFreeze, Thero sent word out that he sounded okay.

"The next week he was told DeFreeze had been picked up and was being helped."

By spring of 1973 there was serious talk of the revolution going on among a small group involved with the BCA. "Thero would talk of his idea of an organization that could be set up to use military force to compel immediate changes in the prison system," explained an inmate friend. "The first step was to somehow set up a group that would set righteous inmates free. Thero felt there would be no change in the prison structure until there was some sort of outside catalyst. He'd say, 'The Man will never give up power over anyone, particularly prisoners, on his own. It will have to be forced.'

"His idea was for something he called the 'People's Army.' He spent a lot of time thinking about it. It wasn't until the inmates began coming down on the guards, starting around 1970 at Soledad, that the prison-reform movement began to make any headway.* The shit started coming down and guards started getting killed and so the prison authorities started saying, 'Okay, back off, we'll make some changes.' They announced some changes, they an-

---

*The CDC parole board experimented with giving inmates on indeterminate sentences a "conditional" parole date in 1971. The board reverted to old policy abruptly in early 1972—and actually cut back on paroles—after parolees were involved in a series of spectacular crimes.

nounced that guys would start getting contingency parole dates, and the inmates backed off. But what no one realized was that they were only policy decisions. When things calmed down the AA [Adult Authority] went right back to the old system, straight indeterminate sentences with no contingency parole dates. Thero would talk about all this all the time.

"What we need, he'd say, is a people's army outside to force changes in the prison system. And then the changes in the prison system would release good men who could start organizing changes in the whole society. It could be the beginning of real change in the whole society. . . .

"In prison you have plenty of time to really think that sort of thing out and plan. Thero had a lot of it planned. At Vacaville he thought you could blow up the gun towers. It's logistically possible. He figured you could blow towers six, seven, and eight and you'd open up the whole side of the joint. He had it all figured. Along the back and side are orchards, and when they're in full bloom you could run right through them and none of the guards could spot you. You go through the orchards and slap a chunk of plastic explosive on each tower. You blow it and then you have vans waiting in the ball park, a quarter of a mile away, to pick up specific prisoners who have been notified in advance where to go. . . and then you'd have your army."

Wheeler even worked out graphs showing the structure of his army. He carefully diagrammed a command structure, support units, and a network of drops and liaisons that would connect each part of the organization. (Graphs of the proposed SLA structure were later found that were almost identical to those Wheeler had drawn up while in prison.)

"Thero's concept," said another inmate friend, "was that it would be an organization of cells. There would be one part of the organization that would act as a military combat unit and another that would be aboveground as the political arm, explaining the actions of the army and organizing around their actions.

"As Thero had it, there would be only one member of each cell who would know how to contact another cell. If that person was killed or busted, contact was lost. You cut it off and forgot it, and either it went off and regrouped on its own and began setting up another network of cells or it was just lost, period.

"Each cell was to have no more than three or four people, and they would be commanded by a war council of no more than nine."

In talking about possible "actions" his people's army could undertake, Wheeler, according to two sources, specifically mentioned kidnapping Patricia Hearst.

"I don't know how he knew she was living in Berkeley," said one convict source, "but I knew he started thinking about Hearst when he read *Blood in My Eye*." (George Jackson's second book of prison writings, *Blood in My Eye*, the New Testament for prison revolutionaries, lists Wallace, Maddox, Hearst, and Hunt as foremost spokesmen for "right-wing traditionalist political ideals.") "Thero mentioned Patricia Hearst by name. He had thought out the whole idea of political kidnapping. He figured it would be no good to rip off the head, because that's the only person who can control the purse strings. So you don't go for someone like Randolph Hearst. He said what you wanted strategically was someone close, but not the main man." Wheeler also mentioned other targets, giving as examples the Vanderbilts, Du Ponts, and Rockefellers, but only with the Hearsts did he have a specific target in mind.

"He said the money would be used to finance the army," continued Wheeler's friend, "to feed and supply the army, but Thero also mentioned the idea of forcing a food handout. He thought that it would be a good idea because you are not asking for the money; you're not asking anything for yourself. It would be coming at them from a direction they just wouldn't expect, and it would make it clear that whatever the army did, it would be for the people, not themselves."

In June, 1973, at a BCA banquet, a prison official remembers Wheeler talking to Bill and Emily Harris, Willie Wolfe, and a diminutive Berkeley lady, Nancy Ling Perry. Nancy Perry had applied for permission to attend BCA meetings, but had been denied because she was already visiting several inmates individually. Wolfe had not been attending the BCA regularly since early spring—around the time DeFreeze escaped—but perhaps that was because he had begun visiting a former Vacaville BCA member, forty-eight-year-old Clifford Jefferson, who had been transferred to Folsom prison the previous December after a wild mop-swinging melee with guards.

On November 4, 1972, Jefferson's homosexual lover—his "punk," in inmate slang—attacked a guard on the first floor of Jenner Unit when the guard, one of the friendlier officers, cursed him out for disobeying an order. The convict was Al Taylor, who had been exchanging romantic letters with Nancy Ling Perry.

"Taylor slugged the guard and the guard went down blowing his whistle," said an inmate witness, "and two guards dragged the kid off to the hole.

"Then in comes Jeff, and he's got to do something 'cause it's his boy, right? So Jeff grabs the lid off this garbage can and slams the guard the kid had hit who's just back on his feet. By then guard whistles are blowing all over, and every inmate is running to see what's happening. It was a real scene. Jeff got out into a corridor with some space and grabs this mop, and he's swinging it round and round, saying he's going to knock the head off any guard who comes at him. One guard, who's got this macho thing, tries to do his thing and gets a broken wrist.

"By then, you know, the inmates are really piling up. There's like two hundred cons there. Then these two guard lieutenants get there and they're saying, 'Now, Jeff, Jeff. Let's reason this out like adults . . .' And they talked him into putting down the mop and walking down to the hole. He'd put on his show, you know, which is probably all he wanted to do in the first place."

Death Row Jeff, as Jefferson is known throughout the prison system, is one of the elder soldiers in the convict ranks in California. Jefferson has been in prison since 1948, when he was convicted for second-degree murder in Bakersfield. While in prison he has been convicted of murdering another convict, accused several times of attacking inmates, convicted of wounding one prisoner with a knife. He spent three years on Death Row awaiting execution (the sentence was commuted), spent five years in the punitive "holes,"—the solitary-confinement dungeons—of San Quentin and Folsom, and is currently serving two concurrent terms of "life without possibility of parole."

With his seniority and reputation for being among the "baddest," Jefferson is one of the "heaviest," most influential convicts in the system. When he was sent to prison, convicts were still being flogged and chained and hung from walls for punishment at Folsom. Through the sixties when prisons were going through their own civil rights battles (actually closer to racial war as blacks refused segregation in prison facilities), Jefferson was a leader among the black convicts. The race wars, the work strikes, the inmate protests—Jefferson had been through it all. And in the raw, racist, and perverse culture within the prisons created with the taxpayers' money, Jeff was a survivor.

"I know what they say about him being so bad and mean," said Corrections Director Raymond Procunier—who personally struck the deal to transfer Jefferson to Vacaville if Jeff, politics aside, would "put up his guns" and stay in line. "But over the years he's always kept his integrity with me personally."

In recent years Jefferson had moved from survival to hope with the awareness of the new prison politics, the heritage of Jackson and all those long wars inside. For Willie Wolfe, for the dream of the SLA, men like Jefferson were important. Death Row Jeff was important.

The SLA wanted Wheeler in its army as well. By August, 1973, Thero, now bleeding internally and still without surgery, had decided to escape. (According to the prison superintendent, the Adult Authority had already set his parole date, but because he was in the stress program had decided not to tell him.) After Wheeler's resignation from Venceremos he was assigned ninety days in the prison book bindery, then reclassified as a minimum-security prisoner. He had already arranged for a "loose job," and was assigned the tasks of cutting the lawn around the gun towers.

"It's the sort of job that looks 'tight,' " said one inmate. "I mean, you're right under the guards, but actually it's one of the loosest. The guards just don't expect a guy who's pushing a lawn mower around their tower to just keep pushing. They don't watch him close.

"So Thero comes out that day and he's 'Bonneroo'—that's what we call it. Everything he's wearing, you know, is fully starched, with pressed pants. 'Bonneroo!' And so right away everyone knows Thero is going to split. It's kind of a thing, you know, if you're going to try it, you go as high class as you can."

The end-of-shift whistle blew at 11:15 A.M. of August 2.

But Thero Wheeler had quit work fifteen minutes early.

3

Emily (Schwartz) Harris .... *Yolanda*

William Taylor Harris .... *General Teko*

Angela (DeAngelis) Atwood .... *General Gelina,*

d. May 17, 1974

A FEW days before Patricia Hearst was kidnapped, Mr. and Mrs. Frederick Schwartz of Clarendon Hills, Illinois, received a letter from Berkeley, a message from their twenty-seven-year-old daughter Emily which deeply worried and upset them. Only the week before they had gotten a more typical note: "We're both fine and so fed up with work we decided to go on a vacation . . . a cabin in the Sierras . . . hope we've not lost our knack for making fires. . . ." But General Teko and Yolanda were already in hiding—and hunted; and not in the Sierras.

DEAR MOM AND DAD,

This letter is long overdue and because of that I am sure it will be somewhat difficult to understand. I'm a very different person than you have known in the past, and I have not communicated that difference to you very honestly. I see suffering all around me—people in prison, people working at unfulfilling jobs that earn just enough money to keep them barely alive; people being murdered on the streets just because they are black and standing on a corner. These are realities. These are realities which exist and which you have chosen to ignore in your life. These realities exist because some people insist on being rich regardless of whether they must utilize the blood and sweat of others. I do not see my freedom and happiness as something that comes when I grab as much as I can from someone else. I will never be free until there are no more rich people and no more poor people. This means that I can no longer relate to the aspirations you have for creating a comfortable life for yourselves because they ignore the tortured lives that others lead in an attempt to survive. Just because you appear successful does not mean you are smarter than another person—instead it means you are white, well-educated and willing to ignore reality in order so that you may do better than others at the expense of others.

I've learned a lot from Bill, from other people here in Oakland, and from people in prison and they in turn have learned a lot from me. One person in particular—a beautiful black man—has conveyed to me the torture of being black in this country and of being poor. He has dedicated his life to eliminating the conditions that oppose people's being able to lead satisfying lives and to replacing these with conditions that make people truly free—so part of the process is to destroy and part is to build.

Bill and I have quit our jobs and have moved with people who are serious about destroying and building. I feel better than I have ever felt because I see myself as a part of a meaningful process that involves more than just myself as an individual—it involves and will affect the way a lot of people live. If I were alone in aspiring to do this I would have little or no effect. But the fact is that more people are dissatisfied than are satisfied so out of their dissatisfaction grows success for the changes that are necessary and inevitable. Bill and I have changed our relationship so that it no longer confines us, and I am enjoying relationships with other men. I am in love with the black man I referred to earlier and that love is very beautiful and fulfilling. I feel like under these circumstances close communication with you all will only be destructive to us all.

I would like to continue to develop in some of the directions I have described here, and I know that much of this will be alien to you. This leaves us little to say to each other. I am not the daughter that you know from the past and that I have pretended to be in the more recent couple of years. I cannot continue to communicate the things I know you want to hear. I love you because of the independence you gave me in the past to get to the point where I am now, but I realize we are headed in totally opposite directions and we can never hope to turn those around and go backwards to a point in the past where we had something in common. I will keep in touch every once in a while but not regularly. Trust that I am well and filled with many aspirations for the future. I do not do this out of any hard feelings, only practical common sense based on no hopes for any real sharing to take place through our communications. None of the changes in me are sudden, but all are part of a process of realization that began years ago. I am a very strong person who is finally realizing their potential. It is truly a wonderful feeling. I only wish I could share it with you but I would be naïve if I thought there was hope for that. One or the other of us would have to negate everything that we lived for. My love for you has not changed, it's just that my love for other people and purposes has far exceeded it. Goodbye to the past, forward with the future.

EMILY

P.S. I don't know how you will react to this but I feel you will be upset. Please don't try to project these feelings on me or to interfere in any way. I will write sporadically to let you know that I am well.

The day after the kidnapping, Fred Schwartz went to the FBI with this letter; worried, "wanting to help Emily." Chicago newspapers later reported that Schwartz was the informer whose tip tied the Harrises to the SLA; and Schwartz's reply was bitter and defensive. (Oakland police had raided the Harris apartment a week before Schwartz received the letter.) But better than anyone, Emily would understand her father's going to the FBI out of concern for her.

Among the SLA, Emily was probably most like Patricia Hearst in temperament, manners, and background. Ironically, after Patty became Tania, there was a sense—strangely common among friends of both women—that they might well have become friends however they met. Even Emily's Oakland apartment was an environment Patty would have liked: painted oyster white, full of plants, tasteful, warm, and always impeccably neat and clean. On the walls there were several political posters—which would not have been in a Hearst apartment—celebrations of Mao and China.

Like Patricia, Emily Harris as a girl had always been close to her father, an engineer active in local politics in the prosperous Chicago suburb where she grew up. Even while attending Indiana University, caught up in the changing values of her generation; even after she had taken up with Bill, a rumpled ex-Marine who taught her a political language with which to express her disquiet, Emily had kept peace on the home front.

"I went with them to the airport one time to meet Mr. Schwartz," remembers a college friend. "He had flown into Bloomington in his private plane to have lunch with his daughter. Bill just laughed at him afterwards; Bill hated his guts." It must have been awkward accommodating both father and lover.

Emily's taste always seemed to lean toward funky guys, men with wit, humor, and energy to match her own. No one who really knew Emily thought of her as weak; a "listener," but not a follower. Emily's intelligence, looks, and exuberance had always been status. Even in high school she was "pep chairman" and a straight-A student. "She was always the smartest kid in class," remarked an early friend, "and teacher's pet in the sixth grade. But everyone liked her." Friends at IU, from which she graduated with a BA in English, thought she and Bill were "an odd couple." Emily was the glossy girl, always stylishly dressed, social chairperson of Chi Omega, one of the elite who set the pace of the campus social life. She met Bill in 1968, on a blind date, after he returned to IU after being discharged from the Marines. She was twenty-one; he was two years older.

Bloomington is a small southern Indiana town totally dominated by the huge IU campus. Like most rural college towns, it is parochial, quiet. College as womb. But it was in Bloomington that both Bill and Emily confronted and were molded by the dissent of the sixties. Bill, first at IU in 1963, rode them all—the civil rights movement, the university *in loco parentis*, the antiwar movement. Emily picked up with the antiwar movement and felt herself reborn in the feminist surge.

The Marines caught Bill Harris on the bounce—he had tried college, and neither had been ready for the other. Bill was a big sports fan and had grown up making the forty-five-minute drive south to Bloomington from Indianapolis to catch home games. There was never any question that he would go to IU; but Bill's idea of college had more to do with the bleachers than with study hall, and the confusion was telling in his grades. He squeaked through two years, for a time on academic probation, before his father refused to continue paying his tuition until he got serious about school. Brash and outspoken, Bill had a full-grin boyish charm and a real sense of humor. "There was a group of people who didn't like him and a whole lot of people who liked him a hell of a lot," said a classmate. Those first IU years were heavy on beer and Bob Dylan and the hip insouciant ennui, but Bill developed a particular concern over what was then happening in the South. "Bill always had a cause," one friend of that time said. "When he got back from the Marines it was the war, but before that it was the colored people." But Bill's best friend stressed "it was something he had gone deeply into, something personal with him." Racism was not an abstract issue in Indiana; the national headquarters of the Ku Klux Klan was just outside Bloomington.

Bounced from school, Bill drifted West and spent the summer and fall of 1965 in San Francisco. The first gusts of the youth revolt were to be seen nearby—the Free Speech Movement and antiwar protest had already shaken Berkeley—but Bill, said his San

Francisco roommate, "seemed oblivious to it all." In the late fall he returned to Indiana and with a close friend, Larry Leach, enlisted in the Marines. "We were both under the impression the Marines were tough physically, and we were both kind of into that at the time," remembers Leach, now a Denver legal-assistance attorney. "And Bill's dad thought it was a good idea. That was really important to him right then." And there was the cultural tradition that a young white middle-class man who had bungled his opportunities should be scalped and uniformed, sworn to the flag, and given a dose of that military discipline to help him "find himself." Bill's mother said she thought it was "a wise move for someone at loose ends with his life."

In the Marines, however, Harris untied a few more knots, unraveled a few more loose ends. He spent two years in uniform, six months in Vietnam. Just before he went overseas, his father died of a heart attack. "He took it hard," said Leach. "His dad had been saying he would never amount to anything," remembered another close friend, "and when he died, it robbed Bill of the one person he wanted to prove himself to." In Vietnam, Harris was assigned to the Marine headquarters at Da Nang. He never saw combat. In a game of touch football he tore a leg ligament—in civilian life he would collect a $28 monthly disability payment—and was shipped out to Okinawa. After he got out of the hospital, he was reassigned to staff the officers' club there.

In the heat of argument Bill was not above exaggerating his Vietnam experience, but to his friends he described a military career in safe, soft jobs. "He used to tell me that when he got to Vietnam he bought this leather bag, cleaned and oiled his rifle, and put it in the bag under his bunk. And he never fired it! Not even for practice. And when there was an inspection, he'd pull out this clean rifle and the officer would look at it and say, 'You men ought to keep your rifles as clean as Harris here.' "

But his stay in Vietnam was enough to sour him bitterly on the war. His letters home expressed his disillusionment, his dawning awareness that Americans had replaced the French in a colonial war. On Okinawa, Bill had to face what many Marines called the "second war." On U.S. military bases all over the world, racial tension was high in 1966–67; but on the island a tense, often violent situation was exacerbated by Okinawans' race hate against blacks. The islanders would attack black Americans on the street, so black Marines largely stayed on base. "The closed setting brought out the worst from both blacks and whites," said a Marine who served with Harris. "It was a real snake pit. Whites wouldn't go to the enlisted club at night, and both blacks and whites walked around only in groups. Bill was there a long time and saw a lot of that."

Later, at Camp Lejeune, North Carolina, where both Harris and Leach spent the last months of their hitches, they found the infection had spread. Leach recalls a painful scene when Bill spotted a Vietnam buddy, a black Marine named Bob Green, walking with two other blacks. Harris went running down the street shouting and waving, but Green was cool and standoffish to them.

"Finally he took us aside," remembered Leach, "and said, 'I really dig you two guys, you're really great, but I've made a commitment and I'm not going to be able to associate with whites.' It really deflated Bill. In Nam they had really been close."

While still a Marine, Harris went to Washington for the 1967 March on the Pentagon—defying general orders at Lejeune. But only after returning to IU did Harris become really vocal against the war. Filled with his experiences, he was bewildered to return only to run headlong into old college drinking values. "A lot of his old friends just hadn't changed," said Leach, who also returned to IU. "They seemed to him to be politically naïve and incredibly ignorant of the social realities. They couldn't understand him and he couldn't comprehend how they could be so conservative and unaware." Bill joined Vietnam Veterans Against the War and became one of the core of campus antiwar activists. Not a leader; often only on the sidelines; but always there. And there he found Emily.

"It was very easy to get down on Bill," said a close friend of Emily, "he was a button man, a slogan man. You'd see him and you'd immediately like him—he had this infectious smile and he was a hell of a nice guy. But away from him, you could really get down on him. He was something of a screamer."

Bill was a theater major, and it was through the Drama Department that the Harrises met Gary Atwood and his girlfriend, Angela DeAngelis. Bill, Gary, and "Angel"—most friends knew only the nickname—were all aspiring actors, part of the backstage clique. They all acted in campus productions, but Gary was the only one considered to have real talent. Bill and Angel eventually opted for teacher training rather than risk the professional stage.

The two couples became part of a small group of friends who got heavily into LSD. "For over a year there were about ten of us tripping a lot," said classmate Charlie Hall. "I mean all the time; every weekend and sometimes just after work during the summer." For a while, too, said Hall, they were into "the whole Ken

Kesey, Merry Pranksters bit"—an exploration of "freaking" for public effect. Once, after taking acid, Bill went out hitchhiking on a truck route. "He had his hair long and frizzy, with this red bandana around his head, and man," said Hall, "he just looked really *strange!* What he was doing was standing out there just to antagonize the red-neck truck drivers. He'd wait for one to stop and scream at him—which several did—and then he'd turn to me and say, '*See,* I told you they're weird!' "

Acid was a big thing in 1969 and 1970, said Charlie, but then everyone just lost interest in it. "Gary and Angel stayed with it longer than the rest of us, particularly Gary." They seemed to need it least; Angel had always been nervous, he said, but Gary was just *electric,* "superanxious."

Exuberant, flamboyant Angel—she signed it with a halo over the g—met Gary playing Perdita opposite him in *The Winter's Tale.* It was the perfect part: "Not too heavy, and she was gorgeous," said another actress. Gary was the IU acting sensation. "The first student considered capable of Hamlet," said one theater professor. He was so skittish that when they first met, he jumped when Angel touched him. "It caught her mother thing," said a close friend. "He was a challenge and she went after him."

They courted in a tempest—the week before the marriage Angel wasn't sure Gary would go through with it—and wed in an extravagant production. They took over a farm, roasted a pig, hosted a revel of wine and skinny-dipping, and married in Elizabethan costumes. But Angela's father refused to attend the wedding.

Angel had been a devout Catholic before IU. She grew up in North Haledon, New Jersey, a small all-white town just outside the ghetto shambles of Newark. Her father was the local Teamsters boss, business manager for Local 999, and their home had the first swimming pool in the neighborhood. Her mother had died when she was fourteen, and as the eldest of three, Angel assumed the role. Bright and popular, she was on the executive board of the local Catholic Youth Organization, captain of the high school cheerleaders, and still earned honor grades. But when she got away from home, she never wanted to return. In her four years at IU she visited home only four or five times.

A story Angela told several friends was that shortly after her mother's funeral in 1963 *Life* magazine published an article on organized crime in the East; reading it and looking at the photos, she was stunned to recognize many of her father's friends whom she had met at the wake. It became an ever more intricate relationship. While she was at IU, her father provided her with a generous allowance. She had her own new car on campus and—always with plenty of pocket money—an almost wanton urge to buy presents for her friends. One couple she baby-sat for said she used to embarrass them by bringing bags of expensive toys for their children. But the allowance was cut off when she married Gary. Gary Atwood was "to the left, way to the left," said her father. Politics became another barrier between father and daughter.

Angel was politicized by Gary. Awed by his intelligence, his poetry, his acting, she accepted him as intellectual mentor. At IU they were very domestic. "She was an Italian mama," said one friend, "always in the kitchen."

"Her greatest ambition," said her best friend back in New Jersey, "was to play Peter Pan," and at IU she worked almost desperately (but unsuccessfully)—to bring off an independent production of the play. Acting friends at IU remember her as "tremendously enthusiastic. She became so involved in what her friends got into that she seemed to become ten times more involved than they—and ten times more disappointed when it fell through." Later, substitute teaching briefly in San Francisco, she taught the most famous lines of J. M. Barrie's classic to her gleeful students for a recital:

> I won't grow up
> I won't grow up
> I will never go to school
> I will never eat my spinach
> Nor obey the golden rule. . . .

Angel's first love was theater, but the economic possibilities discouraged her, so she took the teacher-certification course. She did her student teaching at an Indianapolis high school. She was reprimanded for allowing students to call her Angel and again for wearing a black armband after the Kent State killings. The kids loved it.

In June of 1972 Gary quit IU. He and Angel moved to San Francisco, where Gary had arranged for an unpaid CO job—alternative service for conscientious objectors in lieu of the military—at a government-funded theater. For any couple it would have been trying; the wife supporting them, the man trapped in an unfulfilling job. For Gary and Angel there wasn't a chance. Politicized twenty-three-year-old Italian mamas change in Berkeley.

When they settled, first in San Francisco, later in Berkeley, Angel and Gary spent most of their free time together. Sometimes they saw three, four movies a week. But Gary was frustrated with his menial theater job and alternately sulked and raged. Angel was none too happy earning the rent as a waitress. They fought continuously and separated, briefly, several times. Angel would sometimes show up at friends' homes, crying and occasionally bruised, to stay the night.

"After a while," said a friend, "they just stopped doing things together. Gary would spend a lot of time home, reading. Angel was much more social—going out to parties and things. He just stopped going places with her; they both thought it was the wisest decision."

In September of 1972 Angela auditioned and won a leading role in *Hedda Gabler,* a play produced by the Company Theater of Berkeley. She played Thea, the married woman whose love for "another man" gives meaning to the lives of both. A young woman named Kathleen Soliah, new to Berkeley, played Hedda, Ibsen's classic portrait of a bourgeois Lady Macbeth. Soliah—whose name would come up again late in the SLA story, during Patty Hearst's year of flight after the LA shoot-out—became Angel's closest friend. Angel arranged for Soliah to get a job waitressing at the Great Electric Underground, the restaurant in the Bank of America world headquarters, where she worked. They commuted daily to work together, then to the theater; working together, playing together.

The two of them became the core organizers of an effort to unionize the waitresses. In the winter of 1972 Kathy Soliah and Angel took a night course in radical politics at UC Berkeley. Angel had been talking about women's liberation even back at IU, but the course introduced her to feminist writer Germaine Greer, and Greer's analysis worked with the Marx and Lenin that Angel had already read with Gary. At home the marriage became guerrilla warfare in the kitchen. A close woman friend remembered, "Angel wasn't saying, 'Look, you have to do your share, do the dishes.' She'd say, 'Fuck it!' If he wanted them done, *he'd* have to do them." She became deeply involved in her theater work and tried with Soliah to organize her own acting company, increasingly focusing on agitprop political theater.

In late 1972 Bill and Emily Harris had followed the Atwoods to

San Francisco, staying for a while with Gary and Angel, then set-tling in Oakland. They had no better luck finding teaching jobs than had Angel. Bill—even with a master's degree in urban edu-cation—ended up sorting mail at the Berkeley post office, and Emily got a job as a clerk-typist at UC Berkeley's Survey Research Center. Both detested their jobs. They quickly became activists in Berkeley-Oakland radical circles; their life was paced and their purpose defined by their politics. The Harrises—particularly Emily—were sympathetic and supportive to the awakening Angel. "It was obvious Angela had taken a lot from Gary," said another friend.

Angela's new self-image demanded an aggressive, confronting manner. But her job as a cocktail waitress in a flashy uptown res-taurant, always on coquettish display, trapped her in hypocrisy. The militant feminist rebelled, bitter and angry. At work, even among the other waitresses, old friends came to avoid her because she was so strident and caustic. At a friend's wedding reception she picked out a straight man among the middle-aged guests and engaged him in a baiting conversation. "He was standing there with his mouth open," remembered a friend. "It was hilarious." She realized her sex life did not satisfy her and began to see other men. She let the hair grow on her legs and sought out comments about it, "opportunities to confront men with their sexism." Some friends were no longer sure whom they pitied most in the mar-riage. Gary and Angela—she no longer wanted to be called An-gel—decided to split. Gary wanted to return to IU, but Angela had no intention of retracing any part of her past.

In July, 1973, Angela went home for her sister's wedding. There was a scene. She told friends later she had been "kicked out." Angela had lectured about racism to her family for years, but this time it was more than race guilt. "She just felt we had too much, she felt *she* had had too much," said her father. "She felt that some of what the family had should have gone to the poor, to save the poor from hunger." Some friends said Angela, having decided to cut loose from Gary, now seemed more poised, confi-dent. "She was finally at ease with herself. A really natural, glow-ing woman," remembers a high school chum she visited. Gary went back to IU alone in August.

Later that month a friend from Oregon visited the Harrises and was invited to sit in on a meeting of their Marxist study group. Angela was just starting the classes. "What I remember most viv-idly now," said the woman, "was Angel standing there saying to a group of people, 'I don't know much about this. You're going to have to help me a lot.'" The SLA was just organizing. Four months later the school superintendent of Oakland would be murdered.

The Harrises had an unusually large number of old friends who kept track of what happened to them after the move to the Bay Area. "A lot of us—Bill and Emily's friends—had been worried about them staying at IU all that time," said Charlie Hall. (Bill had spent nearly seven years in Bloomington.) "We were afraid they were becoming two of those nondirectional people," he explained. "Colleges have their own sort of casualties, the people who sit around quoting quotables and never dirty their hands with the real stuff of life. We were afraid Bill and Emily would end up like that."

Hall had watched—from Washington State, where he works as a paramedic—as their politics became more revolutionary. "The same thing has happened to a lot of us," he noted. Bill and Emily regularly mailed him leaflets and posters about Venceremos and the prison movement. He was happy for them. "With the prison thing," he thought they were finally getting their teeth into something real.

In December, Angel moved into the Harrises' spare bedroom. And just before Christmas both she and her friend Kathy Soliah quit their waitress jobs at the Great Electric Underground with a five-page letter sent to all employees and a local radio station that denounced the restaurant managers as "agents of the ruling class."

In January, a week before the Hearst kidnapping, General Teko and Yolanda—already on the run—called Charlie Hall. "It was a strange and difficult conversation," he remembers. "I knew something was happening, but I didn't know what. They thought they were in trouble with the law and it was clear it wasn't something like traffic tickets. But they were very happy, very excited. The die-is-cast sort of thing.

"I kept asking what had happened, but over the phone they wouldn't tell me anything."

"You *know* . . ." Emily kept saying. She was giggling.

"Emily, I don't. Really!" replied Charlie.

"Well, what do you think it is?" she teased.

Charlie couldn't guess. "I told her to stop mind-fuckin' me, but she wouldn't. Neither of them would tell me what was going on."

"Read the papers," said Emily. "You'll find out." Bill asked

Charlie for a loan. Charlie mailed him $75.* "Like I told the feds," said Hall, "I thought the worst it could be was that they had busted out some prisoners."

---

*Hall sent the money to Harris care of "C. Hall" at a Berkeley address he couldn't recall.

4

Birth of the SLA

THE California Correctional Facility—legendary Soledad prison—squats in the middle of the long flat Salinas Valley; three stories of beige brick surrounded by sunbaked lowland given over to gigantic fields of corn, barley, lettuce. Around the prison the land is sparsely settled. San Francisco is more than 100 miles north up California Highway 101. Without help, escape from both the prison and the valley is rare.

Donald DeFreeze, alias Cinque, #A-25219, escaped from Soledad on March 5, 1973. After a lifetime in and out of jails, he was free of them; he would never be arrested again.

DeFreeze had been transferred from the state prison at Vacaville to Soledad in December, 1972; he had been reclassified as a minimum-security prisoner, "trusty" status for inmates unlikely to attempt escape. The transfer and the new classification indicated parole consideration; his disciplinary record had been good: only one minor infraction in the prior year, three minor infractions the year before. He had been assigned to a new job, light security, working on the boiler in the correctional officers training school outside the main prison. March 5 was his first and last day on the job.

A little before midnight DeFreeze had walked out the main gate with guard sergeant Jim Tucker and climbed into a pickup for the ride to the training facility, three-quarters of a mile away. It was the first time Tucker had met DeFreeze, whom he recalls was chatty and amiable. DeFreeze told the guard he had been a deputy sheriff back in Ohio (untrue); Tucker did not know whether to believe him, but he had heard stranger tales from inmates. At the so-called south facility DeFreeze relieved the man on the four-to-midnight shift in the boiler room and was left alone while Tucker drove the other inmate back to the main prison. All prisons run

87

with this sort of calculated risk. Inmates do everything but open and close the main door in most prisons, with trusties trimming the lawn and clipping the hedge outside the walls.

Before Tucker returned, twenty minutes later, he made his regular checks at two other unguarded posts, the snack bar and the firehouse. While Tucker was on those rounds, Donald DeFreeze simply walked out an unlocked door, through an open gate, and scaled an unguarded six-foot fence. The sergeant sounded the alarm, but DeFreeze was a minimum-security "walkaway"; no big thing, not like a mad-dog killer on the loose. Most Soledad walkaways are picked up within twenty-four hours.

DeFreeze said later he approached a Chicano family living in the valley and talked his way into a change of clothes. He hitchhiked north, avoiding the highway patrol, and one ride took him up the peninsula that frames San Francisco Bay against the mainland. Thirty miles south of the city, he stopped in Palo Alto and made fruitless contact with Venceremos members. North and across the Bay, in Oakland, he found James Mayfield, the young radical black serving as outside coordinator for the Black Cultural Association at Vacaville.

Mayfield—a family man with a wife and three kids—is not talking to reporters or to the FBI. He never went underground when the SLA was on the run, although many acquaintances of the fugitives—casual and intimate—suddenly took trips. In DeFreeze's original scheme Mayfield was to be the contact for ex-cons or escapees to connect with the Field Marshal, with the underground army. Cinque planned to appoint him an SLA colonel. But all this was in the future when DeFreeze arrived, unannounced and unexpected, at the Mayfields'. Several sources say Mayfield drove DeFreeze around Oakland and Berkeley while Cinque tried to convince various friends and acquaintances to shelter him. "He must have gone through his whole address book," said one woman. At least a dozen people refused to aid him. A San Francisco black activist said DeFreeze contacted several black women he had met through the BCA, asked them for help, and was refused. "They barely knew him," the man said. "They told him, 'Why should we risk so much for you?'" DeFreeze did not want to stay with Mayfield; both figured Mayfield's home was "hot," a likely place for the cops to check. Neither thought Peking House much better—and DeFreeze felt Dave Gunnell was "kinda freaky"—but when all other doors slammed on him, he ended up seeking refuge at the Chabot Road commune.

It was apparently coincidence that on March 3, two days before DeFreeze escaped, Russ Little, one of Gunnell's tenants, ran into a friend named Chris Thompson in Oakland and bought Thompson's pistol, a .38 Rossi. Thompson had lived at Peking House in the fall of 1972, then went to New York for two months—owing Gunnell $65 and leaving his revolver at the house. Thompson explained later that he had been avoiding Peking House, after he returned, because he could not pay Gunnell the money he owed. When he met Little on the street and Russ offered to buy the Rossi, he decided to sell it for $65—Little would pay off Gunnell. They checked at the pawnshop where Thompson had bought the gun to see what type of document could legally transfer ownership, but in the end, Little just gave Thompson a receipt for the gun—not a document of legal transfer—signed in the name of Alicia Croft.

Thompson accepted that, although he later bitterly regretted it. In the black militant circles he had moved in for several years, names—particularly ones which might someday interest police—were handled gingerly; signatures were not much questioned.

Thompson was a former New York Black Panther; in the 1970 BPP split, between Eldridge Cleaver and Huey Newton, he had sided with the paramilitary Cleaver faction. He helped edit their paper, *Right On.* Later he split from them, drifted West, opened a Berkeley food stand called Harlem on My Mind, and became involved with local activists. He liked the Bay Area. In militant black politics, he said, "New York was like the front lines. Here it's much more mellow."*

---

*Despite his affiliation with the Cleaver faction, Thompson saw the Panther schism as much a clash of personality as ideology. This led him to become involved rather casually with Oakland's Newton-faction Panthers when he moved to California: he worked quietly, avoiding debate about Cleaver. Months later the FBI—perhaps to keep the feuding teams straight, but more likely to stir the broth—left a message for Thompson at a Berkeley office he shared with several radicals, asking that he phone the local FBI office. "When I called, the agent said they'd noticed my car at one of the Panther houses and he suggested—for my health—it would be wiser if I not hang around with the Oakland Panthers because they might find out about my work with the Cleaver people in New York," said Thompson. It may have been a threat, but Thompson didn't understand it that way. "I figured when the FBI starts looking after my health, I'm really in trouble. So I just cooled it." With the paranoia endemic to the radical Left, the bureau well knew that a call from the FBI would start rumors that Thompson was an informer. And it did.

At Peking House DeFreeze was restless and worried; he wanted a more secure hideout. Shortly after Cinque arrived, Russ Little sought out Thompson, telling him that he had a friend, a black escaped con, who needed safe shelter. Thompson suggested Little approach Mizmoon Soltysik, a young Berkeley activist and, said Thompson, one of his ex-loves. (Soltysik had actually jilted Thompson in a bitter scene just the week before—but only after their drawn-out affair had ruptured.) Mizmoon, said Thompson, wasn't openly involved in anything dangerous, but she was "politically together"—and she "dug" black men. Thompson thought they might get on together.

Little had already met Mizmoon. She had been among several of Thompson's girls introduced to the Peking House collective while Chris lived there. Another, Nancy Ling Perry—who worked at yet another Berkeley sidewalk stand—had become a regular visitor at Peking House after Thompson moved out. Nancy Perry was now a close friend of both Little and Wolfe, a trusted courier in the outlaw prison network Wolfe had organized. Thompson's suggestion sounded good.

The introductions were made, and Mizmoon said yes. Donald DeFreeze moved into Soltysik's Parker Street apartment in Berkeley about two weeks after he escaped. There were only two bedrooms and Mizmoon's roommate, Judy D., claimed the second. Mizmoon and Cin were lovers almost immediately. And between the two—almost immediately—there was the magnetic bonding of Berkeley rhetoric and the gunpower politics of the prisons.

Mizmoon's sister Sue, two years younger, arrived in Berkeley on March 23—en route from Hawaii's surf to the ski slopes of Colorado—and visited for three days, staying at the apartment with Mizmoon and DeFreeze. There was a brief family reunion on the twenty-third, when Mizmoon's older brother, Fred, drove up from Santa Barbara. For some time, Fred had been urging Mizmoon to move out of Berkeley and pick some sort of target for her life; law school, perhaps. The metamorphosis of sister Patricia into Mizmoon—she had legally changed her name—had already convinced the family that Berkeley's tangle of politics, personalities, and sex was a volatile social laboratory. But both Fred and Sue had been surprised and pleased to meet the intense quiet black man, obviously Mizmoon's new lover, introduced only as Cin.

Mizmoon had been seriously ill and deeply depressed when Fred had last visited her in January—she had irritated him once again by talking military politics, how a group could not be "picked off" as easily as a lone rebel—but her physical and emotional health had worried him more than the politics they had so often argued about. The family had accepted the fact that Mizmoon was bisexual; her sex life didn't bother Fred, but he was concerned about her depressed spirits. From his mother, whom Mizmoon wrote and visited regularly, he had learned that Mizmoon had broken up with her longtime lesbian lover Camilla Hall only the month before, fighting about Chris Thompson—and now Thompson was gone.

"I liked Cin right away because I could sense that he was making Mizmoon happy," recalled Fred. DeFreeze, he said, was a trim, muscular, good-looking man, with a short rounded Afro. DeFreeze was wearing dark aviator-rim sunglasses, indoors as well as out, and seemed very much at home; shirtless, wearing a pair of old army fatigue trousers. In January, said her brother, "Mizmoon had been going through a rough period . . . she seemed to hate herself; hated her body. She was just getting over a case of gonorrhea, and she had been really depressed.

"With Cin she seemed much more assured. And I noticed right off how nice he was to her. There was a rare parity in their relationship; they seemed to treat each other as equals." Cin told Fred he had just come from New Jersey, leaving a job in a day-care center. "He told us about how one day he had to bring all these kids from the preschool program to an amusement park," recalled Soltysik. "He filled out this whole story; there seemed to be no contradictions between the story and what he was. He seemed to be the sort of gentle guy who would like working with kids."

Fred, a Peace Corps veteran of Malaysia, had only recently returned from a stint in Algeria with the International Voluntary Services, and Cin was curious about his experience. They talked about racism in Malaysia, Arab culture, the Peace Corps. "Cin was particularly interested in the Algerian government's treatment of Eldridge Cleaver," said Fred, and was apparently disappointed with Soltysik's report. When Cleaver wasn't under virtual house arrest, Fred told Cin, he was being shipped around the country in a well-guarded limousine. Algeria used Cleaver as a propaganda tool. "I was so used to being defensive with Mizmoon I probably related to him in the same way," recalled Soltysik later. "But there were no arguments; he asked questions insistently, but he was willing to listen. His questions were the sort where he seemed to be willing to listen to any answer—no matter where they came from or what sort of politics I had. . . .

"When he asked about the Peace Corps, I knew where he was

coming from—you know, how could you work for an agency of the 'corporate government'—but he was willing to listen. He had leftist politics, but without the slightly hysterical edge in Mizmoon's rhetoric." DeFreeze impressed him as an intelligent man, said Soltysik, "not in the academic sense—I mean, he seemed to be stretching for polysyllabic words—but his thought sequence was good, the way he phrased and followed up questions." Sometime during the afternoon, Fred picked up that Cin had once been a pimp back East. Mizmoon was very proud of it. That a man once a pimp could turn around and become a man like Cinque—it meant a great deal to her. "That was the image he projected, something of the bad man turned mild," mused Fred. "I got the feeling that he had come to Berkeley to mellow out. . . ."

Fred Soltysik stayed only a few hours, but Sue's longer visit left her with similar impressions—qualified by a vague worry and suspicion. Not about Cin—more about all that serious and secretive political stuff they were both involved in. The two of them worked hours daily writing some sort of documents—Mizmoon at the typewriter, Cin behind her, talking and peering over her shoulder. Sue recalled them all joking one night: Mizmoon wanted some sort of slogan with punch behind it, and the three of them were tossing all sorts of crazy rhymes back and forth. But the documents were serious—and private. Mizmoon asked Sue not to interrupt when they were working on the papers.

Sue Soltysik remembered another night—after a vegetarian meal cooked by DeFreeze—when there was an after-supper gathering at the apartment for a film showing. Chris Thompson brought the movie, a Cuban color film about the Frelimo guerrilla movement against the Portuguese Army in colonial Mozambique, and eight or so people came to see it. One of them, Sue thinks, was Emily Harris. After the film Mizmoon asked several people—both Sue and Thompson among them—to leave while she and Cin met with the rest of her collective.

Much later Fred Soltysik discovered Mizmoon's notes from that meeting among her possessions; scribbled comments about the film and the group's reaction:

> . . . La Lutia Continua . . . beautiful . . . women and men shown living and struggling in creating the changes we identify with, though in a technologically different environment. We know what happens to your [feeling]. What to brace up to expect. It will sometimes (maybe many times) be hard. But the "payoff" [pig

word] enjoyment of being free and enjoying like we could be doing.

On the reverse of the page, she wrote: "You don't arrive at a
fixed spot and say this is it; there is no more ahead. There is not
an ultimate. Government must always be what people need when
they need it. . . ." Along the margin to the right, there was
another note: "Changes have now been experienced. Death is not
our goal. We are affirming life; an affirmation of life."
There were already links between most of the people who
would later enlist in the SLA, but as yet there was no army. At
least through the spring there were two separate cliques, and several of the later recruits were peripheral to both. When DeFreeze
escaped, Wolfe, Little, and Nancy Perry were already involved
with another prison-based revolutionary terrorist group. A group
that did not include Donald DeFreeze. Cin's arrival in Berkeley
was timely; the Revolution almost started without him.
Cin had landed at Peking House by chance, a last resort, after
several of his black acquaintances had barred him refuge. Prior to
his escape, in the three months between his transfer from Vacaville and his departure from Soledad, neither Wolfe, Little, nor
any of their prison-visiting friends had seen DeFreeze at Soledad.
None of them had even written to him. Cin's fateful connection
was again chance. Yet, within three weeks of his escape, DeFreeze
seems to have stumbled upon two independent groups readying
themselves for the do-or-die commitment of revolutionary terrorism. For DeFreeze, Berkeley lived up to all the prison myths.
And within three weeks of escaping, DeFreeze, with Mizmoon,
had apparently already begun writing out the long elaborate documents that codified and proclaimed the Symbionese Revolution.
A personal vision can be as important as the rare visitor to a prison inmate, and in the politicized prisons it is not rare that the
dream is of an army, the new society, a new life, another chance.
There is no patent on revolution, but DeFreeze abandoned all
modesty and more. His was the grand illusion; he wanted not a
band of guerrilla fighters, but a "nation"—and here and now a
"federation" that would truly represent all races of the People.
DeFreeze—sheltered so long, never involved with politics outside
the prisons—and his friends, oddly as sheltered as he, believed
the time was right. The people ready. Revolution awaited only the
fuse.
In April, Cin moved from Mizmoon's apartment to a hideout in

East Oakland. Mizmoon commuted for about a month; then, in June, they took a place together on East Seventeenth Street in a ghetto section of Oakland. Bill and Emily Harris, if not members of Mizmoon's "collective" then, were at least close friends. (Mizmoon's diary reminds her in early April to repay $10 borrowed from the Harrises.) Angela Atwood was as yet unconnected, still caught in her terminal marriage crisis. Mizmoon's sometime lover Camilla Hall was then still estranged—having broken off because Mizmoon would not pledge fidelity—but Mizmoon was trying to lure her back (even asking sister Sue, during the March visit, to approach Camilla as a go-between). Another who was perhaps still an outsider, although a friend of both Wolfe and the Harrises, was Vietnam vet Joe Remiro. Remiro was then the Venceremos weapons trainer for the East Bay, holding "self-defense" gun classes for radicals in Berkeley and Oakland.

Willie Wolfe, the youngest of all of them, was a central figure—then, perhaps *the* central figure, the connector. But Wolfe, Little, and Nancy Perry were still deeply involved in *another* army, a still-mysterious group of black inmates and ex-cons "sworn to urban terrorism," who called themselves the Partisans' Vanguard Party. As an idea, a cellblock dream, the Symbionese had uncounted precursors—but most, like Vanguard, apparently died in that nether world between plot and reality. For a time, Wolfe and Little didn't need DeFreeze, they thought they already had their black leadership. It would not be until midsummer, after Vanguard was clearly nothing more than a paper revolution, that Wolfe and his friends turned to Cinque. It was in August, 1973, that Nancy Ling Perry moved in with Cinque and Mizmoon.

The people were ready.
Revolution awaited only the fuse.

When Wheeler escaped from Vacaville in August, 1973, DeFreeze met him in Palo Alto. Wheeler said later he had arranged a "pickup" through his BCA/Venceremos connections. "I didn't know DeFreeze had anything to do with my escape until, you know, I saw him," recalled Wheeler in a Texas jail-cell interview after his arrest in Houston in mid-1975, "but I thought anyone who showed up there, well, he was okay, I'd found out where he was coming from. . . . That was the first day I seen the seven-headed cobra."

It was not DeFreeze who picked him up at the prison (Wheeler refused to identify his escape contacts); Cinque met him later, but the rescue at Vacaville had its own melodrama. "At the time," said Wheeler, "I didn't know who was gonna pick me up, I didn't know anything about it . . . [then] the people who did come to get me drove up to the penitentiary and drove straight off into a ditch. They saw me and drove right into it. The prison authorities had to help them get out of the hole. Then they came back up the road and got me and we split."

Hiding out with Wheeler, Mizmoon, Nancy Ling Perry, and Thero's girlfriend—twenty-four-year-old Mary Alice Siem, a Redwood City radical, Venceremos associate, and heiress to a California lumber and real estate fortune—DeFreeze laid out the plan. "He handed me this book, you know, with all these cobras on the cover," remembers Thero. "He asked me to read it. I did and I thought, man, this is really shit. I told him it was a bunch of garbage, it wasn't realistic as far as revolution was concerned. Actually, it was bullshit, it was suicide." DeFreeze was apparently nonplussed at Thero's first reaction (if Wheeler's story is true); it is known that the five stayed together for some time, for about a week in Palo Alto, moving on to Berkeley, then to Mizmoon's Oakland apartment. Wheeler said later he disagreed with Cinque's SLA "concepts," but other reports indicate he at least made some suggestions on how to structure the organization—and perhaps even suggested "targets," Patricia Hearst among them. Still, said Wheeler, DeFreeze's politics and his own "didn't coordinate."

"He became awfully frustrated with me because I wouldn't get the support for him that he wanted, that I had the potential to get. I wouldn't get people to deliver guns, I wouldn't get people to join the organization, I wouldn't talk to people to support the SLA. I had a lot more contacts than he did," said Wheeler. "The people I was talking to that were feeding me and helping me as far as my medical problem was concerned, they would do almost anything I asked them to. But they wouldn't accept the SLA."

(Wheeler's story becomes confusing as to this period; he implied that his "contacts"—he referred to some of them as "those professors"—were wealthy suburban radicals associated with Venceremos, and that although they initially rejected the SLA, they moved to support DeFreeze when they thought they could influence him. Wheeler refused to discuss the SLA connections inside the prisons, claiming that Cinque and "the young white kids" were the whole organization.)

At the time Wheeler's first concern was for himself and the

medical aid he desperately needed.* "I went to these radical doctors, right? They were all scared to help me, they just gave me a bunch of painkillers. What I needed was an operation." Stomach cramps were becoming unbearable; he was bleeding internally and found it difficult to walk. His "contacts" supplied him with money, an alias and false IDs, and Wheeler flew to New York to get his operation. He said he stayed in a penthouse owned by "heavies, real heavy people. I was given the name of some doctors that I was told would help me, but they were scared too. All I got was more pills." Wheeler said he spent the last week of August in a Chicago hotel, too sick to leave his room. (He was finally to get surgery late that fall in Texas). In the first days of September, said Wheeler, he returned to San Francisco just in time to veto the SLA's first planned assassination.

"DeFreeze wanted so bad to get the SLA started he was gonna kill this dude Montgomery,† was gonna write a letter to Montgomery—shit, he already wrote it; he was gonna mail it the next day. Montgomery wrote an article about me, in the *Examiner* I think, and DeFreeze wanted to kill him." Wheeler said he told DeFreeze that if he sent the letter, which would claim Thero was under the protection of the SLA, he, Wheeler, would send another denying it.

Still, Wheeler stayed in the SLA commune. His girlfriend later told the FBI that between Thero's escape on August 2 and October, she had attended about twenty meetings in Oakland at which DeFreeze lectured on the structure and politics of his nascent Liberation Army. Wheeler's lover, Mary Alice Siem, is beneficiary of a $250,000 trust fund, family money from the Coggins lumber fortune of Northern California. Siem's money apparently supported the early SLA collective. Close friends explained that Mary Alice gave Wheeler "a couple of thousand dollars" which he shared with the group. (Ms. Siem, a divorcée with a small child,

---

*Wheeler's defense committee had filed suit to force Vacaville authorities to give him proper medical care, including surgery if necessary, for a severe intestinal inflammation. Vacaville medics had been uncertain of a diagnosis and delayed treatment (which Wheeler would later use as his defense on the escape charge). While a fugitive, he had surgery in Texas for regional enteritis, an inflammation analogous to a serious ulcer.

†Ed Montgomery, a veteran reporter for the San Francisco *Examiner* known for his contacts with local and federal police, had published an article on August 26, 1973, which claimed that a lawyers' commune associated with Venceremos had aided Wheeler's escape.

had become involved with Wheeler while he was still a convict. Her sister, a leading Venceremos activist, had brought Siem in and introduced her to Wheeler during a prison visit; Mary Alice returned alone, then became Thero's most faithful visitor. Her tie with the SLA lasted only until October, she told the FBI. Frightened by DeFreeze's "megalomania," she split and went into hiding from both Wheeler and the SLA.)

When the SLA later described itself in published manifestos, the authority structure seemed a bewildering tangle. The Symbionese Liberation Army was separate from, yet one and the same with, the Symbionese Federation, the Court of the People, and the Symbionese Federated Republic. And each of the above was a united front coalition "of different races and people and socialist political parties of the oppressed people . . . who have under black and minority leadership . . . agreed to struggle together."*

In an unpublished early draft of their "terms of military/political alliance," they describe the SLA as neither an organization or group. It materialized with the active grouping of the combat elements from different revolutionary organizations or groups and parties whose leadership have joined together in the Symbionese War Council.

"We follow the principle that those who fight can talk, because political unity grows from military/political action against the enemy." Implicit and explicit in all the early SLA documents is the singular doctrine which ultimately both defined and doomed the SLA: The federation in all its manifestations is "totally an alliance of war." The combat unit under General Field Marshal DeFreeze was to be absolutely preeminent. It was the Symbionese *War* Council (to be "set up on the level of a Revolutionary United Nations") which was to be the ultimate authority of the federation, and DeFreeze was to be chairman of the council.

In their Oakland apartment DeFreeze and Mizmoon Soltysik

---

*In the dogma of Venceremos, as in that of the SLA, the predominantly white group was sworn to follow "black and minority leadership." The justification for leadership appointments on the basis of race rather than ability was that (a) any successful revolution in America would have to rely heavily on the oppressed racial minorities, and (b) racial minorities should not be expected to follow white leaders, members of the oppressing race; thus, a true revolutionary group must commit itself to minority leadership. In Venceremos the tension and hypocrisy bred by this creed—with actual leadership often exercised by those other than the titular leaders—was one of the many causes of the group's disintegration.

had labored over the proclamation by which the United Symbionese Republic would secede and declare revolutionary war on the U.S. government and the capitalists—pursuant, they noted, to the U.S. Declaration of Independence. Should they call themselves, they wondered, the SLA International People's Army, the Federation Liberation Forces, the United Forces of the SLA, or simply the SLA?

Stories are told of DeFreeze approaching leaders of radical groups in the late summer with a simple and forthright proposal: Ally with the federation and the SLA will put the authoritative accent of terrorism on each of the revolutionary demands of the Left. An activist Oakland attorney said that he knew of several local leftist leaders DeFreeze had approached. "In each case," he said, "they rebuffed him. They thought he was a provocateur or simply crazy. A lot of people just didn't take him very seriously."

For DeFreeze there must have been a sense of incredulity as one after another of those he had counted on to be seated at the War Council refused him; amazement first, then anger, then disgust. For the others, veterans of the East Bay Left, it was probably much less of a shock. For them the binding glue of the SLA was frustration with the factionalized and stagnant Left.

By fall of 1973, said Wheeler, Cinque, Mizmoon, and "Ling" Perry were still the SLA high command, and the high command was still the whole army. "None of the black people from the streets would join, and the people from the Black Cultural Association wouldn't help him. Some of the college kids would come by—Willie Wolfe, and Emily Harris, and her old man came about twice." But none of them were yet members, he said.

The SLA came together as a collection of stragglers; each individually had somehow shaken loose from a prior niche. All but Angela Atwood and Mizmoon's lesbian friend Camilla Hall had been caught in the collapse of Venceremos that summer—but even then perhaps only Joe Remiro was paying dues; others had been deeply involved in Venceremos projects but avoided the group's internal discipline by rejecting membership. Deeply committed, but usually to someone else's revolution.

(Wheeler is probably mistaken in his memory of just when "the college kids" joined DeFreeze, and the distinction he so carefully makes between "members" and sympathetic and knowledgeable associates seems negligible once the group moved into criminal conspiracies.) Wheeler recalls Remiro and Little enlisting in the SLA in October, the fourth and fifth recruits, but other reports indicate they, and others, were deeply involved well before that. Willie Wolfe and Russ Little stopped paying rent at Peking House in September, said landlord and friend David Gunnell, "but we saw little of Willie in that last six weeks and almost nothing of Russ after mid-August. They just weren't around."

August was the crucial month in the formation of the SLA. Perry moved in with Cin and Mizmoon. Thero Wheeler escaped and joined them. Angela Atwood finally split with her husband and began dating Little—and then, after attending Berkeley gun classes taught by Joe Remiro assisted by Wolfe, both Remiro and Little. And it was in August that the East Bay Venceremos, torn by internal feuding, dissolved. In the void of organization, the Coalition, a new group of former Venceremos members and associates, was formed to continue political organizing until some successor to Venceremos was created.

"What happened," explained Remiro, testifying in his own defense much later, "was when we first got together we decided to split the collective into three groups." One group was to work on community organizing; another was to focus on industrial and labor organizing; the third was a prison group. Of the six to eight people who opted to work on the prison project, he said, six—himself, Wolfe, Little, Bill and Emily Harris, and Angela Atwood—would eventually become SLA cadre. "Eventually the collective fell apart, because the other two groups weren't doing anything and couldn't think of anything to do. They all wanted to get into the prison group and . . . we didn't think it would work as well with all these people in it." As the rest of the Coalition turned to prison organizing, he said, the core six of the original prison project spun off independently.

"See," said Remiro, "it was like, working with a person in a collective didn't mean you actually knew the person outside of political work. And what happened was . . . six of us became really close outside of political work. We went out and partied together, and had beers together, and ran around Lake Merritt together, and we just became good friends. And we felt that rather than just working with people who we only know through common political interests, that we would rather work together. We liked each other. We got along well. We had no big personality clashes, nothing like that. We just kind of struck off on our own with our own little group."

Since February, Willie Wolfe and Russ Little had been regular visitors and correspondents to Clifford "Death Row" Jefferson at

Folsom Prison, where the lifer had been transferred in December after his brawl at Vacaville. Wolfe and Little remained his most regular visitors, but by spring the Harrises and Little's girlfriend Robyn Steiner were also visiting Jefferson. "Death Row" had been Wolfe's link to the Vanguard Party, and even later it was apparently through Jefferson that Cinque and the others hoped to become affiliated with the Black Guerrilla Family, a secret communist organization of black inmates of great influence within the California prisons. Wolfe, Little, and Jefferson exchanged an extraordinary series of letters, several of which police found later, which had been "kited" in and out of the prison. In some of these smuggled letters, Jefferson identified himself as a leader of the Black Guerrilla Family (BGF) and "party chief" of the Partisans' Vanguard Party, allegedly a black convict terrorist wing of the BGF.

According to Jefferson's letters, the Vanguard Party, which was later to enter into an alliance with the SLA (or at least allow DeFreeze to claim ally status), was to be the successor of the BGF, a small group which would organize a new stage in "the struggle," guerrilla war in the cities. Death Row Jeff claimed that the plans for the group—and the thirteen-page "party manual"*—were drafted by "me and George Jackson," the black prison hero whose writings made him a legend even before he died in an attempted prison escape in 1971.

The alliance with the SLA is never referred to directly in the Jefferson letters (although some refer cryptically to the Foster murder). There are also implications that Wolfe and Little—perhaps as representatives of the SLA or, more likely, as representatives of a larger group of white radicals associated with Venceremos,† a few of whom would later join the SLA—were

---

*The party concepts: "class struggle, equality, liberation, world revolution, collectivism, communalism, political-interconnected-with-military Maoism, socialism, unity, dialectical materialism, centralism, people's revolutionary war. . . . We shall destroy racism, fascism, bourgeois democracy, idealism, liberalism, monopoly, capitalism, imperialism, competition, disunity." Each member met while in prison, says the manual, and is now a committed "USA Urban Guerrilla." To be a "terrorist" is to have "a quality that ennobles any honorable man or woman because it is an act worthy of revolutionary engagement, armed struggle against the shameful capitalist Amerika and its monstrosities." The document urges a "true internationalism" and alliance with dedicated white revolutionaries.

†Jefferson asked Little, in one letter, to take the party manual and "get Frances, Venceremos or Popeye and have it printed up in little booklets."

brought into a coalition of black terrorist groups that predated the SLA.

In a letter of April 30, 1973—two months after DeFreeze's escape—Little and Wolfe were told to contact another ex-convict, identified as "U" (Ulysses McDaniels, a black convict who had recently been paroled, a former cellmate of George Jackson and allegedly a member of the BGF). Little and Wolfe had not yet met McDaniels, but Jefferson told them to contact him because they had been appointed to the party's five-man central committee.

Jefferson also wrote that he had appointed two field marshals, a chief field marshal, a deputy chief of staff, and a deputy chief for intelligence—all well-known black prison revolutionaries.

After mentioning the appointment of Geronimo Pratt and Wild Man Stevenson, Jefferson wrote: ". . . those are my two for the month of April, if you have yours that great, so please push most others you contact to get theirs." It was, it seems, to have been a multisided coalition, a joint command.

His appointments aside, Jefferson went on in that letter to list other prisoners and ex-convicts—most well-known activists—to whom he wanted copies of the "program" distributed. Most of the men allegedly had already been recruited, but Jefferson made clear that at least some were to be shown the program in an attempt to interest them in the group.

Within an SLA context, the list was an odd one. Although most are known as fiercely political convict militants, several of the Vacaville inmates mentioned are described by both prison and inmate sources as so psychotic they have little touch with even their inmediate prison reality. Several others are known to have decried the SLA as impractical and absurd, in both style and tactics, and spoken disparagingly about DeFreeze. In more than one case the recruits could not even pronounce the full name of the SLA.

With interpolations by the authors, Jefferson's handwritten letter of April 30 reads:

GREETINGS COMRADE WILLY,

I received you most sought letter of April [unclear] 1973, the date you have on the letter, but I received it on 30th of April. I thought you would never write. Anyway, I hope it not so long before your next letter. I heard over the radio that a Wilber Jackson got shot in leg, a few days ago. Was that Popeye? [Popeye Jackson, a veteran of nineteen years "inside," became a Venceremos member once released and the outspoken leader of the United Prison-

ers Union.] I hope Hasting have help you find Junior or someone, the rate it taking in time, he will have died of old age before
we find him. Get his help, so let's get some success there. It good
you have the job [Wolfe got a job in a Berkeley die-casting plant],
but I hate you will not be able to make it up for a month. But your
organizing shall make up for that. So work hard on that, and I
shall expect Russ [Little] up [unclear]. Also would like you to find
me a nice aware girl, stallion-type, tall, any race, between 20 and
50 years old, can come up twice a month on different weeks than
you & Russ. I need this, so work on it.

I am not sure I know Septima Clark, if he's friend of Comrade
Al [Taylor's] I know him, anyway, I hear a guy with name close to
that is okey, so he is okey. Now Ray Ray [Raymond Sparks, Folsom inmate] know you are legit, he at first didn't know Nancy Perry. So he ask me and I give him the scoop on everybody out there.
But anyone writing must use *Da Da o Mi* on letter, then there is no
doubt. Now I wrote Russ a long letter yesterday. Want you & U. to
check it out at once and have the program printed up in a small
pamphlet form at once. See Gloria, she know printer. Now I want
five copies sent to Scott [Raymond Scott, inmate in the psychotic
ward at Vacaville] for him, A. Gibson [Arthur Lee Gibson], Chilli,
Lil John, L.C. all there with him, & I want four copys sent to Ray
Ray [at Folsom prison] for him, Carter, Whiteside, Madhous, and
three copys sent to J.P. Trotter at Soladad Central, for him, Howard, Lil D, also send three to James Lindsey, Quentin, for him
Yogi [Hugo Pinell, reputed leader of the BGF, charged with murdering three guards by cutting their throats during the aborted
George Jackson escape attempt], Lil Tate, also send [unclear]
three copys, send me five copys, give U. a few copys, also Dave &
other comrades copys, you & Russ keep plenty copys, also give B.
Wells & Baby Rayburn copys, send my friend Frances copy, at her
office, also Hasting & Junior copys & Popeye. Send Venceremos
prison union address in Palo Alto, also tell Ray Ray [Sparks], Al
[Taylor], Scott, U. that Geronimo [Pratt] now Deputy Chief of
Staff, and Wild Man [Stevenson] is Deputy Chief Intelligence,
those my two for the month of April, if you have yours that great,
so please push most others you contact to get theirs.

I got a letter from U. and I wrote him back, telling me about the
toilet bit, he seemed to be pretty angry about that, but the Comrade is alright, so you all get in touch with him, if he has not got in
touch with you all yet. Also he is put out with Sugar, so you must
have Sugar call all of us down from each place, this is a must. Also
U. told me about the pretty topless and bottomless girl he has.
They are good to have around, that why I want one, to visit carry
word back and forth. We are going to move now.

Oh yes, did Frances phone you and tell you about what I said about Sacramento, trying to get [action?] for me, phone her about this. Have you heard from Al [Taylor] lately, give him my love in struggle when you write him, also the card I sent to him was returned. Did you give the nut Steve [unclear] & Bob [unclear] my best regards, how are they doing. Also give Cecil my best, always my best to Scott and the fellows, tell Scott to tell A. [Arthur Lee] Gibson he is now a Field Marshal. He is a very good man. Also tell Ray Ray to tell [Edward] Whiteside he is now Chief Field Marshal and Carter is a Field Marshal. Those are our General Staff, that should be enough for him to know you are all legit, but I know he allready know. I was able to contact him two weeks ago, when I gave him complete rundown. He is now in hospital from hurting his leg playing basketball. I hear not to bad & will be out in a day or so. Bonewell is one of us, a good man in Los Angeles. I would like you all to be in touch with.

No, you can not send me cigars here [in isolation], but on Christmas if on main line [the main prison compound].They will keep for about six months in sealed box, in open box about two weeks. What did Hasting himself say about helping us? Now be sure he get a copy of our program, so see Russ get program printed up. [Look?] this letter over good & do this I ask at once, and don't wait two weeks or more to let me hear how things are going. In order for us to be effective, I have to get word all the time & have visit at least every other week, and you know you & Russ, U. are three of the five on Central Committee, read the program close and all have to live up to it or go. Give my love to Dave, [unclear], Russ, Robyn & all comrades.

Da Da o Mi,

COMRADE JEFF

The actual relationship between the SLA and the Partisans' Vanguard Party is still unclear (despite Jefferson's later claim to be a cofounder of the SLA); indeed the actual existence of any organized group within the prisons under Jefferson is in some doubt, despite his impressive roster of prison heavies. Nine days after his letter of appointments to Wolfe, Jefferson sent another to Russ Little, announcing that Ulysses McDaniels was now "out as deputy chief commander." It was a brief note, without explanation, but Jefferson added a requisition that seemed strangely inappropriate for sworn terrorists: "I want printed cards made up for all officers with their rank and party." (Prison officials would later argue that Jefferson's Vanguard Party was largely a figment of his imagination—part of an elaborate exchange of illusion and hope between the dreamers inside and the dreamers outside. ("Can you imagine Vietcong officers with calling cards?" said one.) Three days later Death Row Jeff sent another letter to Little, a "purge letter of some of our reactionaries," which summarily dismissed half the high command. "Chili Red" was kicked out for "lying to Geronimo about me"—and apparently for believing Chili, both Wild Man Stevenson (the Vanguard's deputy chief for intelligence) and Geronimo Pratt (Vanguard's deputy chief of staff) were purged as "cowards and damn lyers [sic]." Chili Red "should be killed as soon as possible," Jeff wrote Little, and as for former Black Panther Pratt, "I can see why [Panther leader Huey] Newton wants to kill him."

In none of his letters did Jefferson mention DeFreeze or the rank of general field marshal. And although Jefferson's letter to Wolfe in the late fall of 1973 indicates a knowledge of the Foster killing and Cinque's SLA, it seems far more likely that it was not DeFreeze himself (whose in-prison credibility as a revolutionary was not high) but the history of prison activism of the young white SLA "soldiers" that gave the nascent SLA credentials with Jefferson and other prison revolutionaries—others perhaps more serious and better organized than Death Row Jeff's Vanguard Party. ("*We do in fact represent the Black Guerrilla Family,*" scribbled Nancy Ling Perry in her personal notebook.)

The prisons remained the anchor for the SLA concept; outside the walls they had difficulty getting anyone else to accept them. The only group that may have been recruited into the SLA "federation" was the Chicano Liberation Front.* On the streets and among radicals, "nobody wanted nothing to do with the SLA," recalls Thero Wheeler. "It just wasn't cool. DeFreeze got really frustrated at that time."

Remiro and Wolfe together moved into a small Oakland cottage on Bond Street on October 1. Friendly neighbors said they were

---

*In the early fall a young Chicano woman accidentally rang the doorbell of the next door neighbor of the Harrises in Oakland and asked if this was where Chicano Liberation was meeting. She was seeking the Harrises. It was a Sunday night, and neighbors of the young couple from Indiana said that every Sunday evening for months there had been an often noisy meeting at the Harrises' apartment.

On June 11, 1974, shots fired through a church window during a community meeting fatally wounded the police chief of Union City, and injured four Chicano bystanders. Ten days later, San Francisco media received an SLA-style communiqué from the Chicano Liberation Front claiming credit for the attack.

not spending much time at home. They did not even bother to get a phone for the first month. Willie Wolfe told one friend he had moved out of Peking House because "there were too many people and he didn't like so many people aware of his activities . . . he didn't feel the people at [Peking House] had common sense on what not to talk about. I just assumed he was talking about things like going to the rifle range and other kinds of things hundreds of people do in the East Bay."

By mid-fall, however, Little and Nancy Ling Perry had begun to rent "safehouses," SLA hideouts. Perry—using the name Nancy DeVoto— rented a three-bedroom tract house in the San Francisco suburb of Clayton. In early October Little rented an apartment near Oakland city hall, a half mile from the school administration building; then, as George DeVoto he moved into the Clayton house with Perry.

Still, rumors of the new Liberation Army drew little interest among the Bay Area Left. In the caldron of the Berkeley counterculture, where new messiahs, tribes, and armies surface regularly, the SLA was viewed with neither much interest nor alarm. In an unaddressed letter DeFreeze denounced "leaders and organizations [who claim] that they must continue to organize new organizations everytime one falls apart, when they fail to understand that the people always organize to fight the enemy, and when leaders fail to start the fight, then people fall apart from the organization.

"To continue in this manner," he wrote, "is totally reactionary, egotistic, opportunistic and anti-revolutionary, since to do so only allows for the continued grouping and re-grouping of the same revolutionary people for the fight that never comes. . . ."

In the early fall, members of the SLA had burglarized the homes of at least three prominent leftist activists, stealing guns, ammunition, and ammo-reloading equipment. They even went so far as to steal the wallet of a prominent Venceremos activist, Janet Cooper, later to use her identification to rent getaway cars for an SLA robbery—possibly an attempt to set her up with the police.

And they were training in the Berkeley hills: "We practiced karate exercises and the proper use of weapons—breaking them down and putting them back together and that," Wheeler said. "DeFreeze was real good at it. I never did see anyone who knew guns as well as he did. He'd be blindfolded and he could take them all apart and reassemble them in a minute."

And still they were polishing up the SLA documents that would later be used to explain their philosophy. Much more careful thought went into organization than into ideology. The future would be shaped in the act of rebellion. Beyond a vague socialism, they had a series of generalized goals—"liberating" monogamous marriage, destruction of the penal system, the rent structure, and quashing "racism, sexism, ageism, capitalism, fascism, individualism, possessiveness, competitiveness and all other institutions that have made and sustained capitalism." There was also a system for breaking up the United States into racially separate sovereign states.*

But DeFreeze had the SLA war machine diagramed and detailed:

MOBILITY UNIT

It is the responsibility of the Mobility Unit to provide for the movement of supplies and military personal [*sic*] and the necessary equipment needed to safely move said personal and supplies. It is responsible for the safe movement of supplies between other units and to and from the combat units, and providing needed hiding places and disguises necessary in the movement of combat elements, and supplies and equipment. It is also responsible for receiving and decentralized stocking of those supplies and equipment under it's authority and which combat forces have found to be in excess of their supplies after expropriation operations.

1. The building of hideouts that will serve from time to time the needs of combat units in operations in different area's of the state and other states as actions allow.

2. The acquiring, building and camouflaging of vans, buses, and other means to allow safe movement of supplies and personal.

3. Arming and armor plating of said type autos and the building of means of concealment for supplies and personal, to also build defense systems into said autos, such as oil, smoke, and nail release systems.

4. Maintaining of autos in top condition and giving them top speed and drive ability at the same time bulletproof and tires ect.

5. Acquiring, decentralized stocking and receiving and provid-

---

*The "National Question"—the question of whether and which ethnic minorities deserve a territorial homeland within the United States—was a major question of dogma up for debate in 1973 among most of the "Maoist" and "Marxist-Leninist" groups in the Bay Area. The concern was a rehash of black nationalist Ron Karenga's proposal for a black homeland secure in "defensive isolation."

ing of phony and real ID papers, uniforms of movement, such as disguises for mailmen, priest, gas man, policeman, nun, army, navy, airforce, wigs, shoes and type said equipment, parts to repair autos, gas and oil facilities, tires, and power generating equipment for tools.

MEDICAL UNIT

It is the responsibility of the Medical Unit to provide medical combat personal when combat units open operations in any area of the state. To provide needed medical care that elements of our forces may need from time to time and to decentralize stocking of medical supplies and equipment under its authority and that may be sent from forward combat troops after expropriation operations against the enemy. It is the Medical Units responsibility to build and find means to safely hide medical equipment. . . . It is the responsibility of the Medical Unit to build and provide underground operating rooms and the needed personal and equipment to run them in all and different areas of the state, both in urban and rural areas.

1. The building of recuperation areas that are security sound.

2. The building of mobile medical teams that are able to be within a 15 mile area from force units in it's operations thereby allowing combat elements aid as soon as possible under war conditions.

3. The building of training facility for medical combat training, warfare and it's medical needs call for military medical training in the areas of gun shot wounds, cuts, shock, gas burns, poison ect. and should be held as the main training priority.

4. Acquiring of generating power equipment for operating rooms and medical equipment.

5. The acquiring, receiving and decentralized stockpiling of medical supplies and equipment across the state in safe and underground areas with only a few security cleared personal knowing the whereabouts of said supplies.

ARMORMENT UNIT

It is the responsibility of the Armorment Unit to provide, stock, build and repair military equipment and to develop new revolutionary weapons. To provide decentralized stocking and hiding areas for weapons and ammo and other type equipment, and supply combat elements with supplies when needed.

1. To build booby traps, bulletproofing, and mines, electric shotgun mines ect.

2. To build facilities for the making of machine guns, reload-

ing equipment, cyanide bombs and bullets, poison and arms to fire them with.

3. Acquiring or building ammo, gas masks, sniper rifles, silencers, mortars, anti-tank weapons, flamethrowers, and explosives.

4. To work with others in the use of the people and the people's creativity to find new means and ways to destroy the enemy better than he can destroy us.

PROVISION UNIT

It is the responsibility of the Provision Unit to provide food and other such supplies as are under it's authority to those units that request it, to see to it that the needs of the Medical Unit are met and that of other units. To form and develop hiding places and underground areas where food and other provisions can be safely stored.

1. Stocking of canned foods and other foods and acquiring of means to maintain the food value of these foods.

2. Decentralized stocking across the state of foods, cooking fuels, equipment for cooking, soap and other equipment necessary.

COMMUNICATION UNIT

It is the responsibility of the Communication Unit to see to it and provide all combat support groups, support units and command sections with communication equipment, to repair said and build it's own equipment if possible to train personal in the use of radio and type equipment and to provide trained personal to combat units and command sections.

1. To build and maintain jamming and monitoring equipment and personal to jam and monitor enemy communications.

2. To build with other units, communication lines between other units, by clear and approved security means, to form teams of communications runners, made up of dogs, birds, women, children, old comrade people, ect., to form areas to aid units in forming dead drops and end cuts for security.

3. To maintain, acquire and receive equipment that has been expropriated by combat units from the enemy, and supply said equipment when needed to other units.

4. To stock by decentralized means across the state these supplies and to also build and set up communication teams across the state with both long and short range radio equipment, thereby giving them the ability to keep all of our units in full contact with each at all times.

INTELLIGENCE UNIT

It is the responsibility of the Intelligence Unit to build and provide means whereby the enemy is always two steps behind us, but never in front of us, it must maintain a ever flowing line of information on the enemy, informers, and supplies that our forces may need. It must intake intelligence and find out clearly the truth of it and pass it on to command sections as soon as possible, it must not overlook any action of the enemy or those who are near the enemy. It must maintain running files and run photo teams to be able to supply the unit and central command with all possible information on the enemy or buildings and terrain that may be needed in carrying out of operations.

1. Building of files on known informers and agents, addresses, family, photo if possible, car color and license number.

2. The forming of information on the movements of police, agents, prison officers and family, photos if possible.

3. Formulating information on movement of money, military equipment, medical supplies, food supplies, arms, explosives, radio equipment, gas and oil and other type supplies.

4. Acquiring of maps of government institutions, jails, prisons, banks, storm drains, communication stations and lines, power plants and lines, oil and gas and other fuel supply tanks areas, airports, navy, army base area and explosive and arms makers locations and security that is used for all these type buildings and areas.

5. Information on movements of police and other military elements, placing of S.L.A. agents in police and military institutions.

6. Forming of counter intelligence agent teams and the forming of means to carry out security checks of S.L.A. personal.

PROPAGANDA UNIT

It is the responsibility of the Propaganda Unit to maintain clandestine press and printing equipment, mimeograph equipment or other type means to provide newspapers, pamphlets, flyers and stamps for propaganda and agitation against the enemy and to allow the people to know both our victories and our failures, to provide the people with truthful information on it's oppression and the need for them to fight against the common enemy as one people.

1. The incorporation of members of the people for the purpose of working in propaganda actions in their community, to train them in the use of walls, tape recordings, loudspeakers, drawings and other forms of propaganda.

2. To provide propaganda to the actions of combat units

against the enemy, to seek to turn enemy soldiers against their officers, to seek to keep unity among our people, while the enemy is trying to divide us.

3. To use radio and other means to bring forth a war of nerves against the enemy, and to give the spirit of struggle to all our people.

4. To by letters sent to government officers attempt to turn them to our side and explaining the meaning of our armed forces actions and that their only hope is to take the side that will win in the end, the people.

5. The misinforming, spreading lies and forming of uncertainty in the enemies forces and personal in local areas, announcing of false information to the enemy, using rumors, information on corruption of government members and all possible means to bring about a war of nerves upon the enemy.

There was imagination, ingenuity, and more than a bit of Ian Fleming in that document. And there was scope. Size. It was for the legions of the future, those who would flock to join his handful of followers, that DeFreeze laid out this plan. The "unit" would become a platoon, the platoon a company, the company a division. *"To Those Who Would Bear The Hopes And Future Of Our Children, Let The Voice Of Their Guns Express The Words Of Our Children's Freedom,"* he boldly scrawled across the bottom of the last page. Time crowded, history waited.

Among several never-issued SLA communiqués later discovered by police, the earliest was dated October 8—marked "Communiqué No. 1"—and was written to claim credit for a planned "attack" on Avis Rent a Car and the General Tire and Rubber Company. The communiqué accused them of serving and supporting the "fascist governments" of Israel, Portugal, South Africa, Chile, and Great Britain.

That attack was canceled—or at least put off. Avis wasn't considered a good enough target; a bombing was not what was needed to introduce the Symbionese Liberation Army properly. It was not bold enough, not overtly revolutionary enough. It did not clearly define the no-quarter stance of the SLA. DeFreeze and his Symbionese wanted to go public with an act that would at once elevate the SLA as a preeminent revolutionary group and separate them from the radicals who had refused to go to war. An execution would do that—an assassination of a public figure in which the SLA would be the fist of the people's rage.

Raymond Procunier, director of the California Department of Corrections, was a priority target. His murder was planned, then canceled, according to police intelligence sources. Rumor had it that convict associates of the SLA vetoed the idea, complaining that murdering "Pro" would only put the prisons into a tight lock-up and install an even more repressive regime.

The Symbionese were not sure whom to target next. Then, as Wheeler recalls: "We was sitting around the house one day drinking wine and somebody started talking about this dude Foster. At the time there was a lot of feeling against him in the community; Bobby Seale was raising hell about him and all. All of a sudden DeFreeze sits up and says, 'Man, we're gonna waste that nigger!'"

5

William Lawton Wolfe .... *Cujo,*d. May 17, 1974
Camilla Hall .... *Gabi,*d. May 17, 1974
(Patricia) Mizmoon Soltysik *Zoya,*d. May 17, 1974

OF the core SLA, Willie Wolfe was the youngest until twenty-year-old Patty Hearst became Tania. He had just turned twenty-three when he died. He was a key figure in the early SLA, but a month after the Foster killing he left the group, saying he planned to leave the country. Weeks later, when it was war and the SLA was on the run after the arrest of Little and Remiro, he returned. It was he who brought his radical friends to the BCA; it was he who became the SLA's courier to Death Row Jeff—but Wolfe is remembered not as the soldier, but as Tania's lover, Cujo.

"Cujo was the gentlest, most beautiful man I've ever known. He taught me the truth as he learned it from the beautiful brothers in California's concentration camps," said Tania mourning and vengeful after the LA shoot-out. "Neither Cujo or I have ever loved an individual the way we loved each other, probably because our relationship wasn't based on bourgeois fucked-up values, attitudes, and goals."

Like most of the SLA, Willie had rejected a great deal. The son of Dr. L. S. Wolfe of Emmaus, Pennsylvania, a wealthy anesthesiologist, Willie had been raised in Connecticut and northern New York, moving several times. When Willie was fifteen, the family was jolted when his father divorced his mother to marry a much younger woman. It became an extended family—his mother had two children by a first marriage and four, including him, by her second; his father had two more by his second and present wife—and sibling relationships were full of rivalries and debate. But Willie stayed close to his mother, and he and all the children had a deep affection for his father.

Willie attended an exclusive Massachusetts prep school, Mount Hermon. A lanky six-footer, he was nicknamed Wee Willie, was sports editor of the paper and a varsity swimmer. Quiet, almost meek, he did not smoke or drink and tried to follow all the rules, and so was the butt of jokes and pranks. His grades were mediocre, but he graduated in 1969 a National Merit Scholar finalist, scoring high 700s in his college boards. But 1969 was a turbulent year, a difficult year for kids of privilege awakening to social crisis. Willie was trying to sort it all out—his family, the war, the relevance of college, success American style. He rejected the family tradition of attending Yale and instead moved into New York's Harlem for a year—living with a black former Franciscan friar who had spent a summer with the Wolfes years before in a program to bring ghetto kids into the country. Shunning his preppie friends, he worked as an insurance-company clerk and bought his clothes secondhand. "He was looking for a life of a little deprivation," said the ex-monk; "when you've had it easy, maybe you feel guilty because you haven't been able to experience life in the raw."

From Harlem, Willie went to London, then off through Europe for nine months. He had borrowed a few hundred dollars from his father and took a budget tour. He stayed with friends, took odd jobs, and bummed around. Always he noted contrasts to American affluence.

Back in the States, he arrived in Berkeley in January, 1971: nineteen years old, a young radical groping for a creed, full of his experiences. He enrolled at UC Berkeley, lived two months in a dorm, then moved into the Peking House commune.

His father was paying the bills, but by the end of the year he was illegally getting food stamps. "I'm looking for ways to ease my dependence on the old man," he explained to his mother in a letter. He asked her to sell his Standard Oil of New Jersey stock. Family money burdened him. He would lecture parents and siblings on the virtue of poverty. On a visit home he told his stepmother, "Your income is outrageous and unjustified—all you need to live on is three thousand dollars a year." (His sister Roxanne remembers how Sharon, his usually placid stepmother, leveled him, replying: "That's right, Willie. Three thousand for you to go to college this year, three thousand for your mother, three thousand for Roxanne to go to school. . . .")

By January, 1972, Willie was writing his mother predicting, "America is heading for either Communism or 1984." His choice was Communism. After the divorce Virginia Wolfe, his mother, had moved to Litchfield, Connecticut, a Yankee-squire town of country wealth that Willie came to detest. He urged her to move—not "to continue to be a passive enemy of the people in their struggle for a decent life." Caught up in the East Bay subculture, he defined himself as a Maoist, a revolutionary. Political friends remember him as shy, seldom speaking up at meetings, but he became deeply involved with the prison issue and the BCA. After one year he decided to drop out of college to devote himself to political activity. When his mother wrote, urging him to reconsider, he replied, "The sick New England, white American standards of success that we've managed to see through are still clogging your brain."

He took karate lessons and began, like many local revolutionaries, to practice at gun ranges. "He was always very disciplined," said a radical friend; "when he said he was going to do something he did it. If a picket line was going to start at four o'clock, he was there at four, not four ten." He was very close with a number of women, but friends remember only one romance—with a Swedish girl whom he had met in Europe, who visited Berkeley and was later deported. He conscientiously wrote his mother—aggressive, caring, demanding letters; urging her to sell her stock holdings ("great complicity in the War") and luxury possessions ("Forget the highboy and other treats/security for your children"). She, too, should live on $3,000 a year, he said.

None of his brothers or sisters, neither older nor younger, accepted the line; they found it simplistic and teased and argued with him.

But by October, 1973, when Dr. Wolfe visited Willie for a week in Oakland, his son had already moved out of Peking House and was living with Joe Remiro. The SLA had formed, and Willie was holding gun classes for small groups of SLA confederates.

Willie introduced his father to friends as "Ace." An Oakland friend later said, "It was clear there was a tremendous amount of affection between Ace and Willie and that Willie was having a hard time with Ace not sharing his political views—but in a much nicer way than most of us deal with our parents about politics. It was kind of a mutual acceptance in which Ace said, 'Well, this is where Willie's at and I accept him and love him'—and Willie saying, 'Well, this is where my father's at and I don't want to be like him in twenty-five years, but I love him too.'"

Dr. Wolfe was a little dazzled by his glimpse of Willie's world: "There were several fantastic things. People kept dropping in every five minutes interested in the Vietnam War, Arabs, Indians on

Alcatraz, women's lib. There was a gal who had decided she would do something for women's lib, so she got a job as a longshoreman. Every night we'd throw her on the floor and knead her muscles back into some sort of shape. . . . I was surprised, given Willie's absolute indifference to skin color, that there were no Negroes who showed up. We talked about Ireland, Israel, lots of causes. . . ."

Dr. Wolfe was impressed by the passion, pace, and variety of Willie's life—but the deeper concerns of Willie, Russ Little, Joe Remiro, and other friends he met went unmentioned. Three weeks later, on November 6, the SLA murdered Marcus Foster.

In early December his stepmother received a letter from Willie saying there was a slim chance he might be home for Christmas. On December 20 he arrived unexpectedly in Emmaus, wearing a blue cotton Mao jacket and a blue skull cap that his sister Roxanne irreverently dubbed "Willie's we-the-people hat." He had left the car his father bought him on the West Coast and hitchhiked East. He was not going back to California, he told Roxanne, to whom he was closest; after Christmas he was going to Sweden to marry, to stay. He went up to visit his mother almost immediately and told her the same thing. His mother accused him of copping out, running away from this country, but he would not answer her. As a wedding present she gave him a "substantial check" (never cashed, according to the family). "I questioned him about his philosophy and how, with his beliefs, he could accept money from me," said Mrs. Wolfe, "but he just told me, 'You wouldn't understand.'"

At his father's house his politics and incessant talk of China had no better audience (although the family was now concerned about and interested in prison problems). Willie's younger brother John, a music student and Buddhist, complained that politics was all Willie could talk about, "but he doesn't really know much, he has a lot of ideas and little information." Sister Roxanne was gleefully introducing him as "Willie my Communist brother." (He snapped at her finally: "Some of my friends are going to be dead in three to five years because they can't keep their mouths shut!") The holidays were busy and the house was full of guests; it was not until January 9 or 10 that Willie told his father of his engagement and plans to expatriate. The two planned a dinner alone Friday night, the eleventh, to talk of the future.

On January 10 Russ Little and Joe Remiro were arrested and identified with the SLA. On the eleventh Willie received three collect calls (later traced to pay phones in Oakland). He told the family he urgently had to go to New York to visit a sick friend. No, he could not wait for dinner.

On February 4 Patty Hearst was kidnapped. Investigators believe Willie was back in California by then, though his mother received a Valentine's Day card—an unusual gesture—signed by her son, postmarked New York, February 11. It was the last the family heard from him.

Only Camilla Hall lingered as long before she, too, went underground with the SLA. She did not disappear until two weeks after the Hearst kidnapping, on February 19—the FBI showed up at her home six days later. Perhaps for Camilla there was doubt, second thoughts; at twenty-nine she was the oldest of the women, Bill Harris' age, with only DeFreeze her elder. An accomplished poet, painter, for years an avowed pacifist, Camilla seemed the least likely of the SLA soldiers, yet invites the most simplistic explanation.

Camilla's first tie with the nascent SLA was more personal than political. It was her intimate friend and sometime lover, Mizmoon Soltysik—who had legally changed her name from Patricia to Mizmoon after Camilla rechristened her in a love poem—who became DeFreeze's protector after his escape, perhaps his first recruit. Camilla and Mizmoon—Gabi and Zoya—the lesbian soldiers of the SLA; on the run, they were always thought of as together. "*Arm in arm in Revolution*," as Camilla wrote, "*Arm in arm in love.*" In a group that took great liberties with rank, neither was ever introduced with a title. And if the media showed unexpected restraint in handling their sexuality, it was more likely due to bewilderment than to tolerance.

In 1968 Camilla had fled to the West Coast from Minnesota, perhaps seeking that tolerance. She lived for three years in Los Angeles, living off her savings and a small income from her art sales, then, at twenty-six, she moved north to Berkeley in late 1971. She settled in an old apartment building on Channing Way; her upstairs neighbor was twenty-one-year-old Pat Soltysik. The Channing Way block was almost a Berkeley legend, a paradigm for communal neighborhoods. The residents were young dropouts and a few students, crowded into a jumble of cheap apartment buildings and decrepit Victorian houses, but the community developed a rare collective identity. There were communal gardens, a block food co-op (the Food Conspiracy), a neighborhood coffeehouse, block parties, street security programs. On a front lawn mid-block stood a ten-foot-high papier-mâché red fist.

Camilla and Mizmoon were soon lovers. "They were very proud of it," said a friend. It was Thanksgiving Day, and one of the neighbors had a feast for forty people with three turkeys. Pat came in "very, very excited," remembers a neighbor. "They didn't come in and announce it to the group or anything, but they were holding hands and that's when they publicly wanted everyone to know. It was almost like an announcement, as if someone were to walk in and announce we're going to be married next year. On our block that was the way it was done . . . when you first fall in love with someone, you walk with your arm around her or him or whatever or whoever it is. In this case it happened to be the two of them."

Channing Way remembers Mizmoon in her T-shirts and peasant blouses and baggy diaphanous harem pants; short, about five feet four inches, with dark hair clipped in a pageboy cut, yet a formidable woman, with a stern strong face. Camilla is remembered as heavyset, with thick granny glasses and short blond hair; she wore green army surplus fatigues or denim overalls and hiking boots. When Camilla arrived, Mizmoon was already a veteran of three years on the block. She had carried the name Patricia for her first twenty-two years, then, with a group of lesbian friends, went to court and became Mizmoon. She demanded that even her family call her Mizmoon. When she became Zoya, she did not go to court.

Mizmoon had been searching to give her new SLA name deeper meaning, explained Tania in the last SLA communiqué; and on her twenty-fourth birthday, May 17, the day of the LA holocaust, she found it. "Zoya," chanted Tania in her fiercest eulogy, "female guerrilla, perfect love and perfect hate reflected in stone-cold eyes."

Pat Soltysik was the third of seven children, the oldest of five girls. She had grown up in Goleta, north of Los Angeles, the daughter of a pharmacist. It had been a close family—Mizmoon always spoke warmly of them, said friends—but her parents had divorced. "Mizmoon was very close with my mother," said her elder brother Fred, but "she and my father didn't get along." She was graduated from Dos Pueblos High School in 1968, senior-class treasurer, popular, and in the top 10 percent of her class. She left Goleta "superstraight," said her brother, but then Berkeley's turbulent years worked their magic.

She arrived in Berkeley on a state scholarship in the fall of 1968. She moved in with her boyfriend, Gene, a computer-science student, who already had an apartment on Channing Way. At the university she was studying French and Spanish (the Soltysik children had grown up speaking French). On the block she and Gene were among the fifteen-odd key people who put time and muscle into developing the Channing community; friends thought them a very close couple. They lived together for two years, but then, as one friend explained, "in Berkeley, you have all these roads to go down. You can become anything. You can take one road and never come back. Gene became really involved in IBM stuff. She was going one way, Gene another." In 1970 Gene wanted out of the Berkeley scene, and in August the two parted.

Whatever happened between Pat and Gene was probably not unlike the failure of many marriages, but it pushed Pat into a desperately liberated chaos. "She was anti-men for a while after Gene; she became celibate toward men," said a close friend, "but then it just became Kellogg's Corn Flakes Variety Time." She became bisexually promiscuous and very active. "I don't think she ever went through a big thing about being a homosexual," said Jesse, a black man who was intermittently her lover. "She was very fond of men, very fond of lovemaking . . . she just dug women, too. She wasn't really heavy politically, but she was aware of the political situation around her. She was into making things, photography, drying plants, a little ceramics." On campus, said a friend, she staked out a table for her feminist friends and was known as a women's activist, but "she was more of a silent doer, not getting out in front of people and yelling." But in 1971 she dropped out of school in her junior year—according to several friends, to work on a photo essay about women, perhaps a book on Japanese women. She had taken a black-studies course and become interested in the prison issue; she began to write to prisoners. Both she and Camilla became supporters of the United Prisoners Union, the radical ex-convicts group, working on a UPU filmscript; but strangely—according to UPU leader Popeye Jackson—both were like most of the "white sisters" in the prison movement, they seemed interested only in the male prisoners, the hoped-for soldiers of the revolution.

Mizmoon's brother Fred, who became the family spokesman, said his sister lived in Berkeley "because it was an ideological ghetto and it gave her the support she thought she needed." He described her as a "gentle person," but said her political rhetoric had become increasingly violent. Fred Soltysik became an outspoken and a bitter critic of the SLA soon after his sister was identified with the group; the only such voice raised from the families of the SLA members. He said his sister had a history of "guilt-tripping herself into relationships with men like Cinque. . . . It's a recorded psychological state of mind that some white women get into," he said. "She took a lot of shit and swallowed every word." Several of Mizmoon's acquaintances and lovers have suggested, like her brother, that the only men she was interested in were black, but little is known of Mizmoon's many turbulent affairs.

Like many of the other SLA members—Bill Harris at the post office, Emily Harris at UC Berkeley, Angela Atwood with her waitresses union, Willie Wolfe at the S-K-S Die Casting plant in Oakland—both Mizmoon and Camilla were deeply involved in union activities. (Perhaps it was not coincidental. The Venceremos organization urged members and associates to get into labor organizing.) In January, 1972, Mizmoon got a part-time job as a janitor in the Berkeley city library and became an organizer for a small group of employees trying to unionize, a struggle that eventually led to a strike that was settled with increased benefits but with a nonunion shop. "She was just learning how to organize women," said one of the strike leaders, "but she acted like a sort of shop steward." Other employees described her as immature, having difficulty relating to older people. It was during the strike that Mizmoon began to study Communist theory.

A black friend remembers her visiting him and his girlfriend in mid-1973, looking around at their nice apartment, and going away "pissed, really pissed." It was middle-class comfort—bourgeois, to her—and "she was anti-middle class one hundred percent," he said. She wrote him an accusing letter, which he got so furious reading he ripped to shreds. "I called her after I got her letter," he remembers, "and I tried to explain that I, unlike her, had gone through a poor thing in my childhood and that now my needs meet my means." And he reminded her, somewhat sardonically, "You can go back anytime to the way you were."

For Mizmoon, her relationship with Camilla seems to have been a stabilizing factor for a while, but within a year the two were parting to become "just good friends." Mizmoon wanted to have relationships with others, and Camilla had become very jealous. But Camilla, for her part, had found something precious in the relationship. "She really loved Pat," said a close friend. "She was really aware of her jealousy and possessiveness and she was working on it, but there were a lot of ups and downs." Finally there were too many. But, said another friend, "her sexual needs had been more fulfilled by Pat than by anyone." While they were together, Camilla "seemed to just glow."

The realization of her sexuality had been awkward and painful for Camilla, the only daughter of a Lutheran minister from Minnesota. She told close friends that only in Berkeley had she decided she was gay; but she had wrestled with it for a long time. Even before she was graduated from the University of Minnesota in 1966, friends said Candy—the childhood nickname she dropped when she moved West—was running with an "artsy-craftsy set of young poets and artists" which included several gay women. A professor friend there remembers Candy tentatively and abstractly bringing up the subject of homosexuality. After graduation she spent two years as a welfare social worker in Duluth and Minneapolis. Camilla would later complain of the frustration of her work with unwed mothers—abortions were unavailable, and her job was to pry for a personal history and set up paternity suits.

Camilla's parents, the Reverend Dr. George Hall and his wife, live now in Lincolnwood, a properous Chicago suburb, where he is pastor of St. John's Lutheran Church. Burdened by tragedy, the family was always close. As a child and in her teens Camilla had watched a brother and a sister die of congenital nephritis, a kidney disorder, and another brother die of polio. She was the only surviving child. Reverend Hall had been director of the African Lutheran Ministry, but the family returned to Minnesota when Camilla was seven, and her father taught at Gustavus Adolphus College. In 1955 Reverend Hall took a new parish in St. Paul, and then in 1960 he was named the Lutheran chaplain to students at the University of Minnesota. After her freshman year nineteen-year-old Camilla and her parents toured South America for four and a half months; she returned horrified by the poverty and deprivation she had seen.

The move to Los Angeles was sudden: She decided and was in LA two weeks later. She shared a home with friends from Minnesota in Topanga Canyon, had her own apartment for a while, then moved in with a bisexual friend. She concentrated on her art—primitive line drawings, often with a Rabelaisian eroticism. (A gallery manager she dealt with remembers best a drawing that first appeared to be a Madonna and Child, but on closer examination was seen as a man hugging his giant penis.) She sold her work—in LA and after she moved to the Bay Area—at the open shopping-center bazaars common in California, pricing a drawing at $30 or $40.

She loved Berkeley at first, she told friends, for "the gentle socialism," the respected lesbian community, and a good market for her work. Radical friends in Minnesota described her politics there as "Peter, Paul and Mary," and LA friends remember her criticizing others for being "too militant," but in Berkeley she picked up the rhetorical cant of the revolution. Openly acknowledged that her sexuality was a release. Her poetry became more explicitly sexual:

> I will cradle you
> In my woman hips
> Kiss you
> With my woman lips,
> Fold you to my heart and sing:
> Sister Woman,
> You are a joy to me.

"She liked the idea," said Mizmoon's brother Fred, that there was another Camilla, an Amazon warrior who fought against Troy, mentioned in *The Aeneid.*

But within a year, in 1972, the glow had dimmed; the spirit and fabric of the sixties counterculture seemed lost. Mizmoon had moved off Channing early in the year, to live with another woman. Camilla had told a friend, "The Berkeley experience is dead." She had enjoyed it, but now it was time to move on. She stayed until fall, to have a benign tumor removed from her breast, then flew to Greece. Just before she left, at the annual Berkeley fall arts festival, friends remember she was visited at her booth by Mizmoon and another young woman, who was introduced as Ling—it was Nancy Ling Perry.

Camilla was in Europe only two and a half months, although she had gone with the intention of staying. She had even talked to friends of the possibility of her parents' retiring in Greece or Spain with her. Like many of the SLA who were known to have traveled in Europe—Wolfe, Soltysik, the Harrises—Camilla sought an ethic, a culture, better than her own. But each returned. "She had expected to find a utopia," said a close friend. She complained that she had been "half cold all the time" because there was no central heating, her father remembers.

Camilla flew back to Illinois, where she had left her car with family, then headed west. Mizmoon flew east to Denver to meet her, and the two reconciled lovers drove back to California, stopping briefly to visit friends at the Duck Lake Commune, a small isolated lesbian collective on 160 acres near the mountain community of Nederland, Colorado. (Mizmoon Soltysik had previously stayed at Duck Lake, and the commune's few cabins in the hills became one focus of the later FBI search for Tania and the Harrises.) On February 15, they arrived at Santa Barbara, giggly and happy, to visit Mizmoon's family and eke out a final few vacation days. Camilla, with her infectious grin, folk guitar, and busy sketchbook, quickly won the affection of Mizmoon's family, but that night the two lovers quarreled, and Camilla drove off for Berkeley, leaving Mizmoon in tears. The issue was an old one: Camilla's monogamy and Mizmoon's bisexual polygamy. It was not the first time Camilla had stalked off to "protect herself," and she would come back, as before. The man at the time was Chris Thompson, but before Camilla's reconciliation, Thompson would be displaced by DeFreeze. Mizmoon's open promiscuity (she admitted to even having an affair with the postman who brought her Camilla's letters from Europe) unbalanced the shared weapon that is every love affair. Mizmoon, who had picked up poetry and watercolors to emulate Camilla, recorded her reactions that evening:

> Why do I justify to you
> the good feelings I have
> with other people,
> with a man especially?
> Do you think I've
> run to a man?
> No momma-----
>   I ain't running
>   to no man-----
> I don't run to someone
>   to escape.
> I go to them to grow,
> to share, to join.*

In Berkeley again, Camilla got an apartment alone and then a job as a gardener with the East Bay Regional Park District, which

---

*The several poems of Mizmoon Soltysik that are published in this work first appeared in *In Search of a Sister* (Bantam Books; March, 1976), a sensitive and loving portrait of Mizmoon, written by her brother, Fred Soltysik, who graciously granted permission for their inclusion here.

had been pressured to hire women. She was assigned to Lake Temescal, one of the smaller parks in the district, where there was only a supervisor and two groundkeepers, Camilla and a very ill old man who could no longer do his job. Her supervisor, Ed Collins, a calloused and graying laborer in his fifties, had been hesitant about hiring her. By doing the work of any two men, she won him over completely. "She really was an incredible woman," he remembers. He was amazed with the ease with which she could enforce the park rules, always a problem. She would go up to a group of black teenagers drinking or smoking pot, he remembers, and in a few minutes they would be calling her sister and a little later would leave laughing. She eventually told him she was gay, that she "didn't own a dress." She told him a great deal about herself; they talked about the park, socialism, the landscaping business—and perhaps to the surprise of each, they became good friends.

Camilla loved her job—planting and landscaping—but it had a built-in crisis. The district board had approved the hiring of a group of women only as six-month "temporaries," and Camilla, working with feminist groups and the municipal employees union, became deeply involved in an unsuccessful fight to get the board to hire them full time. She became the women's organizer and spokesperson in demonstrations and before the district board and the press. "She was an organizer's pay dirt, a leader, and just an excellent person," said the business manager of the union. She was infuriated, he said, when another employee reported to her and union officials that he had overheard a senior park official remark that she would never be hired because of her union activism. She was terminated as of September 30. She worked that last day with tears in her eyes, said Collins.

Ten days later Mizmoon quit her job at the library. The SLA was gearing for its war. Foster was killed in November, and Patty Hearst kidnapped in February. Despite her occasional visits and notes, Mizmoon had refused to give her family a mail address since May, deeply worrying them. Her Christmas card, a black-and-white of an African mother with child, carried a fearsome poem, a jarring challenge to the season's spirit:

TO MY FAMILY

do you walk
where people are poor

do you pretend
you are one of the rich
by "knowing" them
    and serving them

do you hide from
asking, searching out
what is happening here?
does Nazi Germany
look like an old-fashioned
    USA
didn't they like today
introduce fascism

in an underhanded quiet
way (and in "someone" else's back yard)
later, when too late
People scream. Yes! Yes! it's here!
Are we hiding? Are we pretending
wishing we are what we aren't
so that we won't be included
    in the genocide?
If I had a black baby
    would you hide him for me?
Please
have you walked
where the people are poor?
do you feel their beauty and strength?
do you too feel married to the free?

Mrs. Soltysik, an immigrant who had experienced the Nazi occupation of Belgium, wept tears of frustration as she read the
card. "Of course I would hide the baby," she told her son, "but
why would I have to hide it? I don't understand."

Through the winter, Camilla had kept in touch with her old
boss; she would call him to tell him jokes and occasionally come
up to the park to visit. Camilla did not go underground until February 19—fifteen days after the kidnapping—but on the nineteenth she went back to say good-bye to Eddie Collins. She ran up
to him on one of the paths and gave him a big hug. She said she
did not have time to stay, but she wanted to say good-bye. She had
found a great gardening job in Palo Alto, she told him, with great
money and a great carriage house to live in.

The Hearst family had just announced the ransom food-distri-
bution plan, and there were reports in the press of poverty groups

and others refusing food bought with blood money. "Isn't it a shame about the poor people not taking the food?" she asked Collins as they walked through the park together. She went on talking about poor people—and "surplus people," like herself, she said. Surplus people are those willing to work, educated and fit for work—and *needed*, as at the park—but whom society would not assimilate. It was the society, she said, that had failed.

The week before, she had visited a young San Francisco couple, Paul and Joyce Halverson, longtime friends from Minnesota. She told them she was moving to Palo Alto, and to their astonishment, she wanted to give them her prize possessions: her furniture, her artwork, even Keya, the cat she adored. Her new home was small and she would not have room, she told them; besides, she was tired of much of it. When she first told them, Joyce joked, "I'll bet you're going to join the SLA." Camilla grinned and gave her a hug. "No, Joyce, I know you wish I were, but I'm not." And on the eighteenth, when Camilla came to say good-bye, Joyce told her with a smile, "Well, I'm glad you're not joining the SLA because you're too old for that kind of idealism." Joyce remembers no reaction but a quick parting hug.

The Halversons could not take Keya, and it is said in Berkeley that Camilla put the cat on the street with a note around its neck begging the finder to give it a loving home.

Camilla was probably the first to die in the shoot-out in LA, from a bullet through her forehead. A letter to her parents was found beneath the crushed and burned body, and beside her in the ashes were the charred remains of the homeowner's pet cat. The letter told her parents that the SLA was managing to stay "several jumps" ahead of the police by virtue of their "creativity and determination to survive and carry on the business of the revolution."

> . . . our support is from the people and will continue to grow with each victory as we prove to the American people that the revolution can indeed be successful. We intend to be around for quite a while to live and see the victories. I know you trust my sincerity even if you haven't come to agree with the course of action I have committed myself to. I am young and strong and willing to dedicate my courage, intelligence, and love to the work. I really feel good about what I am doing and I want you to also. . . .

The letter, even if mailed, would not have reached her parents. Like a previous letter, it was addressed to a close friend of Camilla's, who lived near her parents, with a request it be delivered by hand. But Camilla did not know any revolutionaries back in Illinois. Her friend probably loved Camilla, but was terrified of the SLA. When the woman received the first letter, she—like several others who were asked to pass on letters from the SLA to parents—immediately called the Federal Bureau of Investigation.

6

Assassination

OUTSIDE, there were three of them. They had taken up their assigned positions and were waiting. Two leaned casually against the building. The third crouched in the foliage.

Upstairs, on the third floor of the Oakland Board of Education building, Deputy Superintendent Robert Blackburn was in his office chatting with Associate Superintendent Andrew Viscovich. Blackburn checked his watch again and wondered if he was going to make it to the polls in time to cast his ballot. It was almost 7 P.M. If Foster did not hurry, Blackburn was not going to be able to vote. The polls closed at 8 o'clock.

Tuesday, November 6, 1973, was General Election Day in California. Shortly before 8 A.M. Blackburn had picked up his boss and closest friend, Superintendent Marcus Foster, and the two had driven to work in Blackburn's Chevy Vega. The office schedule was crowded; the two had even had a working lunch, meeting with the labor arbitrator who three weeks before had helped avert a teachers' strike with a last-minute wage settlement. After lunch the two men worked through the afternoon at the office. At about 4 P.M. Foster hurried over to city hall, where the Oakland City Council was in session. In a budget squeeze, the council had cut recreation funds, and the high schools were no longer to be kept open for after-school use by students. Foster urged that the funds be restored. More than in most communities, he argued, the program was needed in Oakland. From city hall Foster had rushed back to chair a meeting of the Oakland Board of Education. It was a brief session, lasting until about 6:30 P.M.

A few minutes after 7 o'clock Marc Foster entered Blackburn's office. He already had his coat on. Blackburn put on his, the two said good night to Viscovich, and, briefcases in hand, walked down the three flights of stairs toward the back parking lot. Almost immediately as they left the building, Blackburn noticed them.

They were leaning against the building, facing each other, a few feet apart. It struck Blackburn that their presence there seemed strange. It was almost an alleyway between the buildings and a temporary portable classroom structure on the lot. It was dark— sunset that day was at 5:06 P.M.—but Blackburn noted that he recognized neither as an employee of the school district. Perhaps, he thought, they had been among the fifty-odd persons who had attended the board's open session. Or maybe they were waiting for someone still inside. He and Foster walked on. As they passed the pair, Blackburn glanced to his right. He got a good look at both of them.

The Vega was parked facing one end of the portable classroom in a stall marked by a small sign reading DEPUTY SUPERINTENDENT. Blackburn speeded up, heading around the back of the car to unlock the passenger door for Foster, who was still a few feet from the driver's side and walking in a direction that would have allowed him to pass by the front bumper of the auto.

Blackburn's recollection is that the first two shots sounded as if they had been fired almost simultaneously. He whirled around and saw the muzzle flashes of two handguns being fired at Foster, who was falling toward the asphalt of the parking stall labeled SUPERINTENDENT. The next instant, Blackburn was struck from behind by a load of double-aught pellets fired from a distance of no more than fifteen feet. The metal balls tore into the left side of his back. Amazingly, it only staggered him. He recalls being immediately conscious of great burning pain and an awareness he had to keep moving, had to get help. . . . "For Marc." He moved to his right. There was another explosion of sound. A second load of shotgun pellets had been fired at him from the bushes. This time only one or two of the ball-bearing-size pellets hit him. The rest of the charge missed and struck the car. He kept going, stumbling, almost falling, lurching, a distance of some sixty feet, finally coming to a doorway. He still had his keys in his right hand, and he fumbled for the one that would unlock the door, found it, opened the door, and only then did he collapse, in the hallway on the ground floor of the Board of Education building.

David Tom was working in the mimeograph room in the basement of the building when he heard the shots. He rushed upstairs and down a corridor. He heard Blackburn cry out, "Help . . . get help," and saw the figure of the deputy slumped on the floor.

Tom raced to his side. "Dr. Foster . . . go help Dr. Foster . . . out there . . . he's been shot." Tom stood up. Down the hallway he could see a janitor running toward them. "Call the police," Tom ordered, and then he rushed outside. He found Dr. Foster lying face down on the pavement. No response. He grabbed a wrist and felt for a pulse, but felt nothing. He ran back into the building to make sure an ambulance had been summoned. Andrew Viscovich passed him in the doorway. When the associate superintendent checked for a pulse, he thought he felt one. He leaned down and put his mouth to the mouth of the black man and tried to give him back his life by breathing for him. But Marcus Foster was already dead.

Blackburn was conscious as attendants placed him on a stretcher and carried him out. He kept reassuring the school-administration staffers crowding the corridor, "Everything's going to be all right." He told one staffer to cancel a trip to Los Angeles because the man would be needed to handle a meeting Blackburn knew he was not going to be able to attend. He gave assignments and made suggestions as to how best to keep Oakland's schools running smoothly until he and Foster returned. An hour later he learned his friend was dead. Only then did he ask for something that would put him out. "I thought that it should be that either we should both be dead or both be alive," he recalls. "Marc dead and myself alive seemed totally unacceptable." Blackburn was taken to Highland Hospital, where he underwent emergency surgery. Foster's body was transported to the Alameda County Morgue.

Oakland homicide detectives had found considerable evidence at the scene of the assassination. There were eight shell casings that showed some of the bullets that had been fired into Foster had been Peters-Remington .380 Auto Super Vel ammunition. The autopsy would reveal a second handgun, a .38-caliber revolver, had also been used in the killing. Two shotgun shell casings—Remington 12-gauge—were also found. There were scuff marks in the earth in the spot where the person with the shotgun had obviously been hiding. Witnesses were questioned. A woman who had been driving by had seen three persons, all about the same height, running toward nearby Lake Merritt. There were a number of descriptions given police by citizens who thought they might have seen the killers. One reported having seen two black men running. That was the initial description of suspects broadcast over the police radio. They hoped a better description would come from Blackburn. An officer searching the area leading to

Lake Merritt made another discovery. Twelve live rounds of .45-caliber ammunition were found scattered in a line down a sloping hill, as if they had bounced out of a pocket of someone running. Two footprints were found along a dirt path, made by a medium-size lug-sole boot.

The City Council was about to convene for an evening session when a police officer entered the chambers, went over to City Manager Cecil Riley, and, in a low voice, informed him of the shootings. Riley turned ashen. He whispered it to Mayor John Reading. *God! Not Marc Foster!* Mayor Reading finally rapped for quiet, broke the news to the audience, and announced the meeting was adjourned. There was a collective outcry. A number of people in the crowd burst into tears.

At 9:45 A.M. the day after the murder, Dr. Allen McNie began the autopsy on Foster's corpse. His report would state that death had resulted from "shock and hemorrhage due to multiple gunshot wounds." Foster had been shot eight times. Five slugs had hit him in the back, two had entered his body from the front, and one had struck him in the leg. Any of several of the wounds would probably have killed him. The slugs had torn through vital organs. One had perforated the heart. Another had severed his spinal cord. Both lungs were punctured and collapsed. Most of the slugs had passed through the body. Not all of them were found. One of the bullets recovered, however, proved an important find.

Part of autopsy procedure in a shooting death calls for a study of how bullet holes in the clothing match up with wounds on the body. The pathologist noted the clothing, piece by piece. Examining the shirt, he observed a mechanical pencil and a ball-point pen clipped inside the left pocket over the heart region. He started to remove them, but as he reached inside, his fingers touched something else in the pocket, a small chunk of metal. He instinctively knew it was one of the bullets that had passed through Foster's body—it had gone through the heart—and exited from the chest, traveling so slowly at that point that it had stopped when it hit the pencil and pen, ending up tidily encased in the pocket. The doctor decided that the bullet should be photographed inside the pocket as it had been found, in case that should become an important point of evidence. When he took his fingers out of the pocket, he noted an odor. Sniffing his fingers, he knew at once he was smelling cyanide.

It was a touch of conscious melodrama awash in a venerable ocean of unintentioned psychodrama. Garlic bullets for the Revolution. When Dr. McNie and Detective Sergeant John Agler, the Oakland cop in charge of the investigation, examined the slug, they could see that the tip of it had been drilled out. Apparently the killers had filled the tiny holes with potassium cyanide, sealing them with wax. It was the bullets themselves that had killed Foster; the poison found in each of the slugs recovered was not sufficient, even the total amount, to cause death. Dr. McNie and the toxicologist who confirmed it was cyanide were sworn to secrecy by Sergeant Agler. He informed only the police chief of the find. He hoped the secret would hold while he worked to make some sense of it all.

In Oakland there was almost a palpable air of shock, pain, and loss. Marcus Foster was not a national figure—except in his field of education—but in the streets of ghetto Oakland elderly black women cried and trembled with rage and grief when they began talking about the murder of "Dr. Foster." Within the next few days the memorial services would give dramatic evidence of the depth of feeling: Literally thousands crowded special services held in all of the Oakland churches; 1,100 at a Roman Catholic cathedral for a mass concelebrated by the bishop and fifteen priests, 3,000 at his funeral at Beebe Memorial CME Temple, 4,500 for a memorial service at Oakland Coliseum Arena, crowds of grief and tears. Yet it was evident in Oakland as soon as word of the murder flashed public: Marcus Foster was being talked of as the ghettos talked of Martin Luther King, Malcolm X, the Kennedys after their assassinations. Blackburn, unlike Foster, was man rather than myth; but in black Oakland even the tight friendship between Foster and his white deputy was part of the myth.

The day after the murder—late—police issued a revised description of the assassins. There were three persons involved, all relatively young—in their late teens or early twenties—one quite possibly a woman. They had "hippie-length" hair. They had been dressed identically, almost as if in uniform. They were clad in dark-colored pants, denim jackets with a white patch sewn on the right breast of each, and dark-colored knit watch caps. Reporters asked if the suspects were blacks. "Possibly," was the answer. "Possibly" they were Latins. "Possibly" they were whites. "Possibly" the assassins were a multiracial group, the cops said. There was something else new. One witness to the killers' flight reported that one of the three sounded as if he—or she—were "giggling" as the trio ran from the scene.

(More than two years later, during her trial in early 1976 on bank robbery charges, Patricia Hearst would testify that she had been told the names of Dr. Foster's killers by Bill and Emily Harris while the three of them were traveling underground. In the Harrises' account it was Mizmoon Soltysik and Nancy Ling Perry [hair tucked under the watch caps] who fired the cyanide bullets into Foster while Donald DeFreeze blasted Blackburn with a shotgun. Joe Remiro and Russ Little were close by the murder scene in a "backup car," Patricia said she was told.)

The Black Panther Party, headquartered in Oakland, demanded the apprehension not only of the persons responsible for this "brutal and senseless murder" but also of those who planned it. Noting Watergate, they suggested the involvement of "powerful fascist elements." Ultraconservatives, including some police, were certain "commies" were the killers and tagged the Panthers as suspect. (Oakland police raided Panther headquarters soon after, and although they had to drop all charges and release the men arrested, they scored a publicity coup by releasing a photo of an arsenal—confiscated several years before—and claiming the guns were found at the Panther office.) Newspapers noted a Nazi leaflet recently distributed at an Oakland shopping center suggesting the murder of "satanic Jews and all their lackeys who are stirring up the niggers against us." The handbill warned: "There might be shotgun blasts into the guts of mixmaster principals and superintendents." Most people just assumed the killers were "crazies." There are a lot of them in California.

Then the deed drew a claim. On November 7, the day after the killing, Berkeley radio station KPFA received "Communiqué No. 1" from the Symbionese Liberation Army—a three-page document, the top sheet bearing a drawing of a seven-headed cobra.

SYMBIONESE LIBERATION ARMY
WESTERN REGIONAL YOUTH UNIT

Communiqué No. 1

Subject: The Board of Education	Warrant Order:
The Implementation of the	Execution by Cyanide Bullets
Internal Warfare Identifi-	Date: November 6, 1973
cation Computer System	Warrant Issued By:
	The Court of the People

Charges: Supporting and taking part in the forming and im-

plementation of a Political Police Force operating within the Schools of the People

Supporting and taking part in the forming and implementation of Bio-Dossiers through the Forced
Youth Identification Program

Supporting and taking part in the building of composite files for the Internal Warfare Identification Computer System

Target: Dr. Marcus A. Foster, Superintendent of Schools, Oak-
land, California
Robert Blackburn, Deputy Superintendent, Oakland,
California

On the afore stated date, elements of The United Federated
Forces of The S.L.A. did attack the Fascist Board of Education,
Oakland, California, through the person Dr. Marcus A. Foster,
Superintendent of Schools, and Robert Blackburn, Deputy
Superintendent.

This attack is to serve notice on the Board of Education and its
fascist elements that they have come to the attention of The
S.L.A. and The Court of the People and have been found guilty
of supporting and taking part in crimes committed against the
children and the life of the people.

This attack is also to serve notice on the Board of Education
and its fascist supporters that The Court of the People have is-
sued a Death Warrant on All Members and Supporters of the In-
ternal Warfare Identification Computer System. This SHOOT
ON SIGHT order will stay in effect until such time as ALL
POLITICAL POLICE ARE REMOVED FROM OUR SCHOOLS
AND ALL PHOTO AND OTHER FORMS OF IDENTIFICA-
TION ARE STOPPED.

Indictment:

No. 1: The Board of Education has taken upon itself the role of
forming and supporting a Special Political Police Force to
occupy and patrol the schools in our cities. The vast
Black, Chicano, Asian and conscious White youth communities of the Oakland-Berkeley area understand that
this newest extension of police surveillance is patterned
after fascist Amerikan tactics of genocide, murder and
imprisonment practiced by Amerikan financed puppet
governments in Vietnam, The Philippines, Chile and
South Africa. We recognize that the school system censors

and controls what we read, and that the Special Political Police Force is to censor and control what we say and do.

No. 2:   The Board of Education has taken upon itself the role of forming and supporting the implementation of Bio-Dossiers through the Forced Youth Identification Program. The Photo Identification Program, with the addition of composite files, is patterned after the system of apartheid in South Africa. The Bio-Dossiers classify our youth according to color and "criminal tendencies" (will to be free) and seek to eliminate all our valiant freedom fighters by "relocating" (incarcerating) them to such concentration camps as Tehachapi Prison. Under the Preventative Crime Act such concentration camps have the authority to incarcerate our youth from the age of 15 for an "indefinite" period of time. The Preventative Crime Act stipulates that any youth displaying violent or "crimminal" [sic] potential or the possibility of violent or "crimminal" potential in the future, in other words, any youth who oppose the current system of censored Political Police-State education and seek to organize against it are to be classified as dangerous and either disarmed, shot or imprisoned for expressing their rights to be free, and defending the rights to freedom of their fellow brothers and sisters.

No. 3:   The Board of Education has taken upon itself the role of supporting and taking part in the implementation of the Internal Warfare Identification Computer System. The Internal Warfare Tapes are based in the FBI's master computer system. Each state is required to feed this main computer system with information from the composite files of individuals who have expressed political views that may be regarded as differing from those of the fascist ruling class. Members of liberation movements and organizations, as well as single individuals, are identified through photographs and bio-dossiers supplied, in the case of our youth, by the Boards of Education and Public School Systems in our cities. The racist nature of the Internal Warfare Identification Computer System is clear since blacks and other minorities who refuse to serve the rich ruling class are automatically classified as potentially violent and "crimminal." The CIA-ITT financed junto [sic] government in Chile uses similar bio-dossiers to murder all identified people who oppose the military takeover there or who do not serve and support the interests of the wealthy. Similar programs are carried out by governments financed by Amerika and its military corporate enterprises throughout the world in the lands of the robbed; Vietnam, The Philippines, Chile, Brazil, Uruguay, South Africa are some prime examples.

The Black, Chicano, Asian and conscious White youth in our communities recognize the importance of the Oakland-Berkeley area to the liberation struggle of all oppressed people. We know that the ruling class must seek to stop the revolutionary community here before the ruling class can regain its arm of control around the struggling and oppressed people of the world.

We understand that the definition of a fascist government necessitates the elimination of all who oppose its controls. We know that the school system does not educate us, but rather it lies to us in an attempt to perpetuate the interests of the rich ruling class. News of the successful liberation struggles of our brothers and sisters throughout the world is stifled because the enemy fears our knowledge of the fact that a truly determined people can never be defeated. We reject totally the ruling class values of personal material gain and competition among ourselves and we know that the enemy fears our understanding of the fact that nothing is more precious than freedom. The myth of a high-style superfly life and fashion show (a capitalist rip-off) does not sway us for we know that the fascist government of Amerika supplies the dope and the clothes and wants us to spend the rest of our lives paying for them. We are well aware that a fascist government will always allow some of us to get high, while the rest of us go to concentration camps, and none of us are free.

It is clear that Dr. Foster and sideman, deputy superintendent Robert Blackburn, represent the rich ruling class and big business, and not the children and youth of our communities. The school system which they represent and serve does not teach us or address itself to the needs of our survival, but rather it does perpetuate the values of big business and the wealthy. Under the current system, the ruling class is educated to exploit, and our children and youth are educated to serve. We are not deceived by the superintendent and deputy. Robert Blackburn is a former director of education for the Peace Corps in East Africa. The Peace Corps, as well as AID, are promoted and financed as a front for the CIA, and have long been arms of Amerikan imperialist and racist oppression and genocide. Dr. Foster is a former member of the Philadelphia Crime Commission and now his advancement within the fascist process found him as initiator, promoter and supporter of Political Police Units, armed with riot shotguns, to patrol our schools.

The Oakland-Berkeley area is considered potentially dangerous to the Amerikan ruling class, that is why it has been selected for the Political Police Force Within the Schools and the Forced Youth Identification Program. Let it be known to those who sign for the implementation of these fascist programs, that the death of our manchild comrade youth, 14-year-old Tyrone Guyton, murdered on November 1st by three goons from the Emeryville Political Police Patrol is NOT FORGOTTEN. Tyrone fell victim to the racist enemy who is instituting programs such as those initiated by Marcus Foster and Robert Blackburn aimed at the control, imprisonment, execution and genocide of blacks and other minorities. Let it be known to those who sign for the implementation of these fascist programs that they sign their own death warrants. We of the black and other revolutionary youth communities have for too long seen the enemy prostitute our mothers, imprison our fathers, shoot our brothers and sterilize our sisters. We have learned from these lessons; therefore notice is hereby served on the enemy political police state and all its lackeys that we hold as an example to follow the courage of our slain comrade-in-arms Jonathan Jackson and we call upon our mothers, fathers, sisters, and brothers saying TO THOSE WHO WOULD BEAR THE HOPES AND FUTURE OF OUR PEOPLE, LET THE VOICE OF THEIR GUNS EXPRESS THE WORDS OF FREE-DOM.

DEATH TO THE FASCIST INSECT
THAT PREYS UPON THE LIFE
OF THE PEOPLE.

S.L.A.

Oakland is not the best of all possible places and the United States is not the best of all possible societies—but each *does* have a reality, vibrant and troubled, and the Symbionese authors of this document had only the vaguest and most biased sense of that reality. Here is the SLA possessed; possessed of a world in which every "fascist" nightmare of the Left is suddenly born into reality. They proclaim the triumph of terror, and then, one by one, they label their fantasies with eerie solemnity: the "Forced Youth Identification Program" feeds "Bio-Dossiers" of children into an "Internal Warfare Identification Computer System" in Washington, D.C., for use by the "Special Political Police Force" which is patrolling the schools with "riot shotguns" to "censor and control." The SLA, not surprisingly, find themselves at the center of this universe, this trippy little vision: The fascist ruling class must quash the "revolutionary community" of Berkeley and Oakland before it can move on to "regain its arm of control around the struggling and oppressed people of the world."

The murder of Marcus Foster: It was a strange way to start a revolution. But the SLA apparently never bothered to research either Foster or Blackburn. Perhaps it was just too threatening to challenge their frozen assumptions about men who achieve power in America.

Robert Blackburn, forty, was a civil rights activist when the soldiers of the SLA were toddlers. In 1955, while attending Oberlin College, he arranged to spend his junior year as the only white student at Hampton Institute, an all-black college in Virginia. Through the early sixties, Blackburn, although not a Quaker, served on and eventually became chairman of the Quaker Southern Programs Committee—the arm of the American Friends Service Committee which coordinated Quaker social-action projects on school and housing integration throughout the South.

From 1960 until 1964 Blackburn was full-time executive director for the Citizens Committee on Public Education, a liberal Philadelphia pressure group credited with being the primary force behind a major reform of the Philadelphia school administration. He met Marcus Foster, then a grammar school principal, in 1960. He served as northern regional director for the Peace Corps in Somalia, in East Africa, from 1964 until 1967, supervising teacher training and public-health projects.

The SLA's "bloody-fang" view of the Peace Corps is not dissimilar to the manner in which the Philadelphia police viewed Blackburn's work with the Quakers and school and civil rights activists. He had been followed, dossiered, and tagged a "subversive" by then Police Chief (and later Mayor) Frank Rizzo's notorious "civil disobedience unit." But when he returned to Philadelphia in 1967, the reform administration quickly hired him. He was appointed director of Philadelphia's Office of Integration and Inter-group Education. In the summer of 1970, when Marcus Foster was hired as superintendent of the Oakland Unified School District, he turned to his old friend and asked Blackburn to serve as his deputy.

Marcus Foster was Oakland's first black school superintendent. In Philadelphia he had risen to become associate superintendent and, in that city, something of a folk hero. He had made his name by transforming two of Philadelphia's worst ghetto schools—building pride and excitement among students and teachers, uniquely involving parents and local businessmen, and shaming the Board of Education into funding new facilities and expanded curricula. He was Philadelphia's Man of the Year in 1968, and in

1969 received the Bok Foundation's prestigious Philadelphia Award and the NAACP's Freedom Award Citation.

Oakland is an industrial city of about 350,000, a grimy sister city across the Bay from glamorous San Francisco, a turbulent community of large minority populations; polarized, alienated, poverty-ridden, a microcosm of urban ills. A majority of the total population is nonwhite—but ingenious election rules and a bare majority of white voters have kept a largely white conservative Republican power structure intact. Oakland is a city of minorities, with an enormous nonwhite youth population (1973 school enrollment was 21.1 percent white, 64.2 percent black, 5.7 percent Asian, 7.7 percent Chicano, and 1.6 Filipino and other minorities), and the city schools are burdened as the primary interface between the poor and the establishment. When Foster was hired, the dropout rate was soaring, school morale was nonexistent; by nearly every criterion, Oakland education was terrible—and worse, there was a prevalent feeling of futility, even despair, over the possibility of change. The selection of Foster by the Oakland Board of Education, then under heavy pressure from the black community, was both a daring choice and a capitulation.

A great urban school superintendent in the seventies is a rare and peculiar blend of politician, educator, and community organizer. Perhaps each must be tailored to a particular city—if so, Foster arrived at Oakland and found the city his. He came in with vision, energy, tact, and an incurable optimism that in three and a half turbulent years fitfully revitalized a crumbling institution. It is a tale of triumph, if not of victory—a story of survival and rebirth, rapprochement between the schools and the community.

His impact on the Oakland schools was almost literally explosive—shattering a fortified citadel that had developed a siege mentality, opening it up to the pressures and energies of the community. He decentralized, breaking up the ninety-school system into three regions, each as socioeconomically similar as possible, and gave each an associate superintendent with an office in the neighborhood. He developed new avenues for community involvement: A citywide Master Plan Citizens Committee was established, and each school set up its own MPCC to "examine critical issues and establish educational priorities." He convinced the Board of Education to hold on-site meetings in the neighborhood schools on rotation. In the three and a half years, he appointed fifty-five new principals—and for each appointment a parent-student-teacher committee interviewed applicants and selected the two or three from which he made the appointment. (For elementary school appointments, the committee was made up of eight local parents and four teachers; but for junior and senior high school appointments, the selection committee included four teachers, four students, and eight parents. "And if you think it isn't a heavy experience for a forty-year-old professional to have to sit and explain his goals to a fourteen-year-old on the selection committee, think twice," said one junior high principal.) It was a level of community involvement perhaps unique; and Foster attracted grants from major foundations to support the program.

Traditionally, "the schools have succeeded only in convincing the poor that they cannot learn," he said, and with a special sensitivity he developed academic tests and adaptive programs to aid children in the transition from the ghetto idiom of Oakland's several minorities into the "proper" English of the education industry. He had his teachers set themselves goals against which they could be judged and brought back a sense of professionalism, progress, and excitement. "He was doing a notoriously difficult job and doing it well," said the executive secretary of the teachers union, the Oakland Education Association. "Oakland was twenty years behind," said Electra Price, a bitter critic of the school board and a key member of Oakland's Black Caucus. "Marcus Foster brought them up ten years. He did a fantastic job—more than could ever be expected of any one man. . . .

"White Oakland as a whole is terrified of blacks, but Foster could talk with them, and because he was so visible and so outspoken, he was the sort of man who could take away a lot of the subtle intimidation felt in many parts of the black community. He had a healthy influence."

Foster was a moderate man, but no "Uncle Tom." In an often-quoted speech before the American Association of School Administrators in March, 1973, he sparked a little furor in Oakland when he charged that it was only the "institutional racism" of the white establishment that made them seek out "superblacks" to salvage situations so hopeless that whites didn't want to risk one of their own on the job. "Black mayors are called in only when the city becomes an empty husk," he said, "and blacks become superintendents only in cities like mine. . . . Don't be deceived by those moves and think they come about by rightness and righteousness." There was some indignation, but Foster by then had credits to spare in both white and nonwhite Oakland.

Nearly 40 percent of the students in the Oakland schools are from welfare-assisted homes, and over half are classified as "educationally disadvantaged." But the Foster Administration had brought national attention to Oakland schools with slow but constant progress. Statewide student proficiency in math and English dropped, but Oakland's rose annually. The search for educational techniques that could break the rigid statistical correlation between family income and a student's educational achievement fascinated Foster. "The most important idea in education," he called it.

"We are going to make it in Oakland," he wrote shortly before his death, "and history may record that our schools led the way. We are achieving success because we are taking risks and have committed ourselves to an approach that is honest and humane. This is the least an institution should do; in the broader sense it may be the most."

Marcus Foster had become one of the most sought-after school administrators in the country, perhaps the nation's leading black educator. Announcing that Foster and Blackburn had signed new four-year contracts in July, 1973, the Oakland Board of Education noted happily that "Marcus Foster is what is known in the trade as a hot item." Foster rejected offers to become school superintendent in several major cities—including Philadelphia and Atlanta—and, according to Blackburn, turned down four states seeking a commissioner of education just in his last year.

What tied him to Oakland was the community of concern he had created around the schools. "Foster reached into the black community and developed grass-roots support deeper than anyone had ever been able to get before," said Price, herself twice an unsuccessful liberal black candidate for the Board of Education. "When the board met in the neighborhood schools, Marc would be down there mingling with everyone, never aloof. If someone wanted to talk with him he'd say, 'Come down to the office and see me.' That had a tremendous impact, parents being able to go downtown and see the top man. There had never been anyone like him in Oakland. But he still had to deal with the board—so he was always caught in between, serving two masters."

Black Oakland is a huge community of contradictions. It gave birth to the Black Panther Party and some of the most militant black voices of the sixties, but the roots of the community go back to the Deep South—Louisiana, Texas, Oklahoma; the Bible Belt—and churches wield enormous influence. Although he himself was a devout Christian Scientist, Foster regularly worshiped in the black churches and made them the backbone of a new black-activist coalition that supported his work.

"The schools were old, musty. Foster opened them up and let air in," said Henry Mestre, executive director of Oakland's Spanish-Speaking Unity Council, "but Marc's real impact was on attitudes." Relations between the black and brown communities in Oakland had a competitive, sometimes bitter edge, but Foster personally reached out: He officially recognized the Chicano and Filipino communities, sought their consultation, appointed the city's first Chicano principal. "I admired him so. It's difficult to speak in generalizations about Marc," said Mestre. "He had this charismatic kind of power; he was able to reach and move people. How can I tell you? I felt more like a human being dealing with Marcus Foster. . . . We seem to have made a game out of killing the most vibrant men in our society. When Marc was killed, I reacted like any fascist—the things I wanted to do to those people. . . ."

The two school issues that the SLA picked up on—"police in the schools" and student ID cards—were both footnotes in the turmoil of the Foster Administration. When Foster arrived from Philadelphia, Oakland junior and senior high school students had been carrying IDs for three years. They were a nonissue; the kids liked them because they could be used for student discounts. But in 1972, on a tight budget, Foster discontinued the ID program as an economy move. A year later Oakland had its first campus murder, a girl stabbed by a nonstudent at Oakland Technical High School, and in the angry reaction, teachers, parents, and some student leaders suggested reinstating the ID program. "The IDs probably wouldn't have made any difference," said Blackburn, "but then, maybe they would have. . . ." Foster reinstated the program for 1973–74, but under procedures drawn up with a defensive eye to liberal concerns: Cards were not numbered, students were not required to carry them, and the single Polaroid photograph taken was put on the ID; the school retained no copy on file.

But school vandalism and violence had become a political issue throughout the Bay Area; it became an emotionally charged firefight between the law-and-order faction and the radicals and liberals with the loudest voices from the two extremes. A county grand jury issued a report in July, 1973, on vandalism and violence in the Oakland schools, suggesting a "communications breakdown" between schools and police and proposing that it might be necessary to post police officers in the schools. Foster replied that he didn't think police in the schools would deal with the problem—but the tensions over the issue were the sort that put him in the position of a tightrope walker in heavy winds.

In the late summer Foster announced that his staff was studying a proposal from the California Council on Criminal Justice to fund a project to reduce truancy and increase school security. Rumor and some press reports connected this with the grand-jury suggestion of police in the schools; Foster explicitly denied this, but he opened the school year with a speech urging teachers to make a "major effort" to help students understand the police role, feel comfortable in their presence, and consider police vocations. Radicals, speaking largely through the Coalition to Save Our Schools, a small black parent group heavily influenced by young white Venceremos radicals, began organizing an angry protest against the ID program and what they saw as a covert effort to bring police spies into the schools.

There was much talk of fascism and a police state. Anything funded by the CCCJ (the local arm of the Law Enforcement Assistance Administration, the federal police technocrats who fund a variety of innovative and sometimes Orwellian police programs) was seen as "fascistic" by many radicals. In neighboring communities there seemed to be reason for these fears: San Francisco almost adopted a plan to set up a school-police-probation department task force to "detect early signs of violent, antisocial behavior among students"—these possible future criminals to be "counseled" and referred to "appropriate agencies" for help. Berkeley brought in police officers as "counselors" in the high schools. In both Berkeley and San Francisco the programs were torpedoed by widespread community protests.

Oakland schools opened with volatile climate owing to a threatened teachers' strike. Despite Foster's disclaimers, the police and ID issues hung fire, repeatedly brought up by Coalition spokesmen. Then, in October, Foster was set up, probably inadvertently. The CCCJ proposal had been worked out and was due for presentation to the board; Foster had reviewed the supposed "final draft," which had then been returned to the county CCCJ for their final review—and there one change was made, a phrase added calling for the civilian security aides that were to be hired to have a law-enforcement or "security background." Foster's staff checked the draft on return and missed the change—"a stupid human mistake," said Blackburn—and Foster picked it up and signed it for presentation to the board. Just before the meeting he caught the mistake. "He called me over and pointed it out," said

Blackburn. "He said, 'Have you seen this? The most incredible thing!'" Foster went into the meeting and announced that he was removing the CCCJ item from the agenda—that there was a clause in the proposal that he had not seen, had not approved, and the program would not be up for vote until changed.

But the draft proposal had already been released publicly. "For his critics," said Blackburn, "this was the triumphant proof that Foster and Company had been lying all along—despite his withdrawal of the proposal and his explanation. The next day Marc called up [the CCCJ project officer] and practically short-circuited the phone line."

An ironic postscript came a few days later. The Black Panthers had tacitly supported Foster generally, but had joined with the Coalition when the police and ID issues became prominent in the media. A few days after the meeting, said an aide, Panther leader Elaine Brown and a companion visited Foster. "She said, 'Look, you say you don't want the pigs in the schools. What you could do is get the money from CCCJ and we'll provide you with people with security backgrounds. Panthers, tough, paramilitary, who won't take any shit.' Foster got angry; then he thought it was funny. He told her if he got any money for security aides, it wouldn't be for Panthers or any Chicano group or the Urban League—they would be parents hired from the neighborhoods."

"The whole issue was a red herring," said Blackburn. "Marc could look at trouble in the schools here from a different perspective. He had been principal of two of the toughest, meanest schools in Philadelphia. In Oakland we'd had one student killing—but in Philadelphia there are two or three *dozen* every year. He had managed schools far worse than any in Oakland and without police. He just didn't think it was effective; he didn't think it was a problem that could be attacked with paramilitary force."

In the jittery aftermath of Foster's killing—with the Board of Education under SLA "death warrant"—Oakland suspended the ID program to "reassess community and student feelings." Two days later, on November 15, the SLA issued a gloating "Communique No. 2" rescinding the death warrant "on this aspect of the fascist enemy state":

> The forces of the Symbionese Liberation Army . . . remind the enemy rich ruling class that the people will always understand the effectiveness and tactics of revolutionary justice, and will never be deceived by the distortions and lies of the fascist news media. Marcus Foster has been likened to one of our slain leaders.

We ask, who has ever heard of a Martin Luther King on the Philadelphia Crime Commission? Who has ever heard of a Martin Luther King having an aide who is a CIA agent, formerly acting as director of education for the Peace Corps of East Africa? We are well aware that the fascist news media seeks to condition us by repressing the truth. . . .

A plaintive note, so oddly out of place, referred to Blackburn's survival. They could not believe they had been less than totally efficient.

> The people have seen no evidence that Deputy Superintendent Blackburn is in fact still alive. . . . However, if Blackburn is still alive, The Symbionese Liberation Army and The Court of the People wish to point out the contradiction between the medical care received by those who represent the rich ruling class and that received by the poor and oppressed communities. . . .

The Philadelphia Crime Commission, renamed the Citizens Crime Commission some years ago, is a private watchdog group concerned with public safety, something like the League of Women Voters. Foster was one of 500 community and business leaders elected to the general membership of the Philadelphia Crime Commission.

For so many in Oakland it seemed incredible, impossible, bitterly frustrating that the murderers of Marcus Foster simply knew not what they had done.

7

Aftermath of Triumph

THE murder of Marcus Foster was an act that the SLA could neither undo nor justify. Later, when the history of the SLA had become the story of Patty, the media would occasionally refer to it, reducing the incident to half a phrase: "murder of a respected educator." But in a fundamental way the assassination set the stage for all that followed by setting the SLA not only apart, as they had hoped—but alone as well. In the "revolutionary" community of the Bay Area, even among those who agreed with the SLA on the so-called military question, the Foster murder damned them as inept and isolated from "the People." It branded them as "adventurist," that term lifted from translations of Lenin and used as the ultimate pejorative. The Symbionese never escaped the shadow of Marcus Foster. Throughout the entire Hearst episode, from the kidnapping to the gunfight in Los Angeles, the SLA never again mentioned Foster. Then, in the nadir of defeat, Bill Harris referred to the "jive ass nigger" whose "execution" had damned the SLA. Even Weather Underground leader Bernardine Dohrn, in a supportive message to the SLA after the Hearst kidnapping, referred to Foster's death in puzzlement: "We do not comprehend the execution of Marcus Foster and respond very soberly to the death of a black person who is not a recognized enemy of his people."

In part, as the leftist *Ramparts* magazine pointed out in a closely reasoned critique of SLA terrorism, the Left's rejection of the Symbionese was pragmatic—the lesson of the sixties was that isolated terrorist acts are simply counterproductive. But also in part, the editorial added, "the Left's coolness to the SLA was not pragmatic at all, but *moral,* and in that way profoundly political." Whatever glib denunciations of Foster had circulated among East Bay radicals prior to his death, the evident rage and gut-level re-

145

vulsion over the crime in the black community deeply impressed the California Left.

There were some, like Deputy Superintendent Blackburn, who would bitterly suggest that Foster's murder was simply an attempt to block a promising liberal effort at reform, to force the system to regress in order to leave more damaged, angry kids as fodder for the revolution. Others—San Francisco radical writer Warren Hinckle was most articulate—suggested that the SLA killed Foster to appeal to the ghetto gang kids, the "East Oakland black kids who matriculate on the streets and see their schools as prisons in an asphalt concentration camp surrounded by a great society with lawns. If these tough young dudes were part of the 'new *lumpen*' the SLA was hoping to reach by its actions, offing the teacher could be seen as one way to go—bad, but a way."

Yet there is little in the SLA history, theory, or practice that suggested reasoning so subtle, little hint that the Foster murder was anything more than what Thero Wheeler had described, a spur-of-the-moment decision. It was the act of murder, the declaration that they were willing to go all the way, that was important. The man was just incidental.

Behind the walls—in the California prisons—news of the Foster murder spread rapidly. As they got some sense of how the Oakland community felt about Foster, convicts who had learned of the man through the BCA were first confused, then bitter and angry over the biased image they had been given of him. News of the outside world is scant, but inside, the grapevine carries what there is everywhere. Al Taylor—in maximum-security psychiatric isolation in the S-3 wing of Vacaville, where the walls are double thick and Taylor had to shout at the top of his lungs to converse with Charlie Manson in the next cell, and with no radio and supposedly no contact with anyone but staff—knew of Foster's death within a day. And he knew more than just that Foster was dead—and he was angry.

"They shouldn't have done that," he blurted out to his psychiatric therapist, Dr. Wesley Hiler.

"Who's they?" asked Hiler.

"The Lebanese Liberation Army," replied Taylor.

Taylor had been brought into the SLA through his friend Clifford "Death Row Jeff" Jefferson, had been visited regularly by Nancy Ling Perry, and had exchanged love letters with her and friendly notes with Willie Wolfe for more than a year. Although he had a little trouble with the name—Nancy had whispered it but once in a visit—Taylor knew what was coming down. And he knew something had gotten twisted. Murdering black liberals was not his idea of the revolution. "He was very angry," explained Hiler. "He felt they shot the wrong man. He felt they should be killing people who were doing a lot of bad things to the country—someone like Nixon, he said." Elsewhere in the cellblocks of several California prisons there were others among the SLA inmate cadre who were also angry. Isolated, living wasted lives, some imprisoned men become acutely sensitive to the nuances of truth and justice. And they judge harshly. For some the SLA did not measure up. There are persistent reports from "connected" prison sources that some SLA inmates actually ordered DeFreeze's execution after Foster's murder; that a message with that order was delivered to Willie Wolfe. That may be why Wolfe, confused and upset, suddenly took off, hitchhiking to visit his family in Pennsylvania. He left his car and belongings with his SLA comrades, but when he arrived home he told his family he was going on to Sweden to marry. He had no plans to return to California.

Thero Wheeler had been living with DeFreeze, Mizmoon Soltysik, and Nancy Ling Perry in a small Oakland apartment on Seventh Avenue until shortly before the murder. When DeFreeze seemed determined to "waste" the school superintendent, Wheeler recalled, "Hey, like that's when I decided to split. I didn't want no part of that shit." Although DeFreeze had finally established his own line to the local radical sugar daddies, he wanted Wheeler's connections to people and money and other organizations. He wanted Thero—and had already christened him with an SLA name, Bayo.

A prison-militant friend of both framed the clash between Thero and Cinque archly: "There were contradictions," he said, "criticisms were made and reacted to defensively." Said Wheeler, much later: "We didn't ever argue, but we had lots of discussions. I wouldn't join the organization because I couldn't accept the concept. I thought it was stupid. It was shallow, you know, a bunch of nice-sounding phrases they picked up from here and there. It didn't have nothing to do with reality, man, all it could do was get you killed. I never did join the SLA."

When the talk veered to murder, Wheeler started backing out. He moved to another apartment with his girlfriend, Mary Alice Siem, in Redwood City, on the Peninsula south of San Francisco. Cinque and Zoya visited him to discuss their differences. "It was October twenty-third when DeFreeze and Patricia [Mizmoon] came to our apartment and pulled a gun on me and Mary Alice," said Wheeler. "They threatened to kill her baby, man. They robbed Mary Alice of three hundred dollars. I left that night. I went and dropped my guns off—they're still just exactly where I left them—and I took the money I'd been given to set up a backup unit. That was my story to keep them from coming down on me, that I'd set up a backup unit—and then I split."

Wheeler's story—told while he was still awaiting trial on escape charges—is doubtless self-serving, yet nevertheless rings true. Mary Alice told friends she fled the Bay Area right after the threatening visit, and without Wheeler. "She and Thero had personal problems for about a month," said a close friend, "and she also realized what the SLA had become." Wheeler, however, was still around when Dr. Foster was murdered, although friends report the SLA was then hunting *him*. On November 15 Wheeler showed up at the home of Mary Alice's parents in Redding, in Northern California, asking for her. Siem's father, Thomas Landles, a wealthy realtor, turned him away. Mary Alice was hiding in the back of the house at the time. Wheeler spent the night at the Redding Lodge motel, registered as Bradley Bruce, and placed three long-distance phone calls to friends of Mary Alice trying to locate her. The next day, allegedly riding a bus out of state, he disappeared. (Using the same alias, Bradley Bruce, Wheeler appeared in Houston, Texas, shortly after that. He got a job installing fire- and security-alarm systems in schools and business establishments. He was at work the day Patricia Hearst was kidnapped and stayed in Houston, even after his picture appeared on page 1 of Texas newspapers as one of the suspected kidnappers.)

While there was all this hassle with the new recruits, the high command of the SLA had other worries, other plans. With the attack on Foster, the crusade had been launched and all hope pinned to the future. Yet the SLA was still a split-level organization, some underground at Clayton, but with the Harrises, Angela Atwood, and Camilla Hall still engaged with the aboveground world, still at home, still working daily at jobs. Nancy Perry, Mizmoon Soltysik, Cinque, and Russ Little had entered the shadows, living anonymously in Clayton, a white middle-class suburb in the East Bay, in a house they called "the liberated zone."

A week after Foster's death, Bill Harris' old friend and Marine buddy, Larry Leach, arrived for a week's visit to San Francisco, spending three nights across the Bay with Bill and Emily. He found them at ease, happy, but living a rigidly disciplined daily life. Early to bed, because Bill had to visit a prisoner in the Alameda county jail in the morning; meetings with different groups practically each evening (they had but one night free that week); Emily would rush home from work, gulp a sandwich, and be off to a meeting. They were into physical exercise, jogging daily. They introduced Leach to Joe Remiro, Russ Little, and Robyn Steiner—who was then living with the Harrises—and a dozen other political friends. Leach recalls his first meeting with Remiro vividly. Bill Harris introduced the two, then said to Leach—lightly, as if it were a comment on police stupidity: "The cops have been investigating Joe about some political murder." (In fact, police then were not investigating Remiro; there was no tie yet with the Foster murder.)

Leach already knew Angela Atwood from Indiana. "Angel didn't really seem plugged in with the group," said Leach. "She was still flighty and a little scatterbrained. Bill said she was just starting to come into her own after finally getting up the nerve to leave her husband. He said she was just getting her confidence back in herself as a woman. He and Emily were really proud of how far she had come."

Robyn Steiner, too, seemed on the periphery. Leach and Robyn talked late into one night. "She was obviously less committed than the others," he said. "Bill and Emily would come down on her periodically, criticizing her, but in what seemed a constructive way. They'd talk about her hang-up about full commitment to anything. Bill and Emily were trying to shake their bourgeois hang-ups and wanted Robyn to shake hers." Robyn, said Leach, talked to him about leaving the Bay Area, going back to school, becoming a nurse or paramedic. He later realized that she was the only one of the group who referred to a "legitimate" future.

The Harrises were still attending the weekly meetings of a Marxist study group, one of dozens in the East Bay area. There were about twenty to twenty-five people in this group. "They were like college seminars," said one of the several occasional visitors. "There would be a couple people appointed to research intensely into one subject and they'd come back and report to the group." The groups, usually led by Venceremos members, spent considerable time discussing the works of Lenin and George Jackson. "Bill Harris seemed the most mature," recalled one guest participant. "He was educated and well thought out." When the Harrises invited Leach to attend a study-group meeting in mid-November, however, it was Emily Harris who seated herself as chairperson.

"Bill told me that they had only been part of this group for a few months and that it was really unusual that someone who had been part of the group for such a short time to be named discussion leader," said Leach. "He was really proud of her. Emily seemed more self-confident and stronger than I ever remembered her. Even Bill said Emily had grown more than he since they had come there." The people in the study group were supposed to be totally open with one another, to escape the "bourgeois hang-ups." But at the time of Leach's visit there was trouble in the group. "There was jealousy among the women over the men," said Leach, "and Bill and Emily were really pissed about it."

The triangles that had the study group quivering involved several people who by this time had become SLA cadre—although the study group itself was separate and apparently ignorant of the SLA. Joe Remiro always liked to have two full-time women, "out front." "Joe was never secretive about that kind of shit," said one friend. "He always hoped the women would get to be friends." In early 1973 Remiro was sleeping with Cindy G. and Karen G., two East Bay activists, and dating another woman, Pat Z. Russ Little at this time was seeing only Robyn Steiner. In the spring Karen demanded a monogamous relationship, Remiro refused, and Karen withdrew. For a while Joe had only Cindy, but "he was very hurt at losing Karen. He expected those kinds of relationships could work," said his buddy.

By July, Russ Little and Robyn Steiner had split up, and Little was soon seeing Angela Atwood—and then Russ was back with Robyn but seeing Angela, too. In August, Joe—still with Cindy—also started seeing Angela. So it was Joe with Cindy and Angela, and Russ with Robyn and Angela.

By the end of September, Angela was calling a meeting of the five of them—herself, Russ, Joe, Cindy, and Robyn—"to work out some of the unfortunate aspects of their relationships," she told a woman friend.

"Angela was the prima donna of the whole thing," said the woman. "She had both men." Angela was much more attractive than she appears in photographs, said friends. "She was not gorgeous, but there was a certain presence about her, like in Dylan's 'Just Like a Woman'—like a naughty little girl. She dressed well—feminine sort of hippie things, like old Indian silk shirts and batik, earrings, jewelry, rings . . . very feminine."

"Angela probably put up with both Russ and Joe because Joe also had Cindy," said a Berkeley friend. "But when Cindy called it quits [in early October], Angela and Joe moved closer together," eventually establishing a monogamous relationship. Meanwhile, however, Russ Little apparently moved in on Cindy, becoming involved with Cindy, Robyn, and at least two other women—one of whom was Nancy Ling Perry. "Robyn had an agreement with Cindy, who was her friend, that if Cindy balled her man, Russ, she wouldn't keep it a secret, but Cindy did keep it a secret." Robyn found out later, however.

When Larry Leach visited the Harrises in mid-November, Russ was living in an SLA hideout with Nancy Perry, but would visit to sleep with Robyn at the Harrises. "Emily would get down on Robyn for being uptight about the relationship," remembers Leach. "She and Bill told Robyn to either firm it up or get rid of him, but not to stay hung up about it." Shortly after that Robyn decided to drop out altogether and return to Florida; her involvement in the early SLA has never been established, although an accusation, publicly made by the SLA four months later, that she had given information to the police certainly implied some knowledge.

In her place, in early December, Angela Atwood moved into the Harrises' spare bedroom. (Angela was perhaps the last to be sworn to arms; convict SLA associates later said she was the only SLA member they had never heard of.) Aboveground and below, the SLA always carried a peculiar burden of unbridled sexuality, a tension of uncommon dynamic. In August, when Nancy Perry moved in with Cin and Mizmoon in their first Oakland hideout on East Seventeenth Street, recalled Thero Wheeler's girlfriend, Mary Alice Siem, a bitter spat flared because both women wanted to sleep with DeFreeze. It was conventional sexist jealousy, offensive to all their liberated mores, but it still took them awhile to work it out, she said. Even farther back, in May, the earthy and experienced Mizmoon sensed a hulking libido in the quiet, boyish Willie Wolfe, everyone's idea of a Red Guard Eagle Scout, and captured it in a poem in her diary:

> Willie . . . . I hate him
> I want to scream
> next time he touches me
> Get your God Damned Hand Off My Body!
> (but his hands never were)
> damned . . . he's bein' only
> friendly . . . I'm not being paid to have him maul me
> Get your damned mind off my body!

Just go away and let me be.
I hate you Willy.
I hate the way you swagger that huge body
and small mind of yours around.
Crushing me in the name of muscle-heated phallic power
because you know I'm good
and I don't want you.

In January, 1974, an Indiana college chum received a letter from Emily—apparently mailed just before the Harrises were forced into hiding—with an enclosure of several old school photos of Emily with her sorority sisters. "It was a strange letter, like an announcement," the woman recalled. "She said she had gotten into an affair with someone, and because of it, she and Bill had decided to reevaluate their relationship. She said they had decided that although they still loved one another—perhaps more than ever—they were no longer going to narrow themselves sexually to one another. She sent the photos because she thought I'd enjoy having them. She said she and Bill had burned everything, all their old photos and letters, in a bonfire in their fireplace on New Year's Eve. She said they didn't need memories recorded on paper—those were her words—they were committed to the present and the future." The Harrises were ready for the fugitive life, ready by decision even before crisis forced the issue.

Meanwhile, at the clandestine SLA headquarters in Clayton, behind tacked-down shades and draperies, the underground members of the group plotted and played in their own little world.

Fahizah and Zoya—Perry and Soltysik—tagged a note for Angela onto a "target surveillance list" with the home addresses of twelve Bay Area businessmen:

> For A.: Understanding that we are all just learning how to do this, and that it takes practice, and that this list [has] suggestions of things, the most important we'd like to know, and realizing that many of them are very difficult to obtain, and wanting to remind you to be extremely cautious and as inconspicuous as possible, also to let you know that the maps & drawings do not require that you be an artist—F & Z

Beginning surveillance was to include:

1. license plates of cars going to the pad and especially coming out of driveway (7-9am/4-6 pm) coming and going from work, and plates of cars frequently parked in front of the pad

2. a drawing of the pad (showing bushes, trees, type of garage door, lites, power lines nearby, cameras on telephone poles)

3. a brief description of the neighborhood (how rich it is, do neighbors peek out of windows, children around, pig patrols)

4. if possible a description of the driver of the cars you get plates for

5. small outline map of streets going in & out of the area where the pad is located (how close are businesses, gas stations, fire dept., pig stations)

In a note to herself, Fahizah jotted down "equipment needed for surveillance: clip bds., paper, pencils, pens, nurse's uniform, wheel chairs, baby carriages, crutches."

Fahizah was the writer; she worked on communiqués. Others worked in the bomb factory in the back room or researched names to add to their growing list of murder and kidnap targets. Everyone probably worked on the arsenal—ordering new guns and parts, drilling and packing dumdum bullets with cyanide, reloading shells.

Neighbors in Clayton thought the new "DeVoto" couple odd— the husband introduced himself to some as George, but to others as Bob. Little things seemed peculiar. The "DeVotos" were strangely uncommunicative, kept all the doors and windows shut, with drawn blinds—even in hot weather—and kept all the lights on day and night. Four members of the SLA lived inside: Cinque, Zoya, Osceola, and Fahizah. No one noticed the black man—but later several neighbors recalled a "white" with Afro hair. (Theater makeup that could lighten dark skin was later found in the house.)

On November 12, 1973, a curious event—totally unconnected with the SLA—brought police and reporters to the "DeVoto" house. A sixteen-year-old boy followed Nancy Perry home from the nearby 7-11 Store; he rang the bell and when she answered, asked, "Is your husband home?" She asked what he wanted, and the kid fumbled in his pocket and brought out a .22-caliber pistol. It was apparently a rape attempt; the boy was apprehended later and charged with several such attacks. But here he was dealing with Fahizah of the SLA. She kicked at the gun and pushed him. The gun fell and discharged one shot. The boy scrambled for the gun and ran. A neighbor forced the reluctant "Mrs. DeVoto" to call the police. "At the time it was just a weird story," said a reporter who followed cops to the scene. "The police thought it was probably a drug thing. Everyone talked on the lawn; no one was invited inside." A news photographer took what was to become a very famous photo of Nancy Ling Perry; long hair blowing, arms crossed, eyes looking somberly into the camera. Several neighbors began to watch the house more carefully; rumors spread that it was a "dope den." What was really going on inside was much more bizarre.

With BB guns they practiced stakeouts and executions; they made up "teamwork games" to rehearse in precise detail:

> For stakeout at restaurant and parking lot:
> Cin's room is our base—there are three of us there
> Zoya's room is Camilla's pad in Oakland
> Osceola's room is the 24 hr. cafe
> The living room is surveillance area
> Pay phone AM is in the hall bathroom
> Pay phone PM is in the hall closet
> Kitchen is another scene. . . .
> The corner table lamp is the bar where targets are
>   drinking.

The emotional texture of daily life must have been incredible. With the glee of solemn children in Indian headdress, they would stalk the table lamp. Then, smoothing her hair, Nancy could go out to hang clothes in the backyard—affecting a New York accent for her neighbors. She could return to join Cin and Mizmoon studying which poisons kill quickest—*"prussic acid; hydro sulfid (H.S); hydrocyanic acid (HCN)"*—or the layout of the Berkeley post office they had cased for robbery, or the house of a "San Francisco pimp" marked for death.

Always there were more targets—a newspaper article with the names of two San Francisco homicide cops was clipped and filed "for action by the People's Court." And there were the laborious communiqués; hours of work on each—for every killing there was to be a lesson for "the People," a message of terror for the ruling classes. The language was both archaic, for dignity, and jive, to tune in the *lumpen*. Days so full, no hours to waste—the burden becomes heavy and life complex when one carries the fate of the People, the seed of the Revolution.

Nancy made little lists to schedule her day:

> —the Communique
> —all these papers
> —the filing cabinet

> —memorize addresses
> —look on the bottom of this pile
> —make a dress
> —molotov cocktails
> —wood cutting
> —buy bolts of material

The communiqués stacked up; the first drafts were all from SLA "Western Regional Unit 10," each with a place for the number in sequence of release. Each condemns a corporation, the corruption of "International Capitalism," the exploitation of economic colonialism—and each dooms men. Individual men are reduced to symbols—and at the same time enlarged to represent conglomerate structures within which decisions are made many levels above them in the hierarchy.

Operation: kidnap and ransom and/or failure to meet

Subject: The T.A. White Candy Co.
             Sub-division of ITT Corp.

Charges: MURDER, GENOCIDE, ROBBERY, and supporting and taking part in crimes against the people of Chile, Brazil, South Africa, Rhodesia, the Philippines and the American people.

Target: Charles W. Comer, President of the T.A. White Candy Co., a subsidiary of the Pearson Candy Co., a division of the ITT Continental Baking Co., a member of the ITT Corporation.

. . . this attack is to serve notice on this corporation and its divisions and its subsidiaries and its executives that they have come to the attention of the S.L.A. and The Court of the People, and have been found guilty of supporting the murder, oppression and robbery of the people of the world. This attack is also to serve notice on the enemy of the people, that the S.L.A. stands in support and in arms with the demands of the Weather Underground and the demands for the release of the Six Freedom Fighters made by the August 7th Combat Forces. . . .*

---

*The August Seventh Guerrilla Movement is a mysterious group which in 1972–73 claimed credit for the murder of an alleged dope dealer and his girlfriend in Monterey, the murder of a prison guard, and the shooting down of an Oakland police helicopter. According to the FAA, the copter crashed because of a mechanical failure; and prison authorities said they never found a note the

Another communiqué targeted D. E. Stanberry, Oakland warehouse director for the Colgate Palmolive Company. ("Charges: MURDER, GENOCIDE, ROBBERY . . . taking part in crimes against the people of Ireland, Brazil, Rhodesia and South Africa, the Philippines, Angola, Mozambique, and Guinea-Bissau.") A third was to announce the bombing of the local offices of the General Tire and Rubber Company. In each there was the promise that executives of that company would be "shot on sight." All communiqués ended with Eldridge Cleaver's phrase: "Death to the fascist insect that preys upon the life of the people."

Another communiqué, "Number 3," apparently was to follow the Foster murder:

Subject:　The Department of Corrections and all its agents, associates, members.
Charges:　Murder, Genocide, Robbery and [illegible]
Target:　The Department of Corrections and all its agents and wives of said elements

. . . this attack is to serve notice upon this fascist institution and its employees and their wives that they have come to the attention of the S.L.A. and the Court of the People and have been found guilty of taking part and supporting the military take over of the United States and the overthrow of the constitutional rights of the American people and taking part in the murder, robbery and genocide committed against the life of our children and freedom. . . .

This communiqué had a strange addendum, most of which would be echoed in a later "open letter" published by Nancy Perry. There was a centered subtitle on the page—"Why do we charge this?"—and then the following:

The Symbionese Liberation Army was born in 1963-64 in the hearts of all the races and people of this nation when we became

---

ASGM claimed was placed in the pocket of the murdered guard. The "San Quentin Six," whose freedom was to be demanded as ransom for Comer and other targets—a ransom Reagan's California government was certain not to pay—are six prison activists, five blacks and one Latino, charged with murder in the wake of an alleged escape attempt in which black militant George Jackson, two other inmates, and three guards were killed in August, 1971. Although three of the five communiqués the SLA had prepared named the ASGM as "comrades in arms," the SLA later condemned the group as "police agents."

aware of the fact that the American nation had suffered a military overthrow of the government and the constitutional rights of the American people.

The coup that occurred in '63-64 was not like those seen in South America and other countries where the military and the ruling class openly take power from the people and removed the constitutional rights of its people, because it was not necessary to so openly warn the American people, when it was clear that the American people were so conditioned that they would try themselves not to believe what they had seen and what had happened to them. The CIA, FBI and Secret Service and the military were well aware that it was no longer needed to apply the old type military coup on the American people, because they were aware that the majority of the American people were so racist and politically asleep that they would believe anything that was stated by the ruling-class controlled government and press. . . .

Another slip of paper among SLA documents later discovered sets out a schedule that illustrates the quick and urgent pace of daily life in Clayton. Undated, and full of references to people never identified, it read:

Meetings with medical people

Meeting with Seara

Meeting with Arco
Meeting with Chicano Brother

Check on River Operation progress, ask why and who informed others of operations without plan?

Check on money for Bro Hi, will return what is left after show or sale

Check on Ammo progress

Remove M-68 until he has time

Give Seara new section of Document and have 15 copies made in full with letter head

Don't call ME this week, give him time to work out problems

CHECK ALL PEOPLE FOR SECURITY CHECK IN THEIR AREA!!! Report anything that they feel is funny or out of place regarding people around them or cars and people near their homes and in the streets while moving around.

RE-CHECK COMMITMENTS OF OUR PEOPLE!!!

Those who do nothing make no mistakes—SLA
—spray-painted graffito on a Berkeley wall

8

Concord, California
January 10, 1974

FOR an instant the van's headlights illuminated Duge's face as he drove through the intersection. The sergeant was not wearing his uniform cap—it was alongside on the seat—but knew that would not fool anyone wise in the ways of the street as to his occupation. The Dodge had that unmistakable look of an unmarked police car. Two radio antennas jutted from its trunk, and there was that spotlight by the driver's door—not to mention the fact that the Polara carried license plates with a diamond-shaped marking identifying it as a tax-exempt "official" vehicle. Duge glanced at the van, returned his attention to the street ahead, hoping he had appeared only momentarily interested. He had learned nothing from the quick look—except that the van's headlights were damn bright.

Duge continued along Ayers Road, keeping watch through the rearview mirror. It was several seconds before the van began moving—slowly—crossing Ayers and continuing—slowly—on Sutherland Drive. Waiting until it was out of sight, Duge reached toward the dashboard, switched off his headlights, executed a quick U-turn, drove back to the intersection, turned onto Sutherland, and began following. By then the van was some 100 feet ahead, traveling—Duge could see by the speedometer—at no more than ten miles an hour. Either the driver was lost, Duge decided, or he was worthy of suspicion.

Dave Duge had been working graveyard shifts in that part of Concord for seven months. It is a quiet residential area right at the edge of town, inhabited by middle-class, middle-income families with ranch-style homes going for $30,000 and up. At one o'clock on a weekday morning it was rare to see lights burning in the homes or traffic on the streets, and the area is an attractive target for auto boosters—fast-working thieves, usually teenage boys, who break into cars to rip off stereo systems and anything else that strikes their fancy. Auto boosters spot likely targets by cruising—slowly—up and down streets, as the van ahead was doing. Duge noted that the rear windows were covered by curtains.

The van continued its crawling pace to the point where winding Sutherland Drive comes to an end. It turned left onto Bonwell Drive, left again on Manchester Drive, and finally right on Sutherland Drive, heading back toward the intersection where Duge had first spotted it. Still driving without lights, he hesitated only briefly. If the driver was lost, he would appreciate assistance. If not, he had some explaining to do. As the van braked to a halt at the stop sign, Duge switched on the headlights and the red spot and tapped lightly on the horn to ensure he had gotten the driver's attention. A man's face could be seen looking back at him. It was the face of a young white male. Duge picked up his radio mike to inform headquarters he was making a routine traffic stop. He gave the dispatcher the location, the license plate—806 GUD—of the van, and asked for a cover unit. It was 1:23 A.M.

Duge had pulled up and parked about fifteen feet behind the van. Leaving the motor running, he got out of the police car and started toward it. The driver was still eyeballing him. As the officer approached, the man leaned out the window. He was smiling. Duge saw there was someone else in the van, another young man, with a dark mustache. He was not smiling.

"May I see your driver's license, please?" Duge asked. The driver got out his wallet, extracted the document, handed it over, and said, "How come you stopped me?" Duge glanced at the license and replied, "Well, Mr. Scalise, the manner in which you've been driving around this area at this hour seemed a bit suspicious. Where are you going?"

"I'm looking for a friend who lives on Sutherland Court," answered the blond man, whose license carried the name Robert James Scalise. Duge asked the name of the friend. Scalise hesitated, then mumbled, "DeVoto." Duge had not understood. He asked again. "DeVoto," repeated the man. When the name was uttered, Duge noticed the passenger seemed to stiffen. His suspicions about the pair increased, and he asked the passenger to show some identification. Duge later emphasized he was careful not to make it an order, but a "request." He knew he had no authority to force a passenger to show him anything. The dark-haired man, scowling, handed over his license. The name on it was Joseph Michael Remiro.

Duge returned to his car and radioed the dispatcher. He read off the names, birth dates, and addresses of the two men and asked for a "wants and warrants" check on them. As an afterthought, he asked the dispatcher also to check the city directory for the address of a DeVoto on Sutherland Court. Duge was just finishing copying down the data from the licenses onto a report form when the dispatcher radioed back, "Both subjects are clear," adding that there was no city-directory listing for any DeVoto on either Sutherland Court or Sutherland Drive. Except for that, Duge might have dropped the matter. Something about Scalise and Remiro—particularly Remiro—rubbed wrong. If they were merely lost, they should have, like most people, welcomed his appearance and asked for directions.

Duge started toward the van, stopped, looked at the clipboard notepad in his left hand, decided it might be wise to have both hands free. He left the clipboard on the hood of the patrol unit. Again he started forward, this time walking to the passenger door. He tapped on the glass of the closed window. Remiro stared out at him, then slowly rolled the glass halfway down. He did not say a word. Duge asked if he would please step outside. Without hesitation, Remiro complied. Once on the street, Remiro stood, feet apart, facing the policeman.*

"Do you have any guns or knives on you?" Duge asked. Without waiting for an answer, he told Remiro, "I'm going to frisk you." He started toward Remiro, hands outstretched to run them down the sides of the man. Remiro pulled open his jacket and quickly stepped back a couple of feet. Suddenly Duge spotted a bulge on Remiro's right hip, a bulge covered by the man's untucked shirt.

---

*The text version of the Concord shoot-out was based on Sergeant Duge's report; Remiro's story—finally told when he was tried for attempted murder of the officer—differed only slightly, although on key substantive points. Remiro said the van's passenger window was jammed so that, when Duge tapped on the window beside him, he opened the door and stepped out. As he turned his body getting out, he said he caught a sideways glimpse of Duge "moving quickly" behind him. Thinking Duge was pulling his gun, Remiro said he jerked his pistol out and twisted to confront the officer—who had *not* drawn. "He made a yelp," recalled Remiro, and ran behind the van, drawing his revolver as he moved. A moment later, said Remiro, Duge fired first, from behind the police cruiser. At the trial the jury acquitted Little and split without verdict on Remiro, apparently in part because Duge's testimony had been marred when the officer burst out with an angry tirade when he was being cross-examined by Remiro, acting as his own attorney. Both Little and Remiro had already been convicted for the Foster murder and faced further charges for two armed robberies and a jail escape attempt.

Duge had no doubts about it or what was going to happen next. Remiro's right hand darted down, clawing for the pistol.

Duge dodged back, behind the van. He could have tried to take Remiro with a lunge, but there was the other one, Scalise. Instinct made him dive for safety, first to the rear of the van, then a sprint past his cruiser, where he crouched to the rear. A still moment; nothing had happened. He glanced at the driver's side of the van: nothing. He moved right and peered around the fender. Remiro was exactly where he had been, gun in hand. Duge heard two shots and saw the muzzle flashes. His own pistol was still holstered. He drew it and snapped off two quick shots. Remiro ducked behind the front of the van, and Duge pulled back. The two vehicles between them, each man wondered which side the other would come from. Duge opted for the left, guessing Remiro would shift. In a crouch he spun to the other side and cautiously peered out.

Two shots from Remiro; Duge ducked and returned two. Neither had got a good sight on the other; neither was hit. Duge rolled to the right side of the car, then stood up quickly, sighting for a target.

Remiro, running down the sidewalk, weaving, twisted and snapped off a shot at the cop, then ducked into a yard, lost in the darkness. Duge had not fired this time. With a squeal and smoking tires, the van shot forward as Scalise popped the clutch—it crossed the intersection and raced down Sutherland.

Duge snatched at his radio mike. "Concord eleven-ninety-nine. . . . Officer in trouble! I've been shot at!" He described the van and ordered a countywide roadblock. He was broadcasting descriptions of Scalise and Remiro when he heard Patrolman L. J. Lee's cruiser. The backup car finally arrived.

Just then, two blocks ahead, it was the van again, cutting back onto Sutherland. The driver, probably thinking Duge had immediately chased him, had circled—and come out two blocks from the police cars.

Perhaps Scalise was as shocked as Duge was—the van paused at the intersection—but Duge reacted first. He gestured to Lee and shouted, "That's it!" and jumped behind the wheel of his car. Lee was already moving down Sutherland; he had snapped the shotgun free from its dashboard clamp by the time he jerked to a stop about thirty feet from the van. In the glare of the cruiser headlights Scalise could be seen through the windshield. Lee could see both his hands on top of the steering wheel, but the cop was bail-ing out the door with the shotgun almost as the cruiser stopped. He ducked to the rear of the car and leveled the shotgun. The van had not moved.

"Police!" he shouted. "Come out with your hands up!" Duge had pulled up behind him and had another gun on the van. The driver's door opened and Scalise slowly climbed out, hands above his head. "Careful, he's probably armed," Duge warned. Lee ordered Scalise to lie stomach down on the street and, with Duge covering, moved up to search him. There was no weapon, but the man's two shirt pockets were crammed with .38-caliber bullets (fourteen in one, thirteen in the other), and on his belt was a black leather holster.

"Where's the gun?" Lee asked.

"In the van, on the engine cover," the prisoner replied.

"Who's the other guy?"

"Remiro. . . ."

"Where'd he go?" demanded Lee. "Where'd he go?"

Scalise did not answer.

Duge, while fastening handcuffs to the man's wrists, first noticed the blood on the shirt and realized Scalise had been hit in the right shoulder. In one of his shots at Remiro, the bullet had gone through the back window of the van, through the driver's shoulder, and out the windshield.

In the van Lee discovered a snub-nosed .38 Colt and a rifle. Duge called for other officers to assist in the search. Then he noticed, for the first time, that one of Remiro's bullets had shattered the rear window of the cruiser. Scalise was taken to Contra Costa County Hospital. His wound, not serious, was treated, and then he was booked for attempted murder at Concord city jail.

During the next three hours dozens of officers searched for Remiro. Nobody thought to check for a DeVoto in any of the houses along the small cul-de-sac called Sutherland Court, located just outside the city limits in an area called Clayton. Not even after one patrolman, looking through the van for other weapons, opened a large paper sack and pulled out a stack of leaflets emblazoned with the seven-headed cobra symbol of the Symbionese Liberation Army. There was an instant connection between the name and the November killing of Marcus Foster. The officer reported his discovery, and the search for Remiro intensified.

It had been going on for some four hours when, at 5:31 A.M., Patrolman Jim Alcorn, staked out in his patrol car, engine off, on Sutherland Drive, thought he spotted someone run along the sidewalk and dart between two houses a couple of blocks ahead. Alcorn radioed for backup and drove to where he had last seen the running figure. Patrolman Oliver Sansen pulled up. The officers left their cars and started cautiously up a driveway. Sansen pumped a shell into the chamber of his shotgun, the cocking snap noisy in the quiet night. Suddenly a voice called out, "I've had it. . . . I give up. . . . I'm coming out." Remiro slowly rose from behind a camper truck. The officers ordered him to raise his hands and walk out—backward.

With Alcorn covering, Sansen had Remiro kneel while he handcuffed him and started searching for weapons. "It's in my right pants pocket," Remiro volunteered. Sansen reached in and pulled out a Walther PP .380 automatic. He put it on safety. Remiro was booked and jailed.

The arrest of two SLA gunmen brought in the homicide cops from nearby Oakland. One of the officers working on the Foster case said it all along. "It'll probably be something like a routine traffic stop that gives us the break," he would tell reporters. They needed a break. There had been two dry months. Oakland cops had collected a long list of suspects—including a few SLA names and many others—but even after compiling hunches, tips, and a few solid leads from prison informants, they were still groping. Oakland police identified "Scalise" as a local radical they knew as Russell Jack Little; an attorney hired by Little's family verified the name. Oakland police readied search warrants and raided Peking House on Chabot Road and Remiro's old apartment on Bond Street. But for all the police brass hustled into the show that day, the SLA survived because of a major police error. If Sergeant Duge's suspicious nature had given the cops their break, the incomplete police follow-through on the DeVoto lead gave the SLA a chance to escape.

The Department of Motor Vehicles identified the SLA van as registered in the name of Nancy Gail Ling at an Oakland address that turned out to be the home of her brother, Gary.* It had been purchased from a private party on August 10, 1973, and reregistered with DMV in Ling's name on October 10. Later, on closer inspection, police traced the motor in the van to a mid-fall robbery in Berkeley. On October 12 a 1969 Chevrolet van had been

---

*Police investigators cleared Gary Ling as innocent of any knowledge of or involvement in the SLA.

stolen at gunpoint off Telegraph Avenue (both the owner, Donald Sullivan, and his passenger would identify Remiro as the hijacker); the engine had been transferred to Ling's van; the license plates off the stolen truck were later found, cut up into sections in the Clayton safehouse.

The scene of Duge's shoot-out and the spot where Remiro surrendered four hours later were each roughly a block and a half from the SLA hideout. It seems possible that Remiro checked with his comrades during those hours. If they were warned, the SLA probably went on alert. The possibility of siege and "defending the pad" had always been with them, and they had planned for it. Each soldier had a defense station. Their written plan, found later, called for riflemen (or women) stationed at the "basement portholes," the air vents in the crawl space beneath the house, protected by the concrete foundation, and behind barricades of bundled newspapers upstairs.

From the SLA defense plan:

—Keep your hand gun with you at all times
—Keep your amo and rifles, etc. together and ready to carry out immediately
—Always know where your shoes are
—Always know where your molotov cocktails are

"Surrender to the enemy" was forbidden by the SLA code; it drew "penalty by death." But why, then, had Remiro, a firebrand among them, been brought to such a meek end? That he still carried the Walther PP that police ballistics would connect to the Foster murder was just dumb, but his surrender may have been a decoy decided on by the group or Cinque. Remiro himself, much later, would deny any contact—probably truthfully; the SLA hatred of prisons would likely bar such sacrifices. Perhaps Remiro simply had second thoughts about fatal heroics. It is clear the SLA was alerted by early morning—the Harrises never showed up at their Berkeley jobs—but none of the neighbors remembered any activity at the hideout until they saw Nancy Perry—"Mrs. DeVoto"—entering the house around 11 A.M. She left and was seen coming home again around 2 o'clock, a small grocery bag in her arms. At around 2:30 Mizmoon Soltysik walked out of the house and down the street. Several neighbors noted it was the first time they had seen her dressed up, wearing a skirt instead of her usual long sweater and jeans. (SLA wall memo: "Dress with class consciousness much more than have been. We can wear pants—but the kind they wear.")

At about 6:15 P.M. a gold Buick Riviera—the car Willie Wolfe left behind when he hitchhiked East—backed out of the garage. Someone—a neighbor spied only "two skinny legs in blue jeans"—slammed the garage door and ran to join the driver in the heavily loaded car. As it backed out the sloping drive, the undercarriage scraped with a loud thump. The car sped off, leaving a huge white cloud of exhaust.

At that moment a six-inch fuse was burning under the closed door between the attached garage and the main house. A few minutes later it reached a puddle of gasoline.

Gunpowder and gasoline had been splashed over the rugs and walls, and there was a puddle trail from the fuse to an open five-gallon can of gasoline in the front hall. It had been a studied arson—almost professional, except for one hitch. The drapes—for the first time—had been tacked back from the windows; the gas explosion was to break the windows to suck in the air that would turn the light wood-frame building into an inferno. That it did not was partly due to chance—but because of the lack of oxygen in the tightly closed house, the result was what the fire inspector called a "flashover fire": a poof of blaze that blistered the paint and scorched everything; a lot of smoke but something far less than an obliterating fire. The first fire truck on the scene ran in one hose and snuffed it.

In an "open letter" a week later Nancy Perry would claim that she had set the fire "only to melt away fingerprints that may have been overlooked. It was never intended that the fire would totally destroy the premises because there was nothing left there that was of any real consequence to us. . . ." (The SLA never—ever—acknowledged a mistake.)

If by their respective foul-ups the SLA and the police had been gift wrapping and delivering presents to each other all day, this was the bonanza. In the house police found an incredible collection of evidence, virtually a blueprint for the SLA. The firemen had called in the sheriff, and the sheriff's department requested the assistance of a Navy demolition team. They removed from the house two six-inch gunpowder pipe bombs; an aerosol-can bomb stuffed with gunpowder and shotgun pellets; a half can of gunpowder; the half-empty five-gallon can of gasoline and—capped and full—other cans containing another fifteen gallons of gasoline. Scattered through the house were about a dozen bottles (imported Akadama plum wine, Cin's favorite) that had apparently been Molotov cocktails—only one had not ignited; it had a Modess sanitary napkin for the wick. From the aerosol-can bomb police technicians lifted two fingerprints.

Oakland cops on the Foster case were at the scene as the fire still smoldered. When the house was cleared of smoke and incendiaries, police slowly (too slowly: the house was left unguarded that night and neighborhood kids and a couple of curious reporters rummaged through the debris) began to realize what a treasure chest they had. Lying around were the scorched files of what had obviously been the main SLA headquarters. (Fahizah would claim it was merely an "information-intelligence" outpost.) The Symbionese apparently had an incredible propensity to take notes, and hoarded everything. If the significance of the find dawned but dimly on the lawmen, the SLA caught on quickly. All of the SLA combat cadre—with the exception of Camilla Hall—dived for cover, going underground.

Only Bill and Emily Harris still had jobs at the time of the Concord bust; all the rest were unemployed, living on food stamps, welfare, unemployment—and at least two armed robberies. On the morning of January 10 Bill did not show up to toss mailbags at the post office, and Emily called in sick at the Survey Research Center.

(Later in the day Emily visited convict Barron Broadnax at the San Luis Obispo prison—a four-hour drive, halfway to LA—and Angela Atwood, using the name Anne Lindberg, went to San Quentin and saw inmate James Harold "Doc" Holiday. Those visits, in the midst of scurrying for cover, must have been to alert the two black convicts to the capture of Remiro and Little. Holiday, an indeterminate-term lifer, was then the reputed leader of the Black Guerrilla Family, according to prison officials, having succeeded to that title after the death of George Jackson. Broadnax reportedly was a chief lieutenant to Holiday in the BGF. Both had been visited regularly by SLA members or their associates. Robyn Steiner, while living at Peking House with Russ Little, had visited Holiday on more than a dozen occasions during 1972 and 1973. Emily Harris had seen Broadnax fifteen times between August of 1973—when the Symbionese Federation was desperately trying to recruit—and the day the SLA went underground.)

The Harrises and Angela fled their Oakland home in haste, leaving clothes, stereo, personal (and incriminating) papers—all their belongings, all their past. They left toothbrushes hanging in the bathroom and drip coffee, ready for the hot water, on the stove. And they left three pistol boxes; one for a Smith-Wesson revolver, two for Mauser automatics. Open and empty, the blue plastic gun boxes bespoke their priorities.

In Emmaus, Pennsylvania, Willie announced to his father on the tenth that he was going to Sweden to get married and become an expatriate. On the eleventh Willie received three collect long-distance phone calls from public phone booths in Oakland. He was upset. He had to grab a bus to New York—"to visit a sick friend," he said.

Perhaps it was from the hideout Bill Harris had rented, under the alias William Kinder, a block from Oakland city hall, that Emily wrote her parents that she was secluded in the Sierras. When it became clear how much the cops had found in the Clayton house, they knew the risk of reemerging in their old lives was too great. Bill and Emily sent in letters resigning from their jobs, citing personal reasons. Emily called their landlord and told him Bill's dad was dying; they had returned to Indiana and were going to stay. She asked him to sell their belongings, throw away the rest, and send the money to her parents. (Only later did he realize that it must have been a local call, not from Indiana; he heard the operator ask Emily to deposit fifty cents.)

Inside the Clayton house police found treasure beneath the scattered and scorched clutter. The house was furnished in crash-pad modern: mattresses on the floor and wooden crates. There were several typewriters, a mimeograph machine, and boxes and handfuls of bullets all around—.30 caliber, 9 millimeter, .38 special caliber, .45 caliber, .30-06 caliber, and 12-gauge shotgun shells. The walls were covered with posters, Mao and Stalin, and pinned with photos of police officers and slogans signed "Cin." Taped to three walls were well over 100 newspaper and magazine clippings about the exploits of foreign guerrillas and revolutionaries. There were gas masks, bandoliers, stacks of gun and ammo catalogues, stolen license plates, and three BB guns. The walls were pockmarked with the little pellets.

Not all that was found has been made public, but police removed more than a dozen cartons of letters, files, address books, and "miscellaneous documents." There were many letters from prisoners— *Da Da o Mi* letters; plans for teamwork games listing code names—Bayo, Cin, James, Norma, Fahizah, Zoya, Osi— some cryptic, some explicit. There were other lists of names, some with scribbled notations like: "It looks like our old friends don't have it anymore." There was a sketch of the Foster ambush scene and another detailing the location of a January 7 armed robbery in Berkeley—both notated in the cramped script of Joe Remiro. (The Berkeley robbery, only three days before the Concord arrests, was a daring daylight holdup of a courier delivering $4,000 cash to the Top Hat bar from a nearby bank. The messenger later identified Little and Remiro as the two bandits.)

On the living-room mantel was a row of charred books, among them *Anti-aircraft Defense, A White Girl, Criminal Law,* and *The Rise and Fall of the Third Reich.*

On the door of one of the bedrooms was a poster-sized message. Fire had scorched it so only part could still be read. It ended: " . . . I say myself in this room because it has become the only one that comes without being asked, because it understands that it is sexist that a man must ask before a woman will come to see or talk with him so if I don't ask, don't you either, just come on in and find out who lives in here and that he's 90% human, the other 10% we are working on." It was signed "Cin."

A box in one bedroom contained *Who's Who in American Industry,* two copies of the *Directory of American Firms Operating in Foreign Countries,* the *California Blue Book—1971, California International Business Directory, The Watchdogs of Wall Street, Who's Who in the West, Who's Who in Business and Finance, Condensed Chemical Dictionary,* and *Police*—all stolen library books. In another bedroom were *The Roots of Guerrilla Warfare, Marksmanship,* Tegner's *Defensive Tactics,* and *The FBI Lab.*

A closet shelf held twenty-two .38-caliber rounds with hollow points filled with cyanide, a plastic container with a liquid marked CYANIDE WATER, and a cardboard box containing two large vials of mercury and bottles of ammonium nitrate, dimethylolurea, and sulfonic-acid salt—a bomb factory.

In the shorthand listing of the police search-warrant report, one can leaf through the papers found on a shelf beside a bedroom desk:

—typed page listing different gun parts as well as different gun distributors, appears to be part to a rifle (m-1)
—one typed page with list of rifle parts. Return address to Salamone, J. Mark of P.O. Box 24553, Oakland. . . .
—one typed page dated 1 Jan 74 and headed as "Shopping List." List of arms material.
—one typed page relating to government conspiracy against the people.

—two paragraphs relating to why Kennedy was killed.

—typed page Dated 1 Jan 74. Heading: "Rise To the Spirit of the Symbionese Liberation Army." Refers to history of the organization.

—one typed page relating to prisoners in the prison system.

—handwritten page relating to "Internal Warfare Identification Program."

—typed page with one paragraph, thought not completed. Refers ruling class.

—handwritten page referring to Del Monte as conglomerate.

—nine pages typed: five of which list the addresses of the members of the Calif. Council on Crime and Delinquency.

—one typed page headed "THE PRESENT." Refers to Nixon Administration and the Watergate affair.

—one typed page headed, "A PRELUDE TO THE PRESENT." Refers to the Nazi regimé, type of government.

—two paragraphs typed and headed "WHAT IS THE PRESENT." Refers to comparison between US and Hitler.

—typed page referring to Wounded Knee.

—two paragraphs regarding US exploitation of the people.

There were schedules for surveillance duty, maps and detailed plans for robberies and ambushes, early drafts of communiqués ("It may not look like it," one SLA soldier scribbled across the top of a page, "but I am working on the communique")—it was almost too much. It *was* too much for the cops assigned to sort through and analyze the truckload of documents found. Perhaps even after the Foster murder they did not take the SLA seriously; perhaps the whole idea of guerrillas in the Berkeley hills seemed just too farfetched. Whatever the reason, police did not bother to warn most of those listed as SLA targets. It was left to the FBI agents to do so, after the Hearst kidnapping, when the bureau first became involved in the SLA case.

A partial compilation of those on the SLA's "target" list included:

Donald T. Lauer, a vice-president of Wells Fargo Bank; seventy-one years old.*

Arthur P. Shapro, a senior vice-president and director of Liberty National Bank of San Francisco; sixty-eight years old.

D. S. Langsdorf, a senior vice-president of Bank of America; fifty-nine years old.

Theodore Louis Lenzen, a retired vice-president and director of Standard Oil of California; sixty-eight years old.

*Ages are as of late 1973, when the SLA was compiling the target list.

Rudolph A. Peterson, retired president of Bank of America; sixty-nine years old.

Robert T. Shinkle, a senior vice-president of Bank of America; fifty-seven years old. (SLA "intelligence" wrongly had him with Crocker National Bank.)

Calvin K. Townsend, a retired ITT executive and director of the First National Bank; seventy-three years old.

James H. Woodhead, corporate secretary for Kaiser Industries ("all 28," the SLA noted); sixty-six years old.

Joseph A. Moore, Jr., a former president of the California State Chamber of Commerce, now a regent of the University of California; sixty-five years old.

John E. Countryman, former chairman of the board of Del Monte Corporation. (The surveillance of the Countryman residence in San Francisco was assigned to General Gelina—Angela Atwood—while Fahizah was working on a communiqué for the kidnapping. But the SLA's predilection for old men misled them in this case. The surveillance list noted Countryman to be seventy years old. Countryman, however, died in July, 1972, of natural causes. He was sixty-nine.)

Edwin A. Adams, retired board chairman of Bank of California; seventy-one years old.

Charles W. Comer, fifty-three, president of the T. A. White Candy Company, a subsidiary of Pearson Candy Company, a division of Continental Baking Company, a subsidiary of ITT—*kidnap or execute; warrant prepared.*

Three mid-level executives with Touche Ross & Company, an international accounting firm (the reason these three were specifically targeted is unknown).

Tyrone T., a twenty-eight-year-old San Francisco bar owner about whom the SLA surveillance file noted: "was a pimp (may still be)."

Robert A. Magowan, chairman of the board of Safeway Stores; seventy years old.

Susan Ford, sixteen years old, daughter of then Vice President Gerald Ford.

Raymond Procunier, fifty-one, director of the California Department of Corrections.

Marcus Foster, schools superintendent of Oakland—*executed.*

Patricia Campbell Hearst, nineteen years old; daughter of Randolph and Catherine Hearst—*arrest warrant issued.*

Almost all of these names were cited as targets in SLA documents discovered by police either at the Clayton hideout or at the

Harrises' residence in Oakland. There were several other lists of names, some of which may have been for target assignment. In most cases it was quite obvious, and in others, clear at least that some precaution was appropriate. On one page of a small green spiral notebook, the crabbed handwriting of Nancy Ling Perry—apparently listing information to be researched at the University of California library—schoolgirlishly outlined her subjects, listing but one individual in an ominous context of institutions and corporations:

AT UC
1) That daughter of Hearst
2) Senate Select Penal Committee
3) Transportation & what's going on where
4) SCIENTISTS
    1. (unclear scrawl)
    2. That bitch
    3. Touche Ross
    4. The legislature
    5. b/of A people (Bank of America)
    6. U.C. Bd of Regents

On another page, near the end of the notebook, a list of daily tasks and immediate concerns brings up a full name:

1. Pay PG&E Bill
2. For Yolanda and Camilla to come up
3. Van has to be registered by Feb. 1st.
4. Picking up things from Lulu, umbrella & mail & W-2 form
    Thurs. Nite Business
    Meeting
4. Have my Sacramento Trip/David & Margareta scene/etc.
    Patricia Campbell Hearst
    —Jr. Art History—
5. Self defense class for . . .

On the opposite page, scrawled at an angle alongside the name of Patrica Hearst, were the cryptic words:

On the nite of the
full moon
Jan. 7th

The identities of David and Margareta have never been positively verified, but Yolanda and Camilla would soon be known to every California police officer. And Patricia Campbell Hearst would be famous after the SLA executed one of their rehearsed "teamwork games" on February 4—the night of another full moon. Apparently because they simply did not realize the significance of what they read, police never warned Patty or her family. Much later the Hearsts first learned of the green notebook and the warning it held, from the authors. The FBI then confirmed the report.

9

Nancy Ling Perry .... *Fahizah*, d. May 17, 1974
Russell Little .... *Osceola* or *Osi*
Joseph Remiro .... *Bo*

AFTER Remiro and Little had been arrested and charged with the murder of Marcus Foster, there was an incredible letter to the news media from Fahizah, Nancy Ling Perry. The only reason the police were able to capture the two SLA soldiers, she claimed, was because she, back at the hideout, had not known they were under attack and because "none of us were offensively armed." The difference between being "defensively armed"—as Little and Remiro were—and "offensively armed" was that offensive weaponry carried cyanide bullets. She spoke of these cyanide bullets as if they were charmed talismans; they would have protected her captured *compañeros*; now they would avenge them. She said that the two were falsely accused, that Remiro's gun was not the Foster murder weapon, that Remiro and Little belonged to "non-combat" SLA units, that none of the SLA combat units even visited the Clayton house. Yet in its tangled skein of lies and bombast the letter was an extraordinary document; a personal statement of the passions and politics of the SLA, it was the only word from the SLA in the month between the Concord bust and the Hearst kidnapping, and it was perhaps the most revealing of all the SLA communiqués*:

> My name was Nancy Ling Perry, but my true name is Fahizah. What that name means is one who is victorious and I am one who believes in the liberation and victory of the people, because I have learned that what one really believes in is what will come to pass. . . .

---

*The full text is included in the Appendix.

For Nancy Perry, the former Nancy Ling, alias Nancy DeVoto, revolution had become an act of faith. It had nothing to do with mass organizing, dialectical materialism, or the trivia of political theory. Revolution was an *act of will*—and that singular premise gave logic to the Symbionese.

Fahizah, twenty-six-year-old Berkeley street freak, became the media's emblematic figure for the SLA: tiny, brave, bizarre, and bewildering. In the famous photo taken after she was attacked at the Clayton hideout, she was also beautiful. She stood four feet eleven inches, featherweight at about 100 pounds, daughter of an upper-middle-class family; her conservative background was turned topsy-turvy in the ferment of the sixties until she was more alien than alienated. She wore green nail polish and wrote "kill the pigs" on Berkeley walls; a quiet, intense, introverted girl who had not yet given up the hope that young America had created its own counterculture of rebellion. Because most of the drafts of the SLA communiqués found in Clayton were in her handwriting, the press, and then the police, tagged her the SLA's "chief theoretician"—heady status announced on the network news, particularly for a dropped-out hippie who had but lately given up squeezing oranges at Fruity Rudy's sidewalk juice stand on Telegraph Avenue.

Her politics mingled Mao with the *I Ching*:

> A revolutionary is not a criminal nor is she or he an adventurer, and revolutionary violence is nothing but the most profound means of achieving internal as well as external balance. . . . The experience of living in Amerikkka has taught me the realities of what fascism, imperialism and genocide mean; and I have discovered the truth about the military take-over and the police state dictatorship, not because I studied it in college, but because I see it everyday, and because truth is something that is honestly known, as easily as beauty is seen. . . .

There was more of the *I Ching* than Mao.

> When I was in high school in 1963–64, I witnessed the first military coup against we the people of this country. I saw us passively sit by our TVs and unconsciously watch as the militarily armed corporate state took over the existing government and blatantly destroyed the constitution that some of us still believed in. I listened to the people around me deny that a military coup had taken place and claim that such a thing could not happen here. The

people I grew up around were so politically naive that their conceptions of a military coup only recognized those that occurred in South America and African countries where the military and ruling class took over the government by an open force of arms. . . . Here the coup was simply accomplished by assassinating the then-president John Kennedy, and then assassinating any further opposition to the dictator who was to take power; that dictator is the current president, Richard Nixon. . . .

She described the evolution of her "consciousness" in the prescribed terms—"Basically, I have three backgrounds: I have a work background, a love background and a prison background"—but she had never been to prison except as a visitor, or held a "straight" job. Actually, her relevant background was in the common crisis of youth in the sixties: self-doubt and moral certitude in a schizophrenic culture that preached platitudes and raped ethics. She had chosen to reject the bourgeois success her education and background could have given her—and now, so long outside, she had no way back into the mainstream of society. The frustrating quietude of the seventies had left her without purpose and with a bin of unfulfilled utopian dreams.

The SLA vision was cramped on all sides, and Fahizah's declaration sets out a classic illustration. She sees a nation of "pawns and puppets," in which those who have "taken over the government were trying to keep us asleep and in a political stupor"; a citizenry that seems determined to remain oblivious of the fact "that they are in immediate danger of being thrown into concentration camps themselves, tortured, or shot down in the streets for expressing their beliefs." The devil is astride us and no one will even pray. It is a perspective that assumes that the proverbial "People" have somehow been temporarily drugged, blinded to their own self-interest (the Revolution), and thus have only to be sufficiently shocked, awakened by some sufficiently dramatic display of courage and possibility (terrorism) before they will rise. In the vocabulary of the SLA study groups, the people had "false consciousness." It is a sophistic formula commonly used to explain away the inconvenient fact that most American citizens, enduring whatever inequities and injustice they do, seem committed to and involved in the political fabric of the culture.

To acknowledge this and still sustain a viable political critique demands a constancy and maturity Fahizah and the SLA did not possess. The New Left had left them trapped with its celebrated isolation from the mainstream culture. Nancy Ling Perry's political career parallels that of thousands who were led to a frustrated despair. Two important ideas in the New Left scripture were *co-optation* and *repressive tolerance*. The first secured the isolation, demanding of the faithful that they remove themselves from the system so as not to be tempted into a compromise of principle. The second, repressive tolerance, was a popular leftist concept that provided the foundation for much of the extremist violence, although it was seldom publicly articulated. It declared, in essence, that the system was designed to withstand any form of dissent that does not threaten its crucial institutions; thus, only actions that are "criminal," or disruptive enough to force the state to repress them, really challenge the status quo. It is an idea that effectively blocks its adherents from any route of "legal" social protest, narrowing the range of "revolutionary options" drastically. Unavoidably, it led to terrorism; to the conclusion, as Fahizah put it, that "there is no flight to freedom except that of an armed projectile."

Nancy Ling Perry described herself in her public letter as an officer in the SLA's "Information-Intelligence Unit," using her "mind and imagination to uncover facts so that when the SLA attacks it will be in the right place." Foster, she said, had been the right target: "Intensely thorough intelligence operations" had determined that Foster's signature was the first to appear on the Nixon-inspired proposal for "armed police in certain Oakland schools and various forms of computer classification of students." The clincher, it appeared, was the "further intelligence" which revealed that Foster had been a member of the Philadelphia Crime Commission. Intense she may have been, but "thorough" she definitely was not; if Fahizah was the pilot fish of the SLA, the Revolution was blind.

Nancy Ling was the daughter of a family locally well known for their conservative Goldwater politics. Her father was the prosperous manager of a furniture store in Santa Rosa, California, and active in local politics. A high school teacher remembers Nancy as "short, pudgy, cute, good-natured, and active in everything . . . one of those kids who questioned all the rules." At sixteen she wore a Goldwater button for the 1964 campaign, but that was family politics, not yet her own. She went off to Whittier College, Richard Nixon's conservative alma mater, for her freshman year, then, with a spurt of independence, transferred to the liberated bustle of UC Berkeley in 1967.

Berkeley is always full of kids trying to break with the past and create or discover a new life. Within a year Ling, as she liked to be called, had shocked and surprised her parents when she married

Gilbert Perry, a black jazz musician six years her senior. (It was a turbulent, off-again-on-again marriage; they separated within a year, reconciled, and split several times more before they ended it in the spring of 1971.) They had settled in the small gray cottage Ling rented, tucked back behind one of the apartment buildings on McKinley Street in Berkeley. The little cottage bears the scars; under the gray paint on the door you can still see the dark outline of the big scarlet *A* Gilbert painted on the door when he moved out. *A* for Adulteress. One neighbor, a friend of Ling's, said Gilbert later realized that was not true.

Another neighbor, an older woman who lived in the apartment building, remembers Ling discussing her marital problems. "She was really oppressed by Gilbert and I sympathized with her," she recalled. "He was really chauvinistic—he was out screwing around with other women and he knew she knew about it. He was extremely possessive and jealous about her, but he felt he could do as he pleased. She had dropped out of college for a while, and she wanted to get a job, but the idea offended Gilbert's masculinity." She got a job after Gilbert stalked out, dealing play-money blackjack in a topless joint in San Francisco's North Beach called Crystal Lil's. The waitresses were topless; the dealers, like Ling, wore see-through blouses. ("What my work background taught me is that one of the things that every revolutionary does is to fight to get back the fruits of her or his own labor and the control of his or her own destiny.")

Ling returned to school and came out with a degree in English literature in 1970. She began a program to get teaching credentials but quit—frustrated, too impatient to get into a classroom and use her own ideas, said her brother Gary, a Berkeley graduate student in mathematics. From teaching she went to medicine. She enrolled for a second BA in 1972, in chemistry, looking to a paramedic career. She was at it six months—working part time in a UC lab cleaning glassware and caring for the experimental animals—before she gave up again. Her science background was so deficient that she could not compete with the younger students, she said. In January, 1973, she quit school for good and went to work at Fruity Rudy's selling juice on the edge of the campus from a gypsy cart. Already she was interested in the prison movement, particularly black prisoners. She told her brother Gary that she had met "people in Berkeley" who had initiated her into writing letters to prisoners; she told him she was writing several prisoners under different names.

When she was living with Gilbert Perry, said her brother, Ling had been exposed to the experience of being black and poor. "It angered her," said Gary. "She felt not only that it shouldn't be that way, but not for another minute." Still later, shortly before she moved into the SLA hideout in the summer of 1973, she told a neighbor at her Berkeley apartment building that she had just seen *Lady Sings the Blues.* "That's it," she said, "that's where it's at for black people in general. And if it's that bad outside, the deal for blacks in prison is exponentially worse."

She had been deeply into drugs for years, dealing lightly and using heavily; a drugstore selection when available, but mostly hashish. The professor who supervised her at the UC lab remembers her as soft and wan, "burned out." A good friend, a graduate student who worked with her, said she became increasingly "strung out" while she worked at the lab, sometimes barely staggering in to work. She looked increasingly unhealthy, sick, worn. She lectured one professor on the qualities of LSD: "She said it was neither horrible nor a great enlightenment, just something else to try. She said she had done a lot of it." Others remember her buying cocaine, "dropping" a handful of codeine pills. Working at Fruity Rudy's, friends said, she sometimes went through a dozen joints of marijuana to get through the day. "Ling didn't mind spending most of her money on dope," said a friend who sometimes worked at the stand. He said he once asked Ling why she worked at Rudy's. She didn't have anything else, she replied.

She began to have trouble with her hands; they became swollen and puffy; she had difficulty picking things up. She saw several doctors. Arthritis, perhaps, she told a friend. To another she said that perhaps all the drugs were getting to her, poisoning her system. Then she cut out drugs completely, suddenly (about the same time Remiro did the same), and went on a health-food kick. "She said she couldn't be any use to the Movement on dope," recalled Rudy Henderson, the middle-aged black former jazz drummer who owns Fruity Rudy's. Henderson was a hard taskmaster; few of his employees stayed with him long; Ling's friends tell how she would mother him, bring him dinner, clean his room. (After her death Henderson began soliciting bids from reporters for an "intimate story" about Fahizah of the SLA. He said he was getting offers as high as $3,000.)

Ling believed in astrology and that the stars had fated her to constant conflict. On her star chart two lines crossed perpendicularly; one representing domesticity, the other, independence. When Ling quit Rudy's in August, 1973, she apparently moved into an SLA hideout. She gave up her apartment and told her brother she would be unreachable, "moving around." Thero Wheeler's girlfriend, Mary Alice Siem, said Ling set up house with Mizmoon and Cinque in Oakland. Up until the spring of 1973 Ling had spoken about her work around the prisons quite openly, said her brother Gary, then suddenly she became secretive. She had described the cesspools that prisons are; now she just said she "was working with a group that thought they could do something about it":

> My prison background means that I have close ties and feelings for our incarcerated brothers and sisters. What they have taught me is that if people on the outside do not understand the necessity of defending them through force of arms, it is because these people on the outside do not yet realize that they are in an immediate danger of being thrown into concentration camps themselves, tortured or shot down in the streets for expressing their beliefs.

In November, after the Foster murder, Ling visited her brother. No, she told him, she did not have a permanent address yet. (In Clayton she was then "Nancy DeVoto," wife of "George DeVoto"—Russ Little.) She wanted to ask Gary's girlfriend, who had studied Chinese, to translate seven phrases—later known as the "principles" of the SLA—into that language. The girlfriend couldn't. (Ling then tried the Chinese girl who worked the *falafal* cart near Fruity Rudy's, but again it was too difficult.) In December, she sent her parents a card: "I wish love and happiness to everyone. Stay well and well informed. I love you, Nancy." Her mother wrote back, care of Gary, a letter Nancy never picked up. Mrs. Ling enclosed some clippings on prison reform from the *Christian Science Monitor* and some stamps. "Please write. . . ."

Like most of the parents—save Bill Harris' mother and Joe Remiro's parents—Russ Little's folks found Symbionese Liberation Army a bewildering phrase, almost unpronounceable, and the idea of their son as an American revolutionary incomprehensible. "This is my only son," Mrs. Little told the San Francisco *Chronicle*. "He's not the kind of boy who would be involved in anything like that. I'm just completely baffled." Her husband, O. Jack Little, later offered himself in exchange for Patty Hearst. The distance from his parents' home in Pensacola, Florida, where Mr. Little is a retired Navy civilian employee, and Russ Little's flat in Berkeley cannot be expressed in miles.

"He always brought joy and honor to us," said Mrs. Little. "I cannot believe that would change." The Littles were very proud of their son. In 1967 Russell graduated ninth in a class of 600 in high school. He went through a year in junior college, then, with a partial scholarship, on to the University of Florida at Gainesville. He studied electrical engineering for three years, then transferred to philosophy.

Little and Remiro both granted exclusive interviews from jail to the San Francisco *Phoenix,* an underground paper, and both stressed their "proletarian" backgrounds. Russ Little described himself as a white Southern cracker. "It was a very backward, racist environment to grow up in," he said. He was raised in a duplex in a government housing project and later in a working-class subdivision. "I got my first shotgun at age seven. I bought it with money I made cutting grass . . . ." Brought up in the segregated South, Little said he was oblivious to the black civil rights movement. "The blacks in our town didn't dare raise much hell because the crackers would come down on them with guns blazing and everyone knew it." He said he went off to the university in 1968 "completely ignorant" about politics and social problems in this country and elsewhere. He said he boozed and played his way through his first years at college, losing his scholarship, staying in with loans, but now "with one foot inside the door of the Good American Life." Then, in the fall of 1968, he took a course in philosophy with a young Marxist professor that he said changed his life, introducing him to Marx, Lenin, Mao, and Eldridge Cleaver.

"I was way behind and started to catch up. . . . Going to marches, rallies, demonstrations! In the spring getting righteously angry about Kent State, Jackson State. . . . When I went home that summer—long-haired, pissed-off radical—my parents and friends didn't know what to think." The following year he was into philosophy and taking an active part in organizing campus demonstrations. He and his friends, "the campus crazies," came North for the 1971 May Day demonstrations in Washington. "We were confrontation-oriented, believing that direct experience with the brutality of the pigs was most responsible for radicalizing people. I was never a true hippie, a peacenik, or pacifist. I was probably a Yippie. . . ."

In the spring of 1972 Russ—with girlfriend Robyn Steiner—drifted to Berkeley, looking for the real world, the revolutionary proletariat. "I decided that the campus was not the place to be learning and spreading revolution—most people were there because they were trying to 'make it' in America." As the era of riots and demonstrations ended, it was becoming obvious that the New Left was floundering. "People started talking about educating the people again. Bullshit to that. What about the people who had been educated in the sixties?" Russ settled in Oakland, in Peking House, seeking action. He became involved with the prison movement to "search out the revolutionaries, political prisoners, and prisoners of war, and see what their thoughts were."

Through the BCA—then the BGF—Death Row Jeff, and Donald DeFreeze, he learned. "Urban guerrilla warfare is a feasible and successful response to the repression here in the U.S.A. In fact, I believe that urban guerrilla warfare is and will spread to every major city in the U.S. and that eventually an army of national liberation will be formed."

Personality and politics often contrast sharply, but the violent, hard-edged voice of Osceola, the SLA terrorist, speaks a different language from that of the warm Russ Little described by his friends in both Pensacola and Oakland. The recollection of many approximates that of David Gunnell, landlord at Peking House, who said, "Russ was a really mild, loving-type dude." A friend in Florida described him as "someone who really, genuinely cared about people. He was maybe the most gentle man I ever knew."

Little became best friend to young Willie Wolfe while the two were living together in the Peking House collective. Many of their acquaintances remember them as virtually inseparable, both quiet, each seemingly sharing confidences only with the other. Little disappeared from Peking House in July, although he paid rent through September. Wolfe left at the end of September, moving into a cottage with Joe Remiro. Occasionally friends would see the three of them together, but they seemed to be avoiding old acquaintances. Radical friends of Little assumed "it had something to do with his prison work." It was understood that no one should ask questions.

Remiro seemed an odd man to make up a threesome with the other two. Since he had come back from the war, Joe Remiro had always been the outsider in any group, the loner. But now the SLA was going to war, and twenty-seven-year-old Remiro was the expert in war, master craftsman to his two young apprentices.

Much later, while Remiro and Little for a time were locked up together in San Quentin's disciplinary "adjustment center" awaiting trial for the Foster murder, the two regularly sent out letters and proclamations to the media. Perhaps revealingly, each of the several messages Remiro and Little sent out to newspapers was written in Remiro's misspelling hand. Little, the college grad, just signed them. When word was brought to them at the Alameda county jail in their medical isolation cell (a judge had ordered them removed from San Quentin) that six of their comrades had died in the LA shoot-out, Little and Remiro were playing gin rummy. Little laid down his cards and cried, a guard reported. Remiro sat stone-faced, showing no reaction.

That was Joe's way, said a friend. When he was hurt by something, he closed up, showed nothing. Yet Remiro was probably the most volatile, explosive personality in the SLA. "Joe was a political heavy," said an Oakland radical who knew most of the SLA. "I mean, he came across that way. I think his theory stunk and he needed a lot more practice, but he came across heavy. Russ was rhetorical and he wasn't a person who made strong statements or commanded a great deal of political respect—whereas Joe demanded that it be given to him."

Remiro was understood best, perhaps, by his few friends who were also Vietnam combat veterans—vets who had turned against the war and returned to civilian life full of a raging guilt and bitter anger; the sense of disorientation and dislocation they call PVS, the Post-Vietnam Syndrome. "Joe had been a grunt in Vietnam," explained one of these friends, "he was directly in combat. He wasn't dropping bombs from five thousand feet, he was killing from five feet, fifty feet. He was good at it and he got into it—then he had to come home and face himself." Remiro had dropped out of college in his first year and enlisted. When he was eighteen years old, he was in Vietnam in the Army's elite recon unit, the Long-Range Reconnaissance Patrol, the LRRPs of the 101st. At nineteen, on voluntary extended tour, he was a squad leader for a six-man commando team, dropped behind enemy lines to scout and locate concentrations of VC forces.

Born in San Francisco of Chicano and Italian heritage, he was raised "white," educated in Roman Catholic schools. He was graduated from Sacred Heart High School in 1964, then enrolled at San Francisco City College. "I wasn't really into any intellectual thing, you know, and then as soon as I heard about the war I couldn't wait to run and enlist," he told the San Francisco *Phoenix*. "I was a reactionary, I was a stone reactionary. The Catholics trained me right, boy. They taught me to hate commies—you know, kill commies for Christ . . . and I couldn't wait to get over there." He spent eighteen months in Vietnam.

Remiro's war had no law, no rules—even the rank discipline of the infantry didn't extend to the rogue LRRP units. In the field a LRRP private could claim authority normally reserved for command officers, calling in jets, artillery, naval gunfire upon shadows in the wilderness. Not uncommonly, Joe enjoyed it, the danger and all the perverse liberties of war. ("We would play games," he recalled for his trial jury, "chase buffalo around, chase people around with artillery and jets and things.") He was, he said, "really comfortable in Vietnam." And the chaos of Nam seemed actually less frightening than the idea of returning to the States, to civilian life, where Joe, unschooled, was perpetually outranked. The readjustment—when he finally shipped back in March, 1968—was brutal. Out of the war zone, memories and a haunting shame smothered the craftsman's combat pride. "I couldn't believe that everything was going on the same way it was when I left a year and a half ago. And all the stuff was going on in Vietnam—nobody, it never affected anyone's lives. . . ." Waiting out the last ten months of his hitch stationed in California, Joe applied for a *CO* discharge. The war, the killing—it was all wrong, he said.

Remiro said he became a pacifist the day before he returned to the States. He was a survivor; he came home walking from a unit that had one of the highest casualty rates among U.S. forces. But there was a final trauma. As Remiro told several friends, the camp he was in came under attack the day before he was to ship out. The VC zeroed in on the ammo dump and there was a huge explosion; shrapnel—bits and pieces of everything—came raining down on his barracks, cutting through the roof and walls. Remiro said he just stood still, letting it all come down around him, and came out untouched. "Somehow that really fucked him up," said a friend. "It left him confused for a long time."

Remiro's family, particularly his father, had been pleased when Joe enlisted, said a former roommate, "and then that was important to Joe." But when he returned in January of 1969—a pacifist, a vegetarian, a habitual dope smoker, with horror stories of murderous search-and-destroy missions—his father threw him out of the house, Joe told the *Phoenix*. He said his father "told me that he was in [a] war and he never saw nothin' like that and I was lying. Nobody believed me. And then My Lai comes out and everybody acts like it was an isolated incident and it wasn't no isolated incident." Joe *knew*, he said, that it was not an isolated incident. "I came to the conclusion that the only reason I went to Vietnam, the only reason I was subjected to what I was subjected to, was because my father forgot what he experienced in World War II, you know. And I was determined never to forget."

Like most GIs in Vietnam, Remiro had used marijuana, heavily, but when he was transferred back to the States, he got into LSD, psychedelics. Every weekend he'd trip. "What happened was that

I developed a psychological dependency on it," he explained, ". . . it is not a habit-forming drug, but psychologically I used to crave it like I crave a cigarette." After discharge, he used still more, to "go back in time, you know, and see why I did something like that." He built up a powerful fury against the government that had taken him—ignorant of any politics and full of John Wayne—and put him in Vietnam to kill. The Vietcong became his heroes.

"It was over a year before I could go outside of my house without being completely drugged out of my head and talk with somebody," he remembered. Old friends couldn't connect: "They were the same way they were when I left, and I had changed a whole lot. . . . I couldn't relate to anybody who hadn't been to Vietnam, for some reason." Joe said there was one exception; he found one person he could talk to, and so he married her. It was a brief rocky marriage, but blessed with a child, a son, in June, 1971. While Remiro attended a succession of schools and worked at several menial jobs, the marriage collapsed. He could rarely hold a job for more than a month (he quit, he said, whenever his boss reminded him of an Army sergeant). He split from his wife several times before they finally broke it off, hitchhiking up and down the Pacific coast, wandering through the counterculture carnival.

Politically, his pacifist beliefs could not sustain his bitter anger. "I started thinking about if somebody jeopardized the well-being of my son, would I continue to be a pacifist, you know, and immediately I didn't have to think about it. . . . I *would* react violently if it was necessary, you know, and from there I just little by little started coming out of all that and realized that I had a moral obligation to myself and everyone else to—to act in the only way I had been taught to act and the only way that made any difference to anybody." Remiro moved into self-consciously revolutionary politics, joining Venceremos. Later he would become one of the founding organizers of the Oakland chapter of the Vietnam Veterans Against the War, a liberal organization nationally, decidedly Marxist in the Bay Area.

"Joe was very hyper, a very high-energy person," said another vet, "almost frenetic. Joe was not a feeling-type person, he was a totally rational thinking-type person—I mean, he rarely confronted and tried to deal with his emotions." Some of the radical vets had so much difficulty dealing with Remiro that they worried that he was a police provocateur. "He was dogmatic and very hotheaded," said one. "In political arguments he would keep pushing, shouting, even squaring off to fight." Remiro pushed a doctrine of maximum militancy, revolutionary activism *now*—and that cut him off even among the radical vets. "He made it difficult for others to relate to him," said a VVAW leader, "and he was very impatient with others who weren't at his level. Maybe if we had struggled more we could have got him to adjust to the level of political work needed today. . . . Joe saw the whole idea of the PVS as a liberal cop-out, an excuse for noninvolvement—but perhaps he was a classic case himself."

Remiro thought that Vietnam veterans should be a revolutionary vanguard, trained soldiers ready now for the new red flag, and when to his bitter anger he found no takers among the VVAW, he turned to the prisons and the blacks, particularly the vets among them. "Out of maximum oppression," he said repeatedly, "comes maximum resistance." At VVAW meetings, before he dropped out in the spring of 1973, he constantly pushed the Venceremos line, disrupting meetings, demanding the organization acknowledge racism and the national question—national homelands for U.S. racial minorities—as the primary political issues. "The brothers just weren't willing to deal with that," said a VVAW coordinator. (Racial national homelands would become a keystone in the SLA program.)

Projecting from his own experience, Remiro declared that GI educational benefits were just another Orwellian government "shuck," part of the plot to keep returning vets "opiated and . . . out of the fucking mainstream of politics and the working class. . . ." VVAW failed him, then Venceremos failed him. "Venceremos politics written down sounded very good," he explained to the *Phoenix*, "but in practice they turned out to be very racist, elitist, and dogmatic and it was a lot of words and that's all. They spoke up . . . but that's about all they did." Remiro wanted to bring the war home now, and this time he wanted to be on the "right" side. It was hard for a political organization not to fail Joe Remiro—and survive.

Around July or August of 1973, said his friends, Remiro quit smoking dope, just cut it out completely. "He became even more wired up," said a former roommate. "Maybe if he had been smoking more he could have worked it out. . . ."

From letters found at the Clayton house it is clear that Remiro warned his parents he was moving to the dangerous side of the law—and that they had argued and begged, but to no avail. Joe Remiro had gone back to war. He expected to end up dead or behind bars—and prison was the better of the two; in San Quentin he was in with the Dragons,* the *real* revolutionaries, who when the time comes. . . .

But perhaps Little and Remiro did not plan to stay. "You have not been forgotten," Fahizah promised them, "and you will be defended because there has been no setback and all combat forces are intact." Intact—and already well into the final planning for the Hearst kidnapping.

---

*"When the prison doors are opened, the real dragon will fly out. . . ." —from Ho Chi Minh's *Prison Writings.*

10

Kidnap

STEVE WEED and his lover, the girl he was to marry, Patricia Hearst, lived by a quiet routine. They were a close couple who preferred each other's company; "almost to an absurd degree domestic," Steve would say later. They spent most of their evenings alone at home in their comfortable two-story town house apartment, in one of more prosperous graduate-student ghettos close by the sprawling Berkeley campus of the University of California.

It was a way of life by now close to domestic ritual, a routine easily discovered by anyone who watched the couple. But the Symbionese had double-checked.

Two days before the kidnapping, Saturday evening, two strangers knocked on the door about 9:30 P.M. ostensibly to ask about available apartments in the building. The porch light was out, but through the frosted-glass sliding door, Weed could dimly make out two unfamiliar figures. Patty, curious, came up behind him in the hallway. Weed hesitated, then slid the door open.

A young woman, wearing jeans and an oversized sweater, stood at the door; behind her, a tall, thin black man hung back in the shadows. The woman—Weed would describe her as "wasted looking" to police—began to ask nervously about the apartment. She claimed the landlord's realtor had told her that the couple in apartment 4 (Weed's) would be moving out soon and she and her friend had come by to see if they could look at the place. Weed, mystified, said there must be some mistake—the wrong address or apartment number, perhaps—but he answered several questions about the neighborhood and the going price for local apartments. The woman thanked him and the couple left.

"What do you think they wanted?" asked Patty after Steve had closed the door. Weed didn't know—but neither he nor Patty accepted the apartment story. The incident left both uneasy. The man had looked "creepy," said Patty. "I could have knocked that guy over with one hand," Steve assured her. (Weed later identified the woman as Emily Harris, but the man was never identified. He was not one of the two male kidnappers, said Weed.)

The following evening, Sunday—a little after 9 o'clock—Weed answered a ring of the apartment telephone. "Is Mary there?" a woman's voice asked. Weed said it must be the wrong number; the woman apologized and hung up.

Monday, February 4, 1974, had been a typically uneventful day for both Patty and Steve. Weed had walked home alone after his late-afternoon class, Professor Myro's lecture on rudiments and philosophy of logic. Tomorrow, he thought, he would meet with his smaller section of the undergraduate class and help them analyze Myro's lecture. Weed was a teaching assistant in the Philosophy Department at Berkeley, a graduate student who conducted discussion groups for underclassmen. He liked working with students; the honed precision of the formal structures of logic intrigued and excited him. But that was tomorrow. Patty was waiting for him when he got home, and tonight Steve planned nothing more strenuous than turning the TV knob. They ate leisurely; a simple meal, but with wine, always with wine. They watched television through the meal—*Star Trek* followed by *Mission: Impossible.*

Patty was in her bathrobe, doing something in the kitchen, when the doorbell rang. It was 9:17 or so. Steve rose and left the tube, going to the door. No one was expected. Patty came out and followed him down the hall. He remembers she was standing just behind him when he unlocked the sliding door, pulled it open a few inches, and peered out into the courtyard.

Before him stood a young woman, shabbily dressed, her right hand covering part of her face. "I've been in an accident," she said excitedly. "May I use your phone?" There was no pause, no time to reply. Suddenly the glass door was jerked fully open and two men darted around the woman and into the hallway. The first plowed into Steve, knocking him to the floor. The second rushed to Patty, grabbing her and clamping a hand over her mouth just as the scream broke from her throat.

Weed had been knocked flat on his back. He started to flip over and rise when he was kicked in the side of the face, first by the man who had bowled him over, then again by the woman who had followed the two in. He lay there, stunned but conscious, while his

hands were roughly secured behind his back with a length of nylon rope the woman had produced. He was lifted by the armpits
and dragged back from the hall into the living room. In a dazed
glance, Weed could see Patty struggling with her assailant, and for
the first time he noticed that both men were armed, one with a
pistol, the other with a short-barreled rifle.

"Where's the safe . . . where's the money?" the woman demanded. "I told them—I found it difficult to talk because of the
kicks in the face I'd received—I said we didn't have a safe, that the
only money was in my wallet," Steve said later. "That seemed to
infuriate him," said Weed. "He grabbed a bottle off the wine rack
and hit me over the head with it, four times, as hard as he could. I
thought my head was going to cave in. 'Take anything you want,' I
told them."

Weed does not believe he ever lost consciousness during the
episode, but he pretended he had been knocked out by the blows
from the bottle. "I lay there, terrified, trying to figure out something I could do. At that point I still assumed it was just a robbery.
The men didn't say much at all. The woman seemed to be giving
the orders," he said.

While Weed was feigning unconsciousness, one of the men left
the apartment, scouting to see if the noise had roused neighbors.
It hadn't. Steve Suenaga, a UC Berkeley student living directly
across the interior courtyard, did not hear a thing, but just then
was on his way out to visit a girlfriend. He closed the door, heard a
noise behind him, turned. A black man was aiming a carbine at
him. "Get inside, motherfucker," the man ordered, pointing
across to the open doorway of Steve and Patty's apartment. Suenaga didn't argue; he didn't say a word. As they entered and started down the hallway he saw Weed facedown on the floor. A moment later, Suenaga, too, was prone, hands tied behind his back.
When he tried to rise—believing he was about to be killed—someone struck him repeatedly with a rifle butt.

Weed was not aware of what had happened to his neighbor,
and other than the muffled scream she had gotten out while being
grabbed, he had heard no sound from Patty. He debated whether
he should open his eyes. He decided it would not be a wise move.
He had no idea of how much time had passed since the three had
burst into the apartment. Probably only a few minutes, he figured.

"Let's go," said one of the men. For a moment Steve thought it
was over; that he and Patty had survived; the "robbers" were leaving. Then the woman spoke: "We've got to get rid of them

. . . they've seen us." The next thing Weed remembers was hearing a metallic thwack, a rifle bolt, he thought. In that moment of total terror, "I figured I had nothing to lose," recalls Weed. He leaped to his feet, "screaming, screaming like I was crazy. I ran around the room yelling my head off," said Weed. "I don't know why they didn't shoot. I guess it surprised them as much as it did me."

Somehow Weed managed to free his hands from the tangle of the rope. He raced across the living room, yanked open a large sliding-glass door and, still bellowing, dashed onto the patio, which was enclosed by a six-foot-high fence. Weed didn't hesitate: He swerved to the left, reached for the top of the wood-slat fence, jerked himself up and over, and fell into the yard of the neighboring house. Behind him he heard gunfire. Across that yard was another fence. He got up, ran, scaled that, then a third, finally finding himself on the sidewalk of Parker Street at the end of the block, shouting, "Police! Call the police!" He didn't even notice the car in which Patty was being carried away as it swerved past him, around a corner, and disappeared. Weed ran up on a porch, pounded on the door, trying to rouse help. Nobody answered.

Dazed, staggering, he made his way to the corner and around, onto Benvenue Avenue toward the town house, before his legs buckled and he collapsed to the pavement. Neighbors carried him home. There he realized, for the first time, that Patty was gone.

The shooting had begun in the courtyard. As the kidnappers were leaving—one of the men dragging the blindfolded victim by her arm—a woman living in the adjoining apartment opened her door to see what the commotion was. Susan Larkey was dumbfounded. Men with guns. Patty in only a bathrobe, kicking and screaming. The man with the rifle spotted her, turned, and snapped off three shots. One slug shattered the glass door, missing her by no more than a foot. It was either a very good shot or she was very lucky.

Patricia was dragged along a narrow cement walkway leading to the driveway, where the white convertible getaway car was parked, motor running, facing the street. "She was screaming hysterically, struggling, trying to pull free," said another neighbor, who had rushed to a window overlooking the driveway when she heard the shots. By now half naked, her blue robe having slipped off her shoulders, exposing her breasts, she was sobbing, crying, "Let me go . . . please, let me go."

Patty's cries were heard by four UC students next door at 2607

Benvenue. George Takahashi, Steve Gausewitz, Mathew Winkler, and Sandy Golden, studying together for an exam, rushed out onto the front porch. They saw the woman kidnapper raise the trunk lid of the convertible and the two men hoist the struggling, screaming girl and literally throw her into the trunk. The woman slammed the lid shut. The two gunmen spotted the students, aimed their automatic carbines, and fired several short bursts; one slug went through a bedroom window where Ed and Ruth Reagan, an elderly couple who owned the student boardinghouse, were watching TV. The students ducked back inside but came out again, down onto the sidewalk, when they heard the convertible, tires screeching, speed off, someone in it still blazing away as the car turned the corner onto Parker. They were even luckier this time. A light green-and-white station wagon—witnesses said it had been double-parked down the block—roared by, someone inside firing wildly. Sandy Golden felt a bullet whiz through her hair, and Takahashi saw sparks fly up alongside him from slugs ricocheting off the pavement. They dived for safety as the station wagon, too, disappeared around the corner.

All along Benvenue, heads were popping out of doors and windows trying to see what was happening. When people realized they were hearing bullets, not firecrackers, most popped their heads back inside. A young woman who lived across the street from the Hearst apartment looked out her door. She saw a blue Volkswagen Bug pull away from the curb fast. It was the same car that had been parked there for a couple of hours, she remembered, the one with that strange couple in it. She ran to the telephone and dialed the Berkeley Police Department. Busy. She dialed again. Still busy. On the fourth or fifth try she got through. "There's shooting going on—" was all she got out. A voice interrupted, "We know, we know, cars are on the way." It was 9:21 P.M.

Berkeley Patrolman Steve Engler was four blocks away taking a routine burglary report when his walkie-talkie squawked: "All cars, all cars, possible two-oh-seven in progress! Shots being fired! The location is Benvenue and Parker." Engler ran for his cruiser. He was the first officer to the scene. Someone pointed toward 2603 and yelled, "In the back . . . somebody's been shot." He rushed up the walk and pushed through a small crowd at the door of Steve Suenaga's apartment. Suenaga, still bound hand and foot, was on the floor. Neighbors had carried him home and were just untying him. "Over here," someone shouted. "Come over here . . . somebody's hurt bad." Engler followed the voice into apartment 4.

Inside, Steve Weed was slumped on the living-room floor, a group of neighbors huddled around, one pressing a blood-soaked towel to his head. "For a second I thought he was dead," Engler recalls. He radioed for an ambulance. "What happened?" "There were three of them—two black dudes and a white girl." Someone else added, "They took off in a Chevy convertible, a white Chevy." Engler radioed the meager descriptions of the kidnappers and their car. The dispatcher put it out over the air and said an ambulance was on the way. Engler glanced over at Weed. Shock had set in, and his face was swollen, huge, the right side an ugly purple, the right eye bulging out. His hair was saturated with blood. He looked terrible, badly hurt. "You're going to be okay," Engler told the young man.

The ambulance arrived minutes later for Suenaga and Weed. Engler and a handful of other Berkeley policemen began a preliminary search of the apartment. Sergeant Larry Lindenau came down from one of the bedrooms holding a newspaper clipping and handed it to Engler. It was a story out of the December 12 San Francisco *Examiner* announcing the engagement of Patricia Campbell Hearst, daughter of the newspaper's president and editor, to Steven Andrew Weed. The two cops looked at each other. "This is going to be a big one," said Engler.

Berkeley police had immediately set up a command post for the search. A patrol unit soon found the convertible. It had been abandoned a half mile away. There were no signs of the kidnappers or the girl. Reporters were already calling headquarters. Was it true? Had Hearst's daughter been kidnapped? Police confirmed, then took the not-unusual step—in cases of abduction—of asking the media to "embargo" the story temporarily. A little lead, perhaps a description the kidnappers did not know the police had, could give them a break. The news blackout held through the night.

The convertible discovered on Tanglewood Road was registered to a Peter Benenson of Berkeley. A sack of groceries was in the backseat of the car, in it a carton of milk still cool to the touch. At Benenson's home on Josephine Street, officers found two more sacks of groceries spilled out on the sidewalk. Benenson's landlady answered their knock. No, he wasn't home. Odd, said the woman, he had gone out awhile ago to do some shopping. She described him: white, thirty-one, not too tall, long-haired, and bearded; a quiet man, a technician at the Lawrence Radiation Lab, just above the campus.

Neighbors on Benvenue told police another Hearst, Patty's sister, lived only a few blocks away. Officers were sent to inform Virginia Hearst Bosworth and her husband, Jay, of the abduction—and to stand by for their protection. Virginia said her parents, Randolph and Catherine Hearst, were out of town, at some function in Washington, D.C., having to do with a U.S. Senate youth program, sponsored by the Hearst Foundation.

Officers went from door to door on Benvenue seeking witnesses; though few people had information of any use, all were anxious to help. The woman with the story about the blue Volkswagen did not wait to be found. She walked up to an officer on the street. "I think I saw something that may be important," she said.

The woman and her roommate had gone out at about seven. As they walked toward the corner, both had noticed a blue Volks. It was parked, with the engine running, almost directly across the street from Weed's apartment. Two people were inside, but neither of the women paid them any attention. Not then. But hours later, a few minutes after nine o'clock, they had come home. The Volkswagen was still there, still with two people inside. They particularly remembered it because the engine was still running. They had wondered aloud if it had been running the whole time. Yes, she was sure it was the same car. The license plate—she had seen only the front one—was covered with mud, "so you couldn't read it." That was strange, she had thought, because the rest of the car seemed pretty clean. She had gone over to the car and asked if everything was all right. The driver told her, "We're just waiting for friends." She had not thought any more of it—not until she saw it drive off, just as all the shooting was going on. Descriptions? A blond woman, late twenties, short hair—possibly a wig—partially covered by a scarf; the driver was "odd-looking." She thought he might be an albino.* No, she had never seen either of them before.

She told the story again to an FBI agent. "Probably a 'scout car,'" he remarked. Officially, the FBI would not enter the case until the following evening. After twenty-four hours it would be "presumed" the kidnappers could have crossed a state line, making the kidnapping a federal crime. Unofficially, by morning, dozens of agents were on the case. The word had come down from Washington upon identification of the victim.

Anne Hearst, the youngest of the five Hearst girls, phoned her

---

*A composite drawing of the "albino male" by FBI artists later turned out to be a remarkable likeness of Camilla Hall.

parents at the Mayflower Hotel in Washington, awakening them with the grim announcement: "Patty's been kidnapped." The parents seemed to take the news with astonishing calm. Randolph Hearst quickly contacted Berkeley police for more details, then telephoned his newspaper. The overnight editor told him a team of *Examiner* reporters was already gathering facts, but no story would be printed until the embargo was lifted. "Be careful, don't do anything that could get Patty hurt," Hearst said. He hung up, dialed once again, and made reservations for two on the first flight to San Francisco. Then they began to learn to wait.

In Berkeley, before morning, evidence technicians were going over the kidnap scene with everything from tweezers to a vacuum cleaner. They tracked down and lifted fingerprints throughout the apartment. They plucked up strands of hair, tucking each in its own plastic evidence bag. Outside, lab men searched for shoe prints, collected .30-caliber shell casings—they found ten of them—and took pictures of damage done by the bullets. Witnesses were requestioned, some three and four times.

Part of the mystery was solved shortly after sunrise. An FBI technician spotted something beneath a bookcase in the entry hallway. It was a box of .38-caliber bullets. He opened it carefully, mindful of smearing prints, and removed one. Something was peculiar. The bullet had a dab of wax on its tip. He examined the others. Ditto. The box was rushed to the Federal Building in San Francisco. An FBI lab man discovered the bullets had been drilled out, filled with some substance, then capped. A chemist quickly determined the filling to be potassium cyanide.

"The SLA," an agent guessed.

By nightfall Berkeley police, on their own, had also linked the SLA to the abduction. Witnesses picked out a picture of Donald DeFreeze as one of the kidnappers.

Nothing about the finding of the bullets or the link to the SLA and DeFreeze was revealed then. Not even the Hearsts were told. (The family waited three agonizing days until the kidnappers identified themselves.)

In midmorning Peter Benenson had contacted police. He, too, had been a kidnap victim, he said; on arriving home shortly before nine o'clock the night before, he was just unloading the Chevy, two sacks of groceries in his arms, when he sensed someone behind him. Turning, he found himself staring into the muzzle of a pistol in the hand of a young woman. "Give me the keys," she said. "We want your car, not you." Another woman, also armed, and a man appeared. Someone grabbed him by the arm, Benenson said, jerking him around, spilling the groceries to the sidewalk. They tumbled him into the rear seat of the car. One of the women suddenly slugged him—three times with a pistol butt—and he was knocked dazed. He was struck twice more, head blows, when he reflexively stirred as the women pulled his arms behind him to bind his wrists. He was blindfolded and gagged, and he felt a blanket thrown over him. One of the women literally sat on top of him as the convertible drove off, and he could hear the three arguing whether he should be kept in the backseat or transferred to the trunk. It was only a short ride before the car stopped; he was told to stay put, and all three seemed to leave the auto.

Minutes later he heard the first gunshots; the trunk opened and slammed, people tumbled in atop him, and moments later the car jerked forward. When they abandoned the convertible on Tanglewood, Benenson said, one of the women told him he'd be killed if he reported what had happened. After the kidnappers left—in a vehicle Benenson had not seen—he freed himself. Discovering they had taken the keys, he walked to his sister's home nearby and spent the night there. He was very frightened. He had only just learned of the Hearst kidnapping. No, he said, he couldn't identify anyone.

In the car, police had found a single glove, brown-and-beige cotton and leather, size six and a half, a woman's glove with the label of L. S. Ayers, a Midwest department store chain. Benenson said he had never seen it before.*

At Cowell Memorial Hospital, on the UC Berkeley campus, both Steve Weed and Steven Suenaga furnished descriptions of the kidnappers. Both found it difficult sorting features and trying to recall details, the way the kidnappers had moved and talked. They groped for anything that might help the police. "I told the police that I thought the guy who came through the door first— not DeFreeze, the other—had probably been to Vietnam," recalled Weed much later. "It was just the efficient way he came

*The glove would soon be linked to Emily Harris, who had clerked in the L. S. Ayers store in Indianapolis in late 1969 and early 1970. The store sold identical gloves during that period, police learned, and an Indiana friend of Emily told the FBI she recalled Emily had once lent her a pair of gloves "exactly like" the one the interviewing agent showed her.

plowing in and then methodically kicking me in the face. I just thought of those Army films, where they're training men how to hit their victim quickly and incapacitate him."

More than a year and a half later the identity of the second male kidnapper was still an enigma. Shortly after the September, 1975, arrests of Patricia Hearst, Wendy Yoshimura, and Bill and Emily Harris, *Rolling Stone* magazine published an "inside" story about the SLA's underground travels in the four months following the Los Angeles shoot-out. *Rolling Stone*'s unnamed source was Jack Scott, a radical author who had helped the fugitives hide, and *Stone*'s version had Scott being told by Patty/Tania that it was De-Freeze, Willie Wolfe, and Nancy Ling Perry who had stormed into the Berkeley apartment and abducted her. Both Weed and Sue-naga dismissed that. Weed, by then well informed about each of the SLA soldiers, was convinced the woman was either Angela Atwood or Emily Harris. "Nancy Perry was just too tiny. She was four feet eleven, and Patty is five feet two. I'm sure I would have noticed if she had been shorter than Patty; she was right in front of me." The logic of Scott's version—naming only SLA soldiers who were dead—had, in fact, convinced him that it was Emily Harris, still alive, who was the woman on the assault team.

(As for young Willie Wolfe being the second male, Weed almost laughed. "I wish it had been," he said. "Wolfe was about my size, lanky, with narrow features. The guy who came through that door was big, muscular. I'm sure myself it was two black men. For an instant I was face to face with the second guy. The features, the face, the hair—and later when he spoke—everything made me sure it was a black man." Steve Suenaga, a Japanese-American and for years a resident in integrated neighborhoods, also had no doubts. Both male kidnappers were blacks, he said. "I live with them, man, and both of those guys were bloods!"

(Two years after being kidnapped, Patricia Hearst testified during her bank robbery trial that it was Donald DeFreeze, Bill Harris, and Angela Atwood who dragged her from the apartment. Weed, even then, was still certain both men had been blacks, but he conceded, "Well, I could have thought Harris at five feet seven was too short. I'm five feet eleven and I thought he was about my height, but I have a habit of looking at people shorter than I and assuming they're about my size. If I had to be fooled, which I don't think I was, I guess I might have been fooled by Harris, who is muscular, with broad features, and—being a former actor—expert in applying makeup. Even with Harris, though, it would have meant they used things like actor's face putty to broaden his nose and alter other features.")

Weed, even when he was interviewed by FBI agents at the hospital right after the kidnapping, assumed that the police and he would have different priorities in the hunt that would follow. They wanted the kidnappers and he wanted his girl back. He told them and reporters that he would not identify any suspects picked up or testify against anyone charged if Patricia were freed. "All I'm interested in is getting her back, alive and unharmed," he said. FBI agents began quietly, routinely, checking out everyone involved, but they showed particular interest in the background of Steven Andrew Weed. They didn't like his attitude.

The morning after the kidnapping, the publisher of the Oakland *Tribune* called the Berkeley Police Department. He said his city desk was being besieged by callers from throughout the Bay Area asking if it was true that a Hearst had been kidnapped. "Apparently," said former U.S. Senator William Knowland, fuming, "everyone knows about it except the readers of the *Tribune*. We are not going to honor the embargo any longer."

Radio station KGO in San Francisco, tipped off about the *Tribune,* put the story on the air at 10:30 A.M.

By midafternoon both the FBI and Berkeley police had assigned extra personnel to handle the flood of calls coming from concerned citizens, cranks, kooks, and reporters from papers and radio stations in places as far away as Europe, South Africa, and Japan. Tips as to where police could find a white woman in the company of black men piled up. In several communities cops raided suspected hideouts, kicking in doors, guns in hand.

On the flight home Hearst began composing mental drafts of a message to the kidnappers. The United pilot, told of the kidnapping, opened one of the Muzak channels and plugged in to news broadcasts. The jet was over the Rockies when the couple heard the bulletin announcing the abduction of Patty. Arriving at the Hearst mansion in exclusive suburban Hillsborough, the Hearsts closeted themselves with Charles Bates, special agent in charge (SAC) of the FBI's San Francisco office.* Hearst then retreated to his study to work out a statement. He went through several drafts, showed it to his wife, polished it a little more. Then he stepped out the front door and solemnly addressed the tangle of micro-

*Bates, too, had been in Washington when the kidnapping occurred. He returned on an earlier flight to head the investigation.

phones and the growing crowd of newsmen. To them—and through them to his daughter's kidnappers—he said:

"Mrs. Hearst and I pray to God that the men who took our daughter will show compassion and return her unharmed. At this point, their only crime is abduction. For their sake and ours—and especially for Patricia—we plead with them not to make it any worse. We do not believe we are clutching at straws when we say there is evidence that the abductors do have a measure of compassion and are not senseless and brutal. They were heavily armed and could have eliminated all witnesses. They did not. Neither did they harm the owner of the car they commandeered. They held him for a few hours and then released him. In short, there are witnesses who saw the men who took our daughter. Thus, Patricia is no more a threat to them than are the others. Doing bodily harm to her cannot help them. It can only add to the seriousness of their crime. We want our daughter back unharmed. If she is released we will not seek to imprison her abductors. We plead with them to communicate with us directly or through the press. Please, we beg of you, do not compound your crime by harming our daughter."

For two more days the Hearsts endured the silence, the quiet, terrible wait; then, on Thursday, the first word came from the kidnappers. At radio station KPFA in Berkeley, a listener-supported station of the Pacifica Foundation, a receptionist slit open a plain white envelope amid the morning mail and pulled out what first appeared to be a news release. Then she saw the name Patricia Campbell Hearst. It was another highly stylized communiqué ("arrest—not kidnap," Nancy Ling Perry had scribbled in her notebook) from the "Court of the People" of the Symbionese Liberation Army. In full, it read:

SYMBIONESE LIBERATION ARMY
WESTERN REGIONAL ADULT UNIT

Communique No. 3   February 4, 1974

Subject: Prisoners of War	Warrant Order:
Target: Patricia Campbell Hearst— daughter of Randolph A. Hearst corporate enemy of the people	Arrest and protective custody; and if resistance execution
	Warrant Issued By: The Court of the People

On the afore stated date, combat elements of the United Federated Forces of The Symbionese Liberation Army armed with cyanide loaded weapons served an arrest warrant upon Patricia Campbell Hearst.

It is the order of this court that the subject be arrested by combat units and removed to a protective area of safety and only upon completion of this condition to notify Unit #4 to give communication of this action.

It is the directive of this court that during this action ONLY, no civilian elements be harmed if possible, and that warning shots be given. However, if any citizens attempt to aid the authorities or interfere with the implementation of this order, they shall be executed immediately.

This court hereby notifies the public and directs all combat units in the future to shoot to kill any civilian who attempts to witness or interfere with any operation conducted by the people's forces against the fascist state.

Should any attempt be made by the authorities to rescue the prisoner, or to arrest or harm any S.L.A. elements, the prisoner is to be executed.

The prisoner is to be maintained in adequate physical and mental condition, and unharmed as long as these conditions are adhered to. Protective custody shall be composed of combat and medical units, to safeguard both the prisoner and her health.

All communications from this court MUST be published in full, in all newspapers, and all other forms of media. Failure to do so will endanger the safety of the prisoner.

Further communications will follow.

S.L.A.

DEATH TO THE FASCIST INSECT
THAT PREYS UPON THE LIFE OF THE PEOPLE

Paul Fischer, news director of KPFA, immediately telephoned Randolph Hearst and read him the text. There was no doubt it was a message from the kidnappers. The SLA had enclosed Patricia's Mobil Oil credit card (actually in her father's name), known to have been in her yellow leather wallet, which the kidnappers had taken.

The absence of a specific ransom demand in the initial message from the SLA bewildered and worried the victim's father. "I hope whatever demands they make are the kind it is possible to fulfill," Hearst told reporters. "If they are political demands, it will be hard to do anything." FBI Agent Bates pledged the bureau would "not take any action to jeopardize the victim . . . our first consideration is the safety of the girl," he said.

The Hearsts' hope that the SLA would quickly respond to their plea for some proof their daughter was alive dimmed as day after day went by with no word from the kidnappers. The search went on. In a remote section of Contra Costa County sheriff's deputies checked out abandoned coal mines after a citizen reported seeing two black men struggling with a white woman in the area. All over the state, police checked out tips.

An FBI sketch artist produced composite drawings of the trio that had abducted Patty. The sketch of one of the men closely resembled Donald DeFreeze; the drawing of the woman in some ways resembled Emily Harris. The drawing of the second man produced an archetypal Negroid face. Police and some reporters guessed it might be Wheeler—but it was a weak identification. The identity of the second man became more and more of a mystery as the case developed.

Weed was released from the hospital on Saturday. He immediately moved in with the Hearst family. In TV interviews he reiterated his promise not to testify if Patty was freed. "I just hope that the Symbionese Liberation Army leadership makes demands that lead to a smooth transaction. I hope they realize that the Hearst family has only a limited ability to effect any political demands that might be made," said Weed. "What I mean is, if they're talking of letting prisoners go, the Hearsts look at the situation as a family problem, but California and the FBI see it in a larger context. And it's the state that has the final word on political demands."

Weed's remarks were in response to growing speculation that the next communiqué from the SLA would be a demand that its two soldiers confined at San Quentin prison, Little and Remiro, be released in exchange for freeing Miss Hearst. The idea of such a trade demand seemed—to the Hearsts—painfully likely. There was the broad hint in Nancy Perry's "open letter," and already in the hands of investigators were drafts of two "warrants," discovered in the Sutherland Court hideout, in which the SLA planned to demand the release of the group of prisoners known as the San Quentin Six in exchange for kidnapped business executives.

From Florida another deal for the kidnappers was proposed. O. Jack Little, the father of Russ Little, offered to take Patricia's place as hostage. It was only the first of several well-meaning but almost surrealistic pleas from parents of the SLA members which showed they had no comprehension of what their children were into, no sense of being part of "the People" the SLA spoke for.

Hearst appeared visibly haggard at another news conference on February 11—one week after the kidnapping. There was still no further word from the SLA. "If it's an attempt to make us feel badly," he said, "they are succeeding very well."

11

"Mom, Dad, I'm Okay"

IT was a painful wait for the Hearsts, yet only the beginning of a family trial no one could have foreseen. For the first few days the two younger daughters, Anne and Vicky, were brought home from school. The stately twenty-two-room family mansion in Hillsborough, which months before had been put on the market for $380,000 now that the family had grown away, was suddenly full and busy.* The eldest daughter, Catherine, stayed in Los Angeles with police protection; but Patty's other older sister, Gina— Virginia Bosworth—and her husband, Jay, an *Examiner* reporter, moved back to the mansion. A cousin, young Willie Hearst (William R. III), also an *Examiner* staffer, moved in and became the all-night chess partner for Steve Weed, who had been invited to stay at the house (for the first time) after his release from the hospital. An FBI agent moved into the den, keeping mostly to himself. A corps of reporters that would grow into a small army encamped on the small crescent-shaped driveway and along the edge of the road, outside the spiked black iron fence that surrounded the acre-and-a-half grounds. Mrs. Hearst busied herself with make-work, supervising two maids, a cook, and a housekeeper; but for the rest, all thought of work was put aside. Everyone picked up on the routine of daily tension. In his study, a book-lined room decorated with antique flintlock pistols and now with a television set to catch the news, Randolph Hearst manned the telephone himself, taking on all the kooks, the tipsters, and the prayer calls. Finally the SLA broke the silence, with a packet containing eight pages of SLA proclamations. A tape recording with the voices of DeFreeze and Patty (and a demand that a transcript of the tape and all the

---

*A year later the mansion was finally sold—for $250,000—and the Hearsts moved into a condominium atop San Francisco's Nob Hill.

documents be published in full by all media) was received by mail at radio station KPFA on February 12.

"To those who would bear the hopes and future of our people, let the voice of their guns express the words of freedom. Greetings to the People, and fellow comrades, brothers and sisters," began the voice of DeFreeze, speaking slowly, portentously. "My name is Cinque and to my comrades I am known as Cin. I am a black man and a representative of black people. I hold the rank of General Field Marshal in the United Liberated Forces of the Symbionese Liberation Army."

Patricia Hearst, said the Field Marshal, had been "arrested" for "crimes that her mother and father have committed against we the American people and the oppressed people of the world. . . ." As a member of the University of California Board of Regents Mrs. Hearst, he said, had shared responsibility for investment of UC trust funds in "such fascist corporations" as General Motors, Westinghouse, Gulf, Standard Oil, and others. As for the girl's father. . . .

"Randolph A. Hearst is the corporate chairman of the fascist media empire of the ultraright Hearst Corporation, which is one of the largest propaganda institutions of this present military dictatorship of the militarily armed corporate state that we now live under in this nation," said Cinque. "The primary goal of this empire is to serve and form the necessary propaganda and smoke screen to shield the American people from seeing the realities of the corporate dictatorship which Richard Nixon and Gerald Ford represent."

He had, said DeFreeze, been empowered by "the Symbionese War Council, the Court of the People," to demand of this "representative of the corporate state" a "token" gesture of "good faith" before beginning any negotiations for the release of the "subject prisoner."

As a preliminary, the SLA's "token gesture" might have been demanded of a Caesar. The Hearst family was to provide for the distribution of $70 worth of meats, vegetables, and dairy products to "all people with welfare cards, Social Security pension cards, parole or probation papers, and jail or bail release slips." The SLA listed thirteen poor communities—most in and around San Francisco, but including Watts, Compton, and East Los Angeles, in Southern California—and demanded that there be at least five "major stores" taken over in each of the thirteen communities to be used as free-food distribution points three days a week for one month.

"The meat, vegetables and dairy products must be of top quality and in ample supply during all store hours," ordered the SLA, adding, "If this gesture of good faith is not met, then we will assume that there is no basis for negotiations, and we will no longer take and maintain in good health and spirit prisoners of war."

The SLA gave the Hearsts a week—seven days—to begin distribution of the food from the sixty-five outlets. The handout, they ordered, "must" begin on February 19. There was no mention of logistics; apparently the SLA expected a "ruling class" businessman to have no trouble commandeering sixty-five privately owned stores, manning them, and supplying them with millions of dollars' worth of food.

The taped voice of Patty Hearst sounded tense but self-controlled:

"Mom, Dad, I'm okay. I had a few scrapes and stuff, but they washed them up and they're getting okay. And I caught a cold, but they're giving me pills for it and stuff. I'm not being starved or beaten or unnecessarily frightened. I've heard some press reports and so I know that Steve and all the neighbors are okay and no one was really hurt. And I also know that the SLA members here are very upset about press distortions of what's been happening." (Speculative press reports had connected the SLA and the insane Zebra random killings of whites by black men. Other reports tied them with the August Seventh Movement, which claimed to have shot down a police helicopter.) But the SLA, said Patty, "have nothing to do with the August Seventh Movement. They have not been shooting down helicopters or shooting down innocent people in the streets."

She said she was kept blindfolded "usually" so that she could not identify anyone. "My hands are often tied, but generally they're not. I'm not gagged or anything, and I'm comfortable. And I think you can tell that I'm not really terrified or anything and that I'm okay. I was very upset to hear that police rushed in on that house in Oakland [a raid by local police seeking the SLA] and I was really glad that I wasn't there and I would appreciate it if everyone would just calm down and not try to find me and not be making identifications, because they're not only endangering me but they're endangering themselves. I'm with a combat team here that's armed with automatic weapons and there's also a medical team here and there's no way that I will be released until they let me go, so it won't do any good for somebody to come in here and try to get me out by force.

"These people aren't a bunch of nuts. They've been really honest with me, but they're perfectly willing to die for what they are doing. And I want to get out of here, but the only way I'm going to is if we do it their way. And I just hope that you'll do what they say, Dad, and just do it quickly. . . . I'm not being forced to say any of this. I think it's really important that you take their requests very seriously about not arresting any other SLA members and about following their good-faith request to the letter. I just want to get out of here and see everyone again and be back with Steve.

"The SLA is very interested in seeing how you are taking this, Dad, and they want to make sure you are really serious and listening to what they're saying. And they think that you've been taking this whole thing a lot more seriously than the police and the FBI and other federal people have been taking it. It seems to be getting to the point where they're not worried about you so much as they're worried about other people. Or at least I am. It's really up to you to make sure that these people don't jeopardize my life by charging in and I hope you will make sure that they don't do anything else like that Oakland house business.

"The SLA people have really been honest with me and I really, I mean I feel pretty sure that I'm going to get out of here if everything goes the way they want it to. And I think you should feel that way, too, and try not to worry so much. I mean, I know it's hard but I heard Mom was really upset and that everybody was at home. I hope that this puts you a little bit at ease so that you know that I really am all right. I just hope I can get back to everybody really soon.

"The SLA has ideological ties with the IRA [the Irish Republican Army], the people's struggle in the Philippines, and the Socialist people in Puerto Rico in their struggle for independence, and they consider themselves to be soldiers who are fighting and aiding these people. I am a prisoner of war and so are the two men [Russ Little and Joe Remiro] in San Quentin. I am being treated in accordance with the Geneva Convention, one of the conditions being that I am not being tried for crimes which I'm not responsible for.

"I am here because I am a member of a ruling-class family and I think you can begin to see the analogy. The people, the two men in San Quentin, are being held and are going to be tried simply because they are members of the SLA and not because they've done anything. Witnesses to the shooting saw black men. And two white men have been arrested for this. You're being told this so that you'll understand that whatever happens to the two prisoners is going to happen to me. [Several witnesses had seen three people run from the scene of Foster's murder and gave at least three varying descriptions of the trio as seen from a distance; one described the assassins as blacks.*]

"You have to understand that I am held to be innocent the same way the two men in San Quentin are innocent; they are simply members of the group and had not done anything themselves to warrant their arrest. They apparently were part of an intelligence unit and have never executed anyone themselves. The SLA has declared war against the government and it's important that you understand that they know what they're doing and they understand what their actions mean—and that you realize that this is not considered by them to be just a simple kidnapping and that you don't treat it that way and say, 'Oh, I don't know why she was taken.' I'm telling you now why this happened so that you will know so that you'll have something to use, some knowledge, to try and get me out of here. If you can get the food thing organized before the nineteenth, then that's okay and it would speed up my release. Today is Friday the eighth, and in Kuwait the commandos negotiated the release of their hostages and they left the country. Bye."

It was not a free statement; obviously her captors had ordered her to say some of those things. And the tape would not have been released if they had not approved of it—but the wording was hers, the phrasing seemed natural. She adopted their language, accepted them for just what they said they were; but in her position she had little choice. And the vague empathy, the legitimacy she granted them, seemed the intelligent way to relate to captors who were to decide if she lived or died.

*Although it was not public knowledge at the time, both Deputy Superintendent Robert Blackburn and another witness, a woman school employee who had viewed the murder from a window, had furnished descriptions which had convinced police that at least two of Dr. Foster's killers were white. Neither Blackburn nor the woman ever positively identified Remiro or Little, but eyewitness identification was not the basis for the murder charge filed against the two SLA soldiers. Police had solidly linked them to the crime through their ownership of the two handguns that ballistics testing proved were the murder weapons and also considerable evidence discovered in the abandoned SLA safehouse in Clayton (including Remiro's handwritten notes on a sketched diagram of the Foster ambush scene). The strong, albeit circumstantial, case presented by District Attorney Lowell Jensen convinced the jury that both Remiro and Little had been part of the SLA conspiracy that resulted in Foster's assassination, and both were convicted of first-degree murder at the conclusion of their April, 1975, trial held in Sacramento.

The tapes and the eight pages of proclamations were, for most, the first glimpse of the SLA ideology. Widely published—in obedience to the SLA demand—the rhetoric, the stilted language, and the elliptical references were probably barely comprehensible to the masses. Studied, the words revealed a groggy blend of racial (black) nationalism and simplified Marxism. That the SLA had chosen to build a platform of supposedly mass appeal on things like communes for the kids, the abolition of monogamous marriage, racial separatism, and the release of all convicted criminals did nothing to bolster the Hearsts' hope that they were dealing with a rational adversary. A political creed that mandated the suppression of "individualism" and "possessiveness" was as fey as it was far from the common American experience.

The Hearsts had been hoping that the SLA were revolutionaries rather than neurotics, "coming from a political place we could deal with"; but the bewildering dogma, the assertion that a military coup had occurred in 1964 and the blindly unrealistic "token gesture" demand indicated a desperate and naïve fanaticism.

The implied possibility of a *quid pro quo* demand—the arrested Remiro and Little for Patty Hearst*—was enough to bring harsh and unequivocal replies from high officials in then Governor Ronald Reagan's administration: Archconservative Reagan was not about to release accused murderers on terrorists' orders, kidnapping or no kidnapping. The demand seemed almost open-ended. Hearst was to give $70 in goods to an undetermined number of people who carried one of nine identification forms—and estimates of the cost of feeding those holding such cards in California was soaring to around $400 million. The mere mechanical difficulties posed by the "conditions" were enormous.

A point which few at the time noted—although it later became a major area of discussion of the SLA on the Left—was the total exclusion of working people. The SLA's concern, at least as indicated by their list of proposed recipients, was wholly focused on criminals and citizens on the dole. If the requirements were held to, there might scarcely have been a working man or woman in the SLA's food line.

In the other documents accompanying the food demand and Patty's tape were the SLA's "Declaration of Revolutionary War" and a list of sixteen generalized goals ("To create new forms of

*According to SLA documents discovered later, the initial goal of the kidnappers had indeed been to trade Patty Hearst for Little and Remiro.

life and relationships that bring true meanings of love to people's relationships . . .") promising socialism, racial separatism, revenge against the ruling classes, and a world of idealism and justice. In the Symbionese Federated Republic, they promised, each racially separate nation "will be able to provide to each person and couple and family free of cost the five basic needs of life, which are food, health care, housing, education, and clothing." Also included in the tinker's bag of rhetoric was the SLA's "Terms of Military/Political Alliance"—a call for volunteers to join the SLA's "tactical support units"—and a list and explanation of the seven principles of the SLA. The principles (identical to the seven principles of *Kawaida,* the code of conduct for members of Ron Karenga's Los Angeles-based black nationalist group, United Slaves, or US) were unity, self-determination, collective work and responsibility, cooperative production, purpose, creativity, and faith.

The day after the tape was received, on February 13, Randolph and Catherine Hearst, holding hands, emerged from the Hillsborough mansion for another news conference on the front steps of the house. Framed by the cameras between the white pillars with yellow and white lilies on either side, it was a picture that was to flash on the network news with monotonous regularity over the next several months. The two of them paused, Hearst gave Catherine's hand a squeeze; then he stepped before the forest of microphones.

"Patty, I hope you're listening. We're really pleased to know that you're okay. You sounded a little tired and like you were sedated, but you sounded all right and I'm sure that the people who have you are telling the truth when they say that they are treating you under the Geneva Convention. I just want you to know I'm going to do everything I can to get you out of there.

"It's a little frightening because the original demand is what I was afraid of from the beginning. It's one that is impossible to meet. However, in the next twenty-four to forty-eight hours I'll be trying my best to come back with some kind of counteroffer that's acceptable. it's very difficult because I have no one to negotiate with except through a letter that generally comes two or three days later than expected. Anyway, you can rest assured that your mother and I and all the family will do everything we can to get you out.

"Tell them not to worry. No one's going to bust in on them and start a shoot-out. And you take care of yourself. I think you'd like to know that everybody is praying for you. I think a few are even praying for the people who have you and we'd like to thank them and I'm sure you'd like to thank everybody who's really rooting for you to get out of there and come home."

Hearst paused, looked at his wife, then, his voice cracking, said to Patricia, "Hang in there, honey."

Catherine Hearst also spoke to Patty and her captors. "We love you, Patty, and we're all praying for you," she said, tears streaming down her cheeks. "I'm sorry I'm crying but I'm happy you're safe, and be strong. I know God will bring you back. I know those people—they had good ideals. They're just going about them the wrong way. They wouldn't make you suffer for anything they thought we did. God bless you, honey. Take care of yourself."

Still holding hands, they went back inside their home. Several hours later Hearst reappeared to "clarify" his earlier remarks. He had not meant, he said, that he was going to make a counteroffer in the sense of trying to bargain down the SLA price, only that he was going to do the best he could to set up something approximating the SLA demand. "Obviously I don't see how I can meet a four-hundred-million-dollar program," he said. "But I just want these people to know, these members of the SLA, I'm going to do everything in my power to set up the type of program they're talking about." He would have a proposal in the next couple of days, he said. "And if it doesn't satisfy them, it won't be because I haven't done everything I can do to make it function."

Three days later, on February 16, came the SLA reply; a short message, a tape from Patty with a few words from Cinque. As the implications were spelled out publicly, even the SLA realized their original demand was unworkable.

"Dad, Mom," said the voice of Patty, "I'm making this tape to let you know that I'm still okay and to explain a few things, I hope. First, about the good-faith gesture. There are some misunderstandings about that and you should do what you can and they understand that you want to meet their demands and that—they have every intention that you should be able to meet their demands. They weren't trying to present an unreasonable request. It was never intended that you feed the whole state. So whatever you come up with is basically okay. And just do it as fast as you can and everything will be fine.

"But the SLA is really mad about certain attempts to make the feeding of food to be the receiving of goods that were gotten by extortion.* They don't want people to be harassed by the police or

*California newspapers had published speculation that the recipients of ransom food could be prosecuted for complicity in extortion.

anybody else, and I hope you can do something about that and if you can't, well, I mean they'll do something about it. So—you shouldn't worry about that too much.

"Also I would like to emphasize that I am alive and that I am well and that in spite of what certain tape experts seem to think, I mean I'm fine. It's really depressing to hear people talk about me like I'm dead. I can't explain what that's like. What it does also is that it—it begins to convince other people that maybe I am dead. If everybody is convinced that I am dead, well, then it gives the FBI an excuse to come in here and try to pull me out. I'm sure that Mr. Bates [of the FBI] understands that if the FBI has to come in and get me out by force that they won't have time to decide who not to kill. They'll just have to kill everyone. I don't particularly want to die that way.

"I hope you will realize that everything is okay and that they'll just have to back off for a while. There'll be plenty of time for investigating later.

"I am basically an example and a symbolic warning, not only to you but to everyone, that there are people who are not going to accept your support of other governments and that faced with suppression and murder of the people—and that this is a warning to everybody. It is also to show what can be done. When it's necessary the people can be fed and to show that it's too bad it has to happen this way to make people see that there are people who need food. Now maybe something can be done about that, so that things like this won't have to happen again.

"Also, the SLA is very annoyed about attempts by the press and by authorities to turn this into a racial issue. It's not. This is a political issue and this is a political action that they've taken. Anyone who really reads the stated objectives of the SLA can see very clearly that this is not a racial thing. I hope there won't be any more confusion about that. [Pause.] I turned over my notes there so. . . .

"I am being held as a prisoner of war and not as anything else and I am being treated in accordance with the international code of war. And so you shouldn't listen or believe what anybody says about the way I'm being treated. This is the way I'm being treated, I'm not left alone and I'm not shoved off. I mean I'm fine. I am not being starved and I'm not being beaten or tortured. Really.

"Since I am an example it's really important that everybody understand that I am an example and a warning. And because of this it's very important to the SLA that I return safely. So people should stop acting like I'm dead. Mom should get out of her black dress. That doesn't help at all. I wish you'd try to understand the position I'm in. I'm right in the middle and I have to depend upon what all kinds of other people are going to do. And it's really hard for me to hear about reports, you know, and—I hope you understand and try to do something. I know that a lot of people have written and everyone is concerned about me and my safety and about what you're going through and I want them all to know that I'm okay. And it's important for them to understand that I'll be okay as long as the SLA demands are met and as long as the two prisoners in San Quentin are okay. And as long as the FBI doesn't come in here. That is really my biggest worry. I think I can get out of here as long as they don't come busting in and I really think you should understand that the SLA does have an interest in my return. And try not to worry so much and just do what you can. I mean, I know you're doing everything. Take care of Steve and hurry. Bye." She added—to authenticate the date—"On Wednesday, Solzhenitsyn was exiled to Germany."

Next came the deep voice of DeFreeze: "This is General Field Marshal Cin speaking. We wish to clarify what your daughter has said about our request for a good-faith gesture on your part. The people are awaiting your gesture.

"You must rest assured that we are quite able to assess the extent of your sincerity in this matter and we will accept a sincere effort on your part. We are quite able and aware of the extent of your capabilities as we are also aware of the needs of the people.

"Death to the fascist insect that preys upon the life of the people!"

Now the SLA had been trapped publicly; forced to admit the first demand was unrealistic; forced to go so far as to say that they would accept as preliminary ransom "whatever" Hearst could "come up with." The SLA had to give up the initiative, but that left Hearst with no guidelines for his compliance—yet it was the SLA which would judge whether the family had made a "sincere effort." Objectively the SLA had surrendered control—the shift went unnoticed in the press; but it was the sort of thing that would gnaw at Bill Harris or Mizmoon Soltysik. Now the ransom had a Catch 22 factor built in.

The insistence of Patty—speaking for the SLA—that the FBI "back off" and stop bird-dogging her kidnappers indicated how the police were cramping the SLA. The unusual brevity and directness seemed to imply it was a rush job—perhaps because not only police but even reporters had begun to identify them. In the two days just prior to the message, TV station KQED and the San

Francisco *Chronicle* had identified DeFreeze, and Thero Wheeler as well, as members of the SLA. (Local editors had refused to run that story until they got an okay from Randolph Hearst and still were holding stories that identified other SLA members and their backgrounds because Hearst was fearful publication might endanger his daughter.) The public was fed all the SLA rhetoric—but little background information—and the image of the SLA was inflated tremendously.

The cell in which her Symbionese wardens held Patty Hearst captive for some six weeks was a bedroom closet in a tract house at 37 Northridge Avenue in Daly City, a suburb that abuts San Francisco. It was owned by James Mazzariello, who on January 20—two weeks before the kidnapping—rented the three-bedroom white stucco dwelling to two young white women who identified themselves as Toni Wilson and Candi Jackson, TWA stewardesses. "They didn't look like hippies," he recalled. They paid him $265 rent for the first month, plus a $50 cleaning deposit. Mazzariello visited them a couple of days after they moved in; their only furniture was a glass coffee table and one chair. The rest, they said, would arrive shortly. A friend, a young blond man, was helping the women install a peephole and extra security locks on the front door and—oddly—locks on each of the bedroom doors. They were "paranoid about burglars," the women said. On February 3, the day before the abduction, Mazzariello received this letter:

> JIM,
>   Thanks for the note and home information. We are certainly enjoying the house. It's becoming more and more comfortable as we each add our own little things. We should be getting our phone this week and we'll give you a call to tell you the number. Thanks for your offer of help—
>
>   CANDI

One of the "litle things" they added to a tiny closet was Patricia Hearst. Patty was kept confined in that cramped space (the closet was two feet one and one-half inches deep, six feet seven and one-quarter inches long, eight feet one inch high) until at least late March, when the SLA decamped Daly City for a new safe house in San Francisco. On April 5, 1974, when that month's rent check hadn't arrived, landlord Mazzariello began trying to contact his tenants. There was no answer to his daily telephone calls. He dropped by on the tenth and found "occupant" mail had piled up; he left a note of his own. By April 15 Mazzariello was worried enough to break in through a window. Inside, he found the place empty, long-spoiled food in the refrigerator. On the front door there were now *six* security locks. The bedroom walls were scarred with hundreds of BB-size pockmarks. The walls of one closet were ripped with holes seemingly caused by pulled-out bolts or screws, perhaps large screw hooks used to hold up something heavy, and (as at the Clayton hideout) all the window shades had been nailed down. Mazzariello, fed up with uncaring renters, repaired the damage and, in May, sold the house.

"Candi" and "Toni" had abandoned a light-green-and-white '64 Chevrolet station wagon in the attached garage at 37 Northridge. Contacted by the authors in July, 1974—after they heard about his strange tenants—Mazzariello still had the Chevy in his possession. It was registered to a Paul Ashford at yet another Daly City address, 514 Winchester Drive. Neighbors on Winchester said the people who had moved in there in January weren't very friendly and hadn't stayed long. The landlord said he'd rented it on January 12 to a Joann James and a Judith Lawrence. After looking at photos of the SLA women, however, he picked out Emily Harris as having posed as "Joann" and Mizmoon Soltysik as the one who called herself "Ms. Lawrence." And a check of Department of Motor Vehicles files showed that the driver's license photo of "Paul Ashford" bore more than a slight resemblance to Bill Harris.

(After conducting their own investigation, the authors tipped Berkeley police whose inquiries then quickly confirmed that 37 Northridge was indeed where Patty had initially been held and that the station wagon was the kidnap vehicle they and the FBI had long been seeking. An expended .30-caliber casing was found in the Chevy wagon; FBI ballistics experts compared it to firing pin marks on shells found at the kidnap scene—they matched. Although Mazzariello was not able to identify "Candi" or "Toni"— "they were wearing wigs and a lot of makeup the times I saw them," he said—his and neighbors' descriptions of the pair again fitted Emily and Mizmoon. The "blond" friend seen installing locks was not identified, but it could well have been Bill Harris with toupee—his fingerprint was found on the cylinder inside the new lock on the closet door behind which Patty Hearst had been kept prisoner some six weeks.)

Right after the kidnapping—however well they managed their public relations—the SLA was undergoing internal crises; several.

They were nearly broke. And sex, sexual roles, and "sexist" practices (male domination)—a constant undercurrent of tension in
this highly sexed marriage of militant feminists, lesbians, and bra-
vo-macho males—had begun to rankle among the SLA collective.

(The sexual dynamic of the SLA underground would not be revealed until nearly two years later, when police would discover
portions of an SLA manuscript, a military history of the Revolution, but even then, in their own words, the account was confusing. The manuscript was not begun until six or seven month after
the abduction, when Bill and Emily Harris and "Tania" Hearst
were the only survivors of the postkidnap collective. And whatever was written then, in the summer of 1974, was apparently subject to growing disagreement among the three and the few allies
they recruited in their attempt to resurrect the SLA. What is apparent, from the various drafts and revisions of the manuscript, is
that its authors looked back upon the early SLA with an increasing critical feminist perspective, rejudging and rewriting their history with an increasingly harsh hindsight.)

A section of the SLA manuscript, apparently written by Bill
Harris—an early draft, affecting a masculine self-righteousness
which would later be criticized in subsequent, more feminist, revisions—describes libido as surprisingly central to the political dynamic of the SLA:

> Everyone had to help everyone else meet their sexual needs.
> Our position was one of conditional practicality. We knew from
> experience what it is like to live in an underground cell. It is a very
> isolated situation sometimes because you don't have as much free-
> dom of contact with people outside the cell. . . .
>
> We were not making a sexual revolution, but merely trying to
> adapt to the needs of all the individuals in the cell. In practice this
> ruled out monogamal [sic] sexual relationships. There was no
> structure to follow, no rules, no systemized rotation of partners.
> We tried not to place demands on each other, but to learn and be-
> come sensitive to each others needs.
>
> Understandably, there were often conflicts and struggle. We
> didn't generally deal with resulting problems (selfishness, jeal-
> ousy, and personal resentments) by calling collective meetings un-
> less the individuals involved couldn't work it out themselves or
> with the help of another comrade who could serve as an objective
> counsel.

Mass meetings to decide who could grope with whom may reveal one side of the SLA, but another glimpse, more earnest and
interesting, is found in the later writings which give a belatedly

"feminist" analysis of how the SLA women, each so full of bitter feminist rhetoric, could have fallen so completely under the macho sway of the early SLA. It's a limiting, struggling analysis—overlooking completely the depersonalized sex system—trying in hindsight merely to understand how the women could have rushed blindly into the militaristic discipline of the SLA, where the men commanded as "the instructors, the political commissars."

Then or later the SLA feminists would never make the connection, but the parallels between the newly "reborn" political criminal and the newly "conscious" feminist are striking: Both emerge with new values, little rooted in personal experience. Neither has easily accessible role models, except of "heroic," historic proportions. Often for both, the process of transformation is rapid—based on personal experience of oppression, but with only half-formed airy and idealistic notions about alternative roles. Both are "reborn" innocent, full of purist concepts untempered by life experience. And without role patterns, acceptable compromises, personal values clash painfully with the social norm.*

The feminist perspective of the later SLA—developed and written perhaps six months after Harris wrote his version, more than a year after the kidnap—mingled explanation and justification:

> The capture of our 2 comrades on January 10, 1974, put us on the defensive, forcing several other comrades underground. Our changed situation compelled us to place primary importance on obtaining survival skills and the atmosphere was intensely military. Struggles against sexism continued on a one-to-one level, but these struggles just weren't as important as getting the men to teach us about weapons. As women our primary focus was on be-

*Just as the "reborn" convict measures his new utopian ideal against the ghetto reality and seethes with rage; the newly "conscious" feminist contrasts an egalitarian ideal with the tradition and daily reality of male-female relationships and recoils in horror and rebellion. The force of that recoil was an unmeasurable energy in the SLA—just as it had been in the great crisis the so-called Woman Question caused in the New Left in the late sixties, a crisis that undermined the leadership [male] and contributed greatly to the disintegration of the New Left. Feminism brought the unyielding brute morality of the Movement into the bedroom, the kitchen, the living room, and "conscious" women, in that bitter recoil, launched into a frenzied search for an alternative they could not yet see, that they could define only with rhetoric and the angry force of their commitment. In the New Left experience, among certain isolated splinter groups—like the combat communes of the Weather Underground in 1969–70—that frenzied search created a sexual dynamic very similar to that of the early SLA, reducing the individual vision of the ideal to the collective's lowest common denominator.

coming strong female guerrillas. But without realizing it, our concept of what a female guerrilla should be was *male defined.*

It was, conceded the Symbionese authors, "a major contradiction." And although Gabi and Zoya (Camilla and Mizmoon), the "radicalesbians" of the SLA, began to criticize the sexist authority structure, none of the SLA women had enough perspective to understand what was happening until much later. "As a result of conditions we created for ourselves the women weren't able to coalesce into a strong unit, and we failed to develop a position for quite a while.

> Struggles against the most blatant forms of sexism took place on a one to one level. Virtually no struggles along this line took place on the collective level. There were 2 reasons for this: first, we mistakenly believed that one-one was more "respectful" and [therefore] more productive, and 2nd, we felt that survival & military issues were more important and deserving of collective attention than sexism and its resulting problems. . . .
> Because of our male orientation we tended to think of the battle against sexism as a secondary struggle. We failed to assert ourselves as leaders—to protect our self-interest as women—instead of seeing ourselves as revolutionary feminists (or perhaps we did see ourselves as such, but we sure didn't act it!). We behaved the way that Fireside* describes as "Ladies Aux. of the Left." We were so selfless—so womanly—that we would put everyone else's struggle for liberation ahead of our own as we fought. This horribly backward way of thinking was, of course, the result of years of "female" upbringing. It was so hard to see what was happening, because we weren't aware of the nature of our oppression in the cell; we were just so *grateful* to the men for taking the time to teach us (so we could help save their asses!).

The struggle to contain and eradicate sexism among the armed forces of the SLA, wrote the underground authors,† was "one of

---

*Fireside Theater, a satirical comedy group.

†The feminist revisionists among the neo-Symbionese group evolved in mid-1975—a year after the death of most of the original SLA cadre, about a year and a half after the Hearst kidnapping—including Patricia "Tania" Hearst and perhaps five or six other women, for a time Emily Harris among them. Although the critique was developed collectively, it was Tania who was apparently chosen to try to write it up. Thus it was, two years after the kidnapping that had made her famous, the jury about to convict Tania Hearst of bank robbery would read the "feminist critique" documents quoted above, written in the clean Palmer script of Patricia Campbell Hearst.

the most difficult and longest struggles" the SLA had to deal with—"because, like racism, sexism is a foundation of capitalist oppression."

Yet even the Revolution needed capitalist money to pay the overhead. On February 14—ten days after the kidnapping—Bill "Teko" Harris wrote his mother asking her to send him money; the SLA was broke and "desperate" for funds to tide them over. Harris said their need was urgent, although only temporary. They expected a large sum of money soon, he said.

The tone of the letter was exhilarated, optimistic—yet even to his mother, Harris wrote as if he were addressing the Fourth Party Congress: "Everybody's really high here now but due to our own creativity we know things are going to change." He wrote that the police were pressing close and the SLA had to stay hidden, temporarily "immobile." He asked his mother to send him $1,500 and —incredibly—he enclosed a stamped, preaddressed envelope for the money. It was addressed to "Janet Cooper," care of general delivery, Santa Clara, California, and marked HOLD FOR PICKUP.

Bill's letter had been forwarded in a sealed envelope within another envelope—mailed by Emily to two close friends who lived near Bill's parents. It was textbook procedure for mail from the underground—except the Harrises did not know any revolutionaries back in Indiana. Surely the two friends (one of Emily's college sorority sisters and her husband, an Indianapolis attorney) were unlikely recruits for the SLA, even for one of the "tactical support units." The note Emily wrote asking that the enclosed envelope be passed on was a masterpiece of understatement: "Bill and I are both better than ever and into some really interesting things," she wrote. "Things are moving very fast around here and our interest in prisons has carried us into many different areas. . . . I need to ask your help in doing a favor. We need to have the enclosed message delivered to Bill's mother. She can't receive it in the mail for reasons which I will have to explain later so if you will just drop it by in person as soon as possible. . . ."

It might have worked, however enormous the risk, had Emily's friends not already been contacted by the Oakland police working on the Foster murder. Detectives had called every name in the address book Emily had left behind when she fled her apartment in January. They asked the people to notify them if they heard from the Harrises. (Camilla Hall could not remember any prorevolutionary friend back in Illinois either. She sent a letter to her parents via an old school chum, who immediately called the FBI. Angela Atwood fared better. She got a letter to her family through her closest high school girlfriend, the fiancée of a New Jersey cop. Only Bill Harris, however, had sent a letter with a preaddressed return envelope.)

Emily's two friends thought the world of her, but they thought the SLA "sheer insanity." The couple hesitated, then opened the sealed letter to Bill's mother. If it was a strictly personal letter, they would just pass it on. When they found the enclosed envelope with the return address, they called the Oakland police. "We couldn't morally take the chance that we would be responsible for Patty Hearst's death," said the woman.

What followed was a comedy of errors. Oakland police and the FBI were tremendously excited about the letter. They conferred, then asked the couple to copy it and deliver the original to Harris' mother. The Santa Clara post office was staked out for the SLA member who would pose as "Janet Cooper." Bill's mother did indeed send money to her son— although only $250, not the $1,500 the SLA needed—but the check was never picked up. It never arrived in Santa Clara. Bill Harris had put the wrong zip code on the addressed envelope he had sent his mother, the FBI didn't catch it, and the mindless efficiency of the postal service deposited the letter in the general delivery box in Santa Barbara, California. The SLA apparently checked by phone with the Santa Clara post office, and a clerk, ignorant of the FBI stakeout, kept telling "Janet Cooper" her letter had not arrived.

(The bureau muffed yet another opportunity that might have led to the kidnappers and Patty. When Camilla Hall's name was added to the list of suspects, one of the things agents learned was that she had a savings account at the Berkeley branch of the Central Bank. The manager was told to alert the Berkeley FBI office—located in an office building across the street from the bank—if Camilla showed up. The agents did not explain their interest in Hall, and the manager did not pass the word down. On March 1 Camilla was in and out of the bank in less than fifteen minutes, closing the savings account and toting away $1,565 in cash. The bureau never explained why it had not assigned agents to stake out the bank. There was also no comment when the media disclosed that in late February Camilla had sold her car—a Volkswagen believed to have been the "scout vehicle" used in the kidnapping—to a car lot which in turn had sold it to a woman clerk who worked in the San Francisco FBI office steno pool.)

But only the SLA and the FBI kept an eye on the box score of errors in their private contest. In public the game was between the SLA and the Hearst family, and that was a contest which seemed as much centered on the front pages, on the six o'clock news, as it was in the fate of teenage Patricia Hearst. Both the SLA and the Hearsts were very conscious of what was left unsaid, as well as of what was said, and each had its pretensions to guard. The style of communication the SLA had chosen, their flamboyant communiqués to media, forced both into an almost ritualistic exchange. It was as if they were passing headlines back and forth. Each in turn would speak with this little dance of verbal gestures, stylized ritual, like some eerie mating dance. What they said was overshadowed by how they said it.

The day after Patty's "they aren't unreasonable" message, a Hearst spokesman said the family was working out the financial details of the food distribution. The following day Randolph Hearst stepped again before the cameras.

"Arrangements have been made," he announced, "for two million dollars to be delivered to a tax-exempt charitable organization approved by the attorney general of California, capable of making distribution for the benefit of the poor and needy.

"Of this amount, half a million dollars represents my own sum. This happens to be a substantial part of my personal assets. The one and a half million is being made available by a foundation at the determination to contribute by its independent board of directors. That happens to be the Hearst Foundation, the William Randolph Hearst Foundation, and was made by the board after members of my family disqualified themselves. We are now working on the mechanics and have consulted the attorney general's office of the State of California." He was counting out the bills for the ransom, but the SLA had planned this to be the Hearsts' humiliation—and there was little of that. Hearst said that as an additional show of good faith, he was retaining William Coblentz, a San Francisco attorney—who was, incredibly, also a member of the University of California Board of Regents—"to see that Russell Little and Joseph Remiro get a fair trial and receive due process in all phases of the proceedings."

By the following day the nature of the Hearst food distribution became more clear. Randolph Hearst announced that Ludlow Kramer, the secretary of state of Washington State, had agreed to administer the effort. Kramer had directed a very successful private relief program—Neighbors in Need—among unemployed aerospace workers in his state, supplying supplementary foodstuffs and basic staples. The Hearst program would be called People in Need. "The model of it has been done in the State of Washington," explained Hearst. He said Kramer felt that "with the two million dollars we can feed one hundred thousand people a month for twelve months. And it's possible for it to become an ongoing program.

"My own feeling is that this can be quite successful," added Hearst. "However, I do feel that the real problems go much deeper than food and go into jobs and job placements. Possibly later we can do something about that, but at this time we'll look into some of it."

12

Patricia Campbell Hearst

THERE was Quality in the life of Patricia Hearst—and in her nineteen years, a shimmer of independence and rebellion in a cloistered world. She had been bred to the substance and pretensions of great wealth, a future of privilege and a past of legend. Particularly in California, the name Hearst conjures up the lavish extravagance of her grandfather's regal life-style—the Hearst villas and estates are landmarks; San Simeon, the grand castle, a $50 million monument to vanity, the most opulent private home on the continent, is now a state park. But history and most of America remember best the screaming headlines of the Hearst tabloids, the newspaper empire that epitomized the cult of sensationalism and yellow journalism. Patricia Hearst was the grandchild of the legend; raised in the vacuum of mannered gentility with which second generations so often quiet the echo of a flamboyant patriarch.

Grandfather William Randolph Hearst—"the old man," in her father's affectionate phrase—was a colorful and shrewd entrepreneur who built a fortune to establish a dynasty. W.R.H. was a towering figure, fickle and willful, who through his publications wielded enormous power in the first four decades of this century. Denounced and applauded by Presidents, he was a czar of Hollywood, a multimillionaire who dazzled his era and all that have followed with his wanton extravagance. His life inspired Aldous Huxley's *After Many a Summer Dies the Swan*, Orson Welles' epic film *Citizen Kane*, and made the name Hearst synonymous with the decadence and magnificence of great wealth and power. After his sons took over the empire, the Hearst life-style changed, but the newspapers still carry much of the shrill sensationalism that was their birthright and remain well to the right politically.

Patty's love affair with Steve Weed began when she was barely out of adolescence. She was nineteen when kidnapped, and she had already put three faithful years into the relationship. Even her family knew that their engagement announcement, only a month before the kidnapping, was the climax of a long campaign in which Patty coaxed, if not led, her former math tutor to the bottom steps of the altar. Steve, said her friends, had still wanted to wait until she was older—but Patty with her mind set was difficult to deter.

Patty and Steve met in 1970, when she was a sixteen-year-old high school junior at Crystal Springs School for Girls, a small, exclusive private school less than a mile from the family home in wealthy suburban Hillsborough. Steve Weed was a math teacher at the school. He was twenty-three, seven years older, a shaggy, hip recent Princeton graduate who had the hearts of half the school fluttering.

Weed was one of three young men on the school's teaching staff, the most eligible bachelor among 200 teenage girls. The competition for his attention among the girls was fierce and embarrassingly obvious. He had blue eyes and blond hair, the lean build of an athlete, a walrus mustache, and the understated, quiet charm of the right social circle. He was the teacher; cerebral, older (with the gulf that separates the teens from the twenties), master of the arcane mysteries of algebra and trigonometry. For many of the students he was a walking, talking, romantic fantasy. But there is no report of Weed as a rake; he seemed to endure the onslaught with humor and some perspective. Later he would talk with self-effacing modesty of his years with the "giddy girls" and their crushes. But Patty, he said, was different.

At sixteen Patty was unusually precocious; mature beyond her years, self-willed, and very independent. At Crystal Springs Patty had privileges few students were allowed. She had special permission to drive to school in the little blue MG sports car her father had given her for her sixteenth birthday. And just generally, said Weed, she seemed to get away with more. She had transferred to Crystal Springs from another school, and she stayed, by choice, it seemed, an outsider. Steve Weed remembers the school as full of petty jealousies and gossip, but Patty seemed coolly aloof from it all.

For her part, Patty had marked Steve's style and methodically set out to snare him. At the school orientation, when she first saw the young math teacher, Patty had turned to a close friend and said, "Uh, oh, I'm in trouble this year." Halfway through the year, she began visiting his apartment in nearby Menlo Park, asking for help with her geometry (although she was not in his classes). At five feet two, Patty thought she was too short, and she hated the tiny hands she inherited from her mother, but she had a confidence in her sexuality rare for a sixteen-year-old, even by the standards of California teenagers. She had been seduced first at fourteen by a Hillsborough boyfriend, said Weed, and she had enjoyed a few other lovers before she settled with him. About a week after she started coming over to Steve's house, they made love for the first time. "I made the initial advance," said Weed, "but it was pretty much expected by both of us." It was only after going to bed with him that afternoon that she stopped addressing him as "Mr. Weed."

By the end of the year they were seeing each other steadily, although still secretly. Patty had good grades—As and Bs—in all subjects except geometry. Weed helped her improve the grade—he built her class project, a sculpture of balsa wood, and filched a copy of the final to prep her—but she still barely got a B on the test. That summer, after graduating a year early because she'd accumulated enough required course credits, Patty had her family hire Steve Weed as her math tutor. From then until she was kidnapped, Patty and Steve were "virtually inseparable."

Patty's early years were "pretty much unhappy," said Weed. All the Hearst girls were brought up with nannies and governesses. At the age of ten Patty was enrolled in the Convent of the Sacred Heart, a Roman Catholic convent boarding school in Atherton, eight miles south of Hillsborough. At fourteen she transferred to another, Santa Catalina, in Monterey, where the discipline of the old faith was forcefully brought into the secular world by Dominican nuns. In the regimen of Santa Catalina Patty—independent and outspoken, if something of a loner—clashed often with the nuns. Classmates remember her doing more than her share of punishment details, cleaning the toilets. Her independent streak was demonstrated at Santa Catalina on a number of occasions. Once, when a group of students, angry at a teacher, banded together and vowed to refuse to take a test, Patty ended up being the *only* one who didn't take it. Later the school initiated what Patty considered a "witch hunt" trying to learn the identities of several senior-class girls who, rumor had it, had attended an off-campus party where "pot" had been smoked. Patty then was adamantly against marijuana, but considered the Inquisition techniques of the Dominican sisters (students were called in one by one and grilled about the grass-smoking party; their rooms and lockers were searched) an outrage—and said so. Finally, Patty complained bitterly to her father, her favored parent, and that fall transferred to Crystal Springs.

Patty's mother, Catherine Hearst, elegant and attractive at fifty-six, a woman of all the social graces, is herself a product of convent schools of the Deep South. The daughter of an old-line Georgia family, Catherine married Randolph Hearst in 1938, when she was eighteen years old. As the Hearsts took their places onstage early in the kidnap drama, Catherine remained discreetly behind her husband. It was the sensible role, proper in every sense, but many who knew the Hearsts found it surprising. Randolph Hearst is a man accustomed to quiet, low-profile power, with a personal style almost unobtrusive, yet confident and expectant of results. He was born to the name, to the power it held, to the corporate positions he inherited. Of the California Hearsts, it was his wife, Catherine, who was the public figure, particularly through the sixties. Universities and the politicians who control them were more visible then, and particularly in California, against the backdrop of campus turmoil.

In 1956 Catherine Hearst was appointed to the governing Board of Regents for the multicampus University of California (to which the Hearst Foundation had contributed many millions), and from that post, which she still holds, she watched, with undisguised horror, the social activism of the sixties seed and flower among UC students. Mrs. Hearst became well known as a California politician of eccentric and strident views; an archconservative who found the campus breeding barbarian hordes, vandals in the heart of the empire. She raised a bitter, outraged voice among the regents. Reporters who covered Berkeley antiwar demonstrations recall Catherine, incognito in babushka and dark glasses, standing just behind the police lines to survey the crowds.

Mrs. Hearst is a devoutly religious Roman Catholic (her husband converted to her faith when they married). She describes herself as a serious student of Greek, Roman, and Egyptian history and of the history of the Hapsburg dynasty, the kings of England, and the Hawaiian monarchy.

He is by no means an objective witness, but Steve Weed offers an interesting glimpse of Catherine. Late in the kidnap scenario, Weed had been quoted several times giving almost gratuitously cruel descriptions of Patty's parents, and particularly of Catherine, but he said he was trying to be fair when he explained, much later, "People like Catherine are different from you, me, most of us. She relates to all this very differently. . . ." The religion? Praying? "Yes," he replied, "there is the praying and all, but that's not what I mean. I understood her fear. I know she loves Patty, but as the story dragged on and got messier, I felt that what really burdened Catherine was the shame and disgrace of it all. The disgrace, particularly the disgrace!"

Of Patty's father, Weed said, "I like Randy, and I think he liked me. But I think that both of us realized that we didn't really understand one another and probably never would."

Randolph Hearst is a big, gruff, barrel-chested man, extremely likable and friendly, but with a disconcerting habit of not quite finishing sentences and wandering off from the subject of the discussion. The Randolph Hearst who emerged to barter with the SLA, strained but firm and confident, had, at least at first, an almost commanding presence quite unlike the genial but distinctly unimpressive persona friends and employees had grown accustomed to. Even his newspaper, the *Examiner*, seemed to acquire an edge under the pressure, although on the subject of the SLA the paper was bridled and gagged. For years the *Examiner* has been considered one of the worst big-city newspapers in the country, a hard-hitting vehicle for real estate and grocery ads. Patty rarely read the *Examiner*; she thought—and told her father—it was irrelevant scribbling aimed at the geriatric set.

Patricia is the middle child of the five girls, something of a family rebel. For a young, bright, spirited girl, her problems with her parents were not really unusual, although particularly in dealing with her mother, there was a clash of wills that resonated with more than generation-gap tension. Perhaps the heart of the problem was that the two were not so dissimilar. Patty was the first of the girls to reject "coming out" as a debutante in the San Francisco Cotillion, and that irked Mrs. Hearst, a woman who prizes her social caste highly. "It was typical of Patty and the way she did things," said a family friend. "She just charged in and announced to her mother that she would have nothing to do with it. 'I just won't do it!' she said. And she was quite blunt about her feelings. I know her older sister Virginia always thought less of her for that. Patty was kind of tactless and impulsive, and would say things— blurt them out—almost to get a rise out of people."

"The Hearst family, as old and wealthy as they are, never went in for country-club parties, never hosted big parties themselves," said another friend of the family. "They had this enormous house with all these servants and silver and these very expensive and plush furnishings, yet they lived a very quiet life themselves. They went out and entertained very infrequently." "I always found them very homey," said a young woman friend of one of the older daughters, "very casual; people felt free to talk openly, even swear—but always there were these reminders they were the Hearsts. . . . They were always flying to New York, Los Angeles, or Hawaii. And Mrs. Hearst was a regent, and she had just been told by Governor Reagan that, you know, the students were all Communists or dope addicts or something. Mr. Hearst was obviously the scion of an enormously powerful family, and yet he was a very human guy, very unimposing. They *seemed* very close. Mr. Hearst seemed to really enjoy his wife, but they were so dissimilar—Mrs. Hearst with her kind of funny, fidgety prejudices and Mr. Hearst with this genial, open-armed tolerance."

"I remember one dinner at the Hearsts'," said another friend of one of the daughters, "when Mrs. Hearst began insisting that George McGovern had been a coward in World War Two . . . that he had not flown a mission or that he had done something that was specifically cowardly, and it had been cited on his record, that there was proof of this, you know. She'd say something like that when there were a group of us there, and everyone would kind of look around at the others and start being very polite. Asking, you know, 'Well, what proof have you really seen, Mrs. Hearst?' All of the young people would sit there and try to start it at some civilized level, but she wouldn't let it ease. She said, 'Well I've *seen* the proof. I've pressed the people who told me, so I don't think there's any doubt it's true.' It became kind of a teasing game, very annoying because there would be no give on her part.

"She'd get very upset—no, she wouldn't get upset, *we* would get upset. Often we'd just drop the conversation, most of us, anyway. Mrs. Hearst could be very domineering in conversations, very opinionated and very sure of herself, yet she played on this Southern belle kind of approach as a hedge. When a caper like that got going, Mr. Hearst would sort of laugh and look down at his dish and say, 'Oh, Catherine, come on,' or 'Isn't this funny, fellows?' or something like that to let us know it was okay, that this was just her way of being herself."

Friends say the family had never been particularly close, and Patty certainly was never the favorite daughter, but if the kinship was strained, the bond was never cut. In the two years prior to her kidnapping, Patty had been tied up with Steve; she had little contact with her sisters, but there was always a line open to her parents. Weed said that he often played mediator, encouraging Patty to be more "tolerant" toward her mother. He himself was insecure and distinctly an alien among the family. He realized he was not the blue-blood catch Mrs. Hearst had wanted for her daughters, and Mrs. Hearst had made no secret of her distaste for their shared bed outside wedlock. Yet Patty, for all the vaunted independence everyone mentions in her relationship to her parents, was not the sort to cut it alone. And Catherine Hearst was not the sort to turn away from even a willful and sometimes brazen daughter. After Patty and Steve settled in Berkeley, Mrs. Hearst would occasionally ask their opinion of something that had come up at a regents meeting; they would come up with a liberal view, and she of course would disagree. Among the regents, said Weed, Mrs. Hearst was "virtually a stand-in for Governor Reagan."

It was only after Patty was graduated from Crystal Springs, while she was a freshman in college, that Patty and Steve began to think of what they shared as "love." Although with her grades and background Patty could have attended any one of several prestigious schools, she chose to enroll in Menlo College in 1971 for her freshman year. It is a small school located in Menlo Park, on the peninsula, near Palo Alto. Steve Weed lived in Menlo Park; he planned to teach for another year at Crystal Springs before going on for his doctorate in philosophy at UC Berkeley. Menlo is known as a "rich kids' school" (the tuition is $3,450 per year), and there are few restrictions on students, many of whom maintain apartments off campus. Although technically Patty lived in a girls' dorm on campus, she had soon all but moved in with Weed. She was eighteen. At Menlo she breezed through her liberal-arts program with straight A's and came out number one in her class, winning the college's "highest honor" award. Falling in love with a teacher had raised her academic goals considerably. Patty would usually leave to meet Steve immediately after a day of classes. Most weekday nights were spent at his small apartment, but obviously she studied.

"She was the ideal student," said Leon Loofbourow, her faculty adviser. "She studied hard, never dropped a course, attended classes faithfully, and was no problem whatsoever to anyone." Quoted in the Menlo alumni bulletin, he added that Patty was "one of the most delightful, feminine young ladies I have ever met . . . she was well mannered, well groomed," and traded not a whit on family reputation.

Biology professor Stuart Olson first met Patty socially through his friend Steve Weed. With Olson's wife, who also taught at Crystal Springs, they occasionally made up a foursome for dinner. Patty, recalled Olson, was a listener, not naturally disposed to initiating conversation or breaking in, regardless of topic. She would wait until one of the others drew her into the conversation. "You'd never suspect she had money if you didn't know," Olson told the bulletin. "She was completely unpretentious, and it embarrassed her to be thought of as a Hearst heiress." Other teachers and classmates at Menlo remember Patty as quiet and reserved, friendly but often distant, with a coolness that friends describe as maturity but others often misinterpreted.

Patrick Tobin, a Menlo humanities professor who taught Patty, in the summer of 1972, after her freshman year, escorted her and six other Menlo students on a European tour to study archaeology and classical art. He was one of the few people at Menlo who actually got to know Patty rather well. He remembers her as warm to friends, articulate, stubborn in her opinions, and very deliberate. He said her sangfroid—"a coolness similar to Nixon's"—was worn like body armor.

Tobin remembers that he had expected Patty to enjoy and be impressed by Milton and Byron and was surprised when she condemned them—not from their work, but from their personal histories. She had read their biographies and judged them "male chauvinists." Milton with his gospel of "divine chastity"; Milton indeed! She identified strongly with feminist values in the abstract and became quite emotional in talking about the inequality of women. There must have been frustration there, for there was little in the daily life of Patricia Hearst that had been molded by the new consciousness. There was her love affair, of course, but even that was subsidized by Daddy.

Both Steve and her parents had urged her to go on the European study tour that summer, to get a little distance from her life, to think things out. Tobin noted that most of the students he has escorted on these summer tours are overwhelmed, awed by one or two of the treasures they visit, the Sistine Chapel or the Medici Palace perhaps. But the heiress of San Simeon was immune. "She was no rhapsodizer." Tobin smiled. "There was no Mary Magdalene in her." Neither did she seem to react to the poverty and social injustice they saw in their travels. Except for a Crystal Springs class tour to Japan—during which seventeen-year-old Patty confided to a classmate that she was on the pill—the European study tour was the extent of her travel abroad.

The trip was good for her, said Weed later. "She learned a lot. She grew up a lot." She returned to San Francisco in late July. Her parents then knew Steve as her boyfriend, but were still unprepared for her announcement that the two were going to live together in Berkeley. "Her father was a little embarrassed about it," recalled Weed, "concerned that we didn't make a big thing of it as far as publicity, and mostly he was concerned that Patty would be happy." Mrs. Hearst, said Weed, "was very grim-faced about it. . . . She's traditional. The old values; very proper, very concerned about what people think. She was very upset about it but did not try to prevent it. . . . Patty is very headstrong and they knew it wouldn't work."

Mrs. Hearst wanted Patty to attend Stanford—anyplace but Berkeley. But Steve was at Berkeley, so Patty was going to Berkeley. In September, 1972, the two moved into the $240 a month duplex on Benvenue Avenue. Weed was earning $400 a month as a teaching assistant in the Philosophy Department, and Patty got her father to raise her allowance to $300 a month. After the trip Patty decided to skip the fall semester, and it was only in January, 1973, that she began at Berkeley, first as a biology major; finding that difficult, she transferred to art history. "She wanted to take a break from school," explained Weed later, "and a lot of it was wanting to do something different." Through the fall she worked as a $2.25-an-hour clerk in the stationery department of Capwell's, an Oakland department store. It was Tania's only job, ever—before the Revolution.

On the periphery of the Berkeley graduate-student circle, Patty and Steve led an unusually secluded life. Their friends were all Steve's friends, in their mid-twenties and thirties. (Few guessed Patty was only eighteen.) Most of their free time was spent home alone together, studying, watching television, listening to baroque or folk music. Occasionally they entertained, mostly Steve's friends from the Philosophy Department. These parties, said a regular guest, would usually break down with one group discussing philosophy and the other not. Steve was always in the philosophy gossip—"and Patty would sit near him, listening, never bored, seemingly interested, yet rarely participating in the conversation."

Patty did the cooking, and he, said Weed, did the housecleaning. Her ambitions were blandly conventional—oddly so for an eighteen- or nineteen-year-old—stable and rooted when most young people her age see change as the future's most exciting promise. "Patty saw her future in home and family with Steve," said a close friend of the couple. "He'd be the professor and she'd be a mommy—and they'd nestle quietly together in the exurbs of academe." Actually, said Weed, the "only thing in the world she wanted then was to have two kids, a collie, and a station wagon. But we both had . . . the means to do a lot more than that." And

Mrs. Patricia Weed would have a career, some sort of career, out there, too.

Weed is a man of several sides—and the faltering, inarticulate, fidgety figure he was later to cut for newsmen and the TV cameras was not his best image. At UC Berkeley, Weed is considered one of the better teaching assistants the Philosophy Department has ever had, with a powerful, if not quite brilliant, mind. Despite all the descriptions of him after the kidnapping as "frail" and "thin," Weed has the credentials of an extraordinary athlete. He is the son of a Palo Alto stockbroker; his parents are divorced. He graduated number one in his 1965 high school class, scored near-perfect college boards, was a record-breaking high school track star and a National Merit Scholar. "He had a natural sense of timing and coordination that you don't teach an athlete," said his high school coach. "The kid was like a Greek god. . . ." Weed was vigorously recruited by several of the most prestigious colleges in the nation, including Harvard, before he chose Princeton. He studied physics and became captain of the Princeton track team. It was only as a graduate student that he began to pursue his interest in the philosophy of science and from there into the formal structures of logic. He was particularly interested in Kant, Frege, and Heidegger.

Weed had opened up new worlds for Patty—and she for him. But there always seemed to remain something of the teacher-pupil relationship. Intellectually, Steve had exploded a constellation of possibilities for her. His age offered experience that must have challenged her and a stability that was reassuring and perhaps, in hindsight, threatening. Somewhere along the way he taught her how to plant and tend marijuana plants and opened Huxley's door with some mild experimentation with LSD. But Steve said, "Neither Patty nor I had much at all to do with drugs since we've been together, very, very little at all by anyone's standards—that's anyone's standards, not Berkeley standards." A number of friends described the two as "strictly apolitical," and one couple close to them said that they had expected Steve to vote for Nixon in 1972. Weed was liberal rather than radical, self-consciously so, as many young people who have matured in the East find themselves in Berkeley. "Only my radical friends realize how conservative I really am," Weed told a friend. He smiled at the fact that many older straight people—including the Hearsts—thought him a radical because of his longish hair and the bushy, untrimmed mustache that almost covers his mouth. (The Hearsts called him Toothbrush behind his back.) Patty and Steve voted for McGovern in 1972, but friends said Steve voted only because Patty pushed him. He had, said a close friend, "an enthusiastic skepticism of all politicians and ideology," and Patty seemed to agree.

Being with Patty drew Weed into the aura of great wealth, introduced him to the fruits of family riches. On weekends the two would often climb into his Volkswagen or her little MG and be off to relax at one of the Hearst cattle ranches—or the family ski hideaway at Sugar Bowl, in the Sierras—or to the family's villa beside San Simeon on the 77,000-acre estate still owned by the family, surrounding the castle, with miles of coast to walk, the largest privately owned chunk of California shoreline. A favorite hideaway was Wyntoon, Grandfather Hearst's gorgeous wilderness estate near Mount Shasta, in Northern California. Now seldom used by any of the family, it is a reconstructed Bavarian village of four multistoried chalets full of antiques, on the banks of the McCloud River.

Patty loved antiques, and she and Steve spent many hours browsing through the warehouses which still store many of the treasures collected by her grandfather, putting aside those she someday wanted to have. Because of the curious trust structure in which her grandfather had secured most of his fortune—isolating it from direct control of her family—Patty would have to buy these antiques from the estate, but she could purchase them at appraised 1950 prices. (Most of the Hearst fortune—the estates, the investments, the Hearst Corporation—will be ceded to the heirs around the year 2000. Until then it is in trust.) Patty had a passion for Oriental rugs; she chose one and persuaded her father to lend her most of the $1,700 price and then store it at Hillsborough until she and Steve had a place big enough for it.

Weed said that when he first got to know Patty she thought of her name, the wealth, and the notoriety as something of a "predicament." Steve didn't share her concern. "She would say a few things about, you know, how it could put her in an awkward position," he remembered, but "after three years she started to realize that if she went about things in the right way, it certainly was an asset rather than a liability. And that's where things were when she was taken." A number of friends at Menlo and Berkeley remember Patty's awkward embarrassment when they realized she was a Hearst. It was not shame; she was proud of her heritage (although she somewhat pointedly told friends that, no, she had never seen *Citizen Kane* or read the great biography of W.R.H., *Citizen Hearst*). She was proud of her parents' association with the famous—Howard Hughes, the shah of Iran, the Kennedys—and proud to have been one of the young hostesses when Prince Charles came to dinner. But her family was something that she talked of only with her closest friends—and they, listening, thought they heard only "the normal strains of a girl her age" toward parents and family.

It was the classic cure that eased the strains: the wedding announcement. Patricia Campbell Hearst was to marry Steven Andrew Weed on the last Saturday in June—June 29, 1974. When the formal invitations had finally been sent out, said Weed, he could see the relief on the face of Catherine Hearst. It was to be a big, elaborate society wedding, and Mother, who loved weddings, threw herself into the preparations. Patty and her mother went together to choose her china, silver, and crystal patterns.

Patricia chose three formal patterns: the Green Darby Panel of Royal Green Darby; the cobalt blue with raised gold stripes on the rim by Hutschenreuther; and the VBOH pattern with hand-painted flowers and butterflies by Herend. For daily use she chose the Hutschenreuther Blue Onion. Her sterling silver would be Towle's Old Master, traditional with a floral design on the handle; her crystal was to be Powerscourt, the thumbcut design by Waterford.

"Patty saw some antique pearl-handled fruit knives and forks that she loved," Catherine Hearst told *Ladies' Home Journal.* "Her father and I gave them to her for an engagement present." In the flutter of preparations, Patty seemed more comfortable with her parents than she had been for years. She even began to visit the mansion more regularly.

13

People in Need

A FEW days before the kidnapping two of the Hearst family maids had asked Patty what she wanted for her birthday. "What with her usual practicality, she said glasses—water glasses," remembered Katherine Kellings, the upstairs maid. Kellings bought four glasses; the housekeeper bought four more. Patty turned twenty years old on February twentieth—sixteen days after she had been kidnapped, two days after her father announced the food program.

In the Hillsborough mansion there had been a faint hope the SLA might release Patty for her birthday, now that the PIN program had been funded and was recruiting volunteers for the first distribution. There were many hopes. As the period of captivity grew from days to weeks, the sense of imminence, the feeling that *something* might happen tomorrow, if not today, slipped away. But still the story had "bulletin" status. Hillsborough—quiet city of the superrich, where neither businesses nor sidewalks are allowed, a community of 2,764 private homes with an assessed value of $67 million—had lost its treasured anonymity. A hundred reporters now camped in front of the Hearst home; few ventured into Berkeley or Oakland to seek the roots of the story; mostly they waited for the next family press conference, now almost a daily ritual.

It did not occur to Randolph Hearst in the first weeks that he was playing into the hands of the SLA by feeding the insatiable appetite of the media; when it did, it was too late. Two TV networks had moved in big dish-antenna microwave relay trucks; several dozen newsmen bivouacked in camper vans parked in front; the telephone company had brought in a special cable, set up a string of temporary pay phones across the street, and installed private telephones on nearly every tree in the Hearsts' front yard.

234

At one press conference Steve Weed became angry at a reporter who asked for more childhood pictures of Patty. Randy Hearst, exasperated, turned on Weed. "Look," he said, "you don't know anything about this business! I do! A picture of her as a child might cause somebody enough of a twinge to come forward and say something." The press got infant photos, toddler photos—the burden of the family album. Reporters on the mansion stakeout developed a friendly sympathy for Randy, but they—like their public—became increasingly impatient with Weed, who was awkwardly fighting to maintain some sort of stance vaguely in the middle.

"Actually," recalled Hearst later, "I think it was a pretty good idea—to at least make it look like he wasn't a member of the family because we were dealing with radicals." The approval came with hindsight. Weed's independence was more than appearance; he wasn't a Hearst, he wasn't comfortable in the family's united front, and only in those first few weeks did he accept Hearst as the sole spokesman for himself as well as for the family. (When he began to speak out on his own, Hearst asked him to move out.) Inside the mansion Steve was the outsider, the critical voice in the family strategy sessions, asking questions the reporters outside gingerly avoided, particularly about the Hearst finances. He worried that the SLA would doubt that $500,000 was a "substantial" portion of Randy's fortune, sure that they wouldn't understand the Byzantine relationships between the Hearst Foundation, the Hearst Corporation, and the various Hearst families. It was a prescient fear, but it was brushed aside in the tension and chaos prevailing in the mansion.

In the nation's capital Attorney General William Saxbe took a potshot, opining at a press conference that Hearst should make no concessions to the kidnappers and that the FBI—if it cornered the SLA—should go in and try to get Patty out. Hearst responded with cold rage: "Mr. Saxbe is not the father of Patricia. I'm going to do what I can to get her out . . . and to make a statement that you're going to bust in and shoot the place up . . . is damn near irresponsible!" (Hearst had successfully argued to police and the local FBI that the situation was one of political terrorism, requiring special caution—what with the SLA threatening Patty if their associates were arrested and vowing to execute her if lawmen raided their hideout.)

At another press conference Catherine Hearst said $1 million had been received from people who wanted to ransom Patty. Her husband came out the next day and apologized for the misrepresentation. "She got the figures from hearing somebody say that if they had a telethon, suggesting a telethon, that they could raise one million dollars," he said. An undetermined amount of money had been received in small contributions (it was returned, with notes of appreciation), along with dozens of pies, cakes, platters of fried chicken—most of it delivered anonymously from housewives in nearby middle- and working-class communities.

With the ongoing tension, the family fell into occasional bickering, with Weed the common target. Mrs. Hearst, ramrod straight in public, sometimes exploded with rage and frustration in private; railing against the FBI for its lack of results, drawing on the Inquisition for examples of what she would do if she could get her hands on the SLA. "Catherine was close to a nervous breakdown," said Weed later. "She kept walking around saying, 'I know Patty's dead. I just know it.' She was lost in this morbid pessimism, often incredibly depressed. At times the only way she could deal with it was to assume the worst."

In one of the several tempestuous scenes between Mrs. Hearst and her prospective son-in-law, Mrs. Hearst turned on Weed and demanded, "Whatever happened to the real men in this world, men like Clark Gable? No one would have carried my daughter off if there'd been a real man there." The animosity between mother and daughter's lover, always latent, became public in the strain. The FBI was leaning on Weed, too. In college Weed had once roomed with the president of the Princeton SDS, had even been brought in as a ringer to play quarterback for an SDS team in an epic campus football game against the Princeton ROTC (SDS won)—but even without his old radical connections (who thought Weed a nice guy but a liberal), conservative FBI agents would undoubtedly have taken a dim view of the former high school teacher who had taken up with a sixteen-year-old rich girl. Seeking a possible link between Weed and any of the SLA members—or Patty and the SLA—FBI agents questioned him for hours, repeatedly, showing a persistent interest in his sex life.

"No, they didn't like me," recalled Weed. "The FBI didn't like me at all. It was my attitude, I'm told. They just couldn't comprehend my world or my values; they couldn't comprehend the lifestyle of any young person in the Bay Area, in California, maybe in the country. I couldn't believe it; all the stereotypes are true! The FBI agents would sit there and ask these sneering questions: how many girls I've seduced, how often I make love to women, how I make love, how many joints of marijuana I smoke a day. Silly, stupid questions; I should have been insulted, but they were too far out to get upset. I mean, Patty and I only occasionally smoked grass, but there was a half-pound of marijuana in the apartment when she was kidnapped. So—of *course*—we must have been in a drugged stupor, having sex all the time.

"I asked them if they knew any young person in the Bay Area who didn't smoke marijuana occasionally. They didn't answer. I mean, Patty and I were pretty straight! You know, I honestly think that if I had told the FBI, 'The revolution is coming next week, so fuck you!' it would have bothered them a lot less than my casual acknowledgment of values that were to them—not even amoral—*immoral*."

Investigators fished and poked around Weed for months ("Yeah, well, Steve's kind of a difficult guy to get to know," volunteered Randolph Hearst in explanation). The FBI even arranged for Steve to take a voluntary "truth serum" test—canceled after some bad publicity—but they apparently didn't finally cross him off the suspect list until after he had passed a lie-detector examination.

The mansion was full of confusion: company lawyers, paid consultants, the FBI, police, friends, free-lance advisers, even a number of psychics who tried to divine the whereabouts of Patty through ESP. Ex-astronaut Edgar Mitchell coordinated the efforts of four psychics on the case from his Palo Alto parapsychology research center, and the strained and sometimes ludicrous attempts of three other mediums who worked their craft at the mansion provided rare levity for Weed and the young Hearsts. One of the "swamis," as Weed nicknamed them, set up an altar in the dining room, groaning purposefully over a California map, a compass, pictures of Patty, and one of her shoes. Another ran up a one-week $500 charge on the Hearst account at the San Francisco Hilton, billing $300 at the bar while meditating on the cosmic possibilities.

The smiles and occasional belly laughs were probably worth the tab to the elder Hearsts. Anxiety blocked most normal pleasures. And right then the primary concern of the family—the People in Need program—was causing a lot of anxiety.

The first food distribution was scheduled for Friday, February 22, and PIN was a shambles: bickering among the PIN administrators and the handful of radical groups the SLA had demanded oversee the program, tangles in the incredible logistics, rip-offs at the warehouse. PIN recruited a corps of selfless volunteers, but $2 million was being doled out, and vultures hurried to get an early piece of the action. Whether the SLA would be satisfied seemed secondary to whether PIN could actually get the food to the people. Then, the day before the first handout, the "Court of the People" exercised its Catch 22 option: Another SLA tape was delivered.

"To those who bear the hopes and faith of our people, let the voices of their guns express the words of freedom. Greetings to the People. . . ." It was the voice of the Field Marshal with an angry message. It had been Patricia, not he, who had said "any good-faith gesture on the part of the Hearst empire would be basically okay," he pointed out. Cinque said he himself had clarified her statement by adding that it must be a "sincere effort," reflecting both Hearst's "capabilities . . . [and] the needs of the people.

"The Hearst empire has attempted to mislead the people and to deceive them by claiming to put forth a good-faith gesture of two million dollars. This amount is not a good-faith gesture but rather an act of throwing a few crumbs to the people, forcing them to fight over it amongst themselves . . . the plan proposed by Mr. Hearst is not at all acceptable as a gesture of good faith in its present form."

To make it acceptable, said Cinque, an additional $4 million had to be added to the already allotted $2 million—"within one week" and distributed within a single month. The $6 million worth of food—"all canned goods and dry goods [to] be matched with equal amounts of top-quality fresh meats, dairy products, and produce"—was to be given out in seven largely nonwhite neighborhoods in San Francisco, Oakland, and East Palo Alto. No cards or other identification were to be required; anyone asking for the food was to get a package—whether he be "needy" or not.

"The Hearst Foundation is a front for the Hearst fortune," Cinque said. "The foundation serves as a loophole for that fortune"—a financial empire worth "hundreds and hundreds of millions."

After having told Hearst to set up his own food program, the SLA had now changed the rules of the game again—not only demanding more money, but condemning PIN in advance. On the model of Lud Kramer's aid-to-the-unemployed program in Washington State, People in Need was set up to provide basic staples and necessities over an extended period. PIN was offering flour, and now the Symbionese revolutionaries had made it clear they wanted steaks. (At the PIN waterfront warehouse nearly a hundred exhausted volunteers were in the traumatic final stages of organizing the first food giveaway. All work stopped as the volunteers gathered around a radio to hear the communiqué. When Cinque blasted PIN as "crumbs to the people," the warehouse echoed with boos and angry catcalls.)

And now there was more than money demanded: Cinque said Hearst's good-faith gesture must demonstrate "a change of interest, regret for his crimes against the people, and a firm decision that they will no longer be a party to such actions in the future." In the SLA argot, Hearst was being told to renounce capitalism forever and somehow prove to the SLA that he intended to live by this renunciation.

If the new demands were rejected, he said, "all further communications shall be suspended and the prisoner will be maintained according to the terms of the international codes of war concerning prisoners of war and will be maintained in that status until such time as the status of our captive soldiers is changed." Exchange for Little and Remiro, the impossible demand that had haunted Hearst, was raised again.

The communiqué was long, Cinque listing some of the Hearst trusts' extensive land and corporate holdings, then turning to lecture the radical groups which had publicly denounced the SLA but had agreed to cooperate in the food distribution in an effort to help free the Hearst girl. Do not grieve for Patricia Hearst, Cinque said, ". . . fight and cry out in defense of millions and save the children. And by this action you will save also the life of one who has never seen the robbed or knew that the riches of her life were the spoils of a robber and a murderer." (It was a curious way to refer to their captive; perhaps the first hint that the SLA had taken it upon themselves to "educate" young Patty.)

It had been Hearst who had blocked news stories identifying DeFreeze and (erroneously) Wheeler when their names were turned up by reporters for the San Francisco *Chronicle* and KQED-TV. Even after those names were revealed, Hearst continued to request that San Francisco media hold back in identifying other SLA members when out-of-town papers—the New York *Times* was one—began tracking them down. The Field Marshal, however, declared: "It is the judgment of this court that the Hearst family and the Hearst corporation seems to be more foolishly concerned with the identities of the supposed SLA elements rather than with the admission to the people of the crimes committed against the people by the Hearst empire." He was building to the end, the dramatic flair with which the SLA liked to close their messages. This would be one of the more memorable: ". . . they have seemingly said that they know me and therefore do not have to repent for their crimes. . . .

"To this I would say yes. You do, indeed, know me. You have always known me. I'm that nigger you have hunted and feared night and day. I'm that nigger you have killed hundreds of my people in the vain hope of finding. I'm the nigger that is no longer just hunted, robbed, and murdered. I'm the nigger that hunts you now.

"Yes, you know me. You know me, I'm the wetback. You know me, I'm the gook, the broad, the servant, the spik.

"Yes, indeed, you know us all, and we know you—the oppressor, murderer, and robber. And you have hunted and robbed and exploited us all. Now we are the hunters that will give you no rest. And we will not compromise the freedom of our children.

"Death to the fascist insect that preys upon the life of the people."

To the SLA, Randolph Hearst had behaved like a blatant caricature of the white, ruling-class male. He had taken their original demand and turned it around—made it his program. Their plan for a food giveaway spectacular had been revamped; it was now his "improved" reform-style basic dietary-supplement program. Hearst was bewildered, frustrated, and near despair. ("I thought this other whole idea was so much better," said Hearst later. "We thought it would enchant them . . . we were really sincere and taking them seriously politically.")

The Hearst Corporation is today possibly the largest privately owned corporation in the United States, with assets including not only the nationwide chain of newspapers, magazines, and radio and television stations, but with the bulk of its holdings in enormous parcels of real estate in the United States and Mexico. In California alone it owns 212,000 acres. Total assets—according to a report published in 1967 in the highly respected business journal *Forbes*—"are well over the $500 million mark, approaching $1 billion in the estimable future."

But this great treasure is "landlocked," isolated from the living family by the terms of the will of William Randolph Hearst, the patriarch of the dynasty, who died in 1951. Before his death, the elder Hearst—to escape estate taxes, and perhaps because he did not trust the financial acumen of his sons—conceived a foundationlike institution called the Hearst Family Trust, which is run by a board of testamentary trustees and which holds all the voting stock of the Hearst Corporation. Of the thirteen trustees, according to the restrictions of the will, no more than five can be members of the Hearst family. The trustees elect the board of directors for the Hearst Corporation, largely from their own ranks. Randolph Hearst is chairman of the board of the corporation; his brother, William Randolph Hearst, Jr., of New York City, is president and editor in chief of the newspapers. But by the terms of the will, the trust is to remain in independent control of the fortune until it is dissolved—probably around the year 2000—upon the death of the last surviving son and/or grandchild who was alive in 1951, when the first William Randolph Hearst died. The trust is the creation of a tax genius; its assets multiply in shelter and will in time guarantee the Hearst heirs perhaps the largest family fortune in history. But for the time being, the living Hearsts are no more than the most influential employees of the living trust. In setting it all up, William Randolph Hearst provided separately for the members of his family, more than adequately, but less than royally.

According to Steve Weed, who claimed he had been given the opportunity to review the family accounts, the personal wealth of Patty's father was about $1.4 million after he had put the $500,000 into the original PIN program, and most of that in assets difficult to convert into cash. (Weed told a friend Patty had wildly overestimated her father's wealth; she had thought him to have in the neighborhood of $15 million.) Hearst himself said privately the half-million he had put into PIN represented about "one-quarter" of his accessible cash assets; a flat million was "what you could get your hands on if you had to scramble."

The other $1.5 million for Hearst's $2 million "gesture of good faith" was made available to PIN by the Hearst Foundation of San Francisco, a charitable foundation (with assets, in 1969, listed at nearly $44 million) under the control of the trust. Because under the law the public is to be the beneficiary of a charitable foundation, Randolph Hearst had to convince both the California attorney general's office and the federal IRS to approve the contribution to PIN. It was approved with reluctance. (Shortly thereafter, at the urging of the state AG, the California Legislature outlawed the use of charitable-foundation funds for ransom, even if indirectly channeled through a legal charity such as PIN.) A young friend of the Hearst girls, visiting the family at the time People in Need was being set up, recalled his surprise at their concern over arranging the money. Why not just let the lawyers fix it up? he suggested. "They said, 'No, no, no, it's a real problem, and besides, we have to convince the Hearst board. It's not this Mickey Mouse Marxism where Randy just flips a finger and everything's done the way he wants. We really have to work through a lot of different people and it's going to take a lot of work and sweat, and it's too bad we can't convince anybody that that's how it works, but that's the case!"

In a later interview with the authors, Randolph Hearst explained that for the trustees "this was a grandchild, so this was a terribly sympathetic thing that was going on. . . . Under those conditions, with those tapes, the feeling was, 'For God's sake, get her out.'" Hearst said only the trustees voted; the five family members abstained. "That two million we thought was certainly a goodwill gesture," he said, "and when they then came back and said four more, well, when they said four, they put me right out of the box. . . ." When the SLA said "goodwill" equaled $6 million—still not mentioning ransom or what else might be demanded before Patty would be freed—Hearst felt he was at the edge of the bottomless pit.

"I really didn't have control over the first one, but I could talk people into it," he said later. "But when they demanded another four, it was strictly up to the company. . . . I mean, I could no longer control it personally."

On February 22, the day after the communiqué, while a despairing Hearst mulled over the new demand, the first PIN distribution disintegrated into a fiasco.

There was a food riot in the Oakland ghetto at one of the four PIN distribution centers. For millions who watched network TV news that night it was a sight not to be soon forgotten: a vision of Calcutta in California. Men and women jumping up into the PIN trucks and on top of them and throwing food piecemeal and by the case into a screaming, pushing mob around them. The TV footage was taken with long-range lenses; the SLA had ordered both the press and police to stay away from the distribution sites. (The police radio announced the locations and ordered patrol cars to avoid the sites.) The crowds had begun to gather as early as 5 A.M. at the PIN "food banks"—which were being "managed" by the Black Muslims—in San Francisco, Oakland, Richmond, and East Palo Alto. By 9 A.M. about 13,000 people were jostling for positions in the long lines, but the first trucks delivering the food did not pull out of the PIN warehouse until shortly before noon. As the trucks reached the Black Muslims' Shabazz Bakery, the PIN site in Oakland, a crowd of several thousand blocked the street. When the lead driver tried to beep his way through, someone heaved a pop bottle through the windshield. The crowd became a mob.

People clambered onto the trucks and began tossing food into the sea of bodies surrounding the vehicles: cans of tomato juice, boxes of biscuit mix and soda crackers, cartons of eggs, quarts of milk, frozen turkey hindquarters—singly and by the box. Pushing and fighting broke out. Several people were injured by the thrown food and cans. Gangs of kids cruised the streets, breaking windows, relieving some people of their armloads of food at knife point. In all, twenty-one people were treated at Oakland hospitals, including a woman, Paula Atkinson, who lost her right eye when someone hurled a rock through the window of her car. (She later filed suit against Hearst, PIN, and the city of Oakland, seeking $1 million in damages.)

The trucks were emptied in less than an hour. Thousands who had waited hours for the free food went home with nothing at all. Hundreds tried to storm the Muslim bakery demanding PIN food that wasn't there. The Muslims said afterward they had been forced to dole out fish and eggs from their own food stocks to prevent the bakery from being looted. (The next day the Muslims submitted an astronomical bill—$154,000, PIN officials said later—for the 150,000 pounds of fish and 820 cases of eggs they said they gave away in PIN's stead. Kramer went through the roof, and even the coalition radicals winced at the claim. But PIN eventually coughed up a check to the Muslims for $99,026. Kramer, at the time, said only: "These are difficult days.") The Muslims were not taken up on subsequent offers to manage PIN centers again.

At the other three centers that first day there was no violence, but much pushing, shoving, and dissatisfaction. PIN had promised a nutritional package. "Now, you explain to me how my kids are going to be healthy eating this," demanded one man, opening a grocery sack containing four cans of tomato juice and six boxes of pancake mix.

PIN was a disorganized shambles. Scores of volunteers recruited in a public appeal slaved all hours trying to make it work, but the program was burdened with inept leadership from Kramer, a ridiculous time schedule, and total inexperience. Hearst wanted the food out quickly, and Kramer had optimistically promised that his volunteers could purchase, transport, distribute, and package food for 20,000 grocery sacks in three days. With pros handling the logistics and an army supply company for manpower, it would have been difficult—with just volunteers, it was absurd. And these were not the United Fund type of volunteers Kramer had relied on in Washington. "At the warehouse," said Paul Andrews, an unemployed Yale graduate who ended up as one of the warehouse supervisors, "we had—working side by side—militant blacks, fashion models, pensioners, hippies, brewery workers, PhD's, architects, ex-cons, society-page sorts, a guy who called himself Cowboy, who was your basic shit-kickin' Nashville stomper type, and, yeah, one really strange man who later got busted for having a bomb factory in his house."

A PIN volunteer who claimed national notoriety over a year later was Sara Jane Moore, a divorcée from Danville, California, who attempted to assassinate President Gerald R. Ford during a San Francisco public appearance on September 22, 1975. (Mrs. Moore, a dowdy forty-five, labored slavishly as the PIN bookkeeper during the program, a key member of the administrative staff. Her stint at PIN introduced her to a circle of Bay Area radicals, and the FBI recruited her as an informant and kept her circulating among the Bay Area Left hunting SLA clues. Unsteady in both politics and personality, Mrs. Moore had revealed her FBI connection in the media and proclaimed herself a revolutionary before she attempted to shoot the President.) PIN collected an odd retinue.

People were just walking into the warehouse and walking out with food during the first few days, then Kramer hired Pinkerton guards. "They didn't last long," explained one volunteer. "One morning we caught four of them loading their cars with food they had stolen from the warehouse." The Pinkertons were fired and Kramer hired Jack Webb, a former San Francisco police inspector, whose staff of security guards tightened up the warehouse— but could do nothing about thefts from delivery trucks or the large-scale rip-offs from the food banks; the distribution sites were manned solely by local volunteers recruited by the coalition of radical groups the SLA had appointed to oversee PIN.

The "community groups" named as the watchdogs for the Symbionese Liberation Army were a mixed bag of activist organizations representing a wide range of philosophies and goals. They included Glide Memorial Church, Nairobi College (a community college for minorities), the National Welfare Rights Organization, the Black Teachers Caucus, the American Indian Movement, the

United Farm Workers, the Third World Women's Alliance, and the United Prisoners Union. The United Farm Workers refused at the outset to become involved and instead sent a message of sympathy to the Hearsts. Few of the others wanted to become publicly associated with the SLA; it was probably only the leadership and persuasion of the Reverend A. Cecil Williams, the activist black pastor of Glide Church, that convinced the others to join in a coalition, playing off mingled sympathies for feeding hungry people and saving Patty Hearst. The first statement of the group totally disavowed the SLA's tactics. (The SLA had also asked the Black Panther Party newspaper and other underground publications to be PIN "observers," but after Kramer rejected what some thought to be a grandstand offer from Black Panther leader Huey Newton to take total charge of the food giveaway, the Panthers withdrew entirely.) Local leaders of the American Indian Movement announced that their followers wanted nothing bought with the SLA's "blood money," but AIM's national leaders—Russell Means and Dennis Banks—agreed to work with the coalition at the pleading of Hearst.

Attending those first stormy coalition sessions, "Randolph Hearst's mind opened up to a lot of things," said Reverend Williams later. "It was incredible seeing him sitting there, his eyes darting from one speaker to the next, the look on his face saying, 'I didn't know any of this existed.'" (Individually, many of the coalition members sought out Hearst to explain and push their organizations. Perhaps as a result of such discussions, Hearst's *Examiner* would soon dispatch a reporter to Minnesota to cover the Wounded Knee trial of AIM's Banks and Means and to launch a lengthy and costly investigation into conditions at the San Francisco county jail.)

In the February 21 tape General Field Marshal Cinque gave a sharper edge to the coalition when it named WAPAC, a hard-line black radical group, to chair the coalition, giving it veto power over all decisions concerning PIN.

WAPAC, the Western Addition Project Area Committee, was a federally funded urban-development project founded in 1968. Involved in community organizing in San Francisco, WAPAC drew a number of radical black activists and had recently been caught up in the violent struggle between Cleaver's East Coast Black Panther faction—out of which the Black Liberation Army was born—and the Oakland-based Newton Panther faction. The Cleaver/BLA faction dominated WAPAC.

When the coalition met after the first PIN handout, WAPAC

leader Arnold Townsend took the lead in attacking Kramer, and other coalition members added their own scathing criticisms. Not only had the distribution been a disaster, but the coalition was finding Kramer's attitude condescending, not just to the coalition members but to the people PIN was attempting to feed. (A PIN volunteer who worked closely with Kramer described his attitude toward the PIN recipients as "a John Foster Dulles 1955 foreign-aid approach—you know, liberals giving food to the natives to get Patty back . . . to fight Communism, if you like.")

Hearst left PIN to Kramer and the coalition; he had problems enough trying to figure out his next response to the kidnappers. His basic rule for dealing with the SLA had been to accept them for what they said they were and to treat them with respect. That was becoming increasingly difficult. Hearst had called in as a consultant Dr. Frederick Hacker, a Los Angeles psychiatrist with an international reputation in the field of terrorist negotiations. In the family councils Dr. Hacker urged that Hearst's next response contain some sort of timetable, some deadline for Patty's release. The FBI stayed at a distance, offering little advice, wanting to avoid any blame over the outcome. Steve Weed repeatedly pleaded with Hearst to make a detailed public accounting of his wealth that would spell out the limits of his personal finances and the restrictions on the estate fortune.*

---

*The distinction between what Hearst could "get his hands on" and the other monies he all but habitually claimed—the legalistic line between his own fortune and the family hoard he and his brothers could manipulate and enjoy but could never actually possess—was something the SLA could never comprehend. It was also something that Hearst himself, in habit and practice, had always chosen to leave ambiguous. (Patty herself had once written her sister Anne complaining that her father had been upset when the son of one of the non-Hearst trustees of the Hearst Corporation visited Wyntoon, the corporation-owned resort estate in Northern California. Patty had told her father that she thought since she and her sisters could enjoy Wyntoon at their pleasure, the sons and daughters of the other trustees, Hearsts or not, had as much right. Her father had responded angrily. "He was saying things like, 'Well, the other men [trustees] are polite enough not to go up there.' Like this should be reserved *only* for Hearsts. As a matter of fact," Patty told Anne, "it's not *like* he was saying that, he *was* saying that. He said, 'Well, your grandfather built it and we're the only ones that belong up there!") Proverbially, possession is nine-tenths of the law. Subjectively, possession is ownership. Perhaps Mr. Hearst resisted the obvious tack of spelling out just what was his, and what not, out of private habit—or perhaps the convoluted legalisms of the whole trust structure relied on a calculated ambiguity, a blurred authority that could sometimes be read one way or the other. The private realities remain unclear.

Weed was perhaps underestimating the difficulty in explaining why Hearst could not draw on the family trust—particularly since the estate had already contributed $1.5 million—but his view of Randolph Hearst's reluctance to open his ledgers to the world is illuminating. "I had the really distinct feeling," said Weed, "and I think I was entirely accurate, that he could just not begin to understand how people—very intelligent people, included—could fail to understand his financial status." To Hearst the distinction between *his* money and the trust/corporation funds was self-evident to the sane—and those like the SLA who assumed it was all one big pile were uneducable.

It was in the midst of the disastrous first PIN distribution, on February 22, that Randolph Hearst, accompanied by Charles Gould, publisher of the *Examiner,* stepped before the forest of microphones and cameras outside the Hillsborough mansion. The SLA's escalated demand—$4 million more—had come two days before, and this was the eagerly awaited response from Patty's father.

Randolph Hearst made only a brief one-paragraph statement ("grimly" was the popular adverb in the press): "The size of the latest demand of the SLA is far beyond my financial capability. Therefore, the matter is out of my hands." With that, the president and editor of the *Examiner* turned his back and stepped aside, and the publisher—his employee, but an officer of the corporation as well—stepped forth in his place.

"I am Charles Gould with a message from the Hearst Corporation," he said. "The Hearst Corporation is prepared to contribute to People in Need a total of four million dollars for a food distribution for the poor and needy, provided Patricia Hearst is released unharmed.

"Two million dollars will be contributed immediately upon the release of Patricia and two million more will be contributed in January, 1975. This January payment will be evidenced by a binding agreement with People in Need.

"Neither the Hearst Corporation nor the Hearst foundations are controlled by members of the Hearst family. No other funds will be committed by the corporation or foundations under any circumstances."

It was the Hearst challenge to the Symbionese Liberation Army, the first formula for Patty's release, the first direct statement of *quid pro quo* in the two weeks of pseudonegotiations—and it was presented with an air of dramatic finality. The Hearst trustees,

again with family members abstaining, had met in New York—
from which distance the SLA picked up the solidity of a distant
nation; the substance of headlines without the ranting irrational-
ity of full exposure—and had approved the $4 million payoff, but
only if it was to be a businesslike ransom. With a mixture of poker-
table tough talk and boardroom legalisms, the corporate directors
offered the California Revolution their pledge for $2 million on
delivery and a note of indebtedness for a delayed payment of $2
million more ten months later. This to the screaming fanatics in
the hills? Even in New York it must have sounded strange; in
Hillsborough it should have sounded silly; in Berkeley it sounded
absurd. To the SLA, wherever they were, it must have sounded as
incredible as their own communiqués did in Terre Haute.

The SLA's noncommittal attitude toward the release of their
victim, the way they avoided any mention of the final ransom,
keeping up the constant threat of the *next* demand, had forced the
initiative on Hearst, just as their stupidity had forced him to come
up with his own plan for the food distribution. The SLA had
adopted the role of a parole board—and they probably expected
the Hearsts to be as resigned to arbitrary power as a state prisoner
and his family must be. But with Patty a captive now eighteen
days, with no release in sight, the Hearsts had decided they somehow had to call the hand of the SLA and force a resolution to free
their daughter.

It was a basic clash of realities. The SLA claimed the legitimacy of
a new nation, an "army" under the Geneva Convention, and all the
arbitrary prerequisites of a state penal system. The Hearsts had to
bow to these illusions in addressing Patty's kidnappers, but, of
course, they never accepted them. The SLA never took a measure
of the family's emotions, never expected such rebellion, never
realized that they had set up a paradigm of the prisons' indeterminate-sentence system—and that Hearst's reaction was the inevitable result. Beyond that, the SLA and Randolph Hearst simply
spoke different languages (the communiqués versus the time-pay-
ment ransom contract); what was real for one was illusion for the
other. The SLA (with their "ruling class" xenophobia) could no
more believe that the Hearst Corporation was truly independent of
the Hearst family than Randolph Hearst (with his bourgeois ethic)
could publicly announce that the SLA was demanding money from
the Hearst estate, not him, and should henceforth address themselves to the trustees.

"I was pushing Randy," recalled Weed later. "I didn't really want the Hearsts to throw open their books—just to get out there and set up some type of believable framework. To beg a little and say, this I can do and this I can't. But begging doesn't come easy to Randy. He went out there talking to the cameras like the chairman of the board, but when he came back in, you could almost see him sag. We didn't know what to do, and the advice we had right along was pretty shaky. You have to remember that at this time the only SLA people we really knew anything about were DeFreeze and Perry—probably the two craziest people in the group! A spun-out black con and a Berkeley doper who cut her finger and wrote 'kill the pigs' on a wall with her own blood! That's all we had to go on! That's all!

"In those first weeks I knew things were going bad. I think I saw the troubles better than most—certainly better than anyone at the house—but I didn't see what I could do or say that would do more good than harm. I kept trying to prod Randy. . . . I'd push him until his temper began to show, then I'd back off." The exasperation evident in his voice even months later, Weed concluded, "I think it's accurate to say that throughout I was relatively perceptive but ineffectual—pretty good description of an intellectual, huh? . . .

"Of course," he mused, "if the SLA hadn't been so scatter-brained, they could have done a number on the Hearst Corporation. The legal things could have tied up the foundations, but if pressed, the corporation could have come up with a truckload of money. Sane revolutionaries could have really bled them. Even Randy could have gotten a lot more money together if he had been pressed. But the way Randy responded to the demands was conditioned by who was making the demands. The Tupamaros or a group like the South American guerrillas could have got a bundle from the Hearsts. The SLA just slit their own throats with their demands."

But because the SLA kept their collective eye on the flesh-and-blood rather than the corporate Hearst, the trustees never had to confront a direct demand from the terrorists. And with the—to them—obvious necessity of forcing a climax, the trustees could set a final price, feeling, quite reasonably, that they were acting in Patty's best interest. Because time rather than money had become most important, the trustees were able to avoid the hideous question of where the cutoff was: At what amount would they declare themselves unwilling to ransom Patricia Hearst? Still, the family and the trustees had agreed to pay the $6 million for the life of

Patty, making her—undoubtedly and certifiably—the most expensive twenty-year-old on the face of the planet.

Now they waited. It would be two and a half weeks before the SLA would respond—a bitter, anguished period of silence for the Hearsts, who were extremely conscious of the SLA's threat to cut off communications if the $4 million wasn't put up immediately.

The PIN distributions went on in those weeks, always with difficulty, but with the administrators and coalition overseers ironing out many of the problems as the program continued. Despite the logistical difficulties in handling the spoilable fresh meats and produce the SLA demanded, PIN was able to upgrade steadily the quality of the food packages. Kramer, however, never learned the dangers of making optimistic promises—after the first giveaway he said again that PIN, when "geared up," would feed 100,000 people a month and continue "month after month after month"— and he constantly had collisions with the coalition, which called him on every exaggeration. He took it as more than personal criticism; he saw it as a plot. "Kramer's paranoia," said one coalition delegate, "reached the point where he believed that not only was the coalition out to destroy PIN—but Lud Kramer as well. When he started going around with a bodyguard and a police dog, I, for one, began to wonder just what sort of person we were dealing with." But among some coalition members, too, bodyguards became fashionable.

The second PIN distribution, on February 28, was a vast improvement over the first. Kramer claimed afterward that 30,000 people carried away sacks of "top quality" foodstuffs. But WA-PAC's Townsend said his observers at the "food banks" estimated the count to be only 15,000 and the value of each grocery sack was but $8. The third giveaway, on March 5—now at twelve sites— doled out between 35,000 (according to Kramer) and 25,000 (said Townsend) bags of food. Warehouse pilferage was under control by this time, but the almost nonexistent structure for responsibility at the distribution centers—and the prohibition against police involvement—left the situation wide open for aggressive and/ or imaginative thieves. Nine truckloads of choice foods were either hijacked or stolen outright, at a loss of from $10,000 to $30,000 per truckload. In one instance a volunteer drove off to an Oakland distribution center with $20,000 worth of canned hams. Neither the driver, the hams, nor the donated truck was ever seen again. The young man had simply walked in, asked for something to do, and a PIN staffer had handed him the keys. No one had asked his name. In another case a truck filled with poultry was hijacked at pistol point en route to a San Francisco center.

California's Governor Reagan had confidently stated at the outset that few people would accept food that was ransom for a kidnap victim. When it became evident that thousands would line up, he publicly accused the recipients—not PIN or the Hearsts—of "aiding and abetting lawlessness." On March 6, addressing a private luncheon meeting in Washington, D.C., of the Bull Elephants, a club of powerful Republicans, the governor touched on the PIN program, glibly suggesting, "It's just too bad we can't have an epidemic of botulism." When a shocked congressional aide leaked the incredible quote to a reporter, Reagan reluctantly admitted having said it. "It was a joking remark," he explained, "but I do deplore the fact that these people are accepting the food." Later Reagan said he did not feel the botulism comment would have any effect on his then-talked-of presidential ambitions. Later still, he publicly apologized.

(Later, when PIN was no longer the sacred ransom, many commentators would turn on the food recipients. It was easy to fault the food lines: Many in the crowds were vulgar and boisterous, thefts were commonplace, big new cars pulled away from the PIN centers, stuffed with sacks of food, with disturbing regularity. But overall, PIN handed out about 100,000 food packages in the poorest communities of the San Francisco Bay Area, and most people in the lines were patient and grateful, a large number of them elderly, particularly in the later distributions.)

After nine days passed with no reply from the SLA to the take-it-or-leave-it offer of the Hearst Corporation, Randolph and Catherine Hearst issued a plea to the kidnappers to allow Patty to communicate with them. Addressing his daughter directly, facing the TV cameras, Hearst played to the SLA's claim that Patty was being held under the Geneva Convention, under the protection of international codes of war: "Of course it's ridiculous to think that under the Geneva Convention that we would be allowed to go in and see you . . . but under the convention you are allowed to write from time to time to other people. See if they'll let you send us a note or something to let us know you're okay." Added Mrs. Hearst: "Patty, honey, your father's doing everything in his power, and I want you to know that millions of people all over the world are praying for you. I know it's been a long time, sweetheart . . . but keep up your courage and you keep praying."

The silence continued. The media had shifted attention to the

PIN effort in the first days of the lull; now the story drew only brief mention on inside pages. The ongoing escalation of the Watergate scandals, the gasoline crisis, and a crippling strike by teachers and municipal workers captured the headlines in San Francisco. Silent, the SLA was less and less real.

The San Francisco FBI chief, Charles Bates, repeatedly denied the persistent rumor that the SLA hideout had been located; another FBI source was quoted as saying the bureau was "still a little away" from picking up any SLA suspects for interrogation. On March 6 Little and Remiro asked their attorneys to seek court permission for a live TV press conference in prison at which they would make "suggestions" for freeing Patty. On March 8 President Richard Nixon, citing the Hearst case, urged reinstatement of the death penalty for kidnappings in which the victim is murdered.

There was a fourth PIN distribution on the eighth; Kramer estimated that 35,000 people received food at the fourteen sites. Ben Lau, volunteer community coordinator for the Chinatown PIN center, said his helpers "gave out more than seven and one-half tons of fresh beef, fresh chicken, canned luncheon meat, fresh produce, dried milk, carrots, squash, and lettuce" in individual packages worth about $20 each. "People were receptive and appreciative," Lau said. But public opinion had turned against PIN; it was considered corrupt and futile, metaphorically equivalent to the U.S. aid program to South Vietnam.

There would be a fifth and final PIN distribution on March 25, but when the SLA finally broke their silence with an angry and bitter communiqué on March 9—a week after Hearst's plea—they effectively ended the food-ransom stage of the negotiations; indeed, there was a question whether they had not ended the negotiations, period.

The day before that communiqué arrived, in New Jersey nineteen-year-old Larry DeAngelis received a smuggled letter from his sister Angela. "It was almost a good-bye letter," he said. "She wrote that this would probably be the last time she'd be able to risk getting in touch with me." The DeAngelis family had been questioned by the FBI, but was still desperately hoping that Angela—as she had told them—was merely traveling somewhere in Canada. Now she wrote, "I think it's about time I told you where I'm at. . . ." There was no direct mention of the SLA, but the implication was clear. "She rapped a lot about the living conditions of the poor in California," said Larry. "She said she could no longer see people eating dog food and do nothing about it." Angela wrote that she and her friends were going to be "liberating the people." And if the fight went badly, she said in that letter, "I'm willing to die for my cause." She bid love to all in the family and signed off with the nickname she had forbidden her Berkeley friends—"Angel," with the halo atop the *g*.

The March 9 tape-recorded communiqué introduced Angela for the first time as General Gelina, and it was she who was the featured speaker of the SLA screed. The voice surprised those who knew Angela; the battered grammar, the broad accent, and the snarled black slang were unlike the speech patterns of the articulate amateur actress who had taken voice lessons to rid herself of a New Jersey twang. More striking still were the voices of two unidentified women chanting incantations against the fascist state—they actually faked, quite effectively to many white ears, black accents. This was the longest communiqué yet, the least decisive, the least reasonable, the most hysterical:

"After extensive nationwide intelligence and analysis by the Symbionese War Council," Gelina said, "it became clear [to us] that the fascist corporate state and its chief domestic agency, the FBI, and other police-state agencies and institutions intended to set up Patricia Hearst for execution in order to discredit and isolate the people's forces.

"This is shown by the deliberate disregard for the health, life, and safety of Joseph Remiro and Russell Little and the plans of the police-state agencies to see to it that Patricia Hearst is killed." (The reference to the imprisoned SLA soldiers apparently referred to the fact they had been held since arrest in the dreaded Adjustment Center—the "hole," where the "worst" of convicts are confined—at San Quentin prison. On March 8, the day before, Remiro and Little had been transferred to the Alameda county jail, in Oakland, by order of a court.)

"Despite FBI claims that they would not do anything to endanger Patricia Hearst's life, they have raided homes throughout the country, knowing full well that to do so would endanger the life of Patricia Hearst.

"The plans of the police-state agency are to see to it that Patricia Hearst is killed and then use her death to further rally Middle America in support of the Nixon-represented corporate dictatorship and against all revolutionary forces.

"The fascist state and the FBI have attempted to manipulate public opinion in support of Patricia Hearst's safety and eventual return while at the same time creating conditions that it knows would force her execution, saving them the embarrassment of doing it themselves.

"But we have repeatedly stated that Patricia Hearst's safety, execution, or freedom is totally her family's and its class' responsibility. . . . U.S. Attorney General William Saxbe's statement that the FBI should bust in to rescue the prisoner was no slip of the tongue, but was in reality a prematurely exposed government policy decision."

There was no room for a rational response, no room for an answer at all.

A major theme of Gelina's long statement was the almost absolute isolation of the SLA. There had been messages of support sent to the media from the Black Guerrilla Family and WO (two revolutionary prison groups), the Weather Underground, and the tiny Black Liberation Army, but since the Foster murder dozens of established leftist, black, and Chicano groups in California—including almost all the active and most militant—had taken stands, many publicly, flatly condemning the SLA as an enemy of the Left.

Russell Means, the militant radical leader of the American Indian Movement who had brought AIM into the PIN coalition over the objections of the local AIM leadership, bitterly denounced the SLA after the demand for the additional $4 million ransom. "My fears have been realized, and it looks like they're going to continue to make demand after demand," said Means, then standing trial for the Wounded Knee occupation. "The SLA is a punk organization; they are a one-shot organization."

Acknowledging "many on the Left who, without a clear understanding, have condemned the actions of the SLA and the people's forces who have chosen to fight rather than talk," Gelina bitterly attacked. "The analysis of these so-called leaders who presume to speak for the people can be traced to one of two qualities: Either they are cowards afraid of revolutionary violence because it is a direct threat to their personal security, or they are opportunists who have personal gains in allowing the enemy to enslave or oppress and tranquilize the people. . . . To this our bullets scream loudly." In great detail she reviewed the early bartering for Patty, managing to overlook completely all the SLA's mistakes and irrationalities, damning Hearst's actions as a single tissue of "lies and deceptions. . . . The people know his words don't make no bag of cabbages into meat," she said.

"Randolph Hearst responded deceitfully that he would not

meet financially the SLA requests . . . [and] as if Hearst had no connection with the Hearst Corporation, the corporation, supposedly out of the kindness of its corporate heart, responded that it would provide the additional four million dollars, but only after Patricia Hearst is released."

Hearst, she went on, must have assumed the SLA was "inexperienced in the area of corporate trickery." Not so: The people had learned "never to trust the words of the enemy."

"Communications and negotiations" are hereby suspended, Gelina said, and the War Council has decided that Patricia will be allowed to communicate with her family "periodically" only if Little and Remiro are allowed to "communicate via live national TV . . . concerning the full scope of their physical health and all the conditions of their confinement."

Then Gelina, in the echo of bedlam, introduced Patricia Hearst—whose statement, to the shock of many, restated and punctuated the SLA's incredible paranoia.

14

"Bye, Bye, Miss American Pie"
The Transformation of Patricia Hearst

THE voice of Patricia Hearst:

"Mom, Dad: I received the message you broadcast last Sunday. It was good to hear from you after so much silence. But what you had to say sounded like you don't care if I ever get out of here. All you want is to hear from me sometimes. Your silence definitely jeopardized my safety because it allows the FBI to continue to attempt to find me, and Governor Reagan to make antagonistic statements, with no response from you.

"I'm beginning to feel that the FBI would rather that I get killed. I'm telling you this now because I don't think the FBI will let any more words from me get through to the media. I hear that people all around the country keep calling on the SLA to release me unharmed. But the SLA are not the ones who are harming me. It's the FBI, along with your indifference to the poor, and your failure to deal with the people and the SLA in a meaningful, fair way."

In all her messages from captivity Patty clearly had in part been speaking for the SLA—spelling out their conditions, their demands, explaining their affiliations and ideology. What she had to say personally and what the SLA told her to say were always interwoven. It had become the expected formula. In the previous communiqués, however, the SLA rhetoric had seemed a burden to her. What Patty had been told to say seemed easily separated from her own brief messages. With this tape, received on March 9, that had changed. And for the first time a haunting question was framed: What had happened to Patty Hearst in the now thirty-odd days she had been held isolated, a prisoner of the Symbionese?

Strangely, the question had been little asked earlier. That it had to be asked—that anything *could* have happened to Patty's beliefs, personal and/or political—seemed to surprise the commentators and the public. From the stereotyped plots of our romantic literature, the police-story TV and cinema fare, there was a common impression that the girl's captivity at the hands of kidnappers who had savagely beaten her boyfriend and dragged her half naked from her apartment was either hostile or impersonal—and a common expectation that her reaction to it was frightened but coldly defiant.

That curiosity alone would dictate an effort to understand her captors; that her fear and her urge to survive would sensibly lead her to personalize her relationship with them; the likely possibility that these political kidnappers would want to explain themselves to her; and the more distant possibility that they would be men and women she could respect and relate to—all this was overlooked, by the public if not by the family. Dr. Frederick Hacker, the Los Angeles psychiatrist Hearst had retained as a consultant, warned the family in his first meeting with them to prepare for the possibility of Patty's developing some identification and affinity with her captors. "It happens all the time," he said. Emotional exposure due to captivity is as bad as if not worse than physical danger, he explained, and particularly in a political kidnapping or hostage situation. It is not uncommon for a victim to be unusually empathetic.

Patty's statement bit deeply with her rejection of her parents; from what she said, she obviously felt deeply betrayed by her father's "hard-line" approach to the SLA:

"I don't believe you're doing everything you can, everything in your power. I don't believe that you're doing anything at all. You said it was out of your hands; what you should have said was that you wash your hands of it. . . . Dad, you can't put the responsibility for my status on the corporation. You seem to be ignoring the fact that you are chairman of the board and Uncle Bill is president of the Hearst Corporation. I know that if anything happens to me, it will be because your corporation advisers and the FBI decided to protect their interests instead of my life.

"I don't know who influences you not to comply with the good-faith gesture. I know that you could have done it the way the SLA asked. I mean, I know that we have enough money. But it seems to me that you told the FBI to do whatever they decide is necessary to destroy the SLA. But it's becoming true, Dad."

Patty believed that her father had simply refused to put his own money up; that he was risking her life to save his purse. "We never sat down and went over personal finances with the kids," explained Hearst later. "Maybe we should have." He said that none of his children understood even the basic intricacies of the family finances. Patty had never asked—and had never been told—and obviously, he said, she had a much exaggerated idea of his personal wealth and his control over the family fortune.

A bitterness seethed through her words. She said she had heard reports about PIN, and "It sounds like you and your advisers have managed to turn it into a real disaster." As if it had been clear all along, she said that what the SLA had demanded was simply that each person get $70 worth of food all at once. She continued:

"Mom, I can't believe that you've agreed with the 'out of my hands' stance of Daddy's program. I just wish you could be stronger and pull yourself together from all these emotional outbursts and see if you can persuade Dad to listen to you and the rest of the family. You seem to be allowing other people to make your decisions.

"Your statements, if I can call them that, have given the FBI the go-ahead to kill me. I wish God would touch your heart and get you to do something concrete to help me. I wish I knew what the rest of my family was thinking and saying. It's hard to believe that my sisters and cousins aren't saying anything.

"If it had been you, Mom, or you, Dad, who had been kidnapped instead of me, I know that I and the rest of the family and your friends would do anything to get you back. It could have been one of you, and how would you feel if you had been written off the way I seem to have been?

"I'm starting to think that no one is concerned about me anymore. I wish that I could hear from the rest of the family. I'd like to hear what my sisters have to say about Dad's decision not to comply with the terms of the good-faith gesture.

"Steven, what do you have to say? Willie, I know you really care about what happens to me. Make Dad let you talk. You can't be silent. . . ."

Only in hindsight is there any near certainty that this was Patty speaking her own mind. But even at the time, there was something in the tone, in the temper of the logic, and in the little personal references, such as the call to "Willie" (William Randolph Hearst III, her favorite cousin), that made family and others close to the girl fear that this was Patty voicing her own opinions—saying things she would never have said before the kidnapping, but speaking her own mind.

Her anger and despair were understandable, particularly from her isolated perspective, but the shock was in where she leaped from there—or where she allowed herself to be led:

"I've heard the reports concerning the FBI investigation and interrogations. Governor Reagan's careless and antagonistic remarks, and the attempt of the federal agencies to maneuver the news media to mentally prepare the public for my death, calling for mass prayers and petitions to the SLA for my release.

"From this I am forced to draw only one conclusion—that the FBI and other federal agencies want me to die. I no longer seem to have any importance as a human being; rather, I have become all-important as a political pivot point for certain right-wing elements. And I can only be used successfully by these people if I am killed.

"As for the constant reassurances by the FBI that my safety is their primary concern, I can only say that the FBI has never been famous for its concern for the safety of hostages. From what I've seen so far this case is no different. Whether consciously or not, the news media has been assisting the FBI in its now overt attempts to set me up for execution. It has done this primarily in two ways.

"First, by promoting a public image of my father as a bereaved parent who has done all he can to meet the demands of his daughter's kidnappers, and who now awaits her supposedly long-overdue release. In fact, the SLA demands have not even been approximated, and they have made it very clear that until the good-faith gesture is completed, negotiations for my release will not begin. Second, the media, with cooperation from my parents, has created a public image of me as a helpless, innocent girl who was supposedly abducted by two terrible blacks, escaped convicts. I'm a strong woman and I resent being used this way. . . ."

The ring of the "strong woman" remark and the exhortation to her mother seemed to indicate that Patty's sense of herself as a feminist had been inflated considerably during her captivity. But, then, most of the Symbionese were feminist extremists. (One of the two phony black voices on the same tape called on "Comrade Sisters" to avenge themselves on the oppressor: "We women know the truth as it has been revealed in our own lives. We turn our rage toward the enemy in a direct line, right down the sights of our guns.") Clearly, Patty had been talking with her captors. No longer was she just the frightened and angry girl who had been kidnapped; for a month now she had been sharing tight quarters with the SLA people, listening, talking, listening—all the while getting more impatient with the ransom delays. She had changed, adopted some of the suspicions of the SLA, and conceded that the world was an unjust place. Those were the first steps, and there were more, of course—each step, each concession less rooted in the daily realities outside her little prison.

Patty's expressed conviction that the FBI would murder her to smear the Symbionese indicates a political paranoia that originated entirely within her SLA experience, the baggage of a tutored captive. The motivation offered is absurd—reflecting the SLA's exaggerated sense of their own importance—but it is clear from where the SLA drew this fear and how they transferred it on Patty. The forces of law enforcement do in fact balance two often conflicting values—protection of the innocent, on the one hand, and the apprehension of criminals, on the other. The record of the FBI in kidnap cases shows a clearly stressed concern for the innocent (less decisive is their response to airplane hijackers, as witness the many daring and risky hijack captures). But in prison revolts, even when hostages are threatened, the lawmen's stress seems invariably to fall on the apprehension of the criminals— even at the high risk or certainty of sacrificing the hostages. (Such cases rarely involve the FBI, but radicals tend to generalize to imply the bureau's ubiquitous influence.) And it is in this context, the cellblock perspective, that the SLA framed their realities.

When Gelina (Angela Atwood) first claimed the FBI was trying to kill Patty, she argued the point with a direct comparison to two of the most infamous assaults on convicts holding hostages—the 1971 charge on Attica prison by New York State Police (in which ten hostages and twenty-nine convicts were all killed by gunfire of the attacking police) and the 1970 incident at the Marin County Courthouse in which California prison guards opened fire on a van containing escaping convicts and hostages. The logic of such vengeful—and usually death-inflicting—attacks eludes most who are not prison officials, and surely the SLA's news clippings and other documentary evidence of these incidents and other penal horrors would be enough to disorient and sow doubt in the mind of the girl Cinque had described as so vacantly innocent, one who had "never seen the robbed or knew that the riches of her life were the spoils of a robber and murderer."

"In the last few days," she said, "members of the Federation have spoken with me. They have given me some newspaper reports to read about the current practices of psychosurgery and the use, daily, of drugs and tranquilizers in prisons throughout the country. I have also been given some journal commentaries about kinds of conditions that exist in prisons in general and in the Adjustment Center at San Quentin in particular. Members of the Federation have also given me a choice of books to read. I have been reading a book by George Jackson called *Blood in My Eye.* I'm starting to understand what he means when he talks about fascism in America.

"Members of the Federation are studying intelligence reports gathered by the SLA on the activities of the FBI. These, combined with discussions the members of the Federation have had with me, and my own observations of the way my father has been conducting himself, have made me afraid; because I realize that the plans are coming from the FBI and the Attorney General's office in Washington to execute the two men in San Quentin. Or, if that cannot be swiftly accomplished, to execute me by seeing to it that even if I am released I will not get home alive. Or by attempting to raid this place where I am being held, then discredit the SLA by saying that they were the ones who killed me.

"Because of these dangers, I have been transferred to a special security unit of the SLA combat forces, where I am being held in protective custody. I have been issued a twelve-gauge riot shotgun, and I have been receiving instructions on how to use it. While I have no access to ammunition, in the event of an attack by the FBI, I have been told that I will be given an issue of cyanide buckshot in order to protect myself. Because it is the Federation's opinion, and my own from observation, that if the FBI does rush in, they will obviously be doing it against the wishes of my family and in total disregard for my safety. In fact, they would be doing it to murder me.

"Under international codes of war I am allowed to communicate with members of my family and, because of the scope of this incident, with the public as well. However, I should tell you that the practice of allowing me to communicate with you will not continue until the SLA hears from the two men at San Quentin. They want to hear what the two men have to say in a live nationwide broadcast, so they can hear all the conditions of their confinement.

"I really want to get out of here and I really want to get home alive. I am appealing to the public and asking them not to assist the FBI in their investigation. Doing so is simply helping them to dig my grave. And I ask those people who say they pray for me and those who sign petitions to the SLA for my safe release to redirect their energies into opposing the FBI's brutal attempts to murder me and the two men in San Quentin.

"I no longer fear the SLA, because they are not the ones who want me to die. The SLA want to feed the people and assure the safety and justice for the two men in San Quentin. I realize now it is the FBI who want to murder me. Only the FBI and certain people in the government stand to gain anything by my death."

She had been captive a month, and it would be nearly another full month before Patricia Hearst would declare herself Tania—and later still before she would demonstrate her willingness to rob, threaten, and perhaps kill to validate her instant revolution. But already she had changed. This was already a very different girl from the nineteen-year-old UC Berkeley junior who had been kidnapped, the rich, conventionally vague liberal who had been living such a quiet life with her fiancé. What was happening to her?

The Tania transformation was so surprising that many could cope with it only by assuming that there had been no change, that she had been a part of the scheme to begin with—all evidence to the contrary. Her shift of politics was one thing—liberals forced to confront personally the reality of poverty and injustice might well think differently of "reforms" that most often are slow and directionless—but there was much more in the "rebirth" of Tania. Here was a bright, mentally healthy young woman who in time would be persuaded to declare that she—"as a member of the ruling class"—had known all along of a "corporate state" plot to automate the nation totally and then to remove the "expendable excess" peoples; that she as a ruling-class teenager had been bred to the knowledge of the grand scheme to exterminate millions. And having known about that, she explained, she should have realized that her "corporate" parents and the corporate state were of course willing to sacrifice her.

How was she brought to accept so quickly—against all experience and education—the political and intellectual depravity of the Symbionese Liberation Army?

The chemistry of her conversion was likely a complex formula—and the extent of its success was perhaps a great surprise to the SLA members themselves. But many of the pressures and conditions that fed into the process can be identified, some psychological, some situational, some almost mechanical (like the elapsing time, days into weeks). Some, such as the improbable middle-aged-married life-style in which she had encased the vibrant years of her teens, were personal eccentricities, the choice of the girl herself. In the experience of Patty there was much that was peculiar to her—the wealth, the upbringing, the family, the burden of the name Hearst itself—that might have bred its own reaction.

But the transformation was so extraordinary, and the result so ridiculous (even in the eyes of the prekidnapping Patty herself), that resentment and rebellion seem inadequate motives. While they might justify rejection of her family and her past, they would not bind her to the SLA.

Several months later she would declare her great love for the SLA's Cujo, young Willie Wolfe, but certainly she must have already opened herself to these people before she would allow herself to love one of her captors. In an army rife with militant feminists, it seems unlikely sex would not be used to lure or punish. Patty would be taken only with her consent. Cujo may or may not have rejoined his comrades by the time of the kidnapping (a Valentine signed by Willie, postmarked from New York, was mailed to his mother in Litchfield, Connecticut, a week *after* the abduction), but in any event it is doubtful that it was love at first sight. The groundwork for that love and for the transformation had to be in her gradual acceptance of the SLA's legitimacy, in her political "rebirth."

Perhaps the most important element in the process—aside from the fact she was a captive, isolated for a prolonged period—was the attitude with which the SLA members approached the girl. The SLA soldiers thought of themselves as pragmatic Maoists, and most were known to have studied intensely the tactics and theory of Chinese Communism; from this study they brought certain attitudes and expectations into their relationship with Patty.

The Chinese attitude toward "class enemies" differed markedly from that of the Soviet Communists; the Soviets marked huge populations of class enemies for extermination or slave labor, but the Chinese Communists concentrated on "reforming" or "reeducating" those designated enemies of the people. In practice and theory the stress was on attacking the "wrong" ideas and salvaging the person for a productive role in society. The concept was developed both out of Chinese tradition and out of the exigencies of the early history of the party. Confronted with a feudal agrarian China, Mao Tse-tung had adapted classical Marxism by rejecting the insistence of Marx and Lenin that only the urban proletariat, the industrial working class, could be the class agent of the Communist revolution. Building his Chinese Communist Party from the rural peasantry, Mao argued that while an individual's political and social behavior was defined by his class origins (as Marx had claimed), these origins do not *irrevocably* fix political attitudes and that "proper" class behavior can be *learned* and *unlearned.*

In dealing with Patty, then, it can be deduced that the SLA both expected that they could influence or "educate" Patty into changing her upper-class values and politics—and that they attempted to do so, if only to validate further their own commitment. (The concept of "thought reform" through indoctrination also gave them hope within the hostile bourgeois society: As they gained power, they could "educate." As Joe Remiro told the San Francisco *Phoenix*: "We have a bunch of people that have to go through cultural revolutions, people who have to go through a lot of education and a lot of learning. The best thing Mao did for the Chinese people was to educate the *hell* out of them, educate the *hell* out of them.")

On the run, the SLA lived collectively, all of them crowded together in small houses or apartments, and it seems likely that Patty was drawn into the reeducation process at least partially by being physically present during the confronting "consciousness-raising" sessions SLA associates said the group constantly held among themselves. Angela, Bill, Emily, Nancy, Willie—most of the SLA, in fact—had also come from "improper" class origins (upper-middle-class, well-to-do families), and once they made their commitment it was through these intense "criticism–self-criticism" sessions that they tried to refine their "consciousness" and educate their daily lives to the values and ideology first of Maoist Communism (in the Venceremos study groups) and then, among themselves, to the weird amalgam of the SLA philosophy.* They were constantly attempting to confront, root out, and destroy the remnants of bourgeois American values within themselves. The impact and intensity of these self-critical "study sessions" can be extraordinary—particularly when they are inte-

---

*One document found in the Harrises' apartment when police raided it was a Venceremos form which was to be used in filling out a weekly progress report; a self-critical psychological and political profile that was to be submitted to "leadership." One of the eight points to be reviewed before writing the weekly "PP" was titled "Ideological Remolding": "What are the specific criticisms cadre and non-cadre have had of you and what have you done about it? Under Ideological Remolding you should deal with your *own* subjectivity towards the area of your work. Also include a criticism of how you have been acting in the two week period (example: mainly talking to others about personal things or other people, gossip, or mainly talking about political work). Also write down what you study and who with."

grated into the daily pattern of life in an isolated, hermetic environment. The SLA set up such an environment within their collective, much as the SDS-Weathermen splinter faction had in 1969–70. (In both cases the nested ideologues drifted further and further out of touch with life on the "outside," although for the Weathermen the shock of the accidental deaths of three of their "soldiers" in a bomb-factory explosion was enough to force them to reevaluate their position.)

For Patricia Hearst captivity was surely a constantly changing, challenging environment, and the debate was always framed within the context of her captivity. She was a prisoner, her life in the hands of her captors—to be freed perhaps only when the SLA decided she was politically *ready* to be freed.

With what can be identified as factors in Patty's situation as a captive, the pieces fall together with a striking resemblance to what Americans have come to know and awkwardly misunderstand as the Chinese process of "brainwashing." The term refers to the intensive program for "reforming" recalcitrant individualists and bourgeois "class enemies," both Western and Chinese, that was part of Communist China's mass-indoctrination program, *Szu Hsiang Kai Tsao,* which translates as "thought reform" or "ideological remolding." The popular American assumptions about Chinese "brainwashing" have been misleading; even the word is misleading. A more explicit and appropriate phrase is that used by a team headed by Professor Edgar Schein, of the Massachusetts Institute of Technology, as the title of their 1961 book, *Coercive Persuasion,* still generally acknowledged as the seminal study of the Chinese thought-reform effort.

Westerners, in horror of the Orwellian collective, grappled to understand the reports of what was happening in the Chinese prisons in terms of our own cultural assumptions. Americans, in particular, were quick to identify thought reform (common in all Chinese penal institutions long before the Korean War) as the almost mechanical product of exotic "scientific" techniques, the brute side of the medical and psychological sciences. But the framework in which we sought to understand the inescapable evidence of phenomenal changes in personality and values among prisoners of the Chinese limited our appreciation of the frightening simplicity of the process; rather than consider the frailty of the individual mind, we looked for a mysteriously powerful tool or technique.

In fact, there is more "bending" than "breaking" of the victim, and the "brainwash" image of torture, drugs—the days-on-the-treadmill idea—is simply inaccurate and inadequate to explain the results: an often drastic and radical transformation of the individual which left the victim grateful and sincerely trying to adapt to the views of his captors. (The practice of the Soviets, in which the end was not individual reform but merely a "purge trial" confession to justify execution or exile, was entirely different.)

The technique used in Chinese coercive persuasion was evolved not by scientists but by political organizers, and the theory and practice developed not from Pavlovian psychology or the "insidious sciences," but rather in the framework of political debate and ideological education within groups. The intensive program that came to be labeled "brainwashing" entailed constant and fervent political debate within a coercive situation in which the individual was levered with the mass sway of a small peer group.

"[Basically] what happened to people was that they were subjected to unusually intense and prolonged persuasion in a situation from which they could not escape; that is, they were coerced into allowing themselves to be persuaded," stated Dr. Schein in his book. Explaining his phrase "coercive persuasion," he went on:

> We are not implying by the choice of this term that the experience of the victim was not painful. What we are trying to underline . . . is that the phenomenon with which we are dealing is a completely understandable one, and that it occurred in people who were not broken or psychotic during or after their imprisonment. By inserting the concept of persuasion we are further asserting that a genuine clash of beliefs and points of view was involved in many phases of the process. . . .

Dr. Schein and his colleagues made in-depth studies of the experiences of American civilians—many of them missionaries—imprisoned by the Chinese Communists between 1950 and 1956. They concluded that "persuasion" by articulate ideologues within a small preswayed peer group, over a lengthy period of isolation, can indeed result in dramatic and sincere political and personal change. No magic, no mystery; simply striking evidence of the delicate balance between man the individual and man the social creature.

Coercive persuasion is often associated solely with the Chinese, but the process is not alien to any culture. The Chinese state program provides a clear conceptual model—and because of the politics of the SLA, this may be particularly pertinent to the Hearst case—but the same sort of intensive social conditioning is used in milder forms through the mainstream of education and, rarely, in the extreme forms on the political and religious fringe.

Just as the "hidden persuaders" of American advertising stroke repressed urges of greed, narcissism, and guilt; just as effective political rhetoric brings out latent feelings of patriotism, idealism, or arrogant nationalism, effective persuasion, even within a coercive context, plays to the repressed values and ideals (the fundamental contradictions, both conscious and subconscious) in the character of the subject.

Any analysis of coercive persuasion must be keyed to the process rather than the "content" of the persuading ideology (whatever its coherence, logic, or justice). It is the coercive context, the *inescapable,* challenging presence of the captors, that is central. But it is also necessary to acknowledge the unstable nature of personality and zeitgeist. The universal frailty of ego.

Patricia Hearst, the teenage "feminist" housewife, proud liberal heiress, renegade debutante planning a society-page marriage, had perhaps more contradictions than most (although her confusions of role and identity couldn't be too different from those of many nineteen-year-olds emerging from postadolescence). And similar contradictions haunt everyone, young or old. What is identity if not a temporary compromise of purist values, an unconscious balance of conflicting urges: the base and the saintly, the generous and the greedy? Ambivalence is at the core of self.

Personal values are defined in compromise—and personal values are further compromised adjusting to the social environment, the real world. The malignant power of coercive persuasion—apart from the threat and reality of captivity—is in the process of utterly isolating a single individual and then insistently confronting him with aggressive ideologues who are aware enough of the value contradictions to exploit them.

(There are obvious parallels between coercive persuasion and some of the behavior-modification programs in U.S. prisons, but there are also important distinctions, philosophical and logistical. Reports on the Chinese experience have repeatedly noted that the absolute isolation of a single individual—the submergence of one victim in a pressure group of several—is a key factor in the process. The presence of a single "ally," a second recalcitrant prisoner [one other person who could affirm the societal values of the victim's culture], markedly lessens the effectiveness of the process. In American prisons, the most ambitious of the "behavior-mod" rehabilitation program have been constantly foiled by the tough camaraderie of the convicts' outlaw culture. Another factor is more subtle: The bandit ethic of the criminal is but a slight perversion of the success ethic in a competitive capitalist society—the distinction between what the criminal "is" and what society wants him to become is often a matter of opportunity and resources, not a question of fundamental change in value scheme.)

Another subtle but important observation on the Chinese experience: The Chinese Communists were much more successful (at least with their white civilian captives) converting men who had no experience with the reality of Communist society. Others, who had seen the way the Maoist regime actually functioned, who could match the rhetorical idealism of their captors against the social reality of the ideal in practice, were considerably more resilient. The technique of coercive persuasion would seem to be most effective when used in service of a theoretical ideal, a utopian philosophy, an ideology of "human possibility," rather than any established social code or state dogma, each with its unavoidably flawed translation of the ideal into social reality.

Americans are more than ever aware of the myriad sects and cults that can spring up along the periphery of the mainstream culture. The alienation of the seventies spawned hundreds of small groups in an implosion of mysticism; groups with creeds often bizarre and alien, certainly many with beliefs no less strange than those of the SLA (although they rarely draw attention to themselves with violence). Virtually all of these groups gather voluntarily—as did the original SLA—but part of the phenomenon is the response to it, and in looking at that response, specifically the widely publicized work of Ted Patrick and his California group, which calls itself the Deprogrammers, one gets another angle on the concept of coercive persuasion.

Patrick, a black ultraconservative who for a time was an aide to California Governor Reagan, hires himself out to "deprogram" or "debrainwash" young devotees of odd religious cults. Over the past several years he has drawn considerable media attention and several lawsuits, although he has been generally protected by the authorities. Usually hired by the parents, Patrick and his assistants, mostly young fundamentalist Christians, literally kidnap the cultist (with the help of the parents) and hold him prisoner for several days in some secluded location, goading him to "use your mind" and reject the "false religion." He has successfully "deprogrammed" several hundred Jesus freaks from dozens of cults, as well as members of non-Christian groups such as Hare Krishna—bringing them to renounce their new faith and reconcile with their parents and family.

Some of the groups Patrick attacks seem eccentric and exploitive, and the leaders seem to exercise extraordinary control over their followers, hence the widespread public and political support his work has received. But with many groups, judgment is difficult—some have weird beliefs and others completely isolate their followers and dictate a withdrawal from family or social ties. But unquestionably their disciples enter them voluntarily, often fleeing home, personal problems, or just the chaos of the world in general. And certainly if anything is basic to the American ethic, however infringed upon by occasional laws, it is freedom of beliefs, freedom of religion. Yet Patrick and his assistants, and the parents of his "clients," have rarely been detained or challenged in court. Local police officers have been overwhelmingly sympathetic. There is widespread public acceptance that there must be something like "mind control"—perhaps Charles Manson is the classic model—and the blunt fact is that American law simply has no mechanism for testing such an accusation or taking it into account when trying an alleged criminal who claims to have been "brainwashed." (It is a very real problem that will haunt the Hearst case probably long after Patricia Campbell Hearst hears the final judgment upon her.) Yet Patrick simply has no idea of how or why he achieves the successes he does, reclaiming "lost souls" for their families and all-American values. In fact, he might be held up as a testamentary witness to the proposition that neither understanding nor comprehension is a necessary tool for coercive persuasion.

Patrick believes that most of the religious cults that have sprung out of the debris of the youth culture are organized and controlled by Communist agents from Cuba. Many of his fundamentalist helpers see the cults as satanic creations. (The first deprogramming of a Hare Krishna devotee several years ago entailed a classical Christian exorcism. The victim, a young woman, escaped through a window of the locked room to rejoin her group.) Patrick also believes that most of the cult members—particularly in the stranger, more authoritarian groups—are seduced by drugs or hypnotism (almost invariably false).

It brings up the question of who is programming and who is deprogramming, and clearly frames the basic question of whether anyone has any right to do either with coercion. Patrick usually succeeds but often fails; in many cases the cult member is successfully deprogrammed—but weeks or months later runs back to the isolated security of the cult. What Patrick sets up—with his helpers, who can often match the cult devotee in scriptural battles quote for quote from the King James Version of the Bible (and the desperate, loving parents who often are risking kidnap charges)—is a situation for coercive persuasion. What he produces, the "reprogrammed" cultist, is invariably a fundamentalist Christian (whatever the subject's family faith or cult dogma), often a militant Christian soldier eager to enlist in Patrick's private anticult crusade.

Professor Schein breaks down the process of coercive persuasion into three stages: what he calls *unfreezing, changing,* and *refreezing.* This is, he explains, a model that is developed from a conventional "theory of influence" with accepted parallels in all cultures, most obviously in totally enveloping institutions like religious orders, mental hospitals, military basic training—institutions that are in the business of influencing self-image or identity. Unfreezing is a process of disassociation, whereby the subject is brought to view his old life and the self that lived it as from a distance, as if dead—defining a psychological and social reality clearly apart from the subject's situation in captivity. The trauma of capture or kidnap, the constant stress, and the enveloping environment, governed by values very different from the precaptive world of the prisoner, can suffice to *unfreeze.* Similarly, the novice of a religious order breaks contact with the outside world, giving up usual clothes, comforts, even physical characteristics like hair. The routine of life is fundamentally altered; the old self mortified. The "fire and brimstone" of the religious revival serves the same function: making the members of the congregation feel their old life so corrupt and sinful that only conversion can restore self-esteem. Even folk wisdom equates isolation with changeful pressure: the disruptive student made to stand alone in the corner; ostracism of social deviants. But a fundamental difference is set up in the coercive context, where the subject has no escape, where the all-powerful captor has unchecked power to apply pressure or ease it to reward progress.

The second stage, *changing,* is a more delicate process, demanding the subject's willful identification and empathy with someone already committed to the changeful values. Schein suggests two models: either an identification with the captor's authority figure or, more likely and easily, identification with a midway figure— another prisoner, recruit, or novice, almost peer to the captive, but already committed to the new value scheme. The Chinese commonly used group cells, mingling prisoners at different stages of conversion and punishing or rewarding the whole cell for the progress of the group. (What usually brings parents to hire Ted

Patrick and his Deprogrammers is a cult-ordered break with family. And Patrick's young "assistants"—arguing the logical justice of filial loyalty and the imperative ideal of traditional fundamentalism—are usually of similar background, and about the same age, as their cultist captive. The rapport established in those sessions is sometimes so strong that deep and loving relationships often develop.) Cultural parallels for the peer model are numerous: the big brother or "buddy" system used in the military, in schools, for new employees in many corporations. In Alcoholics Anonymous (AA) the key change agent is the person assigned to be responsible for and closest to the new member. Yet again, the "coercive context" brings in a magnitude of difference—when the captor has unfettered power to increase or lessen punishment, stress, or discomfort according to whether he is pleased or displeased.

The importance of stage three, *refreezing,* reinforcing new values and roles, is implicitly or explicitly acknowledged by all "institutions of influence." Mental hospitals and prisons both consider transition and follow-up system integral parts of their rehabilitation programs—and blame negative socialization for their recidivists. Religious groups reinforce their clerics' self-images with elaborate ritual as well as the role expectations of the flock. Medical doctors have taxable evidence of the social support that reinforces the uncommonly intrusive personal manner they are taught in medical school. The key here is the *ritualization* of a new role. What is learned, in school, for instance, is often forgotten unless used in daily life. Ted Patrick urges all of his newly deprogrammed converts to become active members in a religious church or group—and sadly admits that only those who do find this sort of reinforcement keep the faith. Those who don't, he said, often fall back to the cults.

Ted Patrick's career has hinted to some of a terror-fiction possibility, a Dial-a-Personality service for troubled parents, but nothing here is so simple. Patrick's subjects are "persuaded," not mechanically tranformed. Patrick can only deflect them from one ideology of religious idealism to another of equal or greater commitment. And the range within which he can redirect his subject is limited by the subject's *prior* assumptions, the victim's unstated (perhaps subconscious) assumptions of what is true or might be true. The end result of coercive persuasion is but a variant of the victim's original beliefs—an often startling change, but still only a juggled version of previously held values.

The process of coercive persuasion is value-free, merely a vehicle. The essence of the coercive context is in the *situation* rather than in any sophisticated "technique"—which is why the Deprogrammers, and probably the SLA, could use it even ignorant of the mechanics. But the "receptivity" of the victim is dependent on his or her *predisposition* to see the social realities sympathetically, through the eyes of the captors.

Fundamentally, it is a question of guilt—and to a lesser extent, of philosophical depth. The pertinent questions in the Hearst case: Was Patricia Hearst, to begin with, a liberal, sympathetic to a radical perspective on social injustice? Did she feel guilty about her wealth? Her upper-class status? Her family history? Her personal life pattern? Her sense of guilt could have become the foundation for her new "revolutionary" perspective. If, on the other hand, she had absolute contempt for the SLA and their radical point of view from the beginning, conversion would be highly unlikely. And the time factor? Patrick works in days, but his subjects are already one step removed from the encultured value scheme. Two months of pressure in captivity, said Dr. Schein, is more than enough time to produce "enormous and dramatic" changes in personality and political attitude.

(The scale of the Tania transformation is subject to some interpretation. Perhaps it is necessary to put aside her outlandish rhetoric of impending genocide and ruling class teenage plots—and define Tania largely by her willingness to stay and join the SLA, to shoot at people. More than a year later, two days after her arrest, Patty—still the revolutionary—would confide to a friend that some of her Tania posturing had been consciously theatrical: "a stage kind of thing, you know." Rhetoric aside, here is still a transformation of a mysterious and impressive sort, but the scale is more human and less bizarre.)

The process of coercive persuasion is an "override" of what we are accustomed to thinking of as free will, but for the victim it may not seem that way. Consciously the victim finds herself bowing to a powerful, uncompromising argument—often not realizing that the coercive context has undermined her ability to apply freely her powers of reasoning.

(Thus, in the early fifties, Christian medical missionaries could stumble into Hong Kong after having been released from Chinese Communist prisons where they had been subjected to thought reform and explain that the Communists had done nothing but "make them aware" of how they had been willfully and purposely exploiting and enslaving the native peoples they had in fact spent years selflessly serving. From the political perspective of the Chinese, the missionaries had been exploiting and enslaving—by promulgating bourgeois values—but through the process of coercive persuasion they had not only brought the victim to accept their "truth" of treason, they had forced on him a betrayal of self, a retroactive devaluation of sincere and generous motive. The concept is difficult—experts call it "semantic redefinition." It involves completely restructuring the subject's understanding of what he had previously said, thought, and done.)

It may have been in the same way that Patty Hearst, in becoming Tania, was brought retroactively to reinterpret her past motives and her past experience—even to the point of giving them such sad and inane twists.

The studies of coercive persuasion clearly indicate that the mind bows to this sort of override of enculturated values only temporarily—although this is not to say that the process did not have a deep and lasting impact on both the personalities and politics of the victims. American missionaries who had been processed through the Chinese Communists' thought reform reverted to much of their original values and perspective rather quickly after they were freed—they had to readjust, in order to deal with the pervasive standards and values of the bourgeois Western experience. For the transformation to be maintained firmly, according to the experts, it seems that the individual must be kept within a reinforcing environment. There is, however, another way of securing the transformed persona; the most obvious, by making it impossible for the victim to revert.

Korean War POWs, for instance, were pushed to make anti-American propaganda statements or false war-crimes confessions—and then the Chinese would use the predictable American denunciation of the "traitor" as another lever on the captive. The effect was to force the captive to burn his bridges behind him and then make sure he realized he had done just that.

If Patty Hearst went through some equivalent of the coercive-persuasion process, then her Tania declaration and the later bank robbery could have had similar purposes. The SLA collective would have become her reinforcing environment—and she was never let out of it—but the declaration and the robbery, and the public hue and cry that rose after those acts, created a past for her new personality and set up barriers against a retreat into her old persona. The way back blocked, she could then only increase her commitment to and investment in her new self. Simply put, the young woman may have had two conflicting identities—Patty versus Tania—and as the first became impossible to return to, the second would have become more firmly planted, more real.

After the Tania tape, public and police sentiment turned against Patty very quickly and with surprising bitterness, almost as if in retribution for the worry and wasted sympathy she had cost them. (The day after the bank robbery, a hand-lettered sign reading GOD BLESS YOU, PATTY was removed from the window of a modest San Francisco home after having hung there for the world to see since the time of the kidnapping.) The Hearst family—fully aware of the impact of this shift on Patty's options if indeed she had been brainwashed—vainly tried to block the resentful backlash in public opinion, begging that it be remembered that this girl had been forcibly kidnapped and subjected to God knows what, stepping up a media campaign to push an evermore innocent and pure image of the prekidnapping Patty. Even the local FBI seemed to be conscious of the danger of reinforcing the Tania persona; after she had participated in the armed robbery, they selectively revealed evidence in order to suggest more strongly that she had been "somehow coerced" and charged her only as a material witness. But the public would have little of it. To talk of "brainwashing," as the Hearsts did constantly, was to disclaim for Patty individual responsibility for her actions—and Americans put great stock in assigning personal responsibility and blame. The voluble Attorney General Saxbe evidently could not resist another hip shot on the case, declaring from Washington that as far as he was concerned, Patricia was "nothing more than a common criminal."

But clearly, whatever "Tania" Hearst was or will become, she is much more than a merely common criminal.

Two years later—after the arrest, trial and conviction of Patricia Hearst for bank robbery—there would be considerably less public resistance to the idea of "something like brainwashing." But then, two years later, the bewildered public had watched Patricia Hearst appear transformed, and retransformed, and retransformed again. The study of this young woman's shifting persona had become a bizarre and Byzantine popular science. Yet there was no science that could synthesize the Patty personalities. There is no logic of uncompromised clarity that defines psychological reality, no cause-and-effect formulas, no sum that is the subtotal of subjective experience. Between her kidnap and conviction there were not one, or two, but at least a half-dozen different "voices" of Patricia Hearst that had been heard. There were three "public" images, each widely promoted yet of startling contrast: the prekidnap Patty; then Tania, terrorist revolutionary and SLA oracle;

and then the Patricia Hearst on trial, who had gone into jail after her arrest giving the clenched-fist revolutionary salute and then—after five months of isolation with family lawyers and psychiatrists—took the stand in her own defense to claim that she detested and feared her former SLA comrades and was certainly *not* a revolutionary. She had been forced to become Tania, she said, and had stayed hidden with the Harrises underground—plotting the Revolution and acting fully the role of the terrorist outlaw—not because she had been converted, not because she ever *believed* in the SLA, but simply because she had been so utterly terrorized that she had become a zombie whose actions she could not now understand.

(It was not hard to surmise that both "Tania" and "Hearst on trial" were governed images, each engineered by others than Patty to meet their own needs and those they thought in Patty's "best interests." Tania was an SLA mouthpiece, and for the Hearst trial, yet another Patty persona had been coached to describe her experience in the appropriate and specific terms of her peculiar *legal* defense. ["Coercive persuasion" being no legal defense, her lawyers tried a variation on theme that denied persuasion and stressed coercion.] Yet the private Patty voices—Patty as she explained herself to those few she trusted at each stage—must have been increasingly less certain, more bewildered, more reflective of the plight and confusion of a young woman struggling with a psychological history that could fit the design of a new pinball machine. There was no continuity among the public images, and only little more in the reports of Patty's private view of her own evolution—although here it was possible to identify an intermediate stage of Patty moving out of the SLA's "Tania" role: Patty as a "revolutionary feminist," part of a breakaway faction of the SLA just prior to her September, 1975, arrest. Whatever the relevance or partial relevance of the theory of coercive persuasion to Patty's *last* transformation, the leap change there was certainly less vast than the transubstantiation that created Tania from the kidnapped betrothed of Steven Weed.)

In personal terms, what could Patty have found among the Symbionese? How could she relate to them? In their common danger, their shared experience and commitment, there must have been a tremendous caring and interdependence in the SLA's tightly insulated world; perhaps Patty found in the SLA collective affection and love that made the daily experience at less dizzy heights seem drab and sterile. As a group they were nearly all her intellectual peers. And (as all armies are murderous and most soldiers quite different) the SLA people are nearly all described by their close friends as warm, loving, intelligent men and women. As Patty's fear—probably her best defense—diminished with time and lenient treatment, she probably had to come to terms with the fact that these people were sincere, dedicated idealists.

And there was much to respect in the Symbionese: their commitment, their selflessness, their "love of the people"—and, of course, their *moral certainty,* no small coin in an ambivalent age. With this certainty, the SLA offered the classic attraction of the cult, an immodest conviction that they were the dozen most important men and women on the face of the earth, agents of historical inevitability. There is great lure in such faith.

Yet it is intriguing to match the vulnerabilities of Patricia Hearst against the ideological strengths of her captors. The almost universal report of Patty's political apathy confronts the inflamed mix of white guilt and idealism among the Symbionese. Racial, social, and economic inequities might be useful levers on a vaguely liberal American aristocrat, but nothing in the SLA rhetoric suggests they could wield argument around these issues with the surgeon's skill necessary to probe Patricia Hearst's vulnerabilities. There was family guilt—her Georgia-bred mother's once-outspoken racism, the legends of Grandpa's hoard, history's claim that the Spanish-American War was a Hearst creation—but the SLA would probably use blunderbuss rhetoric of the sort the girl had heard, rationalized, and dismissed so often in the past.

To exploit the conversion possibility, the SLA needed an argument honed like a scalpel, an ideal Patricia Hearst could recognize and grasp. And with their crude and contradictory mixture of anarchism, communism, tribal collectivism, and dictatorial militarism—their Fifth Prophet, prison myths, and incredibly unrealistic vision of the power realities of the American class elite—the SLA simply *had* no coherent political analysis of any but the most simplistic sort.* What, then, could have been the fulcrum of the Tania process? What sharp, subtle, and passionate argument

---

*Political theory demands a structural analysis of authority and responsibility, developed historically. The SLA—plotting to kill wives of prison guards and the president of a candy company (a subsidiary, of a subsidiary, of a subsidiary of ITT) to punish the prisons and the multinational corporations, claiming that democracy died in the United States with the last flourish of JFK's Camelot and that every police officer is a Gestapo "insect"—substituted twisted romance for history and random vengeance for responsibility.

could they have used to uncover what Patty herself must recognize as a bitter truth—one side of a value contradiction she had repressed and compromised, something that could make her shake and eventually tumble her entire pyramid of values?

One possibility presents itself. Perhaps the most impassioned "line" in the SLA dogma, one of the rare few drawn from the personal experience of most of the SLA "soldiers," emerged not from the classic state politics of revolution, but from the new and rather distinctly American "personal politics" of sexism. Feminism, self-justifying philosophy of female equality and self-possession, is the most volatile and vital idea in contemporary America's chemistry of change. (A not unrelated statistic is that 1974, the year of the SLA, saw an all-time high in the American divorce rate.) Young women can attempt to integrate the new ideal into their life-styles, but for those but a half generation removed—those who grasped it late and then had to rip apart already-set life patterns to adopt the tyrannical morality of the new ideal—the collision with the feminist consciousness can be a brutal and traumatic experience. Angela, Nancy, Emily, Mizmoon, even Camilla—five of the SLA eight—were all self-transformed feminists with bitter histories of rebellion against traditionally constrictive female roles.

And if one were to scan for the most likely tension in the pre-kidnap life of Patricia Hearst, surely it would be in the contrast between her intelligence and mild feminism and the almost humiliating inequality of her relationship with her man, her former high school teacher, Steven Weed.

(A year later, Patty, still hiding "underground" with the Harrises, wrote, with them, a Tania Interview—a question-and-answer essay that was to be part of a manuscript the SLA hoped to publish. In it, Tania describes her "sudden conversion" as a "process of development," much the same as "a photograph is developed onto paper": the closet as darkroom. While the "interview" encapsulates several classic leftist critiques of capitalism and spews bitter—and oddly depersonalized—invective on her family, the active logic of her transformation seems to be expressed in largely feminist terms, reflecting on bitter memories of a sterile, claustrophobic life as Weed's betrothed and housemate. A relationship in hindsight seen doomed by its degrading imbalance.

(The PIN program showed her that "revolutionary action accomplishes the most," wrote Tania. The SLA taught her about the prisons, explained capitalism and colonialism, told her of white law in black ghettos, but still, she wrote, her "class background" made it "easy for me to think that violence wasn't the way to change things." The SLA gave her a crash course in poli sci, but even that wasn't enough to convert her to the politics of the gun. It was only the fierce beautiful poetry of Angela Atwood, wrote Tania, that finally "moved me to start thinking about ideas that were new to me, about revolutionary violence.")

Angela—"General Gelina"—was the SLA captor who first got close to Patty, perhaps the one that got closest, according to the SLA manuscript. Talking, reading poetry, casually asking questions, it was Angela who probed Patty and got her talking about herself, said the Harrises later. It may have been just coincidence, but it was a fateful pairing: Angela's relationship with her husband—from which she had broken with such anguish and anger—had a close parallel to Patty's relationship with Weed. Atwood must have seen her own history in Patty's submissiveness to Weed. And as the parallel became more clear, she certainly must have expressed a vicarious rage; at least a condescending pity and sympathy. Patty was everything Angela had been—before her feminist enlightenment. Gelina (who had so plaintively confessed her ignorance at a Marxist study group only months before the Foster killing) was no Marxist dialectician, despite her generalship. Angela's rhetorical passion was in her attack on the role of woman as spouse, the role that she, as much as Patty, had once completely absorbed.

In her long SLA interview, Tania writes warmly, intimately, only of Angela and Cujo, Willie Wolfe—and while for Wolfe she has but clichés and heroic labels, only Angela claims bittersweet memories. She writes as if all the others were already revolutionary warriors when she was kidnapped, and Angela the only novice among them. Only Angela was still learning, there to grow alongside Patricia. "It was really heavy," wrote Tania, "for me to see part of her development as a revolutionary. . . ."

Patty as Tania eventually turned on Weed, but not at first. Not when she turned on her family, not when she accused the government of trying to kill her, not even when she first became Tania. (Then her one regret in joining the SLA, declared Patty, was that Steven was not "a comrade.") Her love for Weed was Patty's last sacrifice to the SLA—which perhaps paradoxically reveals both how central he had been to her previous life and how important her betrayal of him was to her final metamorphosis. Only after the bank robbery, when Weed continued to say he did not believe she had freely joined the SLA, did Tania curse him. She called him a "sexist, ageist* pig." Not that this, she added, was "any sudden change from the way he always was."

(A full two years later Weed—having passed through cyclic periods of rage, regret, and resignation—could finally address the question with some rueful self-awareness. "Our relationship had just an enormous amount of ammunition for any concerted attack by intelligent feminists . . . but neither Patty nor I had perceived it that way when we lived it," he admitted. "Patty wanted to get married much earlier; I was the one who said wait, at least till you're twenty. But think what they could do with that! 'Here he was stringing you along—and you staying up all night cooking him Duncan Hines cookies!'

("Superficially, I don't think I was a sexist—I was the one who scrubbed out the toilet, not her. All she did was cook. But I was twenty-three and Patty was only seventeen when we got together . . . and there was still this severe inequality and dependency of her upon me. I even towered over her physically. I *didn't* value her opinions much, and I guess she knew it.

("Hell," he added with a bitter laugh, "I talked to her like a little kid. I would play with her like a little kid. I would yell at her like a little kid. I would even almost *kick* her like a little kid! But it wasn't any permanent thing. It wasn't any long-term situation. It couldn't be, because Patty was growing up. It was changing even when she was taken. It was just a workable arrangement that allowed us to build an enjoyable sort of relationship. We could have grown past it; we just never had the chance. But think of what they could do with that!")

Yet from Patty into Tania there was more than wholesale rejection of her past. Tania accepted and embodied beliefs wholly alien to Patricia. The alchemy of the Tania transformation remains mysterious, incomprehensible, explained only in terms of Patty's background, the sundry attractions of SLA idealism, or even the contextual framework of situational stress: "brainwashing." Like the angular faces of a gem, they define shape, but only reflect light; abstractions lack persuasive strength divorced from the gritty, brutal force of the actual experience.

An objective report on the conditions of Patty's confinement is nonexistent. Ms. Hearst herself, on trial two years later—having admittedly joined the SLA, served as a "soldier" in the underground, tramped back and forth across the country, hiding from

*Discrimination based on age.

the law, often alone and usually armed—argued that it was the unmitigated and unrelieved brutality of her early captivity that had so shocked and terrorized her that (having enlisted in the SLA because she thought it the only way to survive) she fell into "playing the role."

That she did it well enough to mislead her captors and others she met in the radical underground for more than a year and a half was only a measure of her fear; she said she never believed in the SLA, never "converted." If that was confusing—if the evidence of her guerrilla career in the underground implied willful criminal intent, enthusiastic revolutionary commitment, seemingly independent, uncoerced, willful criminal acts—Patricia Hearst told the jury she could explain it no better. Did she think she had been brainwashed? the prosecutor asked. "I'm not sure what happened to me," Patty replied softly.

(The Harrises, from jail, predictably denounced Patty's testimony. Tania, they swore, was a willing convert who had simply betrayed them as soon as she ended up in prison. Patty as captive had been "treated extra-humanely," said General Teko. "The last thing the SLA wanted was Patricia telling horror stories about the conditions she was held under. . . .") The defensive context in which Ms. Hearst detailed her experience—the trial, her obvious bias facing charges—made it difficult to take her description of even her early captivity, uncorroborated, at face value. Yet there was corroboration for much of her story. Even the Tania Interview, part of the manuscript found in the Harrises' last hideout (edited and with interlineations in the script of Emily Harris), sketches a story of crude, brutal, and perverse imprisonment—conditions much harsher than those assumed from the early SLA tapes. A second account—a published "inside story" from allies of the SLA underground—describes a young woman battered into physical and emotional exhaustion, then offered crumbs of freedom, "friendship," and hope of survival itself, life doled out by the handful to reward her step-by-step concessions to her captors.

According to the Tania Interview—the SLA propaganda version, written for publication while the three were safe and free; surely a calculated revelation to add weight to the rest of their tale—"for about six weeks" Patty was kept locked in the small bedroom closet at Daly City, a hot, windowless, stuffy closet with a single burning light blub. (Shaped like a tall coffin, the closet was two feet one and one-half inches deep, six feet seven and one-quarter inches long, and eight feet one inch high.)

"How did this affect you physically, being in a closet for six

weeks?" asks the unidentified questioner in the SLA "interview."
Replied Tania:

> Well, it was pretty cramped in there. At first I didn't get much
> exercise and certainly didn't move around much. After about a
> month I couldn't stand up without feeling dizzy and like I was go-
> ing to faint. For about two weeks I had a blindfold on all the time.
> I had different kinds until we hit on one that was easy to keep on
> and relatively comfortable. The first time I took the blindfold off
> to take a bath, I couldn't focus very well. Everything was out of
> proportion. My eyes hurt—I couldn't open them for a couple
> minutes because they hurt so bad. In fact, I even had to put my
> hands over my eyes while they were closed because the light com-
> ing through my eyelids was too strong. Whenever I took the
> blindfold off, the SLA wore ski masks.
>
> Everyone started to get worried about my health, because they
> weren't out to blind me or damage my eyesight or make me so
> weak that I couldn't stand. They did have the intention of releas-
> ing me, and they didn't want me to go back with all kinds of physi-
> cal problems. When they realized that my physical condition had
> really deteriorated, I was taken out of the closet more often to do
> exercises; in fact, if I didn't do exercises they would jam me
> around it [sic] to make sure that I did do them.
>
> People in the cell didn't realize how oppressive it was being in
> the closet until they started going in there to make communiques,
> practice running rounds through the shotguns, things like that.
> Once they found out that they didn't want to be in there because it
> was so hot, and cramped and dark; then I was out of the closet
> most of the day sitting and talking with the cell members. And it
> didn't take long for me to get back in good physical condition
> again.

The SLA version of the closet experience—like much the rest of
the Tania Interview—has the tone of a woman explaining that the
man who mugged her, and beat her badly, just accidentally happened to rape her in the process. When Patricia Hearst stood trial,
having shed Tania and turned bitterly against the Harrises, there
was none of that—only anger and horror at the memory of those
first weeks in the closet. The night of the kidnap, she said, she felt
only fear, bewilderment, and pain. Her legs were scraped and cut
from being dragged downstairs, and her cheek swollen and
bruised from where one of the kidnappers had slugged her with a
rifle butt. DeFreeze had pulled open the closet door to inform her
brusquely that she was a "prisoner of war." Her captors called
themselves the SLA, he said, and they used "cyanide bullets . . ."

and if she made any noise, they'd dangle her from the ceiling. Other voices, women outside the closet door, whisper-shrieked threats and taunts: "They said that I was a bourgeoisie* that it didn't matter if I got killed or not." In the emotional shorthand of the trial testimony, Ms. Hearst described herself plunged into a Kafka vision of *Alice in Wonderland,* terror in a bizarre and topsy-turvy world.

Sleepless, blindfolded, hands still bound, she was put through a grueling interrogation the next morning, she said—and then again, the next day. The Symbionese simply could not believe she knew so little about her family's business affairs. Cinque read her the SLA's codes of war and the SLA's revolutionary declaration and program. He told her that she was the chosen victim of the Symbionese national "war council," the "court of the People," that she was being held for the "crimes" of her parents. Over the following days the pressure eased, but the scope of her reality had drastically narrowed. Slowly she learned to differentiate between the voices of her captors, and as the days seeped into weeks, they talked with her more and more. She said the SLA offered her food—and "mint tea" to drink—but for the first ten days she couldn't eat or move her bowels. They would take her out to go to the bathroom, and then once a week they allowed her a bath. She had to listen to long lectures on the sins of her family, the imminent revolution—and always there was the constant death threat.

"I could hear a lot of clicking and noises," Ms. Hearst told the jury." It sounded like clips going in and out of the guns and sometimes they'd make noises like they were shooting and I could tell like that they were standing right in front of the closet and doing it to me. . . ." She heard the tapes the SLA made, adding her bit to each to authenticate that they still had a hostage to kill as they threatened—more, she had been told from the beginning that her final ransom would be an exchange for Remiro and Little. And she didn't think the government would go along.

The second generally corroborative account of Patty's first month—and a version of the dynamic of the second month that produced Tania—was based on the recollections of Jack and Micki Scott, authors and radical sports activists, who hid the SLA survivors after the May, 1974, Los Angeles shoot-out. The Scotts'

*The bourgeoisie is defined socially as the class between the aristocracy or very wealthy and the working class—the middle class, the merchant class. In Marxist doctrine, however, the bourgeoisie was redefined generally as "the capitalists," the social class of interests antithetical to the proletariat, the working class.

version of the story they were told by Tania and the Harrises was presented in a stylish journalistic exposé in *Rolling Stone,* a hip rock-politics biweekly of the counterculture based in San Francisco. (The report was written but not yet published in September, 1975, when Patty and the Harrises were arrested.) Although generally sympathetic to the SLA, the Scott version, while it differs in tone and emphasis, gibes remarkably well with the Hearst defense story of Patty's early imprisonment: the weeks in the closet; DeFreeze's constant drumbeat of rhetoric and threats; being told her parents had abondoned her; fear, terror, dismay, and despair.

In the closet Patty lost track of time and was unable to eat, according to Scott/*Stone.* DeFreeze did not physically molest her, but he "kept up a constant intimidation. He berated her and her family for being part of a ruling class that was sucking blood from the common people. 'Your mommy and daddy are insects,' he yelled. 'They should be made to crawl on their hands and knees like insects if they want you back.'"

At first, according to the Scotts, Patty tried to defend her parents, but then she herself became angry with the delay. Patty was terrified of DeFreeze. She fully believed him when he told her that she would be killed if the Hearsts did not comply with all the SLA demands. *Stone* described a process of change. By degrees— her own impatience with the ransom demand; her anger when her father's representative visited Remiro and Little at San Quentin and declared their solitary-confinement quarters "satisfactory"; her fear of retribution when her mother accepted another term on the UC Board of Regents—a disillusionment grew. And with it, "a sympathy" for her captors (or at least a sense that her survival depended on her *own* relationship with the SLA— independent of whatever her parents did—a change in attitude that could be interpreted as "sympathy").

According to both the SLA "interview" and *Stone,* after a month with the Symbionese Patty was so reduced emotionally and physically that she could not walk, could stand for only a few seconds before collapsing to the floor.

It was at this stage, the Scotts' version recounts, that Patty's "sympathy" for the SLA began to jell. DeFreeze opened the closet as a reward, allowing her, for the first time, to walk about the small apartment hideout. One of the Scotts recalled Tania explaining: "[To] be able to walk freely from one room to the other seemed to be the world's greatest pleasure." DeFreeze let up on his baiting rhetoric—"tempered his frequent beratings of her"— and Patty was "urged to attend" the SLA's daily political study group. She was given textbooks, statistics on wealth and poverty in the United States, articles about the holdings of the Hearst family—and in argument and debate the SLA soldiers "encouraged her radicalization. They hugged her, called her sister, and ended her loneliness." Concluded *Stone*: The Tania transformation was "as much emotional as political."

Although the Scott/*Stone* story doesn't make the point—and the SLA Tania Interview is literally blind to it—both descriptions of Patty's weeks in the closet surely argue that her initial confinement gave her something to escape. And trapped as she was, the ransom stalled, she had nothing but her own resources (whatever relationships *she* could build with her captors) to guarantee her survival. And she had nothing to barter with but herself: her body, her allegiance, her commitment.

Despite the intense and undoubtedly deeply felt feminism of the SLA women, it was probably inevitable that sex and sexuality would be tangled in the Tania transformation. They had simply lost the ability to contrast rhetoric with reality; they had little sense of their own roles within the dynamic of the collective (as the SLA manuscript would acknowledge with self-critical hindsight), and they were utterly insensitive to the pressures inherent in the situation of their captive.

The timing of Patricia's decision to become Tania is subject to some dispute; the Hearst defense version seems too cagily engineered. Jack Scott's story and the several versions of the conversion in the SLA manuscript all time her decision—with some logic—in the week and a half after the "shotgun" tape: just before the SLA moved from the Daly City hideout to another on Golden Gate Avenue in San Francisco (six weeks and three days after the abduction). Testifying at her bank robbery trial, Ms. Hearst claimed that it was two weeks later, just about April 1 (one day short of eight weeks in captivity).

The SLA would seem to have little interest in the specific timing of her decision; they were more concerned with the decision itself. Hearst on trial, however, had a defense posture that could only be helped by the claim that Tania was only two well-guarded weeks out of the closet before the bank robbery—rather than the almost full month in the SLA version. (Moreover, in order to accept Ms. Hearst's story that she was held in yet another closet at Golden Gate for another week and a half, one had to credit her claim that after she had so helpfully and caustically lambasted her family and the FBI in the "shotgun" tape, while the SLA was trying to persuade her to voluntarily join them, they kept her blindfolded and locked in an even *smaller,* more uncomfortable closet at Golden Gate [one foot six inches deep, five feet nine inches long] for another ten days.)

Patricia Hearst on trial brought sex into her tale early, recounting a gratuitously cruel attack by Donald DeFreeze four days after the kidnap, allegedly right after she had taped the first recorded SLA message (telling her family she was not being "unnecessarily frightened"). Cin came into the closet, she testified, "and he said, 'I heard from some of the sisters that you were not cooperating' and . . . and that I better not do that any more." With that, she said, DeFreeze reached up under the shirt they had given her and pinched a breast, clutching at her pubic area through her pants with his other hand. It was the only such incident, she said, until—about a month after the kidnap—when, she told the court, she was raped, first by Willie Wolfe, then Cinque. (Patricia did not use the word "rape"—she said only that she had been "sexually assaulted" against her will; she had not resisted, she said, because she was helpless. But when the prosecutor bluntly asked her if she had been raped, she said "yes.")

It was Angela Atwood, she testified, who pimped for the SLA. "She said I was going to sleep with William Wolfe . . . and so I did. She said that she and everyone else wanted me to know more about what it was like being in the cell with them . . . that everybody had to take care of the needs of other people and sexual freedom was part of the functioning of the cell. . . ." That night Wolfe came into the closet, closed the door, stripped her, and had sexual intercourse on the closet floor. About a week later, she said, DeFreeze "did the same thing."

The "rapes" in Ms. Hearst's story occurred shortly before she was "forced" to record the "shotgun" tape. She said neither man took her out of the closet (odd perhaps, for group-sanctioned sex in a three-bedroom safehouse, the six-foot-four Wolfe allegedly raped her in the two-foot-narrow, six-foot-seven-inch-long closet), but they did allow her to remove her blindfold.

The Tania sex tale in the SLA manuscript is very different, but even here it's conceded that Symbionese sex—"nonexclusive" and "nonmonogamous"—became an issue in Patty's captivity some time before she became Tania. A portion of the manuscript, which seems to have been written and edited by Bill Harris, explains:

> From the beginning, we provided for Tania's basic needs: shelter, food, clothing, medical attention and news from the outside.

Although we considered sex a basic human need, our commitment not to exploit her sexually coupled with her overall status as
a POW denied Tania the freedom to have sex with another person. But later these conditions changed, partly due to her own initiative but also because of our growing love and respect for her.
As she became more integrated into the day to day aspects of cell
life we tried to treat Tania as an equal. It was only natural that
with the increased personal interaction between Tania and members of the cell these relationships would also develop sexually.

"We were all aware that a closeness was developing between
Tania and Kahjoh [Cujo *] which we wanted to see progress in a
revolutionary way." Patty's attempt to establish some sort of rapport with Willie Wolfe, the youngest among the Symbionese, the
one closest to her own age, was obvious, so the group decided that
she should be educated to the revolutionary realities. "We wanted
Tania to understand how we felt about building close personal relationships within the cell and the revolutionary responsibility of
comradship [sic] we all had to each other."

Our position was one of conditional practicality. . . . You can't
just let people drop by a safehouse to socialize. So far as sex was
concerned we had to get all of our sexual and personal needs met
by comrades within the cell. Everyone realized that at this time
there was no room for exclusive relationships because each of us
had to help the other comrades meet their sexual needs and
maintain harmony within the cell. We wanted to learn to love each
other on an equal basis and on many levels, including sexually.
We tried not to focus on just one or two people who we might
have subjectively liked best. We had a need to develop collectively
in many areas and sex was just one of them.

Because we still intended to release her if our demands were
met there was skepticism within the group that Tania might mis-
represent the sex question upon her release. Some comrades
feared that the pigs and the media might say we raped her or
forced her into sexual activity because she was afraid not to cooperate. However, it soon became clear to everyone that Tania's understanding of this problem and her commitment to struggle with
us decreased the potential for reactionaries to exploit this issue.

---

*The first mention of the SLA name of Willie Wolfe came in a June, 1974,
taped message from Tania Hearst and the Harrises, and it was incorrectly transcribed by the media as "Cujo" and spelled that way for more than a year. It was
only after the September, 1975, arrests of the three, with the discovery of the
SLA manuscript, that the spelling "Kahjoh" came to light. Because "Cujo" has
become the more familiar to the public, the authors have used it in this book.

There are many people who still cannot comprehend Tania's swift evolution from sheltered bourgeois to freedom fighter. A perfect example of the decadence of the present social order is the sick notion that revolutionary consciousness can be attained at the price of a mere fuck. We who witnessed the evolution of Tania's revolutionary commitment wish to lay this absurd notion to rest. We wish to end all metaphysical speculation around brainwashing and sexual enslavement. To do so we feel it will be necessary to provide a candid explanation of the events that transpired. It would be too easy to say that Tania did not interact sexually with cell members prior to being a member of the SLA, that her relationships broadened only after her decision to stay and fight. This is not the case. Therefore, it would be inexact to contend that her decision was totally free of any personal consideration of her relationships [sic], sexual or non-sexual, with cell members.

Even General Teko realized that a smile and sex from a captive under threat of death is not exactly willful and free.

However [he wrote], only the most foolishly naive bourgeois mentality could deduce that Tania decided to stay because of some magical sexual satisfaction or because of a strong personal attachment to an individual. Anyone who would use this rationale to pick up the gun would be sadly fooling themselves and their prospective comrades. We have seen this happen to people, but they soon become disillusioned with the life of a freedom fighter because their commitment is so shallow. Tania has certainly by her actions proven that her commitment was forged from a political rather than a personal outlook.

Another section of the manuscript—written, like the rest, apparently about six months after the kidnap—is in several drafts, heavily edited and scratched up, with both typed and handwritten versions scribbled, crossed out, changed, and changed again. In writing the SLA history, the three then-remnant Symbionese and the few allies they found apparently had great difficulty dealing with SLA sex, the seduction of Tania, and other questions relevant to feminism. In this section Harris tried to describe Angela's approach to Patty on sex.

In one draft, he writes: "After about four weeks, she [Patty] casually mentioned while talking about sex with Gelina that she 'was horny' and that she would like. . . ." He breaks off in midsentence.

He tried again, in longhand: *"At one point about a month or so af-*

ter her arrest, Gelina asked Tania if she ever got horny." He crossed out part of that until it read: *"Gelina asked Tania if it bothered her not being able to* [he crossed out "have sex"] *fuck. Tania responded that it* [crossed out "should be obvious"] *obviously bothered her,* [crossed out "that the question"] *just like anyone else in a similar situation. Gelina then asked her, again not knowing what to expect, if she* ["ever thought" crossed out] *was attracted to anyone in the cell."*

In a different pen, perhaps at a different time, the last lines were again crossed out, and the sentence is rewritten in the spidery handwriting of Patricia Hearst: *"Gelina then asked if she wanted to fuck anyone in the cell."* A line was added, again by Patty: *"She said that she would like to sleep w/Kahjoh."*

OFFICE OF THE DIRECTOR

UNITED STATES DEPARTMENT OF JUSTICE

FEDERAL BUREAU OF INVESTIGATION

WASHINGTON, D.C. 20535

April 19, 1974

RE: **DONALD DAVID DE FREEZE**   **PATRICIA MICHELLE SOLTYSIK**   **PATRICIA CAMPBELL HEARST**
      NANCY LING PERRY   **CAMILLA CHRISTINE HALL**   **MATERIAL WITNESS**

TO WHOM IT MAY CONCERN:

The FBI is conducting an investigation to determine the whereabouts of these individuals whose descriptions and photographs appear below. Federal warrants charging robbery of a San Francisco bank on April 15, 1974, have been issued at San Francisco, California, for Camilla Hall, Donald DeFreeze, Nancy Perry, and Patricia Soltysik. A material witness warrant in this robbery has been issued for Patricia Hearst, who was abducted from her Berkeley, California, residence on February 4, 1974, by a group which has identified itself as the Symbionese Liberation Army (SLA). The participants in the bank robbery also claim to be members of the SLA.

DONALD DAVID DE FREEZE
N/M, DOB 11/16/43, 5'9" to 5'11",
150-160, blk hair, br eyes

PATRICIA MICHELLE SOLTYSIK
W/F, DOB 5/17/50, 5'3" to 5'4",
116, dk br hair, br eyes

PATRICIA CAMPBELL HEARST
W/F, DOB 2/20/54, 5'3", 110,
lt br hair, br eyes

MATERIAL WITNESS

NANCY LING PERRY
W/F, DOB 9/19/47, 5', 95-105, red
br hair, haz eyes

CAMILLA CHRISTINE HALL
W/F, DOB 3/24/45, 5'5", 125,
blonde hair, blue eyes

If you have any information concerning these individuals, please notify your local FBI office, a telephone listing for which can be found on the first page of your directory. In view of the crimes for which these individuals are being sought, they should be considered armed and extremely dangerous, and no action should be taken which would endanger anyone's safety.

Very truly yours,

C. M. Kelley

Clarence M. Kelley
Director

The FBI "wanted" poster, issued after the bank robbery in San Francisco
on April 15, 1974

Bill Harris

Emily Harris

Nancy Ling Perry (*photo: Eric Rahkonen, Contra Costa* Times)

Camilla Hall *(photo: Rick Mc-Closkey)*

Patricia Soltysik

Patricia Hearst's first communion, age eight *(photo: courtesy Hearst family)*

Patricia Hearst, age nineteen *(photo: Steven Weed)*

Patricia Hearst and Steven Weed *(photo: courtesy Hearst family)*

Dr. Marcus A. Foster, first victim of the SLA *(photo: courtesy Oakland Public Schools)*

Tom Dean Matthews, kidnapped by the SLA in Los Angeles *(photo: Los Angeles* Times)

The April 15 robbery of the Hibernia Bank in San Francisco

Catherine and Randolph Hearst (*photo: San Francisco Examiner*)

"Tania" Hearst posters on the University of California, Berkeley, campus (*photo: Wide World*)

An SLA document with the familiar seven-headed cobra emblem

May, 1974: FBI agents and "Patty dogs" in a Los Angeles search *(photo: Wide World)*

A dramatic moment from the May 17 shootout *(photo: Wide World)*

May 17, 1974: aftermath of the shootout and fire in Los Angeles *(photo: Wide World)*

The Los Angeles ''safe house'' in flames *(photo: Los Angeles* Times)

Los Angeles County Coroner Dr. Thomas Noguchi showing where he found the fatal bullet wound on the body of Donald DeFreeze *(photo: Wide World)*

15

Tania

WHATEVER mortification and debate accompanied Tania's rebirth among the Symbionese, Patricia Hearst's second month of captivity was publicly a quiet time, a tense stalemate, with each day, each week, seemingly burdened with the silence. There was no message from the SLA, and the family stood by the "final" $4 million offer from the Hearst Corporation. If Patty had felt abandoned before, the feeling must have deepened.

After the "shotgun" tape Steve Weed broke with the family and issued his own statement, but that served only to underscore the lack of response from the Hearsts. It was a full week before Patty's parents said anything. They had promised comment early—then delayed; they said they would hold a news conference—then delayed again. What could they say? How could they respond to their daughter who now said she feared, not her captors (who had repeatedly threatened to murder her if the police tracked them down), but only her parents, the FBI, and "certain people in the government"?

The immediate reactions of the family were not unlike those common among the bewildered public. Randolph Hearst was certain that Patty had somehow been coerced into making the statement. Catherine Hearst believed her daughter had been "brainwashed." It would not be long before Randy, too, would conclude that "it must be some form of mind control."

Two days after the communiqué, March 11, Steve Weed held a press conference, making it clear he was not speaking for the family but only for himself. He had, in fact, already moved out of the Hillsborough mansion. Gingerly, Weed conceded that he could understand why Patty "might be irritated. The two weeks of silence on our part was very unpleasant," he explained, but "we really didn't know what to say or do at the time." From Patty's comments, he said, "it's clear she's reading something. The rhetoric isn't hers, but a good part of it is what she sincerely believes . . . from her point of view, it might look like we've made a mess."

In his reaction to the tape, and as part of a deliberate campaign in the weeks that followed, Weed went out of his way to separate himself from the Hearsts, candidly describing for the first time some of the bickering that had gone on, talking about the disagreements he and Patty had constantly had with her parents, family jealousies, political differences. Gelina (Angela Atwood), in the same taped communiqué, had again brought up Mrs. Hearst's role as a University of California regent. Weed had picked that up, and he pointed out that "neither Patty nor I would have appointed her, and certainly we would never have voted—in almost all cases—the way she voted." Yes, he answered reporters, Patty probably "to a degree" believed that the FBI wanted her dead; he himself did not believe it. But he suggested that the bureau be forced into a "very, very public position" in their handling of the case as a precaution.

In his alliance with the family Weed had felt little more than a pawn; his tactical suggestions were ignored, he had no say in the money matters, and he simply had never gotten along well with the elder Hearsts. He set out alone trying to build some sort of life insurance for Patty by publicly giving her an identity as something more than the daughter of a Hearst, while establishing his own position as an innocent party unaffiliated with the Hearsts, molding a public stance that would force the SLA to take him into account. In the following weeks Weed began carefully to leak stories to reporters about how he had been mercilessly grilled by FBI agents, stories about the truth-serum test, the lie-detector test. It was conscious and effective media manipulation. Weed projected an image of Patty as the liberal innocent and family rebel that was both more accurate and more sympathetic in the eyes of the radical community than the girl-child the family described. (In the end, when Patty declared herself Tania, the one regret she had was that Steven was not "a comrade.")

Despite the cautious posture of the family, Weed's statements apparently spurred a reaction from Catherine Hearst—a reaction that could, and was, read as significant by the SLA and their captive. Governor Ronald Reagan announced on March 13, two days after Weed's press conference, that Mrs. Hearst had accepted reappointment for another sixteen-year term as a regent of the

University of California. Randy Hearst first heard the announcement on the radio, said a family friend, and was furious with his
wife for approving Reagan's announcement without checking
with him. He feared, with reason, it turned out, that the SLA
would react angrily; but Catherine had her pride.

On March 16 Randy released a brief written statement to the
press, explaining that he had not responded sooner because "this
last message is more complicated than the previous messages. . . .

"I have not broken my word to the SLA, and I am doing everything I can to carry out their demands. The one thing I want
above all is to get Patty home as quickly as possible, and, I repeat, I
am doing all I can to bring this about.

"I would rather not hold a live news conference at this stage because there comes a time when open discussion can become detri-
mental to a situation."

(The cryptic reference to "a situation" that could be threatened
by open discussion marked a rather dramatic secret development.
Hearst had been contacted by a small group of SLA associates
from within California's prisons, and they, led by Clifford "Death
Row Jeff" Jefferson, had said that they were willing to try to help
free Patty. Hearst had already met once with Death Row Jeff at
Vacaville, where Jefferson had recently been transferred, and the
two men were attempting to negotiate ground rules for Jeff and
other SLA-connected inmates to appeal to Cinque to free the girl
without undermining the SLA's position. All this, however, was
still secret. To the public, and in the eyes of Patty and the SLA,
there was just the silence.)

Two weeks after the communiqué, on March 21, Hearst held a
news conference, in which he again stressed that he personally
had done all he could to meet the SLA's demands—but that the
corporation offer still stood.

Hearst said he had ordered the PIN program suspended temporarily, and it was being revamped in an attempt to meet the
SLA's specifications (he directed that the remaining $750,000 be
spent all at once in a single distribution). He listed court and police officials he had talked to urging that Little and Remiro be
allowed their press conference, but said frankly that it did not
look hopeful. (Two days before, a Superior Court judge refused
permission for the TV appearance, saying it would make a fair trial impossible. Appeal attempts failed.) Said Hearst: "We're still
doing everything we can—talking to people in authority—to see if

they can't relent." Hearst even went so far as to offer himself as a substitute hostage. "Any father would," he said. "I love her. I want her back and Catherine wants her back. The whole family does."

Still in secret, Hearst had met a second time with Death Row Jeff at Vacaville. They had started groping for common ground, at the outset cautious and formal in their own ways. Now they began to speak candidly about what could be done. "He was a very interesting kind of character," said Hearst later, "and he was honestly worried about the [SLA] people getting help, more worried about them getting help than he was about Patricia." But, in the interests of the SLA, Jefferson said, he was willing to try to help set up negotiations to end the stalemate. Prison officials had been informed of Jefferson's connection with the SLA from documents found at the Clayton house. In fact, back in February they had arranged a midnight meeting of federal agents, Jefferson, and Little and Remiro. Before that meeting began, the lifer convict and the two captured SLA soldiers were led through the gas chamber at San Quentin, then into a room where they were asked if they were willing to help in the Hearst-case investigation. None of the three was interested in "cooperating." After conducting their own investigation, the prison officials had concluded that, whatever the structure of the SLA on paper, it was an "outsiders" operation in which inmates had been recruited as window dressing. They were probably correct—but now some of the inmates who had been recruited into the group had developed a sense of responsibility for what was happening.

The manner in which Death Row Jeff connected with Hearst is revealing. It might never have occurred without the intervention of a rather eccentric psychiatric therapist at Vacaville prison, Dr. Wesley Hiler, who had gained the confidence of many inmates. Hiler had been steered to Jefferson by two convicts he had been counseling who had admitted they had been recruited into the SLA. One was Al Taylor, the friend of Nancy Ling Perry, who had thought what he had joined was the "Lebanese Liberation Army." Taylor told the psychiatrist there was now an inmate SLA faction, which included Jefferson, which was becoming increasingly worried over the way the situation was developing on the "outside." All three convicts, according to Hiler, thought the SLA had made a mistake in killing Marcus Foster and feared that Patricia Hearst—whom they viewed as an innocent—was in danger of being killed, either by the SLA or the FBI. (Jefferson, for one, was certain the FBI would kill Patty to smear the good name of the

SLA.) Death Row Jeff was also afraid the SLA might be trapped by holding Patty too long—"pinned down in the field," as he put it—and find themselves unable to escape. He was concerned, too, that by continuing to hold Patty after Hearst had paid out $2 million for the PIN program and the Hearst Corporation had offered $4 million more, the SLA was undermining the goodwill they had created through the food distribution. (Even within the prisons, at least in Vacaville and San Quentin, there had developed a backlash, in the inmate newspapers and on prison bulletin boards there appeared anti-SLA statements, and the grapevine was rife with talk of threats to kill Little and Remiro if Patty were harmed.)

Both the other inmates and Jefferson himself told Hiler that Death Row Jeff was the nominal leader of the SLA, but Jefferson explained that the authority structure of the "Army" was vague and that Cinque's unit acted autonomously. Still, with all his fears about the kidnap action, Jefferson was unwilling to deal with Hearst until after several long talks with Hiler. Jefferson had developed his revolutionary politics wholly within the isolation of prison. His last memories of free life are from his train trip from Bakersfield north to San Quentin in the 1940s, looking out at the shanty towns alongside the tracks. He had been a leader in the struggles to break down segregation inside California's "correctional" institutions, and he had endured waves of prison crackdowns and reforms—but he had very little idea of what had been happening in the outside world in the past several decades. For him Randolph Hearst was a member of the "ruling class," and, said Hiler, "Jeff had developed this monster image of the American ruling class." Jefferson at first refused to believe that a big-name capitalist like Hearst did not have access to unlimited amounts of money or that Hearst did not have the power to put a leash on the FBI and police and pull them back off the trail of the SLA. Hiler said it was only after many long discussions that he was able to cast enough doubts on those assumptions so that Jefferson agreed to meet Hearst. And it was only after his talks with Hearst and Reverend A. Cecil Williams, the black-activist minister brought into the meetings as an intermediary, that Jefferson began to accept a more realistic perspective. After meeting Hearst, said the prison therapist, Jefferson was "much less paranoid," much more aware of the limitations on any individual, capitalist or not. While Randolph Hearst and Death Row Jeff were talking, Hiler tried to arrange a meeting between Al Taylor and Catherine

Hearst. Both were willing, but prisons director Procunier vetoed the idea. "He [Procunier] said that Taylor was, after all, a mass murderer and there was no telling what might happen," said Hiler.

On March 25 the fifth and last PIN distribution went relatively smoothly. The same day, Randolph and Catherine Hearst flew to New York for a Hearst Corporation board meeting. Someone had finally convinced Hearst that the SLA required some sort of guarantee of the $4 million, something more than a corporation spokesman's press-conference promise. Hearst got the board to approve putting $4 million in escrow and naming three prominent California liberals as trustees empowered to release the money if Patricia was returned unharmed. In a widely reported New York interview, Mrs. Hearst said that she was "beginning to lose hope" for Patty's safe release. "I can't think of anything we can do right now. I don't know how you can deal with those kind of people."

On the twenty-eighth, back from New York, Hearst announced the escrow plan. That same day, Joe Remiro and Russ Little sent an open letter to the news media, a long rambling diatribe accusing "the judges, D.A.s, and sheriffs, with the supervision and support of federal law enforcement agencies," of blocking the TV appearance as part of a conspiracy to keep them from speaking to "the People"—"as has constantly been the case since we were attacked and arrested on Jan. 10." They said that they, too, realized the FBI was trying to kill Patty to "discredit the strategy and tactics of the SLA," adding quickly that they were sure their comrades would be able to protect and guard her from outside harm until she could be released and safely returned to her fiancé. The letter continued:

> We do not hold Patricia Hearst responsible for the actions of the Hearst Corporation or the part it plays within the ruling class. We do, in fact, admire the level of courage and objectivity she has displayed and send her our warmest regards. . . .

Addressing themselves directly to Patty, Remiro and Little wrote:

> We feel confident that the SLA will release you unharmed. . . . We hope that when you are released you will continue to speak your mind! . . . Who knows—you might even look back on this as a worthwhile experience where people were fed and

you and the public were exposed to the cruelty and inhumanity of the corporate powers who rule this country.

The following day, Hearst, FBI Special Agent Bates, and California Prisons Director Procunier met with Death Row Jeff and another SLA inmate associate, Raymond Scott. Now was the time, argued Hearst, for Jefferson to make a statement. Jefferson bartered; he wanted something to offer the SLA, perhaps the option of leaving the country. Would it be possible for them to fly to Algeria? When Death Row Jeff brought that up, Hearst recalled later, Bates said that that would depend on what sort of specific proposal the SLA had for freeing the girl.

"Bates then turned to me and said, 'What about it, Mr. Hearst?' and I said, 'Look, I can put a plane at the end of the runway, but I can't get them there. To do that, I think you're going to have to have the support of somebody from the police, because what's gonna happen is, you know, what might happen is they get stopped at a red light or something going to the airport!'" It was decided to wait for the SLA to make a proposal, but Jefferson and Scott clearly understood that such a deal was possible. "The FBI either pretended to go along with it or agreed, and Hearst went along with it," said Hiler, "but of course nothing was released publicly." There was, however, a message. Randolph Hearst tapped it out on a prison typewriter as Death Row Jeff spoke the words:

> Greetings to the poor and oppressed people of the world.
> Greetings to Comrade Field Marshal Cinque and to the combat units of the SLA.
> Greetings to comrades Russell J. Little and Joseph M. Remiro now prisoners in the tiger cages of the Alameda county jail.
>
> Your comrade Death Row Jeff wishes to express solidarity with the communiqué issued by my comrades Russell J. Little and Joseph M. Remiro on March 28, 1974. You brothers and sisters are truly soldiers of the people and are more beautiful than life itself to me.
> In furtherance of my comrades' communiqué of March 28, 1974, I hereby suggest to General Field Marshal Cinque that it would be for the best interest of the poor and oppressed people to start negotiations as soon as possible with Randolph Hearst to release the prisoner of war Patricia Hearst.
> I have been assured that upon the release of the prisoner of war

four million dollars will be placed in the appropriate organization for the purpose of feeding the poor as per the instructions of the SLA.

Negotiations should deal with any combat unit that may be pinned down in the field.

Dare to struggle . . . . Dare to win but do not forget the cry of the people.

The letter was signed by Jefferson, Raymond Scott, and Al Taylor and witnessed in the corner by Randolph Hearst and Reverend Williams. A photo copy of the document was published in the Sunday joint edition of the *Examiner & Chronicle* on March 31.

"They had wanted to say some other things, that an arrangement had been made for the SLA to leave the country," Hiler recounted later, "but the FBI didn't want that specifically mentioned in the letter. Even so, Death Row said afterwards he was sure the SLA would understand that some preliminary arrangements had been made for them to leave the country. He said they were used to communicating in that sort of vague double-talk."

Whatever the message was that got across, the two letters from the "inside" provoked an immediate response from the SLA. On April 2 a florist delivered a bouquet of roses to John Bryan, the editor of the radical San Francisco *Phoenix*. The "underground" weekly in its previous issue had published what was purported to be another SLA manifesto, but which in reality had been a hoax not too skillfully composed by Bryan himself. (Few had taken the alleged SLA document seriously; the rhetoric was too pat, and there was none of the Patty Hearst ID cards accompanying it that had validated the prior written SLA communiqués.) But this time there was no doubt. With the roses and "Communiqué No. 7" came half of Patricia Hearst's driver's license. For Bryan there was also a comic birthday-greetings card showing a stork delivering a package that opened up to the wry exclamation "Happy Birthday! Scared The Hell Out Of You, Didn't I?" and a two-page document described as the SLA's "Codes of War" (see Appendix). But it was the brief communiqué enclosed with the bouquet that drew all attention. It was dated March 29 and headed "Subject: Negotiations and Release of Prisoners."

Herein enclosed are the Codes of War of the Symbionese Liberation Army, these documents as all S.L.A. documents are to be printed in full and omitting nothing by order of this court in all forms of the media.

Further communications regarding subject prisoner will follow in the following 72 hours, communications will state the state, city and time of release of the prisoner.

I.I. Unit 4
Gen. Field Marshal Cin
S.L.A.

Bulletins cut in on TV shows, and headlines barked the excited message: Patty Hearst was to be freed! The Hearsts were ecstatic. Death Row Jeff was pridefully certain his letter had tipped the scale. Checking with the florist who had delivered the roses, FBI agents and news reporters were told that a short but otherwise nondescript young woman had walked in the day before, picked out the $3 bouquet, paid an additional $1.50 delivery charge, and asked that an envelope she handed over be enclosed with the flowers. The florist said the young woman had insisted the flowers be delivered the same day—April 1—and had been assured they would be, but the delivery truck had broken down and delayed the order by a day.

Reporters are notorious cynics, and there were not many who did not realize immediately that the communiqué had been meant to be delivered on April Fools' Day, but their reports made no mention of their fears—this message had been too long and desperately hoped for.

Radio station KSAN in San Francisco received the follow-up communiqué the next day, April 3. It was a far cry from the eagerly expected announcement of when and where the kidnap victim would be released. It opened with the defiant voice of Patricia Hearst herself:

"I would like to begin this statement by informing the public that I wrote what I am about to say. It's what I feel. I have *never* been forced to say anything on any tape. Nor have I been brainwashed, drugged, tortured, hypnotized, or in any way confused. As George Jackson wrote, 'It's me, the way I want it, the way I see it.'

"Mom, Dad, I would like to comment on your efforts to supposedly secure my safety. The PIN giveaway was a sham. You attempted to deceive the people, the SLA, and me with statements about your concern for myself and the people. You were playing games, stalling for time—time which the FBI was using in their attempts to assassinate me and the SLA elements which guarded me. You continue to report that you did everything in your power to pave the way for negotiations for my release—I hate to believe that you could have been so unimaginative as to not even have considered getting Little and Remiro released on bail. While it was repeatedly stated that my conditions would at all times correspond with those of the captured soldiers, when your own lawyer went to inspect the 'hole' at San Quentin he approved the deplorable conditions there—another move which potentially jeopardized my safety.* My mother's acceptance of the appointment to a second term as a UC regent, as you well know, would have caused my immediate execution had the SLA been less together about their political goals. Your actions have taught me a great lesson, and in a strange kind of way, I'm grateful to you.

"Steven, I know that you are beginning to realize that there is no such thing as neutrality in time of war. There can be no compromise, as your experiences with the FBI must have shown you. You have been harassed by the FBI because of your supposed connections with so-called radicals, and some people have even gone so far as to suggest that I arranged my own arrest. We both know what really came down that Monday night—but you don't know what's happened since then. I have changed—grown. I've become conscious and can never go back to the life we led before. What I'm saying may seem cold to you and to my old friends, but love doesn't mean the same thing to me anymore. My love has expanded as a result of my experiences to embrace all people. It's grown into an unselfish love for my comrades here, in prison, and on the streets. A love that comes from the knowledge that 'no one is free until we are all free.' While I wish that you could be a comrade, I don't expect it—all I expect is that you try to understand the changes I've gone through.

---

*San Francisco attorney (and UC regent) William Coblentz, at the behest of Randolph Hearst, had "inspected" on February 20 the Adjustment Center at San Quentin where Remiro and Little were being held in small, separated cells. At the request of their attorneys, Coblentz said, he did not talk with the two SLA members, "but I did discuss their situation with the warden, I checked the conditions of the cells, and saw—and tasted—the food being served." Afterward Coblentz issued a brief statement in which he concluded that Remiro and Little "seemed to be receiving the same treatment as do other prisoners whose situations require special measures for their personal security." On March 8, a federal judge ordered the two men transferred to the Alameda county jail to await trial on the grounds that only persons already *convicted* of a (felony) crime could be held in a state prison. Although Coblentz's visit to San Quentin received considerable media coverage at the time, two years later Bill and Emily Harris were insisting to interviewers that the attorney had lied, that he had never gone to the prison, that it had been "a propaganda ploy by the Hearsts."

"I have been given the choice of, one, being released in a safe area, or, two, joining the forces of the Symbionese Liberation Army and fighting for my freedom and the freedom of all oppressed people. I have chosen to stay and fight.

"One thing which I learned is that the corporate ruling class will do anything in their power in order to maintain their position of control over the masses, even if this means the sacrifice of one of their own. It should be obvious that people who don't even care about their own children couldn't possibly care about anyone else's children. The things which are precious to these people are their money and power—and they will never willingly surrender either. People should not have to humiliate themselves by standing in lines in order to be fed, nor should they have to live in fear for their lives and the lives of their children, as Tyrone Guyton's mother will sadly attest to.*

*Patricia Hearst's reference to Tyrone Guyton came at a time when Oakland's black community was demanding a reinvestigation into the killing of the fourteen-year-old boy by Emeryville police. Some facts of the incident: Shortly before 10:30 P.M. November 1, 1973, officers Dale Phillips and Thomas Mierky, dressed in civies and in an unmarkd car, spotted Guyton and another black youth near a parked auto, acting in what the policemen described as a "suspicious manner." When Guyton, alone, suddenly drove away from that scene (in what was only later determined to be a stolen car), the two cops pursued with red light and siren. Guyton speeded up, leading a half-dozen squad cars on a wild ten-minute chase that zigzagged through industrial Emeryville and across the city line into adjoining Oakland. When one police car smashed into Guyton's auto, the youth leaped out and fled on foot. Officer Phillips later stated that he believed Guyton had had a pistol and had shot at the pursuing police, and that Phillips had then fired at the boy. Phillips' shot struck Guyton in the buttocks, knocking the youth to the ground. Another Emeryville patrolman, William Matthews, said he then saw Guyton's prone body move and, believing the teenager was armed, assumed Guyton was going to shoot at him. Matthews, from a distance of six feet, fired one shot into Guyton's back that killed him. What had aroused Oakland blacks was the fact that Guyton apparently had not had any weapon; there had been no justification for police to fire at him. But even lab reports of chemical testing that indicated Guyton had not fired a gun failed to make a dent in the police version. The official report clearing the officers theorized the running youth had thrown the weapon away and that some unknown person had retrieved and hidden it before investigators could find it.

Three grand juries investigated the incident, but no indictments resulted even after it was revealed during another and independent criminal investigation that a witness who had told the grand juries that Guyton owned and carried a pistol—crucial supportive evidence for Emeryville police—had previously been arrested by one of the Guyton case officers, Phillips, for possession of heroin, but had not been formally charged. The new investigation was seriously considering the possibility that the witness, Dolores Wysingle, was "in debt" to Phillips before the Guyton killing and perhaps offered testimony favorable to him in payment. As

"Dad, you said that you were concerned with my life, and you also said that you were concerned with the life and interests of all oppressed people in this country, but you are a liar in both areas and as a member of the ruling class I know for sure that yours and Mom's interests are never the interests of the people. Dad, you said you would see about getting more job opportunities for the people, but why haven't you warned the people what is going to happen to them—that actually the few jobs they still have will be taken away.

"You, a corporate liar, of course will say that you don't know what I am talking about, but I ask you then to prove it. Tell the poor and oppressed of this nation what the corporate state is about to do, warn black and poor people that they are about to be murdered down to the last man, woman, and child. If you're so interested in the people, why don't you tell them what the energy crisis really is? Tell them how it's nothing more than a manufactured strategy, a way of hiding industry's real intentions. Tell the people that the energy crisis is nothing more than a means to get public approval for a massive program to build nuclear power plants all over this nation. Tell the people that the entire corporate state is, with the aid of this massive power supply, about to totally automate the entire industrial state, to the point that in the next five years all that will be needed will be a small class of button pushers; tell the people, Dad, that all the lower class and at least half the middle class will be unemployed in the next three years and that the removal of expendable excess, the removal of unneeded people, has already started. I want you to tell the people the truth. Tell them how the law-and-order programs are just a means to remove so-called violent—meaning aware—individuals from the community in order to facilitate the controlled removal of unneeded labor forces from this country, in the same way that Hitler controlled the removal of the Jews from Germany.

"I should have known that if you and the rest of the corporate state were willing to do this to millions of people to maintain power and to serve your needs, you would also kill me if necessary to serve those same needs. How long will it take before white people in this country understand that what happens to a black child hap-

---

of publication, the new investigation was continuing. The SLA made mention of the Guyton shooting on several occasions (terming it "murder" carried out "by three goons from the Emeryville Political Police Patrol"), including mention in the first communiqué in which the SLA announced itself and claimed credit for the November 6, 1973, assassination of Dr. Marcus Foster.

pens sooner or later to a white child? How long will it be before we all understand that we must fight for our freedom?

"I have been given the name Tania after a comrade who fought alongside Che in Bolivia for the people of Bolivia. I embrace the name with the determination to continue fighting with her spirit. There is no victory in half-assed attempts at revolution. I know Tania dedicated her life to the people, fighting with total dedication and an intense desire to learn, which I will continue in the oppressed American people's revolution. All colors of string in the web of humanity yearn for freedom!

"Osceola and Bo [Little and Remiro]: Even though we have never met I feel like I know you. Timing brought me to you and I'm fighting with your freedom and the freedom of all prisoners in mind. In the strenuous jogs that life takes, you are pillars of strength to me. If I'm feeling down, I think of you, of where you are and why you are there, and my determination grows stronger. It's good to see that your spirits are so high in spite of the terrible conditions. Even though you aren't here, you are with other strong comrades, and the three of us are learning together—I in an environment of love, and you in one of hate, in the belly of the fascist beast. We have grown closer to the people and become stronger through our experiences. I have learned how vicious the pig really is, and our comrades are teaching me to attack with even greater viciousness, in the knowledge that the people will win. I send greetings to Death Row Jeff, Al Taylor, and Raymond Scott. Your concern for my safety is matched by my concern for yours. We share a common goal as revolutionaries knowing that Comrade George lives.

"It is in the spirit of Tania that I say, 'Patria o Muerte, venceremos.' "

Accompanying the tape was one of the extraordinary poster photos of revolutionary camp: Tania, posed like a mannequin in a tan jump suit, complete with a beret; legs spread as if in a crouch, and slung from a strap around her neck—what appeared to be a cut-down M-1 carbine loaded with a full automatic banana clip, with either a scope or a flashlight attached atop the gun barrel. Her face was solemn, her eyes quiet, almost glazed in the flash, gazing out past the Polaroid for a horizon, perhaps, or a future.

On the ring finger of her left hand, where a woman would wear a wedding or engagement ring, there was a single golden band. It was not a ring that Steven Weed had given her. She had worn no ring when kidnapped.

16

General Field Marshal Cinque

IT would not have been the Field Marshal himself who placed the ring on Patricia's finger—at least not in pledge of union as in marriage; Tania's later announcement that she had loved Cujo, Willie Wolfe, drew a sensible connection to the ring. Yet in another sense, the ring, and the transformation it marked, was indeed dowry for DeFreeze. When Patty declared herself Tania, Donald David DeFreeze had finally achieved the humiliation of the Hearsts he had so single-mindedly sought. This was the unspoken demand that echoes through all his long diatribes. The money, the food, even the blood of the "fascist insect" would not be enough. He kept repeating that the food was to be a gesture of good faith "and regret," not a ransom or a payoff, but a "form of repentance." Cinque wanted to rob the spirit, to make the Hearst family—who for him represented the state, the society, the jailers—hurt as he had hurt; to have to give up something of themselves; to be filled with a frustrated rage and yet to be powerless, castrated.

The conversion of Tania was his greatest triumph. It was, in fact, the high point of the SLA, a catalytic moment full of opportunity, and to exploit it they openly rejoiced in their power. They were the new nation, the revolution come, those who could lead and govern us—and DeFreeze, the Field Marshal, was now the "Chairman" of the Symbionese, no less than a prophet, surely more than a man, no longer a leader, now *the* leader.

With but a pause in the tape, after Tania declared herself, came the voice of Fahizah, Nancy Ling Perry, the SLA "Information-Intelligence" officer, with a long paean to the General Field Marshal. "Cinque is a black brother who spent many years of his life in fascist Amerikkka's concentration camps: man-child years in prison cells and man years in prison cells. Cinque met literally thousands of black, brown, red, yellow, and white freedom fighters

302

while he was locked down; courageous Comrade George Jackson was one among them.* Now the spirit of all the brothers Cinque knows lives in him [as well as] the spirit of all the sisters Cinque never had the opportunity to meet, but knows by common bond—like Assata Shakur, Lolita Lebron, and Bernardine Dohrn—is always in his heart.

"When Cinque escaped alone on foot from Soledad prison, he did so for one reason only: TO FIGHT WITH THE PEOPLE AND TO LEAD THE PEOPLE IN REVOLUTION. [Capitals in the official SLA transcript.] He did not escape so that he could kick back and hide and get high; he did not even escape so that he could satisfy a deep and longing personal ache to simply see the people and be on the streets and reunite with his family and be a father once again to his children. Cinque escaped so that he could actively stalk the fascist insect that preys upon the life of the people. . . ."

While in Vacaville, DeFreeze had cast away his given "slave name" and took up first the nickname Cinque, then the formal Swahili "reborn name" Mtume. Said Fahizah: "Cinque Mtume is the name that was bestowed upon him by his imprisoned sisters and brothers. It is the name of an ancient African chief who led the fight of his people for freedom. . . . The name means Fifth Prophet, and Cin was many years ago given this name because of his keen instinct and senses, his spiritual consciousness, and his deep love of all the people and children of this earth.

"This does not, however, mean that Cinque is from God or someone that is holy or that he has an extreme ego problem, but simply that he to us and to oppressed peoples is the instilled hope and spirit of his people and all peoples. . . .

"We are speaking to the people now because we all know that we cannot afford the loss of another leader; and we want the people to know that in spite of the enemy's technology and prestige of terror we DO have a leader that loves the people, and lives and fights for the people. . . .

*The inference that DeFeeze had met George Jackson is contradicted by records of the California Department of Corrections which show they were never in the same prison at the same time. In 1970, when DeFreeze actually began serving his sentence for a 1969 robbery and shoot-out in Los Angeles, he was initially sent to Vacaville; Jackson by then was being held in the infamous Adjustment Center at San Quentin awaiting trial for the January, 1970, murder of a Soledad prison guard. DeFreeze was still at Vacaville when Jackson was killed leading the bloody August 21, 1971, escape attempt from the Adjustment Center.

"The oppressed peoples of this nation have and will continue to bring forth their leaders, prophets, and fighters until they are free. The people brought forth Malcolm X, who came to unite the people and warn the enemy of what would inevitably happen if the people were not freed. The enemy answered by murdering Malcolm. The people then did again bring forth another prophet, that prophet was Martin Luther King, who with nonviolence and humanity pleaded to the enemy to free the people. And just when King was ready to declare that nonviolent protest would accomplish nothing but the further enslavement and degradation of the people, the enemy murdered King. George Jackson was a prophet and leader from the streets, and when the enemy imprisoned him, George received his education in the raw; he learned firsthand that there can be NO compromise with the merciless pigs. George Jackson came from the prisons of Amerikkka and, love-inspired, he boldly fought the oppressor. When the fascist insect locked him down and murdered him, the people knew that they had suffered a great loss, but they failed to unite in immediate retaliation.

"Now, once again, the people have brought forth another prophet and leader. This leader comes not to beg and plead with the enemy, he comes not to warn of violence, but is himself the bringer of the children of the wind and the SOUND OF WAR. He has ONE WORD to the children of the oppressed and the children of the oppressor: COME."

In the echo of his praises came the voice of DeFreeze, the prophet himself. Since the corporate state and the Hearst empire were not willing to deliver, the SLA had decided to take no more prisoners: "All corporate enemies of the people will be SHOT on sight at any time and at any place," he said. "This order is permanent, until such time as all enemy forces have either surrendered or been destroyed."

Somberly, he issued three SLA "death warrants," declaring two former friends and a longtime adversary priority enemies of the people. He condemned Robyn Steiner, Russ Little's twenty-year-old girlfriend, who had fled Berkeley to Florida in December; Chris Thompson, the young black radical who had introduced several of the SLA members but who had gone to the police after he realized a pistol registered in his name was one of the SLA kill-guns; and Colston Westbrook, the Vacaville BCA coordinator, who had made no secret of his distaste for the SLA and the "stupid Maoists" who had infiltrated his prison group. Steiner, said

Cinque, had informed on the SLA to the FBI; Thompson was accused as a "paid informer"; and Westbrook was credited with being a former CIA torturer in Vietnam and "other countries," now working "for military intelligence while giving cross assistance to the FBI." The three, he said, should be "shot on sight by any of the people's forces."

Turning from the "business of the Revolution," he then spoke to his own family, a long message more poignant to hear than to read: "I would like to take this opportunity to speak to my six lovely black babies. Victor, Damon, Sherry, Sherlyne, Dawn, and DeDe, I want you to know that just to say your names again fills my heart with joy. . . . I want you to understand that I have not forgotten my promise to you, that whenever you needed me I would be there at your side, and so I am now even when you may not see me, I am there; because no matter where I am, I am fighting for your freedom, your future, your life. Daddy wants you to understand. . . ."

He ended the tape with an incredible symphonic finale: "In closing," he said slowly, "I will play the national anthem of the Symbionese Liberation Army." There was a pause, then, wafting slowly from the background, there came a light jazz riff with a spiced saxophone, part of "Way Back Home," a cut on the new album by the Crusaders, *Scratch*. From the background, DeFreeze spoke again—pausing deeply between the phrases, with a reversed crescendo, his voice steadily deeper:

"My People . . . My Brothers . . . My Sisters . . . FREE THE PEOPLE . . . FREE THE LAND . . . AND *SAVE* THE CHILDREN!!!"

The SLA simply had no sense of when they were ahead. The transformation of Tania was an unparalleled propaganda stunt. It put them in the eye of the world—perhaps the food giveaway plus Tania would have given them credits nearly to offset the Foster murder. There would have been no queuing up at the recruiting booths, but perhaps they could have opened lines of support in the still largely hostile radical community. The annunciation of the Fifth Prophet exploded all the possibilities—blew them to pieces. Serious American radicals differ endlessly, but with a handful of cultish exceptions, there is emphatic agreement that the last thing they want is a revolutionary messiah.

Poor Robyn Steiner, a young radical who wanted as little to do with the FBI as she did with the SLA, had in fact repeatedly refused to give information to the police. The SLA intelligence unit must have done its research in tea leaves. After the death warrant Steiner went into hiding from both the FBI and the SLA. Berkeley radicals had their own suspicions about Westbrook and Thompson, and it was public knowledge that both had talked to the FBI about the SLA, but few were willing to nominate them for *Mod Squad* Emmys. Sure, he had talked with the cops, said Thompson privately—the SLA had boxed him in—but Little and Remiro, he said, "*know* I'm not a police agent . . . they would never have gotten as far as they did if I had been. . . ."* Both Thompson and Westbrook went into hiding for a while; with Berkeley full of free-lance crazies, the death warrants were no joke. In character, Westbrook left a message on his automatic telephone-answering machine: "*Hello, this is Colston Westbrook speaking. I am not dead yet, but I still remain high on the SLA hit list. If the caller is a terrorist, please include your affiliation so the credit for my demise can be properly awarded . . . BEEP.*"

The day after the death-warrant message there was a statement issued from prison by Little and Remiro. The SLA was so ill informed that their imprisoned soldiers—after checking with their families and lawyers—felt they had to speak up. They said nothing about Westbrook or Thompson, but they asked Cinque to rescind the death warrant on Robyn Steiner. "She has, in fact, on several occasions refused to talk to the FBI," said Remiro. "We think further investigation into the matter is necessary."

Three days later they sent out another message. Inside, the boys had a lot of time to think. They said that "out of revolutionary love and concern," they felt they had to criticize the "counterrevolutionary trends" in the latest communiqué. While "true revolutionaries" could now have no doubt that Cin was a "military/political genius," those "who attempt through mystical rationalizations to build a superstar jeopardize everything." Mysticism, they said, is a "dead-end street," and "the people have learned through lessons of blood that such superstars, uncriticizable images, can lead toward counterrevolutionary opportunism. The people do not want one prophet, one revolutionary leader—they want a rev-

---

*Thompson later did lay claim to the several rewards that had been offered in the Foster case, eventually collecting $10,000 from the Oakland *Tribune*. But both the state of California and the city of Oakland, each of which had also offered $10,000 for the killers, rejected his claims, and in mid-1976 Thompson was suing to collect. If Thompson had ever been a "police agent" prior to his informing on Little, he did not attempt to bolster his case for the rewards by revealing it; no evidence that he had been an agent was ever found by the authors.

olution! There are many capable revolutionary leaders . . . . "
The Fifth Prophet replied to neither message. The death warrant
on Robyn Steiner stood. (And perhaps even in the eyes of two of
their own, the SLA had become more cult than comrades.)

Donald DeFreeze was selling a used Revolution—no cash down,
little credit needed—but the time was wrong, the politics were
wrong, probably it was the wrong country, certainly it was the
wrong army. In the mellowing of the seventies the gurus and the
shamans had scoured clean many of the corners in which Cinque
earlier might have found followers. Perhaps, in the eerie fatalism
of his message to his children, a shadow of this had come to him.
With Tania's debut, the SLA had peaked. His was not a deep or
subtle mind, but he had been a loser so often that perhaps he was
familiar with the territory.

On a five-to-life sentence, Donald David DeFreeze had spent
only three and a half years in the California prison system—but
there DeFreeze discovered Cinque Mtume within himself, the
prison militant "reborn." The Field Marshal was an eminently
foreseeable man. Prisons continue to clone others like him, newly
politicized rebels who have found in a neo-Marxist analysis an explanation for their crippled personal lives, their class experience,
their racial history.

The SLA world view—life inside the murderous fascist state—
defines more or less accurately life inside the maximum-security
prisons, repression under which the guerrilla has the only dignity,
where the guerrilla mentality best keeps one alive. The SLA was
born when this bitter and determined man emerged into the outside world with his prison zeitgeist intact and chanced across a
group of crippled misfits whose personal frustrations were such
that they could empathize and adopt as their own this vision so far
from the realities of the "outside." A man like DeFreeze had a
great stake in holding to his prison-guerrilla persona, the man of
dignity who had been "born again" in cellblock communism. It
was perhaps the only positive self he had ever known. To let it
slip, to acknowledge a more mundane reality, to see America as
something less than a *Star Trek* prison with Hitler as warden,
would rob him of heroic choice and leave him the human shell he
had been before. It was revolution as an act of will, desperation of
personal rather than collective sort. As Fahizah wrote: "Revolutionary violence is nothing but the most profound means of
achieving internal as well as external balance." At thirty years of
age Donald DeFreeze needed a whole revolution for balance.

If the Field Marshal had not the intellect to edge his passion with logic, the pragmatic vision to rise above his hate and desire for revenge, if he was murderous, wanton with his "death warrants" and bloated with star trip—he was a limited man primed through life to explode just so. From his past there emerges a bewildering series of profiles: DeFreeze as a fundamentalist Jesus freak a mere four years before he emerged as the Field Marshal; DeFreeze as a minor-league police informer, the petty hood, the beaten man, the loser, the betrayed husband who plotted his own arrest because prison offered refuge from his demanding wife— and beneath them all, the desperate fear, in his own words, of "becoming a nothing."

> Woe is me! for I am as when they have gathered the summer fruits, as is the grapegleanings of the vintage: there is no cluter to eat: my soul desired the firstripe fruit. . . .

In April, 1970, DeFreeze waxed biblical writing a long testimonial of his fundamentalist faith. It was sent to the judge who had just sentenced him to five years to life, after DeFreeze was convicted of armed robbery, two counts of assault with a deadly weapon, and possession of a forged check. It was his third felony conviction; he got the maximum.

> The good man is perished out of the earth: and there is none upright among men: they all lie in wait for blood; they hunt every man his brother with a net.
> That they may do evil with both hands earnestly, the prince asketh, and the judge asketh for a reward; and the great man, he uttereth his mischievous desire: so they wrap it up.

In the two years from 1968 to 1970 DeFreeze had been spieling off jive scripture to police, courts, and probation officers. Many thought it was sincere; some thought it further proof of his mental instability; perhaps it helped in his charmed career through the courts in the late sixties.

> The best of them is as a brier: the most upright is sharper than a thorn hedge: the day of thy watchmen be their perplexity.
> Trust ye not in a friend, put ye not confidence in a guide: keep the doors of thy mouth from her that lieth in thy bosom.
> For the son dishonoureth the father, the daughter riseth up against her mother, the daughter in law against her mother in law; a man's enemies are the men of his own house.

This was not the affected voice of the con man begging leniency— the judge had finished with him, sentenced and remanded him— and this was the voice in which DeFreeze responded, the prayer- ful lament but the prelude to an angry message of revenge:

> I told you that God would bring you down. I don't understand its meaning, But there is a meaning for you, I fear that my God will come to you when you are not ready to go.
>
> Maybe you say I have Sinned and must pay, But even you will ask for forgiveness, But you will not forgive and as you have done unto others so will be done unto you. . . .

The letter was long, threatening, bitter; it was not a message of pretense.

During that 1970 trial—his last appearance in open court— DeFreeze had preached and lectured the jury, declared police records forgeries, witnesses liars. Acting as his own attorney, he stood in the court and prayed aloud for the Lord to reveal some- how that "Dear Dumb Donald" was innocent—but it was an open- and-shut case. Spotted with a stolen check in a Los Angeles bank, DeFreeze had run into the street and engaged in a gun battle with police. The judge, in sentencing him, publicly urged prison au- thorities to note that the defendant "needs help and needs a lot of it."

When he wrote the judge, he had already been committed to Vacaville for psychiatric therapy. At the time, the Lord was still with him, the Revolution ahead of him.

Donald David DeFreeze was born in 1943, the oldest of eight children, in the ratty ghetto of Cleveland, Ohio. He hated his fa- ther; he told a prison therapist that as punishment his father had broken his arm on three occasions, twice when he was ten, again when he was twelve. He dropped out of school at fourteen, after the ninth grade, and (according to his various stories) either ran away or was sent away by his mother to protect him from his fa- ther. In Buffalo, New York, he roomed with a fundamentalist minister, the Reverend William Foster, and became involved with a street gang called the Crooked Skulls. In August, 1960, he was arrested trying to rob a parking meter and nine days later was ar- rested again trying to steal a car and a pistol. He was sixteen. He told a psychiatrist later he had planned to return to Cleveland and kill his father. He was committed to the Elmira state reformatory; he did two and a half years.

"Life in the little prison," DeFreeze later wrote, "was nothing but fear and hate day in and day out. The hate was mading [sic], the only safe place was your cell that you went to at the end of the day. . . ." He got out when he was eighteen and returned to Buffalo, where he asked Reverend Foster for permission to marry Foster's daughter, Harriet, then fourteen. When he was refused, DeFreeze left New York State for New Jersey. Reverend Foster said he never heard from the boy again.

Investigating DeFreeze's early past is difficult; while free, he was a loner and a drifter, with few friends. Even after he married, he never put down roots. An extraordinary if somewhat suspect source is from his own hand, a fourteen-page autobiography written early in 1970, while he was awaiting trial for the bank shootout. It was part of a plea for leniency sent to yet another California judge, who was then considering revocation of suspended sentences he received for his two previous felony convictions. The scribbled booklet is laced with piety and self-justifications and full of self-serving excuses, but there is much of it that has the ring of bitter truth, explaining confusing facts already known—and even the lies reveal.

In 1962, he wrote, he had settled in Newark. Girls would disappear when they heard of his record, and he said he was very lonely until he met beautiful Gloria Thomas, twenty-three, mother of three children. "I was 18 and in love and life really became real to me. I asked Glory to marry me and she said yes, we had just one month before we were married." As a minor he needed his parents' consent; they agreed but told him he was a fool.

"Things were lovely all the way up to a few months," he wrote, then in a fight his wife told him "she didn't love me at all, but that she needed a husband and father for her kids." Although deeply hurt, he said he smoothed things over. But seven months later "I came home sooner than I do most of the time from work and she and an old boyfriend had just had relationships [sic]." Furious, he said he offered her to the boyfriend who said he did not want her. Husband and wife fought and talked, and at length he decided to forget the incident and try again. But then he found out "that none of my wife's kids had the same father and that she had never been married," contrary to what she had told him. "I was a little afraid but I said I would give her a good chance. . . .

"I really put faith in her, but somehow, little stories kept coming to me, one was that my boss had come to my home looking from [sic] me and that my wife had come to the door in the nude."

He had hoped their first child would bring them closer, "but as soon as the baby was born it was the same thing, I had begun to drink very deeply, but I was trying to put up with her and hope she would change. But as the years went by [she] never did." Once, he said, he just abandoned the family for two months and went to Canada; he returned to find his wife pregnant. He thought it was his child, he said, and worked at two jobs to provide for the newborn; but he began to hear stories about his wife with other men while he was in Canada and realized that the new child was not his. His wife left him for four months to live with another man, then returned and begged him to forgive her; he did. He was twenty-two years old, legal father to five kids, alternating between welfare and menial jobs, always pressured financially. He wrote:

> I started playing around with guns and fireworks and dogs and cars. Just anything to get away from life and how unhappy I was. I finely [sic] got into trouble with the police for shoting [sic] off a rifle in my basement and for a bomb I had made out of about 30 fireworks from fourth of July. After I went to court and got Probation I was really ashamed of myself. I had not been in trouble with the police for years and now I had even lost that pride.

In his autobiography DeFreeze goes on to place the blame for all his past and present troubles on his marriage, a more than small overstatement—but odd bits of information buttress much of his story. In one of his first SLA communiqués DeFreeze describes himself as the father of *two* children, but later acknowledges the six who bear his name. The two would be the first and third born of the marriage—the four others were the three he adopted when he married and the child he thought not his. DeFreeze writes about how he hid his family and personal life; and the Orange, New Jersey, painting contractor who employed him intermittently over several years—and thought of himself as one of Donald's closer friends—said that in all the time they worked together, he never knew DeFreeze and his wife had children. DeFreeze, he said, was unusually quiet. "He kept strictly to himself, just didn't talk about himself." Another thing the man remembers vividly was Donald's fascination with guns. "He'd talk about them all the time, this one and that one, about how much he'd like to go hunting." (When DeFreeze moved to California, he turned to his friend and old boss and borrowed $60 for a stake. He never repaid the money.)

Working off and on for other painting contractors, DeFreeze tried to open a little house-painting business on his own. House of DeFreeze, he called it, but he overextended his credit and the company went bankrupt. On top of business and the marriage he had other problems. His fascination with guns and bombs had him constantly in trouble with the law. In March of 1965, while under New Jersey indictment for possession of the firecracker/gunpowder bomb, he decided to visit California alone. On March 31 he was stopped by police while hitchhiking through Los Angeles on the San Bernardino freeway. When DeFreeze reached for his identification, the cops spotted a sharpened butter knife and a tear-gas canister tucked in his waistband; searching him, they found a sawed-off rifle in his suitcase. He was arrested and charged with illegal possession of the gun and tear-gas bomb; he was in the county jail three months awaiting trial and when convicted, he was sentenced to "time served." In New Jersey, his family was on welfare. Two weeks after his release in California, he went on trial for the bomb charge in New Jersey. The judge continued the case for a year and in June, 1966, put DeFreeze on two years' probation.

"All my friends and family knew of my wife's ways," wrote DeFreeze, "and of my foolishness in believing her and forgiving her, it was just too much to face, I had to get out." He writes nothing of his own failures. "I moved all over New Jersey but everywhere I went someone knew me or my wife or about my kids, I just couldn't take it anymore, I was slowly becoming a nothing." He said he first planned to move to California alone, but then, because of his wife's pleading, decided to move the whole family. "I put my age up so no one would think about me having so many kids. . . . I hoped it would be a new start for both of us, no one would know me or her or anything about my family."

In Los Angeles, in 1967, another child was born. Donald was twenty-three, now father to six. The marriage got no better. Wrote DeFreeze:

> More and more I was unhappy with everything. I started back playing with guns, drinking, pills, but this time more than I had ever before did. . . . I really don't understand what I was doing. She wanted nice things and I was working and I was buying and selling guns and the next thing I know I had become a thief.

In the spring of 1967 he had been working at a Los Angeles car wash, but was laid off. Unskilled, unschooled, he could not find work. State welfare turned him down because he was not a resident; the manpower training program rejected him because he had a police record.

On June 9, 1967, Los Angeles police officers stopped DeFreeze for running a red light on a bicycle. He gave a fictitious name to the cops and they spotted it. He was arrested and searched; police found a homemade bomb in one jacket pocket and a second bomb and a .22-caliber pistol in a bag in the bike basket. He pleaded guilty to a felony, violation of the deadly weapon control law, and came up for sentencing in September. Arnold Kaye, the court probation officer who investigated DeFreeze's case, wrote in his confidential report to the sentencing judge:

> The [probation officer] has found himself deeply troubled by this case. First, he feels that the difficulties which the defendant has encountered in his life are real and serious. He feels his responsibilities deeply and is overcome when he cannot meet them. . . . The type of behavior encountered in the present offense appears to be the defendant's way of compensating for feelings of inadequacy and powerlessness.

Kaye said he worried about DeFreeze's mental stability and felt that perhaps the defendant should be committed for a short-term psychiatric evaluation, but urged leniency. He noted the irony of the fact that only after DeFreeze was arrested did the welfare department help the family financially, and only then, with DeFreeze on bail, did the job-training manpower program find a priority slot for him. He quoted DeFreeze: "If I had known that we could have got help by me going to jail I could have did a lot of lesser things like broke a few windows or something. It would have been worth it to help my wife and kids." The judge gave him a suspended sentence and put him on probation for three years.

It was only three months later, however, that DeFreeze was again arrested. Again it was guns, but this time the charges were more serious. On December 2, 1967, at 3:30 A.M., a Los Angeles prostitute named Gloria Yvonne Sanders picked up DeFreeze as a trick in downtown LA. They checked in at a motel, had sex, and then DeFreeze pulled a small derringer pistol and put it to the woman's head. He took back the ten dollars he had given her and robbed her of the rest of her night's earnings. After DeFreeze again used her and "performed unnatural acts," Sanders told police, she was shivering and told DeFreeze she was cold. When he allowed her to get up and put on her coat, she snatched the opportunity, ran out the door and down the street. At a pay phone she called the police.

Apparently sure the whore would never go to the cops, De-Freeze dozed off in the motel room. He was sleeping, gun under the pillow, when Sanders returned with two LA patrolmen. It was a new gun, with the serial numbers obliterated. As the cops were leading him handcuffed from the motel, DeFreeze stopped and pointed out his car to Officer L. J. Henricks. He did not want it stolen, he told Henricks, and asked that the police not leave it at the motel. The car was impounded. Incredibly, in the trunk of the car police found twelve stolen handguns in a blue canvas bag—both the bag and the pistols were part of the loot in a major gun theft the month before. More than 200 guns had been stolen in a burglary at the Western Surplus Store, a major LA gun shop; the break-in was the subject of a major police investigation.

The cops put the squeeze on DeFreeze. After wrangling and threatening, they worked a deal: DeFreeze would finger the man who sold him the guns in exchange for a recommendation of leniency. Two days after his arrest DeFreeze led two detectives to his home. He had promised them his wife would be able to tell them where the gun seller lived, a man he said he knew only as Ron. No one was home. While they were waiting, DeFreeze suddenly scrambled, ran through the apartment, and dived out a second-story window. He landed with a roll, jumped up, and ran, escaping. He was free only two days. Acting on a tip from DeFreeze's wife, police raided a friend's apartment and recaptured him. Now the cops put the screws on him, and with a stack of charges against him, DeFreeze tried to salvage his deal. He not only identified Ronald Coleman, later charged with the theft, he set him up. DeFreeze told police Coleman still had in his possession two stolen guns which he, DeFreeze, had sold him earlier. DeFreeze said Coleman was a neighbor and a friend of his. With the police beside him, DeFreeze then telephoned Coleman, asking if he still had the guns. According to the police incident report, DeFreeze hung up and told the three detectives with him, "Ron is at his apartment . . . let's hit him." DeFreeze then led police through the apartment, pointing out where Coleman had hidden a stash of marijuana and several dozen stolen guns.

In neither his autobiography for the court nor in any of his several other pleadings for leniency in 1970 did DeFreeze bother to mention his assisting police. Although, according to his wife, DeFreeze was regularly asked for information by police through the next several months while he was awaiting trial, DeFreeze was a small-scale tipster with a court hearing over his head—not a valuable informer the police would go out of their way to protect. (According to some published reports, this was allegedly a period in which DeFreeze was boring through radical black militant groups as a police superspy; but in the LA ghetto the word was out on DeFreeze; he could not have infiltrated a black militant cub scout pack.)

In August, 1967, DeFreeze pleaded guilty to the armed robbery of the prostitute. He was to be sentenced in September, but while still free on bail was again arrested—for stealing a motorcycle. The charge arose out of an overdue rental and was later dropped, but since he was awaiting sentencing, the cops simply locked him up and kept him with a high bail. His wife, writing his judge in August to complain, said that ever since the Coleman incident, "police officers have been running to and from the house just to talk to [Donald]," but that the police had refused to give DeFreeze or his family any protection from constant harassment in the neighborhood. "As a result of his cooperation in Nov. of 67," she wrote, "he has been shot [at] twice, I have been shot at, & our family has been threatened. We haven't had any police prot. nor would they even come to the apt." In October the court committed DeFreeze to the Chino state prison for a two-month psychiatric evaluation. The staff at Chino recommended that he be sentenced to the state prison, noting an "apparent disorganization of his thought processes," the escape, and his "penchant to possess firearms and bombs." Perhaps because of his assistance to police, the court instead chose to place him on a highly restricted and intensive probation program, with a mandatory program of psychiatric therapy and a provision for a probation officer to search his home regularly for guns and bombs. The Probation Department records note that they recommended the intensive street supervision over prison largely because of DeFreeze's "warm and meaningful family relationship," his apparent religiosity, and the "lack of assaultive or violent behavior" in his criminal record. He was freed in December, 1968, after spending four months in jail.

Looking back, DeFreeze wrote to the judge of a marriage that was anything but warm and meaningful. "I started to tell you to send me to jail and that I didn't want to go home . . . but you should never have sent me back to her." He said his wife was driving him crazy. They had both realized their marriage was loveless; they stayed together for mutual exploitation. He said he had long before realized that he was "too weak" and too afraid of loneliness to leave her on his own. He had mentioned divorce once before, but she had frightened him out of it, saying that he would still have to pay support for her and the six kids. Divorce would only increase his money worries. And now his "loving family" was his probation ticket.

When he got out of jail, he said, his wife began pressuring him to take the family back to New Jersey, where she had family and friends. He asked his probation officer for permission to move, but was refused. His wife demanded that they move anyway, he said, and threatened to wreck his probation by leaving him if he did not. Everything closed in; he felt trapped.

On March 20, 1969, three months after his release on a probation that absolutely forbade him to possess guns, Donald DeFreeze was arrested with a loaded 9-mm semiautomatic rifle. He had bought the gun legally in his own name—he had even registered it with the police department in his own name. One of the few possible explanations for his behavior was the one offered in the autobiography a year later. More than anything else, he said, he wanted to get out from under his marriage. He decided the best way to do it would be to go to jail—so he blatantly violated his parole to arrange his own arrest. "I thought you would really send me to jail [and she would go] to New Jersey, that's why I didn't hide anything, not because I am crazy like I've led people to believe. . . ."

After the gun arrest a hearing was scheduled for the revocation of the probation. It was a good plan; if he had gone to court, he undoubtedly would have been sent to prison. But then prison seemed as frightening as his marriage. He bolted. Free on bond, he, his wife, and the children fled to New Jersey.

In his autobiography, when he writes about the last half of 1969—the period leading up to the bank incident for which he was then facing charges—DeFreeze is vague and less than coherent, awkwardly skipping over anything that might reflect poorly on himself. He describes himself as a marionette, with his wife pulling all the strings. It is known that DeFreeze first spent several months in the Newark area, then brought his family to Cleveland, then returned alone to California. He wrote that his wife had expected that they could live with her family in New Jersey until they got settled, but that did not work out, and "my wife and kids ended up in the streets."

When they could not make a go of it in New Jersey, wrote

DeFreeze, he brought the family back to Cleveland, where his mother and family still lived. He said the family lived with his mother while he took on two jobs to try to build a stake for them. Of course, he insisted, he planned all the time to return to California and give himself up on the probation violation once he had set them up. Then came a crisis. As DeFreeze describes it, he stole $100 from the cash box of a restaurant he worked at, and when he brought it home, his wife was furious with him for not taking more when he had the chance. "Sir, what she said really did something to me, it opened my eyes to what she was and what she had made me become." That night, he said, full of righteous rage, he jumped into his car and drove two days and nights to get to California to turn himself in . . . only, before he could turn himself in, before he "got a chance," he was involved in this crazy incident in a bank and had to defend himself against a bunch of police officers shooting at him. He was arrested, he said, and charged with all sorts of crimes, crimes of which he was innocent, totally innocent. . . .

Actually, the true story of his departure from Cleveland was as melodramatic, but certainly not as virtuous as he described it. On the night of October 11, 1969, Cleveland police investigating a report of a man on the roof of the Cleveland Trust Bank arrested DeFreeze running from the building. He had a knife and two loaded pistols tucked in his belt and was carrying a briefcase in which there was a bomb as well as a number of burglary tools. DeFreeze identified himself as Steven Robinson, a Cleveland man for whom the police had only a traffic citation on record. His mother put up surety for the $1,000 bail, and he was freed. Before police and the FBI were able to identify "Robinson" as DeFreeze, Donald had skipped town.

On November 15, in Los Angeles, a tourist from Hawaii, Mrs. Milagros Bacalbos, was sitting in her car in downtown LA when a man she later identified as DeFreeze approached her and put a gun to her head and demanded her money. He grabbed her purse, pushed her to the floor of her car, and clubbed her with the gun.

On November 17 DeFreeze appeared at a branch office of the Bank of America in Los Angeles and tried to cash a $1,000 cashier's check made out to Milagros Bacalbos which had been in the stolen purse. DeFreeze presented some identification in the name of Bacalbos, but the teller spotted the check as stolen. DeFreeze ran from the bank, chased by the bank security guard. The guard fired several shots at DeFreeze, and DeFreeze began shooting back at the guard and police officers who joined the chase. DeFreeze emptied his .32 automatic at the police but hit no one; he himself was wounded in the left hand and left foot and arrested.

DeFreeze's long-winded but futile defense at his trial consisted of denying the armed robbery, claiming he had found the stolen purse with the check in it, and as he was attempting—admittedly—to cash the check, he suddenly remembered that his car was illegally parked and walked out of the bank to move it. As he was walking out, he said, the "gun-happy" security guard pulled his pistol and fired at him. He said he ran to his car, in which he had a gun, ducking and dodging bullets fired by the security guard and the police, grabbed his pistol, and began to fire in "self-defense." After he was convicted and committed to Vacaville, he appealed the conviction on the grounds that the jury had not been instructed on the particulars of the law concerning self-defense. Appeal was denied.

It was, in a sense, as if the patience of the California criminal-justice system had been stretched like a rubber band. Now it snapped. Both the patience and the efficiency of the system left their mark; both the lies and the truths of this odd man's crippled vision shaped his notorious destiny, his army, and his revolution. Still, the wonder is not that a "Field Marshal" emerged from all this, but that—even in the torrid incubation of Berkeley—the chance mating of personalities could have provided him with a cult.

An unlikely interview that took place in March of 1970 documents just how different Donald DeFreeze was from the General Field Marshal he was to become. In January, 1970, DeFreeze was indicted in New Jersey for allegedly joining with Ralph Cobb, a leader of the New Jersey Black Panther Party, to kidnap the black caretaker at a Newark synagogue, in May, 1969, as part of a plot to extort money "for the Black Panthers" from a prosperous rabbi. (The charge was later dismissed by both police and the district attorney's office as groundless, a false accusation by the caretaker, and charges were dropped. Newark police sources conceded the case would never have been brought to trial had there not been hysteria in New Jersey over the Panthers. Cobb, however, was tried—he denied ever knowing DeFreeze or anything about the incident—and quickly acquitted. Police surmise the caretaker simply linked the name of a well-known Panther, Cobb, with

DeFreeze, a young hood he knew slightly.) Just before the Cobb case went to trial, the defense attorney for the Black Panther located DeFreeze in prison in California and demanded that a deposition be taken from him.

The attorney and his prosecution counterpart flew to California and interviewed DeFreeze in the Los Angeles county jail. Milton Friedman, the Panther attorney, remembers a truculent, defensive Donald DeFreeze who obviously wasn't willing to go an inch to help his client. "He was just a cheap young hood," recalls Friedman, ". . . paranoid. He thought we were somehow trying to set him up. DeFreeze had an alibi; he was working in Cleveland at the time of the alleged kidnap, he didn't know Cobb, he didn't know anything about it—but he was suspicious of everyone, particularly the young woman from the Watts Black Panthers whom I had brought in with me."

The official transcript of the interview, submitted to the New Jersey court, details a long discussion that focused on DeFreeze (to the surprise of both the defense and the prosecutor) identifying the synagogue caretaker as an intimate friend of his wife and her landlord during a brief period when she lived alone in New Jersey and DeFreeze went to arrange for the move to Cleveland. Friedman recalls that DeFreeze got "very agitated" talking about this. At the end of the interview, "Donald just reached over and grabbed the stenographer's notes and ran like hell down the corridor—brushing past the Manson girls, who were holding a session with Charlie in the adjacent visiting room—and into the bathroom, where he tried to flush them down a toilet."

The interview transcript, salvaged by jail guards, quotes DeFreeze talking about black militant politics. "I have," he said, "I think, the reputation of supposed to be a Black Panther or something, because I been hit with this three or four times—with the Black Panther bit or the military bit—but I am not!" The prosecutor asked what he meant by "hit." Said DeFreeze, "I have been questioned about being a member of the Black Panthers or US [United Slaves] or a member of the Muslims—and I never been a member of anything but a church!" Repeatedly asked about the alleged kidnapping, he finally snapped, "I don't walk around slapping people in the face and talking and sticking them up. This ain't my bag! I'm too nervous to be slapping people because they might slap back. . . ."

Said attorney Friedman after the SLA case exploded, "I have difficulty reconciling my image of DeFreeze, à hustler, with

Cinque . . . with any concern for the black people. He certainly indicated to us that he had little sympathy for black political defendants."

The man who described himself at his trial as "Dear Dumb Donald" must have undergone a huge transformation to emerge three years later as the General Field Marshal of the Symbionese Liberation Army, and surprisingly, little information is known about the "reborn" Cinque. A number of former convicts interviewed describe him as quiet, very much a loner; but most of DeFreeze's prison friends have been silent, fearful of being linked with the SLA. Leftist prison activists, trying to discredit the SLA early in the case, have spread rumors that DeFreeze was known as a snitch, an inmate informer, before he escaped, but inmates and ex-cons formerly prominent at Vacaville said that was not true.

Thero Wheeler, interviewed by the authors after he had been arrested in Texas, long after DeFreeze and most of the SLA were dead and shortly before Patty Hearst was captured, kept referring to DeFreeze as "being used" by certain unnamed monied radicals who, while not SLA members, were "affiliated with the SLA." "They used DeFreeze," said Wheeler, funding the SLA and advising him, then cutting him off when he went too far. "They used DeFreeze . . . they tried to use me, too. I think he was being used by a lot of other people that felt certain things should be done but they didn't have the nerve to do—and because he was an escaped convict and was mad, you know, at the world and what was happening to him, they used him."

At least in the early stages of the SLA, said Wheeler, "DeFreeze was being dictated to." Cinque, he added, just was not the sort of leader who could have planned the SLA. "Donald DeFreeze was locked up in jail, messed up like thousands of others that go in and out of there. He was bitter, he was uneducated, and he was trying to find a way out. It's easy if you can find a person that's embittered to convince him to do something. . . ." Wheeler would not identify the persons or person. Once he used the singular "he" talking about the early guardian of the SLA, implying "he" was a known Bay Area radical. It is not a person who had been publicly linked with the Symbionese, he said.

(Switching again to the plural, Wheeler implied that the people who had helped him with money and hideouts after he escaped— presumably his Bay Area Venceremos connections—were some of the same people who gave DeFreeze his direction. These behind-the-scenes people, Wheeler told San Francisco's *City* magazine, "were just playing, you know, playing at revolution. It was like a TV show they could watch. . . ." He was in Texas when the SLA held up the bank, but, he said, "I knew their money had been cut off when they robbed the bank. They wouldn't have done that if they didn't need to. They were just broke, I think.")

Not even Wheeler, however, challenges the fact that individual "soldiers" of the SLA—the Harrises, Remiro, and Little, and those who died in Los Angeles—followed DeFreeze as their commander. Whatever connection there may have been to another leader or leaders ended sometime after the Foster murder, he said. And although he characterizes the SLA as naïve, unaware that "revolution is a long, slow process . . . an evolutionary process," he does not gainsay the allegiance DeFreeze claimed from them.

It's clear that the personality of Donald DeFreeze underwent a great change while he was in prison, a change that became particularly evident when he began to connect with white radicals visiting the prisons. David Gunnell, the Peking House landlord and BCA activist, described DeFreeze as forceful, eloquent, and "charismatic." A "heavy" black Oakland radical who was recruited by DeFreeze for the Symbionese Federation described Cinque as a "wonderful, magnificent man." And from his psychiatric isolation cell at Vacaville, SLA recruit Al Taylor described the Field Marshal as "a very dynamic leader, a hypnotic leader . . . with an ability to stir, excite, and lead people." Taylor said DeFreeze "relates particularly well to women; they sort of get captivated by his personality."

None of this would seem to apply to the Donald DeFreeze who plotted his own arrest to escape from his wife—and certainly charisma is no common trait among even the newly politicized "reborn" prison militants. General Field Marshal Cinque emerged from a deeper transmutation, rare but not unique. In his cellblock protocommunism DeFreeze found a cause that made everything meaningful, that gave him moral certainty, a newfound integrity both personal and political—and among his young white radical friends he found people searching for a black leader, willing to believe deeply in him, willing to be led by him. Probably one without the other could never have created him; but in the mixture of the two, with the certainty of cause and the *process* of leadership, the SLA forged a leader in its own likeness.

17

Tania Goes to the Bank

CAMILLA HALL was at the wheel, steering the green LTD station wagon out Noriega Street through the Sunset District toward the ocean. Mizmoon Soltysik sat alongside Camilla, riding shotgun.

General Field Marshal Cinque and Nancy Ling Perry, each with automatic rifle, were in the backseat. Beside them, behind Mizmoon, was Tania Hearst. She, too, had a weapon. A cut-down M-1 carbine.

As they approached Twenty-second Avenue, someone spotted a police car. Camilla continued past the low white building, turned a corner, then another, then again, circling—twice—before finally pulling up and parking, illegally in a bus zone, on Twenty-second just off Noriega.

Moments before, a brand-new red Hornet Sportabout had taken up position, motor idling, in an abandoned service station directly across the street from the Hibernia Bank. In the car were Willie Wolfe, Angela Atwood, and Bill and Emily Harris.*

The Symbionese Liberation Army—nine now with the recruitment of Patricia Hearst—was about to begin an "action."

Zig Berzins was in a hurry. He had a service call to go out on, but first he had to get across the street and make a deposit. That shouldn't take long, he figured. Not many people knew about the bank's new, earlier opening hour—9 A.M. instead of 10 A.M. He would probably be in and out and on his way in five minutes or so. He strode out of Tweeters 'n' Woofer, his stereo shop, heading catty-corner across Noriega. A beautiful sunny morning, he noted, rare for that often-foggy section of San Francisco. Income tax day, he mused, happy his return had been mailed off well before the deadline. It was 9:50 A.M., Monday, April 15.

*Scenario described by Patricia Hearst during her trial.

322

Through the glass doors Berzins saw that nobody was lined up at any of the tellers' cages. He pushed one door open and, as he went through, gave it a shove backward. He heard a "thud," then the clinking sound of metal objects. "Christ," he remembers thinking, "I've slammed the door on a little old lady and everything's spilled out of her purse." He turned. Kneeling in the entranceway was a young woman, busy at the task of picking up two clips of ammunition and a scattering of bullets strewn around her on the sidewalk. Cradled across her knee was a sawed-off carbine. The girl, he said, was Nancy Perry . . . or Patricia Hearst.

Dashing past whoever it was came a strange procession. More women, all carrying guns. Then, following close, a bearded black man wearing a short leather coat and a floppy hat, armed with a machine gun. The Symbionese—nonplussed by the bowling over of a comrade—stormed into the bank. "SLA . . . SLA . . . " one of them shouted. "Everybody down on the floor and you won't get hurt." Mizmoon, pistol in hand, ran toward the money, vaulting the counter behind which startled tellers were darting for cover.

There were eighteen employees and six customers inside the Sunset branch of Hibernia Bank when the holdup occurred. One was security guard Ed Shea, sixty-six, a retired railroad payroll clerk stretching his pension check as a $2.06-an-hour rent-a-cop. He had been at the bank several months, and he carried a .38-caliber revolver in his holster, but he had never fired it. He considered himself a showpiece, his weapon a decoration. He stood at his post near the door, greeting customers, answering such questions as "Who do I talk to about a loan?" He was there by the door when the SLA trooped in. For some reason the robbers seemed not to take notice of him, and though he heard the order to get down on the floor, he didn't. Shea stood, hands high above his head, a few feet from DeFreeze, who in a loud voice announced, "This is a holdup," paused, then added, "The first motherfucker who don't lay down on the floor gets shot in the head."

The bank had been cased, each soldier's role assigned. DeFreeze stood closest to the single entranceway, swinging his sawed-off automatic rifle in a narrow arc, barking orders. There is little doubt he was the one in command. The women herded customers and employees into one group, forcing them to lie face down on the rust-colored carpeting. One teller did not move fast enough. DeFreeze dragged her through a waist-high swinging door, past Shea, still standing, hands up. Shea turned slowly so

DeFreeze could see he had a gun. "When he spotted it," Shea said later, "he made a grab for it, pulled it out of the holster, and stuck it in his jacket. Then he motioned me to get down. He didn't say one word." Berzins, sure there was going to be shooting, tried to pick out a spot close by a desk, figuring he could roll under it if it became necessary. Fahizah grabbed his shoulder and pulled him over with the others. Then she took position at the far end of the bank, her carbine trained on those on the floor. Patricia stood between DeFreeze and Nancy, closest to the prisoners. Shea and several others said they heard Patricia say at one point, "Keep down or we'll shoot your motherfucking heads off." Berzins did not hear that, but he and others agree she announced at one point—"in a soft drawl," Berzins said—"This is Tania Hearst." Behind the counter Zoya and Gabi—Mizmoon and Camilla—were emptying out two cash drawers.

The SLA had missed someone in their roundup. Upstairs in a small room where employees take coffee breaks was branch manager Jim Smith, sixty-two, reading the San Francisco *Chronicle*. Hearing a commotion downstairs, "some woman screaming and a man's voice shouting," he recalls, he went to a tiny window overlooking the floor. He saw the four women—and their weapons. Smith was astounded. It was his first bank robbery. After forty years with Hibernia, twenty-three as manager of the Sunset branch, it had finally happened. A holdup, and the robbers, from his vantage point, all seemed to be women. Moving away so he would not be spotted, Smith found the silent-alarm button and punched it. Instantly two high-speed cameras with wide-angle lenses began snapping pictures of what was happening below, each shooting 150 feet of Kodak 400 surveillance film at the rate of four frames per second. Simultaneously the button flashed a "211" (holdup) signal by leased telephone line to Commercial Fire Dispatch, five miles away in downtown San Francisco. When the alarm came in, Willie Noonan looked up at a location board, then reached for a hot-line telephone linked to the police radio at the Hall of Justice. "Two-eleven at the Hibernia Sunset, Twenty-second and Noriega," Noonan announced. A police dispatcher immediately put out a citywide broadcast: "Attention, all units . . . attention, all units . . . in the Taraval, a two-eleven in progress, Twenty-second and Noriega, the Hibernia Bank." In the Taraval police district, officers inside the station ran for their cars, and those on patrol headed for the scene, routinely checking watches to note the time. It was 9:51. Most figured it was going to be a false alarm. They thought the bank did not open until 10 o'clock. Nobody had bothered to inform police of Hibernia's new hours. One pair of patrolmen admitted later they drove toward the bank at a leisurely speed—until their radio announced that shots had been fired. Only then did they hit red lights and siren.

Pete Markoff knew about the 9 o'clock opening and had also decided to get his banking out of the way before 10. He stuffed the weekend's receipts into a small canvas bag, picked up some letters that had to be mailed, told his wife he would be back in a few minutes, walked out of his store—Noriega Liquors—toward the bank, two blocks away. As Markoff, fifty-nine, a diminutive silver-haired man, neared the bank entrance, he remembered the letters and continued on to the corner mailbox. Behind him he heard a voice call his name, turned, and saw his friend Gene Brennan. Brennan, seventy, a pensioner, was also on his way to the bank. Markoff dropped the letters in the mailbox, and with Brennan just ahead, the two men walked into the Sunset branch.

Just as the door closed behind him, Markoff caught sight of DeFreeze. Afterward he said he could not tell if he had been looking at a white man or a black man—all he knew was that he was staring into the barrel of a gun. Markoff turned, scrambling to get out of the way, out the door. Nancy Ling Perry began firing, squeezing off shots from her machine gun. A .30-caliber slug tore into Markoff's right buttock, came out the front of his right leg, and drilled a neat hole in the glass door. Two other shots missed; one hitting the metal frame of the door, the second punching another hole in the glass. A fourth shot slammed Brennan in the hand as he, too, tried to get out the door. Markoff stumbled through the door, collapsing on the sidewalk. Brennan, for a few seconds unaware that he had been hit, staggered out. Then he felt the blood and the pain. In shock, Brennan began walking slowly home, calling out, over and over, "I've been shot . . . I've been shot," until he, too, fell.

Up the street, at Greg's Cocktail Lounge, Ken Outland, sixty-two, a pharmacist, was nursing an early-morning Bloody Mary and chatting with Greg Higuera behind the bar. Two other customers were sipping beers and watching an old Spencer Tracy movie on TV. Outland was recovering from a broken ankle—the cast had been off only a week or so—and had been stopping by mornings to visit Higuera, a friend. Suddenly they heard a series of sharp, cracking sounds. At first they thought it was just a lumber truck dropping off another load at the lumberyard down the street. Then they heard shouting outside. Both headed for the door. Higuera saw a figure slumped in front of the bank. Someone across the street yelled, "I think he was hit by a car." Outland, who as a pharmacist has given first aid many a time, rushed toward the bank. He was perhaps twenty feet from the entrance, with Higuera a few steps behind, when he saw women with guns come running out, heading away from him, around the corner onto Twenty-second. Then came an armed man, who turned and spotted Outland and Higuera running toward him. Cinque swung around, carbine at hip level, and fired. Outland threw himself against the wall of the bank. Higuera ducked into a driveway. The bullet missed Outland by only a few inches. DeFreeze disappeared around the corner where the getaway car was parked.

Outland ran to the crumpled form. He shook Markoff's shoulder, asked, "Where are you hit?" The man groaned. "In the hip." "I'll be right back," Outland told him. The pharmacist ran on to the corner, stopped, peeked around the side of the building. Halfway down Twenty-second he saw a green station wagon speeding away, followed by a small red sedan. Both cars, tires screeching, turned left onto Moraga Street, heading toward the beach. Outland tried to note the license plates, but the cars were too far away. A minute or so later the first patrol car arrived. Outland's description went out over the police radio. Suddenly another officer came out of the bank and announced to the world: "Holy Jesus, they're saying it was that SLA bunch that did it." Minutes later a patrol car radioed it had located the getaway cars parked near an elementary school at Thirtieth Avenue and Lawton Street, ten blocks away. They had obviously changed vehicles there, but not a soul had witnessed the switch. People on Noriega gave conflicting versions of what they'd seen. Some said there had been four white men in the red sedan; others said there might have been a woman, maybe two women, with two men. Nobody had paid attention to it before the shooting started; then all eyes had focused on the bank itself. One woman said she had seen someone in the red car aim a rifle out a window and fire toward the bank just before the auto screeched off, right behind the green station wagon.

The witnesses in the bank concurred on one point: The holdup team had performed with military precision and considerable coolness—at least up to that moment when Fahizah opened up with her weapon. "They acted like commandos," said security guard Shea. "They said only what needed to be said. They looked at times like they were giving signals to each other with their hands." The fact that all four women were similarly dressed—in three-quarter-length pea coats, dark-colored flared slacks and hiking boots—added to the illusion that the witnesses had been watching soldiers in action. The SLA had seemed totally unconcerned about the cameras, plainly visible just above the door. "Cool as cucumbers they were," Shea said of the SLA.

By noon Noriega Street was swarming with reporters trying to find out if it was true: Had Patty Hearst been among the bandits, and, if so, had she—as witnesses were saying—been carrying a weapon, shouting out words like "motherfucker," and giving the appearance of being a willing participant? They questioned the growing number of high-ranking FBI agents and police officers gathering at the scene. The reply for several hours was "no comment." The two Mosler Photoguard cameras were unloaded, and the film was rushed to the Federal Building, where it was developed, producing 498 pictures. The photos made it clear Patricia had been among the SLA group, and it even looked as if she had played as major a role in the holdup as witnesses said. Nobody, however, was willing to say so flatly, and the media was spoon-fed a story suggesting "Miss Hearst" might have been forced to go along, that the guns of DeFreeze and Nancy Ling Perry might well have been covering her as well as those on the floor. The next morning's banner in the *Chronicle* read: TWO SHOT IN S.F. BANK RAID—PATRICIA HEARST IN PHOTOS, followed by the subhead SHE MAY HAVE BEEN COERCED. The story quoted James Browning, U.S. attorney for the Northern District of California. "I think this is the first time in the annals of legal history that a kidnap victim has shown up in the middle of a bank robbery," he said. "If she was involved and investigation proves it, we're going to charge her as a bank robber. But it's clear from the photographs she may have been acting under duress."

The abandoned getaway cars turned out to have been rented by two young women, the one signing the contracts calling herself Janet Cooper. The station wagon, a 1973 Ford LTD, had been obtained through an agency in a town a few miles south of San Francisco. The red sedan, a 1974 AMC Hornet Sportabout, had been rented from Continental Rent-a-Car in downtown San Francisco the previous Thursday. Clerk Phil Goldbeck remembered the girls well. "Janet Cooper" was a tall brunette who said she was a nurse at Kaiser Hospital, in San Francisco. She had shown a driver's license with that name and a city address. He had checked the phone book and found a Cooper listed at that address, and so when she handed him $40 cash as a deposit, he had handed her the keys. The other woman was a blonde. He'd paid her little attention other than to ask if she wanted her name added on the contract as a possible driver. "No," she had replied with a shy smile, "San Francisco traffic scares me." Goldbeck was shown a sheaf of photos of known SLA members. He said he did not recognize any of them.*

By evening dozens of FBI agents and plainclothes policemen were pounding the pavement of the Sunset district, knocking on doors, showing pictures of the SLA, asking if anybody resembling the photos had been seen around the area. The assumption was that somewhere close by must be a safehouse, out of which the SLA had operated while casing the bank for the spectacular hold-up in which they had made off with, a count of the cash showed, $10,692.51. Some merchants pointed to pictures of Camilla Hall, saying she had shopped in their stores. Other people picked out pictures of Mizmoon Soltysik, Bill Harris, and Willie Wolfe as people they had recently seen around. Nobody, however, came up with any possible SLA hideout. Near where the getaway cars had been found, agents did get one tidbit. Aldo Ricci, retired machinist, told how, over a period of a week or so, he had seen a dark-colored station wagon pull up at the corner of Thirtieth and Lawton each night precisely at 9 o'clock. There were always several people in it. "They'd pull up and stop for four, five minutes—always with the lights on—just sitting there, then they'd drive off," Ricci said. What he had seen, obviously, was an SLA rehearsal. Interesting, but not much help since he had no idea of the license numbers. It had been more than interesting, however, to learn that Willie Wolfe might be back among the group. It had been suspected, of course, but never established for sure, that he had made his way west on leaving Pennsylvania on January 11, the day after the Concord arrests.

Randolph and Catherine Hearst were ending their eighth day in semiseclusion in Mexico when word of the bank robbery reached them. Patricia's scathing denunciation of her parents, the declaration that she had "chosen to stay and fight" as a soldier of the Symbionese, had staggered and bewildered the Hearsts. The Tania announcement had sent the media army rushing once again to Hillsborough; reporters bombarded the couple with questions they could not answer. The transformation from terrified victim to apparent comrade seemed to defy explanation.

*During her bank robbery trial, Patricia Hearst named Emily Harris and Camilla Hall as the persons who rented the getaway cars; presumably it was Emily Harris who posed as "Janet Cooper."

Visitors to the mansion at the time say Catherine Hearst was on the verge of total collapse. When close friend Desi Arnaz offered his villa in La Paz as a retreat, the Hearsts quickly accepted. Their departure was kept secret until they were aboard an airliner, and their destination was not given out; but it was only hours before the location of the hideaway was discovered and reporters were dispatched to La Paz. "We came here to recharge our batteries and refuel our mental energies to await the next explicit and exotic torture the SLA might dish out," Randy wearily told an Associated Press reporter. "I think they're just cruel people, and I think they fundamentally hate this society so much they think anything's fair."

Hearst understood that the SLA hunt was slipping beyond the point where he had any influence. He had heard of Attorney General Saxbe's response to the Tania tape ("Now that the lid is off," said Saxbe, "I think we're going to see some results.") Never had the SLA's "ruling class" label seemed so inappropriate. Unaware that he was even then being secretly watched by FBI agents—who thought his daughter might contact him in Mexico—Hearst said, "I know I cannot hope to control the FBI, but I certainly hope that even if they know where Patty is, they will not go in with guns blazing and get my daughter killed."

The couple had rested, soaked up sun, and tried to make sense of it all. Randy had given several interviews, then begged for a few days' peace, and newsmen backed off. But when Patty's participation in the Hibernia robbery was flashed on the wire services, a reporter in Mexico City rang up the Arnaz villa. Mrs. Hearst answered.

"I'm so upset I can't talk to you," she said. "We just heard it over the radio. It's so bizarre. I just can't believe it." Hearst would not comment at all that night. Early the next morning the couple boarded a chartered Grumman Gulfstream II jet and flew home. Landing at San Francisco International Airport, they were immediately surrounded by a hundred or so reporters. "How do you feel about this latest development?" a television newsman shouted. "How do you think anybody would feel?" Mr. Hearst replied angrily. "It's terrible. It's something that I think is one of the most vicious things I have ever seen or ever had happen to me. Sixty days ago she was a lovely child. Sixty days later there's a picture of her in the bank with a gun in her hand." Another reporter asked if he thought Patricia had been forced to take part. "I have no idea," said Hearst. "I can't answer that until I talk with the police and find out exactly what happened." Mrs. Hearst, wearing sunglasses to cover the signs of a sleepless night and tears, climbed into a waiting car without saying a word.

Steve Weed, driving to Hillsborough to meet the Hearsts, felt he was trapped in a hallucinogenic nightmare. "I had this mental game," he remembered later. "I had these cutouts, these hollow outlines in my mind—they were the SLA people I didn't know. I had been trying to fill them in, to see them as real people. Now, suddenly, all the shading dropped out, all of them were just black holes, wraiths. The SLA suddenly seemed inhumanly cruel, infinitely malevolent.

"Before I left, I had written down all my options. The FBI wouldn't give me anything more than the five photos they gave the media. I didn't know what other evidence there was. I had filled ten pages in my notebook, writing out things I could say and then thinking of what the SLA response would be. If I do this, they do that—that sort of thing. At the time I was most worried that we would never hear from them again . . . or that this would be the first of several things that would set her up to be killed for the Revolution.

"I finally decided that if she had not been forced, if it had been free will, then I had nothing to lose. . . . But if she had been coerced and nobody called them on it forcefully, then they might kill her and just fade away. I thought if I attacked them, they would have to respond. I wasn't sure of anything, but I didn't see what I could lose. I didn't see, didn't even think about the possibility that she would be insulted and turn around and attack me. . . ."

At Hillsborough he talked briefly with the Hearsts, then spoke to the TV cameras from the steps of the mansion. His voice was dripping with sarcasm. "It was a strange way to convince people that Patty had become a revolutionary, when all they would have had to do was to let her go to say so," he said. "If the bank robbery doesn't serve to convince people that Patty is indeed a revolutionary, they'll embark on some new action. Next time, they'll not be so clumsy as to be photographed with guns trained on her."

Had he noticed anything else in the pictures? "She's lost a lot of weight," he said, "more than anyone five feet two can afford."

But in Washington Attorney General Saxbe opined that Patricia Hearst was now just a "common criminal." The injudicious statement got Saxbe flayed on the editorial pages and caused red faces at FBI headquarters. Newly appointed FBI Director Clarence Kelley tried to take some of the sting out, saying his agents were "proceeding on the assumption" that "Patricia is the victim of pressure or coercion," and that in any event the bureau would be "guided by facts, not by opinion." Yet Saxbe's reaction seemed more accurately to reflect the gut opinions of the cops and FBI agents working the streets in the Hearst case.

Randolph Hearst, although enraged by Saxbe's comments, did not respond until after he had consulted Dr. Frederick Hacker, who urged that something must be said publicly to blunt the prejudicial remark. Hearst blasted the AG: "We happen to know our daughter better than Saxbe does. . . . I don't see that the statement does anything except confirm my original view that the man makes irresponsible statements and obviously talks off the top of his head when he should be listening."

Hacker told Hearst, (and recounted again in a confidential memorandum to the family which the authors obtained), "The chances of capturing and recovering Miss Hearst are not increased by name-calling." Better, the psychiatrist suggested, the Attorney General should concentrate on "finding out why a bank can be robbed at 9 o'clock in the morning and the robbers disappear into thin air, instead of playing amateur psychologist." What the SLA had done was "not really very surprising. . . . One of the frequent rites of revolutionaries such as the SLA is initiation," Hearst was told. "You involve the hostage in an act of violence. The guilt is thus shared—and it greatly increases the difficulty for the hostage to return to the outside community. It is a participation and a bond sealed by blood." The SLA, wrote Hacker, most certainly must be aware that Patricia's value as a hostage—a shield against all the lawmen lined up on the other side of the chessboard—had virtually evaporated.

"There is a backlash about all this," he added. "It is a feeling resulting from the emotional pain the public feels Patty has caused them . . . the question they seem to be asking themselves is 'Why do we have to go through all this pain to have *this* happen?'" He was convinced the SLA did not care about the effect the holdup had on the girl's public status. Producing Tania out of Patricia Hearst had scored a propaganda coup.

Hacker's assessment was on the mark. Media coverage of the case shifted emphasis. "Miss Hearst" was no longer the pitiable victim. Stories were less sympathetic to her, although the slant of the reporting as it concerned Randolph and Catherine Hearst continued to be quite sympathetic; now *they* were the victims. (In Brazil the military censors for the dictatorship spiked all further stories on the Hearst case; the girl's apparent defection to the SLA "set a bad example," said authorities there.)

Yet there was another side, defining an ambiguity that would stand unresolved. Captain of Inspectors Mortimer McInerney of the San Francisco police, after "personally examining" all 498 bank photos, said it appeared to him Patricia Hearst had been a "willing participant. . . . The pictures show her holding a weapon in both hands and pointing it at one of the individuals who was shot," McInerney said. "The pictures also show her yelling at the time of the shooting and apparently smiling after the shooting."

Because there was no witness identification of anyone in the bright red Sportabout—at least nothing strong enough to stand up in court—other members of the revolutionary army escaped federal robbery charges. It was the State of California that tagged them as wanted, too. The Harrises, Angela Atwood, and Willie Wolfe were accused of having fraudulently obtained drivers' licenses by using phony names—a felony. State Attorney General Evelle Younger said he expected the entire SLA band would soon be "rounded up." Saxbe echoed: "We're going to get them." The FBI issued a "wanted" poster bearing Patricia's picture. It immediately became a collector's item. Blowups, printed as a counterculture poster, sold for $2 on the sidewalks of Berkeley.

A week before the bank robbery Steve Weed had flown to Mexico City to talk to Régis DeBray, the French Marxist intellectual. DeBray had been friend and confidant of Che Guevara, Cuba's most famous revolutionary export to South America, and the real Tania Burke, the Argentine woman who had died with Guevara in the Bolivian hills. The connection was made through two prominent Berkeley radicals with whom Weed had been conferring, activists who thought the SLA was beginning to pose a real danger to the legitimate Left. Weed gave DeBray a long update on the story, played a tape of the latest Tania communiqué, and evidently impressed the French writer. DeBray offered to dictate an open letter to the SLA urging Patty at least to deliver irrefutable proof of her free decision to join the SLA. Weed recalls DeBray, in his precise and formal English, wondering aloud if the American Left had not fallen into the hands of imbeciles. "Usually they do nothing," he said, "and when they finally do something, it comes out like this!"

DeBray's letter was published on the front page of Hearst's *Examiner* on April 12, three days before the bank robbery; a cautious, careful letter that asked Patricia "only to assure me that you have consciously and freely chosen to take the name and follow the example of Tania. If such is indeed the case, we can do nothing but respect your decision—no matter how questionable it may seem." He urged her to contact an intermediary, a common friend of Weed and herself, to offer proof of her "real situation" and "relieve the anguish of your friends who fear for your safety and your life." DeBray scored the SLA with a subtle critique. The fierce dedication of Tania Burke, he said, was the result of "years amongst the workers" and the study of "the theory of scientific socialism and the reality of the actual world." It was only a long and difficult apprenticeship, he wrote, "which permitted Tania to create her own revolutionary morale," and he—as Tania Burke's comrade—felt called upon to speak out if any group sought to mar his friend's memory by "dishonestly and cynically" forcing a kidnap victim to claim Tania's name and heritage. "You," he wrote Patty, "will understand that we must be cautious to protect the moral integrity and international purity of her commitment."

DeBray had touched a nerve; pointing out the shallow experience of these "revolutionaries"—in particular, Patty—he clearly framed the radical critique of the Symbionese. It may have been this letter which pushed the SLA, always sensitive and reactive, into the propagandistic theater of the bank robbery. Perhaps, too, Weed, having arranged for the letter and then bluntly calling the Tania transformation a hoax after being told by the FBI that the cameras showed SLA guns covering Patty, set himself up for the final brush-off.

("I was pretty pissed," recalled Weed later. "They were debating whether there was a grin or grimace on her face when the men were shot, but they wouldn't let me or anyone who really knew her see the film. I went to the FBI, they sent me to Browning, the U.S. attorney. He sat me down with three or four of his assistants, and I talked and they listened, but no one would let me see the photos. One guy said, 'Steve, you're not a lawyer, so you wouldn't understand.' Hell, I understood. Even then they were more interested in building their case against her than in possibly helping her!")

But the federal authorities, when they filed "wanted" charges in the holdup, hedged in dealing with Patricia. They made no announcement that they now had a witness who claimed Tania was the *last* to enter the bank, the woman who had collided with the glass door. Shortly after the robbery Zig Berzins had identified that woman (from FBI pictures) as Nancy Ling Perry, but the next day, after studying the bank photos beneath the blaring Hearst headlines, Berzins had decided he was "certain" it had been Patricia Hearst.

DeFreeze, Nancy Ling Perry, Mizmoon Soltysik, and Camilla

Hall were charged with bank robbery, and bail—should they be picked up—was set at a half million dollars each. The FBI issued a "pick up and hold" order for Patricia, but the arrest warrant identified her merely as a "material witness." Perhaps the tip-off to what the FBI and U.S. Attorney Browning privately believed was the fact that the bail figure set for Patty was identical to that for the SLA soldiers—$500,000.

The nation seemed caught between Attorney General Saxbe's quick condemnation and the Hearst family's defensive claim of coercion. Opinion settled with Saxbe after April 24 with the issuance of the next taped communication from the SLA. In an emotionless drone the new warrior heroine addressed the world:

"Greetings to the people, this is Tania. On April 15 my comrades and I expropriated $10,660.02* from the Sunset branch of Hibernia Bank. Casualties could have been avoided had the persons involved kept out of the way and cooperated with the people's forces until after our departure.

"I was positioned so that I could hold customers and bank personnel who were on the floor. My gun was loaded and at no time did any of my comrades intentionally point their guns at me. Careful examination of the photographs which were published clearly shows this was true. Our action of April 15 forced the corporate state to help finance the Revolution. In the case of expropriation, the difference between a criminal act and a revolutionary act is shown by what the money is used for. As for the money involved in my parents' bad-faith gesture to aid the people, these funds are being used to aid the people and to insure the survival of the people's forces in their struggle with and for the people.

"To the clowns who want a personal interview with me—Vincent Hallinan, Steven Weed, and Pig Hearsts—I prefer giving it to the people in the bank. It's absurd to think that I could surface to say what I am saying now and be allowed to freely return to my comrades. The enemy still wants me dead. I am obviously alive and well. As for being brainwashed, the idea is ridiculous to the point of being beyond belief. It's interesting the way early reports characterized me as a beautiful, intelligent liberal while in more recent reports I'm a comely girl who's been brainwashed. The contradictions are obvious.

"Consciousness is terrifying to the ruling class, and they will do

---

*The discrepancy between the amount the SLA claims it stole ($10,660.02) and the amount the bank says was stolen ($10,692.51) has never been explained.

anything to discredit people who have realized that the only alternative to freedom is death and that the only way we can free ourselves of this fascist dictatorship is by fighting, not with words but with guns.

"As for my ex-fiancé, I'm amazed that he thinks that the first thing I would want to do, once freed, would be to rush and see him. I don't care if I ever see him again. During the last few months Steven has shown himself to be a sexist, ageist pig. Not that this is a sudden change from the way he always was. It merely became blatant during the period when I was still a hostage. Frankly, Steven is the one who sounds brainwashed. I can't believe that those weird words he uttered were from his heart. They were a mixture of FBI rhetoric and Randy's simplicity.

"I have no proof that Mr. DeBray's letter is authentic. The date and location he gave were confusing in terms of when the letter was published in the papers. How could it have been written in Paris and published in your newspapers on the same day,* Adolf? In any case, I hope that the last action has put his mind at ease. If it didn't, further actions will.

"To those people who still believe that I am brainwashed or dead, I see no reason to further defend my position. I am a soldier in the people's army. *Patria o muerte, venceremos.*"

DeFreeze and Bill Harris also spoke in the communiqué of April 24. The General Field Marshal talked in what he conceived to be military parlance. He justified the wounding of the two "civilians" as many another general has justified some wartime action in which innocent persons were hurt. Said Donald DeFreeze: "To those who would bear the hopes and future of our people, let the voice of their guns express the will of freedom.

"Greetings to the people and all sisters and brothers behind the walls and in the streets, elements of the Black Liberation Army, the Weather Underground, and the Black Guerrilla Family, and all combat forces of the community.

"I am General Field Marshal Cin speaking.

"Combat operations: April 15, the year of the soldier.

"Action: appropriation. Supplies liberated: one .38 Smith and Wesson revolver, condition good; five rounds of 158-grain .30-caliber ammo. Cash: $10,660.02.

---

*DeBray, worried about offending the Mexican government during his visit, had predated the letter and told Weed not to release it until April 12, when he would be back in Paris.

"Number of rounds fired by combat forces: seven rounds.

"Number of rounds lost: five.

"Casualties: People's forces, none. Enemy forces, none. Civilians, two.

"Reasons: Subject one. Male. Subject was ordered to lay on the floor face down. Subject refused order and jumped out the front door of the bank. Therefore the subject was shot. Subject Two. Male. Subject failed or did not hear warning to clear the street. Subject was running down the street toward the bank, and combat forces accordingly assumed subject was an armed enemy-force element. Therefore the subject was shot.*

"We again warn the public. Any citizen attempting to aid, inform, or assist the enemy of the people in any manner will be shot without hesitation. There is no middle ground in war. Either you are the people or the enemy. You must make the choice. . . ."

The remainder of what DeFreeze had to say focused on Operation Zebra. He described Zebra as being "far more" than a "normal counterinsurgency operation to attempt to entrap the SLA forces."†

---

*DeFreeze apparently was unaware his shot had missed and that the two victims had been wounded by Nancy Ling Perry.

†San Francisco was in the grip of panic at the time of the SLA's April 24 communiqué. In contradiction to Cinque's heady claims, however, Operation Zebra had nothing to do with the search for the Symbionese. Fourteen persons had been killed and seven others had been wounded in a series of seemingly motiveless street shootings that had begun the previous October. That the random attacks on chance victims—men and women, old and young, from all walks of life—were linked to one another had been established by ballistics tests. Even more chilling, as the slayings came to dominate the attention of the city through the media, was the realization that there seemed to be a racial basis for the attacks: In every instance the victims had been whites; in every case where there were survivors or witnesses the gunmen were described as blacks.

By April the public fear had reached the point where San Francisco's streets were virtually deserted after dark. Police brass, under fire from City Hall to capture the killers, drew up Operation Zebra, an ill-conceived plan that was endorsed by Mayor Joseph Alioto. Over a period of a week more than 600 black men were stopped and questioned (and usually, without cause, searched) by police officers. A coalition of leaders of the black community, supported by civil rights advocates and church groups, filed suit against the city in U.S. District Court; a federal judge quickly ruled that such indiscriminate stops were clearly unconstitutional and ordered Operation Zebra be immediately halted.

A few days later an informer named the killers. Four men—Black Muslims who had formed their own kill cult they called the Death Angels—were arrested and charged with the multiple murders. (Police suspected, with only circumstantial evidence, that the Death Angels were responsible for a number of other Bay Area murders, including several savage slayings in Berkeley and Oakland in

The search for the killers was actually a "planned enemy offensive against the people to commit a race war." Cinque's reasoning: "This could possibly be the only way the enemy can stop the SLA from bringing all oppressed people together against the common enemy."

Teko—Bill Harris—in his message on that tape, also described Operation Zebra as a plot to bring about a race war: "The pigs hope to manipulate the fear and racism of the broad mass of unconscious whites in order to eliminate black revolutionaries, and by black revolutionaries we mean black people in general. Pigs like [Mayor Joseph] Alioto wish to maneuver these white people into allowing the fascist army to sweep the ghettos and machine-gun and imprison the people. But anyone who by their racism and government-manipulated fear supports genocide makes the glaring error of forging his or her own slave chains, and if white people in fascist America don't think they are enslaved, they only prove their own foolishness."

Randolph Hearst's depression deepened. He is said to have "shuddered" when he heard the voice of Tania refer to him as "Adolf." Mrs. Hearst remained convinced Patricia had been put under a spell.

Had it all been prophesied in, of all places, a poem by the bard of the Beat Generation, Lawrence Ferlinghetti? Three years earlier, in a work he titled "Las Vegas Tilt," Ferlinghetti had used the medium of imagined newspaper headlines and written these lines: "Hearst's Daughter Castigates Hearst's America/Attacks Absolute Spiritual Bankruptcy." "I don't know where that idea came from," Ferlinghetti said. "I guess it was just wishful thinking at the time."

The SLA again vanished—a step ahead of the posse. When the FBI finally discovered one of their hideouts, it was not the result of detective work, but because of the keen senses of a blind woman.

Lolabelle Evans had concluded that her new upstairs neighbors were "mighty peculiar" right after they moved into the third-floor apartment at 1827 Golden Gate Avenue in late March. Mrs. Evans cannot see, but her hearing is perfect. "They was up to all hours of the night," the elderly woman remembers, "making all kinds of

---

which shaven-headed black men had butchered their victims with machetes.) In March, 1976, after a trial that lasted more than a year, the second-longest trial in California's history, Larry Craig Green, J. C. Simon, Jessie Lee Cooks, and Manuel Moore were found quilty of the San Francisco killings and sentenced to multiple life terms in state prison.

noise, funny kinds of noise. One time it sounded like they was dragging something like machines across the floor. Another time it was like they was drilling through the floor. I worried maybe the ceiling was going to come down on me." Occasionally she could hear voices. One night, just before the noisy tenants moved out, Mrs. Evans said, "It sounded like they was counting money."

The SLA left the Golden Gate apartment one evening in late April, shortly after the bank robbery. The young white woman who rented it on March 20 had called herself Louise Hamilton, a secretary, and paid $250 for two months' rent. Other tenants say several young white women and a black man were seen entering and leaving the apartment. Several quickly picked out pictures of DeFreeze and Nancy Ling Perry after police and FBI agents raided the place on May 2. Lolabelle Evans had discovered her apartment was swarming with cockroaches and complained. The manager guessed they were coming from upstairs, forced his way into the apartment—there were *six* locks on the door—found SLA debris, and called police.

The place was a mess. Spoiled foodstuffs had produced the plague of cockroaches. The walls were covered with graffiti penned by various SLA soldiers, including Patricia Hearst, who wrote, "Freedom is the will of life," and underneath that, "Patria o muerte—Venceremos," signing the slogans with a flair, "Tania." On another wall someone had written, "Books, once read, make good bulletproofing." Emily Harris wrote, "January 1, 1974 . . . A New Year's Resolution . . . Is it real? To load a gun with a magazine of dreams? NO!" The phrase "DA DA O MI," which Death Row Jeff had used in his letters to Willie Wolfe, was scrawled across another wall.

The SLA before leaving had filled the bathtub with a variety of caustic chemicals into which they had dropped a mass of documents and half a dozen keys, including two for the cars they had hired for the bank robbery. On the wall of the bathroom was a message:

WARNING TO THE FBI, CIA, DIA, NSA, NSC AND CBS— There are a few clues in this bathroom. However you will have to wait until they are dry. An additional word of caution: ½ (one-half) lb. (pound) of cyanide (potassium cyanide) crystals has been added to this "home brew"—so, pig, drink at your own risk. There are also many additional juicy SLA clues throughout this safe house. However, remember that you are not bulletproof either. Happy Hunting, Charles.

The gibe at the end was for the FBI's Bates.

Several storekeepers in the neighborhood identified photos of Patty Hearst as a "nice young lady" who had shopped in their stores. One remembered having told the girl, "You know, you look a lot like that Hearst girl who got kidnapped." The young woman had laughed and replied, "A lot of people think that." Later, however, the FBI said it doubted the validity of these reports.

The provisioning of the Golden Gate safehouse—after the Hibernia robbery—had been carried out by four Black Muslims, neighbors in the ghetto district, recruited, by their accounts reluctantly, into giving aid to the squad-size army. It was a brief enlistment, said twenty-one-year-old Jamellea Muntaz. It had begun in early April with a mid-evening knock on the door of her apartment at 1743 Golden Gate. From pictures she had seen flashed on TV, she had had no doubts that the caller was who he said: Cinque. DeFreeze spent about ten minutes with Muntaz, explaining the dreams of the SLA and his personal mission in behalf of "the People." He said the Symbionese needed assistance, someone to run important errands. The young woman agreed to help—out of "fear," she would later say.

About a week later, around noon, "two white girls" (Emily Harris and Angela Atwood) who had called themselves Yolanda and Gelina had dropped by, bearing "a letter from Cin." It was an invitation to Muntaz to come calling at the safehouse in the next block. Jamellea went, bringing along a Black Muslim sister, Retimah X, twenty-six, for support. After being introduced by Cin to his "soldiers," Tania among them, Jamellea and Retimah said, they were sent out on their first mission: a trip to the nearby Foodland supermarket for groceries.

On their next visit the Muslim women brought along two friends, Ali Bey and Rasheem. Cinque said the SLA needed new transport, and over the next couple of weeks Ali Bey and Rasheem, with cash given them by DeFreeze, purchased three vehicles: a $600 station wagon, a ten-year-old Buick sedan, and a red-and-white Volkswagen bus. Ali Bey, with Jamellea posing as his wife, counted out $1,800 cash for the Volks at a used-car lot, registering it in the phony name Rickey Delgato at a nonexistent San Francisco address.

In late April, maybe a week after the bank robbery, Muntaz said, the SLA asked her to find a new hideout. DeFreeze thought that 1827 Golden Gate was both too small and (only twelve blocks from the FBI office) getting too hot. After safehouse hunting for a week, she put down a month's rent, $375, for a run-down two-bedroom flat at 1808 Oakdale Street, in another ghetto section of the city. The next night the four Muslims helped the SLA move. The transfer of weapons and supplies required two trips in the station wagon, which Cinque then gave to Retimah X. It was about May 8, Muntaz thought, when DeFreeze told her the SLA was leaving San Francisco. He didn't tell her where they were going. On May 10, after buying the morning *Chronicle* (which they left behind), the Symbionese decamped.

The visits of the Muslims were later described by Patricia Hearst after her arrest. Tania, however, had not felt the four were "reluctant" helpers at all. Once, after Xeroxing copies of comminiqués for the SLA, she said, the Muslim women brought along Retimah's two daughters (seven and nine years old, Patty estimated) and Jamellea's little girl (who seemed no more than three). Retimah lined the children up in front of DeFreeze, and on signal, the youngsters began reciting—in Swahili, Patty said—the Seven Principles of the Symbionese Federation.

Retimah then told Cinque that she had come with "a code name" for him. The code name, Ms. Hearst said, was "Jesus."

18

Blunder

TONY SHEPARD glanced up at the large convex mirror above the doorway of Mel's Sporting Goods out of habit. That's how he happened to see Bill Harris—General Teko of the Symbionese Liberation Army—stuff a bandolier up his jacket sleeve. Shepard might have ignored the indiscretion had he known who Harris was or what was going to occur during the next several minutes; but all the twenty-year-old security clerk was aware of was that he had a rather inept shoplifter to deal with. Shepard, a second-year police-sciences major, kept pistol and handcuffs ready for such situations.

There seemed nothing out of the ordinary about the couple who had strolled into the sporting-goods store in the Los Angeles suburb of Inglewood a little past 4 P.M. on Thursday, May 16, 1974. They had browsed in the camping supplies and clothing section and picked out a number of items. It was while the woman, later identified as Emily Harris—Yolanda—was carrying the merchandise to the checkout counter that Shepard spotted the man tucking the cloth ammo pouch into his sleeve. Harris then joined his wife at the counter.

Shepard did not confront Harris right then. In California a shoplifter cannot be accused until he physically leaves the premises with stolen merchandise. Once outside he can be arrested—or simply asked to pay for what he stole. That is the common practice of many small businesses which cannot afford the time, expense, and energy involved in making a petty shoplifting a police and court matter. The policy at Mel's was to try to get the thief to pay up or, failing that, bring in the police.

The purchases were rung up on the cash register. A sweater, sweat pants, several pairs of sweat sox, and a watch cap. With tax it came to $31.50. Emily paid with two twenty-dollar bills. The clerk handed her back $8.50 and bagged her purchases. As Yolanda and Teko started toward the door, Shepard got his gun and cuffs and signaled his boss, Bill Huett, to follow him.

341

The Harrises were starting to jaywalk across Crenshaw Boulevard when the young black clerk caught up with them.

"Hey, you—how about coming back and paying for what you didn't pay for?" he demanded.

Harris angrily denied he had stolen anything and continued walking away. Shepard responded, "You're under arrest," and grabbed Harris' arm. A fierce struggle began between the two men. Emily, screaming curses, kicked Shepard's shins. Harris lost balance and fell onto the sidewalk, Shepard atop him. Emily leaped on the clerk's back and beat on his head with her fists. Huett and two other clerks who had rushed outside pulled Emily off. Harris reached into his jacket and came out with a snub-nosed revolver. Huett grabbed it away and stuck it in his pocket while the others kept wrestling. Shepard had just managed to lock a cuff on Harris' left wrist when the shooting started.

From across Crenshaw came a staccato burst of .30-caliber bullets fired from a submachine gun. It was Tania. Shooting in bursts, she sprayed Mel's plate-glass storefront with twenty-seven slugs and put three more into adjoining buildings.

The most recognizable of the SLA (even though at that moment disguised in a curly black wig), Patty had stayed behind—alone—in a Volkswagen van parked in a shopping-center lot. Curled up in the back of the van reading a newspaper, she had heard shouting and looked out. Seeing two comrades in trouble, Tania grabbed a machine gun, leaned out a window, and fired toward the store across the traffic-busy street. That no one was killed or seriously wounded was sheer good fortune: One ricocheting slug struck the chest of a clerk with enough force to bend a ball-point pen in the man's breast pocket, and Huett's wife, Carol, was cut on the forehead by a shard of shattered glass.

"Let us go . . . let us go or you're going to be killed," Harris shouted. The four men ducked for cover. Dashing across the boulevard—Patty firing a final covering burst—the Harrises leaped in and the three drove off. Shepard fired two shots at the disappearing van with his pistol. He missed.

The red-and-white Volkswagen sped up residential Ruthellen Street, a half mile away, and squealed to a stop alongside a Pontiac sedan that had just parked. General Teko and Tania alighted, each armed with an automatic weapon. They had no trouble persuading the occupants, Ken Pierre and Marva Davis, to get out. "We're the SLA. We need your car. I may have to kill someone and I don't want to kill you," said Harris. The couple fled. Emily Harris handed out an armload of weapons and the SLA took off in the Pontiac.

The scene repeated itself two blocks away. A father and son, Tom Patin senior and junior, were standing on West 115th Street when the trio pulled up in the stolen LeMans. Bill Harris emerged with his gun and demanded, "We need your car. We need it right now. We're the SLA." Patin senior handed over the keys, and the Harrises and Patty Hearst drove off in his blue Chevy Nova station wagon. It was now a few minutes past 4:30 P.M. By 6 o'clock every cop in Southern California was looking for them.

At 7 P.M. Yolanda knocked on the door of Tom Matthews' home in Lynwood, an LA suburb. Inquiring about his Ford van parked outside with a FOR SALE sign, she asked to test-drive it. Matthews, an eighteen-year-old high school student, said sure, and the two started off, Emily at the wheel. Driving around the corner, she stopped alongside the appropriated Nova, pointed at Bill and Patty, and said, "These are two of my friends. I'd like to take them along." It was okay with Matthews. As soon as the two got in, Matthews found himself facing a gun. "We're from the SLA and we need to borrow your car," Harris told him, adding, "Don't do anything stupid and you won't get hurt." As they drove off with Matthews, the test drive now a kidnapping, Harris gestured and asked, "Do you know who this is?" Tom looked, and shook his head. "This is Tania," said Harris. "Then they both smiled," Matthews recalled.

On Ruthellen Street police and FBI agents tore apart the abandoned SLA van hunting clues. They got a big break with the discovery of a crumpled-up parking ticket showing the Volks had been tagged three mornings before by the LAPD for illegal parking in front of 835 West Eighty-fourth Street, in a black ghetto neighborhood. Black undercover officers were ordered to that area during the night to begin some quiet checking. Gun-registration records in Sacramento revealed that the .38-caliber revolver taken from the shoplifter had been purchased by Emily Montague Harris at an Oakland gun shop on October 13, 1973.

The SLA van turned out to have been purchased in San Francisco, at a used-car lot only four blocks from the FBI office. The buyer had given a phony name, Rickey Delgato, and an address that did not exist. He was described as a black man in his thirties (Ali Bey) who had been accompanied by his wife (Jamellea Muntaz) and a little girl. The salesman, after studying FBI photos, said it wasn't DeFreeze.

Matthews was kept captive through the night, covered up much of the time by a blanket. After the frightening first few minutes, Tom recalled, he figured "they didn't plan to kill me or anything," and his kidnap became an adventure.

The first couple of hours were spent driving through sprawling Los Angeles county in search of a hacksaw. Two stores Emily checked didn't carry them. The third did. Matthews sawed at the cuff, freeing Harris.

Tania showed off her familiarity with a rifle, deftly unloading a round from the chamber, fitting the bullet into a clip, shoving the clip into the weapon. "She said there had been some stories that [the SLA's] cyanide bullets didn't have enough [poison] in them to kill anyone," recalled Tom. "She said they did, and she showed me a bullet. It had a dented tip."

Matthews asked why the SLA had robbed the bank. "Bill Harris said they needed money because they were fighting guerrilla warfare and it wasn't easy, what they were doing," Tom recalled. "And then Patty Hearst said she'd heard a lot of publicity about the bank robbery, that she was supposedly tied to her gun and couldn't fire it, and that people were pointing guns at her, her own SLA members, and she said that all was false."

Had she really been kidnapped? Tom inquired. Patty assured him she had been. But she had changed when she realized "her father wasn't doing enough in the food giveaway." Tania called the PIN effort a sham, said PIN was merely "a subsidiary fund that the Hearst Foundation" could give money to "as a tax write-off." Patricia Hearst had told him that after she'd fired with her gun at Mel's, "it was a good feeling to see her two comrades running across the street."

The radio was kept turned to an all-news station for bulletin updates on the growing police manhunt. Harris became furious with the first report that he had blown the SLA's Los Angeles cover by stealing a 49-cent pair of sweat sox. "It wasn't sox," he explained to Matthews and the women. "It was a bandolier." (Later, speaking on tape as General Teko, he denied having stolen anything. Shoplifting, he said, was against Symbionese "policy.")

Around nine o'clock, Tom heard talk of a rendezvous, at midnight. A short while later the van pulled up at the ticket booth of the Century Drive-in. Emily paid the admission. The teenager remained hidden in the back while Patty and the Harrises watched *The New Centurions* (a film about the Los Angeles Police Department) and munched on junk food from the snack bar. The meager meal was shared with Matthews. Several times that night, Tom said, Tania reached down and patted him on the head, asked if he was all right, reassured him he wouldn't be hurt.

Midnight came. The SLA three had marked their location by putting a large paper cup upside down atop the speaker stand next to the van. But nobody showed. It was 1 A.M. when Bill said "it would be a good idea if we got some sleep." A long drive took them high up in the Hollywood Hills. Emily pulled off and parked on a little-traveled stretch of Outpost Drive. Matthews, concerned about a baseball game he had to suit up for that afternoon, promptly fell asleep.

He awoke to the three discussing how to get another vehicle. Harris was for "just jumping out in front of a car at a stop sign" and commandeering it. Patty and Emily wanted to pose as hitch-hikers and then "pull their weapons on the driver." The women won. Emily's revolver went into her purse, but Patty had trouble deciding where to hide her pistol. "In the front of her pants or in back?" Yolanda and Tania were back in fifteen minutes with a car and another kidnap victim. Bill Harris bundled up the two car-bines in Matthews' blanket. Teko told Tom to stay put for ten minutes, thanked him, and tossed him the van keys.

"Bill Harris even offered me gas money," said Tom. Matthews declined the offer. By the time he drove home he'd made a decision. Tom told the cops two of his kidnappers had been the Har-rises, but he didn't know who the girl with them was. Not until the next day did he identify Patricia Hearst and relate what she had said to him. And even then he neglected to mention he had kept the sawed-off cuff as a souvenir.

The SLA was riding now in a 1973 Lincoln Continental. Frank Sutter, a building contractor, had made the mistake of stopping for two pretty girls. Patty and Emily both pulled guns and or-dered Sutter into the backseat. "We need your car for a couple of hours," Tania told him. "You're not going to get hurt if you do ex-actly what we tell you." Yolanda added, "We'll kill you if you don't." Sutter did what he was told.

After picking up Sutter, the three drove aimlessly around Los Angeles for some six hours, stopping once to buy a newspaper, then several times to make calls from pay telephones. They finally released Sutter at a little before 1 P.M., telling him where he would be able to find his car. It was right where they said when he walked to the spot fifteen minutes later. He telephoned police. The $250 he had been carrying, Sutter told the FBI, had been liberated by General Teko.*

Back on West Eighty-fourth Street, tracing down the parking

*On August 9, 1976, a Los Angeles jury found William and Emily Harris guil-ty of the kidnappings (with use of firearms) of Matthews and Sutter, the armed robbery of Sutter and two counts of felony auto theft. The Harrises were acquit-ted of six charges of assault. Patricia Hearst was scheduled to be tried in connec-tion with the same Los Angeles charges in January, 1977.

ticket, one of the black detectives was told of two "white chicks," driving a red-and-white van, who had recently moved into a small cottage at 833 West Eighty-fourth Street. He immediately reported; it was shortly before 6 A.M. By 7 o'clock on the morning of Friday, May 17, the block was surrounded by some 125 Los Angeles policemen and FBI agents. Marksmen were posted on roofs, sniper rifles trained on the house.

An FBI SWAT team (Special Weapons and Tactics), the bureau's combat-assault unit, was deployed with semiautomatic rifles, flak jackets, and gas masks. By 8:30 A.M. the number of lawmen at the scene was nearly matched by reporters and photographers tipped that the SLA was under siege.

At 8:55 a police sergeant bellowed through a bullhorn, "To those inside the house at eight-thirty-three West Eighty-fourth Street, this is the Los Angeles Police Department. We want you to come out the front door with your hands up. We want you to come out immediately. You will not be harmed." There was no response. Eight minutes passed. A signal was given.

Several FBI agents rushed the cottage, fired a barrage of twelve tear-gas canisters through the front windows, then retreated to wait as the gas spread through the house. Not a sound came from the small wooden building. Five minutes went by. On signal, the FBI men charged the cottage—the lead man kicking down the door—and several disappeared inside. A minute later an agent emerged, ripped off his gas mask, threw it down, and shouted, "Shit!" The cottage was empty. Yet another SLA safehouse had been abandoned one step ahead of the posse. This time the Symbionese had left behind three suitcases filled with clothing. There were also stacks of SLA documents; a half-dozen gas masks; three purses; two wigs; a sack of medical supplies; two boxes of shotgun shells; a shortwave radio; and a carton of groceries. There was a schedule posted for lookout duty—with nine SLA soldiers traded off two to a watch. A notepad, reportedly that of one of the Harrises, had a list of rations—survival items like beef jerky, chocolate bars, kippers, and sunflower seeds—and beside each its weight. The weights were totaled and divided by nine—probably for backpacking.

A poem written by General Gelina—Angela Atwood—was also discovered.* It read:

> Reality
> You're hard to find

*Revealed later by Patricia Hearst.

We've looked a long time.
A new born babe could tell,
They bid you farewell
And stuffed cries of jive in your place.
Face it, Comrade
Now is the time—we're all alive.
Eat it Pig!
In our minds
The bigger the trigger
The better the target.
The cool, calm palm will smear heavy on the hit.
Sucker pay—
MALCOLM, we're here to stay.

Kyle Jones, who managed the property, said he had rented it on May 9 to two young white women, one calling herself Ms. Rivera, who had found the place through an ad in the Los Angeles *Sentinel*, a black community paper. "Ms. Rivera" had paid $70 for a month's stay. Jones and other neighbors said they had seen the women drive up at different times in several different vans. One was red and white. Another was faded blue in color, with curtains covering the windows and front-end damage. A third was red except for a narrow white stripe around the middle. One neighbor remembered seeing the blue van drive off from in front of the Eighty-fourth Street cottage late the night before.

From the field, police and FBI agents filed their assessments, concurring that they had a hot trail. Apparently the Harrises and Patty Hearst had made no attempt to return to Eighty-fourth Street to warn their comrades, and there was no telephone in the cottage. It was assumed that the rest of the SLA had learned of the shooting at the sporting-goods store and the subsequent chase from a radio news report. Perhaps one among the six remembered the traffic citation and knew the cottage was now too dangerous; more likely it was just caution. Whatever it was, shortly before midnight Donald DeFreeze, Nancy Ling Perry, Mizmoon Soltysik, Camilla Hall, Willie Wolfe, and Angela Atwood fled in haste from West Eighty-fourth Street in search of a new refuge. The LAPD was excited at the prospect of cashing in on the biggest manhunt in the state. With the shoplifting and then the telltale parking ticket left behind (in a pocket of one of Bill Harris' shirts), the SLA appeared to be lightweights from up north. And now they were flushed, off-balance. If they stayed in Los Angeles . . . if they made just one more mistake. . . .

The SLA contingent in fact made no attempt to escape from the city; it was night, traffic on the road was thin, it was too dangerous. Fleeing Eighty-fourth Street, they probably spent the next several hours cruising the streets of black Los Angeles—where DeFreeze was on familiar turf—desperately looking for a place to hole up while they awaited news of the fate of Bill, Emily, and Patty. None of the six apparently had anyone they could rely on to take them in. It seems clear it was sheer chance that led them to 1466 East Fifty-fourth Street at about 4 o'clock on the morning of May 17.

19

Shoot-out

IT was a small stucco house, one of many similar homes built during the 1940s. The neighborhood had once been all white. It is now almost entirely black. Possibly what drew the SLA's attention to 1466 was the fact that at that early hour all the lights were on. They may also have taken note of the four-foot-high stone fence running across the front of the property. A natural shield, should one be needed.

Inside the house were six people: four adults and two sleeping children. Christine Johnson, thirty-five, and Minnie Lewis, thirty-two, lived there. John Smith* and seventeen-year-old Brenda Daniels were visitors. They had dropped in, separately, the evening before "to play dominoes and drink a little wine," Brenda said. They had all done a lot of drinking by the time the SLA arrived on East Fifty-fourth Street. The four were in the front room listening to the radio when someone knocked on the door.

What occurred inside 1466 during the next thirteen hours is constructed from interviews by the authors, other reporters, and LAPD and FBI investigators of the nearly twenty persons who spent varying lengths of time in the house while the SLA was there. Some of these people have given conflicting stories, changing their accounts from interview to interview. The version that follows seems closest to what happened.

Christine and Minnie answered the knock. A handsome black man was on the porch. He spoke in a soft, self-assured voice.

"I saw your lights, sisters. My name is Cinque. I need your help."

---

*The name John Smith is a pseudonym. He is the one person inside 1466 that day interviewed only by the Los Angeles Police Department. The LAPD has refused to identify him other than as John Smith.

Stepping inside, DeFreeze told the women he and "some friends . . . white friends" were being pursued by the police, that they needed a place to stay "for a few hours." At first the women hesitated. Minnie recalled having heard the name Cinque, but wasn't sure just why it stuck in her mind. DeFreeze offered them $100 and promised there would be "no trouble." The women had a whispered conversation, then told Cinque he and his friends could stay "for a little while." The $100 changed hands.

DeFreeze asked John Smith if he would help bring "a few things" into the house. The two went outside, where the rest of the SLA group was waiting. Smith remembers it took a good twenty minutes to unload the vans, for besides suitcases, a footlocker, sleeping bags, and cardboard cartons filled with documents, the Symbionese Liberation Army carried inside enough weapons to outfit an infantry platoon.

In all, nineteen rifles, shotguns, and pistols—and well over 4,000 rounds of ammunition for those weapons—were transferred from the vans to the house. DeFreeze chose the kitchen to store the arsenal. It included:

—Four M-1 .30-caliber carbines. All had been "converted"—capable of being fired only as fully automatic weapons, as machine guns.

—A Browning semiautomatic rifle (Sports Model), .30-06 caliber.

—A Remington semiautomatic rifle, .244 caliber.

—Seven sawed-off 12-gauge shotguns (manufacturers included Mossberg, Ithaca, and Winchester).

—Two Mauser HSc double-action automatic pistols, .38 auto/9-mm caliber.

—A Colt .45 automatic pistol (the military model).

—Two .38-caliber revolvers; one a Smith & Wesson snub-nosed Chief's Special (DeFreeze's personal sidearm), the other a blue-steeled Rossi with a three-inch barrel—the gun Oakland police say Russ Little bought, one of the guns that killed Marcus Foster.

The ammo, some in bandoliers, the bulk in boxes stacked neatly on the floor, included a few rounds that were the SLA's terror trademark—cyanide bullets.

The unloading completed, DeFreeze turned his attention to security. The vans had to be hidden. Smith said he knew just the spot, off the street, behind a two-story apartment house, empty because it was fire-gutted and condemned. And it was only a block away. The General Field Marshal inspected the location. Then he and Smith moved the vans to the rear of 1451 East Fifty-third. They walked around the block, back to the hundred-dollar safe house on Fifty-fourth. It was nearing 6 A.M.

DeFreeze introduced his companions as "soldiers of the SLA," then the six conferred among themselves for a while, much of the time loud enough for their uneasy hosts to overhear. They needed a place to lie low in for a couple of weeks, a place close by. Minnie Lewis quickly suggested a vacant house around the corner on Compton Avenue. Smith led Cinque to the address. It looked okay. DeFreeze made plans to contact the landlord.

Back inside 1466, Christine, Minnie, and Brenda were starting to worry. The SLA soldiers were all packing pistols. There were more guns in the kitchen. And boxes and boxes of bullets. Christine and Brenda had seen one of the white girls (believed to be Nancy Ling Perry) fill several bottles with gasoline. The three huddled in the kitchen and talked of their fears while they washed down what they later described as "nerve pills" with the last of a bottle of wine.

A car pulled up in front of 1466 and honked. It was Smith's boss and a co-worker. He went outside and told them to go on without him. The SLA, explained John Smith, was staying in Minnie Lewis' place and he had a chance to make himself a few bucks, "helping Cinque."

About 7 o' clock DeFreeze asked Brenda if she would go to the store. He gave the girl a twenty-dollar bill, and she walked two blocks to a grocery, returning with beer, bread, cold cuts, and, for DeFreeze, two packs of Camels. Camilla Hall took charge of making sandwiches. Brenda remembers her well. "She was acting like she was the woman of the house."

Minnie Lewis was growing more concerned. Her children were awake and hungry. She gave the two of them sandwiches, sent them off to school, popped another nerve pill, drank a beer, and went to her bedroom for a nap. Her three other children were not there; they lived with their grandmother, Mary Carr, a couple of blocks away. Christine, too, took another pill, a beer, and a nap.

The SLA stayed on alert during the morning hours. DeFreeze and Willie Wolfe traded off half-hour shifts watching the street out the front windows. The four women soldiers took their turns at sentry duty and talked among themselves or with Brenda. Occasionally one would catnap on the wooden floor. There was no need for covers. It was already in the eighties, a beautiful blue-sky smogless day, fast becoming an LA scorcher.

There were two radios and a TV in the house. But apparently the SLA never learned of the 9 A.M. raid on their abandoned West Eighty-fourth Street hideout.

At 9:30 A.M. or thereabouts, DeFreeze asked Smith if he would go out and buy a cheap van or station wagon for the group. The vans hidden on Fifty-third might be hot. A few minutes later Smith departed with $500 handed him by DeFreeze. He went to a pay phone and called around to friends asking to "borrow" a car. He offered up to $40 for the use of one for a day or so. No luck—not even when he explained it was for Cinque and the SLA. He came back with the bad news, said he would try again later, and had a beer.

On West Eighty-fourth Street the LAPD was trying to pick up the SLA's trail. Neighbors around the raided cottage showed no hesitancy in telling what they knew about the strangers who had lived on their street for a week. Kenny Johnson, seventeen, said he had chatted with two of the girls on their front lawn while they sat "smoking a reefer." He and others remembered the various vans, and their several descriptions jibed. A locate-but-take-no-action bulletin was broadcast.

During the late morning several people dropped in at 1466. The SLA made no secret as to its identity; in fact, a few visitors that day say they were given recruitment pitches. One girl asked Cinque what he was doing in LA. DeFreeze took time from handing out carbines and bullets to the others to explain their mission. The SLA had come to Los Angeles to "start a revolution" and "get the police," the girl later told LAPD investigators. No one stayed long. Once outside, each hurried to spread the word: The SLA was right there on Fifty-fourth. By 11:30 it was being talked about over backyard fences and at Sam the Burger Pusher's food stand two blocks away.

Sixty-three-year-old James Reed stopped by about noon with some fresh-picked collard greens for Christine. He found her sitting on the edge of her bed. Reed thought she looked "pretty sick." Suddenly he noticed two white girls, wearing guns. They smiled cordially at him and said "hi" as he hurriedly exited.

At 12:20 P.M. two Metro Squad cops—SWAT team members back on regular duty following the West Eighty-fourth Street raid—decided to check out the rear of 1451 East Fifty-third. It was a regular stop for them, a routine check of a well-known drop spot for stolen-and-stripped cars. The officers knew as soon as they spotted the blue one with the bashed-in front that they had stumbled on the SLA's vans. The discovery of the vans targeted the neighborhood. Black officers in civilian clothing were sent into the area. Gang kids quickly pegged them as cops and passed the word.

The Man was around.

A teenage girl—a friend of Brenda's—dropped in at 1466 a little after 1 o'clock. John Smith was on his way out again with Cinque's $500 in search of a vehicle. He never returned. By that time the LAPD and FBI were gearing for a 3 P.M. strategy session at Newton Street Station to plot out Operation SLA. They were working from the assumption that the Symbionese Liberation Army was somewhere close by those vans. Reporters picked up on the rumors, checked their best sources, and the media began making their way to Compton Avenue "around Fifty-third."

At 2 P.M. a female voice telephoned the FBI and said she had seen the SLA. She mistakenly gave the hideout address as 1462 East Fifty-fourth (next door to 1466). An hour later another anonymous woman caller told the LA police operator she had just seen "two white girls" sneaking through backyards into the rear of a house at 5311 South Compton. Three addresses now had to be checked out.

By 3:30 P.M. the SLA must have been aware that they had been cornered. Even from inside the house DeFreeze had somehow sensed the presence of cops. A young black girl recalls him asking why so many "pigs" were in the neighborhood. He did not seem satisfied with her explanation that it was probably just another dope raid or the LAPD hassling one of the area's several youth gangs. At one point, said the girl, DeFreeze told one of the white women, "Trish, we got to get out of here, it's getting too hot." The woman replied, "Why? It's hot everywhere." If the girl heard the name correctly, then it was to Zoya—Mizmoon (Patricia) Soltysik—that DeFreeze addressed the remark. DeFreeze also told a black man, Clarence Ross, who had wandered in early in the afternoon, "The station wagon should be here by now."

Shortly before 3 Minnie's children began arriving at 1466 from nearby schools. Minnie was passed out on her bed when eleven-year-old Timmy came home. He walked into a houseful of strangers. Rifles and ammo boxes were stacked around the living room, and the SLA women were then loading cartons of cartridges into backpacks.

"Who are you?" Timmy demanded. "We're your mama's friends," DeFreeze replied. "No, you're not. I know all my mama's friends," said Timmy. DeFreeze told the youngster to "sit down." Suddenly Timmy recognized the man. "Are you Donald DeFreeze?" he asked. Cinque said, "No." Timmy dashed out the back door a few minutes later. He saw the elderly James Reed and told him what had just happened. "I'm afraid," the boy said. Reed told him, "Go fetch your grandma."

Two more Lewis youngsters arrived at the house. They told LAPD investigators afterward they had seen Brenda and Christine fighting in a bedroom and that a "white lady" had pulled them apart. Brenda says one of the SLA women asked her to join up, that they "liked the way" she fought.

At Newton Street Station the LAPD and FBI traded intelligence and planned for the soon-to-start SLA sweep. It would be another task for SWAT—but this time it would be the Los Angeles police SWAT team—and LAPD made it clear to the FBI that *they* were going to be running the show. Plans were set out: Only a small number of officers would be directly involved in any confrontation with the SLA. Many more would be needed to "secure the perimeter"—three square blocks—control the anticipated crowds, and divert and direct traffic. The Los Angeles SWAT officers suited up and reported to a field command post set up near the target area.

Around 4 P.M. Mary Carr stormed into 1466. A glance told her Timmy's tale about Cinque and the SLA had been true. "Where's Minnie?" the fifty-two-year-old grandmother demanded. Brenda pointed to the bedroom. Mrs. Carr found her daughter passed out on the bed. Christine was awake but in an alcoholic daze. "Is everybody here drunk?" Mrs. Carr asked. Brenda took her aside and whispered that there were two white women in the other bedroom, that they had "bombs" in there with them. Mary Carr exploded, strode into the kitchen, and confronted DeFreeze.

She told him to get himself and the SLA "out of this place, right now!" DeFreeze said something to her about "black people sticking together." Mrs. Carr did not reply. Rounding up two of her grandchildren, she left—unaware that eight-year-old Tony was still inside. She took the youngsters to her place, fixed them a bite to eat, and, with Timmy along to back up what she had to say, went out in search of "an officer."

A little before 5 P.M. Brenda went to the grocery again with another of DeFreeze's twenties. He wanted two more packs of Camels. On her way back a policeman stopped Brenda. Nobody was being allowed past the perimeter lines.

Minnie Lewis left her house to "go see a friend." She did not come back.

Clarence Ross and young Tony were in the living room. Tony was watching cartoons on TV; Clarence was drinking from a pint bottle of whiskey.

DeFreeze spent some time in the kitchen talking with another eighteen-year-old black girl, who had come over to "see the SLA." She says he told her he was aware police were in the area, that there was probably going to be a shoot-out, and that he was pre-pared to die. But, he told her, "We're going to take a lot of moth-erfucking pigs with us." She also told LAPD investigators DeFreeze was drinking from a jug of Boone's Farm wine during their conversation, but that he appeared—in the stiff words of the police report—"sober and in full control of his faculties."

The girl said Christine stumbled into the kitchen and started to say something. Before any words came out, however, Christine passed out, fell to the floor, and began snoring. DeFreeze lifted her gently and carried the woman to her bedroom. The neighbor went home shortly before 5:30.

At 4 o'clock the command post, set up in the offices of a tow-truck business a few blocks from East Fifty-fourth Street, had gone into operation. An LAPD "tactical alert" was called. That allowed the field commander of Operation SLA to order in cops from throughout the city, as many officers as he needed. SWAT teams One and Two, eighteen policemen under the command of an officer in charge (OIC), reported for duty shortly before 4:30. At 4:20 perimeter boundaries had been established. Eventually 218 LAPD cops and 127 FBI agents would be handling the task of traffic and crowd control.

Until Mary Carr pinpointed her daughter's home as the sanctu-ary the SLA had chosen, the LAPD had had three other suspected hideouts under surveillance. Although it was decided that at-tempts would be made to evacuate homes near all four suspect dwellings, the LAPD ruled out a mass evacuation of the area as being too dangerous. If the SLA soldiers caught on to what was happening, they might try a breakout in the midst of an evacua-tion effort.

The LAPD says it evacuated "a number of residents" prior to the start of the shoot-out, but that "others refused" to leave their homes; in one instance, police reported, occupants of a house called the officers trying to talk them into leaving "motherfuck-ers." Most residents of the area and community leaders as well contend that little or no effort was made to get people to safety.

At a little after 5 o'clock the LAPD had targeted 1466 East Fifty-fourth as the house where the SLA was staying. Final attack plans were mapped.

At 5:40 SWAT officers were in position, armed with semiautomatic carbines, sniper rifles, shotguns, tear-gas launchers, and personal sidearms. Team One was at the front of 1466, Team Two at the rear.

(Thirty-two miles to the southeast, in a motel room across the street from Disneyland, Bill Harris had just clicked on a TV set, switching channels until he found one broadcasting live from the East Fifty-fourth Street scene. Checking in at the Anaheim motel [Emily had spent a college summer working at Disneyland and knew the area well], Harris had overheard someone talking about the SLA, about a house being surrounded by police, that it was on television.*)

"Ready to give the surrender announcement," radioed Team One leader. "Go!" ordered the OIC. It was 5:44.

"*Occupants of fourteen-sixty-six East Fifty-fourth Street, this is the Los Angeles Police Department speaking. Come out with your hands up. Comply immediately and you will not be harmed,*" Team One leader commanded by bullhorn. A few seconds' pause. He repeated the message. Behind the house, some seventy feet away, Team Two leader reported he had heard the broadcasts clearly. There was no response from inside. A minute went by. Team One leader spoke again: "*People in the yellow frame house with the stone porch, address fourteen-sixty-six East Fifty-fourth Street, this is the Los Angeles Police Department speaking. Come out with your hands up. Comply immediately and you will not be harmed.*" Another minute went by.

"The front door . . . somebody's coming out," Team One leader reported suddenly.

A tiny form came through the doorway. It was Tony. He had heard the bullhorn over the noise of the TV cartoons. He had not understood the words. Tony had come out to see what was going on. He walked down the steps, started toward the sidewalk—and froze. All around him were gas-masked figures with guns. "Come this way, over here," Team One leader called. Tony just stood there. Team One leader darted into the open and scooped up the eight-year-old. Tony was crying, screaming, "Mama, Mama." An officer carried him to the corner. Detectives began questioning

---

*From accounts of Patricia Hearst and Bill and Emily Harris given after their capture.

him about who was in the house, whether they had guns. It was several minutes before Tony stopped sobbing long enough to give answers.

Two more surrender announcements. Another figure appeared in the doorway. It was Clarence Ross. He had understood the order. Ross walked out, hands clasped behind head, onto the sidewalk. He balked when Team One leader yelled, "Come this way, slowly." The SWAT officer again exposed himself. He dashed out, collared Ross, dragged him to the corner. Questions were fired at the man. Was the SLA in the house? Was DeFreeze? Were the white women inside 1466? What weapons had he seen? Ross shrugged. He had seen a black lady inside, but no one calling himself DeFreeze or any white women or any guns. He stuck to that story.

Young Tony, however, had given the LAPD a good idea of what it was up against. SWAT knew it was facing at least five, possibly eight, heavily armed soldiers of the SLA. The SWAT OIC decided a quick move had to be made if appeals for surrender failed. He was concerned about the approaching nightfall—an escape attempt by the SLA under cover of darkness would be a likely move; that would greatly increase the chances of people—cops and civilians—getting killed or wounded. There was even the possibility the SLA might try to escape by "tunneling" to another dwelling, the OIC noted later in his report.

Unnoted in any report, but certainly a consideration, was the fact that with night falling, police might have to deal with "hostiles" both in front and behind them. In the Los Angeles ghetto— perhaps in any black ghetto—police are on a limited visa. Crowds could gather—perhaps angry crowds—during a police siege of radicals led by a black man. The LAPD had previously had nasty experiences in such situations. The SWAT officer in charge decided to move in. Tear gas would be the next approach; he radioed his intention to the command post.

Team One leader continued bullhorning surrender commands. In the nine-minute period between the first broadcast and the firing of the first gas canister, "a minimum of 18 separate surrender announcements were made," the official LAPD report of the events of May 17 states.* (Eleven more surrender appeals were made during the shoot-out.)

---

*Although one of the authors watched from a half block away, much of the detail in this report necessarily relies on the official police account. Several newsmen were right at the scene, however, and verify numerous surrender demands

As calls for surrender continued, SWAT officers on both sides of 1466 reported hearing movement inside, sounds like furniture being pushed across the floor, sounds of people shouting to one another. There was no indication there would be a surrender. The LAPD, latecomers to the drama, did not know the SLA code forbade the act. The eighteenth appeal went ignored. At 5:53 the OIC signaled Team One leader.

A front window shattered as two Flite-rite rockets *whooshed* through it into the house and exploded into white clouds of eye-searing, throat-choking CS tear gas.

A burst of machine-gun fire from the house was the SLA's response to the tear gas. The automatic M-1 sprayed .30-caliber bullets into an apartment house directly across the street. SWAT officers instantly answered with their semiautomatics. The battle was joined.

For the next few minutes firing from both sides was intense, almost continuous. The cops and the SLA stopped shooting only when emptied guns forced them to reload. The gunfire drowned out the screams of other residents on the street who suddenly found themselves in the middle of a firefight. Weapons were firing out of 1466 from several windows, hitting all over the place, ricocheting off the street, off buildings, miraculously neither killing nor wounding anyone. Police bullets drilled into the house. (An additional eighteen men from the SWAT reserve were deployed to reinforce the two SWAT fire teams around the house.)

The FBI, miffed at being kept on the sidelines serving as traffic cops, saw a chance to get into the act after the battle had raged for twenty minutes. When the LAPD ran short of tear gas (some 100 canisters of CS and CN gas were lobbed into 1466 during the gunfight), the FBI asked if its own SWAT team could lend a hand. Approval was given, reluctantly. Seven agents spent the next half hour shooting tear gas (sixteen canisters) and bullets (sixty rounds) at the house from a spot across and down the street. The LAPD finally told the FBI no further help was needed.

6:30 P.M.: Heavy firing from the house still continued. Team One leader climbed to the roof of 1468 and crawled to the edge overlooking 1466. He took aim with a gas launcher at a side win-

---

by police bullhorn. The authors went to great lengths to verify details; even to the point of synchronizing various taped news reports and police radio calls against a beeping time-tape to pinpoint time to ten-second intervals, searching for material discrepancies in the official account.

dow and pulled the trigger. Nothing happened. The weapon had misfired. He loaded another Flite-rite into the gas gun, raised himself up, and leaned over. An SLA automatic weapon fired at him. The slugs hit low, raking the stucco wall just below the roof line. The officer threw himself backward onto the rooftop and lay there for several seconds. A thousand feet above, a police helicopter radioed that a "possible wounded officer" was atop 1468. Team One leader was not hurt, however. He jumped to the ground, leaned around a corner, and fired yet another rocket of tear gas into 1466.

Three SWAT officers smashed through a window of 1468 at 6:35 and climbed into what they supposed would be an empty building. They found three black women huddled on the floor. The interior walls of 1468 were pockmarked with bullet holes. The officers immediately began evacuating the women, lifting them through a window. It was Mattie Morrison's house, and as the fifty-eight-year-old woman was being handed through, she begged the policemen, "Don't leave my dogs behind." She said afterward the cops had told her they did not have time "to go around saving animals." Mattie Morrison's three pets—"they was my family"—died in the fast-spreading fire that erupted in the SLA's fortress a few minutes later.

It will never be determined just how the fire started. The SLA had a two-gallon can of gasoline inside 1466, carried in with the weapons and ammunition. Christine and Brenda both say they watched an SLA woman fill bottles with gasoline from that can. If Molotov cocktails were in 1466, one could have burst into flame on being hit by an exploding tear-gas canister.

At 6:40 a Team Two SWAT man tossed a couple of Federal 555 riot-gas canisters into a window on the east side of 1466. A minute later black smoke could be seen pouring out windows at the rear of the house. Within another minute flames started shooting up through the roof. Team One leader radioed, "Cease-fire," and called into the burning building with the bullhorn, "Come on out. The house is on fire. You will not be harmed." There was no response. He ordered "breathing apparatus" readied for expected "smoke-inhalation victims."

In less than four minutes the whole of the rear of the house was aflame and fire was spreading throughout the small structure. There had been no response to the latest surrender appeal. A TV reporter theorized live to the nation that probably all in the house were dead or dying. Just then Christine Johnson burst through the doorway. She stumbled down the concrete-block steps. She was screaming, hysterical.

Christine, apparently only slightly less intoxicated than terrified, lurched onto the sidewalk. A SWAT officer ran out, grabbed the woman, and began pulling her toward the corner. Christine lost balance, fell, and was dragged on her stomach the rest of the distance to the intersection. As she was being handcuffed, Christine started yelling, "They held me, they held me," at intelligence officers bellowing questions at her. (The LAPD report describes Christine as being "hysterical and hyperactive" at that point, the reason they cite for why an officer "placed his foot firmly but lightly on her back to stop her voluntary and involuntary movement.") It was not until after she had been cuffed, searched, and put in a cruiser that the cops discovered Christine had been wounded—not seriously—by a shotgun blast and had sustained minor burns in the blazing house. She was treated —and arrested—at the University of Southern California hospital prisoners' ward. (The felony charge of harboring fugitives was later dropped.)

Christine explained later where she had been during the hour she spent in the midst of the fierce shooting. Oblivious to the siege, asleep across her bed, she had been totally unaware of the battle until the bed caught fire.

At about the time Christine emerged from the burning house, a patrol car was arriving on the scene with four automatic weapons from the LAPD's special-equipment arsenal. Two M-16s—the gun mass-produced for Vietnam—went to Team One; Team Two got the pair of 9-mm Schmeissers. Bursts of machine-gun fire were still coming from 1466.

There was a lull in the gunfire at 6:47. Team One leader broadcast the final surrender call: "*Come out, you will not be harmed. The house is on fire. It's all over. Throw your guns out the window. You will not be harmed.*"

An SLA soldier answered with an M-1.

Three minutes later the SLA's bunker was a sea of orange flame out of which a coal-black pillar of smoke rose a hundred feet or so and then, bent by the wind, drifted northeast across Los Angeles. The SLA guns were still firing.

No longer able to withstand the flames and smoke within the house itself, the SLA chopped a hole through the floor and sought shelter in the eighteen-inch-high crawl space beneath. The Symbionese M-1s were now being fired out narrow air vents in the foundation. Suddenly Team Two leader shouted excitedly into his radio: "We've got one down under the house . . . came out . . . went back in . . . possibly hit . . . still firing."

Fahizah and Gabi had taken the fight to the enemy. Nancy Ling Perry, clad in combat fatigues, hunting knife sheathed on web belt, gas mask discarded, came out of a crawl hole in the foundation at the rear of the house. Russ Little's .38 Rossi was in her hand. She began crawling toward the house next door. Team Two, the LAPD report says, held its fire.

Fahizah was several feet out when Camilla Hall emerged through the crawl hole firing an automatic pistol ("toward members of SWAT Team Two," states the LAPD report). The SWAT officers opened up on her with several weapons. One slug hit her—in the center of the forehead—and killed her instantly. A comrade grabbed the ankles of the lifeless Gabi and pulled the body back inside. Machine-gun fire from the crawl hole resumed.

Fahizah had not come out to surrender, according to the official account, which was corroborated by monitored police-radio instant reports. (The incident was one of the few apparently not witnessed by one of the newsmen who crowded in on what one television anchorman called "the greatest domestic firefight in the history of television news coverage.") The official police report—a blue-bound, mass-printed 138-page book entitled *The Symbionese Liberation Army in Los Angeles*—describes the death of Fahizah, the only SLA soldier to escape from the building:

> Nancy Ling Perry then turned to her right and fired a revolver toward members of SWAT Team Two. Members of Team Two returned weapon fire toward the crawl hole and Nancy Ling Perry. She fell to the ground approximately ten feet from the crawl hole. . . .

The autopsy report states that Nancy Ling Perry was killed by "two gunshot wounds to the back, one severing the spinal cord and the other penetrating the right lung."

It was almost over. For a minute or so longer one soldier of the SLA continued firing out the crawl hole. Team Two blazed away at the opening with automatic weapons. Then the last gun of the SLA fell silent. (In all, some 9,000 shots had been fired by both sides; again, according to the police report.) The final cease-fire command was given at 6:58 P.M. as the walls and roof of the house collapsed. Four minutes later LA firemen began pumping streams of water into 1466 and three adjacent homes, which were also ablaze. They stood back a safe distance. Ammunition and pipe bombs were still exploding. (Fire apparatus had been standing by since the beginning of the siege, but when the blaze broke out, the battalion chief on the scene declared that his firemen could not safely position their hoses with shots still coming from the house. It was, in the official slang, a "let-burn situation.")

The bodies of DeFreeze, Soltysik, and Wolfe were found close together in the right rear corner of the crawl space beneath the structural floor. Nancy Ling Perry's body, just outside the building, had been buried beneath the falling wall. Angela DeAngelis Atwood died just inside the crawl-space portal from which Ling and Camilla Hall had rushed. Camilla—Gabi—who had been fatally shot as she stepped out and then dragged back into the crawl space by her comrades, was buried deep under the charred debris. Her body was not found initially, resulting in a mistaken body count. Five bodies were removed that night—all badly burned and crushed, gas masks melted on their faces. Camilla was found two days later as investigators continued to sift through the charred rubble.

With white nylon cords, police and coroner's investigators charted out the ruins into fifteen square grids, double-sifting debris, collecting evidence, charting the location of everything found. Police even collected all shell casings and identified the guns that had fired them by the firing-pin impressions. (Los Angeles Police Chief Davis later had some of the big double-aught shotgun shells found in the search encased in Plexiglas cubes. He distributed them as mementos to reporters who had covered the shoot-out.)

No police officers, FBI agents, or bystanders were hit by SLA bullets, although the houses all around 1466 East Fifty-fourth bore evidence of the heavy outgoing fire from the house. Five police officers sustained injuries related to the incident. One police officer strained his back carrying a heavy wooden case of gas projectiles; another strained his lower back and right shoulder evacuating citizens from nearby houses; and three others were injured working "perimeter crowd control"—one hit by a thrown brick, one injuring his arm making an arrest, the third pulling a leg muscle in another arrest. Thirty-five persons filed a total of $150,000 in damage claims against the city for damage done to cars and buildings by bullets and fire.

According to the official police report on the siege, only twenty-nine of the thirty-seven SWAT officers actually fired (thirty-eight) weapons—but the "prolonged gunfire at 1466 East Fifty-fourth Street caused the barrel riflings of [twelve] weapons to completely wear out and the magazine springs to become unserviceable." The LAPD allocated $1,450 for the replacement of two M-16 and ten AR-15 rifle barrels. The SWAT siege team fired a total of 5,371 bullet slugs (cost: $1,010.13) and seventy-five tear-gas rockets ($975) and tossed eight tear-gas canisters ($99.60). The cost of two police helicopters hovering over the scene for four hours was billed at $415.53; 321 police vehicles were assigned to the scene and related area patrol (mileage cost: $1,435.98), and $3,386 worth of damage was done to police equipment (half weapons damage, half vehicle damage). Personnel costs were substantial: The LAPD assembled a task force of 410 officers for the siege. On the day of the shoot-out, 305 received assignments and 105 were held in reserve. The following day, Saturday, 196 officers were assigned for crowd control and traffic and "crime scene security." (Through the early-morning hours, into the day and night, a crowd often in the thousands gathered at the scene.) On Sunday 157 officers were again assigned to crowd and traffic control in the area. Associating the cost of all three days with the incident, the police report billed personnel costs (over half in overtime pay) at $59,581.81. Adding all expenses, the LAPD report tallied the cost of eradicating the SLA in Los Angeles at $67,576.55.

The coroner's announcement that Patty Hearst was not among the victims was received as a public-relations godsend at the Parker Center headquarters of the LAPD. A second plus came by way of a subtle comment on the character of DeFreeze: LA coroner Thomas Noguchi, famed for his handling of the Robert Kennedy and Tate-LaBianca murders, issued a verbal report claiming that the Field Marshal had committed suicide, noting powder burns in the head wound. (Noguchi also promised an unusual "psychological autopsy," an investigation into the "compulsive" elements in their refusal to surrender. Never in all his experience, he said, had he seen such unyielding behavior in the face of flames. Yet several months later, when the formal coroner's report was legally filed—detailing the autopsies performed the day after death—it was clearly stated that DeFreeze's wound was *not self-inflicted* and that no gunpowder residue was found. Noguchi, severely criticized in the press for the misleading earlier statement, refused to discuss the discrepancy. More than a year later no "psychological autopsy" had been issued.)

In the hours, days, and weeks following the shoot-out, there were numerous, scattered, and contradictory reports of Tania, Teko, and Yolanda being seen in the Los Angeles area. The three had quickly slipped from sight.

Then, three weeks later, from an unknown hideout there came another communiqué, the last taped message ever received from the "Malcolm X Combat Unit" of the Symbionese Liberation Army. Speaking with evident rage, pain, and grief, Tania—Patricia Hearst—gave the SLA eulogy for the six victims. General Teko—Bill Harris—also gave his version of the battle of Fifty-fourth and Compton. Rather incongruously at the time, Teko announced that the SLA now took up the banner of the New World Liberation Front.

20

Eulogy

LOS ANGELES radio station KPFK broadcast the messages from the surviving Symbionese soldiers immediately upon receiving the recording on the morning of June 8.* Stations throughout the country "patched in," and millions listened to the words of Tania, Teko, and Yolanda. Said Patricia Hearst, in a voice cold and angry:

"Greetings to the people. This is Tania. I want to talk about the way I knew our six murdered comrades because the fascist pig media has, of course, been painting a typical distorted picture of these beautiful sisters and brothers.

"Cujo [Willie] was the gentlest, most beautiful man I've ever known. He taught me the truth as he learned it from the beautiful brothers in California's concentration camps. We loved each other so much, and his love for the people was so deep that he was willing to give his life for them. The name Cujo means 'unconquerable.' It was the perfect name for him. Cujo conquered life as well as death by facing and fighting them. Neither Cujo or I had ever loved an individual the way we loved each other, probably because our relationship wasn't based on bourgeois, fucked-up values, attitudes, and goals. Our relationship's foundation was our commitment to the struggle and our love for the people. It's because of this that I still feel strong and determined to fight.

"I was ripped off by the pigs when they murdered Cujo, ripped off in the same way that thousands of sisters and brothers in this fascist country have been ripped off of people they love. We mourn together, and the sound of gunfire becomes sweeter.

"Gelina [Angela] was beautiful. Fire and joy. She exploded with

*KPFK said a phone call directed them to a cassette that had been hidden beneath a mattress atop a rubbish pile behind the station.

365

the desire to kill the pigs. She wrote poetry—some of it on the walls of Golden Gate, all of it in the LA pig files now—that expresses how she felt. She loved the people more than her love for any one person or material comfort, and she never let her mind rest from the strategies that are the blood of revolution. Gelina would have yelled 'Fire Power!' to the people if there wasn't the need to whisper the words of revolution. We laughed and cried and struggled together. She taught me how to fight the enemy within, through her constant struggle with bourgeois conditioning.

"Gabi [Camilla] crouched low with her ass to the ground. She practiced until her shotgun was an extension of right and left arms, an impulse, a tool of survival. She understood the evil in the heart of the pig and took the only road that could demoralize, defeat, and destroy him. She loved to touch people with a strong— not delicate—embrace. Gabi taught me the patience and discipline necessary for survival and victory.

"Zoya [Mizmoon] wanted to give meaning to her name, and on her birthday she did. Zoya, female guerrilla, perfect love and perfect hate reflected in stone-cold eyes. She moved viciously and with caution, understanding the peril of the smallest mistake. She taught me, 'Keep your ass down and be bad.'

"Fahizah [Ling] was a beautiful sister who didn't talk much but who was the teacher of many by her righteous example. She, more than any other, had come to understand and conquer the putrid disease of bourgeois mentality. She proved often that she was unwilling to compromise with the enemy because of her intense love for freedom. Fahizah taught me the perils of hesitation—to shoot first and make sure the pig is dead before splitting. She was wise, and bad, and I'll always love her.

"Cinque loved the people with tenderness and respect. They listened to him when he talked because they knew that his love reflected the truth and the future. Cin knew that to live was to shoot straight. He longed to be with his black sisters and brothers, but at the same time he wanted to prove to black people that white freedom fighters are comrades-in-arms. Cinque was in a race with time, believing that every minute must be another step forward in the fight to save the children. He taught me virtually everything imaginable, but wasn't liberal with us. He'd kick our asses if we didn't hop over a fence fast enough or keep our asses down while practicing. Most importantly, he taught me how to show my love for the people. He helped me see that it's not how long you live that's important, it's how we live; what we decide to do with our lives. On February 4 Cinque Mtume saved my life.

"The Malcolm X Combat Unit of the SLA was a leadership-training cell, under the personal command of General Field Marshal Cinque. General Teko was his second in command. Everything we did was directed toward our development as leaders and advisers to other units. All of us were prepared to function on our own, if necessary, until we connected with other combat units. The idea that we are leaderless is absurd as long as any SLA elements are alive and operating under the command of our General Field Marshal.

"It's hard to explain what it was like watching our comrades die. Murdered by pig incendiary grenades. A battalion of pigs facing a fire team of guerrillas, and the only way they could defeat them was to burn them alive. It made me mad to see the pigs looking at our comrades' weapons—to see them holding Cujo's .45 and his watch, which was still ticking. He would have laughed at that. There is no surrender. No one in that house was suicidal—just determined and full of love.

"It was beautiful to hear Gabi's father. He understands. Gabi loved her father, and I know that much of her strength came from the support he gave her. What a difference between the parents of Gabi and Cujo, and my parents. One day, just before making the last tape, Cujo and I were talking about the way my parents were fucking me over. He said that his parents were still his parents because they had never betrayed him, but my parents were really Malcolm X and Assata Shakur.* I'll never betray my parents.

"The pigs probably have the little Olmec monkey that Cujo wore around his neck. He gave me the little stone face one night.

"I know that the pigs are proud of themselves. They've killed another Black leader. In typical pig fashion they have said that Cinque committed suicide. What horseshit! Cin committed suicide the same way that Malcolm, King, Bobby, Fred, Jonathan, and George did.† But no matter how many leaders are killed, the pig can't kill their ideals.

"I learned a lot from Cin and the comrades that died in that

---

*Assata Shakur is the reborn name of Joanne Chesimard, a black woman associated with leadership in the outlaw Black Liberation Army.

†Malcolm X, Martin Luther King, Bobby Hutton, Fred Hampton, Jonathan Jackson and George Jackson—murdered black militant leaders, the latter four killed by police or prison guards.

fire, and I'm still learning from them. They live on in the hearts and minds of millions of people in fascist Amerika. The pig's actions that Friday evening showed just how scared they really are. They would have burned and bombed that entire neighborhood to murder six guerrillas.

"The SLA terrifies the pigs because it calls all oppressed people in this country to arms to fight in a united front to overthrow the fascist dictatorship. The pigs think they can deal with a handful of revolutionaries, but they know they can't defeat the incredible power which the people, once united, represent.

"It's for this reason that we get to see—live and in color—the terrorist tactics of the pigs. The pigs saying, 'You're next.' This kind of display, however, only serves to raise the people's consciousness and makes it easier for our comrade sisters and brothers throughout the country to connect. I died in that fire on Fifty-fourth Street, but out of the ashes I was reborn. I know what I have to do. Our comrades didn't die in vain. The pig lies about the advisability of surrender have only made me more determined. I renounced my class privilege when Cin and Cujo gave me the name Tania. While I have no death wish, I have never been afraid of death. For this reason the brainwash/duress theory of the Pig Hearsts has always amused me.

"Life is very precious to me, but I have no delusions that going to prison will keep me alive. I would never choose to live the rest of my life surrounded by pigs like the Hearsts. I want to see our comrades in this country's concentration camps, but on our terms, as stated in our Revolutionary Declaration of War, not on the pigs' terms.

"*Patria o muerte, venceremos!* Death to the fascist insect that preys upon the life of the people."

Emily Harris also eulogized the dead and scorned public reaction to the fiery LA shoot-out as expressed in media editorials:

"There's been a lot of talk about wasted lives, referring to the six dead bodies of our comrades and to Tania, Teko, and myself. There are no editorials written for the wasted lives of the brothers and sisters gunned down in the streets and prisons. The present uproar of white America over the fate of Patty Hearst was barely a murmur as hundreds of young men, mostly black and brown, went off to die in Vietnam. . . ."

The most bizarre of the three was the diatribe of Bill Harris:

"To those who would bear the hopes and future of our people, let the voice of their guns express the words of freedom. Greetings to the people, the Black Liberation Army, the United People's Army, the Black Guerrilla Family, the Weather Underground, and all freedom fighters of the United Symbionese Federation and the New World Liberation Front.

"This is Teko speaking. Yolanda, Tania, and I extend profound feelings of revolutionary love and solidarity to General Field Marshal Cabrilla* and all soldiers of the United People's Liberation Army; to Bitin [sp?] Commander and all elements of the Anti-Aircraft Forces of the SLA; to Combat Unit #4 of the Black Liberation Army; to comrade Martin Sostre and all other comrades, brothers, and sisters in Amerika's concentration camps.

"To our beloved comrades-in-arms, Osceola and Bo, we echo the words you could have often left us with: *A lucha continua . . . venceremos.*

"We have come together in many different cells, squads, and military political units. We have taken many different meaningful names. But we are not hung up on names, for, as comrades-in-arms, we are one in our struggle for freedom. The determination to eliminate our common enemy by force of arms has united us. To our comrade sisters and brothers of the Black Liberation Army and all other fighters, let it be known that the Malcolm X Combat Unit of the Symbionese Liberation Army proudly takes up the banner of the New World Liberation Front.

"The Malcolm X Combat Unit of the Symbionese Liberation Army left the San Francisco Bay Area in a successful effort to break a massive pig encirclement. It had become clear from other SLA elements and from the people in the community that the pigs were preparing to trap us on the San Francisco Peninsula. We knew there was a great risk in setting up a base of operations in San Francisco, which is a natural defile, a trap. The area was very small, surrounded by water, and with limited choices for breaking a major encirclement. However, we accepted this potentially dangerous condition because we saw the importance of making solid contacts in the oppressed communities of this city. We considered ourselves to be an underground unit; however, the majority of our unit's members moved about freely, and in the five months we were there, we made many good contacts.

*The author of a communiqué from the United People's Liberation Army, she claimed the rank of general field marshal of the SLA in a message sent to the media in early June. The body of the communiqué was devoted to citations honoring each slain member of the SLA with "The Mark of the Shao Lin Dragon."

"We decided to move our base of operations to Southern California, concentrating on the Greater Los Angeles area with its vast oppressed communities and more favorable terrain. In April the War Council dispatched an Intelligence and Reconnaissance Team to Los Angeles. Its mission: to make some additional contacts and survey the area. Based on the favorable results of this mission and the concentration of pig activity in the San Francisco Bay Area, our unit slipped out of San Francisco and into Los Angeles on May Day, 1974.

"On Thursday, May 16, 1974, three members of the Malcolm X Combat Unit of the SLA were sent out to buy a number of items needed by the unit. At Mel's Sporting Goods store in Inglewood, a pig-agent clerk named Tony Shepard, attempting to show his allegiance to his reactionary white bosses, falsely accused me of shoplifting. It was impossible to allow a verifying search by a store security guard because I was armed, and therefore we were forced to fight our way out of the situation.

"The pigs originally said that a forty-nine-cent pair of sox were stolen and that this was what caused the shoot-out at the store. The people found this very difficult to believe when it was pointed out that we had already purchased over thirty dollars' worth of heavy wool sox and other items. This, apparently, became increasingly confusing to the pigs, who later charged that an ammunition bandolier was the item taken, supposedly to make the accusation more believable.

"The policy of the Symbionese Liberation Army has always been to avoid shoplifting, because of the heavy risk involved to the whole unit. We cannot afford to have soldiers busted on humbug charges. However, we realize that the combat and support elements run a great risk of being jammed whenever we move about aboveground. The most unfortunate aspect of this situation was that the pigs then learned that SLA elements were in the Los Angeles area. It appears that even with this knowledge, the pigs would not have located our comrades if a collaborator named Mary Carr had not snitched to the enemy.

"On Friday, May 17, 1974, a CIA-directed force of FBI agents, Los Angeles City, County, and California State pigs, with air support and reserve assistance from the United States Marine Corps and the National Guard, encircled elements of the Malcolm X Combat Unit of the Symbionese Liberation Army. The result of the encirclement was that the people witnessed on live television the burning to death of six of their most beautiful and courageous freedom fighters by cowardly, fascist insects. In most cases when an urban guerrilla unit is encircled by the enemy, it can expect to take great losses, especially if the enemy has time to mobilize a massive force.

"Our six comrades were not on a suicide mission, as the pigs would have us believe. They were attempting to break a battalion-sized encirclement. By looking at the diagrams of where their bodies were found, it is clear that they had split into two teams, moved to opposite sides of the rear of the house, and were pre-paring to move out of the house by force. The heavy automatic weapons fired from the front of the house was a diversionary tac-tic to force the pigs to concentrate some of their forces in the front. The two dynamite-loaded pipe bombs were to be used as fragmentation grenades to clear a path through the cringing pigs who had started the blaze by firing incendiary grenades into the house.

"Cin, Fahizah, Zoya, Cujo, Gelina, and Gabi died of smoke in-halation and burns before they could get outside. The pigs want us to believe that the fire was started by the SLA, that it was caused by SLA Molotov cocktails, or by accident from pig tear-gas gren-ades. This is pigshit. The SWAT squad, FBI, and LAPD would have had to go into the house themselves to clear it out. They showed their true cowardice by using incendiary grenades to cause the fire that killed our comrades.

"For those that don't know, incendiary grenades burn at such an incredible temperature that they melt steel and armor plate in a matter of seconds and are impossible to extinguish.

"The pigs want the people to believe that the bad-ass tactics of the SLA guerrillas drove the fascists to use such barbaric force. But we say that the SLA is a reaction to fascism. The SLA uses au-tomatic weapons and homemade bombs because the pigs have au-tomatic weapons, artillery, and hydrogen bombs.

"The pigs want the people to believe that General Field Marshal Cinque Mtume committed suicide. To this absurdity, the SLA re-sponds by quoting our beloved comrade brother. He often said, 'We must not fear death, for to fear death is to put our fear of pig terror before our love of the children and the people's struggle for freedom.' The pigs have historically focused on eliminating Black leaders. Many have been murdered and imprisoned in Amerika's concentration camps.

"For over a year the pigs couldn't find Cin to murder him, so they attempted to isolate him from the people with pig propaganda. First they worked on the most blatantly racist Whites with their traditional 'crazy-Black-nigger, escaped-convict-rapist' routine. Next we learned that Cin was a plum-wine alcoholic. This obviously was the White racist, Liberal answer to the logic that a Black revolutionary leader could order and assist in the assassination of a jive-assed, pig-agent school superintendent.

"It followed that the White supremacists and bourgeois Black elements of the revolutionary left so-called leadership would be pimped with ridiculous tales of links between the SLA and the CIA—that Cin was and had been a paid informer for the Los Angeles Police Department and the California attorney general's office. If this were true, we dare these fools and collaborators to explain Cin's reward for his deeds—a life term in California's concentration camps.

"White, sickeningly Liberal, paranoid conspiracy freaks and spaced-out counterculture dope fiends proved their naivete and amateurish research skills as they rambled on and on and on about the California Department of Corrections. Bizarre stories about Cin having been programmed and electrodes implanted in his brain while at Vacaville began to appear in the so-called underground press.

"Cinque Mtume: the name means 'Fifth Prophet.' Cin was indeed a prophet. The pigs would have the people believe that Cin was just, as they would say, another dumb nigger. They continually attempted to undermine his leadership by propagandizing that Cin was being offed by Whites; that he wasn't smart enough to be the brains behind the planning and execution of the successful SLA actions.

"To this display of racism we say, go on into the Black community and ask the people if Cinque Mtume was not a prophet. Ask the people if they think he was being used by Whites. The people know that a Black man in Amerika does not need conscious Whites to push him into leading a revolution. Racists cannot believe that middle-and upper-middle-class Whites and a daughter of a superfascist ruling-class family would ever have reason to follow the lead of a beautiful Black genius, revolutionary warrior and give their lives for the people. Sick-assed racists would have us believe that White women who follow the lead of Black revolutionaries are only mindless cunts enslaved by gigantic Black penises.

"The cringing pigs who faced the firepower of Gelina, Gabi, Fahizah, and Zoya know much better.

"Racists believe that it is impossible for white men to denounce

White racism and follow the revolutionary leadership of Black men, but the SLA proved this theory to be a sick delusion. Cinque Mtume, himself, was the spirit of Frederick Douglass, Gabriel Process, Denmark Vesey, Marcus Garvey, the Scottsboro boys, Medgar Evers, William E. Burghardt Du Bois, Malcolm X, Martin Luther King, Emmett Till, little Bobby Hutton, Fred Hampton, L. B. Barkley, Jonathan and George L. Jackson, Mark Essex, and every other Black freedom fighter who came before him.

"To racist slander, the SLA and all the people say: Death to the fascist insect that preys upon the life of the people.

"And now, after our comrade brother fought valiantly against a battalion of pigs—a battle witnessed by millions—these same chickenshit pigs are trying to have us believe that General Field Marshal of the Symbionese Liberation Army Cinque Mtume killed himself. Cin was so determined to kill pigs that as long as his heart was beating and that there was any air in his lungs at all, he would fight, even if his only weapon was his body. We all know that revolutionaries do not kill themselves. Revolutionaries kill the enemy.

"Cin was the baddest member of the SLA and therefore our leader. Our five White comrades who died with him were among his students and had learned well. They, too, showed incredible determination and courage. Cujo, Gelina, Fahizah, Zoya, and Gabi did not commit suicide, as the pigs would have us believe. Pigs tell us it is suicidal for Whites to join Blacks and other oppressed people in making revolution. To this oinking we say, it is suicidal for the ruling class and all its pig agents to believe that they can continue to oppress, exploit, murder, and imprison an undivided revolutionary army of people. White Amerikans who follow the example of our beautiful comrades and join the fight for the freedom of all oppressed people will not do so because they wish to die, but because they wish to be free.

"The pigs boast that they have broken the back of the Symbionese Liberation Army. But to do this, the pigs would have to break the back of the people. The military/political leader of the SLA and five top cadre have been killed by the fascists. However, the SLA is not dead and will not die as long as there is one living, fighting member of any oppressed class, race, sex, or group left on the face of this earth. The pigs have won a battle, but the war of the flea is not over. As our dear comrade Ho Chi Minh once wrote from an imperialist prison, 'Today the locust fights the elephant, but tomorrow the elephant will be disemboweled.'"

21

Refuge I

THE Symbionese Liberation Army suffered their first blood in the Los Angeles ghetto, their first casualties, and it seemed it was there the SLA's Revolution died. Three refugees survived, but these three could never re-create the strange chemistry that had made eight an "army." Too much around them had changed. De-Freeze was dead, and it had been he who catalyzed and directed their furious passion. Teko wore his command as a little man; there was no longer a magic, no longer a dancing illusion of a nation teetering on the edge of revolution. The remnant SLA was able to retreat and find refuge, but only by chance. Later they tried again to recruit and re-form—they found allies, bought new guns, and again they would kill—but never again would they raise banditry as the specter of revolution, probably not even among themselves.

After the fiasco at the sporting goods store, the flurry of flight—failing to make contact at the drive-in (apparently because the theater was in the area of Mel's, Cin and the others avoided the rendezvous)—Bill, Patty, and Emily knew they were on their own. But the trio had been sent out together because they were a self-sufficient "fire team"—one of the three subunits of the cadre nine. There was another meet set two weeks hence; all they had to do was lie low.

They abandoned the hijacked Continental only after Emily purchased a small sedan compact in Los Angeles, tracing down newspaper ads until they found a private owner willing to take cash and give up the car on the spot. Emily bought food and new wigs for herself and Patty; then the three took to Southern California's labyrinth of freeways, driving southeast into Orange County.

They must have heard the radio bulletins about the raid on West Eighty-fourth, heard that the others had escaped, that the

374

police were now sweeping the city. They had the textbook theory of escape: chase the tourists, lose yourself in a natural and diverse crowd. They drove for Anaheim, where Emily had spent one college summer; for Disneyland, the famed California amusement park, with its mob of May vacationers.

They drove right up to the big-gated entrance of Disneyland and found a motel across the street. It was late afternoon, about 5:30, when Emily checked in for the three of them. A single room. Patty stayed with the car, but Bill wandered into the lobby. Minutes later—just as Patty and Emily were opening the room—he came rushing back. He had overheard something about the police surrounding a house in LA—that it was on television. Bill turned on the color TV, spun the dial—and there Tania, Teko, and Yolanda watched the scene unfold at East Fifty-fourth Street. "It was so unreal," recalled Emily much later. "I said, 'It couldn't be them—it's just a mistake—like the raid on Eighty-fourth Street this morning.' Bill said kind of flatly that he recognized the sound of their weapons—the automatic carbines." They watched it all: the police platoons, the smoke, the fire. Listening to the steady crackle of the gunfire and then the soft roar of the wind-sucked flames. Patty recalled everyone screaming, crying, almost hysterical. The Harrises would recall only *Patty* crying: She wanted to go back to LA, they said, to attack the police from behind, full of a vengeful rage.

But they stayed and shared a night of pain, panic, shock, and loss. (None of the three mentioned the bandolier or Mel's, said Patty, "until later. . . .") They stayed at the Anaheim motel two, three days, then drove fifteen miles west to Costa Mesa. Another motel, for a week. They kept inside as much as possible; Patty never left the room. Those must have been long, close, claustrophobic days. They drove north then. Away from the sunny, friendless city that had so briefly been the southern base of the Revolution. Up the valley route on Interstate 5, back to Berkeley, back to the cultural womb that had created them.

Even in the Bay Area, even with the radical community shocked into new sympathy for the SLA by the televised barbecue in Los Angeles, they found no easy refuge. The horror of the Fifty-fourth Street shoot-out had deeply shaken a precious delusion, the white middle-class sense of invulnerability which had been so central to the gun-waving rhetoric of "armed struggle." And personal politics rather than mass politics had created the SLA. The Symbionese had never had a base of their own, never a network of support. Now, desperate, the fugitive three had no connections, few friends who could or would help them. They were in the Bay Area for at least a week before they made safe contact—and that with a woman who was but a friend of a friend: twenty-seven-year-old Kathleen Soliah, bosom buddy to Angela Atwood in the months before Angel became General Gelina.

The three checked into a downtown San Francisco motel for two days, then—with the last of their money—rented a cheap apartment on Walnut Street in Oakland and began an urgent search for a patron. They must have taken heart when, a couple of days later, on May 31, the Weather Underground bombed the California attorney general's Los Angeles office—dedicating the attack to "our sisters and brothers" of the SLA. Two days after that they had found Kathy Soliah. It would have been difficult to miss her.

A memorial rally for the SLA was held in Berkeley's Ho Chi Minh Park on June 2. The rally was small by Berkeley standards, about 400 people, many there just out of curiosity. The notable absence of any California leftist luminaries—the single exception being Wilbur "Popeye" Jackson, leader of the United Prisoners Union—reflected the critical and mixed emotions with which the Left and even Berkeley viewed the SLA, even in the common outrage over police tactics in Los Angeles. Jackson lambasted the "armchair revolutionaries" who scorned the SLA, but even Kathy Soliah, in the most impassioned speech to the crowd, bespoke the ambivalence.

She had watched, she said, unknowing, as Angela became Gelina: "When I first met her she wasn't very political, but she was always on the right side." They had lost touch the winter before; Kathy had returned from a Mexico vacation to discover Angela on the run and the SLA in the headlines. A lot was happening that she could not understand. "There were many times when I wanted to talk to her and ask her what the hell was going on with her and the SLA. Certainly there were times when I felt they made serious mistakes and should have connected more with the people they were supposedly fighting for." Still, she argued, Angela, Camilla, Mizmoon, and Nancy Perry were "among the first white women to fight so righteously for their beliefs and to die for what they believed in.

"I believe that Angela was a truly revolutionary woman," she said. "And the amazing thing is that she and her women comrades came from the same background as many of us here. They were white middle-class people with a lot of advantages who had gotten into the women's struggle and then generalized that struggle to include all people." The TV cameras panned the crowd, then zoomed in on Soliah at the microphone as she roused the crowd with a chanted salute. To Bill, to Emily, to Tania she cried, "Keep fighting! *I'm* with you! *We're with you!*"

Kathleen Soliah had been the prime mover in organizing the Berkeley memorial, and she had already begun to gather another group, which would call itself the Bay Area Research Collective, a pro-SLA propaganda group to republish the SLA communiqués and drum up radical support for the fugitive underground. (The organizing leaflet for BARC also suggested—rather belatedly— that they might research Marcus Foster in an attempt to justify his assassination.) Soliah had virtually enlisted in the SLA before the TV cameras, and if she was not an uncritical acolyte, her speech had rather precisely captured the egocentricity that had informed the original SLA.

The possibility that Kathy Soliah would become helpmate to the SLA was apparently so obvious (particularly after the SLA rally) it was considered unlikely. Like the proverbial butler, Kathy Soliah was too prominent—thought police—too public, to be in direct contact with the fugitives. By any logic it was true, but Yolanda, Teko, and Tania, destitute and desperate, had nowhere else to go. It was apparently a day or so after the memorial rally that Emily Harris contacted Kathy Soliah.

Steve Soliah, Kathy's brother—himself a key figure in the SLA renaissance four months later—said Emily appeared at his sister's home one evening, alone, uninvited, unannounced. But she surely didn't have to introduce herself. (Kathy's name and phone number were in Emily's address book left behind for police to find when the Harrises went hurriedly underground.) It was like a lost spider finding a web weaver. While Soliah had never been politically "heavy," never more than a follower on the fringe, she had access to everything the SLA had always lacked: contacts; resources; experience. Perhaps only now, in the aftermath of Los Angeles, was it available for an SLA connection, but upon the alert of Kathy Soliah, there was a tight and effective network of friends mobilized to save the SLA.

Soliah was nearly a Berkeley veteran; she had arrived in the Bay Area only in 1971, but 1971 was the last of a bitter three years that had transformed many young liberals infatuated with idealism into radicals motivated by a burden of conscience. Something died in 1968: with Martin Luther King's murder, Robert Kennedy's assassination, the "children's crusade" for McCarthy, the bloody Democratic convention in Chicago. Soliah had been schooled at the University of California at Santa Barbara, graduating in 1970, and with most of her generation she still had scars, memories, and friends from the years of dread: 1969, 1970, 1971. They were years of imperial war in Vietnam, years with the scent of domestic fascism. Suspicions that it would take Watergate and its cathartic aftermath finally to validate five years later.

They were years for conspiracies; years when the phrase "good German" became the radical's curse upon the liberal.

Nixon was inaugurated in 1969, and his "secret plan for peace" called for escalation in Indochina. Antiwar demonstrations became bigger and more bitter. SDS split; the "Days of Rage" in Chicago gave birth to the Weather Underground. In Berkeley an attempt to claim and plant a "People's Park" on a vacant, barren, ugly University of California lot spiraled into a National Guard mobilization and days of vicious street battles, tear gas, the shotgun-blast death of a young demonstrator fired on by a sheriff's deputy.

Cambodia was invaded by the United States in 1970, and the response was a National Student Strike—and the Jackson State and Kent State students murdered. In August, Jonathan Jackson, kid brother to George, raided the Marin County courthouse and died with his hostage judge, and others, in a bullet-riddled van. At UC Santa Barbara, where Kathy Soliah was then a senior, antiwar demonstrators burned a Bank of America office—and police struck back with a brutal rampage through the off-campus Isla Vista student ghetto. In 1971 there were mass arrests in the nation's capital during the huge Mayday antiwar demonstration. On August 21—a day many blacks and California radicals recall with the livid memories others associate with JFK's assassination— George Jackson led his murderous revolt in San Quentin's Adjustment Center and was cut down by guards' bullets, alone in the middle of the prison yard. And Nixon, seeking "peace with honor," sent B-52s to carpet-bomb civilian Hanoi during the Christmas holidays—as antiwar Vietnam veterans took over the Statue of Liberty in New York harbor to fly the Stars and Stripes upside down in the international signal of distress.

Those three years that turned the decade were among the nation's darkest since the Civil War. The SLA was but sad spectacle because it was fundamentally irrelevant, irresponsible, and amoral, born of its own incestuous narcissism. But in those three terrible years a large part of a generation teetered at the edge of treason, caught up in the contradiction between the American reality and American ideals.

It was a small network of friends from that era who responded when Kathy Soliah asked for help for the SLA. The Los Angeles burnout was like a flame from the past, igniting a fuse not yet too old to burn. Samaritans and "soldiers," different people were drawn in at different times—some infatuated with the electric sensation of the SLA; some caught up in a spasm of reaction to the old smell of revolt. All, it seemed, took the Tania transformation at face value.

Kathleen Soliah was an outspoken feminist and an actress, as Angela had been. She was a strong, dominating woman, tall and blond, whose love of theater had only slowly—and recently—been overshadowed by her commitment to the Revolution. Kathy was the oldest of five children, daughter of a high school track coach and English teacher in Palmdale, on the high desert thirty-five miles north of Los Angeles. Of the five Soliah siblings, the three oldest—Kathy, Steve, and Josephine—would be drawn into the SLA conspiracy. (In fact, of all the names later connected with the SLA's refuge and rearmament, Kathleen Soliah would be the most evident link between them.) In the ironic mold that had become the SLA routine, the Soliahs were quiet American middle-class stock, a conservative family. And Kathy's *vita* was resplendent wth teenage honors: Girl Scout counselor, junior high yearbook editor, churchgoer, "pep chairman" for Palmdale High, from which she was graduated with honors.

Kathy Soliah had come to Berkeley in late '71, moving up from Los Angeles with her boyfriend, twenty-four-year-old Jim Kilgore. Son of a prosperous lumber dealer in San Rafael, just north of San Francisco, James Kilgore had dropped out of his graduate program in economics at UC Santa Barbara the year before, when Kathy graduated with her BA in theater. The two traveled; settled for a while in a commune in Monterey, then LA. They moved north at the urging of a new friend, Jack Scott, then a prominent Berkeley activist who had made a name for himself with a controversial mix of politics and athletics. Scott had come out of the late sixties as perhaps the leading advocate of the "Jock Liberation" movement, protesting the authoritarian nature of coach-dominated sports and the pressure of commercialization on college and professional athletes.

Kilgore, a sports enthusiast and one time college sports writer, had corresponded with Scott and then met him in Los Angeles. At the time Kathy and Jim were already thinking of moving to San Francisco. Live theater is almost nonexistent in Los Angeles, smothered perhaps in the aura of Hollywood. Kathy hoped for a chance to get on stage with one of the myriad small theaters in the Bay Area. Kilgore, having discarded ecometrics, was hoping for a career as a free-lance photographer or writer, perhaps a sports-writer. Scott encouraged the move, and when Jim and Kathy first arrived in September, 1971, he had them stay at the apartment he shared with Beverly "Micki" McGee, on Fifty-eighth Street in Oakland. They were Scott's guests for three weeks, until they got a place of their own on Shattuck Avenue in Berkeley.

Steve Soliah, Kathy's brother, arrived in Berkeley in the end days of that year. Steve, then twenty-three, a year younger than Kathleen, had been a star athlete, a record-breaking runner at Humboldt State College in Northern California, but had dropped out in his junior year and slowly drifted south for the Berkeley scene. Steve connected well with Scott's circle of self-questioning athletes. He stayed with Jim and Kathy for a month; then moved—with a new girlfriend, Emily Toback—into a small Berkeley Way commune to live with two new friends he met through his sister and Scott: Michael Bortin, a twenty-three-year-old San Francisco native, graduated from Berkeley the previous June, and Bortin's longtime sweetheart, Pat Jean McCarthy, twenty, a granddaughter of former San Francisco Mayor Henry "Pinhead" McCarthy. Bortin was a busy Berkeley activist, an officer of the campus SDS chapter in 1969, but while still a student, he had started his own private contracting firm, and he hired both Steve and Jim Kilgore to work with him as house painters. It was a casual, itinerant profession, and both Steve and Jim took to it rather well.

Josephine Soliah had followed her brother and sister to the Bay Area in 1973, two years later. Jo, then twenty, had dropped out of the California State University at Long Beach, in Southern California, during her senior year, deciding she no longer wanted teaching certification. She was intent on a new vocation, nursing, but when she couldn't get into a training school immediately, Kathy persuaded her to come north. The two sisters moved together into an Oakland commune—Kathy and Jim had chosen to separate for a period. Kilgore and Steve Soliah were still working together as house painters, and Jim still had a close relationship with Kathy, but Kathy had become deeply involved in the women's movement, said friends, and wanted to live independently.

But the four of them—Kathy and Jim, Steve and Jo—saw a lot of one another, and each of them, by the spring of 1974, had come to share a vague empathy for the SLA outlaws. After the shoot-out, all pitched in to arrange the memorial rally. Kathy's pain and outrage at the death of Angela had shaped the response of the other three. And when Emily Harris recruited Kathy, the others—Jim, Steve, and Jo—were ready to be brought in on a draft.

(Martin Soliah, Kathy's father, returned home from a fishing trip to learn from friends in Palmdale that his daughter had been on television giving a pro-SLA speech in Berkeley, and he immediately telephoned to "chew her out." Kathy was not there, but sister Jo was. Josephine had always been the dutiful daughter, writing faithfully, keeping everyone aware of the family doings. Jo was then working at Oakland's Children's Hospital. She told her father that brother Steve had advised Kathy not to speak at the rally, but Angela Atwood had been Kathy's best friend and Kathy was "very, very upset" over her death. Later Kathy herself called home. She explained to her father that she had given the eulogy for Angela out of "personal" rather than political feelings—politics they might argue, she said, but her personal feelings "are none of your business." Much later her mother would wistfully recall the incident and remark that only Kathy of all the kids had the spunk to stand up to their father when he was angry.)

Angela Atwood and Kathy had first met in September, 1972, during auditions for a production of Ibsen's *Hedda Gabler* with the Theater Company of Oakland. They both won lead roles, and working on the play, they quickly became friends. When Kathy said she needed a job, Angela got her hired as a waitress at a downtown restaurant-lounge, the Great Electric Underground, where she herself worked. They began to hang out together all the time, said friends.

Angela and Kathy took a night course together in radical feminism, and at the restaurant they tried to organize a waitresses' union. For an acting class Angela took, the two of them created a one-act play called *Edward the Dyke.* Kathy played Edward, a lesbian; Angela was a psychiatrist who tried to convince her that all her problems could be solved by a soft bed and a sexy man. ("They had a strong sisterly love, but I think that's as far as it went," confided a close friend.) Angela's marriage was then floundering, and she was exchanging her wifely image for a tough feminist identity. "Angela became more outspoken about women's liberation eventually," recalled an actress who worked with both, "but her expression of that—and being outspoken—seemed to come from Kathy. They were both into women's liberation when they met, but Kathy much more so."

Angela's mix of politics and feminism had the edge and tumult of a new convert—at least that's the way Kathy and mutual friends saw it. "She was just getting into it all, all at once," said one woman friend of both. "Kathy thought she would level off with a little time and experience." But time and experience is just what Angela did not have.

Waitresses who worked with them at the Great Electric Underground recall both Kathy and Angela as "the organizers"—picking up on every little issue, often fighting battles for other employees who would as soon let matters lie. Although the two were a team in "office politics" at the restaurant, it was Angela who seemed to grate on the nerves of her co-workers. "When Angela got into the social classes and that stuff," said one, "that plus her feminist rap became just all-consuming . . . she was always miserable and upset about something. It just became unpleasant to be around her."

As Angela became involved with the early SLA, in the late summer of 1973, she began to drift apart from most of her old theater chums—but not, apparently, from Soliah. Angela and Kathy kept working together at the Great Electric Underground until late December, about three weeks before the SLA took to cover following the arrests of Remiro and Little. Both were caught up in their rapidly collapsing union effort at the restaurant.

The focus of the organizing drive—a running feud with management over the hem and cleavage of the waitresses' uniform—was not the sort of bread-and-butter issue that created the Knights of Labor. Just a few days before Christmas both Kathy and Angela quit—with a bombastic four-page denunciation of management and their co-workers:

> We consider our employment situation a microcosm of the working world at large. Our actions here are a reflection of our beliefs in the radical political spectrum. At GEU, we have gone as far as we can. We have no support from our peers. No one is willing to take chances . . . . we leave to find areas in which our concerns and actions are productive. . . .

By mid-January Angela would be a fugitive, General Gelina of the SLA, but before then, over the Christmas holidays, Kathy Soliah had left for a long vacation in Mexico (with a woman friend she introduced to her parents in Palmdale—and whom they, hesitantly, describe as "overly masculine"). Despite reports to the contrary and despite Soliah's later protestations, it seems a strong possibility that Kathy knew something about Angela and the SLA.

Both Angela and Kathy had been utterly committed to theater—at one point in 1973 they talked with friends about starting their own—but even then, for Angela theater had become a political tool, while Kathy seemed intent on polishing an art. The producer for the Oakland theater that put on *Hedda Gabler,* Jerry Roth, describes Angela as "a nonentity, and not very bright either." But for Kathleen he had only rave reviews. "An excellent actress," he said. "Kathy had emotions, could feel love, hate, anger. . . . Angela seemed apolitical—you ever see somebody who was totally blank? You got the feeling there was nothing there." More likely, Angela's politics outside the theater had come to engross her, while Kathleen could balance and discipline her energies.

When she returned from Mexico, Kathy had taken several odd jobs: working in a bookstore; for a while painting with her brother and Kilgore. Then she got another acting job, with the Emeryville Shakespeare Company. Right after the Los Angeles shootout, she quit. From her stance in arguments among the cast, "we knew she was an SLA supporter or something," said one actor in the group. "But onstage she did beautiful work," he lamented, "she made it all happen. . . . She was fine before the killings in LA, but after that there was a real change. When Angela Atwood died, she wilted like a flower out of water."

When Patty, Bill, and Emily had made contact with Kathy Soliah, their most urgent need was money, but nearly as important, they wanted to get out of the Bay Area—then again being swept by a tight dragnet of police and FBI agents. Patty said during her trial that the Soliahs and others, "friends of the Harrises," provided funds. And Kathy Soliah said she thought she could arrange a hideout refuge.

Steve Soliah later said that Kathy and Jim Kilgore told him two weeks after the Berkeley SLA rally that they had been contacted by the Harrises. Steve claimed he warned them the whole scene was too hot: "I told them they were crazy. I advised them to get out." But he gave his sister $100 for the rescue fund, and a few days later, when Kathy asked him if he wanted to meet the three, he jumped at the chance. He said he went, alone, to an address Kathy had given him, unlocked an empty apartment in North Berkeley, and waited as he was told. If it was a rendezvous, the SLA team apparently staggered crosstown with full armament.

Steve said the Harrises and Patty arrived with heavy bags, which they immediately unpacked to unlimber "lots of weapons." Steve said the only thing he could really remember about the conversation was Bill Harris urgently explaining that the three of them *had* to get out of the area. To stay would be suicide, and there had been enough death.

(The late history of the SLA—the period between the LA shootout and the arrests a year and a half later of the Harrises, Steve Soliah, Patty Hearst, and Wendy Yoshimura—is difficult and confusing to trace. Several of the principal actors have offered guarded, contradictory, and highly selective accounts of their experiences during this period; and though we use this information for elaboration and contrast, the factual scheme offered here is largely based upon the full confession of Patricia Hearst—a much more detailed, revealing, and self-incriminating version than that offered publicly in her trial testimony—and the results of the authors' independent investigation.

(The "inside accounts" which have been previously published—Patty Hearst's own trial testimony; Bill and Emily Harris' tale in a *New Times* magazine interview; an early *Rolling Stone* article ["Tania's World"] which although unattributed was substantively based on interviews with Jack and Micki Scott; and another *Rolling Stone* article ["The Lost Year of the SLA"] which, although published without credit, was largely based upon information provided by Steve Soliah—were all defensively skewed and misleading. Each account offered conflicting stories, contradicted earlier versions offered by the same sources, and the authors' independent investigation revealed major inaccuracies in each.

(The SLA had fractured bitterly, and each of these accounts reflected those new antagonisms among the group. By the time the stories were published, each of those involved had too much to hide: too many loyalties to keep, too many enemies among former comrades. Each feared several of the others, feared what they might say more than what they might do; so while they spoke disparagingly of each other, they avoided serious allegations against the others even as they sought to minimize their own criminal liability. Too much truth, then, seemed dangerous for *everyone*. Patricia Hearst agreed to "tell all" only after she had been convicted of the Hibernia Bank robbery, only after she had been conditionally sentenced to thirty-five years' imprisonment. And when her sentence was later reduced to seven years, making her eligible for parole in early 1978, that cooperation was a major factor in the court's decision.

(Relevant material from the *Rolling Stone* and *New Times* articles is cited—with credit, some qualification, and direct attribution where possible—to help trace the shifting alliances within the group and the evolution of divergent political philosophies among them. The two *Rolling Stone* pieces—"Tania's World," which relied heavily upon information provided by the Scotts; and "The Lost Year of the SLA," which was largely based upon interviews with Steve Soliah—were written by Howard Kohn and David Weir and published as unattributed "inside reports" with no caveat; but where the authors were able solidly to confirm the source of the information quoted here from those articles, that information is cited as to source.

(History is the final judge of those who call themselves revolutionaries, but for the remnant SLA the media, although a frail substitute at best, became the court of first appeal. Yet it was only with the trial testimony of Patricia Hearst that the shadowy personalities of the post-shoot-out SLA began to be revealed, and it was only with Patty Hearst's confessions to the FBI, after her own conviction, that the details of the SLA's last year were unveiled. During her trial, Patty had begun to name names, but even then, she had loyalties that she discarded only after her conviction. She did not, for instance, recall Steve Soliah's being involved with the group in 1974. And although she admitted Soliah had been her lover in late 1975, when both were arrested, on trial she steadfastly refused to give any information about that last year, claiming her Fifth Amendment protection against self-incrimination, and extending that protection, de facto, to several of her underground comrades.)

Patty testified at trial that she recalled staying two weeks, perhaps longer, at the Oakland hideout on Walnut Street, and it was there that the last SLA tape was made. Later, she said, at the Berkeley apartment—owned by a friend of either Kathy Soliah or Kilgore (one of them had a key because they had to "feed some turtles" while the friend was away)—she for the first time was introduced to Jim Kilgore, Kathy Soliah, and Jack Scott.

Scott, she said, was the SLA's ticket East.

When Kilgore and Kathy Soliah first met Jack Scott, he was still finishing his PhD in sociology at UC Berkeley but was already perhaps the best-known graduate "teaching fellow" in American academics. He had already published the first of two books he developed out of his thesis, *Athletics for Athletes* (it would soon be followed by *The Athletic Revolution*), and had become a minor guru for thousands of amateur and professional athletes who had begun to search for a more positive self-image than the traditional brawn-and-bonehead stereotype. Scott was one of the first to offer an alternative and to challenge the sacrosanct authority of the coach as the Lord's stand-in. He had been *Rampart*'s sports columnist; in 1967 he had raised such a furor with an article sympathetic to Harry Edward's proposed black boycott of the Olympics that his house had been firebombed. Within a couple of years, many of his complaints would seem common sense—but he had grabbed America by the jockstrap, and the initial reaction had been explosive. In 1971, after he received his doctorate, he was hired and then fired by the University of Washington; he collected a full-year salary without working a day, but a revolt of the coaches had made the university back out of his contract. Scott's private research group, the Institute for the Study of Sports and Society (ISSS), became a national clearinghouse and hot-line contact for maverick college and professional athletes.

In 1972 Scott had been named director of athletics at Ohio's Oberlin College (over the unanimous objection of the Oberlin coaches) and launched a brief, stormy career in college sports. He hired Tommy Smith, famed for his black-gloved 1968 Olympics salute, as his assistant athletic director and track coach and brought in Cass Johnson as the first black head coach at a predominantly white college.

Tall and gangly, warm with friends and bitterly sarcastic with critics, himself a former track star of national stature, the earnest and articulate Scott had helped numerous professional athletes shape and express critiques of their sports. The Scott ISSS helped prepare and publish Dave Meggysey's *Out of Their League*, Gary Shaw's *Meat on the Hoof*, and Paul Hoch's *Rip Off the Big Game*—as well as Scott's own writings. He was a gadfly on the powerful American sport industry, and sportswriters around the country valued him as a source. In 1973, after Scott had criticized Alabama football coach Bear Bryant, then Vice President Spiro Agnew loosed a verbal barrage, publicly denouncing Scott as "an enemy of sport!"—as if the industry were the game—and suggesting that Scott's heroes, if not the likes of Bryant, were Fidel Castro and Che Guevara. (On the latter point, Agnew was not far wrong, although Scott's liberal critique of American sport had long predated his continual and gradual slippage left.)

With rank and title from Oberlin, Jack Scott had been testifying before congressional committees investigating the use of coach-prescribed drugs among athletes—a subject on which Scott, the critic-coach, was a walking encyclopedia. Scott had carried his institute to Oberlin, and the school became a center in the national debate on American sport ethics. But the tall, balding Scott had a brusk, often offensive personal manner that rivaled his theories for creating enemies. In early 1974 a new Oberlin president forced Scott out, buying the remainder of his four-year contract for $40,000. Flush with cash, but dismayed and discouraged by his loss of position, Jack, his mate, Micki, and the ISSS moved to New York City.

It was there, in the flow of headlines, that Scott's interest in the Hearst case and the SLA germinated. Two months after the kidnapping it was enough to spur him to write a Boston sportswriter to complain of the harsh line on the SLA being published in the left-liberal Boston *Phoenix.* It may have been, as Scott later claimed, that he decided in June, 1974, to return to Berkeley and seek the roots of the SLA for a book, but it seems unlikely. Scott's SLA connection was certainly more direct than the slow blind grope through the Berkeley Left he would come to describe so dramatically. Scott knew, intimately, virtually all those who would later become involved in the SLA renaissance.

Patty testified that it was not Scott but Bill Harris who first began talking about an SLA book, shortly after they arrived in Oakland. "It was," she said with bitter recall, "supposed to be a propaganda thing about the SLA, their politics, and just how great they were." Scott, she said, was introduced by Kathy Soliah as "a writer and some kind of sports director" from New York. "He said that he was going to help get the three of us across country and that he felt that being in the East was the best place for everyone to be," recalled Patricia at trial. "He said he was going to pay for everything and I think what he said he wanted out of it—at first—was a chance 'to struggle,' as he put it, with the people of the SLA."

Scott, said Patty, arranged for Emily's transport first, calling in an old friend, thirty-one-year-old Phil Shinnick, a former University of Washington athlete, an ISSS associate, and member of the 1964 U.S. Olympic team, now an associate professor at Rutgers University's Livingston Division. Patty said she met Shinnick* the night he picked up Emily at the Berkeley apartment to drive her to New York, where Scott's now-common-law wife, Micki, was already arranging for a farm country refuge.

Patty herself went next—in late June, she said—with Scott himself, the two of them driven by Scott's elderly parents, John and Louise Scott.* The Scotts, both in their mid-sixties, were then living in Las Vegas, where Mr. Scott managed a motel apartment complex. Patty said she rode in the backseat with Jack; Mr. and Mrs. Scott up front. She was but thinly disguised, with a wig, new clothes, and glasses, and virtually every state trooper on the interstates had received a special SLA alert—but no one was looking for Tania in the company of such a sedate elderly couple. For the four- or five-day trip, they always ate in the car or in motel rooms, said Patty. Mr. Scott would register himself and his wife in one room; Patty and Jack in another. They reached New York and went directly to Jack's Upper West Side apartment, and there Tania was reunited with Emily and introduced to Micki Scott and a close friend of the Scotts, Wendy Yoshimura, a twenty-nine-year-old Japanese-American woman. Patty said Wendy was first introduced as "Joan Shimada" (Patty herself was introduced as "Pearl"), but Jack Scott had explained en route that he had arranged for Wendy, a fugitive on Berkeley bomb charges since 1972, to spend the summer with them. He wanted the SLA to learn some of the subtle arts of survival on the run. Jack, testified Patty, said he and Micki had done this all once before—when they shuttled Wendy cross-country, one step ahead of the posse, two years before.

Mr. and Mrs. Scott stayed at the apartment for only an hour, said Patty. Jack apparently stayed a day or two, then flew back to California to drive Bill Harris East, leaving Patty, Wendy, Emily, and Micki to get to know one another.

Much later Jack Scott would describe his role in the Hearst case as that of a "human Switzerland," and the phrase—prospective book aside—seemed accurately to characterize his motives for initially getting involved with the fugitives. A surprisingly small number of Scott's personal friends expressed surprise when rumor first linked him to the SLA. Jack, said some, had been lately talking about the futility of peaceful reform. Others emphatically argued that whatever Jack did, it was only to forestall another Los Angeles massacre and indicated "only sympathy, not approval, of the SLA."

Scott himself—in the colorful, albeit sometimes inaccurate account he gave *Rolling Stone* magazine for its first "inside story" of his SLA experience—claimed to have stumbled over the fugitives in Berkeley, researching his book, and cut a bold deal for his assis-

---

*Neither Shinnick nor the elder Scotts had been indicted on or convicted of any harboring charges. All three refused to testify before a grand jury, but each publicly denied any knowledge of the SLA or association with Patricia Hearst.

tance. *Stone* said Scott told the Harrises and Patty he had money and was willing to help, but only on the condition that they disarm. Reluctantly, after some bitter argument (Tania the most indignant at the request), they agreed. Scott claimed he had covered himself on all the angles. Not only did he force the trigger-happy SLA to put down their guns, but he also offered Patty her freedom as soon as he got her away from the Harrises. As *Stone* described it, Jack stopped his car just outside San Francisco as he and Patty, alone, began their trip to New York. It was, as far as Jack knew, Tania's first hour apart from the SLA since her kidnapping. Jack allegedly pulled to the side of the road and told the girl that she didn't *have* to go with the Harrises; he told her he would take her anywhere, even to Hillsborough. Patty allegedly turned to him, incredulous, on the verge of panic, and demanded to go "where my friends are going." Patty thought the offer "inexcusable," reported *Stone*.

(Patty gave her trial jury a different version: She claimed Scott had never made any such offer, and although she said the SLA guns had been left behind with the Soliahs, Scott had other guns in New York which he brought down to the farm hideout.)

Whichever story is true, it is apparent that despite the risks they were taking, Jack and Micki still had an ambivalent attitude toward the SLA—a contradiction that would soon place them at odds with their new dependents. But there is another tangled story in the Scotts' connections with the Soliahs, Yoshimura, and a little-known Berkeley group called the Revolutionary Army, a tiny 1970-vintage Berkeley bombers' club that suddenly went defunct in early 1972. It was difficult to be an activist at UC Berkeley during those years and not at least to *know* some of the people who dropped into the underground with the Weathermen or an assorted variety of "armed struggle" collectives, but the Scotts seemed to be unusually knowledgeable.

On March 30, 1972, police discovered what was described as a "massive" bomb factory in a Berkeley garage while investigating a complaint of gas fumes. The garage had been rented by an "Anne Wong"—later identified as Wendy Yoshimura. Police evacuated the area and removed several hundred pounds of various chemical explosives, gunpowder, fuses, blasting caps, a large quantity of ammunition, and a small arsenal of rifles and pistols (including an AK-47 machine gun, probably of Vietnam War origin). Also found was a fused pipe bomb, a partially completed beer-can grenade (particularly vicious: gunpowder and heavy carpet tacks, a deadly crowd bomb), and a three-gallon oil-ammonium nitrate chemical bomb.

Police staked out the garage and that night, at about 3 A.M., three men in a small blue Volkswagen drove up, unlocked the garage, and went in. Trapped by the cops, the three surrendered: William Brandt, twenty-four, Wendy Yoshimura's roommate and lover; Michael Bortin, twenty-three, painting partner of Steve Soliah and Jim Kilgore (then sharing communal living quarters with Pat Jean McCarthy, Soliah, and Emily Toback); and Paul Rubenstein, twenty-two, a Lawrence, Kansas, SDS-Weatherman—a new roommate sharing the Shattuck Avenue home of Kathy Soliah and Jim Kilgore.

Brandt refused to give police his name or address—which allowed Yoshimura her opportunity to escape—and Bortin, while giving his name, gave a false address. Only Rubenstein gave his true name and address (police subsequently raided the Shattuck Avenue apartment, but no charges were pressed against Soliah or Kilgore). All three of the men had been armed, dressed in dark clothing, and they carried flashlights and a glass cutter. In the car, police found a ready-to-mail communiqué from "The Revolutionary Army," claiming credit for an arson bombing of the UC Berkeley Naval Architecture Building, apparently scheduled for that night. ("Any stage in the production of the Empire's death machines is a legitimate target of revolutionary war, including the training school for the technicians of Death," the communiqué declared.) Also found in the garage were plans and notes for a planned RA bombing of the UC Berkeley Space Sciences Laboratory and a detailed multipage plan apparently for the kidnap or assassination of former Secretary of Defense Robert McNamara. The McNamara plan included maps of the former Cabinet member's Aspen, Colorado, ski camp, detailed descriptions of the McNamara family, and extensive notes on the Aspen area, with lists of "hostile" residents and possibly sympathetic supporters.

(After bargaining with the district attorney's office, all three pleaded guilty to charges of possession of materials for the manufacture of explosives, but the DA's men—apparently in part based on information later provided by Rubenstein—associated the group, and particularly Brandt, with a long series of Bay Area bombings, ten during 1971, one in late January, 1972. Most of the targets were allegedly banks, but also included was a tack-grenade bomb—housed in a beer can—tossed into a bar across the street from the San Francisco Hall of Justice frequented by cops and court personnel. The 1972 bombing—an ammonium nitrate mix in a container identical to the one that held the prepared oil-and-chemical mix found in the raided garage—was exploded in the Berkeley office of the Control Data computer firm.

(Bortin and Rubenstein were each sentenced to one-year county jail terms—although Rubenstein got out in eight months—but
Brandt got slugged with a one- to fifteen-year state prison sentence. Brandt was alleged to have threatened Rubenstein and attempted to attack him physically in jail, warning him not to give
evidence that would incriminate others. Bortin served a full year,
until released in the spring of 1973 on probation for an additional
three years. Brandt's parole was refused repeatedly in 1974 and
1975.)

The arrests of Brandt, Rubenstein, and Bortin occurred only a
few months after Steve Soliah arrived in Berkeley, about six
months after his sister and Jim Kilgore settled on Shattuck Avenue. Police at the time believed that additional evidence had been
removed overnight and destroyed from both the house Bortin
shared with Steve Soliah and the Brandt-Yoshimura apartment.
They had no evidence to charge anyone but the three arrested—
and Wendy Yoshimura.

Patricia Hearst would say in court that Jack Scott had told her
that, on the night of the 1972 arrests, Micki Scott had gone to the
Brandt-Yoshimura apartment and "helped clean it out." And that
he, Jack, had "taken Wendy Yoshimura"—to LA she thought—
and then arranged to get her transport to the East Coast. Details
remain unclear, but it seems certain that Kathy Soliah knew she
could trust the Scotts long before she contacted Jack about sanctu-
ary for the SLA.

Both the Scotts, Kathy Soliah, and Jim Kilgore were among
Brandt's visitors at Soledad prison. In 1973 Kathy Soliah had
been Brandt's most frequent visitor, usually making the hundred-
mile drive south to Soledad once a month; when she missed a
month, Jim Kilgore usually visited. Jack Scott had written to the
court* in behalf of Brandt, describing himself as a close friend,
urging release consideration, and in June, 1973, Jack and Micki
Scott, visiting California from Ohio, had driven down from
Berkeley to see Brandt. (And much later, as the SLA three and
Wendy Yoshimura prepared to return to California from their
summer retreat, Jack Scott made a lone visit to Brandt in August,
1974.)

Wendy Masako Yoshimura, brought in by Scott to be "senior
adviser" to the SLA trio, was a woman of unusual background.

---

*"William has been sickened by the Vietnam war for years," Scott explained in
the letter, "and I would often be deeply concerned about him when he would go
into deep depression after reading about the daily horrors in Vietnam." As Nixon escalated the war, Brandt's despair "grew even greater," wrote Scott, and his
"compassion for the Vietnamese" caused him to be "consumed by anguish."

She was one of a generation of Japanese-Americans who had been born in U.S. concentration camps in California during World War II. Although both her parents were American-born and her father had attempted, unsuccessfully, to enlist in the U.S. Army after Pearl Harbor, the Yoshimuras were imprisoned in the infamous Manzanar "detention camp" in Southern California as part of the national program to jail Japanese-Americans during the war. After the war her parents fled the United States and went to Japan—her mother for the first time—where Wendy was brought up in the A-bombed city of Hiroshima. In 1957, when Wendy was eleven, the family moved back to the United States, to Fresno, in California's Central Valley. Her parents were returning home, but their daughter was a native-born foreigner; unable to speak English, she was dropped from the seventh to the second grade. She was seventeen when she entered high school, but she was a prizewinning artist as a student and at Fresno State College and in 1965 transferred to the California College of Arts and Crafts in Oakland. She was apolitical, socializing largely within the Bay Area Japanese community, for the first three years she was in the Oakland-Berkeley area. In a short biography she wrote much later, Wendy recalled the sequence of her political education:

> In 1969 at [Oakland's] Merritt City College I took an evening philosophy course in order to graduate. I met a man who opened my eyes to social injustice. (Obviously, it usually is a man, isn't it?) Now that I think back I was aware of it but never stopped to think of the whys. I didn't like what I saw but I simply accepted it. Then I met another man (again!) who had the time and patience to help me understand about the Vietnam War, capitalism, colonialism, imperialism, racism, classism, sexism, etc., etc. This was in the spring of 1969. With my new awareness I found myself less interested in art. . . .

The second man had been Willie Brandt, with whom Wendy fell in love. She joined the second Venceremos brigade of young Americans harvesting sugarcane in Castro's Cuba in 1969 and became a Berkeley antiwar activist. In 1970 the UC Berkeley football season had been marred with a series of "Jock Lib" demonstrations: in the highly inimitable Berkeley style, the protesters called themselves the People's Athletic Commission. Although Jack Scott was not the leader of the group, he was involved, and it was reportedly then that Scott first met Brandt, Yoshimura, Mike Bortin, and Pat Jean McCarthy.

Bortin and McCarthy were two names apparently deliberately omitted from the long list of people Patricia Hearst identified in her trial testimony as assisting the SLA shuttle eastward. ("It was a selective list," explained one leftist source, intimately familiar with the story. "She named those she had come to distrust or dislike—or whose names were already public—but she protected others.") After Bortin was released from jail in early 1973, he had gone back to work painting houses with Jim Kilgore and Steve Soliah—Able Painting they called the firm. Kathy and Jo Soliah would often join the three of them painting their bigger projects. Pat Jean McCarthy had waited for Bortin and rejoined her lover when he was released under conditions of parole. Bortin, McCarthy, the three Soliahs, and Kilgore were all close friends, and although there is no direct evidence that Bortin and McCarthy were brought into the rescue plot after Emily Harris contacted Kathy Soliah in June, 1974, the close daily association of all of them and the background they shared strongly suggest that Bortin, at least, had been introduced to General Teko before they went to the East Coast—probably before Harris' proclamation that the SLA was joining the New World Liberation Front.

During the trial of Patricia Hearst, in early 1976, the authors briefly interviewed (and were interviewed by) both Bortin* and McCarthy. (This was after the Soliah sisters and Kilgore had gone underground, but sometime before Patty, in her postconviction revelations to the FBI, named both Bortin and McCarthy as key figures themselves in the latter-day SLA, the first to split from the group in violent disagreement with the Harrises.) Both claimed to have known "nothing at all" about the Soliah clan's SLA involvement, but from their longtime friendships with nearly all the participants in the rescue operation, they offered some sense of the motivations that effected it.

In 1972, when he and Brandt were involved with the Revolutionary Army, argued Bortin, the Soliahs and Kilgore were "intel-

---

*Although he had briefly talked with the authors shortly after the arrests, Bortin approached them again in the latter days of the Hearst trial—as an emissary, he said, from the Soliahs and Kilgore and the other former SLA fugitives. He wanted to talk with us, to look at what we had been writing. He said that he had been commissioned to locate someone to whom "the people underground" could send a tape cassette giving *their* side of the widely disputed last months of the SLA. Bortin read most of this book in draft form and said he was "impressed." He said he would recommend (through his "unknown and unidentifiable" telephone contact with the fugitives) that the Soliah group send us their story. When it was given, it was a heartening compliment—and it remained that, but became more confusing after Michael Bortin was named by Patty as the only recruit in the SLA renaissance who vied with Bill Harris for leadership. The intense interest of the FBI in both Bortin and McCarthy apparently blocked further negotiations for yet another side of the story.

lectually radical but not practically." They knew nothing, he said, of what was going on. But with the SLA, "Kathy was just driven after Los Angeles," said Bortin, "and I think guilt had a lot to do with getting her involved. Kathy was just caught in between a second time. She had seen us go into armed struggle and get busted in '72—two of her close friends—and after Angela went with the SLA, I guess she just felt she had let it go by again. I think she just felt she had watched, twice, as her closest friends committed themselves, and it was time she joined them, made her own commitment." It was, lamented Bortin, "sad" that the group she got tangled with was the SLA: "It was the most unreasonable of all the options."

(Both Bortin and McCarthy had known Angela well through Kathy, they said. Pat McCarthy confirmed what for the authors was still a working hypothesis: "Angela would have been the one who would have related best with Patty Hearst, both with their Catholic school backgrounds and their complicated relationships with their fathers. Of all of them, Angela was still the loosest. She liked to sing, she liked to dance. She believed in their ideas—which were a little strange—but she was still more human, you know." It was a validation that took on considerable weight after Patty told federal authorities that she had spent a lot of time talking with Mike and Pat Jean.)

In the first weeks following the Los Angeles shoot-out a whole new cast of characters had moved onstage, and it would be these people who would play out the final act of the SLA's psychodrama. It would be they who would organize and effect the Symbionese renaissance in California that began in late 1974, after the rest-and-recuperation sojourn on the farm. But they were new personalities, with different beliefs, different assumptions—and although they would be enough caught up in their infatuation with the SLA myth to participate in varying ways in the SLA's final violent spree, their different perspectives would introduce a conflict into the SLA that would eventually lead to an internal schism, a shattering of the SLA that preceded, and perhaps foretold, the arrests in the fall of 1975 and the confusion of stories that followed.

In the welded collective of the original Symbionese Liberation Army, in their heedless and headlong rush to their fate, there had been no time, no relaxation of pressure, no opportunity for all the blatant and bizarre conflicts in the beliefs they expressed to come back to haunt them. Whatever their professed creed, the SLA had so tangled their militarism, their economics, their dogma and neo-dada fury in a combination of total abnegation and alienation that knew no master—neither Marx nor Mao—that their faith was defined in a conflict of furies: a "totalitarian anarchism" that was no less absurd for the havoc it wreaked.

The "second team" was no mainstream group themselves, but they carried certain fundamental ideals—a more humanistic sense of self, feminism among the women, that could not be smothered in the Luddite militarism of the SLA—and the tensions that evolved in that conflict would eventually lead to the SLA's self-destruction even before the bureau closed in on its quarry. The retreat East was an epilogue for the first SLA story—what began in the fall that followed, the apparent renaissance of the SLA, was a different story, perhaps a different book, but it was then that all the twisted contradictions that had been carried along in the furious plunge of the original SLA were exposed among their successors. It would be said later that the SLA story was clearest when it was all a mystery—before people began to sort and define the threads of their belief, before it all unraveled. That may be so, but only because the whole of the SLA experience could then be written off as a nihilistic absurdity—and there is, perhaps, more to be learned tracing its devolution than describing its predictable evolution.

After Jack Scott returned to California to ferry Bill Harris East, Micki Scott, Emily Harris, Patty Hearst, and Wendy Yoshimura reportedly set off on their own for the farm Micki had rented to shelter the fugitives. Patricia would say in testimony that she had spent only two or three days at the Scotts' New York apartment. An advertisement in the New York *Times* had offered thirty-eight acres in the Pennsylvania Poconos as a summer rental. The landowner, Timothy O'Sullivan, a New York City fireman, had got but one reply, from Micki Scott, who said that she and her husband were writers who needed a "quiet place to work." O'Sullivan said he went up to the Scotts' West Ninetieth Street apartment himself to give Micki a three-month lease (July through September) and to collect her $2,000 check. The farm was unoccupied, and apparently there was no complaint if the new tenants moved in a week early. And so, as the heat of summer began to settle on New York City, this part of the last detachment of the Symbionese Liberation Army decamped for rural Pennsylvania.

22

Refuge II

IN the rubble of the Los Angeles massacre, somehow preserved in the smoldering heap of wood, tile, and stone, scavengers found a few scraps of paper that had survived the inferno. One of these was a Polaroid photograph of seven people.

On the wall behind them had been draped a cloth the size of a sheet, on which had been painted the shadow form of the *naga*, the SLA's seven-headed cobra. The group was posed. Directly in front stands Donald DeFreeze, centered so that the splayed necks of the cobra encircled his head and settled like some plumed crown. To the right of Cin stands Nancy Ling Perry, and beside her is Bill Harris, glasses and beret, with a dark goatee. On the other side of DeFreeze, to the left, is Patty Hearst; next to her, only a shoulder and the edge of a face visible along the charred side of the photograph, stands a short and stocky figure, perhaps Camilla Hall.

Neither Angela Atwood nor Willie Wolfe is shown—one apparently held the camera—but in front, crouched or kneeling to the right and to the left, are Zoya and Yolanda, Mizmoon Soltysik and Emily Harris. The photo has a quality of rigid formality; the Court of the People. Each of them holds a gun. Teko has a pistol, each of the others an automatic rifle or shotgun. All are dressed in black, almost in uniform, but with various types of shirts and jerseys. Emily has perhaps the involuntary glimmer of a smile, but Mizmoon, beside her, glowers fiercely. There is a solemn air about all but Tania.

Patty is wearing what appears to be a short blond wig, and while the others have on shirts buttoned high or turtlenecks, her black blouse is unbuttoned low and pulled back to expose one shoulder. She is grinning broadly.

The new SLA garrison was an isolated farmhouse in the village of South Canaan—some twenty miles northeast of Scranton, where Jack Scott had grown up. As a hideout it was ideal; as a refuge it was idyllic. The house itself was a tall, dingy two-story white-frame building. It sat on a bluff overlooking miles of gently rolling countryside, with the ridge of the mountains crowding the horizon. There were four bedrooms, a kitchen, a living room, and a dining room—inside and out, more safe space than the Harrises had seen in nearly a year. Behind the house were a barn, three small ponds, and a windmill. There was a screened porch on the first floor of the house, and on the second, a long open balcony curbed by a low wrought-iron railing in which four letters were worked in blocked iron scroll: P-A-I-X—*paix*—French for "peace."

The house was well situated for privacy, and with many of the nearby farms abandoned by absentee landlords, local people had become accustomed to young transients renting houses for the summer. Few noticed the quiet group at the old farm. "There were two men and two women," recalled Mrs. Louis Prati, who lives in the closest occupied house. One man, who called himself Alan (thought to be Bill Harris), told her he and the two women were assisting a writer, a sportswriter; "Alan" was a proofreader, the two women, secretaries. A local gas man, who delivered a tank of propane soon after "Alan" and his companions arrived, recalls seeing seven people at the farm: three young white men, two men he thought were black or Oriental, a very attractive Oriental woman, and another woman, who just lay on a cot with a blanket pulled over her head while he was in the house.

"For two hours she was under that blanket," he said. "She just moved a little bit, but she didn't uncover her face. Even after it got warm."

Patty Hearst testified at her trial that she thought the group had stayed at the South Canaan farm only two or three weeks before shifting the hideout, for unexplained reasons, to another camp about twenty miles northeast, just across the New York-Pennsylvania state line, in the small village of Jeffersonville. John Fullwood, a substitute mail carrier from nearby Hamlin, recalled delivering mail to the South Canaan farm sometime in July. He said he saw Wendy Yoshimura and another woman, possibly Emily Harris, sunning themselves in the field beside the house and stopped to chat briefly with Bill Harris, who met him in the yard. He recalls Harris saying something then about "moving on soon." The neighbor, Mrs. Prati, could make no positive identifications, but said one woman she remembered was a redhead, the other Oriental. "The Oriental girl was really, really, pretty," she said.

"The redhead had freckles all over her." Although she only occasionally saw the people over at the old farm, she did not when first questioned think she had seen Patty Hearst. But an eleven-year-old girl who lives nearby identified a photo of Tania as a woman she had met picking blueberries near the farm. The Oriental woman was Wendy Yoshimura, and by several accounts, the redhead was Patty—hair dyed, body freckled with makeup, occasionally even appearing pregnant.

Scott's *Rolling Stone* memoirs were selective and undoubtedly defensively skewed, but however uncertain the source, they offer a rare glimpse of the psychological state of Patty Hearst and the Harrises that summer. During the ride East, Scott had soured on Patty's paranoia (a highway construction man *must* be a pig! She was sure of it!) and her random curses on anyone who had not wholeheartedly supported the SLA. All the liberals and virtually all the Left were "pigs." Scott himself was a borderline case. Sports, Jack's avocation, was irrelevant—no use at all to the Revolution.

The Harrises, Scott recalled, were tense and exhausted when he first met them in Berkeley. There was a sense of hysteria on a hair trigger, but they were still determined and capable. Patty seemed a blustery echo of Bill and Emily: tense, explosively temperamental, adept at grabbing a rifle and rolling into firing position at a sound in the midnight darkness. The manic image of Patty sharpens in Scott's recollections of the first weeks in Pennsylvania: Tania grabbing the daily New York *Times* to X out photos of corporate pigs and political enemies; Patty trying to pull rank on Scott—since *she* was number three in the SLA, anyone associated with the SLA was under her command when Bill (number one) and Emily (number two) were elsewhere.

"Pearl," the tense and troubled Patty Hearst who arrived at South Canaan, might have been reduced to such a fevered freak by the experience of watching six comrades incinerated in Los Angeles (as the TV announcers and police sadly prophesied that she, Patty, was probably inside), but in the recollections of both Scott and Wendy Yoshimura, the "Pearl" of the farm seemed an almost logical product of the closet captivity that transformed Patricia into Tania. (Scott made no explicit connection; in fact *Rolling Stone*'s account seemed almost to disassociate the brutal captivity, although the experience is well detailed, from the personality that emerged.) Yoshimura—some fifteen months later, having watched Patty seemingly regain, redevelop, a personality and independence in an evolution "unimaginable" when she first met her—would recall Hearst in refuge as "a fuckin' vegetable."* (Looking back, Wendy would write her imprisoned lover Willie Brandt, referring to that evolution: "I hope you'll have a chance to meet P.H. She is incredible! She amazes me! I swear only the toughest could have come out of it as she did. What an ordeal she went through!!") Yet it remains difficult to get a fix on Patty's psyche.

As the summer months passed, reported *Stone*, the sun, space, and safety of the farm slowly mellowed all three. They read the scriptures: Marx, DeBray, Fanon—architects of other revolutions in other nations. They skinny-dipped, sunbathed, picked berries, and romped in the fields. Yes, Patty was number three, "a sister," confided Emily, "but she's still learning." Even on sabbatical, they maintained a military regimen: daily calisthenics, jogging, sprinting, thirty minutes to an hour of daily practice with a BB gun, and—echoes of Clayton—antic duels of cops 'n' robbers. (Bang! Bang! Ducking through the kitchen dodging for cover; leaping over the dining-room table to escape ambush.)

The Scotts apparently paraded a number of their friends out to the farm to review the ranks, and General Teko kept trying to recruit for the number four slot. But outside the Bay Area the violent fanaticism of the SLA was more a curio, a tourist attraction. Even the Scotts, while willing to hide them from "Amerikkkan justice," kept up an insistent challenge to their past. (Jack Scott claimed he tried to argue with the Harrises over the murder of Marcus Foster, but the most they would concede was that the killing had been bad public relations.)

On July 2 Scott brought Jay Weiner, a young summer-intern sportswriter for *Newsday,* a Long Island newspaper, up to the South Canaan farm. It was Weiner's twentieth birthday, and Jack Scott, his old professor and friend, had a gift surprise. Weiner reportedly just smiled as he was introduced to "Alan" and "Judy" (the Harrises), "Joan" (Yoshimura), and "Susie" Hearst—pretending not to know who they were. *Rolling Stone* reported that Scott took Weiner for a walk and began to explain the situation when Weiner interrupted, saying he didn't *want* to know what was going on: "I don't want to get involved." Weiner, who would be the first of the farm visitors tracked down by the FBI, told a different story to a federal grand jury.

Jack Scott had been Jay Weiner's mentor. While still a college

---

*Quoted by a San Francisco attorney, one of the very few people who had privately discussed the SLA experience with the reticent Ms. Yoshimura.

student, Weiner had transferred from Temple University in Philadelphia to Oberlin to study with Jack and work with the ISSS. "Weiner thought Scott brought him to the farm for two reasons," explained a federal source. "Jack wanted to buff his fingernails a little, to show he was still a pretty sharp guy. Secondly, he wanted Weiner to go out and do some fund raising for the fugitives. He saw himself going through that forty thousand bucks he got from Oberlin and he wanted Weiner to go out and buzz around the radical athletic community and raise some cash. Weiner told him, okay, he'd go back to Philly and New York and see what he could do—but to himself he was thinking, 'Screw this, this is *too heavy.*' He said Scott kept bugging him for money but that he never did much about it."

The move from South Canaan to Jeffersonville, in rural New York State, was apparently sudden, just as the group had begun to settle in Pennsylvania. It may have had something to do with the casual visit of landlord O'Sullivan, the New York City fireman—Berkeley rumor would later explain that the fugitives had been "spooked" when they realized O'Sullivan worked "for the government."

The Jeffersonville safehouse was another summer rental; a large one-room camp built alongside a ramshackle abandoned cheese creamery which had gone out of business in the twenties. The place was even more isolated than South Canaan, screened by heavy woods, and again up a little used dirt road off a minor county highway, twenty-two acres of privacy. Jeffersonville is a tiny hamlet in Sullivan County, along the edge of the Catskills, between Callicoon Center and Kenoza Lake. It's an old-country German community—settled by refugees from the Revolution of 1848—the stable population is in the hundreds, but it's another area favored by big-city dropouts, and the locals have a tolerant attitude toward hippie hermits and strange newcomers.

One of the several related owners, Beverly Nerenberg, told local reporters the place had been rented—through an ad in the New York *Village Voice*—to a tall, thirtyish woman with short blond hair and a "pointy nose." The woman, apparently Micki Scott, had an "unconvincing English accent" and told Ms. Nerenberg she had just arrived in the United States from Britain. Despite reservations, Nerenberg rented the property, but she came to rue the decision long before the SLA was ever associated with the creamery. When the group cleared out after Labor Day, '74, she said, she discovered they had left the place "incredibly filthy," the woodwork scarred and chipped, old food encrusted all over the kitchen—and with a circular track, apparently from the jogging exercise, worn into the lawn around the buildings. (When a male "friend of the Englishwoman" called to request she return the security deposit, she refused, citing the damages. The man, Nerenberg said, flew into a rage, called her "a motherfuckin' capitalist pig," and threatened that he knew where she lived. Frightened, the woman called local police, but they said they could do nothing unless she could identify the man.)

There were at least two "Patty sightings" reported to the police and the FBI while the fugitives were living at the creamery. In one case a resident called the local New York State Police barracks and told the duty sergeant he thought he had just seen Patty Hearst in what passes for downtown in Jeffersonville. Later, about midsummer, Jim Owens, the owner of the One-step Inn, a tavern in Youngsville, just a little up the road from Jeffersonville, called the Sullivan County resident agent of the FBI, Leyland Lowery, to say that he was almost certain Patty Hearst had been in his bar the night before. It was a Tuesday night—he remembered the weekday long after he forgot the date because he picks up his copy of the *National Enquirer* on Tuesday, and it was while reading an *Enquirer* story on the FBI search for the SLA, looking at the pictures, he suddenly realized the Hearst girl had been one of the four people who had been playing pool and drinking in the bar that night. They had come in about 11 P.M., he recalled, and left about an hour later, driving off in a small foreign car. Neither report (if either was investigated at all) resulted in any threat to the SLA sanctuary.

Patty said that it was at Jeffersonville that the group began target practice with Scott's guns, general weapons training—still keeping up the calisthenics, the obstacle-course combat training— and, taking advantage of the heavy forest, a study in *Last of the Mohicans* woodsmanship. "The point/slack manoeuvres" were the most fun "though strenuous," recalled Harris, General Teko, for *New Times*. There would be an objective chosen some distance away, a split into two teams. One group would get a five-minute head start, then would try to ambush the one that followed, which in turn would try to circle and ambush the one ahead. "The idea," he explained, "was to try and locate each other in a surreptitious manner and make counter-manoeuvres—there was a lot of sneaking around, low crawling, things like that. We tried to learn how to move quickly, stealthily, quietly, pick up the kinds of instincts that people who grow up in the suburbs don't have." Emily at one point visited Grossinger's, the "Borscht Belt" resort at the far end of Sullivan County (checking it out as an emergency hideaway in case police closed in), and Bill got himself a yarmulke to become "one of the fish in the sea" as he hiked the Catskills.

And they worked on a book. It was to be a military history of the SLA as well as a statement of politics like the Weather Underground's *Prairie Fire*—it would have a question-and-answer format and two sections: personal interviews with Tania, Teko, and Yolanda and then a collective discussion of the SLA career and politics. The manuscript was never finished apparently because of increasingly serious dispute among the group after they returned to California—arguments about the political line, accuracy, and attitude of the portions of the manifesto written back East. (Revealingly, virtually all the manuscript segments—including the Tania Interview—would later be seized at the Harrises' apartment. Most of the feminist critiques, also apparently written for the book, were found at the apartment shared by Patty and Wendy.)

Teko Harris' version of the SLA history might have touched several nerves among the others. In the manuscript, Harris still couldn't face up to the truth about the shoplifting incident at Mel's that triggered the Los Angeles police search and led to the fatal confrontation of the shoot-out ("What happened in reality was that we had gone out that day to buy combat clothing that the cell needed immediately," wrote Teko. "We were amazed that we were being jammed around shoplifting when there was no reason for it. . .."). And Emily's explanation of why the men had been shot during the Hibernia Bank robbery offered something less than a revolutionary sensitivity: "We felt that these men, by their actions, had attempted to interfere with us being able to carry out the operation successfully. . . . We can never hesitate to stop someone who actively attempts to fuck us up during an operation."

Yet the most fascinating portion of the manuscript later seized was the Tania Interview. Studied, it seems to reveal far more about Patty's psychological state and position within the group that summer than it was ever intended to. It's an incredible portrait. With its internal inconsistencies, the contradictions between it and other portions of the manuscript, the deadened emotions, tunnel vision, and the *utter* lack of subjective presence—the disassociation, the way Tania talks about Patty, the girl kidnapped and closet captive, as if Patricia Hearst were a pet hamster, lacking all natural emotions, feeling no anger, no resentment, not even *fear*—the SLA's Tania is a stand-up figurine, a cardboard character. If there was no other evidence, the Tania Interview would suffice to throw a strong suspicion upon the SLA's transformation of Patty Hearst. This is the voice of Yoshimura's "fuckin' vegetable."

Patty would testify at her trial that the interview was a group effort—involving not only the two Harrises, but an editorial consultant Jack Scott had recruited, Paul K. Hoch, a PhD from Brown University then teaching at Dawson Junior College across the border in Montreal. Hoch was a friend of Scott from Berkeley and Oberlin days, an author of several books: one describing student unrest at the London School of Economics in the late sixties (a student at LSE himself, Hoch had been deported from Britain), and another on football, *Rip Off the Big Game,* in part sponsored by Scott's ISSS.

Preparing the Tania Interview was the first task of the summer, said Patty on trial, and it became a major group effort. They discussed all the questions and answers before they began: "First I went over it with the Harrises . . . the question and how it was going to be answered, and then I went over it with Paul Hoch." They began with seven hours of tape-recorded Tania, transcribed that onto about 200 pages, then boiled that down—with considerable revisions—into this neat little 34-page package profile. For the final version, "I sat down with the Harrises and they made up the questions and then we did like an outline of how the question was going to be answered," said Patty. ". . . they took certain facts and I knew how I was supposed to answer the question. And, if it wasn't right, they'd correct it and I'd answer it the way it was supposed to be answered."

That, with all the editing, this incredible profile could result says something about the Harrises, but that the interview could be written as it was, blind to so many things, silent about so many others, says a great deal about the character of Tania.

The objective facts are there; it's the subjective facts that are missing. "How did this affect you physically, being in a closet for six weeks?" asks the interrogator. Tania answers:

> Well, it was pretty cramped in there. At first I didn't get much exercise and certainly didn't move around very much. After about a month I couldn't stand up without feeling dizzy and like I

was going to faint. For about two weeks, I had a blindfold on all the time. . . . The first time I took the blindfold off to take a bath, I couldn't focus very well. Everything was out of proportion. . . .

According to the interviewed Tania, it was only after the SLA "realized that my physical condition had really deteriorated"—apparently when she could no longer stand—that the Symbionese took her out of the closet to exercise. "Everyone started to get worried about my health because they weren't out to blind me or damage my eyesight or make me so weak I couldn't stand. . . . They didn't want me to go back with all kinds of physical problems." This, then, was the objective situation—in the SLA's *own* version—of Patty's first month (perhaps even the first six weeks, it's unclear): a girl physically crumbling, painfully enclosed in a six-by-two-foot cell, "hot and cramped and dark."

What was the psychological reality, what was Patty thinking during these first brutal weeks? Tania tells us:

> . . . After only a couple of weeks I started to feel sympathetic with the SLA. I was beginning to see that what they wanted to accomplish was necessary, although at that time it was hard for me to relate to the tactic of urban guerrilla warfare. But how can someone disagree with wanting hungry people to have food? It was like Arnold Townsend [the WAPAC spokesman for People in Need] said at a news conference, "We will help distribute the food because we have people who need the food—the real tragedy here is that there are so many poor and hungry people in California." It's pretty hard to see that starvation and hunger are the real tragedies, and not the fact that one person had been kidnapped and might get killed. I'm not trying to say that I was super brave or anything—just that I could see my situation clearly. I would have been dishonest with myself if I hadn't agreed with the goals of the SLA. At the same time there were so many ideas that they talked about that I couldn't understand . . . yet.

There is such a thing as generosity, Christian charity, even revolutionary self-sacrifice—but that "one person" who might get killed is *she herself!* In the Olympian perspective, one life against many, her equation has a certain validity, but even if she had the "clarity" to see that, is it reasonable that two weeks into the closet captivity, her single emotion toward her captors was "sympathy"? The mention of that "person" who "might get killed" is the *only* reference in the Tania Interview to the death threats that she heard on each SLA tape message. But she wasn't worried about the nice people who had locked her in the closet hurting her.

> Q: Did you know that they intended to release you, or was there some doubt in your mind that you'd get back alive?

> TANIA: I could tell from their concern for my physical health that they did not intend to release me, and they didn't kidnap me to kill me. At the same time, I definitely had my doubts that I would stay alive. I told Cin right away that I didn't think that my parents would cooperate—that they had no love for me, and I had none for them. I realized that they would have to do something to secure my release, if only to save face, but I was totally unprepared for their bullshit response to the SLA's demands—their bad-faith gesture.

The description of the first weeks of her captivity gets more and more complex—two weeks into the experience we have Tania physically debilitated, approaching the point where she cannot stand, her vision blurred, but able to see her situation "clearly"; certain because of the SLA's "concern for my physical health" that her kidnappers meant her no harm, feeling an increasing "sympathy" for the SLA, and worried more about the "fascist" government's agents than the kidnappers who kept threatening to kill her.

> There was no doubt in my mind that if the feds were lucky enough to find me I would "get it." They had no intention of letting me stay alive. In the face of the first political kidnapping in this country, what could have been better for the pigs than if the victim was killed? I would instantly become an Establishment martyr. It wouldn't have mattered who killed me—the pigs, through the media, would have said that it was done by the SLA, and for all anyone would have known this so-called terrorist group would have murdered an innocent young woman.
> Because of this, at the end of two or three weeks Cin asked me if I wanted to have a class on how to defend myself with a shotgun. After he proposed the class he let it go to see if I would pursue it—to see how interested I was. That was the way he did things—he wanted to see where I would take his suggestion. For a few days I kept asking, "When are we going to work with the shotgun?" Finally, when he was convinced that I was interested and wanted to learn, we had the class. . . .

As one reads the Tania Interview, it's the disembodied voice that becomes haunting. The way in which the voice of Tania talks about her former self, Patty, in such a weirdly condescending way—as a separate person, almost subhuman. At one point the interrogator asks her to describe how the media portrayed her during her imprisonment:

> Well, that kind of depended on what was happening at the time. At first, I was an "innocent child." My parents released baby pictures in an effort to rouse public sympathy for a multi-millionaire whose little white girl had been taken away in the night. However, it finally came out that their little girl had been taken away from an apartment which she shared with a man, and the image had to change.
>
> The media was able to exploit its sexism and racism to the highest degree. I began to be portrayed as a "liberal-minded young woman who was abducted by crazy black escaped convicts." My mother appeared at press conferences dressed in black to urge me through her racist tears to "keep praying honey . . . God will bring you home." It was incredible.
>
> During this period when this type of propaganda was being spread, Catherine and Randy solicited sympathy through a devious "bandwagon" method which exaggerated public support for my family's plight. . . .

More than the tone, more than the stupefying inability of the SLA to believe that there could have been any genuine public pain felt for a "ruling class" mother and father whose "little white girl" has been kidnapped, what is really incredible is the missing perspective, the absent "voice" of that girl who was locked in that closet (her "family's plight"!). Where is Patty Hearst in the voice of Tania?

The only visual image in the whole of the interview comes when Tania dwells on the memory of her SLA lover, Cujo, Willie Wolfe, but it is quite a stunning picture. It was the beginning of their relationship, apparently the birth of the romance, in the first week or so after the kidnap. Nineteen-year-old Patricia Hearst is locked inside the closet, in the dark, and Willie Wolfe is sitting outside, reading Stalin's *Dialectical and Historical Materialism* aloud to entertain her.

> Cujo was an incredibly patient, loving and dedicated person. His experiences with the brothers in California's concentration camps played an important role in his political development, and they were always in his heart. He taught with the patience he

learned from the brothers inside. . . . He explained everything as he read, and never got frustrated if I asked a "stupid" question. In fact, everyone in the cell would always take the time to make sure that I really understood what they were all about. Cujo was a beautiful and gentle man, and at the same time a strong and ruthless guerrilla soldier.

Although Bill Harris, in his section of the manuscript, cautiously admits that Willie Wolfe and others had sex with Patty while she was still captive, the Tania of the interview denies it outright. Presumably the contradiction would not have been there when the manuscript was finally published, but we learn something from it in the contrast. Said Tania:

> My personal relationship with Cujo was based on a political and military relationship. The strong personal relationship did not develop, could not develop, until after I joined the cell because there would have been no common understanding and therefore no basis of trust between us. I had a lot of good feelings for him before I was accepted into the cell; but I had those same feelings for other comrades, too.

And after Cujo . . . there was the "revolutionary responsibility of comradship [sic]."

> People in the cell didn't have exclusive relationships. There was no room for bourgeois types of personal relationships. The cell couldn't function like that on a military/political level. . . . Everyone in the cell had the attitude, and for very good reasons, that personal/sexual relationships could be dangerous.

With an absolutely mind-boggling frankness, Tania explains that it was "about four or five weeks" after the kidnap—precisely about the time she found she was no longer able to do anything but *crawl* out of the closet—that Cinque "seriously" suggested to the group that Patty might want to join them. And it was only a week or two later that Tania was "reborn" with the realization that "I had come to feel too strongly about the need for revolutionary change in amerikkka, about the need for revolutionary violence directed against the capitalist ruling class, about the need to organize the people into a fighting force to destroy imperialism and the racist-class society which keeps the people enslaved. . . .

> My decision to struggle to become a guerrilla fighter wasn't one that was pried off the wall. What some people refer to as my "sud-

den conversion" was actually a process of development, much the same way that a photograph is developed onto paper. You've got the picture there because you've used light and the negative to begin the printing process. All you have to do after that is put the paper into a bath and the picture comes up. You could destroy what is already there before it's printed by taking the paper out into the light—but if it's done right, the picture gradually comes up.

(It was perhaps a measure of the Hearst trial defense that the Tania Interview had weight with the jury only as prosecution evidence—proof that Patty had been a "willing" recruit into the SLA. It was not the description of her captivity, or the bizarre synchronism of events within that captivity, that became important—the issue instead became whether Tania's descriptions of the Hearst family and Patty's relationship with Steve Weed—all couched in bitter, unmitigated hatred [see Appendix]—was "accurate" or at least accurately described Patty's feelings.)

By August the alliance between the Scotts and the SLA had become very uncomfortable. The Scotts had spent a fortune, risked themselves—but not once, said *Rolling Stone*'s report, had anyone said thanks. What began as debate between them was reduced to bickering. Tania and the Harrises had become openly scornful of the Scotts' moderation. The SLA was sworn to guns, and Jack and Micki could not finally accept a political horizon so limited. The Scotts decided to help the Harrises, Hearst, and Yoshimura return West—but after that go their separate ways. Jack and Micki had been invited to join basketball star Bill Walton in Portland, Oregon, to share his home and house their peripatetic institute in the Pacific Northwest. And General Teko no longer felt so bereft and isolated; the East might be barren, but back in the Bay Area he had recruited another "team." Bill had been regularly in touch with Kathy Soliah over the summer, and she and several of her friends had agreed to reorganize the SLA. Now Teko wanted to get back to California, back to the front lines.

Patty testified that the group left the Jeffersonville creamery and returned in early September to spend about two weeks at the still-leased South Canaan farmhouse before they began the trek westward. The SLA's "second team" apparently did not wait for the General's return before launching their fall offensive. The new banner that the SLA had raised in their post-shoot-out communiqué—the New World Liberation Front—was already establishing a Bay Area battle presence. The first NWLF bomb, planted in the Burlingame office of the General Motors Acceptance Corporation on August 6, had failed to explode, but it was the beginning of the promised campaign. The accompanying communiqué, the first from the New World Liberation Front, sent "greetings and love to the Symbionese Liberation Army."

In mid-September Bill Harris mailed a secret letter postmarked from Boston to his mother in Indiana. (Harris may have traveled there and mailed it himself; more likely it was funneled through a friend.) It was a "general communiqué" to his family and old friends. The SLA, he wrote, was preparing to return to armed action. He and Emily were well, still committed to the long-term fight—"sanely, calculatedly." His daily physical exercises now left him too weary even for sex, he said. Harris admitted that the SLA had miscalculated; "conditions" were obviously not perfect. But, he urged his mother, "don't let your concern for my life and safety make you weak. Pull for us, support us because in the end we are going to win."*

The Scotts were eager for the parting. They had closed down their New York apartment, and Jack Scott had already surveyed Oregon (stopping to visit Willie Brandt—Wendy Yoshimura's boyfriend—at Soledad prison on August 28). Soliah and Company were to have handled SLA transportation, but there were several delays. Teko's second team had not yet mustered enough revolutionary courage to cart Patty Hearst, the nation's most wanted fugitive, cross-country. Scott's recollections for *Rolling Stone* again cast him as the hero of the situation. Jack, to extricate himself from the underground, consented again to be drafted for the job.

Unmentioned in the *Stone* article was a curious incident involving the Scotts' tan Volkswagen, allegedly stolen in New York City. Micki Scott reported the '68 VW Bug stolen on September 6; thirteen days later it was discovered, badly damaged, in an isolated section near Seelyville, Pennsylvania, just seven miles from the South Canaan farmhouse. The car was so badly damaged that it was sold for scrap, and the Scotts claimed $1,160 in insurance

---

*Mrs. Betty Bunnell, mother of Bill Harris, had been the only parent among the SLA families to make an open statement of support for the SLA—although even Mrs. Bunnell, in comments to personal friends, made it clear she disagreed with the SLA's tactics and was confused by their dogma. Her letter to "Teko," published in the Berkeley *Barb* in June, 1974, was a message of love. "You are always in my thoughts and I am proud of you," she wrote. She said she had carefully listened to the last SLA communiqué and finally "could begin to understand your total commitment to the fight against oppression of all kinds."

money from Ohio Casualty. (Later the VW was searched by police, and a slip of paper was found in the glove compartment that seemed to describe a highway route cross-country through Canada.) On September 19, the same day the VW was located by the Pennsylvania State Police, Micki Scott rented a yellow van from Ryder Truck Rental in Manhattan. The van was to be returned on October 18 in Denver, Colorado. (It was not, however. The truck turned up in a Ryder parking lot in Portland, Oregon, on October 18. The lot was unattended when the van was dropped off. It had been driven 4,040 miles.)

Steve Soliah said later that his sister Kathy told him—after talking with Teko long-distance—that "they wanted to come back to California, near the Bay Area but not in it . . . they said Sacramento looked good," and that in September he and Kathy had gone to Sacramento to locate a new safehouse for the SLA. (Distance from the Bay Area was apparently not the only factor. After long delay the trial of Joe Remiro and Russ Little for the murder of Marcus Foster had been scheduled for an early 1975 date, and because of the enormous media coverage of the SLA in the Bay Area, the two accused men had obtained a change of venue. They were to be tried in the California state capital, in Sacramento, seventy-five miles northeast of Oakland. Until the trial began, they would remain in custody in the tenth-floor jail of the Alameda county courthouse. The SLA followed the case of their captured soldiers closely; the "liberation" of Osceola and Bo—if possible—would be among the first items on the agenda of the resurgent Revolution.)

Each of the fugitives was reportedly driven West separately. Patty started off with the two Scotts in the rented van, along with the Scotts' dog. But on reaching Cleveland, Micki had caught a plane West, leaving Jack and Tania a less conspicuous "married couple" for the rest of the route. Wendy Yoshimura drove with Margaret Turcich, a friend Wendy had met while a fugitive living in New Jersey; Bill Harris reportedly with Kathy Soliah; and Emily Harris with an unknown driver. According to *Rolling Stone*—reporting Scott's story straight—Jack drove Patty to Las Vegas, where his parents live, and left her at a secluded motel, carefully avoiding any introduction to the members of the SLA's "second team." But Scott needed no introduction to Teko's new recruits. The details of the rendezvous and the shuttle, first to the Bay Area, then up to Sacramento, remain unclear. But shortly after he arrived in Las Vegas, Jack Scott placed a call from his parents' telephone to a San Francisco number listed to "Alexander Berk-man." "Berkman" was actually an alias—among several—of Mi-chael Bortin, still on probation status from his conviction in the 1972 Berkeley bomb factory case, who was then sharing a flat in the Outer Richmond district with girlfriend Pat McCarthy.

Confidants of Wendy Yoshimura later claimed that she decided to withdraw from the group when they reached the Bay Area. (Wendy would later explain, in a letter to be smuggled in to Willie Brandt at Soledad, that her experiences over the summer had made her realize that the Harrises were "very different" from her—"and that personally I did not much like them.") As "Joan Shimada" she moved into a Hyde Street apartment on the fringe of San Francisco's Tenderloin district, with Mary Margaret Tur-cich, twenty-three, and another friend from her underground days in New Jersey, twenty-two-year-old Peter Fittipaldi. (Yo-shimura apparently met Fittipaldi when she worked for a time for a trucking firm in Westfield, New Jersey, owned by one of Peter's older brothers; Mrs. A. R. Fittipaldi, Peter's mother, said the two had dated. Wendy had met Margaret Turcich while baby-sitting for a professor at a small college where Turcich was a student. The two became friends—for a time Wendy even lived with the Turcich family in Delanco, New Jersey, paying board and room with baby-sitting—and Wendy at some point had brought Marga-ret into her confidence. Margaret's brother, Joe, told reporters that his sister was an antiwar activist "now into women's rights." "She just tried to help people with favors who really needed help," he said. Although they shared an apartment with Yo-shimura until February, 1975, said investigators, apparently nei-ther Fittipaldi nor Turcich was ever more than a peripheral char-acter in the building drama, largely isolated from the new SLA/NWLF combat squad.

Colorado State Police believe Patty and Jack (or one or all of the other cars in the SLA caravan) may have stopped in Colorado, at the Duck Lake Commune, the lesbian collective at which Miz-moon and Camilla had once vacationed. By unlikely coincidence, Cecil Moody—the convict who had beaten out DeFreeze as presi-dent of the Black Cultural Association at Vacaville—happened to be in the area when the radical community in nearby Denver was whispering of an SLA presence.

Moody once had been considered a prime suspect as the second male on the scene at the Hearst kidnapping. Although technically still a convict, Moody had been out of prison on a work furlough at the time of the kidnapping and was living in a Department of Corrections halfway house in Oakland. At CDC halfway houses regulations require a convict to return directly after his work day, sign in and stay in. The records showed that Moody signed in the night of the snatch, but ex-cons said such things could on occasion be "arranged," and several SLA investigators had never been satisfied that Moody could not have been a mere five miles away in Berkeley for the kidnapping. When neither Weed nor any of the other witnesses could identify him, however, Cecil Moody was paroled on February 26, 1974.

He walked out of prison directly into the arms of the FBI. Moody was only one of several ex-convicts and former friends of DeFreeze pressured into becoming FBI informers on the Hearst case, but Moody was considered of unusual value because of his ties to the nascent SLA through the BCA. (Moody's friends claim he played a game with the bureau, collecting their money and telling tall tales.) Moody was still on the FBI payroll when he was arrested on May 5, 1974, for the brutal beating and robbery of an elderly Berkeley man. Moody's jailers decided he was psychologically disturbed and transferred him to the Napa State Hospital, from which he promptly escaped on May 25.

Four months later, in the early fall, Moody appeared in Colorado. He played guitar in the Tombstone Bar in Denver and reportedly traveled regularly to Nederland, a small mountain town near the Duck Lake Commune. He stayed in Colorado through autumn, launching a late-fall spree of armed robberies with two teenage girls as sidekicks. (In late January, 1975, he fled Colorado for San Francisco. Colorado troopers tipped the FBI after they arrested the two girls, who claimed Moody had bragged of being a member of the SLA, and on February 12 an FBI SWAT squad captured him in a raid on a San Francisco apartment.)

The FBI's investigation had run long and empty through the summer . . . and through the fall. Publicly, the FBI had stated early in the summer that it was certain the SLA trio had fled California. Privately, agents admitted they were certain of damn little else. The SLA never made the FBI's Ten Most Wanted list—but only because the list was nothing but a publicity device, and the SLA needed nothing to draw attention to it. Still, a stream of exclusive interviews with FBI Director Kelley and key FBI officials kept the fires stoked. The *American Legion* magazine ran the SLA "wanted" poster, and—at the bureau's request—the *Journal of the California Dental Association* reproduced the dental records of the

three fugitives, with photographs to the side. The FBI had even
printed 60,000 "wanted" posters in Spanish (the first ever for the
bureau: *Buscados por el FBI*) for distribution in Mexico and Central and South America. The FBI was trying. Hard.

Public interest had perhaps peaked, but it was still the American crime story of the year, perhaps the decade. And the FBI was
becoming dangerously overinvested in the Hearst case. A national
police dragnet of virtually unprecedented proportions had been
organized, but to no avail. In preparation for the February anniversary of the kidnapping, the FBI even had a film crew preparing a TV documentary on the case (the project was eventually
canceled, but again it was an FBI first). Tania was a trinket that
still fascinated millions. At every press conference, every ceremo-
nial dinner, FBI Director Clarence Kelley could expect rote questions on the investigation. *Why* couldn't they find her? How soon
did he think the FBI could find her? What *was* the FBI doing all
this time?

Watergate and the darker secrets of J. Edgar Hoover's FBI regime had already stained the bureau's once-burnished image, but
now, improbably, the success of this twenty-year-old socialite terrorist in eluding capture had become an important measure of
the FBI's capability in their mandated police function. In political
cases, in which radical fugitives could disappear into a sympathetic underground network, the FBI had a sorry record. (Six of their
Ten Most Wanted fugitives were then self-declared revolutionaries.) But this was a case it simply had to close; failure would not
be ignored. Perhaps more than ever before, the FBI's credibility
depended on the apprehension of a single fugitive.

San Francisco Agent in Charge Charles Bates tried to explain
his problem to Middle America. "In the past ten years finding
some kinds of people who agree with certain ideologies has become more difficult," he told reporters. "We have a group of people who agree with certain ideologies. We have the phenomenon
of communal living. Very few people would hide an ordinary
bank robber or murderer, but many will help conceal someone
for ideological reasons."

At FBI headquarters in Washington, the *Village Voice*, of New
York City (a left-liberal weekly that would have had trouble nego-
tiating for a public tour of the building during Hoover's reign),
was granted a rare informal interview with the two agents charged
with coordinating nationwide kidnap investigations. Ten months
into the case, Special Agents Ellie Turner and Tony Murray

claimed that the FBI had already spent more than $3 million, invested 270,000 man-hours, and interviewed 25,000 people—or tried to. In a revelation as astonishing for the source as for the fact, the FBI said that more people had refused to cooperate with their agents than had agreed.

The myth of the radical underground is vastly overblown (middle-class radical fugitives simply find it easier to blend with "respectable society" than do most criminal elements), but there *is* a loose network of old friends and comrades from the decade of resistance. And here with entrée, political fugitives ranging from draft resisters and military deserters to "retired" protest bombers of the sixties find refuge, but it is a principled subculture of sanctuary. It is rarely open to the violent fringe of the Left; until after the debacle in Los Angeles, it was not open to the SLA. Revolutionary groups like the Weather Underground have their own small support networks, but the "underground" of media myth is more accurately described as a conspiracy of silence, speechless witnesses. Leftists who bitterly disagreed with the SLA felt still bound by principle to refuse to cooperate with the FBI and police investigators. America as a nation is held together by shared ideas and ideals (rather than the tie of individual men to the actual soil); "Americanism" is a state of mind, a commitment of consensus—but the sixties had seen that cloak of consensus ripped. Agencies of government, and particularly the FBI, came to represent "illegitimate authority" and tainted power to an unmeasured but sizable minority of American citizens.

"It's a popular idea to be a revolutionary these days," Agent Murray told the *Voice*. "Not a bad life, I guess. The underground has manuals now saying what to do when we come to the door. We're 'pigs,' you see. We represent authority, and people won't talk because of that." As kidnap specialists, Turner and Murray had perhaps the most ironic perspective on the Hearst case.

The agents showed the *Voice* reporter the two most widely circulated photographs of Patty Hearst; one showed Patty walking happily alongside Steve Weed; the second was of Tania, with beret and machine gun, against the *naga* backdrop. "Look how she's changed," exclaimed Turner. "From a radiant, full-faced girl to those hard chiseled features. . . . She went from Patty to Tania. Where does she go next?

"She was an heiress," he said. "How could an heiress go from that plateau to the degradation of living in these pads? That's what I can't fathom. The filth, the menial squalor. No heat, the shabbiest kind of existence. No beds, no furniture, just filth. This is a gal who is used to the finest things in life, all her life. Now, with six or eight other people, she's living like a pig! What causes that? What makes her become a bank robber? How often does a victim of a kidnapping become a kidnapper?" (A generation that had driven itself silly trying to escape its own "radiant, full-faced" features could laugh at Turner's bewilderment, but his was the voice of the proverbial silent majority. America is—still—a middle-class state, a nation that respects and envies wealth far more than it fears or resents the wealthy.)

The months ticked off with an unnerving silence for the Hearst family, a silence more painful for the uncertainty it held. Two of the Hearst daughters had enrolled in Midwestern colleges under assumed names. The elder Hearsts had moved out of the Hillsborough mansion to a condominium atop San Francisco's Nob Hill. The mansion "has got a lot of memories that are rather painful for us," explained Randolph. "It's easier for me than it is for Catherine because I have a job and she hasn't and so she has more time to think about it. . . ."

Mr. Hearst's message to Patty—through public interviews—had become less assertive, more tentative and cautious. "If I say come out because you're worth more out than you are underground, I'm talking as a capitalist to a radical," he complained to one reporter. "I can make a lot of sense to the average guy in the street or to the mother and father that's sitting out there, and so can Catherine. But I keep thinking: What is Patty thinking all the time? Can I have any effect on her?

"I believe she's alive. I just hope she's well. I hope she comes out of her own accord and doesn't remain a fugitive for years. I have to assume that she's underground. . . . If she does come out, we would help her, of course. If she doesn't want our help, she might use some of her own funds. She has a small fund—enough to defend herself.* If she wants to get a group together to have a defense fund for her, fine, she can do that.

"We'd like to see her free and we'd like to see her living her own life any way she wants to live it. At least so we know she's all right and isn't going to spend the rest of her life hiding from law enforcement."

Behind the scenes, Randolph Hearst kept probing for lines to the SLA and his daughter through the radical subculture. His

*Patricia had a $35,000 trust fund left to her by her grandmother.

personal contact with poor blacks, convicts, militant Indians, and other underclass groups seemed to make a deep personal impact on him, certainly on his newspaper. The *Examiner* began to report the problems and concerns of social-outcast groups with enterprise and sympathy and tact—quite unlike the Hearst tradition of tar-'n'-feather politics. Hearst himself acknowledged the paper's more liberal bent, but insisted the changes reflected plans made long before the kidnapping. He admitted his recent experience had "accelerated" the shift; but, he said, "if I hadn't felt that way before, the change would have been in the opposite direction."

The public got one glimpse into Hearst's strange odyssey in October, when reporters learned that the Los Angeles police had detained Randolph and Catherine Hearst at the LA airport to inquire why they had met with Mickey Cohen, an eccentric retired mobster who had once been a kingpin of organized crime in California. As Cohen later told the story, the Hearsts had asked him to use his contacts in the black underworld to try to trace the Harrises and Patty. When Cohen thought he had been successful—locating the SLA in Cleveland, hidden by black nationalists—the Hearsts had flown down from San Francisco to discuss his plan for "freeing" Patty. After dinner in a posh LA restaurant, recalled Cohen, a depressed Catherine Hearst had worried aloud if it "'might not be a mistake bringing Patty back . . . to thirty, forty years in prison.'" Cohen, a convict himself for nineteen years, was astonished the "fix" wasn't in. "I say, 'Hey, what do you mean? . . .' I says to Catherine Hearst, 'If that's the case, Catherine, I'm not going to bring Patty in at all. I don't bring nobody back to go to prison.'"* (Having already heard Cohen's plan, the Hearsts were undismayed. Cohen had reportedly arranged for an ambulance and two black gunmen in Cleveland. He wanted Catherine Hearst to dress as a nurse and remain in the ambulance while the two men, toting tommy guns, rushed the hideout and dragged Patty to her "rescue.")

Most of Randy's efforts were less ambitious but more serious. One of Hearst's regular contacts was Popeye Jackson, the leader of the Venceremos-oriented United Prisoners Union, a tough black ex-con who had spent nineteen of his forty-four years in prison. Hearst had first met Jackson during the PIN food program, when Popeye was one of the radical leaders the SLA asked to oversee the handout. "Jackson didn't really disagree with the

---

*Michael "Mickey" Cohen, *In My Own Words* (Englewood Cliffs: Prentice-Hall, 1975).

idea of terrorism or revolutionary kidnaps," recalled Steve Weed, who also kept up contacts on the circuit. "He just thought the SLA was stupid."

Even before the PIN program started, Jackson—on parole—had been arrested and charged with possession of heroin found in his car. (Jessica Vodquen, a UPU activist close to Jackson, later testified in court that she was an informant of the San Francisco police and the FBI; that she had overheard her police superiors plot to "frame" Popeye; and that she—at their request—had borrowed Jackson's car and delivered it for police inspection shortly before the arrest. Vodquen, twenty-two, was taken into police custody shortly after her testimony and soon recanted, but Jackson was acquitted of the heroin charge after police admitted that Vodquen had been a paid informant.) When the PIN program began, Hearst learned that the state parole board was considering revoking Jackson's parole despite his acquittal—which was within their authority—and he brought personal and editorial pressure to bear to keep Jackson on the street. After an article and editorial favorable to the UPU, Jackson's parole was reinstated. The two men talked often, albeit agreeing less. "Popeye believed that Hearst had respect for him as a man," explained Jackson's mistress.

The Jackson-Hearst relationship had a strange and fatal pivot. A messenger occasionally used between them was forty-seven-year-old Sara Jane Moore, the former PIN bookkeeper and comptroller whom Hearst had kept on after PIN ended, in an attempt to straighten out the chaotic records. Moore was a woman of several sides, with a foot in several camps. Playing on acquaintances she had made through PIN, she became an odd but ever-present regular on the fringe of Berkeley's revolutionary circles. Then, playing on her radical contacts, she gained personal access to Randolph Hearst. And through it all, she was a paid informant for the Federal Bureau of Investigation.

"Sara Jane was one of those people who became just completely obsessed by Patty," recalled Steve Weed. "For months, right up until she herself was arrested, she would call me up at odd hours, often in the middle of the night, to talk about Patty, the SLA, whatever was happening. I think I might have been her only friend at the end. I'm pretty sure it was the strain of the whole thing that eventually pushed her over the edge."

Ms. Moore was a white suburban matron, a widow with some money of her own. (It is a combination the FBI has often found oddly effective for infiltrating secretive radical groups. Older "working class" converts are particularly prized among revolutionaries.) For months after PIN closed down, Sara Jane took to hanging around the UPU office, tailing after Jackson "like a puppy dog," said one UPU staffer. The street-wise Jackson played it for what it was worth—reportedly borrowing several hundred dollars from her—then openly accused her of being a police agent. Denying the charge, Moore retorted that Jackson was "selling out the Movement" for favors from Randolph Hearst. Months later—an outcast among the Bay Left but still in regular attendance at public rallies—Sara Jane went public. Yes, she admitted, she had been an FBI informer, but she had been converted—*now* she was a true revolutionary. And now, again, she charged that Popeye had dishonored the cause—selling out for "money and middle-class life." Implying that Jackson had become a police snitch was no way to guarantee her own credibility—Sara Jane remained a pariah on the edge of the Bay Left—but her accusations, despite the source, were apparently believed by some. Popeye Jackson was murdered on June 8, 1975. Both Jackson and a young woman friend, Sally Voye, were shot and killed by an unidentified young man as the two sat and talked in a car in front of Jackson's San Francisco apartment at 3 A.M.

(Only days before, an NWLF communiqué had demanded that Jackson publicly answer charges virtually identical to those circulated by Sara Jane Moore. The day after the murders another "NWLF" communiqué claimed responsibility for the killings, charging Jackson with being a police informer. That was followed by yet another message, also allegedly from the NWLF, claiming that the first had been fraudulent but lauding efforts to "create a snitch-free base." Another message, signed by the "Strategic Command" of the SLA, defended and praised Jackson. Yet another communiqué followed—from the Weather Underground—also praising Jackson. Three months later, on September 22, 1975 (just four days after the arrest of Patricia Hearst), Sara Jane Moore attempted to assassinate President Gerald Ford in San Francisco. She shot at him and—narrowly—missed, was disarmed and captured. At the time of her arrest, Ms. Moore was still working as an informant for the U.S. Treasury's Bureau of Alcohol, Tobacco and Firearms—and perhaps, still or again, for the FBI.)

For the return of the SLA, Kathy and Steve Soliah had rented a shabby one-bedroom duplex in downtown Sacramento, at 1721 W Street, less than a mile from the state capital buildings. The lease began on October 1, and it was apparently shortly thereafter that "Mr. and Mrs. Carroll Simmons"—Teko and Yolanda—moved in.

Accompanied by Tania Hearst. The apartment was cramped, smelly, and dirty; three small rooms, $80-a-month. Busy Interstate 80 crossed just alongside the building, and so even inside there was a constant racket of highway noise. Patty reportedly shared the single bedroom with the Harrises—cohabitant, daughter, and disciple in one. But the SLA, coming down from the hills, had walked into a swirl of new people, and soon there was high tension among even the three.

It is difficult, if not impossible, to trace the subtle pressures amid the group; even more difficult to attempt to identify the new face of Tania that was then emerging. What is clear, from several reports, is that Patty began to squabble more and more with Bill Harris—and when it came to outright disputes, Emily would always side with Bill. Why Patty then began to speak up, what brought her now to react against the discipline and daily paternalism she had accepted unquestioningly through the summer, is unclear. Part of it may have been the counsel of Wendy Yoshimura; part may have been bitterness that Yoshimura, because of the Harrises, had decided to stay in San Francisco rather than Sacramento. And part of it may have been Steve Soliah, and the new sexual triangle—or quandrangle—he set up among them.

Inside information on what was happening among the group is extremely limited—and all from highly suspect sources. Patty's postconviction FBI interviews confirmed for the first time that Bortin and McCarthy and several others were then deeply involved with the SLA fugitives, but their impact is unclear. The only glimpse into the SLA dynamic in Sacramento was in the unattributed interview Steve Soliah gave *Rolling Stone* in early 1976. (The article was a response to an interview given *New Times* by the Harrises, in which they denied there had been any internal disputes in the SLA and claimed that Patty Hearst, then on trial, was betraying the love and trust of faithful comrades. Soliah/*Stone* made it clear that there had been a bitter schism in the group and that the Harrises had been abandoned by virtually all the rest of the group shortly before the September, 1975, arrests.) Soliah traced the beginnings of the split back to the first month the SLA had been in Sacramento, when a sudden and spontaneous spark of resentment in Patty had set off an angry and continuous round of bickering among the three.

Rolling Stone's account has Soliah making a rare visit up to Sacramento in late October—allegedly the first since he and Patty had had a brief affair right after her return to California the month before—and Tania dragging him aside to blurt out angrily how she hated living with the Harrises, particularly Bill. "If I had any alternative at all, I'd jump at it," she is quoted as saying. Harris, she said, had "some sort of complex. He acts like he's a coach or drill sergeant or something." At the time, said Soliah/*Stone*, Teko was still the unquestioned commander in chief of the SLA—drillmaster for the calisthenics, discussion leader in the daily political study sessions, tactical commander for strategy. A bull moose disciplinarian who wielded all the authority of a spit-'n'-polish general over the noncoms in the motor pool.

It's a striking image, but it seems overplayed and mistimed. It's certainly true that Harris' leadership and the authoritarian style he affected became major issues in the internal squabbles the following year—and may have even been part of the tension that fall. But Soliah understates the sexual dynamic in his whole story.

(The logic of Soliah's narrative was apparently designed to buttress his claim that none of the Berkeley group ever got caught up in the renaissance SLA crusade, for who would follow an arrogant wimp like Harris? It was perhaps wishful hindsight, but it didn't happen that way. In a letter to Willie Brandt, Wendy Yoshimura would confess that *everyone* had been "spellbound into submissiveness" by the Harrises. The sensational media play on the SLA had daunted all, she said, "making us unable to think clearly of them as people with strengths and weaknesses but as leaders who knew *everything*." Patty would later tell her FBI interrogators that virtually all of the Berkeley group had been initially swept away with the Harrises' grand design for a resurgent SLA—and the contact between the Soliahs, Bortin, et al and Bill Harris was much more regular and continuous than Soliah acknowledged.)

Although there are but scant details, it's also apparent from SLA documents later seized that the "cell" was undergoing "tremendous changes" as it absorbed the Berkeley group. What tangled Patty's relationship with the Harrises may have been more personal than political. All summer Harris had his two-woman army to himself (in a "nonexclusive" relationship of sexual comradeship) but almost as soon as Patty arrived in California again—the second night, according to Soliah—she and Steve Soliah became lovers. It seems more than coincidence that it was just then that the Sacramento trio suddenly began to spat. Another factor may have been the influence of the Berkeley women, which seems—according to both the captured SLA documents and Patty's FBI confessions—to have brought Emily's star into an ascendancy and pushed Bill, at least temporarily, to one side.

As sisterhood developed the women became the motive force in the collective. There was tremendous strength and energy coming from us that had been suppressed before, and because of this the whole group was really moving ahead with incredible speed. But we still weren't moving as a collective as fast as we should have been. The men were dragging their feet. Their sexism had made them afraid of our strength in spite of the fact that they could intellectualize about how great it was *objectively,* subjectively they felt threatened. . . .

We had been too isolated to solve the problem ourselves and only in the last year have we begun to understand the problems and contradictions of the past and really started to deal with them. It takes struggle and study for us to unite and support each other—because it's a fact that the men feel threatened by us, not because they consciously want to oppress us with their machismo, but because subconsciously they still have leanings toward relating to women in a traditional (i.e. sexist) way. We realize, however, how much we can accomplish as a group of strong, unified revolutionary women struggling against sexism in a cell situation.

Whatever the internal tensions, they were not sufficient to disrupt the new SLA's "urban guerrilla" plots.

There was work at the library. Poring over the Bay Area *Social Register, Moody's* and *Standard & Poors,* clipping from newspapers, they began to gather a new list of target candidates for "future actions." It was work that employed certain talents that only Patty had, according to Emily Harris in *New Times.* "She was different from anyone else in the SLA. She knew people personally in corporate America, some of the same families whose daughters had gone to the same private schools and country clubs. She knew these people so it was logical for her to do the research on them."

There was work on the book, honing arguments that would be broadcast to the nation as the voice in the wilderness. "Believe it or not," wrote General Teko, "many aboveground Left groups and organizations do *not* think that fascism is the order of the day in amerikkka. The purpose for studying this question is to understand the historical and present contradictions which have led us to agree with George Jackson's analysis and say that fascism is *here now,* thereby understanding why we are underground. . . ."

And there were the bombings. Even before the SLA trio left Pennsylvania for California, the "second team" had launched a series of New World Liberation Front bombings that had state and federal cops in a frenzy in California. The first NWLF bomb—

planted at the Burlingame GMAC office in August—had been a dud, but by September they had improved their ordnance.

On September 3 a bomb exploded shortly after midnight in the downtown San Francisco office of Dean Witter and Company. An NWLF communiqué said the brokerage firm was targeted because it profited from selling stock in "corporations that exploit people." Similar NWLF messages, redundant and of expressive length, claimed seven more bombings through the fall: one at the Palo Alto office of Dean Witter (September 13); another in the warehouse of an ITT subsidiary in San Leandro (September 28); in a women's rest room of the ITT-owned Sheraton-Palace Hotel in San Francisco (October 2); at the Sheraton Airport Inn in Los Angeles (October 6); and at the Los Altos Hills home of retired ITT president Robert Halleck (October 30). Other targets were seven meter maid three-wheeled motorcycles in a Berkeley parking lot (November 6) and the downtown San Francisco office of General Motors Corporation (December 19).

The NWLF claimed responsibility for each bomb in a communiqué, and each—when necessary—was preceded by a phone warning. There were no personal injuries. Although the obvious connection to the SLA's last message—the June eulogy tape—was immediately made, there was nothing to indicate the original SLA was back in the area.

According to Patty's postconviction FBI confessions, it had been decided among the group that they would keep the SLA low profile. They used the NWLF signature for all their bombings and planned to send no communiqués at all for their "heavier" high-risk operations. They had apparently learned something from the intense negative public reaction over the two men shot during the Hibernia Bank robbery—and they felt they could well do without the increased police attention that would be brought to bear if the seven-headed cobra resurfaced. The grand plan called for the liberation of Remiro and Little—Bo and Osceola. Perhaps then they would crow, but not yet.

Joe Remiro and Russ Little were still being held in the Alameda county jail in downtown Oakland pending transfer to Sacramento—with all the pretrial motions scheduled, it appeared that the trial would be delayed at least until March. The Harrises made contact with Joe and Russ inside—reportedly through an attorney—and passed the word that they were back and trying to plan a breakout scheme, trying again to do what they had originally hoped the kidnapping of Patricia Hearst would achieve. Patty later told the FBI that the escape plan involved a sizable group—the Sacramento three; the Soliahs; Jim Kilgore; Mike Bortin; Pat Jean McCarthy; a cousin of Remiro's Patty knew only as "Sally" (later identified as a San Francisco woman, a cousin of Joe Remiro, who had regularly visited Russ Little); and another woman, a longtime Berkeley friend of Mike Bortin, whom Patty knew as "Bridget." (Both women were apparently introduced to Tania with pseudonyms. No charges have been filed, and Steven Soliah, Bortin, and McCarthy have denied Patty's accusation.)

The Alameda county courthouse is an imposing structure, 1930-style cement Gothic, with the county jail on the tenth floor. The Alameda Sheriff's Department headquarters is in the same building, along with most of the county offices. The location is downtown Oakland, center city, only blocks from the Oakland school building outside which Marcus Foster was killed. The plan called for the SLA assault teams to hit the place commando-style, get to the tenth floor, wreak bloody havoc with automatic weapons—and escape. It was not a modest plot.

Inside, Remiro and Little drew up a detailed diagram of the jail, pacing out the distance between gates, noting the exact time of each of the jail routines, the number of guards on duty when and where, and smuggled both the diagram and their description of the jail routine out to "Cousin Sally"—again, "through an attorney," Patty told the FBI—who in turn brought it to "the Soliahs," who then ferried it to Sacramento. Emily Harris, said Patty, redrafted the diagram and began to design scenarios for the breakout. Emily was apparently the "operations officer" for the project. In early December she assigned others to place the courthouse under surveillance, particularly watching the tunnel entrance. Beneath the building, running east to west, is a basement-level tunnel used to deliver supplies to the courthouse—and by prisoner vans delivering or picking up jail inmates. There is a special elevator from the tunnel directly up to the tenth-floor jail, and that would be the main entrance for the assault squads which would use a kidnapped sheriff's deputy to gain entrance.

For at least a week, the two tunnel entrances were watched. Surveillance notes later found charted the movements of "pig cars" and "pig deputies" in and out of the tunnel on December 9, 10, 11, 14, 15, and 16. The plan called for a simultaneous break from the inside by Remiro and Little, according to Patty's tale to the FBI. It would be timed for a weekend, when there were only four deputies on duty in the jail. The two SLA soldiers inside were to arrange a joint conference with one of their attorneys; then, at the designated hour, they were to attack the two guards in the area with sharpened pencils, stab them, and get the key to the jail gun locker from the duty officer. Armed, they would become another "assault team."

Patty told the FBI that there were two lengthy meetings in Sacramento going over details of the plan, meetings reportedly chaired by Emily. She, the Harrises, Kilgore, the Soliahs, Bortin, and McCarthy attended both, Patty said: "Bridget" sat in on only one, and she wasn't certain if "Cousin Sally" attended only the first meeting or both. Just what was said and by whom is not known, but according to Patty, at the conclusion of the second meeting it was Emily who made the final decision. Such an attempt would be "suicide," she ruled, they didn't have enough people, they couldn't muster "enough firepower."

Yolanda's veto message was received angrily by Remiro and Little, Patty said. From the jail they sent back a response "that was something like 'Fuck you—we're going to try anyway!'"

23

Renaissance

RE-CREATING the SLA, even reclaiming the name of the SLA, involved some very fundamental problems. The mystique of the Symbionese had been shaped in the heady aura of Cinque's convict fury. The others had been middle-class whites scratching at the outside of the prison walls for a rush of authentic cellblock rage. Without the black connection, without the prison connection, the SLA had lost their precious legitimacy. No longer were they the vengeful fist of the oppressed, the chosen champions of the underclass. Teko had no claim to the heritage of George Jackson—nor did any of the others. All were disqualified by class privilege and white skin.

They were trapped in their own ethnocentric dogma. They were white so they could "represent" only whites. They were middle-class, so they were effectively classless, spiteful rebels among the elite. In their own terms, the political reality of the SLA had been reduced to their public image. They were sworn to follow only nonwhite leadership, but they had a lily-white army. The contradiction was so blatant they apparently tried to draft another black field marshal.

Ulysses McDaniels—the former cellmate of George Jackson and the man Death Row Jeff referred to as "U." in his letters to Willie Wolfe—had been "deputy chief commander" of Jefferson's Partisan Vanguard Party. In April, 1973, Jefferson had named McDaniels, along with Wolfe and Russ Little, members of the Vanguard Central Committee, but it was only a week and a half later, in a letter to Little, that Jefferson declared "U." purged. (There was perhaps some protest from the others; at any rate, a few days later, Jeff sent another note explaining, "Ulysses is out our thing, 'fired,' and that 'final.' Because he can't get along with anyone and hasn't done a damn thing he said he was.")

425

McDaniels, forty-four, on parole and living with his girlfriend in Palo Alto, apparently did not take Jefferson's Vanguard very seriously, but then McDaniels himself was one of the few ex-convicts with a prison reputation and political stature to match Jefferson. (George Jackson, when he wrote his critique of Eldridge Cleaver's stance in the Black Panther Party split, had asked only Jefferson and McDaniels to cosign it, and he described them in *Blood in My Eye* as "two of the oldest [time spent in prison] and most respected black partisans in the California concentration camp system.") If the SLA was seeking an heir to Cinque, McDaniels was a more than likely choice. There is no evidence that DeFreeze had tried to enlist McDaniels when the SLA formed, but shortly after the Los Angeles shoot-out Teko may have contacted him.

McDaniels was being pressured by someone. Right after the shoot-out, said one friend, Ulysses and his twenty-year-old lover, Barbara Kessler, "began acting strangely." Ms. Kessler—the "topless and bottomless" girl Jefferson wrote of with such envy—was working at the Green Door massage parlor in Palo Alto, forty miles down the Peninsula from San Francisco. McDaniels told friends he might have to leave Palo Alto quickly "even though Barbara was making good money." Somehow the threat passed, and for several months McDaniels appeared unconcerned and at ease.

Then, in early October, right about the time the Harrises returned to California, Barbara Kessler suddenly quit the Green Door and told a close friend that she and Ulysses had to leave Palo Alto. "When she told me they were buying guns and planning to split because of the SLA, I offered to let them stay with me," the friend recalled. "Barbara was really afraid that somehow the cops would find out about the guns and bust Ulysses for violating parole, but Ulysses was more scared of the SLA than his parole officer." McDaniels apparently feared a siege or attack from the SLA, and he had assembled a small arsenal of weapons, said the friend, at least three semiautomatic rifles and a shotgun. In late October neighbors recall Ulysses spending an afternoon burning letters and documents of some sort in a vacant lot near his home. Then, on October 31, McDaniels and his lady left Palo Alto for Canada, explaining cryptically to another friend that the "SLA was leaning on him."

The SLA had done little to commend them to any serious prison revolutionary. They had largely alienated the Left. They had reduced the issue of prison reform to a stage setting for their personal star trips. And the letters they left behind at Clayton had branded most of their convict allies by name and number. (On October 20, just before McDaniels fled the Bay Area, convict Raymond "Ray Ray" Sparks—another key figure in Death Row Jeff's letters to Wolfe—had killed himself after committing himself to the Folsom prison hospital in deep depression. Sparks had bitterly protested being linked with the SLA, swearing to prison officials that he knew nothing about DeFreeze or any "army," but when he was again rejected for parole, he became certain that the SLA tie would keep him in forever. He hanged himself.) In the media games of modern terrorism and "armed propaganda," symbol becomes substance. And the SLA—for both symbol and substance— had in the end created nothing more than Tania. Always the cult, it had finally become the cult of its best-known victim.

On the anniversary of the kidnap, Emily Harris wrote a commemorative essay for the SLA book—and dedicated it to Tania.

> My life really changed a year ago today. On Feb. 4 I proved to myself and we all proved to each other that we were guerrillas and that the revolution will be made by determined people who do determined things and don't let anything stand in their way. It was really a turning point in history because it kicked the whole intellectual movement out of their armchairs and it showed all those beautiful people on the streets that the SLA is another material reason for them to hope for change. . . .

She recalled "the food program, Randy and Catherine, the pigs and all their harassment clues, all the tension of being 8 fugitives holed up in a tract house." It was, she wrote, "all such frustrating shit, especially knowing we weren't going to get Ossie and Bo out. I mean the only highs we got were from looking forward to the next action, from seeing the few responses of righteous people . . . on TV, and from seeing you change to become a comrade." Yet even in this celebration of the Tania transformation —on a manuscript page festooned with cobra drawings and the slogan, "Just as the caterpillar becomes a butterfly so the man (woman) child becomes an armed combatant"—there was a hint of the struggle then current among them:

> It's clear that conditions aren't going to fall into our laps and nothing's going to be easy. We aren't even close to sharing revolutionary relationships with each other because we don't even know

what those kinds of relationships should be—we only have hints and hopes. But what's talked about and fought about between these four walls don't amount to shit compared to revolutionary action. . . .

According to both Steve Soliah and friends of Yoshimura, the three weren't even sharing "four walls" in Sacramento—the squabbles between Patty and the Harrises had become so bitter by January that the Berkeley group had to finance a second hideout, on T Street, also in downtown Sacramento, which Patty reportedly shared with Kathy Soliah.

(Varying reports give confusing versions of this. *Rolling Stone/* Soliah claimed Patty moved alone to T Street, but it also claimed, inaccurately according to Patty's FBI confessions, that the Berkeley group was only seldom in touch with the trio. Soliah himself, when he went on trial for bank robbery, testified that by early spring 1975 Emily and Patty were living together and it was *Bill* who was living alone.) The Harrises, in their *New Times* memoirs, have a bitter recall of Tania's disaffection, but that seems to be a final verdict on the whole last year. The neighbors of "Mr. and Mrs. Simmons" on W Street remember the Harrises living there through the winter, but being regularly visited by a young woman, believed to be Patty, often in the company of Steve Soliah.

"We just needed to get away from each other sometimes," Emily told *New Times*. "She'd get tired of our habit of patronizing her and we needed relief from her stupid bourgie rebelliousness. She had that whole problem of her class background. She didn't do an about-face—one day an heiress, the next day a revolutionary. She had aspects of both in her personality." But was there a "revolutionary" personality—for Emily any more than Tania? Somewhere in that nexus of the personal and the political—the struggle to capture in one's personal life, in the very fabric of the personality, the rigid and moralistic tenets of "proper" class, sexual, and social politics, the new Symbionese collective was being caught up in circular dialectics very similar to those which marked the incestuous squabbles in the latter days of the New Left. Notes from SLA study sessions later seized by police list the dogma knots they pondered ("Is the struggle of white people—the oppressor nation—for natonal liberation and self-determination?" If middle-class U.S. whites aren't oppressed by imperialism, is the black bourgeois?), but the disruptive dynamic was in the "personal politics" of sex and gender role:

While we all had a degree of consciousness about progressive ways of relating to men, as heterosexual women we still had subjective fears of relating to men in a strong and undependent way. . . . We women struggled to build close personal relationships among ourselves. We wanted to be able to go to each other for love and support instead of feeling we had to go to our "main man" for this. We had to smash the dependencies created by monogamous sexual relationships, and to do this we had to destroy monogamy within the cell. Monogamy serves only to reinforce male supremacy and the oppression of women. Monogamy means that "the men wear the pants."

(It was the first stage of what would become the feminist dynamic of the new SLA, an undercurrent of tension and turmoil that would influence and often dictate the evolution of the SLA in their last year. The "nonexclusive" sexual pattern that Bill Harris had explained as necessary because of the isolation of the early SLA collective, now became "party line" as the new women's clique among the group tried to adapt classical Marxist concepts on the oppression of women—schemes of class and economic role—to the interpersonal relations among the "second team." It was an ironic replay of the experience of many communes and collectives in the late sixties: an egalitarian line loosening the relationships between men and women; then an independent women's clique demanding "recognized leadership" in the group; then a declaration that women—as "the most oppressed class"—are *the* leadership, the "vanguard" of the Revolution. In the end, it was all circular. What began as an effort to overlap the personal and the political spiraled into the realization that a socioeconomic "class" revolution would not suffice to address the needs of the women within the classes; the political revolution and the restructuring of sexual roles might be parallel, but they were not necessarily interdependent.)

It was the underside of the SLA dynamic—sometime in the spring, according to Patty's postconviction story to the FBI, Emily Harris and Kathy Soliah became lovers, and by May the SLA women had decided they all wanted to live separately from the men in their own collective—and yet it was only one level of the SLA reality. Even as they wrenched themselves into properly "liberated" roles, the group remained successfully active "on the streets." In fact, the NWLF would begin to achieve what the early SLA had only dreamed of: an armed and disloyal "opposition"—isolated, illegal, but almost established by its constant presence.

The New World Liberation Front bombings had continued into the new year; three explosions seemed almost timed to celebrate the anniversary of the Hearst kidnap—although the NWLF communiqués focused on global politics and made no mention of Tania, the Hearsts, or the SLA. On February 3, the eve of the anniversary, the San Jose office of General Motors Corporation was bombed. On February 4 the NWLF claimed responsibility for two explosions (their only double bombing): one at the Pillar Point Air Force Radar Station near Half Moon Bay and the second at the Vulcan Foundry in Oakland. Another, protesting news coverage of the previous three, came on February 6, when an NWLF pipe bomb exploded at the local KRON-TV station in San Francisco. Not unnoticed, the New World Liberation Front now had adopted a familiar signature phrase in their communiqués: "Death to the Fascist Insect That Preys upon the Life of the People."

For a decade, California has led the nation in bombing statistics, but by February, 1975, the Bay Area alone was averaging one bombing every sixteen days. "It's been like this for a year," the San Francisco *Chronicle* complained, "and lawmen are embarrassed and chagrined that they have not been able to make a single arrest—and they are not even sure whom to suspect. . . ." The NWLF messages had a standing invitation to other groups to adopt the name, and there were apparently one or more independent "NWLF" units that became active in bombings—but according to Patty's FBI confessions, it was Bill Harris and the "second team" who were behind most of the two dozen NWLF bombings over the following nine months. ("The Harrises *were* the goddamn NWLF!" said one Patty-briefed source, mixing admiration with exasperation.)

The SLA shuttle on the ninety-minute route between Berkeley and Sacramento must have been busy in January and February. (Overcrowding may, in fact, have been the real reason they rented the second Sacramento hideout.) Precisely who was spending time where is unclear, but on top of the bombing campaign there were several percolating plots. Steve Soliah applied for a phony driver's license (in the name of "Victor Silva") and in mid-January filled out state transfer forms "selling" his 1962 Corvair to an imaginary Oakland man—apparently because the Harrises were using the car so much. Michael Bortin got permission to take a month's vacation out of state—to visit friends in Mansfield, Ohio (who claim he never arrived nor told them he was coming), and from January 9 to February 9 he was released from his probation-reporting obligations.

The meetings on the Remiro-Little breakout plan apparently took place in January; it was February before they received final word from Joe and Russ that the two of them would attempt escape from the Oakland jail on March 1. But even before, it must have been clear they needed more funds—money in amounts that can only be quickly obtained at gunpoint.

Once they decided on a bank robbery, it must have taken at last a week, perhaps more, to plan for the heist. (Wendy Yoshimura, still in San Francisco but in touch, brought the wrath of the Harrises upon herself when she bluntly refused to join the "fund-raising team," Patty told the FBI, and Pat Jean McCarthy, Bortin's girl, had drawn nearly as much criticism when she defended Wendy's right of choice. McCarthy, said Patty, would be the first ejected from the group by the Harrises.) The FBI would later seize, at the Harrises' San Francisco safehouse, a long and detailed checklist—euphemistically titled "Bakery"—describing how to rob a bank. It was a fifty-nine-point outline that focused largely on the preliminary planning and the details of the advance work.

The planning team chose the "general area" largely on the basis of local police activity, then made a list of "all good possibilities" from the yellow pages of the telephone book; each of those was surveyed, and then the list was narrowed to "the three best." Those three were carefully diagrammed—each building and its locale photographed; the neighborhood, possible escape routes, "backup" gun stations and "switch-car" locations all carefully mapped out—before the team leader made a final choice.

The "Bakery" list was meticulous and thorough; no plan can foresee the unexpected, this left little room for mistakes:

  VI.   Final Surveillance
        A. Retreat
           1. detailed maps of the area
           2. knowledge of main access routes, natural barriers, de-
              files, parks, schools, dead-end streets, stop signs, stop
              lights, shopping centers, parking lots
           3. initial planning of route
              a. bakery to switch point
              b. switch point—visibility, proximity to target
              c. switch point to home
           4. final planning of route
              a. first plan for route isn't always the best
              b. dry run
              c. initial route changed because of dry run; initial route

didn't utilize the terrain (hills) the best way it could and switch points were too apt to be detected by neighbors

    d. final dry run with all drivers

  5. checking area at proposed time of heist for traffic and available parking, number of people on the streets, etc.

B. Interior of bank

  1. detailed floor plans . . .

  2. positions of members of assault team

  3. time inside (not being greedy)

  4. entrance and exit of assault team

  5. where assault car was parked

C. Backup

  1. firepower

  2. position of backup, number of teams, number of people on each team

  3. teamwork—working together, covering and assisting each other

  4. backup's role during the retreat

D. Cars for the operation

  1. all possibilities of getting them

  2. types—what kind of cars

  3. coordination of getting them and placing them at switch point, picking up people etc.

  4. disposal of cars

VII. Assigning people to team positions and designating leadership

A. Responsibilities of each position

B. Team discussion of responsibilities and coordination

C. Inter-team rehearsal

D. Final dry-run—total rehearsal

It was a commando handbook. They followed the procedure step by step, and when they went into action, everything fell into place like the intricate gearworks of a Swiss-tooled clock. At 9:30 A.M. on February 25—a week before the scheduled Oakland break—the Revolution requisitioned a treasury at the Guild Savings and Loan branch in suburban North Sacramento.

Guild Savings is a small banking operation, located in a busy shopping center called Arden Plaza. Two men walked in quietly together, split and positioned themselves; then the one closest to the door announced in a loud and businesslike voice, "This is a robbery." Ordering customers and employees to lie on the floor, he began to count off the time, glancing at his wristwatch every few seconds. The other bandit, a burly redhead, face half hidden by a pulled-up turtleneck sweater, calmly rifled the tellers' drawers, stuffing the money—$3,729 cash, the bulk of it in fresh $20 bills—into a blue cloth tote bag with a white drawstring. "Traveler's checks! Where are the traveler's checks?" he demanded. One teller spoke up to say they didn't carry them—but pointed out a stack of money orders. He snatched up thirty-nine blank American Express money orders, shoved them into the bag, and vaulted the counter, shouting for everyone to "stay down for ten minutes." The two ran out, leaped into an old Chevy in which a third man was waiting with the motor idling; then they were gone.

It was swift and neat, but the precision didn't indicate the sort of military teamwork that had a backup team poised. The investigating Sheriff's Department deputies never thought of the bandits as an assault team; it was just another robbery. They were in and out in less than three minutes, but there had been no violence; it wasn't even clear if the two had been armed. No one saw any guns, although the men had each kept one hand in a pocket and poked it about in a way that gave every indication of a pistol.

The bank had no surveillance camera; there were no photographs, and descriptions were the usual, vague and varying. Employees and witnesses who had seen the car outside could offer little beyond the fact that the three robbers were white, probably in their late twenties. It would be seven months before police would even connect the SLA to the crime and a full year before they would get the full story from Patricia Hearst—when she finally decided to talk to the FBI with a thirty-five-year federal prison sentence hanging over her head, after she had been convicted of the Hibernia Bank robbery. According to Patty, the two men inside Guild Savings had been Jim Kilgore and Mike Bortin; the getaway driver had been Steve Soliah. (Both Bortin and Soliah deny the charge.)

After the three had fled, said Patty, Kathy Soliah calmly sipped coffee in a restaurant across the street, timing the police response. The assault team had five minutes "clear" before the first sheriff's cars arrived—long enough, they thought, and more time than they'd get in the city. For the next job, a bigger bank, Patty said, the group decided to stay in the jurisdiction of the Sacramento County Sheriff's Department, in the suburban communities just outside the city limits. Then they began again, with a list from the yellow pages. . . .

The day after the holdup, on February 26, Steve Soliah was stopped by a highway patrol officer and given a ticket for speeding northbound on California Interstate 5—near the village of Castella, nearly 200 miles north of Sacramento, but only 20 miles south of the turnoff for the vast (and often virtually deserted) Hearst wilderness estate of Wyntoon. The car he was driving was registered to Mike Bortin's mate, Pat Jean McCarthy.*

Back in Sacramento, also on the twenty-sixth, a young white couple (Bill and Emily Harris), introduced themselves as Mr. and Mrs. Elliott Burton when they purchased a 1966 Chevrolet station wagon from a Sacramento wholesale produce firm—Harris bartered the price down to $400 and paid for it, cash, with a stack of fresh twenties. (The next day they brought the car in for a quick paint job—Sahara tan—at the Earl Scheib auto-paint shop in Sacramento. Another man, unidentified and using an alias, picked up the car later—and paid the $40 tab with two fresh twenties.)

Newly funded and still unidentified, the SLA must have felt secure and self-sufficient in Sacramento. Ironically, it was on that very Wednesday, the twenty-sixth, that the fates began to tilt against them, as the FBI moved against the Scotts.

Two FBI agents delivered a subpoena to sixty-six-year-old John Scott, Jack Scott's father, at his Las Vegas, Nevada, home. The subpoena ordered him to appear for questioning before a Pennsylvania grand jury investigating the SLA's South Canaan refuge. (Jack Scott said later he just happened to be visiting his family when the FBI arrived. While the agents talked to his father at the door, said Jack, he was in the living room, behind his father— standing on his head doing yoga exercises, and the agents apparently did not recognize him upside down.) Acting on an anonymous telephone tip, the FBI had attempted to talk to Jack and Micki about the SLA in late January at the Portland, Oregon, home of Bill Walton. The agents had been rebuffed, but that was neither uncommon nor even particularly suspicious in this investi-

*In November, 1974, Jim Kilgore also received a speeding ticket, in another car registered to Ms. McCarthy. Later, in the spring of 1975, after the Scotts had been publicly linked to the SLA refuge, the FBI reported that Ms. McCarthy's 1974 Toyota—the same car Soliah had used—was used by the Scotts in San Francisco.

gation. But now the FBI had something more solid. And now they had subpoenas. One can refuse to talk to the FBI, but a grand jury can compel testimony—even self-incriminating testimony, with a grant of immunity—and to refuse can mean jail for criminal contempt of court.

Probably already suspecting, if not certain, where the leak had come from, Jack Scott called Micki, who was then visiting friends in San Diego, and arranged to meet her in California. Both flew to San Francisco the next day; together they rented a car from the Trans Rent-a-Car in suburban Burlingame, and—shadowed by a FBI car—they drove to Berkeley. There, at the corner of Ashby and San Pablo avenues, the Scotts jumped a yellow light and left the FBI car trapped by a line of cars that stopped for the red light. The Scotts abandoned the rented car in an Oakland parking lot and walked away. They disappeared for five weeks: "visiting friends," said Jack later.

The FBI had finally gotten its "Scott Connection" on January 31. Walter Scott, Jack's forty-one-year-old older brother, wandered drunk into the Scranton, Pennsylvania, police station at 2 A.M., babbling that he had information of where Patty Hearst had been hiding. Walter had demanded to see an old high school chum, Scranton police captain Clem Ross. Scranton—only twenty miles from the SLA farmhouse—had been the Scott family's hometown before the elder Scotts moved to Nevada; both Jack and Walter had been star athletes for Scranton high schools. "Even three-quarters drunk," said a Scranton police officer, Walter was sufficiently convincing that the duty officer called in detectives to question him. As Walter became more sober and began to flesh out his story, Scranton PD called in the local FBI. By dawn Walter was being interrogated by a team of FBI agents.

Police sources said Walter told a long involved story outlining the basic tale as he had heard it from his kid brother, Jack, but embellishing it with melodrama (perhaps also from Jack) and family gossip. Jack, said Walter, had bragged to him of hiding Patty and the SLA. Walter did not know exactly where the farm was, but from what Jack had told him, he could describe it and he knew it was somewhere in Wayne County. Agents were able to locate it and put it under surveillance within days.

Walter Scott is a complex personality; an unusual man acting under unusual stress in an extraordinary situation. Walter was then living in Syracuse, New York, but he was a well-known figure in the Scranton bars as a heavy drinker, usually broke, famous for making up fabulous stories about himself. Yet there seemed to be more to Walter's stories than imagination; he had often implied that he was working for the government in some secret capacity, and he was often off to or returning from some distant and exotic land. Privately Walter described himself as a computer expert "with an IQ of 139" who had worked at NATO intelligence headquarters, Xerox, and RCA—then free-lanced for various American spy agencies on classified assignments. A West Point dropout, an ex-Marine and very proud of it, Walter would later be described as an alcoholic, often manic-depressive. Walter, in fact, would admit that he had several times voluntarily committed himself for treatment of severe depression. Jack Scott later claimed Walter had worked as a hit man for the CIA and other U. S. spy agencies—a charge that not only fed the slew of rumors around Walter but unleashed speculation as to why Jack chose his brother, of all people, to confide in. (*Rolling Stone* claimed Jack had spilled the story of his SLA adventures trying to match his brother's tales of derring-do during an all-night drunk in Las Vegas.) Much later, after Walter returned from a long European vacation sponsored by the FBI, the New York *Times* reported that the freshly wounded Walter Scott claimed to have been one of several hundred civilian gunmen, presumably under CIA contract, flown in to Phnom Penh to provide security for the evacuation of the U.S. embassy in Cambodia. Even after Walter was identified as their key witness in the Pennsylvania investigation, the FBI refused to comment on the more exotic rumors surrounding the man.

(Walter implicated his brother, his sister-in-law, and his parents in the federal crime of harboring fugitives, but after he had given the FBI a fresh scent on the SLA, Walter seemed to set out to discredit himself as a prosecution witness. He was quite successful; cunning, neurotic, or confused, Walter made such a public fool of himself that he disabled himself for the witness stand and left the government with no case against the elder Scotts and a much more shaky case against Jack and Micki. Walter did not go to the police for money; at least twice he had tried to tip the FBI to Jack's SLA connection with anonymous phone calls—the calls that had sent the FBI to interview the Scotts in January—claiming no reward. His motives appeared confused and subject to constant change: an embittered mixture of rage, jealousy, patriotism, and sometimes common sense. "Bill and Emily Harris and Patty Hearst, they shoot up people," he told one group of reporters.

(By late spring, when Walter returned from his overseas tour, the Scott connection had become a media sensation, and Walter strutted in the center of the storm. First he appeared to reporters in "protective custody" with an FBI escort, cursing brother Jack: "That son of a bitch went and got my sixty-six-year-old mother and father involved in a commission of a crime. . . ." Weeks later he was with Jack and Micki denouncing the FBI for "incompetence" and "harassment"—and retracting all previous charges he had made against his brother. He played the headlines like a trampoline, bouncing back and forth from the FBI to his family. With his hyperkinetic flip-flops, Walter was a one-man carnival. He wanted to serve two conflicting loyalties—and, in the end, he may have managed it, but only by bringing the scorn and ridicule of both upon himself.)

Whatever his difficulties as a court witness, Walter Scott had given the FBI their first good lead on the SLA in a long seven months. The SLA trail had seemed stone cold. Agents had investigated all leads, checked out each of several thousand "sightings"—all to no avail. The case files had been checked and rechecked, and seemed perpetually sterile. Now the investigation was localized again, in California, and the FBI had two fresh leads: Jack Scott (and his friends, and associates) and Wendy Yoshimura. Walter had not known about Wendy Yoshimura on the farm, but FBI technicians, when they finally searched the farmhouse in late February, found the fingerprints of both Bill Harris (on a discarded piece of broken glass) and Wendy (on a newspaper stuffed beneath a mattress). The FBI's "Patty dogs," flown in from California to identify Tania's scent, yelped at the bed she'd used.

(It was when the San Francisco newspapers headlined the discovery of the farm and the Yoshimura link that the formerly reticent Wendy threw her lot with the SLA. "She was scared, she thought they'd be searching for her in the Bay Area, and she didn't know where else to turn," explained a close friend. Apparently shortly after the Guild robbery, Wendy fled to Sacramento.

(The Harrises had carefully overseen what they thought was a very thorough "wipe down" of the farmhouse before they trekked West. The FBI found Bill's prints on the broken glass in the trash, but the telltale newspaper—the Labor Day issue of the Sullivan County *Democrat,* carried from Jeffersonville when the SLA abandoned the creamery—had a history that became all the more ironic as the Yoshimura lead became the most important clue in the case. "It was really kind of stupid," said a Yoshimura confidant with a grimace. "Wendy had been asleep, and she woke up to find a bug crawling in front of her, on the bed I guess. She had cleaned the whole place, and so she got up to see if she could find where the bug had come from, and she found this hole under the mattress. So she grabbed this newspaper and stuffed it under there to block the hole. And then when they wiped the house down, they never saw it. Can you believe it? All because of a bug!")

Everything seemed to come down at once. The Scotts went underground (whether they were in touch with Sacramento or not is unclear), and then, shortly before 5 P.M. on March 1, Remiro and Little made their breakout bid from the Alameda county jail.

Little and his attorney, John Bain, were in the lawyer's interview room when Bain requested that Remiro be brought in for a joint conference. It was a Saturday; the jail had only four guards on duty. Sheriff's Deputy Lawrence Franks escorted Remiro from his cell, and Duty Sergeant Robert Jensen opened the conference room to let them in. When Franks brought in another chair for Remiro, Little met him at the door, suddenly slashing up with one hand and jabbing a sharpened lead pencil four inches into Franks' throat.

Remiro brushed aside the attorney and jumped the sergeant, slugging Jensen, dazing him, then leaping on top of him to gouge one eye. The four struggled on the floor, a tangle of arms and legs; then Remiro snatched the sergeant's keys and dashed to the nearby jail weapons locker. The other two guards were at the door by now. They shouted to Bain to push the door button to let them in, but Bain, who had not been harmed at all, was off in a corner, screaming for help, seemingly in hysterics. Deputy Franks, the pencil still jutting from his throat, managed to break free of Little and punched the electric door-lock button—and the other two deputies burst in. It was a close thing. Remiro had already found the right key and inserted it into the locker full of loaded guns when he was tackled and overpowered.*

(Jail officials assumed it was an inside job, probably a hostage plot; apparently there was no attempt to check the area around the building for any possible confederates. While the escape attempt was routinely investigated, Remiro and Little were kept un-

---

*A jury found Little and Remiro guilty of the escape and assaults at their trial on those charges held in June, 1976. Already imprisoned for the Foster murder, each received additional prison terms of from five years to life.

der tighter security until their transfer a month later to Sacramento, where the Foster murder trial was held. There, the county courthouse was held under extraordinary armed security. The two SLA soldiers apparently had no hope of a courtroom rescue; for the first month of the trial, both chose to absent themselves from the courtroom and listened to the testimony through an intercom in their cells.)

There was now a full-press SLA hunt again in California—and across the country (Jack Scott, if he hadn't told his brother about Yoshimura, apparently did tell him of several other friends, including Shinnick and Weiner, involved in the SLA refuge East, and they were all rousted by the FBI). Yet even on the night of the Oakland jailbreak attempt, there was another NWLF bombing, damaging three Pacific Gas and Electric (PG&E) transmission towers in the hills above Oakland. Two days later, in San Jose, fifty miles south of Oakland, Steve Soliah got into a car accident—and was painfully if not seriously injured, breaking five ribs. (Soliah would later claim that the Harrises had ordered him and sister Kathy to rent a South Bay safehouse, in San Jose, for the SLA. The accident apparently scuttled the plan to move from Sacramento—if Soliah was telling the truth—but it was only two weeks later, on March 18, when the Harrises quickly abandoned their first Sacramento hideout and temporarily moved to another on Capital Avenue, also in downtown Sacramento.)

A flip of chance, it seems, brought the Sacramento police to "interview" one of the SLA—probably Emily Harris—on the eighteenth. Investigating the unrelated murder of a man beaten to death and robbed in a vacant lot close by the W Street hideout, a detective routinely canvassed the neighborhood for witnesses. A woman answered the cop's knock at the door of the SLA duplex. ("She opened the door only about two inches," he said much later, explaining that he never got a real look at her.) No, she told him, nobody there had seen or heard anything. The detective thanked her and departed, not even bothering to ask her name.

That same afternoon, wearing a nurse's uniform and identifying herself as "Jessica Henderson," Emily Harris rented another tiny $85-a-month utility apartment in an eleven-unit complex at 2728 Capital Avenue. (Neighbors would identify Jim Kilgore and perhaps Bill Harris as living there, along with a seldom-seen and unidentified woman, probably Emily.) And it was only the next day, March 19, that "Art Peterson"—James Kilgore—rented the first of a series of garages in Sacramento that would be used to stash SLA vehicles for "future actions," several already well into planning.

(The FBI would later seize a detailed diagram and surveillance notes—in the handwriting of Patricia Hearst—for the Bank of America branch in Marysville, thirty-five miles north of Sacramento, apparently one of the preliminary surveys the SLA did as they narrowed in on their next robbery target. "There are 2 picture window size openings in the wall separating the work area from the teller area—no glass," jotted Patty, "3 tellers were open during a *busy* period so the 4th Window may never open . . . saw 7 employees, 5 women & 2 men, one young and nervous; manager is fat and Black.")

In the recharged FBI investigation, the Scott lead took first priority and brought an immediate grand jury inquest. The Scotts were potential defendants on harboring charges, but the thrust of the investigation was still directed toward the SLA fugitives. The Scotts had led a public life easy to backtrack, but most of their close friends were radicals hostile to the FBI—and the trail had inherent limitations. Walter Scott had told agents that Jack and Micki had split with the SLA and knew nothing of their whereabouts.

(On March 11 the FBI had independently corroborated this part of Walter's story when they brusquely swept Jay Weiner out of his car in the Oberlin College parking lot to detain and interrogate him. Earlier, on the same day they had subpoenaed the elder Mr. Scott, agents had tried to interview Weiner, and he had refused to talk with them. Now they were no longer polite, and they had a subpoena. "They scared the livin' bejesus out of him," said one friend, and Weiner talked, first to the FBI, then, two days later, to a federal grand jury in Pennsylvania.)

The Scott investigation was one thing, but the second lead from the South Canaan farmhouse, Wendy Yoshimura, was a much more intricate study. Wendy had been underground for nearly three years, with friends and associates unknown, and police intelligence reports indicated—inaccurately, according to Yoshimura's friends—that she traveled in the most secure of political-fugitive circles, with the Weather Underground. (The California attorney general's office reported that Wendy had been known to travel personally with Weather leader Bernardine Dohrn.) Jay Weiner's FBI interrogation had produced one important new clue—he knew that Yoshimura had been using the name "Joan Shimada" underground—but even that, until well into the summer, didn't connect with the FBI circuitry. The Yoshimura link may have been pushed to a back burner—or perhaps the bureau was focusing on trying to trace her (and the SLA) through the Weather Underground—but certainly the leads from Yoshimura's past were not followed up for several months.

A review of the Yoshimura case certainly should have quickly brought up the name of William Brandt, and Brandt's visiting list was a virtual *Who's Who* of SLA associates. Signed in on Brandt's Soledad guest book were Jack Scott, Micki Scott, Jay Weiner, Pat Jean McCarthy, and Kathy Soliah and Jim Kilgore, then well-known to the FBI as two organizers, perhaps the prime movers behind the Bay Area Research Collective, now the SLA propaganda voice in California. But no one seemed to be studying the roots and tentacles of the 1972 case.

Brandt had been something of a loner in Berkeley radical circles before his arrest—street rumor had it that for a time the Revolutionary Army was he alone—but since he had been jailed, his obvious intelligence and articulate politics had made him a popular contact for prison reform .people. He had a lot of visitors. At Soledad Brandt was considered almost a model prisoner; he was a member of the prison bridge club, the choir, the Junior Chamber of Commerce, and the inmate council on higher education. He is described as "very intelligent" by prison officials who, at the time, seemed to look favorably upon his hope for a December, 1975, parole. His political background and the fact that his politics had led to the bomb conviction had been cited as factors when he was twice before denied parole, but in interviews with CDC counselors Brandt swore that his political ideology had "matured" and he no longer advocated violence to seek change. (In confidential interviews, Brandt had admitted to several bombings he had not been charged with but said that none had been designed to kill anyone. He described his younger self as politically naïve, pushed into political violence by peer pressure.)

From Yoshimura to Brandt to Soliah and Company there was a trail like a five-lane interstate. The FBI was neither hasty nor inspired—it would be midsummer before they pressed the Soliah connection (and then the key was a lead on Mary Margaret Turcich, from Wendy's life underground in New Jersey, not from the '72 Revolutionary Army case)—but in its diligent, plodding manner the bureau began to trace back from South Canaan to Berkeley.

The NWLF bombings continued. There were four more bomb-

ings in late March and early April directed against the Pacific Gas
and Electric Company. On March 21 three PG&E towers were
bombed in the Oakland hills, and on March 27 a PG&E substation
in San Jose was bombed—and after the damage was reported as
"slight," the NWLF made a return visit. First, on the twenty-ninth,
they bombed another PG&E installation near Sacramento; then
they went back to San Jose, to the same substation, and on April 8,
exploded five powerful pipe bombs. And there were more communiqués:

> PG&E, if you inhumane dogs won't realize that you're draining
> the lives of poor people, we the People's Forces of the NWLF will
> continue to haunt you parasites. You cause misery and suffering
> to millions of poor people daily as you line your greedy-ass pocket
> with money. Pure and simply blood money! Dogs!

Jack and Micki Scott had stayed "underground" only just shy of
six weeks. On the night of April 8 San Francisco television
viewers received a titillating news scoop that Jack and Micki were
at the very moment en route to Algeria by jetliner. (The report
was picked up nationally. The AP wire service posted its corres-
pondent at the Algiers airport for the night.) The next morning,
the ninth, the Scotts, with their attorney, hosted a surprise press
conference in San Francisco. They issued a statement that reiterated the message they had telephoned to several reporters while
in hiding. Vietnam, Watergate, the economy, and the almost daily
revelations of CIA and FBI illegalities had convinced them that
the U.S. government was morally bankrupt, they said, and thus
made them willing to "struggle alongside all progressive people,"
despite "profound" disagreements.

"Our actions over the past year are completely defensible," they
argued. "If we somehow acted to avert bloodshed and killing, we
certainly find that nothing to apologize for. We want to make
clear that we find the tragic and senseless killing of Marcus Foster
to be morally and politically intolerable—but no more so than the
execution without trial last May of six alleged members of the
SLA in Los Angeles."

It was a position Randolph Hearst thought he might be able to
relate to. Through the Scotts' attorney, Hearst contacted Jack that
afternoon and asked if Jack and Micki would be willing to give a
worried father any information. Scott was willing—or at least intrigued initially—but before he agreed to meet, he played a little
game with Hearst. Scott typed out a three-sentence statement
praising himself and Micki as "non-violent sincere people" who

had helped the SLA for "humanitarian reasons," and he demanded that Hearst issue it as his own before he would meet with him. On the morning of April 11 a front-page story in the *Examiner* quoted the statement as Hearst's personal opinion.* On the night of the twelfth Jack and Micki met Randy for dinner at the luxurious Pacific Heights town house of the Scotts' attorney, Michael Kennedy. Speaking in cryptic unspecifics, Jack assured Hearst that Patty had been in good health when last he'd seen her, and that no, she was not pregnant by Cinque, although she had been using a pregnant stomach as a disguise. Details of whatever else Scott said are unknown, but Hearst was grateful. Events, however, were quickly overtaking Scott's summer reminiscence.

On Monday, April 7, in Sacramento, a car—a 1965 blue Ford Mustang—was stolen from where it was parked only four blocks from the SLA safehouse on T Street. The following night, April 8, the NWLF made its second bomb attack on the San Jose PG&E substation.

The next day, April 9, a very nervous gum-chewing Emily Harris, calling herself Janet White, rented another Sacramento garage for the SLA. The owner, Richard Roller, recalled that "Miss White" had been accompanied by a young man, never introduced, who let her do all the talking. She said she was going to store her mother's car, that she would be dropping it off in a few days. But she also asked—and checked to be sure—if the garage had an electrical outlet. Roller thought that strange, and suspicious. He called an old friend, Sacramento PD Officer James Cooke. Because of the unexplained concern over the electrical outlet, the cop figured he'd perhaps stumbled onto a workshop for an auto-stripping ring. Cooke told Roller to call him again as soon as the young woman brought the car in.

On the night of April 12, at a large drop-in party in Oakland, a guest discovered her purse missing—and with it, the keys to her car. Outside, the car—a 1967 Pontiac Firebird—was also gone. Two days later, on the fourteenth, "Janet White" parked the Firebird—"Mother's car"—in the Sacramento garage. Landlord Roller watched her padlock the door, then drive off with a young man (a different one this time, he noted) in a newly painted Chevy station wagon. He jotted down both the license numbers of the Chevy (the car bought the day after the Guild Savings and Loan

---

*In the *Examiner* version Hearst prefaced the statement with his own phrase; "While I do not necessarily agree with Mr. and Mrs. Scott's political philosophy, I have no reason to believe them to be other than. . . ."

robbery by "Elliott Burton") and the Firebird, and rang up Officer Cooke. Cooke punched the license numbers into the stationwide police computer system and got an instant hit on the Firebird: stolen . . . Oakland . . . April 12. Roller asked what he should do. Nothing, he was told; the police would handle it.

The Sacramento PD put a "loose surveillance" on the garage (passing checks by patrol units) and hoped to catch the gang when they came back to strip the car. They missed. On the evening of April 20 the Firebird was moved and parked overnight on a residential street about a mile from the branch office of the Crocker National Bank in Carmichael, a suburb seven miles out of Sacramento. Early on the morning of April 21, a Monday, it was driven to a shopping-center parking lot, just behind the bank. The Carmichael Crocker branch had just recently begun to open for business at 9 A.M. (as had the Hibernia Bank shortly before the SLA holdup in San Francisco a year before). The trial of Remiro and Little was going into its fourth week at the Sacramento county courthouse.

At precisely 9 A.M. the bank doors opened. A minute later Mrs. Myrna Opsahl, forty-two, mother of four teenage sons, got out of a car and, with two women friends, walked across the bank parking lot to enter. The three women were all members of the Carmichael Seventh-day Adventist Church and had volunteered to deposit the weekend church collections for their pastor. Mrs. Opsahl was carrying a small plug-in adding machine with both hands.

One of the women noticed four figures ducking through a large hole in the cyclone fence separating the shopping center from the bank lot. She noticed, with mild curiosity, that all four seemed to be wearing bulky, heavy coats—"hunting clothing," as she described it later—and wool knit caps. Odd attire, she thought, for such a warm, though cloudy, spring day.

One of the church volunteers, the eldest of the three, held the door for Mrs. Opsahl and her other friend. The four others had walked up just behind them. The woman glanced toward them. The first of the four, Mike Bortin, said Patty, reached out and grabbed the door, holding it for her to enter. Surprised and pleased at the courtesy, she nodded, smiled and said, "Thank you," as she bustled past him and into the bank.

It was but a long instant later—now in the bank—she heard a harsh, woman's voice behind her shout out, *"Everybody hit the floor. . . . Move!"*

All three of the church ladies spun around, shocked, to stare at the four bandits who had followed them inside. The robbers—three men and a woman, it seemed—were now masked. Each held a gun. Three were wearing ski masks; the woman had a knit watch cap pulled low on her forehead and a green scarf covering her mouth and nose, cowboy-style.

The woman, the apparent leader, screamed at them again, adding curses and obscenities. Mrs. Opsahl jerked in a quick turn, flustered. Her friends thought she was trying to put the adding machine down on a counter. She never got the chance. The woman—who still stood by the door as the others had fanned out—swung her sawed-off shotgun slightly to the right to cover Mrs. Opsahl's sudden movement, her finger tightened on the trigger, there was an explosion, and Myrna Opsahl flipped backward and fell. The full load of heavy buckshot had caught her in the stomach and left torso, ripped open her body, lifted her slightly and tossed her to the floor like a bleeding rag doll. "I saw the pellets hit her side," the elder churchwoman recalled, "and I just stood there, horrified. . . ." The sudden bloodshed left everyone paralyzed for a moment; then a man shouted, *"Get your noses to the carpet!"* Mechanically, the bank employees and customers lowered themselves to the floor.

Obviously according to plan, three of the robbers spread out in the lobby and took positions to cover the people on the floor while the fourth—a short man with a pistol, dressed all in Navy blue—vaulted the counter and began looting the cash drawers. In a husky phony-Southern drawl he demanded of a clerk, *"Where are the traveler's checks?"* When they were pointed out, he stuffed them, with the cash (some $15,000), into a blue cloth tote bag with a white drawstring. No one went near the fallen woman, who lay bleeding profusely. When several of the men and women face-down on the carpet lifted their heads, craning to see if Mrs. Opsahl was alive, one, perhaps two, of the bandits standing guard kicked at them and growled, *"Keep down!"*

The woman with the green scarf over her face kept glancing at her wristwatch, giving a countdown aloud: "One minute and thirty seconds . . . one minute and forty seconds . . . two minutes. . . ." At the three-minute count she shouted out, *"Time's up . . . let's get out of here!"* The four fled through the door they had entered—at least one spritely leaping over the body of Myrna Opsahl.

Just an instant before the robbers burst from the bank, a blue Ford Mustang parked directly across the street drove off quickly. The manager of a nearby variety store had noticed the driver earlier, dressed so strangely in a bulky, heavy jacket, pacing back and forth beside the car. "He was either mumbling to himself or talking into some type of walkie-talkie," the man recalled. He also remembered, as did several other witnesses, the stolen license plates on the Mustang—916-LBJ. (It was perhaps the most recognizable set of plates in Sacramento; the local telephone area code is 916, and who could forget LBJ?)

Sheriff's cars were already on their way. A woman walking past the bank had glanced inside, seen guns and masked bandits, and dashed to the corner gas station to call the alarm.

The robbers had fled through the bank parking lot, back through the hole in the fence, leaving a trail of fifteen 9-mm bullets which spilled as they ran. From a distance, witnesses outside saw them unmask as they tumbled into the green-and-black Firebird which sped off moments later. The bank had no security cameras, and witness reports were confusing: Three men? Four men? Four men and a woman? Reasons why became more apparent a year later when the convicted Patricia Hearst finally told the FBI of her own role in the murder–bank robbery and identified the seven other persons she said had been involved.

According to Patty's account, Bill Harris, with an automatic rifle, had been with Steve Soliah in the backup car, the LBJ-plated Mustang across the street, although witnesses noted only one man. The four robbers inside, said Patty, had been Michael Bortin, Jim Kilgore, Emily Harris, and Kathleen Soliah.* Emily had fired the first fatal shotgun blast—by accident, said Patty. Emily and Mike Bortin both wore false mustaches, and the plan was for both Emily and Kathy Soliah to be mistaken for men. Emily's voice, despite its hoarse and harsh inflection, sounded feminine; but Kathy Soliah, consummate actress, had fooled all the witnesses.

Hearst and Wendy Yoshimura had been assigned to drive the "switch cars," said Patty. When Bill Harris and Steve Soliah abandoned their Mustang in an apartment-complex garage about two miles from the bank, Patty said Yoshimura, wearing a blond wig, picked them up in a rented Pinto. Patty was parked, in a rented VW van, by a funeral home only blocks from the bank. When the escaping Firebird, with Bortin at the wheel, passed her, she pulled out and followed in the van. A mile from the bank, the Firebird pulled over and the other four scrambled into Patty's van. One of them was shouting, "Go! Go! *Go!*" Patty recalled.

The VW headed for the T Street safe house in Sacramento, where they were to meet the other three. Kathy Soliah was sputtering something to the effect that a "woman teller" had been

---

*Bortin denied all charges.

shot, said Patty, and Patty asked how it happened and who did it.

"I did," said Emily. "Let's not talk about it."

"Maybe the woman will live," Kathy said hopefully.

"No," replied Kilgore. "I looked at her."

An ambulance was then rushing Mrs. Myrna Lee Opsahl to Carmichael American River Hospital, where Dr. Trygye Opsahl, the woman's husband, worked as a staff surgeon. The emergency room frantically paged Dr. Opsahl when the woman was identified, but his wife was dead before he could reach her bedside.

All of the Symbionese had returned safely to the safe house, said Patty, but everyone was upset as they listened to the radio reports. Bortin said angrily that *he* should have been in charge of the assault team, recalled Patty; that Emily, who had been "operations officer" for the heist, was "nervous and incompetent." Kilgore sullenly agreed; he drew a diagram for Patty and explained what the others already knew: When the shot was fired, Jim had already moved around behind the customers, into Emily's line of fire. "If it hadn't been for good ol' Myrna," Bill Harris told Patty, "One of our comrades would be dead; she got all the buckshot."

Teko snapped the expended shell casing out of Emily's shotgun and held it up for the others to see. "This is the murder round," he told them. And now, he said, all of them would be wanted for murder—"a gas chamber offense." Harris took the cartridge and went out. When he returned a short while later, he said he had buried it under a tree near the duck pond in Sacramento's McKinley Park.

Through the afternoon they listened to the constant radio reports: the early obits for Mrs. Opsahl; random details from the police, the FBI; there was no mention of the SLA; sheriff's cruisers found one getaway car, then two; a pregnant teller had been kicked; the Firebird linked to the rented garage . . . Myrna Lee Opsahl . . . Opsahl . . . Opsahl. . . . After one report, Patty remembers Kathy Soliah's turning to Emily and quietly saying how badly she felt for her; that she knew how much it must bother her.

Emily tried to explain what had happened. "The safety must have slipped," she said; the trigger lock on the shotgun must have accidentally been snapped off. Then she lashed out angrily: "It didn't matter anyway," she told the others. "The woman who was killed was a bourgeois pig—her husband was a doctor!" An expendable member of an expendable class.

On the LBJ Mustang, police found two fingerprints not

identified until months later. (On the back side of the stolen rear plate there was one print from Steve Soliah; on the back side of the front plate, another, from Jim Kilgore. With no suspects and only the two individual prints, there was no way of matching the fingerprints, even against prints on file.) There was no overt connection to the SLA. No flags, fireworks, or revolutionary pronouncements from the underground. The commando style and the fact that a woman had seemingly led the robbers did spur speculation about the SLA, but with no communiqué and the sheriff's investigators stating flatly that they had "no evidence whatsoever" to support an SLA theory, the Symbionese faded as suspects—at least in the public eye. Privately, both the FBI and the locals still considered the SLA a strong possibility, but the Sacramento Sheriff's Department, fearing a panicky public response, decided to underplay the SLA possibility.

When the getaway Firebird was identified as the stolen car the Sacramento police had staked out so loosely a week before, there was a statewide alert for the tan Chevy station wagon Richard Roller had seen his erstwhile tenant drive off in. Roller, as conscientious as he was curious, had noted the car's license plate—TDC-315—but could make no identification of the woman. The registered owner, "Elliott Burton," was nonexistent.

A day or so after the robbery, Patty told the FBI, the Chevy wagon was quietly stored in the empty Sacramento garage "Art Peterson," Kilgore, had rented a month before. The car gathered dust, undisturbed for nearly a year, until Patty's FBI confessions gave federal agents a map to the hideaway garage. Month after month, the $15 rent had been promptly paid by mail. Even after the Harrises and Patty Hearst were arrested, in September of 1975, the rent kept coming in—right through the Hearst trial, until March of 1976. From within the much sought tan Chevy, FBI technicians lifted nine fingerprints of Steven Soliah's.

24

The New World Liberation Front

IT was in the aftermath of the Carmichael bank robbery that the SLA went into its greatest period of turmoil (although in none of the versions that have been given of those troubles has the murder of Mrs. Opsahl been a major factor). It was just after the April bank robbery that the SLA-Berkeley alliance began to fall apart and a feminist rebellion among the women led them to separate themselves from the men. Within a couple of weeks Emily had stalked out on Bill in Sacramento, and within a month the whole operation had moved down to San Francisco—apparently because that was where Emily and the other women decided to base *their* collective.

Tensions seemed to explode on several levels. General Teko's aspirations to remain the undisputed commander in chief of the SLA—and the tension that this set up with his SLA underling, Emily—were part of the problem. Tactics were another; according to friends of both Yoshimura and Steve Soliah, the Harrises were still committed to political assassination as a terrorist weapon, and the Berkeley recruits were fitfully coming to the decision that however willing they were to be an NWLF bombing team, they would *not* support assassinations à la Foster.

Steve Soliah offered one version of what happened in court testimony one year later (when he was tried for, and acquitted,* of

*Steven Soliah was acquitted of the Carmichael bank robbery charge on April 27, 1976, by a Sacramento federal court jury which weighed four weeks of testimony. FBI investigators had linked Soliah to the crime both through fingerprints (found on two getaway cars used by the SLA in the heist) and eyewitness identification—two tellers picked out his photo as one of the bandits *inside* the bank. Soliah pleaded not guilty, asserting he had done nothing more criminal than help the SLA fugitives hide from police. Even before Soliah's trial began, U.S. Attorney Dwayne Keyes was told by Patricia Hearst—in the first of her "discussions" with government agents—that the eyewitnesses were wrong. Soliah, the Carmichael robbery), and he gave another, more detailed account in his interviews with *Rolling Stone* for the article published just after his trial jury had been chosen. Soliah sought to blame the strain among the group solely on Bill Harris' monomania for being head honcho. Soliah described Harris as a sort of Symbionese Captain Queeg, a petty martinet—foot stamping, throwing tantrums, giving Patty a black eye in a squabble over wording in the manuscript, and screaming running-dog-lackey-type curses at anyone disagreeing with him.

One account he gives of a fight between Tania and Teko had Bill Harris screaming. "You little bitch. What do you know about the struggle of the people—you grew up in a fucking mansion." To which Patty spat back, "Kiss my cunt, Adolf!"

With Emily, said *Rolling Stone*/Soliah, General Teko was no more lenient. At one point (apparently about the time of Carmichael), Teko was trying to reestablish his authority, over his wife as well as his army. For one of the still-regular gun practice sessions, Emily wanted to use a favorite rifle, but Bill demanded she take another. When Emily said she was going to take the gun *she* wanted, Teko "tried to kick her," reported *Stone*/Soliah. Emily, in turn, "jumped on him and pounded away on his back."

Two weeks or so after Carmichael, Emily had walked out on Bill, moving south to bed and board in Berkeley with Steve Soliah. Possibly as some test of nonmonogamous therapy, Patty moved back to provide solace for Bill. But sex between Tania and Teko was "brief and mechanical," explained *Stone*/Soliah. (Patty later told the FBI Harris was "often impotent.") She stayed only a week with him, both of them bitching—before Patty moved to San

---

said Ms. Hearst, had not been in the bank, rather, she explained, he had been across the street acting as a lookout.

Although Patty was willing to testify against her former comrade and lover, Keyes declined to put her on the stand and instead based his case on the two "eyewitnesses." The tellers' identification of Soliah during the trial, however, was more than slightly blunted when the defense produced a surprise witness—a customer who had happened into the bank in the midst of the holdup who bore an amazing resemblance to Soliah. The government's case was further weakened when Soliah's longtime girlfriend Emily Toback gave testimony supporting his claimed alibi that he had been ninety miles away, at Toback's San Francisco apartment, at the time of the robbery. (Ms. Toback's tale did not stand up long; a check of records showed she had been visiting a Folsom prison inmate at the moment the crime in Carmichael was occurring and could not possibly have known Soliah's actual whereabouts at that hour. By the time Toback's testimony was exposed as a lie, however, the jury had already begun its deliberations.)

Francisco with Wendy Yoshimura. Bill Harris then arranged a meeting with Soliah to tell him he didn't like Steve sleeping with his wife, and Steve, finding the affair "too uncomfortable for his easy-going nature," explained *Stone,* asked Emily to move out. But Emily wasn't one to be pushed, certainly not back with Bill, so, in late May, she moved in with Wendy and Patty to form an SLA women's collective. The women then "assigned" Bill Harris, Steve Soliah, and Jim Kilgore to live in another San Francisco apartment. Emily, said *Stone*/Soliah, "urged them to convene their own meetings with the other men in the group."

Now that is Steve Soliah's version, and it apparently omits more than a few people in all the dizzy bed shuffling. At some point in all this, according to Patty's tale to the FBI, Kathy Soliah and Emily Harris became lovers. And then with Kathy and Jim Kilgore again broken up, Wendy Yoshimura and Jim became lovers. And then a couple of weeks after the women organized their collective, Steve Soliah and Patty resumed their romance. For all that and more, it was a busy month of May.

On May 1 the NWLF bombed a California Department of Corrections parole office in Sacramento. On May 9 another NWLF bomb exploded in a Berkeley PG&E office building (a block from the Berkeley PD). On May 19 an NWLF device destroyed a shack on the prison guards' rifle range just outside the walls of San Quentin. And there was a new recruit: Bonnie Wilder, twenty-eight, an old high school chum and close friend of Kathy Soliah. Bonnie apparently enlisted in April (although Patty said she didn't meet her until May). In late April she moved from her Alcatraz Street address in Oakland to an unknown location, refusing to give friends or family her new address, although she continued working as a clerk for an Oakland construction company until midsummer. On June 6, however, Wilder applied to become a woman police officer in Oakland. (Her police application was approved, and Ms. Wilder was scheduled to take a written test on September 16. She did not appear. Two days later she was a fugitive; when the Harrises were arrested, her personal papers and effects were found in their apartment.) The SLA long-held fantasy plan for an "inside man" at police headquarters had apparently been attempted—and it was only an ironic measure of the evolution among the Symbionese that the inside man was to have been a policewoman.

Despite all the hoopla in the media, the FBI had allowed Jack and Micki Scott quietly to withdraw to Portland. Although the

Pennsylvania grand jury was still investigating, there were no indictments yet. Jack, however, was considering ways to collect on his new reputation, searching for an author to ghost-write a Scott-SLA memoir, using his material and sharing the profits, but allowing Jack to remain disassociated from the published book for legal protection. According to Scott business associates involved in arranging the deal, Jack had propositioned the team of *Rolling Stone* reporters in early April, shortly after he emerged publicly from hiding. Before the project got under way, however, in early May, Scott received word from Bill Harris in Sacramento, offering an even more lucrative book project: the manuscript Patty and the Harrises had been working on since Scott's SLA summer the year before. An SLA manuscript and the Tania Interview; Patty's own story.

The SLA needed someone to front for them to publishers (and had apparently been impressed by Scott's refusal to talk to the FBI), and Jack Scott, despite his "principled" and "profound" disagreements with the Symbionese, was sorely tempted by the fifty-fifty royalty split Teko offered. (Scott said later he had spent nearly $20,000 helping the SLA.) In June, Scott flew to New York and contacted editors at McGraw-Hill and Doubleday, two major publishing firms, and sounded out terms for an SLA self-portrait. He was agreeably surprised; a legitimate SLA manuscript partially written by Patty Hearst could bring several hundred thousand dollars.

Scott returned to the Bay Area very excited at his new prospects—only to get word from an SLA messenger (perhaps Pat Jean McCarthy, whose car Scott occasionally borrowed, according to FBI) that there were some internal problems among the group. There would be no manuscript soon, possibly not at all.

Depressed and angry, Jack decided again to do his own book. He recontacted the New York publishers, particularly McGraw-Hill, and pressed for a contract for himself (secretly) and Kohn and Weir (publicly) to do an SLA memoir. His wife, Micki—still sympathetic to the fugitives and upset at Jack's mood and the security threat such a book might be to the SLA—flew off to Portland, leaving Jack alone in Berkeley.

Through the end of May and most of June there were no further NWLF bombings, then at the end of the month there were two in the Bay Area. On June 27 the New World Liberation Front bombed the Alameda offices of the U.S. Bureau of Indian Affairs. Two days later gasoline bombs were thrown into the backyard of a suburban Piedmont home owned by George Jamieson, a partner in the Rhodes-Jamieson Construction firm in Oakland. Then, all through July, the group was dormant; it was the longest period since the return to California in which there had been no SLA-NWLF attacks. Internal problems absorbed their attention, then there was a flash of danger as the FBI nipped too close.

The male SLA collective had held together for only a couple of weeks, according to *Stone*/Soliah. By mid-June Bill Harris was living alone, probably at a Lyon Street San Francisco apartment; Jim Kilgore had apparently moved back to his old apartment in Daly City, and Steve Soliah was living either with Jim or at the Berkeley commune in which he had kept a rented room. The women's collective—Wendy, Patty, Emily, probably Kathy Soliah, and perhaps Jo Soliah and Bonnie Wilder—was still together, but the sexual "separatism" that had been the political "line" among the women in May had apparently been compromised. Emily and Kathy Soliah had begun their affair, and perhaps in reaction, Jim Kilgore had become involved with Yoshimura and Patty had taken up again with Steve.

It was a confusing period. According to *Rolling Stone,* the rest of the group had "ostracized" Bill Harris, and Emily was working desperately to try to mediate between Bill and the Berkeley group. Yet, according to Yoshimura, Harris was still able to order a purge sometime over the summer, kicking out Pat Jean McCarthy, putting Mike Bortin on "probation," then kicking him out, too. Whether General Teko still had any authority among the group is unclear—Wendy wrote Willie Brandt that even she "was once thrown out," but that obviously didn't disassociate her from the group. (In fact, it may have been that Bill, and Bill alone, was the SLA—and the rest of the group had independently taken over the NWLF operation.)

The dispute was apparently multisided: There was General Teko's macho style of leadership, and there was his commitment to terrorism, political murder. Harris, said *Stone*/Soliah, felt the group should kill cops, "because the police were to blame for the six deaths in Los Angeles and because he was convinced the silver badge was a symbol for black rage." The Revolution would begin in the ghettos, argued Harris; the fuse just needed the right spark.

Bill—and apparently Emily, too—still clung to what had been perhaps the fundamental assumption that had galvanized the original SLA. White Americans were, in Bill Harris' phrase, the "racist punks of the world"—white America was too racist and corrupt to be saved; it could only be destroyed. The "revolutionary" aspect of both the white SLA and the white New Left of the sixties had been defined not by their "class origins," but by their *rejection* of their middle-class status. It was a conundrum that had plagued all their attempts to apply Marxist class-war theory to the American reality. The SLA (as the Weathermen SDS group did in 1969) had ducked the question by equating their isolation with purity—they, a tiny group of white outlaws, were like renegades in Nazi Germany. The white nation had to be destroyed, and they—as "representatives" of the oppressed nonwhites—would begin the process. It was the only attitude that could justify random terrorism in a nation where the white middle-class majority was obviously not interested in revolution. It was a creed burdened with more than a little self-hate. (Even the Weather Underground had recanted with a new doctrine in 1971 that "reclaimed" the white society from which they had sprung and shifted from tactics of terrorist murder to "armed propaganda" bombings similar to the NWLF campaign.) Harris apparently couldn't turn his back on the code of Cin and the original SLA— and the Berkeley "second team" brought the doubts of the seventies to bear on the sixties certainty of the SLA.

But there was no blinding flash of illumination. Several of the people Steve Soliah would later credit as arguing most strongly against the terrorist murders the Harrises advocated were— according to Patty's confessions to the FBI—themselves deeply involved in kill plots over the summer of 1975. Among the documents seized by police when the Harrises were arrested was a detailed diagram and map—drawn and labeled by Patty—of a small San Francisco coffee shop called Miz Brown's, located in the city's Richmond District and frequented by police officers off-duty and on meal breaks. Patty told the FBI that at one point the group considered a raid in which SLA commandos would burst in with "machine guns," line up the cops, and shoot them down in cold blood. Just when the plot was hatched, how it was justified, who vetoed it and why is unclear, but certainly it was a long way from that type of thinking to the letter Yoshimura wrote in September spelling out a critique of the Harrises' terrorist politics. (Even Soliah admitted to *Rolling Stone,* in a rather spectacular understatement, that the group had on occasion "equivocated" on the question of terrorism.)

Despite Miz Brown's, however, the fact remains that the NWLF bombers carefully avoided injuring people, and by September Wendy was scornfully separating the Harrises from the rest of the group as "doctrinaire Marighelaists"—advocates of terrorism as an end in itself, independent of politics and social realities. She and the others had been misled for a while, she wrote Willie Brandt, but "we've come to the conclusion that we do in fact disagree politically very drastically" with the Harrises. "These people are totally unable to check out the objective situation and deal with it," Wendy wrote. "They simply do not know how to take a theory and apply it to the reality that exists."

They never went beyond where the New Left dropped off; instead, seemingly oblivious to the past, they plowed up old theory, discovering the wheel again and again, reliving the past rather than resolving it. Even the move into the sexual stockades and the new feminist critique of the group seemed part of an inexorable logic that had them programmed to repeat the past. Like so many of the feminist collectives of the New Left, confronting sexism within the group led to sexual separatism, which led to experimentation with lesbianism (Kathy and Emily), which led into a whole dynamic that turned back upon the male leader. It had all happened before.

There is no way precisely to date SLA documents later seized by the FBI, but it seems certain that the "feminist revisions" of the SLA history and dogma were written during this period. There was an extensive collection of notes, essays, and manuscript sections—many in the handwriting of Patricia Hearst—that came out of the women's collective, but they seem to have a logical progression and illustrate the unfolding of a new SLA dogma.

At first there was the attack on monogamy. "We began to destroy the attitudes that had made us think we *had* to be monogamous," wrote Patty in one essay, "fear and passivity, the false sense of security, jealousy, and power trips." But trying to restructure relationships by changing only the form, not the process, was apparently unsuccessful. Despite all their efforts, a truly liberated feminism was difficult to find within themselves, so they turned their focus to the group: ". . . breaking down traditional sex roles and establishing recognized women's leadership as a group/class within the cell [was] one of the most difficult and longest struggles. Because like racism, sexism is a foundation of capitalist oppression . . . "

It was a formula that married the personal and the political: Bad psychology is a product of sexism, sexism is a function of monogamy, monogamy is "class behavior" between men and women, class behavior is governed by economics, and American economics is capitalism. Ergo, if people are unhappy, it's because they have been corrupted by capitalism. Even in the text, Patty admitted, "It all sounds too simple the way it's been run down. . . ." It was Marx out of context. Marx had argued that the social structure of the modern family had become a "reproductive" system to produce laborers for industrial work. It probably is true in a sense, but to take the theory stark literally, to assume economics governs the hormones, is to blink at everyday reality; to deny Freud to salute Marx. But the feminist theory was even more productive for the SLA. The women, among themselves, finally declared a vanguard, the seed carriers for the revolution:

> Out of the Women's Movement we see emerging the potential leadership of white people in the coming revolutionary struggle. Throughout the past ten years among white people, women have shown consistently the most initiative and creativeness. They have effectively united the personal with the political, a crucial aspect to revolution in a culturally alienated and economically unbalanced society.

In the language of "vanguard theory," they declared sexism the *primary contradiction,* the "basic form of oppression": ". . . the freedom of women equals the freedom of all people because it ends the basic power imbalance in human relationships, which is the sanctioned domination of one-half of the people (women) by the other half (men)."

An analysis at last. There was something here of the welcome for the girl Wendy among the lost boys on Peter Pan's island: *"We have a mother. At last we have a mother."*

> As oppressed people, women have a real stake in revolution (much more than white men) and can, therefore, better identify with and understand Third World and class struggles. Although the pig media characterizes the Women's Movement as white and middle-class, and, to a great extent it is, we consider Feminist Revolution to be a unifying platform for all races and classes of women.
>
> It is a basis for fighting closely with groups who have other primary focuses of oppression. We fully understand that if we fight a revolution in this country we may gain a socialist economy and abolish racism and classism but unless women push, shove, and

fight like hell for a Feminist Revolution, sexism could very well flourish after that revolution. . . .

Feminist Revolution means (a) freedom and self-determination for all women, (b) cultural and economic (socialist) revolution, and (c) recognizing the need for armed struggle to win a revolutionary war.

In late June a family reunion in Palo Alto, just south of San Francisco, brought Martin and Elsie Soliah north from Palmdale to see the relatives and their kids. Kathy, Steve, and Josephine arrived together and joined in the laughing and joking. Josephine talked of her teller's job at a Wells Fargo Bank branch. Steve said he was still recovering from the rib injuries suffered in the auto accident in March, but he was planning to go back to work painting within days. Kathy said she was working, too, another stint as a waitress, but the tips were good. An uncle asked the name of the restaurant, saying he would like to drop by, but Kathy refused to give it. It was odd, but she joked her way past it. Late in the evening Kathy took her father aside. "We've always been a close family," recalled Martin later, "but not one that shows our affections with a lot of kissing. Hugs, yes. But that day Kathy came up, put her arms around me, kissed me full on the lips, and said, 'I love you, Dad. I love you so much.' It was," the father said, "the first time she'd ever done that."

The elder Soliahs drove home to Palmdale feeling "more in touch with the kids—Kathy especially—than we had in years," said Martin. A week or so later, "Jo telephoned. She said she had quit her job and that she and Kathy were moving into a new place together, an apartment house in San Francisco." Josephine gave them the address—625 Post Street—and said she would let them know the telephone number soon. She never did, and that caused the parents some mild concern. Of the three, Jo had always been the most dependable, the one who regularly called, who always wrote home.

On June 29 two part-time deputies with the San Mateo County Sheriff's Department were on rescue patrol along Highway One, the coast road that winds down the Peninsula south of San Francisco. It was a beautiful, sunny, almost cloudless day—one of the "high people-density" days that had climbers, swimmers, and city-boy hoofers scattered all over the beaches and along the coastal cliffs. About 5:30 the two deputies were driving past a stretch of cliff called Devil's Slide when they spotted a man and a woman be-

ginning the rugged climb up the slide from Gray Whale Cove
beach. The rescue team pulled over. It was too late to stop them;
the deputies just watched the couple's progress. They had seen
the climb attempted before, but only skilled and experienced
climbers usually made it. These people weren't climbers.

Midway up, 200 feet above the rocky shoreline, now obviously
exhausted, the couple was stuck. Up was out of the question;
backing down even more dangerous. The rescue team moved in
with gear.

Shouting to get the couple's attention, one deputy slung down a
line. It was quickly grabbed. Following the shouted orders from
the deputies, each looped the rope around them and then—one at
a time—the rescue team pull-walked them up the cliff. The girl
was first. One deputy checked her out for injury or shock. She
seemed okay, he recalled, but still scared. Understandably; it had
been a close thing. When they pulled the man up, a tall sandy-
haired fellow, he too seemed "shaken but all right."

Devil's Slide is one of the posted danger areas along the San
Mateo coast, and it's a misdemeanor—as well as dangerous—to ignore the signs and climb. But arrests are very rare. When the rescue squad had to come in, usually the culprits have been frightened enough to learn a lesson. These two looked worried enough.
The man identified himself as Victor Silva; the girl Nancy Ann
Silva, his wife. Both twenty-six, out for the day from San Francisco. One of the deputies gave them the standard warning lecture;
then they were allowed to go. They did, quickly.

The deputies watched them drive off, noting the time on the
brief rescue report they filed. It was six o'clock. The rescue team
returned to patrol status. Neither of the deputies ever suspected
that for half an hour Tania of the SLA, and a friend and comrade, Steve Soliah, had been in the custody of the law.

It was early July, and whatever was happening internally
among the "new team," the fates were about to deliver a new twist
to the FBI's investigation—a turn that pivoted on Jack Scott's increased frustration and sliding fortunes. Scott's initial advances to
McGraw-Hill had been well received at first, but when the publisher offered $125,000 for an insider's SLA manuscript, Jack put
up a fuss and demanded $300,000. Confronted by a greedy and
an increasingly agitated prime source who was not willing to put
his name to the book, McGraw-Hill began to rethink its proposal.
They had been burned badly on Clifford Irving's Howard
Hughes book hoax, and they did not want to get caught again. On

reflection, McGraw-Hill backed out entirely. Scott was nearly broke, desperate, and—according to *Stone*—increasingly swayed by a perverse and angry bitterness that focused more on the Hearst family than the SLA. If anyone owed him something, he felt, it was Randolph Hearst, whose bratty daughter he had hid from trigger-happy police while she played revolutionary.

Scott decided to play a daring and risky new card. His apparently regular discussion with his SLA contact had informed him that Patty was showing some sort of independence, defining herself as "revolutionary feminist," and balking at General Teko's military regimen; not openly defiant, but now critical of the SLA tradition of macho militarism. Scott was told (again, according to *Stone*) that Patty had even talked of trying to visit secretly her parents and sister. With this new information, Scott made an appointment to meet Randolph Hearst again. If Patty wanted to see her parents, her family certainly wanted to see her. And Scott thought it was a deal he could perhaps cash in on. There was even the possibility that the Hearsts could arrange something to keep Patty out of jail; perhaps Tania could go public. Playing with these possibilities (and without checking with Patty, and ignorant of the Carmichael killing), Jack Scott met Randolph and Catherine Hearst for dinner at the Señor Pico, a well-appointed San Francisco restaurant, on July 11. There, and into the early-morning hours, at the Hearsts' Nob Hill apartment, Randolph listened to Scott trying to edge a corner on what was obviously a proposition for Patty's coming out.

Scott was interested in money—a lump sum for his "expenses" and legal fees—according to *Stone*, perhaps a long-term contract as a sports columnist for the Hearst papers. Something that would not stink of a sale, but a deal nonetheless. According to the Hearsts, Scott was talking in terms of making an "appeal" for Patty's surrender—but at the same time making it clear he had a way of contacting the SLA and Patty. Randy was interested in talking out the possibilities, but Catherine had just had one too many "revolutionaries" trying to collect a capitalist buck with an offer to contact Patty. Scott left with a vague proposal hanging in the air, a "suggestion" that if Catherine resigned from her post as a UC regent, Scott could get to Patty. "I'd do anything for Patty," said Catherine the next day, but Scott had become just another radical trying to get money, playing his own angle. Could he really be speaking for Patty? For the SLA? "It is a very sticky proposition," she decided, and Scott a rather slimy character.

The FBI had watched with interest as Scott came out of the background to huddle with the Hearsts. The following day agents visited Nob Hill and asked Catherine what had happened. She told them. And yes, she said, Scott seemed to imply he had recently been in touch with the SLA. Later the same day Los Angeles *Times* reporter Jerry Belcher—a veteran on the Hearst case who had only recently switched to the *Times* from Hearst's *Examiner*—called Catherine at home to check a tip he had received on the Scott offer. The next day the Sunday *Times* carried the explosive exclusive quoting Catherine's version of the meeting. Mrs. Hearst said she would resign if she were sure Scott "was really in touch with Patty, and that any of these things would affect her one way or another." But after a year of this, how could she be sure of anything? It put her "in a difficult position," she said. "It's really a sticky one. . . ."

If Catherine felt she was in an awkward position, Jack Scott was suddenly pushed into an absolutely untenable one. Catherine had been diplomatic enough not to mention Scott's open palm, but Scott's "secret" meeting with the Hearsts was now slugged under headlines on page 1 across the nation. Scott was scared. General Teko would not take kindly to unauthorized negotiations; in fact, he might have a violent reaction. Scott vehemently denied making any offer and frantically demanded that Randolph Hearst publicly do the same. Without a blink, the following day's papers quoted Hearst contradicting Mrs. Hearst.

Catherine Hearst's estimation of Scott—and her report that Scott had a line to the SLA—kicked a nerve at the FBI. Agents had been lagging on the Scott investigation; they had concluded that it was a cold trail with an interesting past, useless for locating the SLA's current whereabouts. Now they wanted to look again more closely at Scott; and Scott and Yoshimura; and Brandt—and all those other names that once seemed peripheral. But first they tried it the easy way. If Scott was for sale, they had a bid. Within a week after the dinner at the Señor Pico, the FBI sent brother Walter to see Jack with a $200,000 offer. Jack, reportedly both frightened and genuinely insulted, turned them down cold.

In the field the FBI's new interest in the Scott-Brandt connection produced a more interesting result. Right after the Scott-Hearst talk hit the headlines, people began to disappear. "That was the significant thing," explained a senior FBI investigator. Working from Brandt's visiting list, "we started coming up with names of people who we felt could help us, really help us, and we

couldn't find them." Others, like Bonnie Wilder, who were not being sought by the FBI were also moving for deeper cover. Two
days after the Scott story broke, on July 15, Wilder—the prospective Oakland policewoman—quit her job at the construction company and dropped out of sight. The same day, or perhaps the day
before, Kathleen Soliah, who was working as a waitress at the
Plate of Brasse restaurant in San Francisco's posh Sir Francis
Drake Hotel—using the alias "Kathleen Anger"—didn't show up
for work. She didn't call in, and she never claimed the paycheck
due her; she just disappeared.

Brushing over all the Scott connections again, the East Coast
Scott-SLA investigators came in with a near bull's-eye. Scott's
friend Jay Weiner had given the FBI the alias Wendy Yoshimura
had used during her first two years underground—Joan Shimada—back in March. FBI agents had tried to check it out, but made
little headway, although they did find that "Shimada" had a New
Jersey car registration. There was an SLA bulletin on the car, and
agents traced down the registered address, but it added little to
the case file. Now, however, agents rechecked the registration and
discovered "Joan Shimada" had sold the car, apparently in New
Jersey, to Cathy Turcich—younger sister of Mary Margaret Tur-
chich, Wendy Yoshimura's friend and former San Francisco
roommate, who was now working with Kathy Soliah at the Plate of
Brasse. On July 19 FBI agents visited the Turcich family residence in Delanco, New Jersey. According to police sources, the
agents were told of the family's long connection with "Shimada"—
and that daughter Mary Margaret, Wendy's close friend, was in
San Francisco, in touch with Wendy, if not living with her, and
working at the Sir Francis Drake Hotel.

Kathleen Soliah had disappeared, but Turcich showed up that
day—July 19—at the restaurant. Sometime midway in the morning shift she received a long-distance telephone call—apparently
from New Jersey—and walked off the job, leaving immediately.
Hours later two FBI agents arrived at the restaurant asking for
her. It was apparently several days later—when agents questioned
the hotel employees about Ms. Turcich's friends—that someone
made the connection to "Kathleen Anger." Anger was apparently
identified as Kathy Soliah from photographs of Scott-Brandt associates. Like beads on a string, pieces were coming together:
Scott to Yoshimura, Yoshimura to Turcich, Turcich to Soliah. . . .

A week later, on July 28, Inspector Terrill Dyer of the Sacramento Sheriff's Department homicide squad asked the state CI&I—Bureau of Criminal Identification and Intelligence—to check latent prints from the license plates of the Carmichael bank robbery getaway car against prints on file for one James William Kilgore, CII # 3–772–066, member of the pro-SLA Bay Area Research Collective, boyfriend of Kathleen Soliah. CI&I fingerprint expert Cornace Sanders made a positive ID on a right-hand thumb print found on the license plate. Scott to Yoshimura, Yoshimura to Turcich, Turcich to Soliah . . . now Soliah to Kilgore to the Carmichael bank robbery and the murder of Mrs. Opsahl. The fingerprint alone was insufficient evidence for even a warrent, but the list of people sought by the FBI for questioning had grown quickly. But still they had to find them.

On August 4 three NWLF fire bombs exploded in the carport of the suburban Woodside home of Charles de Brettville, chairman of the Bank of California, a director of Pacific Gas and Electric, Shell Oil, Western Union, and Safeway Stores, Inc. De Brettville's Jaguar sedan was damaged. On August 8 an unclaimed pipe bomb was discovered under a parked San Francisco police car and defused. The bomb had probably been planted to explode the night before—August 7, the fifth anniversary of "manchild" Jonathan Jackson's attack on the Marin county courthouse. (George Jackson's seventeen-year-old younger brother had freed and armed three black convicts and seized several hostages who were to be exchanged for the "Soledad Brothers," including George Jackson. Guards fired on the escape van, killing young Jackson, two convicts, and a judge held hostage.)

Six days later the NWLF claimed a similar bombing of an Emeryville police cruiser:

> August 13, 1975
> REAL DATE: 5 years, 6 days
>
> WE RECKON ALL TIME IN THE FUTURE FROM THE DAY
> OF THE MAN-CHILD'S DEATH
>
> The explosion at the Emeryville Station of Fascist Pig Repression is a warning to the rabid dogs who murder our children in cold blood. Remember pigs: everytime you strap on your gun, the next bullet may be speeding towards your head, the next bomb may be under the seat of your car. The people and the people's armed forces will no longer quietly submit to the occupation of our communities and we will never forget the executions of Tyrone Guyton, Clifford Glover, Claude Reese, Alberto Terrones and Derrick Browne.

THERE ARE TO BE FUNERALS? LET THERE BE
FUNERALS ON BOTH SIDES.
LONG LIVE THE GUERRILLA
DEATH TO THE FASCIST INSECT THAT PREYS UPON
THE LIFE OF THE PEOPLE

Jonathan Jackson/Sam Melville Unit
New World Liberation Front

The bomb had been planted by Emily Harris and Steve Soliah,
Patty would later tell the FBI, and in a nearby restaurant parking
lot, waiting for the explosion and watching the reaction, were
Kathy Soliah and Jim Kilgore.* Who wrote the communiqué is
not known, but the explicit threat of police killings documented
but one side of the debate among them—a month hence only the
Harrises, Yolanda and Teko, would argue for cop killing.

Perhaps "funerals" was bombast—or perhaps for the moment,
the group was swayed toward Teko's bloody grand strategy. (The
distinction between radicals who bomb buildings, "armed propaganda," and those few who make the leap from destroying property to political assassination is often blurred in the media, but in
the closed world of American revolutionaries, among those committed to "armed struggle," there is a threshold between bombs
and blood lust many refuse to cross.)

To sort out the alignments then, to separate the politics from
the flux of personality and passions, is particularly difficult—
probably even for the participants—because the group was again
caught up in shifting sexual liaisons. The affair between Emily
and Kathy was apparently breaking up or had broken up, Yoland-
a was about to return to Teko, and Jim Kilgore—then Wendy Yoshimura's lover—would again pick up with Kathy. Over the next
several weeks there emerged a flip-flop pattern of sexual triangles
and rectangles that must have played some kind of hell with the
new code of feminist revolution.

A couple of days after the Emeryville bombing, Kilgore and
Kathy and Josephine Soliah (perhaps with one or two others) took
off into Northern California on a scouting trip, apparently seeking a mountain stronghold in Mendocino County. They were
gone for a little more than a week, bringing back maps of the
Mendocino outback, lists of old abandoned mines—trail notes for
future Ches of California. And while Wendy waited for her man

*None of the four have been charged or indicted.

to return, Jim and Kathy, up in the hills, were apparently redis-covering each other.

Some of the tumult of this—the last month of the SLA—was captured in a diary Wendy Yoshimura kept, later seized by police. It begins the day of the Emeryville bombing, just before the scout team went north, and the last entry is dated September 15, three days before the arrests. The entries are intensely personal rather than political, but she had tried so hard to weld the two that her most private passions are imbued with her politics. She writes frankly of her increasing disaffection within the group. (And al-though it seems personal—she alone against the others—it be-comes clear in the end that not only she but most of the others feel similarly. Then she recasts the sense of personal dislocation in a stinging rebuke for the political premise and practice of the SLA. But the diary is different; it is a rare glimpse at the underside of the politics: personal, poignant, sometimes precious. While Kil-gore's away, she bemused herself mooning over him, shamed at her own jealousies, confused at the conflicts between emotions and political propriety. A hunger for authenticity, an illicit posses-siveness, wrestle with the mandated instability of the political code, and she catches it all with ironic innuendo:

> My love for him is very honest and I do so want to deal with it in a most progressive way I know how (at this point in my life) but without the cooperation of the other two involved, it is impossible and very impractical for me—for my mental well-being.

Yet, while Kilgore is still away, she, Patty, and Emily are visited by another friend, probably Mike Bortin, who stays more than a short while. "My friend finally fucked her," she writes the next day. "I guess I'm happy for him—mixed feelings—though I feel a little threatened—wonder if he is still interested in fucking me—he says he is but can't trust his words." She has the tangled syntax of the girl from Hiroshima for whom English is a second lan-guage, but it's expressive; by turns whimsical, hopeful, bitter and anguished—and always earnest.

She visits Turcich and Fittipaldi, her two New Jersey friends suddenly jerked into the underground, and finds them "de-pressed, isolated and alone," and lashes at herself. "Why wasn't I more sensitive toward that feeling they're experiencing!?! It really makes me furious to have been so insensitive." Wendy is writing the day the Emeryville communiqué makes the papers: "Felt low and depressed when I returned home. 'Those people' [the Harrises] were buzzing and high because of 'it' and it made me feel more down and out of it. . . ."

> What is it—something is off. Maybe I am off. Why do I relate to men so fucking closely and I don't with women? My conditioning—but why am I still dealing it the same way? Why do I feel so close to [Jim] and not to other women? Why do I feel so defensive around C? Why do I feel as I understand him better. . . . Am I fucking up? I'm afraid to ask other women, including C, all the doubts and questions. I have fear of them saying I'm fucking up. I know if I asked C or T they'll tell me I'm not. . . . What is it? I know that I'm not that different from other women in my fucked up behavior towards men but at the same time I am different in a lot of ways—my behavior—being able to say what I'm feeling, etc., etc. So where do I draw the line? I can't put myself down and think my sense of how I relate to men are totally fucked but at the same time I have to see when I do fuck up. What is the solution? Where do I clearly draw the line? I feel so confused.

She has an argument with Emily, who apparently suggested that the FBI went after Margaret Turcich because she changed her phone number. Wendy is infuriated: "That's ridiculous. She [Emily] is off the wall. My small friend [Patty] has a good sense of things—I appreciate her the more I get to know her. Why do people seem so crazy to me? Do I come off like that to some people too? I wonder."

She awakes one night with a "weird" nightmare: "The dream was about him but very strange—with all those characters, Reggie, Archie, Veronica, and Betty." There is a tender, joyous recall of her imprisoned lover, Brandt, but there are nearly daily notes for Kilgore: "I love him and miss him but not at all in a hopeless, helpless way—Thank goodness." She writes of close, tight, loving relationships with four comrades—but they seem to be old ties, old comrades. Those around her share something less:

> How different these people are to me. I don't feel comfortable with them nor do they with me. I am alone—being able to be alone with myself—because I am high—they're in the other room eating. I don't feel like eating—because I am high. I know I'm getting on their nerve [sic]—well, so are they on my nerve.
>
> They're here with me and do I feel uncomfortable. I guess I'll leave the room soon.
>
> Why can't I get high & happy with these people. Am I up tight

or are they? I guess we both are. So she eats because she feels up tight and nervous and I drink—what's the difference. So she (the little one) doesn't like the music, well, I don't like it either when TV is on constantly!—after 5:00 News.

For the revolutionary, the Revolution has many faces: one for the private soul; one for the public to be led; one for the comrades in struggle; one for the mother and father left behind. Found in the notebook pages of the diary, unmailed, was a letter Wendy wrote to her parents in Fresno.

Dearest

How are you? Fine I hope—yes, with all my heart you two are doing well. I am doing just fine. I am with dear friends and, other than not being able to see you two . . . I am happy, mentally, and very well physically. I want to thank you very much for sticking by me, loving me and trusting me. You know me, M and D. You know I have strong principles. You're right, M, maybe I would [not] have been in "trouble" (as you call it) if I had stayed in F and remained ignorant. (What a waste of good principles that would have been. ☺) I wouldn't trade anything in the whole wide world (even freedom) for what I know and feel now. What I believe in now—to correct the injustice being done to the people—seems at this point very idealistic, but I know that it will be a reality. I know more people will feel the same as I do and will participate in correcting the wrongs. There must be people like we are, however small the number now, who must start the process or it will not happen. Don't you read the paper. . . ? It is happening everywhere—all over the world.

We aren't idealistic—we are realistic. A day does not pass by my feeling outraged by seeing what wrongs are done to people. I am speaking of basic, simple thing [sic] as people being hungry, drunk (to numb their pain and frustration), going mad (driven to madness, unable to cope with this irrational society) and many other symptoms [sic] of this insane and unjust society. My love for the people, the humanity, is intensely strong. I feel it so strongly that I cannot ignore it and "live happily ever after. . . ."

Don't think for twice that I am being unhappy or my personal needs are not being satisfied. All my needs are satisfied (other than not being able to talk, touch & see the 2 dearest people I so intensely love . . .). I have friend whom I love dearly . . . I have not, not in my whole life, has [sic] friends like I have now. They are not like S, N and the rest of the apolitical friends I have had in the past. Those old friends were good people but they always came first for themselves. No matter how much they loved me—they always came first (& of course, I was the same way; I came first). The friends I have now are different. . . . Their love for me is not only personal but also political. They love me for my personality but also for what I believe it [*sic*]. And yes, I do love them the same way. It is probably hard for you to understand the whole thing as you never had the chance to experience such friendship. All I know is I feel fortunate to have such friends.

Please, please, M & D, don't worry about me. I *am* really doing very very well . . .

So Much Love, Respect & Trust

25

Quest, Capture, and Questions

FAR from the front lines, distant from both the violence and the rhetoric, the SLA throughout its career had a second class of casualties—back on the home front. The families of the SLA soldiers were all victims, irretrievably trapped between love and confusion. Although four of the original ten—Angela DeAngelis, Nancy Perry, Remiro, and DeFreeze—had married and divorced, it was the parents who bore the burden. It seemed that none of the parents were any better informed about the SLA than the average newspaper reader, but out of love and their own desperation to, comprehend, each struggled to settle a logic to the Symbionese. After the campus rebellions it was a rutted pattern: middle-class parents shocked at the allegations raised against their children, uncertain of what their son or daughter might be capable, utterly confused as to the politics, equating the SLA with naïve and youthful idealism. Only DeFreeze had escaped the rebel-child image; his age and prison blurred the equation; but for each of the others it was the most obvious analysis for the public, the media—and even the parents themselves.

Politically, perhaps the most profound critique of the SLA was dramatized among the families; the SLA had goose-stepped to war, leaving even those who loved them most as ignorant and unconvinced of their cause as the mass public to which they addressed their blustry broadsides. Disbelief and bewilderment had been the first reactions from the families. Donald DeFreeze's mother and ex-wife both told reporters they thought Donald had a "mental problem," but neither could believe he was Cinque, the SLA leader. Joe Remiro's father blamed "the pills the Army gave him" for changing his son's personality. Some of the families found no SLA logic and sought instead the root of illogic. Mizmoon Soltysik's family explicitly condemned the narcissist guilt of

468

the Berkeley subculture—but perhaps all of the families blamed Berkeley.

None of the families tried to explain or defend the SLA, none could see the SLA as anything other than suicidal; but after the Los Angeles shoot-out, anger, fear, pity, and guilt exploded in vague justifications and bitter condemnation of "the John Wayne approach to law enforcement." There was a sense of personal failure and loss, but there was also an impressive dignity about each family as they claimed their dead. Each of the Symbionese was buried with love, pride, and great sorrow. These families deserved more than to have been written off, in Nancy Perry's phrase, as "racist and politically asleep"—and perhaps that was a core tragedy of the SLA.

The families of both the SLA and its victims had been integral parts of the story. History will record Tania, Randy Hearst, and the men who stood apart from family—Cinque and Marcus Foster—as the dominant figures in the case; but in real terms, in human terms, the burden of the SLA had always rested on the home front. And in the fall of 1975, as the police closed in on the last of the Symbionese, yet another family was trapped.

Two days before the Marin County Courthouse bombing, on August 18, Martin and Elsie Soliah had received their first visit from the FBI. Special Agent Curtis Holt, the local resident FBI man, arrived alone at the Soliahs' stucco tract home in Palmdale shortly before Martin got home from playing golf at the country club. Holt told Elsie Soliah he was making general inquiries about a young woman and then proceeded to give a careful and detailed description of Kathleen. "You must be talking about our Kathy," Mrs. Soliah exclaimed. The agent conceded he apparently was. Martin's car had just pulled up in front, and Elsie, somewhat flustered, immediately deferred. "You better talk to my husband about this," she said.

The elder Soliahs were not really shocked—the television report of Kathy's pro-SLA speech in Berkeley the year before had caused quite a furor in the neighborhood—but the idea of a federal agent investigating their daughter was still disturbing. At the June reunion Martin had talked with the kids briefly about the SLA, very briefly; he had been satisfied when Kathy swore outright that she "had never been a member of the SLA." Seen from Palmdale, the SLA had a spectral quality, distant headlines and hoopla, more of that Berkeley foolishness. And for all the affection in the family, neither Kathy nor any of the other kids had ever tried to explain their politics to their parents. Dialectical materialism was not dinner-table conversation, and it had been many years since the kids thought they could share everything with their father. Martin Soliah was a sensitive if rough-hewn man; he could sense the distance, but it seemed no greater than a generation of parents had to endure. His children knew his values, he had never been meek expressing them. A former World War II fighter pilot, a graduate of Luther College, a Nixon supporter, he wanted his children to be honest people and good Americans—and that was the phrase he would use.

Martin was still trying to adjust to the new morality that had Kathy sleeping with Jim Kilgore; the SLA was beyond him. He was not the sort of man to read an NWLF communiqué, and certainly they were not addressed to him. When Kathy had begun living with Jim Kilgore, her father had been outraged and had told Kathy so in no uncertain terms. For a while Kathy had stopped calling and writing home, but her sister Jo had passed reports back and forth, maintaining the connection and eventually bringing about a reconciliation. It was a kin bond; warm and caring. It was not structured to allow parents to understand their kids, but until now Martin had thought it normal and sufficient. Until now, there had been only the common confusion of a parent confronting the shifting values of the second generation; until now there had been nothing inexplicable.

Now the FBI was trying to find Kathy, Steve, and Josephine— and was unable to locate them. Special Agent Holt was from nearby Lancaster, and Martin knew him as a distant acquaintance. "He told us," recalled Martin later, "that our kids weren't in any trouble, that the FBI just wanted to *talk* to them about a couple of other people they were looking for." Just to talk—"he told us that several times." The agent said the FBI was looking for two women, Margaret Turcich and Wendy Yoshimura. "I'd never heard of one of the names he mentioned, but the other, Wendy Yoshimura, rang a bell. I said, 'Didn't her name come up in the Hearst case?' and he said yes, but that this investigation didn't have anything to do with the Hearst case."

The FBI apparently knew quite a lot about the kids, Martin discovered. As they talked, the agent began to tell him things he didn't know. About the Bay Area Research Collective, about Kathy's restaurant job at the Plate of Brasse. According to the FBI, Kathy had been working under an alias: Anger, Kathleen Anger. The Soliahs were deeply worried, but certain still that there was some confusion, that "the kids would straighten this whole thing out." Yes, they had an address in San Francisco. They showed the agent a letter from Josephine with 625 Post Street as a return address. He jotted it down, thanked them, and left.

That evening the Soliahs tried to contact their daughters. Mrs. Soliah dialed for San Francisco information, asking for a telephone number listed for 625 Post Street. The operator replied that she could not give out that information. "Tell her we have to reach our kids. . . . Say there's been a death in the family," Martin urged his wife. She did, and moments later a telephone-company supervisor informed Mrs. Soliah that the Post Street address was not an apartment house; it was a business, a rug company of some sort. "I didn't sleep much that night," Soliah said.

The same day, August 18, the Harrises, together, moved into a new apartment; a $180-a-month second-floor flat on Precita Avenue in San Francisco's Bernal Heights section. There had apparently been something of a blowout among the group. Jim Kilgore and Jo and Kathy Soliah were still up in Mendocino, but among the others, something had happened the day before. Wendy's diary entry for the eighteenth has day-after relief: "Very anticlimactic day, indeed! . . . I can't wait for him to come back. This living situation is getting too crazy for my mental well-being."

Wendy's report for the nineteenth is cryptic but prescient. She writes as though she were marking time. Something big is in the works, among the group ("everything" is about to change), and something else: "Picked up her thing, my thing, a little hassle over that as he, again, didn't speak his mind until we paid for it. . . ."

On August 20—the eve of the fourth anniversary of George Jackson's death—the New World Liberation Front exploded a bomb in the parking lot of the Marin County Civic Center, gutting two sheriff's patrol cars. Like the Emeryville bombing, this too was claimed by the "Jonathan Jackson/Sam Melville Unit" of the NWLF. (Nine different NWLF "units" had claimed various bombings with communiqués, and of the nine, eight—according to agents briefed by Patricia Hearst—were but masks for the latter-day SLA.) The Marin bombing communiqué was left in a phone booth in San Francisco's financial district, per usual—taped to the bottom of the booth's table ledge—and a radio station tipped for the pickup:

> . . . The rebellions of San Quentin, Attickkka and the Women's Correctional Center, Raleigh, North Carolina, have become symbols of the flames of resistance that burn throughout

Amerikkka's concentration camps. On the streets the fire also rages because the barbaric conditions in the prisons are merely the reflection of our brutal, inhumane society. . . .

The communiqué went on to include a famous quote from George Jackson:

"Violence is not supposed to work in Amerika. For no one, that is, except the omnipotent administrator. But this has yet to be proven to my satisfaction since I know that a bomb is a bomb; it twists steel, shatters concrete and dismembers men everywhere else in the world. Why not those made in Amerika? A bullet fired from an assault rifle in the hands of a Vietnamese liberation fighter will kill a pig in Vietnam. Why won't it kill a pig in the place where pigs are made?"

A witness anonymously telephoned police the day after the Marin bombing to describe a "sun-bleached blue Buick" station wagon, containing four or five people, several of them women, which he had seen speed from the scene just before the blast. (The bombers, Patty told the FBI, were Hearst herself, Michael Bortin, Steve Soliah, and Wendy Yoshimura.)* Yoshimura's diary for that day has the cool tone of a professional after a job well done: "Intellectually very satisfying day but not so personally—and I know why. I was, indeed, very happy but at the same time I couldn't get caught up in the whole thing. I guess these people don't satisfy my personal needs."

The day after there was apparently another hassle with the Harrises, and Wendy rages in her entry:

Bad! Started out very badly this morning. I didn't like the way the whole thing came down—"Fuck!" & etc. At times like such we must maintain objectivity, especially dealing with people like "them." Knowing "them" I know "they" already feel badly enough. We all know when we make *mistakes*—Yes, of course, we must discuss it so it won't happen again—but WE MUST DISCUSS IT.

Then she notes something pleasing and painful: a phone call from Kilgore. ("It was so nice. I miss him so. Is it fucked up to miss him? I don't know—it all get so confusing sometimes. . . .") But it's a bad season for couples, and Wendy feels "a little appre-

---

*None of the four have been charged or indicted.

hensive" about his return. "All one has to do is be honest and sincere," she reminds herself, "no games whatsoever. It seems so simple—so easy. But then people keep telling me those things do come much easier for me. . . ." She talks with a woman friend—apparently not one of the core group—and returns home, worried again about her balance of energy between men and women: the feminist obligation "to communicate and relate to women."

> . . . I agree but it is so difficult [for] me. None of the women I relate to now would . . . be the ones I would choose to relate to if I lived freely. I know that much and it makes it very difficult for me to deal with it practically as well as progressively. Her criticism around that was she didn't think [Jim] was not much different than those women—and in a sense that's true. But how much—it isn't even clear in my head. I am probably putting more energy toward [Jim] because I fuck him. Disgusting but I don't know how to deal with it.

But she is faced with dealing with it when Jim, Kathy, and Jo return. Wendy immediately senses something has changed. Personal crisis crashes atop political crisis.

> All the senses I have—is it all off? I can't figure it out. What is the matter with it? Am I off or are they?? I don't know. Do "they" all have the same kind of problem? Do "they" really? Who creates it—who WHO??? If he goes what's that to me? Am I being "a man oriented?"
>
> Come off it! He *does* make more sense to me! Not because he happens to be the man I fuck with. I have that sense (of course, I don't know it for sure). What I have to say to them is the truth—"I feel no support, understanding or communication with nobody . . . and 'a little bit' from a couple of people just ain't enough!"
>
> I can't tell him "NO" (for my sake) as much as I can't toward C. I, at the same time, maintain a clear perspective on what I feel—my senses of things.
>
> Maintain myself—my feeling & senses must be trusted by me—who in the fucking world is going to trust it if I don't?!? Just keep it cool. I MUST FOR MY SANITY.
>
> So he had to do some thinking. (I bet he fell right asleep.) . . . Bull Shit—what can he think about—it's all a big *muck*. Yes, that's why he'll fall right to sleep. The lady—where is her head at—I don't know—all I know is where mine is at. NOWHERE!
>
> I'm ready to take on anybody—the all of *you*. If you still maintain your position, then I am off—off I go!

For the Soliah parents there was not even the emotional release of Wendy's raging melodrama. They could only wait and suffer the silence, the isolation imposed on them by their children. Worried, fearful; but not even knowing what there was to fear.

They had received a letter from Josephine on August 23, almost a week after the first FBI visit—a chatty, affectionate letter home that briefly allayed their fears of the worst. Jo said she and Kathy had just returned from a wandering fishing trip, casting for salmon in the upcountry streams of Mendocino and Sonoma counties, north of San Francisco. It hardly seemed a letter from a kid in trouble. In fact, thought Martin Soliah with some pride, the trip was just the sort of thing *his* girls would try. But there was still the mysterious return address on Post Street—and that still made no sense to Martin and Elsie. It was like a loose clue, and try as they might, they couldn't fit it into a natural scenario.

Four days after the letter, the FBI returned. Curt Holt, Martin's FBI acquaintance, appeared at the door with two unfamiliar men, agents who had come up from the Los Angeles field office. The two LA agents did all the talking. "They were all questions, not the least bit friendly," recalled Martin. He told them about Jo's letter, showed it to them. "They said agents had checked and found 625 Post was a mail-holding outfit; you know, for people who don't have a permanent address, like merchant seamen. I told them we'd also learned it wasn't an apartment house, and I said, 'Look, I want to talk to my kids as badly as you guys. . . . What can I do to help?' They looked at each other, and then one of them asked, 'Will you go to San Francisco and try to find your daughters and ask them to talk with us?"

Neither Martin nor the FBI men had mentioned Hearst, but Martin was certain it was all connected with the SLA case because of the Yoshimura name. Even his own granite faith in the kids' innocence must have trembled. "I told them, 'You're asking a hell of a lot. You're asking me to put a tail on my kids!' 'No, no,' they said, 'we just want to talk to them, to find out if they know anything about Wendy Yoshimura or Margaret Turcich.'" Martin recalled that the FBI had talked to Kathy once before, talked to her for some four hours after the SLA rally, in mid-July, 1974. The FBI had "nothing on her" then; apparently they had nothing on her now. It was just a mixup of some sort. He sat quietly thinking; then he told the agents bluntly that he was certain his kids were not "involved in anything"—so certain that, yes, he would go to San Francisco and ask them to talk with the FBI . . . at least with Agent Holt.

The next day, Thursday, August 28, Martin Soliah and Agent Holt flew to San Francisco. Soliah said later he had set only one condition in agreeing to assist the FBI. "I asked their assurance that if the kids didn't want to talk that nobody would harass them or follow them or anything like that. They told me, 'Absolutely not, Mr. Soliah'—and if they didn't want to talk, well then, that would be it and thanks for trying." It was a fool's demand, and Soliah knew it. Kathy, Jo, and Steve were not the FBI's quarry, and while agents would surely have liked to debrief them, the FBI was more interested in finding them, watching them, and seeing where, and to whom, they might lead. (There were numerous contradictions in Mr. Soliah's story, told a number of times, which indicate that he agreed, at least at first, to *locate* the kids for the FBI—without tipping them off that the FBI was on to them.)

In San Francisco the FBI put Soliah and Holt up in adjoining rooms at the Embassy Hotel, close by the Federal Building in the Civic Center. "I offered to pay," said Soliah, "but they told me it was the least the FBI could do for my helping them." He left a note for Josephine at the 625 Post address—"It was a small storefront in a sleazy part of town; dog manure all over"—and returned to his hotel to wait. Holt was there, and two San Francisco agents checked in with him regularly; Martin couldn't understand why one of them was so abrasive and surly. ("It must have been because of the Carmichael thing," he mused later, "but I didn't know anything about that. It didn't even make the papers down in Palmdale.")

Friday morning, the twenty-ninth, he went back to the mail drop, redated the note, and returned to the hotel to wait with the agents. Soliah said he and the agents had cooked up a cover story to explain his visit to San Francisco (surely an unnecessary subterfuge if he was only to invite them to talk with the FBI). In the note he left for Jo he said he had stopped by for a surprise visit at their Post Street "apartment," only to find it didn't exist. The FBI was apparently certain enough of Martin's mission that they agreed not to shadow his rendezvous; they would leave it up to him to find out where his kids were staying. But Soliah was into this to clear his kids, not to catch them for the FBI.

Friday afternoon, around four o'clock, the phone finally rang. "It was Jo," recalled Martin, "really excited, happy. Asking what am I doing in town? And is Mama with me? And that she and Kathy would be right over and they'll leave a note for Steve who's out house painting so he can meet us as soon as he gets home." The girls arrived twenty minutes later, and the three went out for a beer. Then, when Steve joined them, Martin took them all to dinner. They walked up the street to the first reataurant and started to go in, but Kathy objected, saying it was too close to the FBI office. The comment startled Martin. "What are you afraid of?" he demanded. They walked to another restaurant and entered, the question hanging.

Martin put aside the FBI's cover story and all that went with it. "If I was going to ask them to be straight with me, I figured I had to level with them." Because he had come alone, the kids knew something was wrong anyway. ("I don't go anywhere without Mama," he explained with a smile.) "I said, 'Look, the FBI's been around. They're looking for some people they think you might know, and they couldn't find you, so they asked me to come up. Now I think you should talk to them, and if you know anything, you should tell them, but if you don't want to talk, okay, and nobody's gonna bother you.'"

There was a moment of shock. The announcement drew differing reactions from the three, but it was unmistakably a bombshell. Josephine began to cry; Steve said nothing, absolutely nothing; but Kathy, "Kathy exploded . . . she was furious." "Daddy! How could you?" she demanded. "How could you do such a thing? Don't you know you can't trust the FBI?" Martin, suddenly desperately worried that he had been used to trap his own children— "like a Judas goat!"—tried to sort out the FBI's story with the kids. He accused Kathy of working under the "Anger" alias—"Aren't you proud of your name now?" Kathy met the accusation bluntly. "They're liars," she said. "I've never been anybody but Kathy Soliah." Kathy acted as spokesperson for the three, denying everything, but she, too, began to sob. She said they did not know any Margaret Turcich or Wendy Yoshimura, that they had nothing to do with the SLA underground or Patty Hearst. The FBI agents were liars . . . liars . . . liars.

Martin confronted his son with the FBI's charge that Steve and Jack Scott had been using the same car.* Steve argued that even if

---

*Steve had been ticketed in Pat Jean McCarthy's car the day after the Guild bank robbery in February. The FBI's interest had been caught when a woman driving the same car had picked up Jack Scott's parents when they flew to San Francisco in April to confer with their son, after Jack and Micki popped up from the underground. Tracing the registration, the bureau got the McCarthy ID, found the record of Soliah's ticket—and, checking further, discovered that in November, 1974, Jim Kilgore had been ticketed for speeding in another car registered to Ms. McCarthy. It took the FBI some time to put it all together, but the circle of SLA associates was so small that they were practically holding hands.

that were so, it didn't mean he was himself connected with the Scotts. Friends often lent out cars in San Francisco. "It isn't like it is at home, where everybody has a car," explained Steve.

Mr. Soliah spent a full seven hours walking and talking with his three oldest children, but the conversation, he said, just kept going around in circles. He asked them to talk to Curt Holt, an FBI man who was a friend, but "they said we trust your friend, but we don't trust the other people in the FBI up here." Then perhaps Martin didn't either. But trust was an elusive quality even among the family now. "They just kept saying that they hadn't done anything wrong, not a single thing—but that they couldn't hurt other people. I felt they knew more than they were saying, but they wouldn't budge, so I gave up arguing with them. . . .

"I begged them to come home with me, right then. I told them I'd put up the money for them to start a business. I said, 'Let's get the hell out of this place. . . . Come back to the desert, breathe some fresh clean air. . . . How can you live here?' I asked them. 'How can you live in a place like this where there's dogshit all over the sidewalks?'" The argument framed the whole evening: fruitless and painful.

"They told me to go on home and it will be all over soon. 'What do you mean?' I said.

"They said we can all be together in a few weeks and be a family again. I said, 'We're a family now!'" The talk, said Martin, just went around and around. In the early-morning hours they ended up sitting on a stone bench just outside the Federal Building; then they parted tearfully. "Don't worry, Dad, there's nothing to worry about," Kathy promised.

When he returned to the hotel, Martin found the FBI waiting. They were disappointed when Soliah told them the kids had refused to tell him where they were living, but at least one agent blew up when Martin said he had asked the kids to talk to Holt and told them the FBI had asked him to come to San Francisco to find them. "If you told them the truth," said the agent, "you blew the whole thing!" (The mail drop was the FBI's only direct lead, and now that was "hot." The Soliah siblings never went back to it. And now they were tipped.) Other agents apparently felt he had done all they could ask of a father. "They thanked me for my cooperation," said Soliah. "They even reimbursed me the thirty-three dollars I had paid for dinner." Saturday morning, August 30, Martin Soliah flew home, worried sick. Shortly after he'd left, the Embassy Hotel had a call for him. Told that he had checked out, Kathy, Jo, and Steve called home to talk with their mother.

"They kept saying they had done nothing wrong, that they weren't in any trouble," recalled Elsie Soliah. But there was something going on, something they could not explain. They promised, again, that it would be "over soon." Then, they said, they would come home to visit.

Yoshimura's diary entry for August 30 carried the impact of the news; the FBI had found the trail to Turcich and now the Soliahs. The aboveground connections were disappearing.

> Well, things look very bad. Where are we to go from here? What or who will feed us, clothe us, and house us? What we had, a little, we had is gone. Where is it to go now? "We" mustn't forget the "units." At the same time we must keep our perspective straight on our life *now*. Totally confusing period.

September 1, the Geneva Avenue safehouse was abandoned in haste. The owner, Eugene Zucker, who runs a cleaner's shop on the ground floor, recalled them leaving because the account ledgers had forced him to spend his Labor Day in the office. It happened so quickly. There were several people; they carted everything out into a couple of vans and drove off, waving good-bye. Landlord Zucker was sorry to lose them as tenants. Quiet, paid the rent on time, "never any trouble," he said.

Already the group had split at the seams. The Soliahs were talking about being free of it all "soon"; Wendy was still writing about preserving the NWLF "units," but she had earlier decided she wanted to get away from the Harrises (and now, the rest of the group, flushed from their old hideouts, crowded together for at least a week, developed bitter personal tensions even among the anti-Harris alignment). As Wendy's relationship with Jim Kilgore dissolved, he apparently used political jargon to push her aside:

> So I'm been too dependent. So he tells me. So fucking what! What I feel now is I feel so low and down and out that I want to be physically near someone I can talk to & relate to. And I thought I could be with [Jim], and I am proven wrong—and he wants no part of it—Fine!
> . . . I guess what it means is that he is too paranoid to respond to my need, which means he won't give me the room to figure it out for myself. To see if *it* means I am being "too dependent," exclusive and being a passive female! Then the conclusion is I don't need *it*. I can find it out for myself.
> As for now all I can be is what I am. I must say and express what

I feel. And if I am rejected as I was tonight then all I'm doing is responding to that. Stay away from me. I don't need it. I don't need it, crammed down my throat. I have to figure it out for myself. What it is! Fuck HIM!

The rhetoric of personal liberation is double-edged; evasion can be the flip side of exploitation. And among this group, "personal politics" apparently drew an uneven tandem with the socialist crusade—and in both spheres, they seemed to envision change by fiat rather than any humanistic process of education, adaption, and social absorbtion. Apparently the political contradictions and the personal conflicts among them blurred only briefly even in the threat and confusion that followed Mr. Soliah's visit; already there had been the schism with the Harrises, implicit, if not overt, and within a week, it seemed the general consensus that even among the anti-Harris faction, personal problems made cooperation impossible. Yoshimura gave up on them all: "I think, in fact I'm pretty sure, that I'm going to Boston. I see no future that is rational or positive in this area. I see no people [who are] positive or progressive. . . . I am going. I am going. I am GOING."

Yet they were able still to sort out the personal from the political enough to spell out their critique of the Harrises and the SLA. The cop-killing debate was only a front for the deeper issue, and among themselves they spelled it out in Marxist terms. It was, ironically, a black-and-white issue. All theories of terrorism assume that there is a social audience that can relate to and understand a given attack. The Harrises were certain the killing of police officers was understood and appreciated in the black community, and for that effect, they were willing to disregard its impact in the white community, among the "working class" from which most police are recruited. It was a twist of "class war" theory that came out of the guilt and alienation that had been the nadir of the New Left, although it was rarely expressed as bluntly as in the SLA dogma. It cast aside the political reality, the political possibility, for the privilege of "purity"—political elitism and principled suicide. For the Harrises, that was enough; that was the heritage of the SLA. But for the others, once they understood, that wasn't enough.

It's strange that it took them so long to understand the differences between them; but the plague of the American Left has always been its language: a rhetoric imported, translated, twice- and triple-used, from Russia, from China, from the thirties. It was painfully evident in the sixties. "To be in the movement you had to master the tongue, for no other language could be understood or respected," Left historian Elinor Langer perceptively noted. "But the fact is that this language could rarely be understood either, because its referents were not concrete. It only rarely corresponded with what we saw or felt or needed to express." Yoshimura, when she spelled out the terms of the schism, wondered at the fact that although it *sounded* as if they all agreed, they had in fact found bitter differences. But then, stipulating point by point the differences, she took the key issue and boiled it down to another word symbol. "Their understanding of [the] importance of international perspective is very shakey to say the least," she wrote, and what she meant, in translation, was that the SLA had been in error writing off the American "working class" out of guilt and sympathy for nonwhite victims of American capitalism and racism.*

Willie Brandt—Soledad convict, former commander of the Revolutionary Army, once Wendy's lover—had for a while become a symbol of sane revolutionary leadership among the anti-Teko group. Patty later told her posttrial FBI interrogators that—to displace Harris—several among the group had schemed a plan to bust out Brandt. The plot called for arranging a court appearance in Salinas, then ambushing the prison transport car carrying Brandt (virtually duplicating the 1971 Chino escape plan that had freed Venceremos convict Ron Beaty). The plot, said Patty, had evolved so far that the group had contacted an attorney to set up the court appearance, but then Emily Harris, who at the time was something of a mediator between Bill and the others, managed to derail the scheme. It is not without irony that the document of dissolution, the autopsy of the SLA, was a letter written by Wendy

---

*"Internationalism" is a totem of Marxist thought, a principle that argues that the cutting edge of the worldwide struggle for socialism is among the oppressed. But Internationalism has a Marxist corollary in the concept of "solidarity," which stresses that—particularly for the individual Marxist in the imperialist society—there is an obligation not only to support foreign liberation struggles, but the domestic struggles to define the more ambiguous class-issue within the bourgeois capitalist society as well.

Struggles against colonialism and foreign imperialism may present the clearest evidence of the evils of capitalism, the Marxist argues, but the prime task of the American socialist is to organize and define the working-class struggle in the United States. Yoshimura's critique hit at the SLA's almost absolute rejection of the white American worker (an interpretation confirmed by Yoshimura's attorney and friend James Larson of San Francisco).

Yoshimura that was to have been smuggled to Brandt at Soledad prison.

DEAREST BROTHER,

It is very difficult for me to begin this letter as it will be very contradictory to the letter I've written you last.

Well, I'd have to inform you that the group has literally ceased to be a group. How could this have happened so suddenly?!? You may even be thinking the letter I've written you previously was a full of bogus—but not so. Every word I've written in the last letter, I sincerely meant it.

Ever since the group came together around those people a little over a year ago, we've had a very trying time. The security was a big factor but there was the sensationalized media play on those people affecting our heads, in effect making us unable to think clearly of them as people with strengths and weaknesses but as "the leaders" who knew *everything*. My experience during the summer made me realize that they (two [Bill and Emily Harris] in particular—not P.H. [Patty Hearst]) in fact are very different from me and personally I did not much like them. In spite of it I decided to stick with it because of their fierce dedication, my knowing there were others waiting to work together, and I was under their spell.

Unfortunately the other people were also spellbound into submissiveness and there began a mass of confusion touched up with fucked up interpersonal dynamics between some of the people. To show you how confusing it was, it began with—some ready to go underground (expecting it to get hot next week) to some pushing for jobs, staying cool and normal; some pushing for totally isolated communal living to some demanding normal separate living arrangements; some demanding fucked up interpersonal relationships be dealt with, to some seeing it as totally unnecessary; some wanting to off pigs to some totally disagreeing. Let me tell you, I can go on forever. It was a psychodrama!

Finally, at one point, we seemed to have found a middle ground and it looked as though we were beginning to coordinate and work together. We finally were able even to do a couple of actions. This was when I wrote you the last letter. Since then it began to get obvious that the security that seemed to be existing was due to total repression, politically as well as personally, on everybody's part to maintain the group together. As you can well imagine, such calm can be maintain for only so long. It began to rattle and once it started the process was very fast. M [Mike Bortin] was put on some bogus "probation" (to which I was the only one who protested in vain). Then M [Mike] quit. After that there were series of incidents that took place which only made it very clear to particularly J [Jim Kilgore], K [Kathy Soliah], P.H. and me that we wanted no part of it. We, those of us who decided to go our own way, discussed the matter and it became obvious to us what the problems were. On the surface it seems as though we all agree and believe in the same thing, but after working with them, we've come to the realization that we do in fact disagree politically very drastically. Let me give you some of the examples:

—They've no understanding of what it really means by "third world leadership." Their blind insistence of third world leadership (Black) is clearly coming from white guilt.

—They continually separate the political from the personal.

—They have very shallow understanding of the Women's question. So shallow that they are like Siamese twins.

—Their understanding of importance of international perspective is very shakey to say the least.

—Their attitude around arm struggle is that it only is valid and anything else (aboveground, etc.) is irrelevant.

And to add to this [there] is the personal aspect of these people. They are two individuals with weak egos lacking very much in sense of themselves. They have so, so little sense of themselves that they literally have to use the old Kantian bullshit—"I think, therefore I am"—to even function. They are doctrinaire Marighelaists. These people are totally unable to check out the objective situation and deal with it. They simply do not know how to take a theory and apply it to the reality that exists.

It's difficult for me to clearly analyze what exactly is the problem with these people but I think, other than their lacking in strong egos they are victimized by the guilt they feel—guilt—[for the] death of their comrades possibly quickened by his fuckup at the sporting goods store (it's true—he fucked up)—guilt they feel for being born white. (And are they so racist that they must put Blacks on a pedestal to even consider them worthy?)

I truly feel that what motivated them to take on an arm action is very different from what motivates me and the others. It's very different.

Unfortunately our vision was clouded for the reason I mentioned before and it took us this long to get it together. Everyone rebel one way or another at different times. I was once thrown out; so was P [Pat Jean McCarthy] and so was M. P.H. was hated by our "leader" for being so "rebellious." J at the end kept having violent verbal fights with him—often almost becoming physical. All of this going on plus trying to survive at the same time—Isn't it any wonder we could do no action to speak of for so fucking long!?!

Well, you may think the rest of us should come together and

deal with them. Of course, that crossed our minds by we see it clearly that they are not dealable. If we tried we will only be doing that and nothing else! I swear!

I wish that I am able to tell you what we are up to now. All of us still want to continue with our work but we don't know exactly where and with whom. Some are definitely leaving the area, others are thinking about it and some like M and P are definitely staying here. I don't know what I am going to do, yet, but within a week or so I should come up with a decision. Either I go to Boston with a woman friend from back east or stay here and work with P, M and possibly others. It's totally confusing at this point for me. Don't even think that we all are going in all different areas tripping off with total pessimism. We definitely plan to keep in contact and have the perspective of working in different areas and coordinating our actions.

I wish that I could talk to you and tell you in every detail about everything. Some day I will. I tell you this is an experience I'll never forget! It was horrendous but at the same time I've learned a hell of a lot. Now I understand more clearly my political views, and, oh, the sense of myself I've gotten out of this ordeal—I wouldn't exchange it for anything! I think most of us came out of this ahead. I hope you'll have the chance to meet P.H. She is incredible! She amazes me! I swear only the toughest could have come out of it as she did. What an ordeal she went through!! What an ordeal all of us went through!! I can write a book about it.

As for how I feel about you have not changed since the last letter—in fact my love for you have increased since then. I have the greatest sense about you, politically as well as personally. Oh, Brother, I have the highest respect for you and feel the deepest love for you. I also have the greatest sense of myself that I know when we see each other you will feel the same about me. I'm sure of it!

I should be able to let you know soon what will happen with everyone involved.

So Much Love, Respect and Power,
me

Only the week before Martin Soliah's San Francisco visit, Bill and Emily Harris had moved into their new Precita Avenue apartment in the Bernal Heights district of the city. Even when they heard of the FBI's renewed interest in the Soliahs, they apparently felt secure. Everyone else bailed out; two safehouses were abandoned immediately. Some of the group crowded into Jim Kilgore's Daly City lodgings; the Soliah sisters and Bonnie Wilder moved in—temporarily—with the Harrises. A week after Mr. Soliah's visit, "Charles Adams" rented a flat at 625 Morse Street in San Francisco's Outer Mission District, a poor working-class neighborhood about two and a half miles from the Harrises' safehouse. "Adams" said he would be sharing the small modern two-bedroom apartment with his Oriental wife, "Emily," and his sister. Two days later, on September 9, Steve Soliah, Wendy Yoshimura, and Patty Hearst were settled in at 625 Morse.

The "Adamses" were an oddly quiet trio. Several neighbors recall Soliah as "a kind of sleepy-eyed fellow with blond hair," but they didn't see him often. The two women seldom came out during the day. One neighbor remembered that, while he had never seen anyone enter or leave the place, "I would walk by and, like, I'd see people peeking out from behind the windows. It was strange."

In the polyglot heavily Latino Bernal Heights, the Harrises blended into the neighborhood more naturally. They were good tenants, quiet, friendly people. They had rented the apartment using the names "Christopher and Nanette Carswell" (and then ordered a telephone under the name of "Mata Mexima"). "Chris" and "Nanette" introduced themselves around and made several casual friends. Emily's downstairs neighbor invited her in for coffee and cake, and "Nanette" asked the woman up for tea. ("She had these green-brown eyes that were very serious, always squinting. We talked about jobs and children and my little boy.") The Harrises jogged daily, around the block and nearby Bernal Park. Occasionally they stopped to chat with park regulars, including several people who exercised there about the same time they trotted. ("They seemed like basic people . . . interested in gardening . . . saving the land, preserving the earth . . . ecology.") Neighbors do not remember many visitors to 288 Precita at first, but after a couple of weeks there were several people who came by almost daily, usually in the evening hours: "young white folks." "There was a lot of activity at night," said a next-door resident. "At twelve thirty or one A.M. they'd be doing things like washing dishes, things most people do a lot earlier." Another neighbor, a seventy-six-year-old widow who guards her window-sill as a hobby, recalled "two really odd-looking young women" who visited the apartment several times. The women seemed furtive, wearing big floppy straw hats clear down over their foreheads, and they were always in a hurry," explained the elderly Leona Forbes. "They were so funny-looking I wondered where they came from."

The Harrises were stocking their little apartment like a National Guard armory. And like Clayton so long before, the house was also becoming a library of SLA memorabilia. They carted in boxes and cases of files, manuscripts, and notebooks, lists of telephone numbers and names that agents would eagerly confiscate a month later. The bombing campaign was apparently to have been a long-term offensive. Teko had a well-equipped and stocked bomb factory: boxes of alarm clocks, reels of wire, batteries, stacks of iron pipe with caps drilled for fuse wires. There were several jugs of gasoline and three pounds of high-explosive gunpowder. (The FBI would later find a half-dozen completed pipe bombs ready for the fuse and an assortment of guns. There were four .38-caliber revolvers*; two 9-mm semiautomatics; a couple of .22-caliber pistols; three military-model M-1 rifles, one with a cut-down barrel and all converted to fully automatic weapons; two 12-gauge shotguns; and—of course—one Marksman twenty-shot BB repeater air pistol.)

Sunday, September 14, in San Francisco's Golden Gate Park, there was a rally for the "San Quentin Six," prison inmates then standing trial in Marin County for conspiracy-murder. The six were convicts charged with the bloody mayhem that accompanied George Jackson's 1971 escape attempt from the San Quentin Adjustment Center, when three guards and two white inmates had been murdered, and Jackson himself killed. Among the crowd were the Harrises, General Teko and Yolanda, and of the rest of the group, at least Kathy Soliah. James "Doc" Holiday was also there. Holiday—thirty-three-year-old former leader of the Black Guerrilla Family at San Quentin—had been a key prison contact for the early SLA. (Back in January, 1974, the day Remiro and Little were arrested, Emily Harris and Angela Atwood had made separate seemingly urgent prison visits before they dropped into the underground. Atwood, at San Quentin, had visited Holiday.) Doc Holiday had been paroled only two months before, July 23, 1975, after serving fourteen years of a life sentence for robbery and murder.

Kathy Soliah approached Holiday at the rally, according to a source who witnessed the meeting, and told Doc the Harrises wanted to talk with him. Holiday was willing. They rendezvoused the next night, September 15, at an Oakland motel. Holiday knew the Harrises—Emily had visited him in prison—and of course he

---

*One of the .38s was the gun DeFreeze had taken from Hibernia Bank guard Ed Shea during the first SLA bank robbery.

knew the SLA. He listened quietly as Teko and Yolanda set out the situation: The "second team" was to hell and gone. But there was a chance of reorganizing, of re-creating the Symbionese Federation—if they had the galvanizing leadership of a famed prison revolutionary. Another black field marshal. A man like Holiday. Their commitment was proved, and they were offering themselves; all he had to do was say the word. Holiday—according to several sources—said no. How he refused, how he explained himself, what later possibilities they discussed is not known.* But when they parted that night, the SLA was still but two lily-white soldiers in search of a black commander.

It was the Harrises' last attempt to revive the past, and purely coincidentally, it was the prelude to the end. That Monday morning, September 15, the FBI had finally found the Soliahs. In July, Mike Bortin had taken on a sizable painting job, a large apartment complex in Pacifica, a coastal bedroom community on the Peninsula just south of San Francisco. There were 200 apartments, and the contract—non-union—paid $80 to $100 per unit. For Bortin, all the Soliahs, and Jim Kilgore, it had been a daily income. (Steve Soliah, in *Rolling Stone*, said even Patty went along to slop paint a few times.)

After Mr. Soliah had told the FBI that Steve and the girls were still contract painting, agents had begun checking independent painting jobs throughout the Bay Area. At a little after 9 A.M. on the fifteenth, Special Agents Jason Moulton and Ray Campos interviewed Bill Osgood, the manager of the Pacifica apartments. They showed him a portfolio of photographs, and Osgood identified one picture: Michael Bortin. Osgood said he knew Bortin as "John Henderson," the contract boss for a crew of "hippie painters" who were working through the units two a day. Yes, he

---

*A little more than a month later, on November 1, 1975, Holiday and another parolee, Michael Cowans, twenty-nine, were arrested by Los Angeles police and charged with the torture slayings of two black men and the wounding of two other persons. The purported motive for the murders of Winston Dowling, thirty, and Matthew Thompson, twenty-five, was that their roles as narcotics informers for the LAPD had become suspected in the ghetto community and "contracts" had been put out on them. Holiday and Cowans were identified by the surviving victims, one of whom claimed Cowans had bragged that he and Holiday were "high up" in the SLA. A few days later LA police announced they had learned Holiday was mastermind of a plot to kidnap Kathleen Brown Rice, the sister of California Governor Edmund G. Brown, Jr., and hold her in exchange for the "unconditional release" of SLA soldiers Russ Little and Joe Remiro, then being held in the Los Angeles county jail while awaiting one of their trials.

said, the crew included a couple of girls. He couldn't identify them, but they'd be arriving for work at any moment.

The FBI men asked Osgood not to mention their visit, then took up position in their unmarked government sedan to wait for Bortin's crew. At 10:30 A.M. they saw Kathy and Josephine Soliah arrive on the job. Jubilant, they radioed the sighting to headquarters. They were ordered to back off while plans were laid for a major surveillance operation.

About 5:30 P.M. Kathy and Jo—and a man, never positively identified, but thought to be Kilgore—quit painting for the day. They climbed into a black-over-beige '67 Ford, drove up onto the freeway, and north into San Francisco. Apparently there was no concern that they might be followed, for—with at least three FBI cars alternately on their tail—they drove directly to Morse Street, residence of the most wanted fugitive in the nation, Patricia Campbell Hearst. They got there a little after six, parked, and all three went into 625 Morse. Agents circled the block for perhaps fifteen minutes; then orders came to break for the night.

The Ford was there in the morning, and—very early—the FBI was, too. It was not until 10:50 that Steve Soliah, alone, came out of the three-story building, patiently warmed up the car engine, and drove off. Steve now led his bureau escorts in toward the center of the city, to Bernal Heights, Precita Avenue.

Steve pulled up in the 200 block of Precita and waited. Moments later Kathy and Jo—dressed for another day of painting—came out of a building agents could not see, got in, and the three proceeded to Pacifica. At quitting time the Soliahs again piled into the Ford,* and again with the FBI cautiously trailing, set out into rush hour. This time, however, the first stop was Bernal Heights, where Kathy and Jo were seen to enter the white duplex at 288 Precita. Steve continued on to Morse Street. The FBI now had two Soliah addresses. Agents assumed they had Kathy and Josephine living at 288 Precita, Steve at 625 Morse. The stakeout would be at Precita. Kathy, agents felt, was the key figure; if there were connections made, it would be through her.

The FBI men moved in to situate themselves early the next morning, the seventeenth. The house was to be watched around

---

*Agents later discovered that Steve Soliah, using the alias "John Matthews," had bought the 1967 Ford—with $400 cash, all $20 bills—on April 29, 1975, in Orangevale, a town near Carmichael. That the purchase was made eight days after the Crocker National Bank robbery was a point raised by the prosecution at Soliah's trial.

the clock; any visitors were to be followed and (if possible without compromising the operation) identified. Cruising surveillance was under way by 7 A.M.—one agent spotted Steve's Ford parked a block away. At 8:10 a light-beige camper truck with Utah license plates slipped into a just-vacated parking spot on Precita with a good view of 288. Three FBI agents were in the van; the primary surveillance post had been established.

At 10 A.M. they had the first sighting: Kathy and Jo came out of 288 and walked around the corner to the Ford. They drove off, apparently headed to work; they were not followed. There was no indication anyone else was inside 288, but there was no way of telling; the second-floor windows were all curtained. At precisely 10:50 agents caught their first glimpse of one of the FBI's Three Most Wanted.

General Teko, clad in cut-off jeans, T-shirt, and sneakers, came out, down the steps, stood for a moment stretching, then vanished back inside.

At least it *looked* like the long-sought Bill Harris. Agents weren't close enough to be sure, but he seemed about the right age, height, and weight. The suspect's hair appeared to be jet black, and Harris' natural color was dark brown. A dye job perhaps? But the details of the man's features were obscured by a bushy black beard. The agents had no pictures of Harris less than two years old, and none with a beard. But still. . . . The FBI's FM frequency crackled with the bulletin, and orders flashed back fast: Get a closer look. The number two man in the FBI office, ASAC Larry Lawler, assistant special-agent-in-charge, was dispatched to Precita.

At 11:30 A.M. a new suspect was seen: Two people had come out of 288, the same man and a woman, short-haired . . . who just might be Emily Harris.

Yolanda and Teko were out for a midday jog, down the block and through the park, then looping back. Agents cruised by them, even timed the run: twenty minutes. The two were just climbing the stairs when Lawler arrived on scene and drove past 288. Radioing his own sighting, the ASAC signaled that he was taking charge. Just after noon the bearded man emerged again and strolled to the corner grocery a block away. He bought the morning *Chronicle* and sauntered back to the apartment, reading as he walked. Through a small peephole in the side of the camper, a telephoto lens tracked him the last half block, catching a series of candid snaps of the suspected—but unsuspecting—SLA general.

At 4:35 P.M. the man came out, again alone, toting a white cloth bag. He walked two blocks to a self-service laundromat and went in. Busy with the shirts and underwear, he didn't look up as ASAC Lawler walked past him and over to the pay telephone. Larry Lawler is thirty-five, six feet, broad-shouldered, jut-jawed, and with a razor-cut wave of thick brown hair—in his suit, white shirt, and tie, he looks like Central Casting's answer to Efrem Zimbalist, Jr. Lawler flipped through the Pacific Tel & Tel directory, but he was concentrating on the brow, the eyes, and lips of the face behind the black beard. ("From the photographs we had of William Harris," Lawler said later, "it appeared that his two front teeth were not lower than the two teeth next to them . . . in the picture we had of him smiling; it gave the indication that the teeth appeared to be arced upward.") Harris, bent to his task, found nothing to smile at.

Then Harris turned, walked over to a woman at the laundromat's service desk and asked for change for a dollar. Lawler was right behind him; his own dollar in hand. Bill turned with his change to confront the biggest, most cheerful grin Lawler could muster. But Harris didn't crack. With a cool stare he turned back to the washing machines.

Lawler left the laundromat a few minutes later no more certain than when he'd entered. But on the man's left knee, just below the cut-off Levi's, he'd noticed what seemed a surgical scar—and when the field office checked Harris' Marine Corps records, agents found that Lance Corporal Harris had had an operation on that knee. The man spent an hour at the washing chore, then hauled the laundry home on his shoulder. An hour later, 6:18 P.M., the door opened again, and the woman, earlier seen jogging, walked to the grocery. She picked up a few things from the shelves, went up to the cash register, paid the clerk, and turned to leave just as Lawler—suit, tie, and smile—walked in. The ASAC got a two-second straight-on look; then she was past him. A couple of minutes later Lawler came out, joined up with Special Agent Leo Brenneisen, and the two of them strolled along the sidewalk comparing notes. Brenneisen wasn't of any opinion about the woman, but Lawler was certain of one thing. "I don't know who that lady is," he said of Yolanda, "but I'll guarantee you it's not Emily Harris!"

Dusk settled in. At 7:10, Jo and Kathy Soliah were dropped off by Steve; they went inside, and Steve drove the Ford off to the Outer Mission, to Morse. There still was no surveillance at the

Morse address, but the Precita stakeout continued through the night. New orders came as fresh agents took over the watch: If it appeared anyone was moving out, he or she was to be stopped and positively identified. At the Federal Building downtown, FBI SAC Charlie Bates debriefed the first stakeout team in an 8 o'clock conference that evening. The Harrises? Some agents were certain; others, Lawler among them, still weren't sure. There had been dozens of "certain" SLA sightings and numerous FBI and police raids that netted only shocked and scared utterly innocent citizens. With all the bad publicity—and several lawsuits as well—the FBI was now trying to tread very carefully.

The meeting broke up and then, at 8 o'clock the following morning, Thusday, September 18, agents gathered again in Bates' office. The general consensus was that if they had the Harrises, Patty was probably inside. If there was anything to the theory of *modus operandi*, all of those that remained of the SLA were probably living together. The SLA had always moved in unit strength, and from the Los Angeles shoot-out on, the bureau had not got any indication that the three had ever lived apart. Bates gave the orders: If they go jogging, take them on and find out if it's the Harrises. Stripped for running, clearly unarmed—that was the time to grab them.

By 9 A.M. Lawler had fifteen agents in the vicinity of Precita. They waited and watched. At 10:02 Kathy and Jo left for work. They were not followed.* At 11:30 a report from the FBI "camper" put the agents at the ready: A young black man drove up in an old truck, double-parked in front, walked up the steps of 288, and rapped on the door. The bearded Harris answered the knock, then stepped out and talked with the stranger. A new SLA member? Teko went back inside, returned almost immediately, and accompanied the man to the truck. Everyone tensed, then, a long minute later, relaxed as Bill walked back upstairs with a fish in hand. The visitor was the local Black Muslim fish peddler.

Twelve-fifty P.M.: Both the man and the woman came out—Bill in purple track shorts and a green polo shirt; Emily all in white, tennis shorts and a T-shirt. At the sidewalk they broke into a slow

---

*The Soliah sisters, with brother Steve and Jim Kilgore, spent the day painting in Pacifica. When the four heard a radio news bulletin about the capture of the Harrises, Kathy, Jim, and Josephine immediately took to the underground. Steve Soliah—hoping to warn Patty and Wendy—rushed to the Morse Street apartment . . . too late. FBI agents grabbed him as he started up the stairs.

lope. Lawler watched them round the corner, then began ordering men into position. Bates himself was parked atop a hill a few
blocks away, listening as other agents gave spot reports on the
progress of the couple.

One-twelve P.M.: An FBI car flashed the word. The suspects,
still jogging, were heading home. A sedan carrying Lawler and
three other agents pulled up and double-parked on Precita a few
doors down from 288. Other agents closed in. Bill and Emily
turned the corner, walking now, chatting. As they came abreast of
the government car, the car's four doors sprang open.

"We're the FBI," announced Lawler as agents surrounded the
pair. Teko stopped in his tracks, surrendering without a word. It
was Emily who moved on fight reflex. The moment she realized
what was happening, Yolanda reared back, wheeled, and tried to
sprint toward the corner. She found herself facing two agents
moving toward her, one with a shotgun; a third was on her heels.
She got ten paces; then they grabbed her; she struggled for a few
moments. *"You motherfuckin' sons of bitches,"* Yolanda raged. *"You
sons of bitches!"* Emily was quickly hustled into an FBI auto and
driven off around the block, they hoped, before her tirade could
alert anyone inside the apartment. Bill was still silent. A senior
agent grabbed one of Teko's hands and peered closely at the
loops and whorls on the fingertips. "It's him," he told Lawler.
"Double-check," he was told. Harris was pushed into an FBI car
where another agent quickly inked Bill's fingers and rolled them
onto a five-by-eight print card. Identification was positive. "He's
Harris!" By radio, Lawler gave the go to hit the house.

Back and front, they rushed the building. The first two agents
up the steps, John Schreiber and Tom Padden, discovered a padlock on the outer door. Schreiber pounded on it: "FBI!
. . . FBI . . . *OPEN UP!*" Padden smashed the window beside
the door with the butt of his shotgun, then reversed the gun to
cover the room inside. Schreiber reached through, unlocked the
window, threw up the sash. *"FBI!"* he cried again as he clambered
over the sill, scrambling through pistol in hand; others followed
and agents fanned out through the apartment.

A minute, two. Then Schreiber came out to report: empty, no
Patty—but there were guns and bombs, cases of papers and
books.

Someone must have cursed; no one was particularly happy.
Still, two out of three was an improvement on the past. Charlie
Bates, now out in front, ordered the Harrises shipped downtown

and gave the customary mop-up instructions—secure the place; get the search warrant; alert the magistrate. He had the office flash Washington—and he ordered teams of agents out to check three other addresses they had connected with the Soliahs: an apartment house a block away, with a FOR RENT sign in a window (where one of the sisters had stopped to inquire about leasing a flat); an address on Masonic Avenue the girls had been known to visit in the past; and 625 Morse Street. Just possibly. . . .

Bates, who had commanded the FBI's "Hearnap" investigation from Day One, was visibly disappointed. Even to the moment of arrest, Bates had kept his poise, reserving doubt. But then it had all come together, and for a moment he, too, was certain that Tania Hearst was in the house. The busts came down at 1:15 P.M. Bates stayed at the Precita scene until 2 o'clock, then headed downtown. His PR assistant had scheduled a press conference for 3 P.M., in time for the evening TV news. The odds were against another arrest, he thought—Patty, so long elusive, had slipped by again.

Special Agents Tom Padden and Jay Moulton drew the Morse Street checkout. As they headed for their car, Padden spotted two San Francisco detectives who had just arrived at Precita. He asked if they wanted to check out another possible safehouse, and Inspectors Tim Casey and Larry Pasero were more than willing. "Hell yes!" said Casey. A lumbering gray-haired veteran from the SFPD robbery detail, Casey wanted Patty almost as badly as Charlie Bates. The Hibernia Bank job was his case, and he'd been chasing Symbionese shadows all over the country for seventeen months. The two teams joined up, G-men and cops, and they rode out to the Mission section in the FBI sedan, listening to Padden recount the story of the Harrises' capture.

Morse Street was a long shot, all agreed. Patty had probably been staying with the Harrises and escaped the sweep just by chance. Still, long shots do come in.

"We drove past the place a couple of times and looked it over," recalled Casey later. "There were only two ways out of it, and we figured we could hit it without any help."

The only sign of people at 625 Morse was a middle-aged man working in one of the two ground-level garages below the two floors of apartments. The FBI did not know whether Steve Soliah was living in the second- or the third-floor flat. The cops decided to talk with the man in the garage. "He looked straight as a string," said Casey. The man was Jerry Prill, the owner of the building. Prill told them nobody was living in the second-floor apartment and that the third floor was occupied by new tenants, a young man and a couple of girls. The girls were upstairs now, Prill said.

Padden flipped out a sheaf of SLA photos and displayed them for Prill. The landlord shook his head at the pictures of both Patty Hearst and Wendy Yoshimura. He had not seen anyone among the photos—except maybe "the older-looking one." He pointed to a picture of Emily Harris. "That one."

The FBI man asked Prill to describe the layout of the apartment and asked advice as to the fastest way in. "Up the back stairs," Prill said; the back door was half glass. It was a federal operation so the FBI ranked in command. Padden chose Casey to accompany him up the back stairway and assigned his FBI partner and the other San Francisco inspector to cover the front.

"They were wooden stairs, and we went up slow and quiet," said Casey. Both men had their guns in hand; Padden his custom-mounted .38, Casey a .357 magnum, the heavy artillery of handguns, capable of putting a slug through an engine block. "I was right behind Padden," recalled the inspector, "and when he got to the top landing, he all of a sudden froze." Padden had found himself looking through the open top of a Dutch door straight at Wendy Yoshimura. And Wendy was staring right back. Padden broke the trance first.

"*FBI . . . Freeze!*" he yelled, lunging with the big gun right through the open top of the door, arm straight. Wendy was standing; Patty was rising from a kitchen table. "*Freeze,*" he yelled again. Tania was up and moving, toward the back, the bedroom, the guns. Padden had his pistol only feet from Yoshimura's head. At Patty, he yelled again, "*Freeze or I'll blow her head off!*" Patty stopped. The door was opened, and the lawmen burst in. "I ran past him, inside, past the Oriental girl, and then I saw her," remembered Casey. "All I could see was her back—she was heading for another room—and I called out, '*Patty!*' and she turned around and I said, 'Don't move!' I looked at her close, and I could see it was Miss Hearst. She looked pale and scared. I went over and put the cuffs on her. She didn't give any trouble."

Prill, who had followed the two up the stairs, reached the landing just as Casey pushed past Padden into the kitchen. Patty had stopped—at Padden's threat or Casey's shout—and turned. Patty, said Prill, "laughed, then giggled, then put her hands up."

Tania was in custody. Patty Hearst was reclaimed—if not for

Steve Weed, if not for her parents, if only for the courts, the psychiatrists—at least for the millions who still harbored a desperate curiosity about her transformation and the personality it had created. It had been 591 days since the SLA had kidnapped her—and they, too, had called it an "arrest."

Padden asked the two women if they had weapons. Patty pointed to her purse. The agent removed a revolver, loaded, from the bag. A pistol was also found in Wendy's purse, loaded. (Another pistol, a shotgun and two sawed-off rifles—one the carbine Tania Hearst had carried into the Hibernia Bank—were found in the bedrooms. And in the refrigerator, neatly wrapped in aluminum foil, nestled next to the eggs, was a packet of eighty-four $1 bills, one among them bearing Serial Number L07097168D; a "bait bill" stolen from the Carmichael bank.)

Yoshimura asked if she could get her contact lenses, and Padden let her take them off the kitchen table. On the table, between a vase of pink flowers, three coffee cups, and a box of envelopes, there—as yet unsent, perhaps just finished—was Wendy's letter to Willie Brandt, the official death certificate of the Symbionese Liberation Army.

"Let's clear out," said Padden. "We're not going to touch anything until we get the warrant." Casey started to lead Hearst out when suddenly, "very politely," Patty asked if she could change her clothes. She had, it seemed, wet her pants.

Postscript

The SLA was almost a cultural test tube, a specimen sample from a bitter side of the sixties that marched apace after virtually all their comrades veered aside. Yet they marked time oddly, retracing rather than resolving the past. Culturally rootless, out of their time, they leaped into the social void—and in the eerie half-life of their plunge, among themselves if nowhere else, they recreated something of the pained and pimpled adolescence of the New Left.

Now the corpse didn't even twitch; the cobra was dead. Crushed—not by the police who trapped them in LA; not by the legion of G-men who tracked them back and forth across the country—but by the earnest and brute morality they lashed upon themselves. It was only the armored quality of their fevered rhetoric, its ability to blunt and foil even the most common sense, that allowed them to survive so long. The shadow of Marcus Foster still stood to measure their isolation and naïveté; the ghost of Myrna Opsahl cursed the cheap pious arrogance with which they sloughed off responsibility. As the symbol of the SLA the mysterious *naga* had been replaced by the crumpled, cellophane-wrapped bandolier the shoplifting General Teko had jammed up his sleeve.

There will be judgments, perhaps better made with time, of just how just had been their rage, how pitifully naïve had been their Justice, how corrupting their self-righteous certainty of moral superiority. Perhaps the arrogance of that certainty will be the final lesson from the Symbionese, for their story was almost a case study: Individuals unattached to any politic—no Movement, no Revolution; frustrated romantics with no liaison to the People they had reduced to such a pocket cliché.

495

The nation from which they sprang is itself a mass of contradictions, and the times are more than usually confusing. But whatever the path of the future, it will not be mapped by kids plotting in dank cellars, and pride, not guilt, will give us leaders.

Appendix

Appendix

A Selection of SLA Documents

Codes of War of the United Symbionese
Liberation Army

PENALTY BY DEATH

ALL CHARGES THAT FACE A DEATH PENALTY SHALL BE PRESENTED TO A JURY TRIAL MADE UP OF THE MEMBERS OF THE GUERRILLA FORCES. THE JURY SHALL BE SELECTED BY THE CHARGED AND THE JUDGE CONDUCTING THE TRIAL SHALL BE SELECTED BY THE CHARGED ALSO. THE CHARGED SHALL SELECT HIS OR HER DEFENSE, AND THE TRIAL JUDGE SHALL SELECT THE PROSECUTOR. THE JURY SHALL NUMBER AT LEAST 3/4THS OF THE REMAINING MEMBERS OF THE CELLS, AND THE VERDICT MUST BE UNANIMOUS.

1. THE SURRENDER TO THE ENEMY.

2. THE KILLING OF A COMRADE OR DISOBEYING ORDERS THAT RESULT IN THE DEATH OF A COMRADE.

3. THE DESERTING OF A COMRADE ON THE FIELD OF WAR.

a. LEAVING A TEAM POSITION, THEREBY NOT COVERING A COMRADE.

b. LEAVING A WOUNDED COMRADE.

4. THE INFORMING TO THE ENEMY OR SPYING AGAINST THE PEOPLE OR GUERRILLAS.

5. LEAVING A CELL UNIT OR BASE CAMP WITHOUT ORDERS.

Any comrade may leave the guerrilla forces if she or he feels that they no longer feel the courage or faith in the people and the struggle that we wage. A comrade, however, must follow the CODES OF WAR in doing this: that is, he or she must inform the commanding guerrilla of their wish to go from guerrilla force. Thereupon, the guerrilla in command will release them in a safe area. The excombatants may only leave with his or her personal side-arm. REMEMBER, this is the ONLY way a comrade may leave the S.L.A., any other way is deserting, punishable by death.

6. ALL PAID OR UNPAID INFORMANTS OPERATING WITHIN THE COMMUNITY AGAINST THE PEOPLE AND THE GUERRILLA FORCES ARE SENTENCED WITHOUT TRIAL TO IMMEDIATE DEATH.

PENALTY BY DISCIPLINARY ACTION

DISCIPLINARY ACTION SHOULD BE PRIMARILY TO AID THE COLLECTIVE GROWTH OF THE CELL, SO THAT THROUGH POSITIVE ACTION THE MISTAKE IS UNDERSTOOD, ALL CHARGES THAT FACE DISCIPLINARY ACTION SHALL BE UNDER THE FULL CONTROL OF THE GUERRILLA IN COMMAND, AND SHE OR HE SHALL WEIGH ALL EVIDENCE AND SHALL DECIDE THE VERDICT, AND IF NEEDED, DIRECT THE DISCIPLINARY ACTION TO BE TAKEN BY THE CHARGED COMRADE NECESSARY TO DIRECT HIM OR HER. EXAMPLES OF DISCIPLINARY ACTION ARE: THE CLEANING AND MAINTENANCE OF ALL CELL ARMS, AMMUNITION AND EXPLOSIVES FOR ONE WEEK, THE UPKEEP OF OUTHOUSES, THE FULL SUSPENSION OF WINE AND CIGARETTES, AND EXTRA DUTIES SUCH AS ADDITIONAL WATCHES, PRACTICE AND STUDY PERIODS, CORRESPONDENCE, FILING, TYPING, WASHING, CLEANING, COOKING, AND PHYSICAL EXERCISES.

1. LACK OF RESPONSIBILITY AND DETERMINED DECISIVENESS IN FOLLOWING ORDERS.

2. NONVIGILANCE OR THE LEAVING OF AN ASSIGNED POST WITHOUT ORDERS.

3. LACK OF RESPONSIBILITY IN MAINTAINING EQUIPMENT OR PROFICIENCY IN ALL GUERRILLA SKILLS, ESPECIALLY SHOOTING.

4. THE USE OF ANY UNMEDICALLY PRESCRIBED DRUG.

THIS RULE RELATES TO THE USE OF SUCH DRUGS AS HEROIN, SPEED, PEYOTE, MESCALINE, REDS, PEP PILLS, WHITES, YELLOW JACKETS, BENNIES, DEXIES, GOOF BALLS, LSD, AND ANY OTHER KIND OF HALLUCINARY DRUGS. HOWEVER, PERMISSION IS GRANTED FOR THE USE OF ONLY TWO TYPES OF RELAXING DRUGS: THESE ARE MARIJUANA, AND/OR BEER AND WINE AND OTHER ALCOHOL. THIS PERMISSION IS ONLY GRANTED WHEN APPROVED BY THE GUERRILLA IN COMMAND, AND WITH VERY RESTRAINING USE ONLY. NO OFFICER MAY GRANT THE USE OF ANY OF THESE SAID DRUGS TO THE FULL NUMBER OF FORCES UNDER HIS OR HER COMMAND. IF THIS PERMISSION IS GRANTED ONLY HALF THE FORCE WILL BE ALLOWED TO TAKE PART, WHILE THE OTHER HALF WILL STAND GUARD DUTY.

THE PAST HAS SHOWN ONCE TRUE REVOLUTIONARIES

HAVE SERIOUSLY UNDERTAKEN REVOLUTIONARY ARMS STRUGGLE, MARIJUANA AND ALCOHOL ARE NOT USED FOR RECREATIONAL PURPOSES OR TO DILUTE OR BLUR THE CONSCIOUSNESS OF REALITY, BUT VERY SMALL AMOUNTS FOR MEDICINAL PURPOSES TO CALM NERVES UNDER TIMES OF TENSION, NOT TO DISTORT REALITY.

5. THE FAILURE TO SEVER ALL PAST CONTACTS OR FAILING TO DESTROY ALL EVIDENCE OF IDENTIFICATION OR ASSOCIATION.

PENALTY BY DISCIPLINARY ACTION

6. KILLING OF AN UNARMED ENEMY: IN THIS INSTANCE THE ENEMY REFERS TO MEMBERS OF U.S.A. RANK AND FILE ONLY AND NOT TO ANY MEMBERS OF THE CIA, FBI, OR OTHER SPECIAL AGENTS OR ANY POLITICAL POLICE STATE AGENTS. MEMBERS OF THE USA MILITARY RANK AND FILE ARE TO BE ACCORDED THIS DISTINCTION BECAUSE WE RECOGNIZE THAT MANY OF THEM HAVE BEEN FORCED INTO MEMBERSHIP EITHER DIRECTLY, THROUGH THE DRAFT, OR INDIRECTLY DUE TO ECONOMIC PRESSURES.

7. TORTURES OR SEXUAL ASSAULT ON EITHER A COMRADE OR PEOPLE OF THE ENEMY.

8. CRIMINAL ACTS AGAINST THE POOR, COMRADES OR GUERRILLA FORCES.

9. MALICIOUS CURSING OR ANY KIND OF DISRESPECT TO THOSE IN COMMAND, A COMRADE, OR THE PEOPLE.

10. DECEIVING OR LYING TO FELLOW COMRADES OR THE PEOPLE. IF ANY OF THESE ACTS ARE COMMITTED ON A CONTINUOUS BASIS, THE CHARGED COMRADE SHALL BECOME A PRISONER OF THE CELL AND SHALL REMAIN IN THIS PRISONER STATUS UNTIL SUCH TIME AS SHE OR HE IS ABLE TO PROVE THEIR RENEWED COMMITMENT TO REVOLUTIONARY DISCIPLINE AND REVOLUTIONARY PRINCIPLES OR THE CHARGED MAY REQUEST TO BE DISHONORABLY DISCHARGED [sic].

CONDUCT OF GUERRILLA FORCES TOWARDS THE ENEMY SOLDIERS AND PRISONERS

1. PRISONERS OF WAR SHALL BE HELD UNDER THE INTERNATIONAL CODES OF WAR, THEY SHALL BE PROVIDED WITH ADEQUATE FOOD, MEDICAL AID, AND EXERCISES.

2. ALL USA MILITARY RANK AND FILE FORCES SHALL BE ALLOWED TO SURRENDER UPON OUR CONDITIONS OF SURRENDER, AND THEREUPON THEY SHALL BE CAREFULLY

SEARCHED AND INTERROGATED. ALL PRISONERS ARE TO RE-
CEIVE INSTRUCTION ON THE GOALS OF SYMBIONESE LIBER-
ATION ARMY, THEN RELEASED IN A SAFE AREA.

3. ALL WEAPONS, MEDICAL AND FOOD SUPPLIES, MAPS,
MILITARY EQUIPMENT AND MONEY ARE TO BE CONFISCAT-
ED AND TURNED IN TO THE GUERRILLA IN CHARGE.

4. UNDER NO CONDITIONS SHALL ANY RANK AND FILE
ENEMY SOLDIER BE RELIEVED OF HIS OR HER PERSONAL
PROPERTY.

CONDUCT OF GUERRILLA FORCES TOWARDS THE PEOPLE

ALL GUERRILLA FORCES SHALL CONDUCT THEMSELVES IN
A MANNER OF RESPECT TOWARD THE PEOPLE, AND SHALL
WHEN ABLE AND SAFE TO DO SO, PROVIDE FOOD AND OTH-
ER AID TO THE PEOPLE. THEY SHALL, WHEN POSSIBLE, IN-
FORM THE PEOPLE OF THE GOALS OF THE UNITED SYM-
BIONESE FEDERATION AND ENCOURAGE OTHER WOMEN
AND MEN TO JOIN OUR FORCES AND TO SERVE THE PEOPLE
IN FIGHT FOR FREEDOM.

ALL COMRADES HAVE ONE MAIN RESPONSIBILITY, THAT
IS TO STRUGGLE AND WIN AND STAND TOGETHER, SO NO
COMRADE STANDS ALONE, ALL MUST LOOK OUT FOR EACH
OTHER, ALL MUST AID THE OTHER BLACK, BROWN, RED,
YELLOW, WHITE, MAN OR WOMAN, ALL OR NONE.

THIS DOCUMENT MAY CHANGE FROM TIME TO TIME, SO
OFFICERS ARE REQUESTED TO FOLLOW THE CHANGES WITH
DISCIPLINE.

TO THOSE WHO WOULD BEAR THE HOPES AND FUTURE OF
THE PEOPLE LET THE VOICE OF THEIR GUNS EXPRESS THE
WORD OF FREEDOM.

Gen. Field Marshall
S.L.A.
Cin

THE SEVEN PRINCIPLES OF THE SLA

[*The seven heads of the* naga *were held to represent the seven principles of the SLA, here presented in Swahili, Spanish, and English. The principles are identical to the seven points of the black nationalist creed of Kawaida, but the text explication was apparently developed by the SLA authors.*]

TO THOSE WHO WOULD BEAR THE HOPES AND
FUTURE OF OUR PEOPLE, LET THE VOICE OF
THEIR GUNS EXPRESS THE WORDS OF FREEDOM

UMOJA—LA UNIDAD—UNITY—To strive for and maintain unity in our household, nation and in The Symbionese Federation.

KUJICHAGULIA—LA LIBRE DETERMINACION—SELF DETERMINATION—To define ourselves, name ourselves, speak for ourselves and govern ourselves.

UJIMA—TRABAJO COLLECTIVO Y RESPONSABILIDAD—COLLECTIVE WORK AND RESPONSIBILITY—To build and maintain our nation and the federation together by making our brothers' and sisters' and the Federation's problems our problems and solving them together.

UJAMAA—PRODUCCION COOPERATIVA—COOPERATIVE PRODUCTION—To build and maintain our own economy from our skills, and labor and resources and to insure ourselves and other nations that we all profit equally from our labor.

NIA—PROPOSITO—PURPOSE—To make as our collective vocation the development and liberation of our nation, and all oppressed people, in order to restore our people and all oppressed people to their traditional greatness and humanity.

KUUMBA—CREATIVO—CREATIVITY—To do all we can in order to free our nation and defend the federation and constantly make it and the earth that we all share more beautiful and beneficial.

IMANI—FE—FAITH—To believe in our unity, our leaders, our teachers, our people, and in the righteousness and victory of our struggle and the struggle of all oppressed and exploited people.

THE SYMBIONESE FEDERATION & THE SYMBIONESE
LIBERATION ARMY DECLARATION OF
REVOLUTIONARY WAR & THE SYMBIONESE PROGRAM
August 21, 1973

The Symbionese Federation and The Symbionese Liberation Army is a united and federated grouping of members of different races and people and socialist political parties of the oppressed people of The Fascist United States of America, who have under black and minority leadership formed and joined The Symbionese Federated Republic and have agreed to struggle together in behalf of all their people and races and political parties interest in [sic] the gaining of FREEDOM and SELF DETERMINATION and INDEPENDENCE for all their people and races.

The Symbionese Federation is NOT A GOVERNMENT, but rather it is a united and federated formation of members of different races and people and political parties who have agreed to struggle in a UNITED FRONT for the independance [sic] and self determination of each of their races and people and The Liquidation of the Common Enemy.

And who by this federated formation represent their future and independant pre-governments and nations of their people and races. The Symbionese Federation is NOT A PARTY, but rather is a Federation, for its members are made up of members of all political parties and organizations and races of all the most oppressed people of this fascist nation, thereby forming unity and the full representation of the interests of all the people.

The Symbionese Liberation Army is an army of the people, and is made up of members of all the people. The S.L.A. has no political power or political person over it that dictates who will fight and die if needed for the freedom of our people and children, but does not risk their life or fight to our freedom, but rather the S.L.A. is both political and military in that in the S.L.A. the army officer, whether female or male, is also the political officer and they both are the daughters and sons of the people and they both fight as well as speak for the freedom of our people and children.

The Symbionese Federation and The Symbionese Liberation Army is [sic] made up of the aged, youth and women and men of all races and people. The name Symbionese is taken from the word symbiosis and we define its meaning as a body of dissimilar bodies and organisms living in deep and loving harmony and partnership in the best interest of all within the body.

We of the Symbionese Federation and The S.L.A. define ourselves by this name because it states that we are no longer willing to allow the enemy of all our people and children to murder, oppress and exploit us nor define us by color and thereby maintain division among us, but rather have joined together under black and minority leadership in behalf of all our different races and people to build a better and new world for our children and people's future. We are a United Front and Federated Coalition of members from the Asian, Black, Brown, Indian, White,

Women, Grey and Gay Liberation Movements.

Who have all come to see and understand that only if we unite and build our new world and future, will there really be a future for our children and people. We of the People, and not the ruling capitalist class, will build a new world and system. Where there is really freedom and a true meaning to justice and equality for all women and men of all races and people, and an end to the murder and oppression, exploitation of all people.

We of the Symbionese Federation and The S.L.A. are the children of all oppressed people, who have decided to redefine ourselves as a Symbionese Race and People. Yet, recognizing the rich cultures of each and enforcing our rights to existance [sic] of our many cultures within a united federation of independant and sovereign nations, each of them flourishing and protected by its own laws and codes of self determination.

We are of many colors, but yet of one mind, for we all in history's time on this earth have become part of each other in suffering and in mind, and have agreed that the murder, oppression, and exploitation of our children and people must end now, for we all have seen the murder, oppression and exploitation of our people for too long under the hand of the same enemy and class of people and under the same system.

Knowing this, the Symbionese Federation and the S.L.A. know that our often murderous alienation from each other aids and is one of the fundamental strengths behind the ruling capitalist class's ability to murder and oppress us all. By not allowing them to define us by color, and also recognizing that by refusing ourselves to also internalize this false division definition [sic] knowing that in mind and body we are facing the same enemy and that we are all comrades of one people, the murdered and oppressed, we are now able to become a united people under the Symbionese Federation and make true the words of our codes of unity that TO DIE A RACE, AND BE BORN A NATION, IS TO BECOME FREE.

Therefore, we of the Symbionese Federation and The S.L.A. DO NOT under the rights of human beings submit to the murder, oppression and exploitation of our children and people and do under the rights granted to the people under The Declaration of Independence [sic] The United States, do now by the rights of our children and people and by Force of Arms and with every drop of our blood, *Declare Revolutionary War* against The Fascist Capitalist Class, and all their agents of murder, oppression and exploitation. We support by Force of Arms the just struggles of all oppressed people for self determination and independance within the United States and The World. And hereby offer to all liberation movements, revolutionary workers groups, and peoples organizations our total aid and support for the struggle for freedom and justice for all people and races. We call upon all revolutionary black and other oppressed people within the Fascist United States to come together and join The Symbionese Federation and fight in the forces of The Symbionese Liberation Army.

THE GOALS OF THE SYMBIONESE LIBERATION ARMY

1. To unite all oppressed people into a fighting force and to destroy the system of the capitalist state and all its value systems. To create in its place a system [of] sovereign nations that are in the total interest of all its races and people, based on the true affirmation of life, love, trust, and honesty, freedom and equality that is truly for all.
2. To assure the rights of all people to self determination and the rights to build their own nation and government, with representatives that have shown through their actions to be in the interest of their people. To give the right to all people to select and elect their own representatives and governments by direct vote.
3. To build a people's federated council, who will be a male and female of each People's Council or Sovereign Nation of The Symbionese Federation of Nations, who shall be the representatives of their nations in the forming of trade pacts and unified defense against any external enemy that may attack any of the free nations of the federation and to form other aids to each others' needs.
4. To aid and defend the cultural rights of all the sovereign nations of The Symbionese Federation, and to aid each nation in the building of educational and other institutions to meet and serve this need for its people.
5. To place the control of all the institutions and industries, of each nation into the hands of its people. To aid sovereign nations of the federation to build nations where work contributes concretely to the full interest and needs of its workers and the communal interest of its communities and its people and the mutual interest of all within the federation of nations.
6. To aid and defend the rights of all oppressed people to build nations which do not institute oppression and exploitation, but rather does institute the environment of freedom and defends that freedom on all levels and for all of the people, and by any means necessary.
7. To give back to all people their human and constitutional rights, liberty, equality and justice and the right to bear arms in the defense of these rights.
8. To create a system where our aged are cared for with respect, love, and kindness and aided and encouraged to become assets in their own ways to their nations and to their communal community. That the life that moves around them is not a frightening and murderous one and where life is not a fear, but rather one of love and feeling and of unity.
9. To create a system and laws that will neither force people into nor force them to stay into personal relationships that they do not wish to be in, and to destroy all chains instituted by legal and social laws of the capitalist state which acts as a reinforcing system to maintain this form of imprisonment.
10. To create institutions that will aid, reinforce and educate the growth

of our comrade women and aid them in making a new true and better role to live in life and in the defining of themselves as a new and free people.

11. To create new forms of life and relationships that bring true meanings of love to people's relationships, and to form communes on the community level and bring the children of the community into being the responsibility of the community, to place our children in the union of real comradeship and in the care and loving interest of the revolutionary community.

12. To destroy the prison system, which the capitalist state has used to imprison the oppressed and exploited, and thereby destroy the love, unity, and hopes of millions of lives and families. And to create in its place a system of comradeship and that of group unity and education on a communal and revolutionary level within the community, to bring home our daughters and sons, and sisters and brothers, fathers and mothers, and welcome them home with love and a new revolutionary comradeship of unity.

13. To take control of all state land and that of the capitalist class and to give back the land to the people. To form laws and codes that safeguard that no person can own the land, or sell the land, but rather the nations' people own the land and use it for their needs and interest to live. No one can own or sell the air, the sky, the water, the trees, the birds, the sun, for all of this world belongs to the people of this earth.

14. To take control of all buildings and apartment buildings of the capitalist class and fascist government and to totally destroy the rent system of exploitation.

15. To build a federation of nations, who shall formulate programs and unions of actions and interests that will destroy the capitalist value system and its other anti-human institutions and who will be able to do this by meeting all the basic needs of all of the people and their nations. For they will be all able to do this because each nation will have full control of all of its industries and institutions and does not run them for profit, but in the full interest of all the people of its nation.

16. To destroy all forms and institutions of Racism, Sexism, Ageism, Capitalism, Fascism, Individualism, Possessiveness, Competiveness and all other such institutions that have made and sustained capitalism and the capitalist class system that has oppressed and exploited all of the people of our history.

By this means and the mutual aid and unity of each nation within The Symbionese Federation, will each nation be able to provide to each person and couple and family free of cost the five basic needs of life, which are food, health care, housing, education and clothing, and in this way allowing people to be able to find and form new values and new systems of relationships and interests based on a new meaning to life and love.

"IF THE QUEST FOR FREEDOM IS DEATH
THEN BY THE DEATH OF THE ENEMY WILL
BLACK AND OTHER OPPRESSED PEOPLE
FIND AND REGAIN THEIR FREEDOM"

THE UNITED SYMBIONESE WAR COUNCIL
TERMS OF MILITARY/POLITICAL ALLIANCE

Our commitment to the revolutionary struggle for self-determination for all oppressed people and races and the international proletarian revolution is total and fully uncompromisable. Therefore, any relationship the Symbionese War Council has with any group or organization is based on their active military/political commitment to the goal of gaining freedom for all oppressed people and races.

1. Our alliance with any group or organization is based upon their firm decision to fight as well as talk in behalf of the people's interest, and once this commitment is clear then we can come together in order to:

   1) collectively develop a common strategy
   2) work together to develop tactical co-ordination
   3) Assist each other in developing the abilities and talents of all the members of the Symbionese War Council and to analyze the strengths and weaknesses of the leadership in order to constantly better all aspects of the ability and actions of the War Council, and its individual leadership from other organizations.

2. Command positions of The War Council are subject to the approval of all members of the council, based upon the military/political thinking and ability of the presented officer to work with others in the interest of freedom for all people and races.

3. Command positions in The War Council are not appointed by who one knows, one's sex, one's color or the group or organization one belongs to, but only by one's Courage, Determination, Intelligence, Aggressive Initiative and Capability as a Leader, and one's Military/Political thinking.

4. All members of The War Council are expected and fully are responsible for the military political leadership of The S.L.A., they must fight and speak for the people and this must be understood clearly by all members.

5. No member of The War Council can elect or select himself or herself to a position such as the head of a government or people's council; the War Council is totally an alliance OF WAR AGAINST THE COMMON ENEMY. The people themselves shall have and hold the ONLY RIGHT to select and elect their governments and government heads of state.

6. It is NOT the policy of The War Council to rip off leadership or membership from other organizations, but rather it is the policy of The War Council to aid and support the development and education of leadership to fullfill [sic] truly its responsibility to the people, and to allow the collective intelligence, leadership and resourcefullness [sic] of the leadership from different organizations and groups to flourish together and grow together; thereby forming an area where the collective interests and needs as well as weaknesses and

strengths of each can benefit each IN THE COMMON STRUGGLE TO LIQUIDATE THE COMMON ENEMY.

7. [word illegible] military force is a necessity for actualizing political goals and must therefore be held as a priority; therefore, the true assistance in the supplying of military equipment, materials, finances, personal [sic] is of the utmost importance, once these forces have fully committed themselves to open and total warfare against the common enemy and members of The War Council must understand this clearly.

8. Leadership of any group or organization who is truly committed and in agreement with the goals of the S.L.A. and the terms of military/political alliance may be presented to The War Council; however, the presented officer's membership is not confirmed until it is verified that prior to presentation for membership a combat action has been taken part in by that group, or organization within the last 12 months.

9. Once The War Council collectively agrees to an action or plan of strategy then that action shall be understood as an action of the S.L.A., and not of any single group or organization. Just as the fingers cannot call themselves a fist, and the fist cannot call itself the fingers. From time to time the membership on the War Council may disagree upon a particular action or strategy. When in disagreement, that particular membership need not participate in The S.L.A. action, but membership on The War Council is maintained only as long as all commitments made to the collective Symbionese War Council are continued to be fully adhered to [sic]. It is the disagreeing group or organization's responsibility to, on its own, prove out their ideas in order to change or modify its own or the collective War Council's direction.

10. It is the policy of The War Council not to involve itself in the internal political affairs or disagreements that may result within different organizations or groups. However, The War Council recognizes and accepts membership to the Council of any military/political unit, cell or organization that qualifies and shall recognize them as true representatives of that particular organization or group. It is the collective policy of The War Council that the failure of the elected leadership to take her or his revolutionary responsibility as far as the War Council is concerned shall be totally the responsibility of the elected leader and not that of The War Council.

11. Organizations or groups that wish to serve in combat units must select two persons, one female and one male (if possible), who have full responsibility and authority to act and represent their group or organization and who will hold a command position in the unified command of The United Symbionese War Council.

12. All members of The Symbionese War Council must clearly understand that our commitment is total and our goal is the total freedom

of the people and children and the destroying totally of the common enemy. Therefore, it is held that any restraining of supplies or other war materials etc. for political reasons or reactionary reasons or political chess games with the enemy, by any officer or other persons in the War Council, that by its actions endangers the lives of the women and men of The Symbionese Liberation Army shall be held as a full and total violation of this alliance pact and compromising with the enemy and the freedom and life of the people and children and therefore is punishable by death.

TO THOSE WHO WOULD BEAR THE HOPES AND FUTURE OF THE PEOPLE, LET THE VOICE OF THEIR GUNS EXPRESS THE WORDS OF FREEDOM.

[*On January 17, 1974, a week after the arrest of Joe Remiro and Russ Little, after the Clayton fire and the discovery of the SLA safehouse, Nancy Ling Perry posted a letter to the media.*]

A LETTER TO THE PEOPLE
FROM FAHIZAH (former name nancy ling perry)

"TO THOSE WHO WOULD BEAR THE HOPES AND FUTURE OF THE PEOPLE, LET THE VOICE OF THEIR GUNS EXPRESS THE WORDS OF FREEDOM."

Greetings, my comrade sisters and brothers, all love, power and freedom to you. I am very glad to have this opportunity to speak to you, even though I know that what I am feeling cannot be completely expressed in words. You may have heard of me, not because I am any more important than any of you, but simply because my former name has been in the news lately. My name was Nancy Ling Perry, but my true name is Fahizah. What that name means is one who is victorious, and I am one who believes in the liberation and victory of the people, because I have learned that what one really believes is what will come to pass. So, my name is Fahizah and I am a freedom fighter in an information/intelligence unit of the United Federated Forces of the Symbionese Liberation Army. I still am that, in spite of the fact that I am now being sought for a political action, and in spite of the fact that two of my closest companeros are now chained in the Adjustment Center (the prison's prison) at San Quentin concentration camp. I am still with other members of the SLA information/intelligence unit, and I am hiding only from the enemy and not from the people. I have no intention of deserting my committment [*sic*] nor would I ever try to run away from it, because I have learned that there is no flight to freedom except that of an armed projectile. Although it is the practice of the Symbionese Liberation Army to act rather than talk, I am compelled to speak because I wish to make clear my position and why I am fighting, what it is I am fighting for, what the purpose and nature of the SLA information/intelligence unit is, and why I will continue to fight.

First of all, I think I should tell you something about my background and the evolution of my consciousness. Basically, I have three backgrounds: I have a work background, a love background, and a prison background. My prison background means that I have close ties and feelings with our incarcerated brothers and sisters. What they have taught me is that if people on the outside do not understand the necessity of defending them through force of arms, then it is because these people on the outside do not yet realize that they are in an immediate danger of being thrown into concentration camps themselves, tortured, or shot down in the streets for expressing their beliefs. What my love background taught me was a whole lot of what love is all about, and that the greater one's capacity for love is, the greater is one's longing for freedom. What my work background taught me is that one of the things that every revolutionary does is to fight to get back the fruits of her or his own labor and the control of his or her own destiny.

When I was in high school in 1963-64, I witnessed the first military coup, against we the people of this country. I saw us passively sit by our t.v.'s and unconsciously watch as the militarily armed corporate state took over the existing government and blatantly destroyed the constitution that some of us still believed in. I listened to the people around me deny that a military coup had taken place and claim that such a thing could not happen here. The people that I grew up around were so politically naïve that their conceptions of a military coup only recognized those that have occurred in South America and African countries where the military and ruling class took over the government by an open force of arms. But the method of taking over the government was different here. Here the coup was simply accomplished by assassinating the then president john kennedy, and then assassinating any further opposition to the dictator who was to take power; that dictator is the current president richard nixon. In 1964 I witnessed these and other somewhat hidden beginnings of the military/corporate state which we now live in. And I heard my teachers and the government controlled media spread lies about what had happened. I saw the Civil Rights protests, the killings and bombings of my black brothers and sisters and the conditioned reactions of extreme racism in my school and home. When I questioned my teachers about how these occurrences related to the meanings of democracy and freedom that we were told existed to protect us all, the answer I got was that we were better off not knowing the truth about what was happening. I told my teachers and my family and friends, that I felt that we were all being used as pawns and puppets, and that those who had taken over the government were trying to keep us asleep and in a political stupor. I asked my teachers to tell me what happened in Nazi Germany; I asked them to tell me the meaning of fascism; I asked them to tell me the meaning of genocide; and when I began to hear about a war in Vietnam, I asked them to tell me the meaning of imperialism. The answer to all my questions then was either silence, or a reply filled with confusion and lies, and a racist pride and attitude that well, after all, it was all for us.

The experience of living in *Amerikkka* has since taught me the realities of what fascism, imperialism, and genocide mean; and I have discovered the truth about the military take-over and the police state dictatorship, not because I studied about it in college, but because I see it everyday, and because truth is something that is honestly known, as easily as beauty is seen. There is no need for me to relate here everything that I have seen, or everything that I am sure you are already aware of. I am sure, my sisters and brothers, that you realize that the government is now in the rapid and steady process of removing the means of survival from the lower class and giving these benefits to the middle class in an effort to rally support from them. And as the government is removing these means of survival from the people, then naturally the people who have been robbed must in turn take back what rightfully belongs to them, and take back what they need in order to survive. This the current dictatorship calls a crime, whether they take food from the grocery store, or take to the streets to make a speech, or take a gun in their hand to defend themselves.

As a member of the Symbionese Liberation Army information/intelligence unit, I fight against our common oppressor, and this I do with my gun as well as my mind. I try to use my mind and my imagination to uncover facts, so that when the SLA attacks it will be in the right place, and that the actions of the more experienced SLA combat units will truly serve to benefit the people and answer their needs. The action taken by the SLA combat unit in reference to the Oakland Board of Education was a specific response to political police state programs and the failure of the Board to heed the rights and demands of the people in the community. The specific program was one of the photo identification (similar to the system of apartheid in South Africa), biological classification in the form of bio-dossiers which classify students according to race and political beliefs, internal warfare computer files, and armed police state patrols within the schools. Intensely thorough intelligence operations carried out by one of the SLA information units was able to obtain factual information that Foster's signature was the first to appear on the Nixon Administration inspired proposal for armed police agents within certain Oakland schools and various forms of computer classification of students. Further intelligence revealed that Foster's background included membership on the Philadelphia Crime Commission. Foster's sideman, Blackburn, is a CIA agent. As director of Education in East Africa he worked to implement test programs against black people there, and he trained other agents to carry them out so that he could return to his country and introduce those same programs here. I feel a need to explain this again because I want to make it clear that the SLA was not indiscriminantly issuing death warrants for Foster, Blackburn and anyone else, but rather we were attacking the programs and proposal of which they were the initiators, supporters and first signers. Such an attack was the only means left open to us to demand that the people's wishes be met, and that all such dangerous, genocidal programs be stopped.

The government controlled media has made some reference to the effect that this action was carried out by white people made up in black face. Members of the SLA do not have to make up in black face in order to defend the black community, since the SLA is a federation formed in the style of a revolutionary United Nations whose commanding leadership is composed of representatives of the black, brown, yellow, red and white communities. We have more than enough members from every race to carry out any operation. As revolutionaries we would never disguise ourselves by race, because we would never deliberately act in a manner that would bring further police investigation onto any one race of peoples [sic]. But I would like to ask, since when does one have to be black in order to care about the murder of 14 year old Tyrone Guyton by political police state death squads, since when does one have to be white in order to feel for the starving children in Appalachia, since when does one have to be an Asian in order to care about stopping the na-palming of children in Vietnam, since when does one have to be brown in order to fight against the mass slaughters being conducted by the military junta in Chile? ? ? ? Since when? ? ? ? Not since we have come to re-alize that we are all one in struggle.

I am a member of the Symbionese Liberation Army information/intel-ligence unit and that means that my responsibility is to aid the combat units with information, and keep myself armed at all times. I am in a race to learn how to fight, because I am in a race to survive. SLA infor-mation/intelligence units have a military/political alliance with SLA com-bat units. What that means is that information units totally support armed struggle. That is to say that all members of the SLA understand that politics are inseparable from struggle, in fact politics have no mean-ing without armed combat and information units to give politics a pur-pose.

The Symbionese Liberation Army is unlike many existing political or-ganizations in this country which support the armed liberation struggles of peoples throughout the world, but when it comes to the struggle here in Amerikkka, they consistently denounce militancy and revolutionary violence, and in so doing denounce the only means left to the people to achieve their liberation.

I believe that whenever people are confronted with oppression, star-vation and the death of their freedom that they want to fight. It has been the history of many political leaders to suppress this will of the people, and to pretend that the people do not have the right to fight, and to pre-tend that the people will somehow achieve their liberation without revo-lutionary violence. But the truth is that there has never been a precedent for a non-violent revolution; the defenseless and unarmed people of Chile can testify to that. All members of the SLA recognize that we, right here in Amerikkka are in a state of war, and that in a state of war, all must be armed, and understand the true meaning of self-defense. When any member of the people's army strikes out at the murderer of our peo-ple and children, we are doing so in self-defense, we are doing so be-cause we are left no alternative, and force of arms is now our only legal means to affect [sic] revolutionary justice. However, the natural instincts of many people in our country have become perverted by the condition-ings to which they have been subjected, they have been conditioned to be afraid of revolutionary violence. I no longer have these fears because as a comrade of mine named Osceola has taught me, "The only way to de-stroy fear is to destroy the makers of fear, the murderer and the oppressor." A revolutionary is not a criminal nor is she or he an adventurer, and revolutionary violence is nothing but the most profound means of achieving internal as well as external balance.

I would like to correct and clarify the information given to you by the regime-controlled media and police-state reports associating the Symbionese Liberation Army with the August 7th. First of all, statements about August 7th literature and original communiques being found in the Concord house are completely untrue. The Symbionese Liberation Army is NOT the August 7th; In fact, the August 7th is a counter revolutionary Oakland City and California State police plot to discredit revolutionaries and confuse the people. Freedom fighters act only in the interest of the people, they do not unnecessarily shoot down a helicopter whose crashing would endanger lives of people in their communities, nor do they credit themselves with events or accidents that occur in which they had no part, nor do they issue threats which they are unprepared to carry out, nor do they expose the nature and whereabouts of their forces, as for example in the recent statement issued by August 7th saying that armed guerilla [sic] units existed inside the prisons. The events and communiqués associated with the August 7th served only enemy purposes: that is, a state wide lock-down went into effect in the prisons and the people began to think of revolutionary action as that which would endanger their lives and homes. As a member of the SLA I can tell you that the SLA takes full credit and responsibility for its actions, we acknowledge everything that we do, and if we had shot down a helicopter, we would say so; and if I had participated as a decoy in the taxi cab incident I would say so. However, I would like to tell you not to rely solely on my analysis that the August 7th and the Oakland and California State Political Police are one and the same, but instead, just take a look for yourselves. Ask yourselves of the extent to which the police state will go to discredit revolutionaries by labelling all street violence as revolutionary activity and by issuing nothing but threatening communiques and then saying that such threats were coming from revolutionaries. It isn't just coincidence that the week the August 7th issued an idle threat against the life of prison official Procunier, was the same week that the California legislature re-instated the death penalty.

The house in Concord, Calif. was a Symbionese Liberation Army information/intelligence headquarters, nothing more. The house was set on fire by me only to melt away any fingerprints that may have been overlooked. It never was intended that the fire would totally destroy the premises, because there was nothing left there that was of any real consequence to us, nor was there any material left behind that could stagnate the functioning ability of the SLA to carry on the struggle. The reports that mass armaments were found in that house is a lie. It is an attempt to frame my 2 comrade brothers and it is an assertion to cover up the fact that there were no weapons found there. All that remained were 3 broken BB guns, a couple of malfunctioning gas masks, a few research books, and several liberation posters on the wall. Also, let me tell you that no one living or coming to that house was a part of the SLA combat forces. This can be easily verified; first of all, everyone in SLA combat forces is offensively armed with cyanide bullets in all weapons that they carry; and up until today this had NOT been the case for SLA information/intelligence units or any support units, at that time all units but combat were only defensively armed with hand guns and carried no cyanide bullets. Secondly, we can easily verify that the ballistics on the .380 now in the hands of pig agents do not match those of the weapon used in the attack on the Oakland Board of Education. Information/intelligence units or any support units were never allowed to possess or have any contact with combat unit weapons. Beginning January 11th however, a directive was issued by The SLA and The Court of the People stating that as of that date, all units of The Symbionese Liberation Army are to be heavily, and offensively armed with cyanide bullets in all their weapons. I would like to convey the word, to my 2 captured companeros: you have not been forgotten, and you will be defended because there has been no set back and all combat forces are intact.

There really are no words available to me to express what I feel about the capture of my two companeros. They are in a concentration camp now because none of us were offensively armed, and because I was not aware that they were under attack. But my beautiful brothers, as we have said many times, we learn from our mistakes, and we learn from our active participation in struggle, not from political rhetoric, so we won't cry, but simply fight on; and right on with that. A comrade of mine, Bo, says something that I'd like to leave you with:

"There are two things to remember about revolution, we are going to get our asses kicked, and we are going to win."

"DEATH TO THE FASCIST INSECT THAT PREYS UPON THE LIFE OF THE PEOPLE."

Fahizah

[On February 12, eight days after the kidnapping of Patty Hearst, a San Francisco radio station received the first taped message from the SLA—this statement from the then-unidentified Cinque and a message from Patty.]

To those who would bear the hopes and future of our people, let the voice of their guns express the words of freedom: Greetings to the people, fellow comrades, brothers and sisters.

My name is Cinque, and to my comrades I am known as Cin. I am a Black man and representative of Black people. I hold the rank of general field marshal in the United Federated Forces of the Symbionese Liberation Army.

Today I have received an order from the Symbionese War Council, the Court of the People, to the effect that I am ordered to convey the following message in behalf of the SLA, and to insert a taped word of comfort and verification, that Patricia Campbell Hearst is alive and safe.

The Symbionese Liberation Army is a federated union that maintains political elements of many different liberation struggles, and of many different races. Our unified purpose is to liberate the oppressed people of this nation and to aid other oppressed people around the world in their struggle against fascist imperialism and the robbery of their freedom and homeland. Since this is the purpose of the SLA, it is therefore clear to us, as it will be to all oppressed people, that our interest is to serve and defend the people and not ourselves, since the people shall always come first, themselves.

The SLA has arrested the subject [Patricia Hearst] for the crimes that her mother and father have, by their actions, committed against we, the American people, and oppressed people of the world. In understanding this charge, we must first understand who the Hearsts are, and who they serve and represent.

Randolph A. Hearst is the corporate chairman of the fascist media empire of the ultra-right Hearst Corporation, which is one of the largest propaganda institutions of this oppressive military dictatorship of the militarily armed corporate state that we now live under in this nation.

The primary goal of this empire is to save and form a necessary propaganda and smokescreen to shield the American people from the realities of the corporate dictatorship that Richard Nixon and Gerald Ford represent. This network of propaganda programs and confusion has succeeded in hiding the truth from the people; that truth being that this nation has suffered its first military coup and that the Constitution, which some of us still believe in, has been overthrown.

The fascist Hearst Corporation, composed of, firstly, a national newspaper syndicate which includes the San Francisco *Examiner*, the *Chronicle*, and others which jump from California and to as far away as New York and Philadelphia;

Secondly, a magazine monopoly composed of over 13 publications, which include, for example, *House Beautiful, Harper's Bazaar, Town and Country* and *Cosmopolitan*;

Thirdly, a TV and radio station empire across the nation, with production and propaganda fields of both national and international use;

Fourth, ownership of vast areas of real estate in the United States and Mexico, forest, grasslands and cattle farms.

All of this is directly connected with Washington and the corporate dictatorship of Richard Nixon and Gerald Ford. That is to say, the Hearst empire is one of the empires of the ruling class and its interests are the rich and in direct contradiction with the interests of the people. Therefore, they are enemies of the people.

Mrs. Randolph A. Hearst is a member of the University of California Board of Regents and is responsible along with others appointed by Governor Reagan, for the lowering of funds and the investment of our California tax money in corporations which have interests and do gain profits from the robbery, oppression, genocide carried out by fascist and racist governments around the world, and within the United States itself.

The Regents, with the support of Mrs. Hearst, have time and time again been requested by we, the people, to not invest our money in such fascist corporations as General Motors, Westinghouse, Gulf, Standard Oil, Bank of America and others, who have and do serve and gain profit in the oppression, robbery and murder that is committed against Black people of South Africa, where 70,000 Black children a year die from malnutrition; against white people of Ireland, where U.S.-trained British soldiers shoot down in the streets Irish fathers and mothers and U.S. manufactured tear gas suffocates Irish children as their older brothers and sisters rot in British concentration camps; against the freedom of the Philippine people that the United States and Marco's [sic] puppet soldiers used U.S. manufactured napalm to attempt to burn away the spirit of freedom from the hearts and souls of the poor and starving [sic].

The U.C. Board of Regents, one of California's largest foreign investors, supports, through its investments, the murder of thousands of Black men and women and children of Mozambique, Angola and Rhodesia, murder designed to destroy the spirit that all humanity longs for.

With all these crimes placed before the Board of Regents and Mrs. Hearst, with all the pleas from the people to stop supporting these corporations and the murders of thousands of men, women and children, the Board and Mrs. Hearst did not raise one voice in protest, or refuse to be part of these crimes committed against these people, and those committed against the American people.

For these acts and others, the Court of the People finds the Hearst family accountable for their crimes and hold that they are enemies of the people.

We of the Symbionese Liberation Army hold the Hearst Corporation and the Hearst family and the Board of Regents, as well as the corporate state which they support and aid, are enemies of the people, and that the people have the legal and human right and duty to attack said enemy according to the forms of war taken by the oppressed people against any enemy or murderer and oppressor to regain their freedom and liberty and to give love to their children and people.

It is therefore the directive of this Court that before any forms of negotiations for the release of the subject prisoner be initiated, that an action of good faith be shown on the part of the Hearst family to allow the court and the oppressed people of this world and this nation to ascertain as to the real interests and cooperative attitude of the Hearst family and in so doing, show some form of repentance for the murder and suffering they have aided and profited from; and this good faith gesture is to be in the form of a token gesture to the oppressed people that aid [*sic?*] the corporate state in robbing and removing their rights to freedom and liberty.

This gesture is to be in the form of food to the needy and unemployed, and to which the following instructions are to be followed to the letter.

In closing, and speaking personally for myself, and as a father of two children, I wish to say to Mr. Hearst and Mrs. Hearst that I, as also the persons under my command for the authority of the Court of the People, are not savage killers and madmen, and we do hold a high moral value to life. We value life very deeply, and with all the spirit that we, as human beings, can bring forth in our hearts.

Speaking as a father, I am quite willing to lose both my children, if by that action I could save thousands of white, black, yellow and red children from a life of suffering, exploitation and murder. And I am therefore quite willing to carry out the execution of your daughter to save the life of starving men, women and children of every race; and I along with the loyal men and women of many races who love the people, quite willingly give our lives to free the people at any cost.

And if, as you and others might so easily believe, that we will lose, let it be known that even in death we will win, for the very ashes of this fascist nation will mark our very grave.

PAEAN TO CINQUE

[From the communiqué of April 4, 1974—the same in which Patricia Hearst was first revealed as Tania, an SLA recruit.]

Love to our sisters and brothers in prisons; courage & faith to our two captured soldiers; greetings to all oppressed peoples; may we connect. My name is Fahizah.

The SLA is taking these opportunities to speak with the people now, because we have been having a temporary period of inactivity while waiting for the completion of our unit's last action. We know that the people want far more than 6 million dollars of food; & we will continue to fight for the total liberation of all oppressed peoples by the only means available, that is force of arms. The Court of the People has issued The Codes of War of the Symbionese Liberation Army and I wish to state that Cinque Mtume is the General Field Marshal of the Symbionese Guerilla [*sic*] Forces, as well as chairman of the United Symbionese War Council.

Cinque is a black brother who spent many years of his life in fascist Amerika's concentration camps: manchild years in prison cells & man years in prison cells. Cinque met literally thousands of black, brown, red, yellow & white freedom fighters while he was locked down, courageous comrade George Jackson was one among them. The spirit of all the brothers Cinque knows lives in him now, and the spirit of all the sisters that Cinque never had the opportunity to meet, but knows by common bond—like Assata Shakur, Lolita Lebron & Bernadine [*sic*] Dohrn—is always in his heart.

When Cinque escaped alone on foot from Soledad prison he did so for one reason only: TO FIGHT WITH THE PEOPLE & TO LEAD THE PEOPLE IN REVOLUTION. He did not escape so that he could kick-back & hide & get high: he did not even escape so that he could satisfy a deep and longing personal ache to simply see the people, and be on the streets and re-unite with his family and be a father once again to his children. Cinque escaped so that he could actively stalk the fascist insect that preys upon the life of the people. The lives both he & the people's fighting forces lead now may be harsh and dangerous, but it is better to work with hard reality, than to play in pleasant, but unproductive, enslaving dreams.

Cinque Mtume is the name that was bestowed upon him by his imprisoned sisters & brothers. It is the name of an ancient African Chief who led the fight of his people for freedom. The name means Fifth Prophet, and Cin was many years ago given this name because of his keen instinct and senses, his spiritual consciousness and his deep love for all the people and children of this earth. This does not, however, mean that Cinque is from God or someone that is holy or that he has an extreme ego problem, but simply that he to us and to all oppressed peoples is the instilled hope and spirit of his people & all peoples, and that he is of the people and from the people. A prophet is a leader and fighter who is one of the people. Leaders are individuals who within themselves feel that it is time to lead and bring us one step closer to freedom for all peoples. A leader is one who is able to help the people understand the swiftness and fierceness with which they must move if they would survive.

Part of the revolutionary process in which we are engaged involves the constant redefining of thought, word, and action. We must deal with all the conditions outside ourselves which oppress and enslave us, and we must deal with the enemy within; we must deal with both these diseases simultaneously, and with an unrelenting commitment and understanding that in reality we are not living to die, but rather all who chose to fight to the death are dying to live. Cin's example to the people has taught us thru his actions and by his own words, that he or she who is scared and seeks to run from death will find it, but she or he who is NOT AFRAID and who actively seeks death out will find it NOT AT THEIR DOOR.

We embrace the concepts of art and spiritual consciousness in material relevant terms based upon the common conditions of all oppressed peoples. We have begun to redefine art as the natural creative reflection of our desperate struggle to survive. Art for us is the total process of sharing and communally using what we learn in order to live and to fight. We recognize Cin as an artist for what he teaches the people, but we also realize as he himself has said, that truth has no author. Another thing which we feel is necessary to clarify is the word spirit & all that which is called spiritual. The spirit is the bodies and souls of all the people, and the spiritual is the intensity of our common instincts, as reflected thruout history to fight for the freedom of all oppressed peoples, to save the earth and the children from the putrid disease of bourgeois mentality and the putrid disease of the corporate fascist military state. In a profound and spiritual sense, as our sisters and brothers in the SLA have said, resistance to this disease is the single greatest human endeavor today.

Comrades in struggle, there is a high price that we have paid and will pay for our mistakes, and there is an even higher price which we have been paying for the loss of our leaders. We are speaking to the people now, because we all know that we cannot afford the loss of another leader; and we want the people to know that in spite of the enemy's technology and prestige of terror we DO have a leader that loves the people, and lives and fights for the people. This example helps to make a love among comrades that gives attention, appreciation, care and protection—from each brother and sister to the other.

The oppressed peoples of this nation have and will continue to bring forth their leaders, prophets & fighters until they are free. The people brought forth Malcolm X who came to unite the people and warn the enemy of what would inevitably happen if the people were not freed. The enemy answered by murdering Malcolm. The people then did again bring forth another prophet, that prophet was Martin Luther King who with non-violence & humanity pleaded to the enemy to free the people. And just when King was ready to declare that nonviolent protest would accomplish nothing but the further enslavement and degradation of the people, the enemy murdered King. George Jackson was a prophet & leader from the streets & when the enemy imprisoned him, George received his education in the raw; he learned firsthand that there can be NO compromise with merciless pigs. George Jackson came from the prisons of Amerikkka & love-inspired he boldy fought the oppressor. When the fascist insect locked him down and murdered him, the people knew that they had suffered a great loss, but they failed to unite in immediate retaliation. Now, once again, the people have brought forth another prophet and leader.

This leader comes not to beg and plead with the enemy, he comes not to warn of violence, but is himself the bringer of the children of the wind and the SOUND OF WAR. He has ONE WORD to the children of the oppressed and the children of the oppressor: COME. We have joined together with love and unity and the understanding that those who would be free, must themselves STRIKE THE FIRST BLOW.

TANIA INTERVIEW

[*During the sixteen months, after the Los Angeles shoot-out, that Patricia Hearst and Bill and Emily Harris were underground, they began writing what was to have been a history of the Symbionese Liberation Army. A portion of the book was to have been question-and-answer interviews in which each of the three described their pre-SLA lives and the reasons that led them to become revolutionaries. The unfinished manuscript—including a lengthy section titled "Tania Interview"— was seized by FBI agents when the Harrises and Patty were captured in San Francisco in September, 1975. Following are excerpts from the Tania Interview.*]

Q. Catherine and Randolph Hearst have been presented in the media both as rich pigs and as plain folks at various times. Can you tell us what your family was really like?

A. My first memories of my parents, or any kind of "family life," start when I was about nine years old. The propaganda that's been spread in the media about how close my family is has no basis in reality. My parents hired nurses and governesses to take care of us because they didn't want to do it themselves, or didn't feel capable of doing it themselves. . . .

. . . My parents didn't live a flashy, flamboyant, "beautiful people" type of life. They spent a lot of money on things like houses, planes, boats, vacations, but they still managed to keep themselves real low profile as far as publicity went. They didn't give or go to big parties, you just didn't see anything about Randolph and Catherine Hearst on the society pages. They left that for other members of the family. My father is a very rich and powerful man, and because he's so powerful it was in his interest to keep a low profile. He benefits from the fact that the public identifies my uncle, William Randolph Hearst Jr., as being *the* Hearst pig and doesn't even know about Randolph Apperson Hearst. In fact most people get the two of them confused because the names are somewhat similar. . . . Everything from my upbringing, due to my class position, was trying to make me declare allegiance to my parents' values and ideas. As a young woman in high school, I was more than anything else embarrassed by my parents' wealth and their class position. I had no support— no one to help me understand why I felt the way I did because everyone I knew was from backgrounds similar to mine and couldn't relate to my confusion.

Q. At what point did Steven Weed come into your life?

A. It was during my last year of high school that I met Steven Weed. I was 17 and he was 23. He was a teacher at the school that I went to and I decided that I was going to have an affair with him. I was first attracted to him because [of] the way he felt about his pupils—he hated the little rich bitches from Hillsborough and Woodside. But as we started seeing more of each other, he began to think that maybe a rich bitch isn't so bad after all. Most of my energies began to go into this relationship, and I started college and housekeeping at the same time. I fell in love with Steve and I felt very secure. I thought that I would be able to avoid any further confrontations with my ruling class upbringing because Steve would change my name and rescue me from being "a Hearst." My escapism was reinforced by going to college because during the time when I wasn't with Steve or his friends, I would hide in my studies.

For about a year and a half, I was content to think about nothing but becoming a "gentle woman" and fitting into Weed's life. But in spite of reactionary attitudes, I was growing. My relationship with Steve was changing and I was becoming resentful of his patronizing attitude towards me—the way he was trying to mold me into his idea of supermate. . . . While part of me was plotting my escape from this relationship, the other part of me was smiling for engagement pictures and cooking dinner—playing out various aspects of a role that I hated.

Steve and I used each other for three years, but we both knew it couldn't last. . . . By January [1974] I'd abandoned my subjective attachment to the idea that everything would be "different" once we were married, but I was still too afraid to break out of a relationship that had once seemed so safe. After I was kidnapped, one of the [SLA] sisters asked me what Weed and I talked about, and I couldn't think of anything except bullshit chatter. Only then was I finally able to admit to myself that our relationship *stunk.* That it totally lacked the mutual respect necessary for people to grow and develop together.

Q. What sort of model did your mother provide for you in terms of a pattern for you to follow?

A. My mother didn't provide a very attractive model for me to follow. She was often on some kind of drug, usually barbituates [*sic*]. I never liked to have friends over to the house mostly because of the drugs. One day when I was in high school, a boy friend came over and she was so fucked up she could hardly talk. I was real embarrassed but he excused it by saying that his mother was an alcoholic. Our parents weren't unusual. The ruling class' pastime [*sic*] activity consists of drugs, booze and divorce. My parents were into dope and alcohol. . . .

. . . Also, Catherine is incredibly racist. My father is too, but he usually isn't as blatent [*sic*] about it as my mother. He puts up his liberal-nice-guy front, or at least he tries to—he couldn't afford to be so obvious, being in contact with people the way he is in the publishing business. He's a real pig, but he usually makes a good first impression. . . .

Q. How did you feel about your kidnappers at first?

A. At first I didn't trust or like them. . . . For a while I didn't trust anything that anyone said to me. But I got over that level of mistrust pretty quickly. I realized that except for security information, I wasn't being lied to anymore. . . .

Q. What was your reaction when it was first suggested to you that you might become a member of the SLA?

A. My decision to join the SLA was the result of process of political development. . . . After only a couple of weeks I started to feel sympathetic with the SLA. I was beginning to see that what they wanted to accomplish was necessary, although at that time it was hard for me to relate to the tactic of urban guerrilla warfare. But how can someone disagree with wanting hungry people to have food? . . . It's pretty hard not to see that starvation and hunger are the real tragedies, and not the fact that one person had been kidnapped and might get killed. I'm not trying to say that I was super brave or anything—just that I could see my situation clearly. I would have been dishonest with myself if I hadn't agreed with the goals of the SLA. At the same time there were so many ideas that they talked about that I couldn't understand . . . yet. . . .

. . . So-called investigative reporters suggest that during these weeks I was falling in love with some member of the SLA. In reality I was falling in love with the masses of people and learning how to struggle with my weaknesses—to fight the "enemy within."

When I was given the choice of either joining the combat unit or returning to my parents' house, I was really worried. I had only read a few books, and was generally lacking the political analysis and military skills that I thought would be a prerequisite for joining the cell. But my comrades were willing to help me learn the military/political skills that I was lacking as long as I was willing to struggle to become a guerrilla soldier. . . .

Q. What was the reaction to the suggestion that you might join the SLA from the other members of the cell when Cin first proposed it to them?

A. . . . I heard that there was a lot of opposition to the idea. Some members of the cell objected to me staying, because they did not want someone with them that had not made a well-thought-out decision. . . . The comrades who objected, though, were the ones who were often gone all day taking care of different business for the cell. I finally got down and talked to each comrade individually so that they could understand what had gone into my decision—so that we could get to know what each other was thinking. When the members of the combat unit decided that I could stay with the cell, the decision was unanimous.

Q. The media has at times put across the theory that you were being brainwashed during this period. How do you feel about that?

A. . . . I couldn't believe that anyone would come up with such bullshit! . . . I feel that the term "brainwashing" has meaning only when one is referring to the process which begins in the school system, and is continued via the controlled media—the process whereby the people are conditioned to passively take their place in society as slaves of the ruling class. Like someone said in a letter to the *Berkeley Barb*, I'd been brainwashed for 20 years but it only took the SLA six weeks to straighten me out.

I'm not sure how many people actually believed the "brainwash-duress theory" that Randy and Catherine cling to—[Attorney General] William

Saxbe certainly didn't. However, a lot of people who didn't think that I was brainwashed decided that there must have been some other equally horrifying reason for my refusing to return to my family. Some thought that there must be all kinds of bizarre sexual activities going down in the cell, and that I have freaked out as a result of being gang-banged. Other sick-ass racists were hoping that I had fallen in love with Cin after getting a "little taste." The idea that I had been kidnapped by Black men really played into a lot of people's fantasies, and many people immediately assumed that I had been raped.

Q. The media has told some pretty outrageous lies when they've discussed your comrades' personalities. How were you generally portrayed in the media?

A. . . . The media was now able to exploit its sexism and racism to the highest degree. I began to be portrayed as a "liberal minded young woman who was abducted by crazy Black escaped convicts." My mother appeared at press conferences dressed in black to urge me through her racist tears to, "keep praying honey. . . . God will bring you home." It was incredible. During the period this type of propaganda was being spread, Catherine and Randy solicited sympathy through the devious "bandwagon" method which exaggerated public support for my family's plight. The media spread outrageous and contradictory lies, saying that thousands of people had volunteered to distribute the food even though it was predicted that no one would go to receive the "blood money" food anyway. . . .

. . . Basically, the media hasn't dealt with me any differently than they have with my comrades. Their invention of our "bizarre personalities" is done in an effort to isolate us from the people—to make the people think that we're crazy. The pigs have to lie about the past lives of revolutionaries because most of us are from backgrounds similar to millions of other young people. We could be *anyone's* daughter, son, husband, wife, lover, neighbor or friend—and that's what really scares the pigs.

Q. I think that it was about the time of your conversion that you began to develop a personal relationship with one member of the cell, Cujo [Willie Wolfe]. Can you tell us something about that relationship?

A. My personal relationship with Cujo was based on a political and military relationship. The strong personal relationship did not develop, could not develop, until after I joined the cell because there would have been no common understanding and therefore no basis of trust between us. I had a lot of good feelings for him before I was accepted into the cell; but I had those same feelings for other comrades, too.

Cujo was an incredibly patient, loving and dedicated person. His experiences with the brothers in California's concentration camps played a very important role in his political development, and they were always in his heart. He taught with the patience he learned from the brothers inside. Before I got a reading light in the closet, Cujo read Stalin's *Dialectical and Historical Materialism* and some other essays to me. He explained everything as he read, and never got frustrated if I asked a "stupid" question. In fact, everyone in the cell would always take the time to make sure that I really understood what they were all about. Cujo was a beautiful and gentle man, and at the same time he was a strong and ruthless guerrilla soldier.

Q. Did you have sexual relationships with other people in the cell?

A. People in the cell didn't have exclusive relationships. There was no room for bourgeois types of personal relationships. The cell couldn't function like that on a military/political level. . . . The SLA had experienced certain difficulties with exclusive relationships in the past, and once I joined the cell some of the comrades were afraid that the personal relationship between me and Cujo might become a problem. As a result, our comrades helped us deal with the potential for problems before a real problem ever came up. . . .

. . . After a while the comrades realized that our personal relationship was working well in the cell situation. Both Cujo and I were becoming stronger because of the reinforcement from each other and the understanding with which we were able to deal with each other's weaknesses. . . . Our cell was divided into three teams . . . our intention was to split up in order to live and work in different areas. . . . Cujo and I were on different teams, not because we were in love and therefore nobody wanted us to be together, but because our military skills complemented different people. . . . We really wanted to fight the enemy together, but more than anything else we wanted to FIGHT THE ENEMY—no matter where we were, or which comrades we were with. . . .

Q. How did your comrades in the SLA compare with the sort of people you knew in your Patricia Hearst days?

A. The sisters and brothers in the SLA are very loving people. They show their love for their comrades not only by giving them a big hug, but by administering a swift kick in the ass when it's necessary. Bourgeois liberalism in dealing with comrades has no place in a cell situation, because we want the people we love to be able to survive. . . .

. . . The people that I knew in my aboveground life had no concern for a friend's survival—no one even thought about things like that. People only worried about whether or not a friend was happy; they had a very selfish and narrow view of the world.

My comrades and I aren't always "happy" in the bourgeois sense, but there is true meaning to our lives. Our joy comes from the knowledge that the people will win their freedom and destroy this capitalist-individualist society, and not from a trinket that someone bought for us.

We live for the people, and some of us died for the people. It was horrible to watch our closest comrades burned alive, but the people were able to see just how fascist this government really is, and what kind of determination revolutionaries must have to bring this motherfucker down. Our own deaths do not frighten us, for death is a reality of life, and we no longer run from reality.

Index